Pro ASP.NET MVC 5

Adam Freeman

Pro ASP.NET MVC 5

ISBN-13 (pbk): 978-1-4302-6529-0

ISBN-13 (electronic): 978-1-4302-6530-6

President and Publisher: Paul Manning
Lead Editor: Ewan Buckingham
Technical Reviewer: Fabio Claudio Ferracchiati
Editorial Board: Steve Anglin, Mark Beckner, Ewan Buckingham, Gary Cornell, Louise Corrigan, Jim DeWolf, Jonathan Gennick, Jonathan Hassell, Robert Hutchinson, Michelle Lowman, James Markham, Matthew Moodie, Jeff Olson, Jeffrey Pepper, Douglas Pundick, Ben Renow-Clarke, Dominic Shakeshaft, Gwenan Spearing, Matt Wade, Steve Weiss
Coordinating Editor: Kevin Shea
Copy Editor: Larissa Shmailo
Compositor: SPi Global
Indexer: SPi Global
Artist: SPi Global
Cover Designer: Anna Ishchenko

Distributed to the book trade worldwide by Springer Science+Business Media New York, 233 Spring Street, 6th Floor, New York, NY 10013. Phone 1-800-SPRINGER, fax (201) 348-4505, e-mail orders-ny@springer-sbm.com, or visit www.springeronline.com. Apress Media, LLC is a California LLC and the sole member (owner) is Springer Science + Business Media Finance Inc (SSBM Finance Inc). SSBM Finance Inc is a Delaware corporation.

For information on translations, please e-mail rights@apress.com, or visit www.apress.com.

Apress and friends of ED books may be purchased in bulk for academic, corporate, or promotional use. eBook versions and licenses are also available for most titles. For more information, reference our Special Bulk Sales–eBook Licensing web page at www.apress.com/bulk-sales.

Any source code or other supplementary material referenced by the author in this text is available to readers at www.apress.com/9781430257882. For detailed information about how to locate your book's source code, go to www.apress.com/source-code/.

Dedicated to my lovely wife, Jacqui Griffyth.

Contents at a Glance

Contents

About the Author

Adam Freeman is an experienced IT professional who has held senior positions in a range of companies, most recently serving as chief technology officer and chief operating officer of a global bank. Now retired, he spends his time writing and running.

About the Technical Reviewer

Fabio Claudio Ferracchiati is a senior consultant and a senior analyst/developer using Microsoft technologies. He works for Brain Force (http://www.brainforce.com) in its Italian branch (http://www.brainforce.it). He is a Microsoft Certified Solution Developer for .NET, a Microsoft Certified Application Developer for .NET, a Microsoft Certified Professional, and a prolific author and technical reviewer. Over the past 10 years, he's written articles for Italian and international magazines and coauthored more than 10 books on a variety of computer topics.

■ ■ ■

CHAPTER 1

Putting ASP.NET MVC in Context

ASP.NET MVC is a Web development framework from Microsoft that combines the effectiveness and tidiness of model-view-controller (MVC) architecture, the most up-to-date ideas and techniques from agile development, and the best parts of the existing ASP.NET platform. It is a complete alternative to traditional ASP.NET Web Forms, delivering advantages for all but the most trivial of Web development projects. In this chapter, you'll learn why Microsoft created ASP.NET MVC, how it compares to its predecessors and alternatives, and, finally, what's new in ASP.NET MVC 5 and what's covered in this book.

Understanding the History of ASP.NET

ASP.NET was a huge shift when it first arrived in 2002. Figure 1-1 illustrates Microsoft's technology stack as it appeared then.

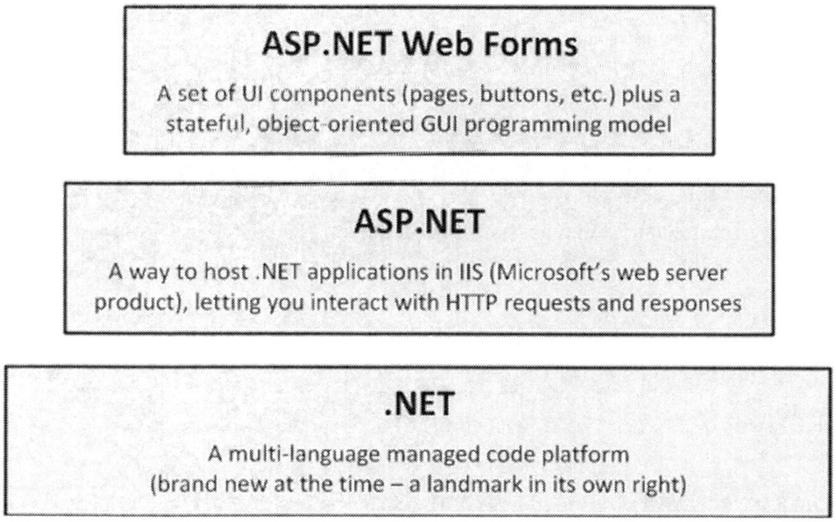

ASP.NET Web Forms

A set of UI components (pages, buttons, etc.) plus a stateful, object-oriented GUI programming model

ASP.NET

A way to host .NET applications in IIS (Microsoft's web server product), letting you interact with HTTP requests and responses

.NET

A multi-language managed code platform
(brand new at the time – a landmark in its own right)

Figure 1-1. *The ASP.NET Web Forms technology stack*

With Web Forms, Microsoft attempted to hide both HTTP (with its intrinsic statelessness) and HTML (which at the time was unfamiliar to many developers) by modeling the user interface (UI) as a hierarchy of server-side control objects. Each control kept track of its own state across requests (using the *View State* facility), rendering itself as HTML when needed and automatically connecting client-side events (for example, a button click) with the corresponding server-side event handler code. In effect, Web Forms is a giant abstraction layer designed to deliver a classic event-driven graphical user interface (GUI) over the Web.

The idea was to make Web development feel just the same as Windows Forms development. Developers didn't need to work with a series of independent HTTP requests and responses. They could think in terms of a stateful UI, and Microsoft could seamlessly transition the army of Windows desktop developers into the new world of web applications.

What Is Wrong with ASP.NET Web Forms?

Traditional ASP.NET Web Forms development was great in principle, but reality proved more complicated:

- *View State weight*: The actual mechanism for maintaining state across requests (known as View State) results in large blocks of data being transferred between the client and server. This data can reach hundreds of kilobytes in even modest Web applications, and it goes back and forth with *every* request, leading to slower response times and increasing the bandwidth demands of the server.

- *Page life cycle*: The mechanism for connecting client-side events with server-side event handler code, part of the page life cycle, can be extraordinarily complicated and delicate. Few developers have success manipulating the control hierarchy at runtime without getting View State errors or finding that some event handlers mysteriously fail to execute.

- *False sense of separation of concerns*: ASP.NET Web Forms' *code-behind* model provides a means to take application code out of its HTML markup and into a separate code-behind class. This has been widely applauded for separating logic and presentation, but, in reality, developers are encouraged to mix presentation code (for example, manipulating the server-side control tree) with their application logic (for example, manipulating database data) in these same monstrous code-behind classes. The end result can be fragile and unintelligible.

- *Limited control over HTML*: Server controls render themselves as HTML, but not necessarily the HTML you want. In early versions of ASP.NET, the HTML output failed to meet with Web standards or make good use of Cascading Style Sheets (CSS), and server controls generated unpredictable and complex ID attribute values that are hard to access using JavaScript. These problems are much improved in recent Web Forms releases, but it can still be tricky to get the HTML you expect.

- *Leaky abstraction*: Web Forms tries to hide HTML and HTTP wherever possible. As you try to implement custom behaviors, you frequently fall out of the abstraction, which forces you to reverse-engineer the postback event mechanism or perform obtuse acts to make it generate the desired HTML. Plus, all this abstraction can act as a frustrating barrier for competent Web developers.

- *Low testability*: The designers of Web Forms could not have anticipated that automated testing would become an essential component of software development. Not surprisingly, the tightly coupled architecture they designed is unsuitable for unit testing. Integration testing can be a challenge, too.

Web Forms isn't all bad and Microsoft has put a lot of effort into improving standards compliance, simplifying the development process, and even taking some features from ASP.NET MVC. Web Forms excels when you need quick results, and you can have a reasonably complex web app up and running within a day. But unless you are careful during development, you will find that the application you create is hard to test and hard to maintain.

> ■ **Note** For complete details of ASP.NET Web Forms, see my *Pro ASP.NET 4.5 in C#* book, also published by Apress. I cover the complete framework and provide best-practice guidance for avoiding the most serious pitfalls.

Web Development Today

Outside Microsoft, Web development technology has been progressing rapidly and in several different directions since Web Forms was first released.

Web Standards and REST

The drive for Web standards compliance has increased in recent years. Web sites are consumed on a greater variety of devices and browsers than ever before, and Web standards (HTML, CSS, JavaScript, and so forth) remain the great hope for enjoying a consistent browsing experience. Modern web platforms can't afford to ignore the business case and the weight of developer enthusiasm for Web standards compliance.

HTML5 has begun to enter mainstream use and provides the Web developer with rich capabilities that allow the client to perform work that was previously the exclusive responsibility of the server. These new capabilities and the increasing maturity of JavaScript libraries such as AngularJS, jQuery, jQuery UI, and jQuery Mobile means that standards have become ever more important and form the critical foundation for ever richer Web apps.

> ■ **Note** I touch on HTML5, jQuery, and its cousins in this book, but I don't go into depth because these are topics in their own right. If you want more complete coverage, then Apress publishes my books on these subjects: *Pro AngularJS*, *Pro jQuery 2.0*, *Pro JavaScript for Web Apps*, and *The Definitive Guide to HTML5*.

At the same time, Representational State Transfer (REST has become the dominant architecture for application interoperability over HTTP, completely overshadowing SOAP (the technology behind ASP.NET's original approach to Web services). REST describes an application in terms of resources (URIs) representing real-world entities and standard operations (HTTP methods) representing available operations on those resources. For example, you might PUT a new `http://www.example.com/Products/Lawnmower` or DELETE `http://www.example.com/Customers/Arnold-Smith`.

Today's Web applications don't serve just HTML. Often, they must also serve JSON or XML data to client technologies such as AJAX and native smartphone applications. This happens naturally with REST, which eliminates the distinction between Web services and Web applications, but requires an approach to HTTP and URL handling that has not easily been supported by ASP.NET Web Forms.

Agile and Test-Driven Development

It is not just Web development that has matured. Software development as a whole has shifted toward *agile* methodologies. This can mean a lot of different things, but it is largely about running software projects as adaptable processes of discovery and resisting excessive forward planning. Enthusiasm for agile methodologies tends to go hand-in-hand with a set of development practices and tools (usually open source) that promote and assist these practices.

Test-driven development (TDD), and its close relative, *behavior-driven development (BDD)*, are two examples. The idea is to design your software by first describing examples of desired behaviors (known as *tests* or *specifications*), so at any time you can verify the stability and correctness of your application by executing your suite of tests against the implementation. There's no shortage of .NET tools to support TDD/BDD, but these tend to not work well with Web Forms:

- *Unit testing tools* let you specify the behavior of individual classes or other small code units in isolation. These can be effectively applied only to software that has been designed as a set of independent modules, so that each test can be run in isolation. Unfortunately, few Web Forms applications can be tested this way.

- *UI automation tools* let you simulate a series of user interactions against a complete running instance of your application. These can be used with Web Forms, but they can break down whenever you make a slight change to your page layout. Without special attention, Web Forms change the HTML structures and element IDs, breaking test suites.

The .NET open source and independent software vendor (ISV community has produced no end of top quality unit testing frameworks (NUnit and xUnit), mocking frameworks (Moq and Rhino Mocks), inversion-of-control containers (Ninject and AutoFac), continuous integration servers (Cruise Control and TeamCity), object-relational mappers (NHibernate and Subsonic), and the like. Traditional ASP.NET Web Forms is not amenable to these tools and techniques because of its monolithic design, and so Web Forms gets little respect from these projects.

Ruby on Rails

In 2004, Ruby on Rails was a quiet, open source contribution from an unknown player. Suddenly fame hit, transforming the rules of Web development. It's not that Ruby on Rails contained revolutionary technology but that the concept took existing ingredients and blended them in such a compelling and appealing way as to put existing platforms to shame.

Ruby on Rails (or just Rails, as it is commonly called) embraced an MVC architecture, which I describe in Chapter 3. By applying MVC and working in tune with the HTTP protocol, by promoting conventions instead of the need for configuration, and by integrating an object-relational mapping (ORM tool into its core, Rails applications more or less fell into place without much effort. It was as if this was how Web development should have been all along. Rails showed that Web standards compliance and RESTfulness don't need to be hard. It also showed that agile development and TDD work best when the framework is designed to support them. The rest of the Web development world has been catching up ever since.

Node.js

Another significant trend is the movement toward using JavaScript as a primary programming language. AJAX first showed that JavaScript is important; jQuery showed us that it could be powerful and elegant; and Google's open source V8 JavaScript engine showed us that it could be fast. Today, JavaScript is becoming a serious server-side programming language. It serves as the data storage and querying language for several non-relational databases, including CouchDB and Mongo, and it is used as a general-purpose language in server-side platforms such as Node.js. Node.js has been around since 2009 and gained acceptance quickly. Its key innovations are as follows:

- *Using JavaScript*: Developers need to work only in a single language, from client-side code, through server-side logic, and even into data-querying logic via CouchDB or the like.

- *Being completely asynchronous*: Node.js's core API doesn't expose any way of blocking a thread while waiting for input/output (I/O) or any other operation. All I/O is implemented by beginning the operation and then later receiving a callback when the I/O is completed. This means that Node.js makes extremely efficient use of system resources and may handle tens of thousands of concurrent requests per CPU. (Alternative platforms tend to be limited to about one hundred concurrent requests per CPU.)

Node.js remains a niche technology. Its biggest contribution to web app development has, rather oddly, been to provide a consistent JavaScript engine on which development tools can be written. Many emerging client-side JavaScript frameworks, such as AngularJS, have good tooling support based on the use of Node.js.

Node.js adoption for deploying web apps has been slower. Most businesses building real applications in limited time frames typically need the infrastructure in full-stack frameworks such as Ruby on Rails and ASP.NET MVC. Node.js is mentioned here only to put some of ASP.NET MVC's design into context against industry trends. For example, ASP.NET MVC includes *asynchronous controllers* (which I describe in Chapter 19). This is a way to handle HTTP requests with non-blocking I/O and scale up to handle more requests per CPU.

Key Benefits of ASP.NET MVC

In October 2007, Microsoft announced a new MVC Web development platform, built on the core ASP.NET platform, clearly designed as a direct response to the evolution of technologies such as Rails and as a reaction to the criticisms of Web Forms. The following sections describe how this new platform overcame the Web Forms limitations and brought ASP.NET back to the cutting edge.

MVC Architecture

It is important to distinguish between the MVC architectural pattern and the ASP.NET MVC Framework. The MVC pattern is not new—it dates back to 1978 and the Smalltalk project at Xerox PARC—but it has gained enormous popularity today as a pattern for Web applications, for the following reasons:

- User interaction with an MVC application follows a natural cycle: the user takes an action, and in response the application changes its data model and delivers an updated view to the user. And then the cycle repeats. This is a convenient fit for Web applications delivered as a series of HTTP requests and responses.

- Web applications necessitate combining several technologies (databases, HTML, and executable code, for example), usually split into a set of tiers or layers. The patterns that arise from these combinations map naturally onto the concepts in MVC.

The ASP.NET MVC Framework implements the MVC pattern and, in doing so, provides greatly improved separation of concerns. In fact, ASP.NET MVC implements a modern variant of the MVC pattern that is especially suitable for Web applications. You will learn more about the theory and practice of this architecture in Chapter 3.

By embracing and adapting the MVC pattern, the ASP.NET MVC Framework provides strong competition to Ruby on Rails and similar platforms, and brings the MVC pattern into the mainstream of the .NET world. By capitalizing on the experience and best practices discovered by developers using other platforms, ASP.NET MVC has, in many ways, pushed forward beyond what even Rails can offer.

Extensibility

The MVC Framework is built as a series of independent components that satisfy a .NET interface or that are built on an abstract base class. You can easily replace components, such as the routing system, the view engine, and the controller factory, with a different one of your own implementation. In general, the MVC Framework gives you three options for each component:

- Use the *default* implementation of the component as it stands (which should be enough for most applications).

- Derive a *subclass* of the default implementation to tweak its behavior.

- *Replace* the component entirely with a new implementation of the interface or abstract base class.

You'll learn all about the various components, and how and why you might want to tweak or replace each of them, starting in Chapter 14.

Tight Control over HTML and HTTP

ASP.NET MVC produces clean, standards-compliant markup. Its built-in HTML helper methods produce standards-compliant output, but there is a more significant philosophical change compared with Web Forms. Instead of generating out swathes of HTML over which you have little control, the MVC Framework encourages you to craft simple, elegant markup styled with CSS.

Of course, if you do want to throw in some ready-made widgets for complex UI elements such as date pickers or cascading menus, ASP.NET MVC's "no special requirements" approach to markup makes it easy to use best-of-breed UI libraries such as jQuery UI or the Bootstrap CSS library. ASP.NET MVC meshes so well with jQuery, for example, that Microsoft ships jQuery as a built-in part of the default Visual Studio ASP.NET MVC project template, along with other popular libraries, such as Bootstrap, Knockout and Modernizr.

■ **Tip**   I don't get into the detail of these "blessed" JavaScript libraries in this book because they are not part of the core MVC Framework and do their work within the browser. Client-side development for MVC Framework applications is an important topic, however, and you can learn more in my book *Pro ASP.NET MVC 5 Client*, which will be published by Apress in 2014. There are some libraries, however, that provide support for core features such as validation and Ajax requests and I describe these in Part 2 of this book. I describe Knockout in Chapter 27 and I use Bootstrap (albeit without a detailed introduction) throughout the book.

ASP.NET MVC-generated pages don't contain any View State data, so they are smaller than typical pages from ASP.NET Web Forms. Despite today's fast connections, this economy of bandwidth still gives an enormously improved end-user experience and helps reduce the cost of running a popular web application.

ASP.NET MVC works in tune with HTTP. You have control over the requests passing between the browser and server, so you can fine-tune your user experience as much as you like. AJAX is made easy, and there aren't any automatic postbacks to interfere with client-side state.

Testability

The MVC architecture gives you a great start in making your application maintainable and testable because you naturally separate different application concerns into independent pieces. Yet the ASP.NET MVC designers didn't stop there. To support unit testing, they took the framework's component-oriented design and made sure that each separate piece is structured to meet the requirements of unit testing and mocking tools.

They added Visual Studio wizards to create unit test projects on your behalf, which can be integrated with open source unit test tools such as NUnit and xUnit as well as the test tools that are included in Visual Studio, which I introduce in Chapter 6. Even if you have never written a unit test before, you will be off to a great start.

In this book, you will see examples of how to write clean, simple unit tests for ASP.NET MVC controllers and actions that supply fake or mock implementations of framework components to simulate any scenario, using a variety of testing and mocking strategies.

Testability is not only a matter of unit testing. ASP.NET MVC applications work well with UI automation testing tools, too. You can write test scripts that simulate user interactions without needing to guess which HTML element structures, CSS classes, or IDs the framework will generate, and you do not have to worry about the structure changing unexpectedly.

Powerful Routing System

The style of URLs has evolved as Web application technology has improved. URLs like this one:

```
/App_v2/User/Page.aspx?action=show%20prop&prop_id=82742
```

are increasingly rare, replaced with a simpler, cleaner format like this:

```
/to-rent/chicago/2303-silver-street
```

There are some good reasons for caring about the structure of URLs. First, search engines give weight to keywords found in a URL. A search for "rent in Chicago" is much more likely to turn up the simpler URL. Second, many Web users are now savvy enough to understand a URL, and appreciate the option of navigating by typing it into their browser's address bar. Third, when someone understands the structure of a URL, they are more likely to link to it, share it with a friend, or even read it aloud over the phone. Fourth, it doesn't expose the technical details, folder, and file name structure of your application to the public Internet, so you are free to change the underlying implementation without breaking all your incoming links.

Clean URLs were hard to implement in earlier frameworks, but ASP.NET MVC uses a feature known as *URL routing* to provide clean URLs by default. This gives you control over your URL schema and its relationship to your application, offering you the freedom to create a pattern of URLs that is meaningful and useful to your users, without the need to conform to a predefined pattern. And, of course, this means you can easily define a modern REST-style URL schema if you wish. You'll find a thorough description of URL routing in Chapters 15 and 16.

Built on the Best Parts of the ASP.NET Platform

Microsoft's existing ASP.NET platform provides a mature, well-proven set of components and facilities for developing effective and efficient Web applications. First and most obviously, as ASP.NET MVC is based on the .NET platform, you have the flexibility to write code in any .NET language and access the same API features—not just in MVC itself but in the extensive .NET class library and the vast ecosystem of third-party .NET libraries.

Second, ready-made ASP.NET platform features—such as authentication, membership, roles, profiles, and internationalization—can reduce the amount of code you need to develop and maintain any Web application, and these features are just as effective when used in the MVC Framework as they are in a classic Web Forms project. The underlying ASP.NET platform provides a rich set of tools on which to build web applications with the MVC Framework.

■ **Note** I describe the most commonly used ASP.NET Platform features as they relate to MVC development in this book, but the platform is a topic in its own right. For complete details of the rich features that the ASP.NET platform provides, see my forthcoming *Pro ASP.NET MVC 5 Platform*, which will be published by Apress in 2014.

Modern API

Microsoft's .NET platform has evolved with each major release, supporting – and even defining – the state-of-the-art aspects of modern programming. ASP.NET MVC 5 is built for .NET 4.5.1, so its API can take full advantage of recent language and runtime innovations, including the `await` keyword, extension methods, lambda expressions, anonymous and dynamic types, and Language Integrated Query (LINQ). Many of the MVC Framework's API methods and coding patterns follow a cleaner, more expressive composition than was possible with earlier platforms. Don't worry if you are not up to speed on the latest C# language features: I provide a summary of the most important C# features for MVC development in Chapter 4.

ASP.NET MVC Is Open Source

Unlike previous Microsoft Web development platforms, you are free to download the original source code for ASP.NET MVC, and even modify and compile your own version of it. This is invaluable when your debugging trail leads into a system component and you want to step into its code (and even read the original programmers' comments). It is also useful if you are building an advanced component and want to see what development possibilities exist, or how the built-in components actually work.

Additionally, this ability is great if you do not like the way something works, if you find a bug, or if you just want to access something that's otherwise inaccessible, because you can simply change it yourself. However, you'll need to keep track of your changes and reapply them if you upgrade to a newer version of the framework. ASP.NET MVC is licensed under the Microsoft Public License (Ms-PL, `http://www.opensource.org/licenses/ms-pl.html`), an Open Source Initiative (OSI)–approved open source license. This means that you can change the source code, deploy it, and even redistribute your changes publicly as a derivative project. You can download the MVC source code from `http://aspnetwebstack.codeplex.com`.

What Do I Need to Know?

To get the most from this book, you should be familiar with the basics of web development, have an understanding of how HTML and CSS work and a working knowledge of C#. Don't worry if you are a little hazy on the client-side details. My emphasis is on server-side development in this book and you can pick up what you need through the examples. In Chapter 4, I provide a summary of the most useful C# language features for MVC development, which you'll find useful if you are moving to the latest .NET versions from an earlier release.

What Is the Structure of This Book?

This book is split into 2 parts, each of which covers a set of related topics.

Part 1: Introducing ASP.NET MVC 5

I start this book by putting the ASP.NET MVC Framework in context. I explain the benefits and practical impact of the MVC pattern, the way in which the MVC Framework fits into modern web development and describe the tools and C# language features that every MVC Framework programmer needs.

In the next chapter you will dive right in and create a simple web application and get an idea of what the major components and building blocks are and how they fit together. Most of this part of the book, however, is given over to the development of a project called SportsStore, through which I show you a realistic development process from inception to deployment, touching on the major features of the ASP.NET MVC Framework.

Part 2: ASP.NET MVC in Detail

In Part 2, I explain the inner workings of the MVC Framework features that I used to build the SportsStore application. I show you how each feature works, explain the role it plays in the MVC Framework and show you the configuration and customization options that are available. Having set the broad context in Part 1, I dig right into the details in Part 2.

What's New in this Edition?

Version 5 of the MVC Framework is a relatively minor upgrade and a lot of the changes are really to do with the way that ASP.NET projects are created and managed in Visual Studio. Table 1-1 briefly describes the new MVC Framework features and details where you can find more information about them in this book.

Table 1-1. *The New Features in MVC 5*

Feature	Description	See Chapter
Authentication Filters	A new kind of filter that can be used to include different types of authentication within the same controller	18
Filter Overrides	A new kind of filter that is applied to action methods to prevent filters defined globally or on the controller from taking effect	18
Attribute Routing	A set of attributes that allow URL routes to be defined within the controller class	15, 16

ASP.NET version 4.5.1, on which the MVC Framework 5 is built, has been enhanced as well. The most important change is the addition of the ASP.NET Identity API, which replaces the Membership system for managing user credentials. I don't cover ASP.NET Identity in this book, although I do explain how authentication and authorization are applied to MVC Framework applications through the use of features like filters.

■ **Note**   I will be covering ASP.NET Identity in my *Pro ASP.NET MVC 5 Platform* book, which will be published in 2014 and cover all of the facilities that the ASP.NET platform provides. That said, I don't want you to have to buy a second book to learn about something as important as user security, and so Apress has agreed to distribute the security-related chapters from that book from its web site for download without charge when that book is published. Those chapters won't be available immediately because I have not written the platform book yet, but it is my next major writing project after this book and my hope is that the delay won't be too long.

A new edition is a chance to go beyond writing about new features and I have made some other changes for this book. I have expanded the SportsStore example to show the basics of responsive and mobile web application development, I added quick references to the start of all the in-depth chapters so you can find easily specific examples, and I added a chapter that shows how one of the open source libraries that Microsoft has embraced—Knockout—can be combined with the Web API feature to create Single-Page Applications (SPAs).

Where Can I Get the Example Code?

You can download all of the examples for all of the chapters in this book from Apress.com. The download is available without charge and includes all of the Visual Studio projects and their contents. You don't have to download the code, but it is the easiest way of experimenting with the examples and cutting and pasting techniques into your own projects.

What Software Do I Need for This Book?

The only software you need for MVC development is Visual Studio 2013, which contains everything you need to get started, including a built-in application server for running and debugging MVC applications, an administration-free edition of SQL Server for developing database-driven applications, tools for unit testing and, of course, a code editor compiler and debugger.

There are several different editions of Visual Studio, but I will be using the one that Microsoft makes available free of charge, called *Visual Studio Express 2013 for Web*. Microsoft adds some nice features to the paid-for editions of Visual Studio, but you will not need them for this book and all of the figures that you see throughout this book have been taken using the Express edition, which you can download from http://www.microsoft.com/visualstudio/eng/products/visual-studio-express-products. There are several different versions of Visual Studio 2013 Express, each of which is used for a different kind of development. Make sure that you get the Web version, which supports ASP/NET applications.

Once you have installed Visual Studio, you are ready to go. Microsoft has improved the scope of the features in the Visual Studio Express in recent years and there is nothing else you need to follow along with this book. I do rely on additional software packages, but these are installed through Visual Studio and don't require separate downloads and installations (and are available without cost).

▪ **Tip**   I have used Windows 8.1 throughout this book, but you can use Visual Studio 2013 and develop MVC applications quite happily on earlier versions of Windows. See the system requirements for Visual Studio 2013 for details of which versions and patch levels are supported).

Credits

In Chapter 10, I use a feature of the Bootstrap CSS library called *Glyphicons Halflings*, which are a set of icons that are not usually available for free, but for which the creator has given an open license for their inclusion in Bootstrap. The only request is that the creator's URL be quoted when it is possible to do so, which seems like a fair and reasonable thing to do. Here is it: http://glyphicons.com.

Summary

In this chapter, I explained the context in which the MVC Framework exists and how it compares to Web Forms. I described the benefits of using the MVC framework, the structure of this book and the software that you will require to follow the examples.

You saw how the ASP.NET MVC platform addresses the weaknesses of ASP.NET Web Forms, and how its modern design delivers advantages to developers who want to write high-quality, maintainable code. In the next chapter, you'll see the MVC Framework in action in a simple demonstration of the features that deliver these benefits.

CHAPTER 2

■ ■ ■

Your First MVC Application

The best way to appreciate a software development framework is to jump right in and use it. In this chapter, you'll create a simple data-entry application using the ASP.NET MVC Framework. I take things a step at a time so you can see how an ASP.NET MVC application is constructed. To keep things simple, I will skip over some of the technical details for the moment. But don't worry. If you are new to MVC, you will find plenty to keep you interested. Where I use something without explaining it, I provide a reference to the chapter in which you can find all the details.

Preparing Visual Studio

Visual Studio Express contains all of the features you need to create, test and deploy an MVC Framework application, but some of those features are hidden away until you ask for them. To enable all of the features, select Expert Settings from the Visual Studio Tools ➤ Settings menu.

■ **Tip**   For some reason, Microsoft has decided that the top-level menus in Visual Studio should be all in uppercase, which means that the menu I referred to is really TOOLS. I think this is rather like shouting and I will capitalize menu names as Tools throughout this book.

Creating a New ASP.NET MVC Project

I am going to start by creating a new MVC Framework project in Visual Studio. Select New Project from the File menu to open the New Project dialog. If you select the Web templates in the Visual C# section, you will see the ASP.NET Web Application project template. Select this project type, as shown in Figure 2-1.

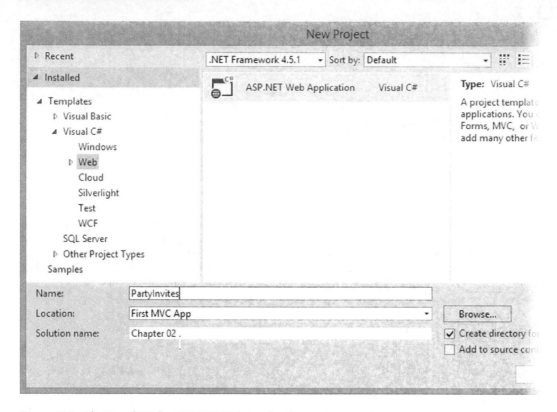

Figure 2-1. *The Visual Studio ASP.NET Web Application project template*

Set the name of the new project to **PartyInvites** and click the OK button to continue. You will see another dialog box, shown in Figure 2-2, which asks you to set the initial content for the ASP.NET project. This is part of the Microsoft initiative to better integrate the different parts of ASP.NET into a set of consistent tools and templates.

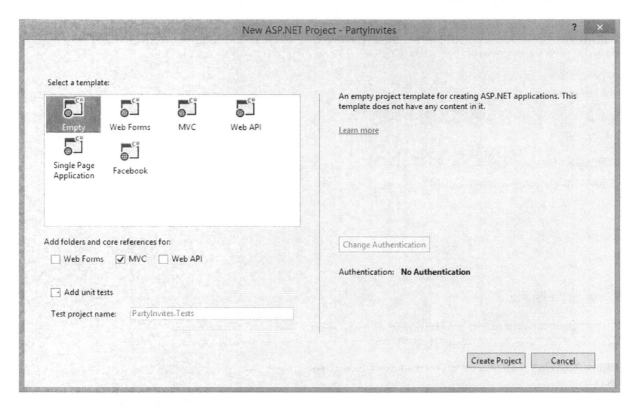

Figure 2-2. *Selecting the initial project configuration*

■ **Tip**   Make sure you select version 4.5.1 of the .NET Framework at the top of the window. This is the latest version of .NET and is required for some of the advanced features that I describe in this book.

The templates create projects with different starting points and configurations for features such as authentication, navigation and visual themes. I am going to keep things simple: select the Empty option and check the MVC box in the *Add folders and core references* section, as shown in the figure. This will create a basic MVC project with minimal predefined content and will be the starting point that I use for all of the examples in this book. Click the OK button to create the new project.

■ **Note**   The other project template options are intended to give you a more complete starting point for your ASP.NET projects. I don't like these templates because they encourage developers to treat some important features, such as authentication, as black boxes. My goal in this book is to give you the knowledge to understand and manage every aspect of your MVC application and, as a consequence, I use the Empty template for most of the examples in the book – the exception is in Chapter 14, where I show you the content that the MVC template adds to new projects.

Once Visual Studio creates the project, you will see a number of files and folders displayed in the **Solution Explorer** window, as shown in Figure 2-3. This is the default project structure for a new MVC project and you will soon understand the purpose of each of the files and folders that Visual Studio creates.

Figure 2-3. *The initial file and folder structure of an MVC project*

You can try to run the application now by selecting **Start Debugging** from the Debug menu (if it prompts you to enable debugging, just click the OK button). You can see the result in Figure 2-4. Because I started with the empty project template, the application does not contain anything to run, so the server generates a 404 Not Found Error.

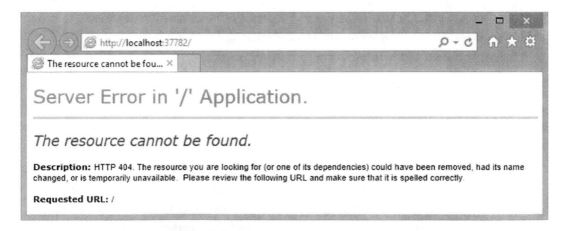

Figure 2-4. *Trying to run an empty project*

When you are finished, be sure to stop debugging by closing the browser window that shows the error, or by going back to Visual Studio and selecting Stop Debugging from the Debug menu.

As you have just seen, Visual Studio opens the browser to display the project. The default browser is, of course, Internet Explorer, but you can select any browser that you have installed by using the toolbar shown in Figure 2-5. As the figure shows, I have a range of browsers installed, which I find useful for testing web apps during development.

Figure 2-5. *Changing the browser that Visual Studio uses to run the project*

I will be using Internet Explorer 11 throughout this book, but that's just because I know that IE is so widely installed. Internet Explorer used to play fast and loose with web standards, but recent versions have been good at implementing the HTML5 standard. Google Chrome is also a good choice for development and I tend to use it for my own projects.

Adding the First Controller

In MVC architecture, incoming requests are handled by *controllers*. In ASP.NET MVC, controllers are just C# classes (usually inheriting from System.Web.Mvc.Controller, the framework's built-in controller base class).

Each public method in a controller is known as an *action method*, meaning you can invoke it from the Web via some URL to perform an action. The MVC convention is to put controllers in the Controllers folder, which Visual Studio created when it set up the project.

■ **Tip**   You do not need to follow this or most other MVC conventions, but I recommend that you do—not least because it will help you make sense of the examples in this book.

To add a controller to the project, right-click the Controllers folder in the Visual Studio Solution Explorer window and choose Add and then Controller from the pop-up menus, as shown in Figure 2-6.

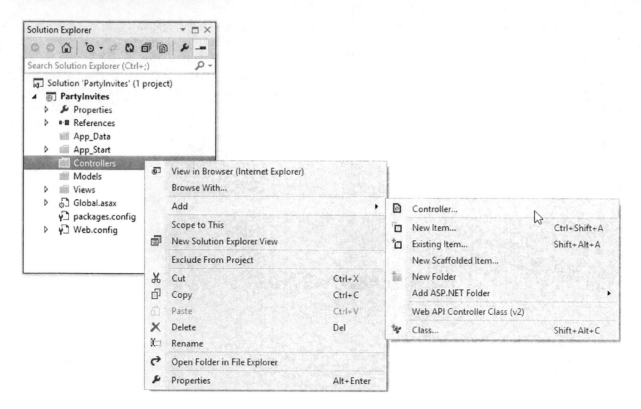

Figure 2-6. *Adding a controller to the MVC project*

When the Add Scaffold dialog appears, select the MVC 5 Controller - Empty option, as shown in Figure 2-7, and click the Add button.

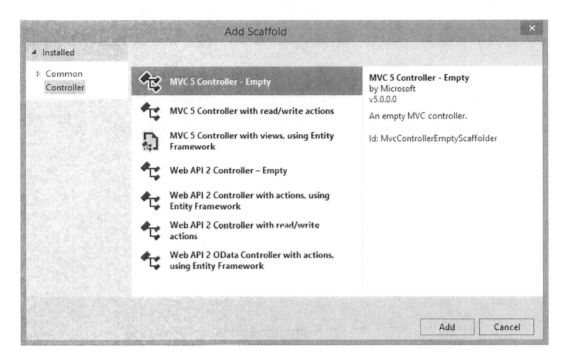

Figure 2-7. *Selecting an empty controller from the Add Scaffold dialog*

The Add Controller dialog will appear. Set the name to HomeController and click the Add button. There are several conventions represented in this name: names given to controllers should indicate their purpose; the default controller is called Home and controller names have the suffix Controller.

■ **Tip** If you have used earlier versions of Visual Studio to create MVC applications, then you will notice that the process is slightly different. Microsoft has changed the way that Visual Studio can populate a project with preconfigured classes and other items.

Visual Studio will create a new C# file in the Controllers folder called HomeController.cs and open it for editing. I have listed the default contents that Visual Studio puts into the class file in Listing 2-1. You can see that the class is called HomeController and it is derived from the Controller class, which is found in the System.Web.Mvc namespace.

Listing 2-1. The Default Contents of the HomeController.cs File

```csharp
using System;
using System.Collections.Generic;
using System.Linq;
using System.Web;
using System.Web.Mvc;

namespace PartyInvites.Controllers {
    public class HomeController : Controller {
```

```
        public ActionResult Index() {
            return View();
        }
    }
}
```

A good way of getting started with MVC is to make a couple of simple changes to the controller class. Edit the code in the HomeController.cs file so that it matches Listing 2-2. I have highlighted the statements that have changed so they are easier to see.

Listing 2-2. Modifying the HomeController.cs File

```
using System;
using System.Collections.Generic;
using System.Linq;
using System.Web;
using System.Web.Mvc;

namespace PartyInvites.Controllers {
    public class HomeController : Controller {

        public string Index() {
            return "Hello World";
        }
    }
}
```

These changes don't have a dramatic effect, but they make for a nice demonstration. I have changed the action method called Index so that it returns the string "Hello World". Run the project again by selecting Start Debugging from the Visual Studio Debug menu. The browser will display the result of the Index action method, as shown in Figure 2-8.

Figure 2-8. *The output from the controller action method*

■ **Tip**   Notice that Visual Studio has directed the browser to port 37782. You will almost certainly see a different port number in the URL that your browser requests because Visual Studio allocates a random port when the project is created. If you look in the Windows task bar notification area, you will find an icon for IIS Express. This is a cut-down version of the full IIS application server which is included with Visual Studio and is used to deliver ASP.NET content and services during development. I'll show you how to deploy an MVC project into a production environment in Chapter 13.

Understanding Routes

As well as models, views, and controllers, MVC applications use the ASP.NET *routing system*, which decides how URLs map to controllers and actions. When Visual Studio creates the MVC project, it adds some default routes to get us started. You can request any of the following URLs, and they will be directed to the Index action on the HomeController:

- /
- /Home
- /Home/Index

So, when a browser requests http://yoursite/ or http://yoursite/Home, it gets back the output from HomeController's Index method. You can try this yourself by changing the URL in the browser. At the moment, it will be http://localhost:37782/, except that the port part may be different. If you append /Home or /Home/Index to the URL and hit return, you will see the same Hello World result from the MVC application.

This is a good example of benefiting from following MVC conventions. In this case, the convention is that I will have a controller called HomeController and that it will be the starting point for my MVC application. The default routes that Visual Studio creates for a new project assume that I will follow this convention. And since I *did* follow the convention, I automatically got support for the URLs in the preceding list.

If I had *not* followed the convention, I would need to modify the routes to point to whatever controller I had created instead. For this simple example, the default configuration is all I need.

■ **Tip** You can see and edit your routing configuration by opening the RouteConfig.cs file in the App_Start folder. I explain what the entries in this file do in Chapters 16 and 17.

Rendering Web Pages

The output from the previous example wasn't HTML—it was just the string "Hello World". To produce an HTML response to a browser request, I need a *view*.

Creating and Rendering a View

The first thing I need to do is modify my Index action method, as shown in Listing 2-3.

Listing 2-3. Modifying the Controller to Render a View in the HomeController.cs File

```
using System;
using System.Collections.Generic;
using System.Linq;
using System.Web;
using System.Web.Mvc;

namespace PartyInvites.Controllers {
    public class HomeController : Controller {

        public ViewResult Index() {
            return View();
        }
    }
}
```

The changes in Listing 2-3 are shown in bold. When I return a `ViewResult` object from an action method, I am instructing MVC to *render* a view. I create the `ViewResult` by calling the `View` method with no parameters. This tells MVC to render the *default* view for the action.

If you run the application at this point, you can see the MVC Framework trying to find a default view to use, as shown in the error message displayed in Figure 2-9.

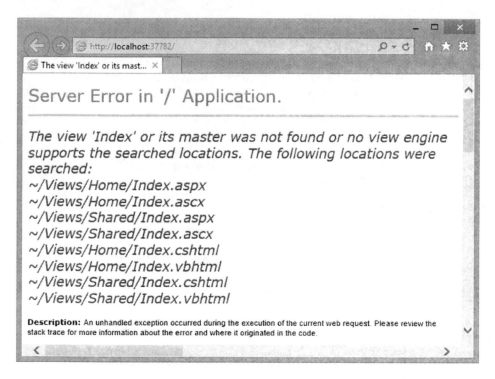

Figure 2-9. The MVC Framework trying to find a default view

This error message is quite helpful. It explains not only that MVC could not find a view for the action method, but it shows where it looked. This is another nice illustration of an MVC convention: views are associated with action methods by a naming convention. The action method is called `Index` and the controller is called `Home` and you can see from Figure 2-9 that MVC is trying to find different files in the `Views` folder that have that name.

The simplest way to create a view is to ask Visual Studio to do it for you. Right-click anywhere in the definition of the `Index` action method in code editor window for the `HomeController.cs` file and select `Add View` from the pop-up menu, as shown in Figure 2-10.

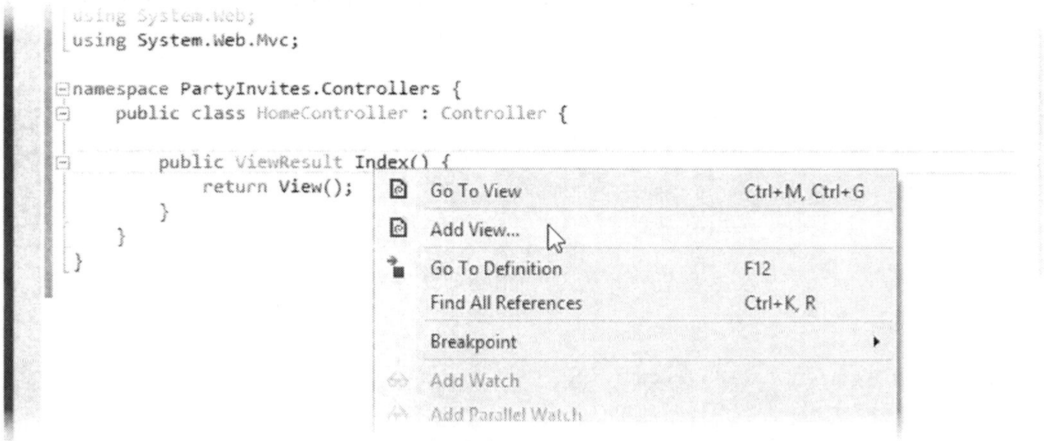

```
using System.Web;
using System.Web.Mvc;

namespace PartyInvites.Controllers {
    public class HomeController : Controller {

        public ViewResult Index() {
            return View();
        }
    }
}
```

Figure 2-10. *Asking Visual Studio to create a view for an action method*

Visual Studio displays the Add View dialog, which allows you to configure the initial contents of the view file that will be created. Set View Name to Index (the name of the action method that the view will be associated with—another convention), set Template to Empty (without model), and leave the Create as a partial view and Use a layout page boxes unchecked, as shown in Figure 2-11. Don't worry about what all of these options mean at the moment—I'll explain all of the details in later chapters. Click the Add button to create the new view file.

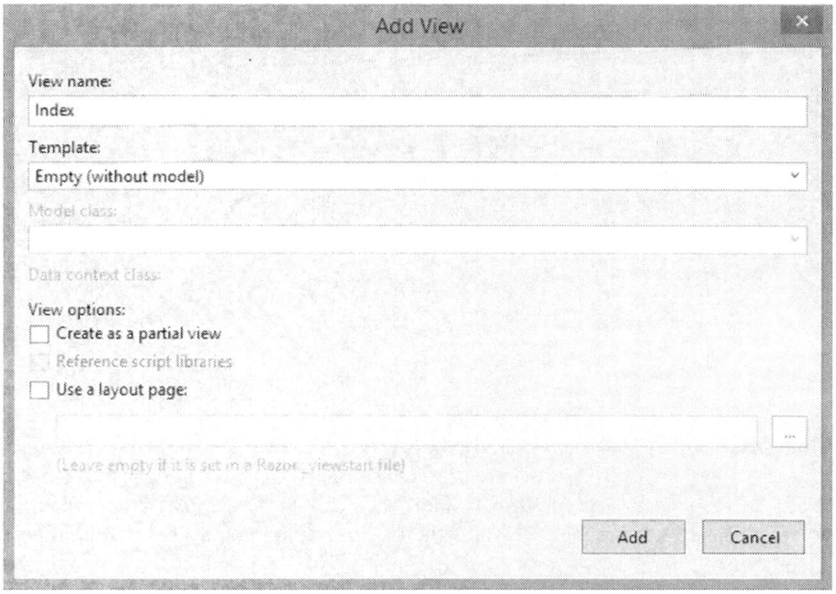

Figure 2-11. *Configuring the initial contents of the view file*

21

Visual Studio will create a file called Index.cshtml in the Views/Home folder. If this isn't the effect you achieve, then delete the file you created and try again. This is another MVC Framework convention: views are placed in the Views folder, organized in folders that correspond to the name of the controller they are associated with.

■ **Tip** The .cshtml file extension denotes a C# view that will be processed by Razor. Early versions of MVC relied on the ASPX view engine, for which view files have the .aspx extension.

The effect of the values I told you to enter into the Add View dialog tell Visual Studio to create the most basic view, the contents of which are shown in Listing 2-4.

Listing 2-4. The Initial Contents of the Index.cshtml File

```
@{
    Layout = null;
}

<!DOCTYPE html>

<html>
<head>
    <meta name="viewport" content="width=device-width" />
    <title>Index</title>
</head>
<body>
    <div>
    </div>
</body>
</html>
```

Visual Studio opens the Index.cshtml file for editing. You'll see that this file contains mostly HTML. The exception is the part that looks like this:

```
...
@{
    Layout = null;
}
...
```

This is an expression that will be interpreted by the Razor view engine, which processes the contents of views and generates HTML that is sent to the browser. This is a simple Razor expression and it tells Razor that I chose not to use a layout, which is like a template for the HTML that will be sent to the browser (and which I describe in Chapter 5). I am going to ignore Razor for the moment and come back to it later. Make the addition to the Index.cshtml file that is shown in bold in Listing 2-5.

Listing 2-5. Adding to the View HTML in the Index.cshtml File

```
@{
    Layout = null;
}
```

```html
<!DOCTYPE html>

<html>
<head>
    <meta name="viewport" content="width=device-width" />
    <title>Index</title>
</head>
<body>
    <div>
        Hello World (from the view)
    </div>
</body>
</html>
```

The addition displays another simple message. Select Start Debugging from the Debug menu to run the application and test the view. You should see something similar to Figure 2-12.

Figure 2-12. *Testing the view*

When I first edited the Index action method, it returned a string value. This meant that MVC did nothing except pass the string value as is to the browser. Now that the Index method returns a ViewResult, the MVC Framework renders a view and returns the HTML it produces. I didn't tell MVC which view should be used, so it used the naming convention to find one automatically. The convention is that the view has the name of the action method and is contained in a folder named after the controller: /Views/Home/Index.cshtml.

I can return other results from action methods besides strings and ViewResult objects. For example, if I return a RedirectResult, the browser will be redirected to another URL. If I return an HttpUnauthorizedResult, I force the user to log in. These objects are collectively known as *action results*, and they are all derived from the ActionResult class. The action result system lets us encapsulate and reuse common responses in actions. I'll tell you more about them and show more complex uses in Chapter 17.

Adding Dynamic Output

The whole point of a web application platform is to construct and display *dynamic* output. In MVC, it is the controller's job to construct some data and pass it to the view, which is responsible for rendering it to HTML.

One way to pass data from the controller to the view is by using the ViewBag object, which is a member of the Controller base class. ViewBag is a dynamic object to which you can assign arbitrary properties, making those values available in whatever view is subsequently rendered. Listing 2-6 demonstrates passing some simple dynamic data in this way in the HomeController.cs file.

Listing 2-6. Setting Some View Data in the HomeController.cs File

```
using System;
using System.Collections.Generic;
using System.Linq;
using System.Web;
using System.Web.Mvc;

namespace PartyInvites.Controllers {
    public class HomeController : Controller {

        public ViewResult Index() {
            int hour = DateTime.Now.Hour;
            ViewBag.Greeting = hour < 12 ? "Good Morning" : "Good Afternoon";
            return View();
        }
    }
}
```

I provide data for the view when I assign a value to the ViewBag.Greeting property. The Greeting property didn't exist until the moment I assigned the value—this allows me to pass data from the controller to the view in a free and fluid manner, without having to define classes ahead of time. I refer to the ViewBag.Greeting property again in the view to get the data value, as illustrated in Listing 2-7, which shows the corresponding change to the Index.cshtml file.

Listing 2-7. Retrieving a ViewBag Data Value in the Index.cshtml File

```
@{
    Layout = null;
}

<!DOCTYPE html>

<html>
<head>
    <meta name="viewport" content="width=device-width" />
    <title>Index</title>
</head>
<body>
    <div>
        @ViewBag.Greeting World (from the view)
    </div>
</body>
</html>
```

The addition to Listing 2-7 is a Razor expression. When I call the View method in the controller's Index method, the MVC framework locates the Index.cshtml view file and asks the Razor view engine to parse the file's content. Razor looks for expressions like the one I added in the listing and processes them. In this example, processing the expression means inserting the value assigned to the ViewBag.Greeting property in the action method into the view.

There's nothing special about the property name Greeting; you could replace this with any property name and it would work the same, just as long as the name you use in the controller matches the name you use in the view. You can pass multiple data values from your controller to the view by assigning values to more than one property. You can see the effect of these changes by starting the project, as shown in Figure 2-13.

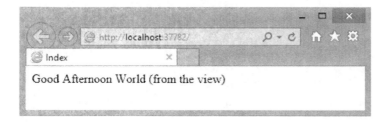

Figure 2-13. *A dynamic response from MVC*

Creating a Simple Data-Entry Application

In the rest of this chapter, I will explore more of the basic MVC features by building a simple data-entry application. I am going to pick up the pace in this section. My goal is to demonstrate MVC in action, so I will skip over some of the explanations as to how things work behind the scenes. But don't worry, I'll revisit these topics in depth in later chapters.

Setting the Scene

Imagine that a friend has decided to host a New Year's Eve party and that she has asked me to create a web app that allows her invitees to electronically RSVP. She has asked for four key features:

- A home page that shows information about the party
- A form that can be used to RSVP
- Validation for the RSVP form, which will display a thank-you page
- RSVPs e-mailed to the party host when complete

In the following sections, I will build up the MVC project I created at the start of the chapter and add these features. I can check the first item off the list by applying what I covered earlier and add some HTML to my existing view to give details of the party. Listing 2-8 shows the additions I made to the Views/Home/Index.cshtml file.

Listing 2-8. Displaying Details of the Party in the Index.cshtml File

```
@{
    Layout = null;
}

<!DOCTYPE html>

<html>
<head>
    <meta name="viewport" content="width=device-width" />
    <title>Index</title>
</head>
<body>
    <div>
        @ViewBag.Greeting World (from the view)
        <p>We're going to have an exciting party.<br />
```

```
        (To do: sell it better. Add pictures or something.)
        </p>
    </div>
</body>
</html>
```

I am on my way. If you run the application, you'll see the details of the party—well, the placeholder for the details, but you get the idea—as shown in Figure 2-14.

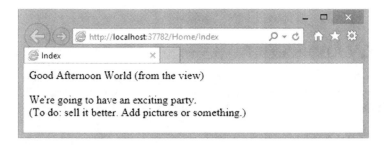

Figure 2-14. *Adding to the view HTML*

Designing a Data Model

In MVC, the *M* stands for *model*, and it is the most important part of the application. The model is the representation of the real-world objects, processes, and rules that define the subject, known as the *domain*, of the application. The model, often referred to as a *domain model*, contains the C# objects (known as *domain objects*) that make up the universe of the application and the methods that manipulate them. The views and controllers expose the domain to the clients in a consistent manner and a well-designed MVC application starts with a well-designed model, which is then the focal point as controllers and views are added.

I don't need a complex model for the PartyInvites application because it is such a simple application and I need to create just one domain class which I will call GuestResponse. This object will be responsible for storing, validating, and confirming an RSVP.

Adding a Model Class

The MVC convention is that the classes that make up a model are placed inside the Models folder, which Visual Studio created as part of the initial project setup. Right-click Models in the Solution Explorer window and select Add followed by Class from the pop-up menus. Set the file name to GuestResponse.cs and click the Add button to create the class. Edit the contents of the class to match Listing 2-9.

■ **Tip**   If you don't have a Class menu item, then you probably left the Visual Studio debugger running. Visual Studio restricts the changes you can make to a project while it is running the application.

Listing 2-9. The GuestResponse Domain Class Defined in the GuestResponse.cs File

```
namespace PartyInvites.Models {
    public class GuestResponse {
        public string Name { get; set; }
        public string Email { get; set; }
        public string Phone { get; set; }
        public bool? WillAttend { get; set; }
    }
}
```

■ **Tip**   You may have noticed that the WillAttend property is a *nullable* bool, which means that it can be true, false, or null. I explain the rationale for this in the Adding Validation section later in the chapter.

Linking Action Methods

One of my application goals is to include an RSVP form, so I need to add a link to it from my Index.cshtml view, as shown in Listing 2-10.

Listing 2-10. Adding a Link to the RSVP Form in the Index.cshtml File

```
@{
    Layout = null;
}

<!DOCTYPE html>

<html>
<head>
    <meta name="viewport" content="width=device-width" />
    <title>Index</title>
</head>
<body>
    <div>
        @ViewBag.Greeting World (from the view)
        <p>We're going to have an exciting party.<br />
        (To do: sell it better. Add pictures or something.)
        </p>
        @Html.ActionLink("RSVP Now", "RsvpForm")
    </div>
</body>
</html>
```

Html.ActionLink is an HTML *helper method*. The MVC Framework comes with a collection of built-in helper methods that are convenient for rendering HTML links, text inputs, checkboxes, selections, and other kinds of content. The ActionLink method takes two parameters: the first is the text to display in the link, and the second is the action to perform when the user clicks the link. I explain the complete set of HTML helper methods in Chapters 21-23. You can see the link that the helper creates by starting the project, as shown in Figure 2-15.

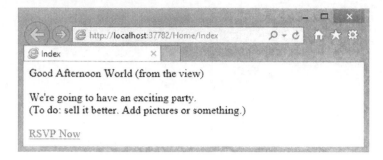

Figure 2-15. *Adding a link to the view*

If you roll your mouse over the link in the browser, you will see that the link points to `http://yourserver/Home/`
`RsvpForm`. The `Html.ActionLink` method has inspected the application's URL routing configuration and determined
that `/Home/RsvpForm` is the URL for an action called `RsvpForm` on a controller called `HomeController`.

■ **Tip** Notice that, unlike traditional ASP.NET applications, MVC URLs do not correspond to physical files. Each action
method has its own URL, and MVC uses the ASP.NET routing system to translate these URLs into actions.

Creating the Action Method

You will see a 404 Not Found error if you click the link. That's because I have not yet created the action method that
corresponds to the `/Home/RsvpForm` URL. I do this by adding a method called `RsvpForm` to the `HomeController` class,
as shown in Listing 2-11.

Listing 2-11. Adding a New Action Method in the HomeController.cs File

```
using System;
using System.Collections.Generic;
using System.Linq;
using System.Web;
using System.Web.Mvc;

namespace PartyInvites.Controllers {
    public class HomeController : Controller {

        public ViewResult Index() {
            int hour = DateTime.Now.Hour;
            ViewBag.Greeting = hour < 12 ? "Good Morning" : "Good Afternoon";
            return View();
        }

        public ViewResult RsvpForm() {
            return View();
        }
    }
}
```

Adding a Strongly Typed View

I am going to add a view for the RsvpForm action method, but in a slightly different way—I am going to create a *strongly typed* view. A strongly typed view is intended to render a specific domain type, and if I specify the type I want to work with (GuestResponse in this case), MVC can create some helpful shortcuts to make it easier.

▓ **Caution**   Make sure your MVC project is compiled before proceeding. If you have created the GuestResponse class but not compiled it, MVC won't be able to create a strongly typed view for this type. To compile your application, select Build Solution from the Visual Studio Build menu.

Right-click the RsvpForm method in the code editor and select Add View from the pop-up menu to open the Add View dialog window. Ensure that the View Name is set as RsvpForm, set Template to Empty and select GuestResponse from the drop-down list for the Model Class field. Leave the View Options boxes unchecked, as shown in Figure 2-16.

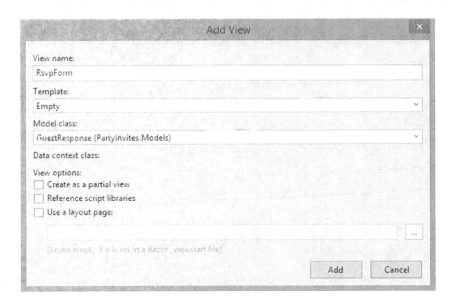

Figure 2-16. *Adding a new view to the project*

Click the Add button and Visual Studio will create a new file called RvspForm.cshtml in the Views/Home folder and open it for editing. You can see the initial contents in Listing 2-12. This is another skeletal HTML file, but it contains a @model Razor expression. As you will see in a moment, this is the key to a strongly typed view and the convenience it offers.

Listing 2-12. The Initial Contents of the RsvpForm.cshtml File

```
@model PartyInvites.Models.GuestResponse

@{
    Layout = null;
}
```

```
<!DOCTYPE html>

<html>
<head>
    <meta name="viewport" content="width=device-width" />
    <title>RsvpForm</title>
</head>
<body>
    <div>
    </div>
</body>
</html>
```

▪ **Tip** The options that you select and check when you create a view determine the initial content of a view file, but that's all. You can change from regular to strongly typed views, for example, just by adding or removing the @model directive in the code editor.

Building the Form

Now that I have created the strongly typed view, I can build out the contents of RsvpForm.cshtml to make it into an HTML form for editing GuestResponse objects, as shown in Listing 2-13.

Listing 2-13. Creating a Form View in the RsvpForm.cshtml File

```
@model PartyInvites.Models.GuestResponse

@{
    Layout = null;
}

<!DOCTYPE html>

<html>
<head>
    <meta name="viewport" content="width=device-width" />
    <title>RsvpForm</title>
</head>
<body>
    @using (Html.BeginForm()) {
        <p>Your name: @Html.TextBoxFor(x => x.Name) </p>
        <p>Your email: @Html.TextBoxFor(x => x.Email)</p>
        <p>Your phone: @Html.TextBoxFor(x => x.Phone)</p>
        <p>
            Will you attend?
            @Html.DropDownListFor(x => x.WillAttend, new[] {
                new SelectListItem() {Text = "Yes, I'll be there",
                    Value = bool.TrueString},
```

```
                    new SelectListItem() {Text = "No, I can't come",
                        Value = bool.FalseString}
                }, "Choose an option")
            </p>
            <input type="submit" value="Submit RSVP" />
        }
    </body>
</html>
```

For each property of the GuestResponse model class, I use an HTML helper method to render a suitable HTML input control. These methods let you select the property that the input element relates to using a lambda expression, like this:

```
...
@Html.TextBoxFor(x => x.Phone)
...
```

The HTML TextBoxFor helper method generates the HTML for an input element, sets the type parameter to text, and sets the id and name attributes to Phone (the name of the selected domain class property) like this:

```
<input id="Phone" name="Phone" type="text" value="" />
```

This handy feature works because the RsvpForm view is strongly typed, and I have told MVC that GuestResponse is the type that I want to render with this view. This provides the HTML helper methods with the information they need to understand which data type I want to read properties from via the @model expression.

Don't worry if you aren't familiar with C# lambda expressions. I provide an overview in Chapter 4, but an alternative to using lambda expressions is to refer to the name of the model type property as a string, like this:

```
...
@Html.TextBox("Email")
...
```

I find that the lambda expression technique prevents me from mistyping the name of the model type property, because Visual Studio IntelliSense pops up and lets me pick the property automatically, as shown in Figure 2-17.

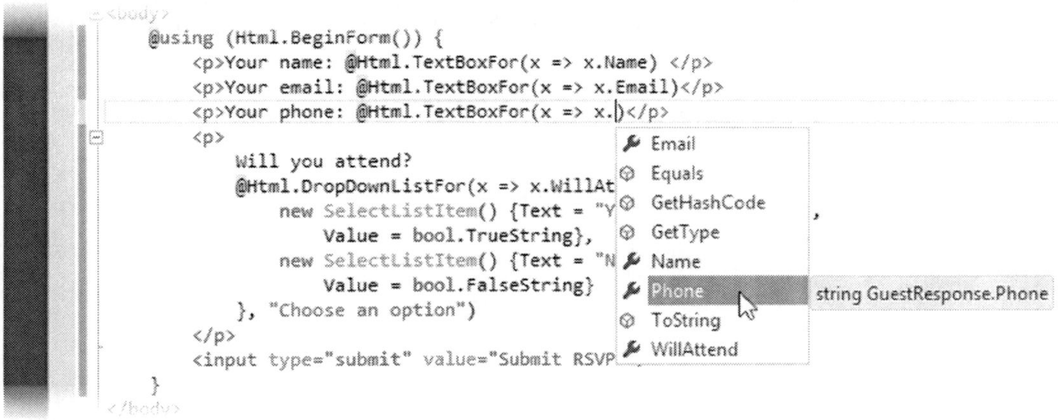

Figure 2-17. *Visual Studio IntelliSense for lambda expressions in HTML helper methods*

Another convenient helper method is `Html.BeginForm`, which generates an HTML `form` element configured to post back to the action method. Because I have not passed any arguments to the helper method, it assumes I want to post back to the same URL that the HTML document was requested from. A neat trick is to wrap this in a C# `using` statement, like this:

```
...
@using (Html.BeginForm()) {
    ...form contents go here...
}
...
```

Normally, when applied like this, the `using` statement ensures that an object is disposed of when it goes out of scope. It is commonly used for database connections, for example, to make sure that they are closed as soon as a query has completed. (This application of the `using` keyword is different from the kind that brings classes in a namespace into scope in a class.)

Instead of disposing of an object, the `HtmlBeginForm` helper closes the HTML `form` element when it goes out of scope. This means that the `Html.BeginForm` helper method creates both parts of a form element, like this:

```
<form action="/Home/RsvpForm" method="post">

    ...form contents go here...

</form>
```

Don't worry if you are not familiar with disposing of C# objects. The point here is to demonstrate how to create a form using the HTML helper method.

Setting the Start URL

Visual Studio will, in an effort to be helpful, make the browser request a URL based on the view that is currently being edited. This is a hit-and-miss feature because it doesn't work when you are editing other kinds of file and because you can't just jump in at any point in most complex web apps.

To set a fixed URL for the browser to request, select `PartyInvites Properties` from the Visual Studio `Project` menu, select the Web section and check the `Specific Page` option in the `Start Action` category, as shown in Figure 2-18. You don't have to enter a value into the field–Visual Studio will request the default URL for the project, which will be directive to the `Index` action method on the `Home` controller. (I show you how to use the URL routing system to change the default mapping in Chapters 15 and 16).

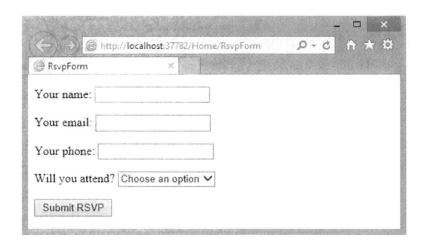

Figure 2-18. *Setting the default start URL for the project*

You can see the form in the RsvpForm view when you run the application and click the RSVP Now link. Figure 2-19 shows the result.

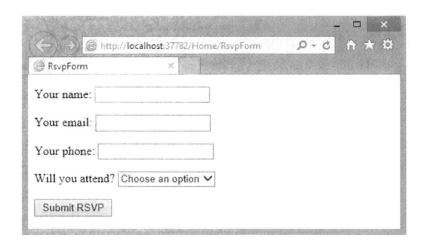

Figure 2-19. *The RspvForm view*

Handling Forms

I have not yet told MVC what I want to do when the form is posted to the server. As things stand, clicking the Submit RSVP button just clears any values you have entered into the form. That is because the form posts back to the RsvpForm action method in the Home controller, which just tells MVC to render the view again.

▪ **Note** You might be surprised that the input data is lost when the view is rendered again. If so, you have probably been developing applications with ASP.NET Web Forms, which automatically preserves data in this situation. I will show you how to achieve the same effect with MVC shortly.

To receive and process submitted form data, I am going to use a clever feature. I will add a second RsvpForm action method in order to create the following:

- *A method that responds to HTTP GET requests*: A GET request is what a browser issues normally each time someone clicks a link. This version of the action will be responsible for displaying the initial blank form when someone first visits /Home/RsvpForm.

- *A method that responds to HTTP POST requests*: By default, forms rendered using Html.BeginForm() are submitted by the browser as a POST request. This version of the action will be responsible for receiving submitted data and deciding what to do with it.

Handing GET and POST requests in separate C# methods helps to keep my controller code tidy, since the two methods have different responsibilities. Both action methods are invoked by the same URL, but MVC makes sure that the appropriate method is called, based on whether I am dealing with a GET or POST request. Listing 2-14 shows the changes I applied to the HomeController class.

Listing 2-14. Adding an Action Method to Support POST Requests in the HomeController.cs File

```
using System;
using System.Collections.Generic;
using System.Linq;
using System.Web;
using System.Web.Mvc;
using PartyInvites.Models;

namespace PartyInvites.Controllers {
    public class HomeController : Controller {

        public ViewResult Index() {
            int hour = DateTime.Now.Hour;
            ViewBag.Greeting = hour < 12 ? "Good Morning" : "Good Afternoon";
            return View();
        }

        [HttpGet]
        public ViewResult RsvpForm() {
            return View();
        }

        [HttpPost]
        public ViewResult RsvpForm(GuestResponse guestResponse) {
            // TODO: Email response to the party organizer
            return View("Thanks", guestResponse);
        }
    }
}
```

I have added the HttpGet attribute to my existing RsvpForm action method. This tells MVC that this method should be used only for GET requests. I then added an overloaded version of RsvpForm, which takes a GuestResponse parameter and applies the HttpPost attribute. The attribute tells MVC that the new method will deal with POST requests. I also imported the PartyInvites.Models namespace—this is just so I can refer to the GuestResponse model type without needing to qualify the class name. I explain how these additions to the listing work in the following sections.

Using Model Binding

The first overload of the RsvpForm action method renders the same view as before–the RsvpForm.cshtml file–to generate the form shown in Figure 2-18.

The second overload is more interesting because of the parameter, but given that the action method will be invoked in response to an HTTP POST request, and that the GuestResponse type is a C# class, how are the two connected?

The answer is *model binding*, an extremely useful MVC feature whereby incoming data is parsed and the key/value pairs in the HTTP request are used to populate properties of domain model types. This process is the opposite of using the HTML helper methods; that is, when creating the form data to send to the client, I generated HTML input elements where the values for the id and name attributes were derived from the model class property names.

In contrast, with model binding, the names of the input elements are used to set the values of the properties in an instance of the model class, which is then passed to the POST-enabled action method.

Model binding is a powerful and customizable feature that eliminates the grind and toil of dealing with HTTP requests directly and lets us work with C# objects rather than dealing with Request.Form[] and Request.QueryString[] values. The GuestResponse object that is passed as the parameter to the action method is automatically populated with the data from the form fields. I dive into the detail of model binding, including how it can be customized, in Chapter 24.

Rendering Other Views

The second overload of the RsvpForm action method also demonstrates how to tell MVC to render a specific view in response to a request, rather than the default view. Here is the relevant statement:

```
...
return View("Thanks", guestResponse);
...
```

This call to the View method tells MVC to find and render a view called Thanks and to pass the GuestResponse object to the view. To create the view I specified, right-click on any of the HomeController methods and select Add View from the pop-up menu and use the Add View dialog to create a strongly typed view called Thanks that uses the GuestResponse model class and that is based on the Empty template. (See the Adding a Strongly Typed View section for step-by-step details if needed). Visual Studio will create the view as Views/Home/Thanks.cshtml. Edit the new view so that it matches Listing 2-15—I have highlighted the markup you need to add.

Listing 2-15. The Contents of the Thanks.cshtml File

```
@model PartyInvites.Models.GuestResponse

@{
    Layout = null;
}
```

```
<!DOCTYPE html>

<html>
<head>
    <meta name="viewport" content="width=device-width" />
    <title>Thanks</title>
</head>
<body>
    <div>
        <h1>Thank you, @Model.Name!</h1>
        @if (Model.WillAttend == true) {
            @:It's great that you're coming. The drinks are already in the fridge!
        } else {
            @:Sorry to hear that you can't make it, but thanks for letting us know.
        }
    </div>
</body>
</html>
```

The Thanks view uses Razor to display content based on the value of the GuestResponse properties that I passed to the View method in the RsvpForm action method. The Razor @model expression specifies the domain model type that the view is strongly typed with. To access the value of a property in the domain object, I use Model.PropertyName. For example, to get the value of the Name property, I call Model.Name. Don't worry if the Razor syntax doesn't make sense—I explain it in more detail in Chapter 5.

Now that I have created the Thanks view, I have a basic working example of handling a form with MVC. Start the application in Visual Studio, click the RSVP Now link, add some data to the form, and click the Submit RSVP button. You will see the result shown in Figure 2-20 (although it will differ if your name is not Joe or you said you could not attend).

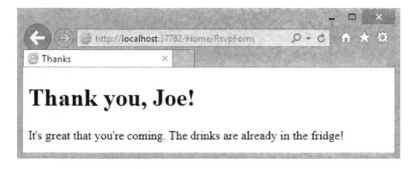

Figure 2-20. *The Thanks view*

Adding Validation

I am now in a position to add validation to my application. Without validation, users could enter nonsense data or even submit an empty form. In an MVC application, validation is typically applied in the domain model, rather than in the user interface. This means that I am able to define validation criteria in one place and have it take effect anywhere in the application that the model class is used. ASP.NET MVC supports *declarative validation rules* defined with attributes from the System.ComponentModel.DataAnnotations namespace, meaning that validation constraints are expressed using the standard C# attribute features. Listing 2-16 shows how I applied these attributes to the GuestResponse model class.

Listing 2-16. Applying Validation in the GuestResponse.cs File

```
using System.ComponentModel.DataAnnotations;

namespace PartyInvites.Models {

    public class GuestResponse {

        [Required(ErrorMessage = "Please enter your name")]
        public string Name { get; set; }

        [Required(ErrorMessage = "Please enter your email address")]
        [RegularExpression(".+\\@.+\\..+",
            ErrorMessage = "Please enter a valid email address")]
        public string Email { get; set; }

        [Required(ErrorMessage = "Please enter your phone number")]
        public string Phone { get; set; }

        [Required(ErrorMessage = "Please specify whether you'll attend")]
        public bool? WillAttend { get; set; }
    }
}
```

The validations rules are shown in bold. MVC automatically detects the attributes and uses them to validate data during the model-binding process. Notice that I have imported the namespace that contains the validations, so I can refer to them without needing to qualify their names.

Tip As noted earlier, I used a nullable `bool` for the `WillAttend` property. I did this so that I could apply the `Required` validation attribute. If I had used a regular `bool`, the value I received through model binding could be only `true` or `false`, and I wouldn't be able to tell if the user had selected a value. A nullable `bool` has three possible values: `true`, `false`, and `null`. The `null` value will be used if the user hasn't selected a value, and this causes the `Required` attribute to report a validation error. This is a nice example of how the MVC Framework elegantly blends C# features with HTML and HTTP.

I check to see if there has been a validation problem using the `ModelState.IsValid` property in the controller class. Listing 2-17 shows how I have done this in the POST-enabled `RsvpForm` action method in the `Home` controller class.

Listing 2-17. Checking for Form Validation Errors in the HomeController.cs File

```
...
[HttpPost]
public ViewResult RsvpForm(GuestResponse guestResponse) {
    if (ModelState.IsValid) {
        // TODO: Email response to the party organizer
        return View("Thanks", guestResponse);
    } else {
        // there is a validation error
        return View();
    }
}
...
```

If there are no validation errors, I tell MVC to render the Thanks view, just as I did previously. If there *are* validation errors, I re-render the RsvpForm view by calling the View method without any parameters.

Just displaying the form when there is an error is not helpful—I also need to provide the user with some indication of what the problem is and why I could not accept their form submission. I do this by using the Html.ValidationSummary helper method in the RsvpForm view, as shown in Listing 2-18.

Listing 2-18. Using the Html.ValidationSummary Helper Method in the RsvpForm.cshtml File

```
@model PartyInvites.Models.GuestResponse

@{
    Layout = null;
}

<!DOCTYPE html>

<html>
<head>
    <meta name="viewport" content="width=device-width" />
    <title>RsvpForm</title>
</head>
<body>
    @using (Html.BeginForm()) {
        @Html.ValidationSummary()
        <p>Your name: @Html.TextBoxFor(x => x.Name) </p>
        <p>Your email: @Html.TextBoxFor(x => x.Email)</p>
        <p>Your phone: @Html.TextBoxFor(x => x.Phone)</p>
        <p>
            Will you attend?
            @Html.DropDownListFor(x => x.WillAttend, new[] {
                new SelectListItem() {Text = "Yes, I'll be there",
                    Value = bool.TrueString},
                new SelectListItem() {Text = "No, I can't come",
                    Value = bool.FalseString}
            }, "Choose an option")
        </p>
        <input type="submit" value="Submit RSVP" />
    }
</body>
</html>
```

If there are no errors, the Html.ValidationSummary method creates a hidden list item as a placeholder in the form. MVC makes the placeholder visible and adds the error messages defined by the validation attributes. You can see how this appears in Figure 2-21.

Figure 2-21. *The validation summary*

The user won't be shown the Thanks view until all of the validation constraints applied to the GuestResponse class have been satisfied. Notice that the data entered into the form was preserved and displayed again when the view was rendered with the validation summary. This is another benefit of the model binding feature and it simplifies working with form data.

■ **Note** If you have worked with ASP.NET Web Forms, you will know that Web Forms has a concept of *server controls* that retain state by serializing values into a hidden form field called __VIEWSTATE. ASP.NET MVC model binding is not related to the Web Forms concepts of server controls, postbacks, or View State. ASP.NET MVC does not inject a hidden __VIEWSTATE field into your rendered HTML pages.

Highlighting Invalid Fields

The HTML helper methods that create text boxes, drop-downs, and other elements have a handy feature that can be used in conjunction with model binding. The same mechanism that preserves the data that a user entered in a form can also be used to highlight individual fields that failed the validation checks.

When a model class property has failed validation, the HTML helper methods will generate slightly different HTML. As an example, here is the HTML that a call to Html.TextBoxFor(x => x.Name) generates when there is no validation error:

```
<input data-val="true" data-val-required="Please enter your name" id="Name" name="Name"

    type="text" value="" />
```

And here is the HTML the same call generates when the user doesn't provide a value (which is a validation error because I applied the Required attribute to the Name property in the GuestResponse model class):

```
<input class="input-validation-error" data-val="true" data-val-required="Please enter your name"
id="Name" name="Name" type="text" value="" />
```

I have highlighted the difference in bold: the helper method added a class called input-validation-error to the input element. I can take advantage of this feature by creating a style sheet that contains CSS styles for this class and the others that different HTML helper methods apply.

The convention in MVC projects is that static content, such as CSS style sheets, is placed into a folder called Content. Create this folder by right-clicking on the PartyInvites item in the Solution Explorer, selecting Add ➤ New Folder from the menu and setting the name to Content.

To create the CSS file, right click on the newly created Content folder, select Add ➤ New Item from the menu and choose Style Sheet from the set of item templates. Set the name of the new file to Styles.css, as shown in Figure 2-22.

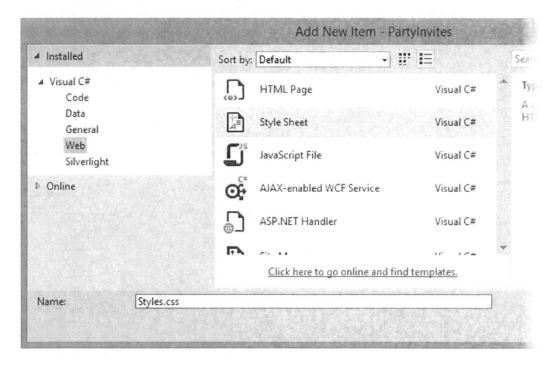

Figure 2-22. *Creating a new style sheet*

Click the Add button and Visual Studio will create the Content/Styles.css file. Set the content of the new file to match Listing 2-19.

Listing 2-19. The Contents of the Styles.css File

```
.field-validation-error      {color: #f00;}
.field-validation-valid      { display: none;}
.input-validation-error      { border: 1px solid #f00; background-color: #fee; }
.validation-summary-errors   { font-weight: bold; color: #f00;}
.validation-summary-valid    { display: none;}
```

To use this style sheet, I add a new reference to the head section of RsvpForm view, as shown in Listing 2-20. You add link elements to views just as you would to a regular static HTML file, although in Chapter 27, I show you the *bundles* feature that allows JavaScript and CSS style sheets to be consolidated and delivered to the browsers over a single HTTP request.

⬛ **Tip**   You can drag JavaScript and CSS files from the Solution Explorer windows and drop them on the code editor. Visual Studio will create `script` and `link` elements for the files you have selected.

Listing 2-20. Adding the Link Element in the RsvpForm.cshtml File

```
@model PartyInvites.Models.GuestResponse

@{
    Layout = null;
}

<!DOCTYPE html>

<html>
<head>
    <meta name="viewport" content="width=device-width" />
    <link rel="stylesheet" type="text/css" href="~/Content/Styles.css" />
    <title>RsvpForm</title>
</head>
<body>
    @using (Html.BeginForm()) {
        @Html.ValidationSummary()
        <p>Your name: @Html.TextBoxFor(x => x.Name) </p>
        <p>Your email: @Html.TextBoxFor(x => x.Email)</p>
        <p>Your phone: @Html.TextBoxFor(x => x.Phone)</p>
        <p>
            Will you attend?
            @Html.DropDownListFor(x => x.WillAttend, new[] {
                new SelectListItem() {Text = "Yes, I'll be there",
                    Value = bool.TrueString},
                new SelectListItem() {Text = "No, I can't come",
                    Value = bool.FalseString}
            }, "Choose an option")
        </p>
        <input type="submit" value="Submit RSVP" />
    }
</body>
</html>
```

⬛ **Tip**   If you have moved to MVC 5 directly from MVC 3, you might have been expecting us to have added the CSS file to the view by specifying the `href` attribute as `@Href("~/Content/Site.css")` or `@Url.Content("~/Content/Site.css")`. As of MVC 4, Razor detects attributes that begin with `~/` and automatically inserts the `@Href` or `@Url` call for you.

With the application of the style sheet, a more visually obvious validation error will be displayed when data is submitted that causes a validation error, as shown in Figure 2-23.

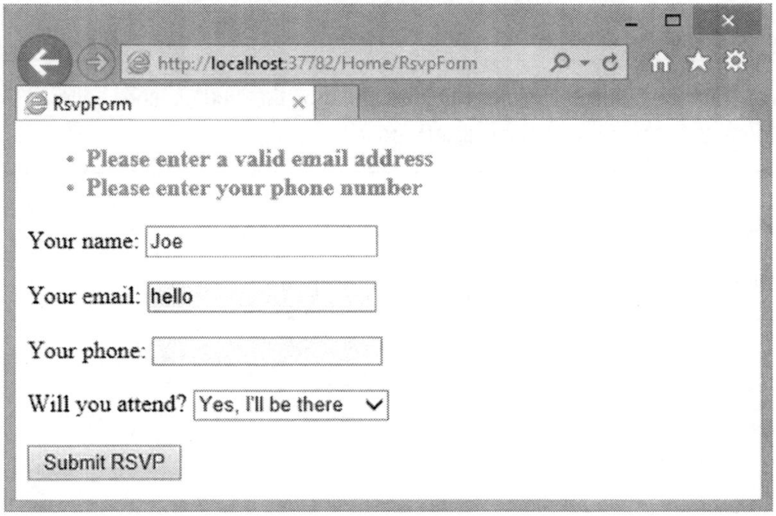

Figure 2-23. *Automatically highlighted validation errors*

Styling the Content

The basic functionality of the application is in place – except for sending emails, which I'll get to shortly–but the overall appearance is pretty poor. Although this is a book focused on server-side development, Microsoft has adopted a number of open source libraries and included them in some of the Visual Studio project templates.

I am not a fan of these templates, but I do like some of the libraries they use and one of the new adoptees in MVC 5 is Bootstrap, which is a nice CSS library originally developed by Twitter that has become widely used.

You don't have to use the Visual Studio project templates to use libraries like Bootstrap, of course. You can download files directly from project web sites or use NuGet, which is integrated into Visual Studio and provides access to a catalogue of pre-packaged software that can be downloaded and installed automatically. One of the best NuGet features is that it manages dependencies between packages such that if you install Bootstrap, for example, NuGet will also download and install jQuery which some Bootstrap features depend on.

Using NuGet to Install Bootstrap

To install the Bootstrap package, select Library Package Manager ➤ Package Manager Console from the Visual Studio Tools menu. Visual Studio will open the NuGet command line. Enter the following command and hit return:

```
Install-Package -version 3.0.0 bootstrap
```

The Install-Package command tells NuGet to download a package and its dependencies and add them to the project. The name of the package I want is called bootstrap, and you can search for package names either from the NuGet web site (http://www.nuget.org) or using the Visual Studio NuGet user interface (select Tools ➤ Library Package Manager ➤ Manage NuGet Packages for Solution).

I have used –version to specify that I want Bootstrap version 3, which is the latest stable version available as I write this. Without –version, NuGet would have downloaded the latest version of the package, but I want to make sure that you are able to recreate the examples exactly as I have shown them and so installing a specific version helps me to ensure consistency.

NuGet will download all of the files required for Bootstrap and for jQuery, which Bootstrap relies on. CSS files are added to the Content folder and a Scripts folder is created (which is the standard MVC location for JavaScript files) and populated with Bootstrap and jQuery files. (A fonts folder is also created–this is a quirk of the Bootstrap typography features, which expect files to be in certain locations).

■ **Note**   The reason that I am showing you Bootstrap in this chapter is to illustrate how readily the HTML generated by the MVC Framework can be used with popular CSS and JavaScript libraries. I don't want to lose my focus on server-side development, however, and so if you want complete details of the *client*-side aspects of working with the MVC Framework, then see my book *Pro ASP.NET MVC 5 Client*, which will be published by Apress in 2014.

Styling the Index View

The basic Bootstrap features work by applying classes to elements that correspond to CSS selectors defined in the files added to the Content folder. You can get full details of the classes that Bootstrap defines from http://getbootstrap.com, but you can see how I have applied some basic styling to the Index.cshtml view file in Listing 2-21.

Listing 2-21. Adding Bootstrap to the Index.cshtml File

```
@{
    Layout = null;
}

<!DOCTYPE html>

<html>
<head>
    <meta name="viewport" content="width=device-width" />
    <link href="~/Content/bootstrap.css" rel="stylesheet" />
    <link href="~/Content/bootstrap-theme.css" rel="stylesheet" />
    <title>Index</title>
    <style>
        .btn a { color: white; text-decoration: none}
        body { background-color: #F1F1F1; }
    </style>
</head>
<body>
    <div class="text-center">
        <h2>We're going to have an exciting party!</h2>
        <h3>And you are invited</h3>
        <div class="btn btn-success">
            @Html.ActionLink("RSVP Now", "RsvpForm")
        </div>
    </div>
</body>
</html>
```

I have added link elements for the bootstrap.css and bootstrap-theme.css files in the Content folder. These are the Bootstrap files required for the basic CSS styling that the library provides and there is a corresponding JavaScript file in the Scripts folder, but I won't need it in this chapter. I have also defined a style element that sets the background color for the body element and styles the text for a elements.

■ **Tip** You will notice that each of the Bootstrap files in the Content folder has a twin with the prefix min—e.g., bootstrap.css and bootstrap.min.cs. It is common practice to *minify* JavaScript and CSS files when deploying an application into production, which is a process of removing all of the whitespace and, in the case of JavaScript, replacing the function and variable names with shorter labels. The goal of minification is to reduce the amount of bandwidth required to deliver your content to the browser and in Chapter 27, I describe the ASP.NET features for managing this process automatically. For this chapter—and most of the other chapters in this book—I will use the regular files, which is normal practice during development and testing.

Having imported the Bootstrap styles and defined a couple of my own, I need to style my elements. This is a simple example and so I only need to use three Bootstrap CSS classes: text-center, btn and btn-success.

The text-center class centers the content of an element and its children. The btn class styles a button, input or a element as a pretty button and the btn-success specifies which of a range of colors I want the button to be. The color of the button depends on the theme that is being used—I have the default theme (as defined by the bootstrap-theme.css file), but there are endless replacements available with a search online. You can see the effect that I have created in Figure 2-24.

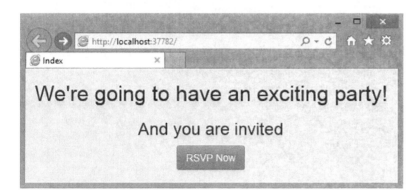

Figure 2-24. *Styling the Index view*

It will be obvious to you that I am not a web designer. In fact, as a child, I was excused from art lessons on the basis that I had absolutely no talent whatsoever. This had the happy result of making more time for math lessons but meant that my artistic skills have not developed beyond those of the average 10 year old. For a real project, I would seek a professional to help design and style the content, but for this example I am going it alone and that means applying Bootstrap with as much restraint and consistency as I can muster.

Styling the RsvpForm View

Bootstrap defines classes that can be used to style forms. I am not going to go into detail, but you can see how I have applied these classes in Listing 2-22.

Listing 2-22. Adding Bootstrap to the RsvpForm.cshtml File

```
@model PartyInvites.Models.GuestResponse

@{
    Layout = null;
}

<!DOCTYPE html>

<html>
<head>
    <link href="~/Content/bootstrap.css" rel="stylesheet" />
    <link href="~/Content/bootstrap-theme.css" rel="stylesheet" />
    <meta name="viewport" content="width=device-width" />
    <link href="~/Content/Styles.css" rel="stylesheet" />
    <title>RsvpForm</title>
</head>
<body>
    <div class="panel panel-success">
        <div class="panel-heading text-center"><h4>RSVP</h4></div>
        <div class="panel-body">
            @using (Html.BeginForm()) {
                @Html.ValidationSummary()
                <div class="form-group">
                    <label>Your name:</label>
                    @Html.TextBoxFor(x => x.Name, new { @class = "form-control"})
                </div>
                <div class="form-group">
                    <label>Your email:</label>
                    @Html.TextBoxFor(x => x.Email, new { @class = "form-control"})
                </div>
                <div class="form-group">
                    <label>Your phone:</label>
                    @Html.TextBoxFor(x => x.Phone, new { @class = "form-control"})
                </div>
                <div class="form-group">
                    <label>Will you attend?</label>
                    @Html.DropDownListFor(x => x.WillAttend, new[] {
                            new SelectListItem() {Text = "Yes, I'll be there",
                                Value = bool.TrueString},
                            new SelectListItem() {Text = "No, I can't come",
                                Value = bool.FalseString}
                        }, "Choose an option", new { @class = "form-control" })
                </div>
                <div class="text-center">
                    <input class="btn btn-success" type="submit" value="Submit RSVP" />
                </div>
            }
        </div>
    </div>
</body>
</html>
```

The Bootstrap classes in this example create a panel with a header, just to give structure to the layout. To style the form, I have used the form-group class, which is used to style the element that contains the label and the associated input or select element.

These elements are created using HTML helper methods, which means that there are not statically defined elements available to which I can apply the required form-control class. Fortunately, the helper methods take an optional object argument that lets me specify attributes on the elements that they create, as follows:

```
...
@Html.TextBoxFor(x => x.Name, new { @class = "form-control"})
...
```

I created the object using the C# *anonymous type* feature, which I describe in Chapter 4 and specified that the class attribute should be set to form-control on the element that the TextBoxFor helper generates. The properties defined by the object are used for the name of the attribute added to the HTML element and class is a reserved word in the C# language, so I have to prefix it with @. This is a standard C# feature that allows keywords to be used in expressions. You can see the result of my styles in Figure 2-25.

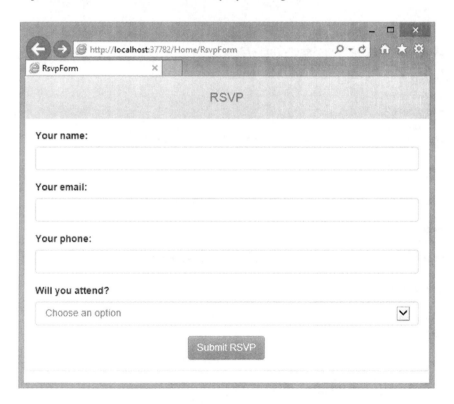

Figure 2-25. *Styling the RsvpForm view*

Styling the Thanks View

The last view file to style is Thanks.cshtml and you can see how I have done this in Listing 2-23. You will notice that the markup I have added is similar to that in the Index.cshtml view. To make an application easier to manage, it is a good principal to avoid duplicating code and markup wherever possible and in Chapter 5 I will introduce you to Razor *layouts* and in Chapter 20, I describe *partial views*, both of which can be used to reduce duplication of markup.

Listing 2-23. Applying Bootstrap to the Thanks.cshtml File

```
@model PartyInvites.Models.GuestResponse

@{
    Layout = null;
}

<!DOCTYPE html>

<html>
<head>
    <link href="~/Content/bootstrap.css" rel="stylesheet" />
    <link href="~/Content/bootstrap-theme.css" rel="stylesheet" />
    <meta name="viewport" content="width=device-width" />
    <title>Thanks</title>
    <style>
        body { background-color: #F1F1F1; }
    </style>
</head>
<body>
    <div class="text-center">
        <h1>Thank you, @Model.Name!</h1>
        <div class="lead">
            @if (Model.WillAttend == true) {
                @:It's great that you're coming. The drinks are already in the fridge!
            } else {
                @:Sorry to hear that you can't make it, but thanks for letting us know.
            }
        </div>
    </div>
</body>
</html>
```

The lead class applies one of the Bootstrap typographic styles and you can see the effect in Figure 2-26.

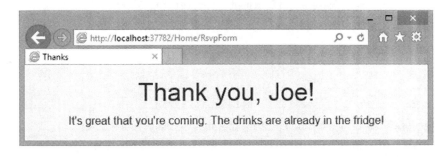

Figure 2-26. *Styling the Thanks View*

Completing the Example

The last requirement for my example application is to e-mail completed RSVPs to the party organizer. I could do this by adding an action method to create and send an e-mail message using the e-mail classes in the .NET Framework–and that would be the technique which is most consistent with the MVC pattern. Instead, I am going to use the WebMail helper method. This is not part of the MVC framework, but it does let me complete this example without getting mired in the details of setting up other means of sending e-mail. I want the e-mail message to be sent as I render the Thanks view. Listing 2-24 show the changes that I need to apply.

Listing 2-24. Using the WebMail Helper in the Thanks.cshtml File

```
...
<body>
    @{
        try {
            WebMail.SmtpServer = "smtp.example.com";
            WebMail.SmtpPort = 587;
            WebMail.EnableSsl = true;
            WebMail.UserName = "mySmtpUsername";
            WebMail.Password = "mySmtpPassword";
            WebMail.From = "rsvps@example.com";

            WebMail.Send("party-host@example.com", "RSVP Notification",
                Model.Name + " is " + ((Model.WillAttend ?? false) ? "" : "not")
                    + "attending");

        } catch (Exception) {
            @:<b>Sorry - we couldn't send the email to confirm your RSVP.</b>
        }
    }
    <div class="text-center">
        <h1>Thank you, @Model.Name!</h1>
        <div class="lead">
            @if (Model.WillAttend == true) {
                @:It's great that you're coming. The drinks are already in the fridge!
            } else {
                @:Sorry to hear that you can't make it, but thanks for letting us know.
            }
        </div>
    </div>
</body>
...
```

> ▪ **Note**   I used the WebMail helper because it lets us demonstrate sending an e-mail message with a minimum of effort. Typically, however, I would prefer to put this functionality in an action method. I will explain why when I describe the MVC architecture pattern in Chapter 3.

I have added a Razor expression that uses the WebMail helper to configure the details of my e-mail server, including the server name, whether the server requires SSL connections, and account details. Once I have configured all of the details, I use the WebMail.Send method to send the e-mail.

I enclosed all of the e-mail code in a try...catch block so that I can alert the user if the e-mail is not sent. I do this by adding a block of text to the output of the Thanks view. A better approach would be to display a separate error view when the e-mail message cannot be sent, but I wanted to keep things simple for this first MVC application.

Summary

In this chapter, I created a new MVC project and used it to construct a simple MVC data-entry application, giving you a first glimpse of the MVC Framework architecture and approach. I skipped over some key features (including Razor syntax, routing, and automated testing), but I come back to these topics in depth in later chapters. In the next chapter, I describe the MVC architecture, design patterns, and techniques that I use throughout the rest of this book and which form the foundation for effective development with the MVC Framework.

CHAPTER 3

■ ■ ■

The MVC Pattern

Before I start digging into the details of the ASP.NET MVC Framework, I want to make sure you are familiar with the MVC design pattern and the thinking behind it. In this chapter, I describe the following:

- The MVC architecture pattern
- Domain models and repositories
- Creating loosely coupled systems using dependency injection (DI)
- The basics of automated testing

You might be familiar with some of the ideas and conventions I discuss in this chapter, especially if you have done advanced ASP.NET or C# development. If not, I encourage you to read carefully—a good understanding of what lies behind MVC can help put the features of the framework into context as you continue through the book.

The History of MVC

The term *model-view-controller* has been in use since the late 1970s and arose from the Smalltalk project at Xerox PARC, where it was conceived as a way to organize some early GUI applications. Some of the fine detail of the original MVC pattern was tied to Smalltalk-specific concepts, such as *screens* and *tools*, but the broader concepts are still applicable to applications—and they are especially well suited to Web applications.

Interactions with an MVC application follow a natural cycle of user actions and view updates, where the view is assumed to be stateless. This fits nicely with the HTTP requests and responses that underpin a Web application.

Further, MVC forces a *separation of concerns*—the domain model and controller logic are decoupled from the user interface. In a Web application, this means that the HTML is kept apart from the rest of the application, which makes maintenance and testing simpler and easier. It was Ruby on Rails that led to renewed mainstream interest in MVC and it remains the implementation template for the MVC pattern. Many other MVC frameworks have since emerged and demonstrated the benefits of MVC—including, of course, ASP.NET MVC.

Understanding the MVC Pattern

In high-level terms, the MVC pattern means that an MVC application will be split into at least three pieces:

- *Models*, which contain or represent the data that users work with. These can be simple *view models*, which just represent data being transferred between views and controllers; or they can be *domain models*, which contain the data in a business domain as well as the operations, transformations, and rules for manipulating that data.
- *Views,* which are used to render some part of the model as a user interface.
- *Controllers*, which process incoming requests, perform operations on the model, and select views to render to the user.

Models are the definition of the universe your application works in. In a banking application, for example, the model represents everything in the bank that the application supports, such as accounts, the general ledger, and credit limits for customers—as well as the operations that can be used to manipulate the data in the model, such as depositing funds and making withdrawals from the accounts. The model is also responsible for preserving the overall state and consistency of the data—for example, making sure that all transactions are added to the ledger, and that a client doesn't withdraw more money than he is entitled to or more money than the bank has.

Models are also defined by what they are *not* responsible for: models don't deal with rendering UIs or processing requests—those are the responsibilities of *views* and *controllers*. *Views* contain the logic required to display elements of the model to the user—and nothing more. They have no direct awareness of the model and do not directly communicate with the model in any way. *Controllers* are the bridge between views and the model—requests come in from the client and are serviced by the controller, which selects an appropriate view to show the user and, if required, an appropriate operation to perform on the model.

Each piece of the MVC architecture is well-defined and self-contained—this is referred to as the *separation of concerns*. The logic that manipulates the data in the model is contained *only* in the model; the logic that displays data is *only* in the view, and the code that handles user requests and input is contained *only* in the controller. With a clear division between each of the pieces, your application will be easier to maintain and extend over its lifetime, no matter how large it becomes.

Understanding the Domain Model

The most important part of an MVC application is the domain model. We create the model by identifying the real-world entities, operations, and rules that exist in the industry or activity that the application must support, known as the *domain*.

We then create a software representation of the domain: the *domain model*. For the purposes of the ASP.NET MVC Framework, the domain model is a set of C# types (classes, structs, etc.), collectively known as the *domain types*. The operations from the domain are represented by the methods defined in the domain types, and the domain rules are expressed in the logic inside of these methods—or, as you saw in the previous chapter, by applying C# attributes. When an instance of a domain type is created to represent a specific piece of data, it is called a *domain object*. Domain models are usually persistent and long-lived—there are lots of different ways of achieving this, but relational databases remain the most common choice.

In short, a domain model is the single, authoritative definition of the business data and processes within your application. A *persistent* domain model is also the authoritative definition of the state of your domain representation.

The domain model approach solves many of the problems that arise when maintaining an application. If you need to manipulate the data in your model or add a new process or rule, the domain model is the only part of your application that has to be changed.

■ **Tip**   A common way of enforcing the separation of the domain model from the rest of an ASP.NET MVC application is to place the model in a separate C# assembly. In this way, you can create references *to* the domain model from other parts of the application but ensure that there are no references in the other direction. This is particularly useful in large-scale projects. I demonstrate this approach in the example I start building in Chapter 7.

The ASP.NET Implementation of MVC

In MVC, controllers are C# classes, usually derived from the `System.Web.Mvc.Controller` class. Each `public` method in a class derived from `Controller` is an *action method*, which is associated with a configurable URL through the ASP.NET routing system. When a request is sent to the URL associated with an action method, the statements in the controller class are executed in order to perform some operation on the domain model and then select a view to display to the client. Figure 3-1 shows the interactions between the controller, model, and view.

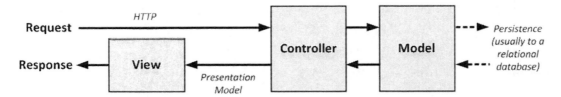

Figure 3-1. *The interactions in an MVC application*

The ASP.NET MVC Framework uses a *view engine*, which is the component responsible for processing a view in order to generate a response for the browser. Earlier versions of MVC used the standard ASP.NET view engine, which processed ASPX pages using a streamlined version of the Web Forms markup syntax. MVC 3 introduced the Razor view engine, which was refined in MVC 4 (and unchanged in MVC5) and that uses a different syntax entirely, which I describe in Chapter 5).

■ **Tip** Visual Studio provides IntelliSense support for Razor, making it a simple matter to inject and respond to view data supplied by the controller.

ASP.NET MVC doesn't apply any constraints on the implementation of your domain model. You can create a model using regular C# objects and implement persistence using any of the databases, object-relational mapping frameworks, or other data tools supported by .NET.

Comparing MVC to Other Patterns

MVC is not the only software architecture pattern, of course. There are many others and some of them are, or at least have been, extremely popular. We can learn a lot about MVC by looking at the alternatives. In the following sections, I briefly describe different approaches to structuring an application and contrast them with MVC. Some of the patterns are close variations on the MVC theme, whereas others are entirely different.

I am not suggesting that MVC is the perfect pattern for all situations. I am a proponent of picking the best approach to solve the problem at hand. As you will see, there are situations where some competing patterns are as useful as or better than MVC. I encourage you to make an *informed* and *deliberate* choice when selecting a pattern. The fact that you are reading this book suggests that you already have a certain commitment to the MVC pattern, but it is always helpful to maintain the widest possible perspective.

Understanding the Smart UI Pattern

One of the most common design patterns is known as the *smart user interface* (smart UI). Most programmers have created a smart UI application at some point in their careers—I certainly have. If you have used Windows Forms or ASP.NET Web Forms, you have too.

To build a smart UI application, developers construct a user interface, often by dragging a set of *components* or *controls* onto a design surface or canvas. The controls report interactions with the user by emitting events for button presses, keystrokes, mouse movements, and so on. The developer adds code to respond to these events in a series of *event handlers*: small blocks of code that are called when a specific event on a specific component is emitted. This creates a monolithic application, as shown in Figure 3-2. The code that handles the user interface and the business is all mixed together with no separation of concerns at all. The code that defines the acceptable values for a data input, that queries for data or modifies a user account, ends up in little pieces, coupled together by the order in which events are expected.

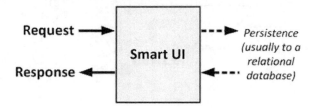

Figure 3-2. *The Smart UI pattern*

Smart UIs are ideal for simple projects because you can get some good results fast (by comparison to MVC development which, as you'll see in Chapter 7, requires some careful preparation and initial investment before getting results). Smart UIs are also suited to user interface prototyping. These design surface tools can be *really* good, although I always find the Web Forms design surface in Visual Studio to be awkward and unpredictable. If you are sitting with a customer and want to capture the requirements for the look and flow of the interface, a Smart UI tool can be a quick and responsive way to generate and test different ideas.

The biggest drawback is that Smart UIs are difficult to maintain and extend. Mixing the domain model and business logic code in with the user interface code leads to duplication, where the same fragment of business logic is copied and pasted to support a newly added component. Finding all of the duplicate parts and applying a fix can be difficult. It can be almost impossible to add a new feature without breaking an existing one. Testing a Smart UI application can also be difficult. The only way is to simulate user interactions, which is far from ideal and a difficult basis from which to provide full test coverage.

In the world of MVC, the Smart UI is often referred to as an *anti-pattern*: something that should be avoided at all costs. This antipathy arises, at least in part, because people come to MVC looking for an alternative after spending part of their careers trying to develop and maintain Smart UI applications.

Although it is a common point of view, it is overly simplistic and it is a mistake to reject the Smart UI pattern out of hand. Not everything is rotten in the Smart UI pattern and there are positive aspects to this approach. Smart UI applications are quick and easy to develop. The component and design tool producers have put a lot of effort into making the development experience a pleasant one, and even the most inexperienced programmer can produce something professional-looking and reasonably functional in just a few hours.

The biggest weakness of Smart UI applications—maintainability—doesn't arise in small development efforts. If you are producing a simple tool for a small audience, a Smart UI application can be a perfect solution. The additional complexity of an MVC application simply isn't warranted.

Understanding the Model-View Architecture

The area in which maintenance problems tend to arise in a Smart UI application is in the business logic, which ends up so diffused across the application that making changes or adding features becomes a fraught process. An improvement in this area is offered by the *model-view* architecture, which pulls out the business logic into a separate domain model. In doing this, the data, processes, and rules are all concentrated in one part of the application, as shown in Figure 3-3.

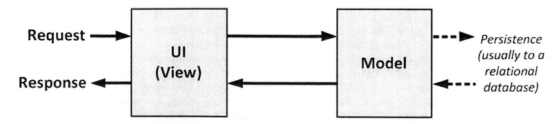

Figure 3-3. *The model-view pattern*

The model-view architecture can be an improvement over the monolithic Smart UI pattern—it is much easier to maintain, for example–but two problems arise. The first is that since the UI and the domain model are closely integrated, it can be difficult to perform unit testing on either. The second problem arises from practice, rather than the definition of the pattern. The model typically contains a mass of data access code—this need not be the case, but it usually is—and this means that the data model does not contain just the business data, operations, and rules.

Understanding Classic Three-Tier Architectures

To address the problems of the model-view architecture, the *three-tier* or *three-layer* pattern separates the persistence code from the domain model and places it in a new component called the *ddata access layer* (DAL). This is shown in Figure 3-4.

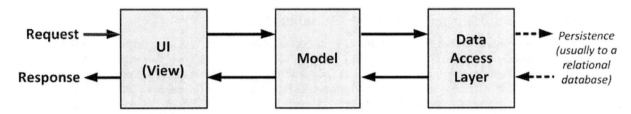

Figure 3-4. *The three-tier pattern*

The three-tier architecture is the most widely used pattern for business applications. It has no constraints on how the UI is implemented and provides good separation of concerns without being too complicated. And, with some care, the DAL can be created so that unit testing is relatively easy. You can see the obvious similarities between a classic three-tier application and the MVC pattern. The difference is that when the UI layer is directly coupled to a click-and-event GUI framework (such as Windows Forms or ASP.NET Web Forms), it becomes almost impossible to perform automated unit tests. And because the UI part of a three-tier application can be complex, there's a lot of code that can't be rigorously tested.

In the worst scenario, the three-tier pattern's lack of enforced discipline in the UI tier means that many such applications end up as thinly disguised Smart UI applications, with no real separation of concerns. This gives the worst possible outcome: an untestable, unmaintainable application that is excessively complex.

Understanding Variations on MVC

I have already described the core design principles of MVC applications, especially as they apply to the ASP.NET MVC implementation. Others interpret aspects of the pattern differently and have added to, adjusted, or otherwise adapted MVC to suit the scope and subject of their projects. In the following sections, I provide a brief overview of the two most prevalent variations on the MVC theme. Understanding these variations is not essential to working with ASP.NET MVC and I have included this information just for completeness because you will hear the terms used in most discussions of software patterns.

Understanding the Model-View-Presenter Pattern

Model-view-presenter (MVP) is a variation on MVC that is designed to fit more easily with stateful GUI platforms such as Windows Forms or ASP.NET Web Forms. This is a worthwhile attempt to get the best aspects of the Smart UI pattern without the problems it usually brings.

In this pattern, the presenter has the same responsibilities as an MVC controller, but it also takes a more direct relationship to a stateful view, directly managing the values displayed in the UI components according to the user's inputs and actions. There are two implementations of this pattern:

- The *passive view* implementation, in which the view contains no logic—it is a container for UI controls that are directly manipulated by the presenter.

- The *supervising controller* implementation, in which the view may be responsible for some elements of presentation logic, such as data binding, and has been given a reference to a data source from the domain models.

The difference between these two approaches relates to how intelligent the view is. Either way, the presenter is decoupled from the GUI framework, which makes the presenter logic simpler and suitable for unit testing.

Understanding the Model-View-View Model Pattern

The *model-view-view model* (MVVM) pattern is the most recent variation on MVC. It originated from Microsoft and is used in the Windows Presentation Foundation (WPF). In the MVVM pattern, models and views have the same roles as they do in MVC. The difference is the MVVM concept of a *view model*, which is an abstract representation of a user interface—typically a C# class that exposes both properties for the data to be displayed in the UI and operations on the data that can be invoked from the UI. Unlike an MVC controller, an MVVM view model has no notion that a view (or any specific UI technology) exists. An MVVM view uses the WPF *binding* feature to bi-directionally associate properties exposed by controls in the view (items in a drop-down menu, or the effect of pressing a button) with the properties exposed by the view model.

■ **Tip**   MVC also uses the term *view model* but refers to a simple model class that is used only to pass data from a controller to a view, as opposed to *domain models*, which are sophisticated representations of data, operations, and rules.

Building Loosely Coupled Components

One of most important features of the MVC pattern is that it enables separation of concerns. I want the components in my applications to be as independent as possible and to have as few interdependencies as I can arrange.

In an ideal situation, each component knows nothing about any other component and only deals with other areas of the application through abstract interfaces. This is known as *loose coupling*, and it makes testing and modifying applications easier.

A simple example will help put things in context. If I am writing a component called MyEmailSender that will send e-mails, I would implement an interface that defines all of the public functions required to send an e-mail, which I would call IEmailSender.

Any other component of my application that needs to send an e-mail—let's say a password reset helper called PasswordResetHelper—can then send an e-mail by referring only to the methods in the interface. There is no direct dependency between PasswordResetHelper and MyEmailSender, as shown by Figure 3-5.

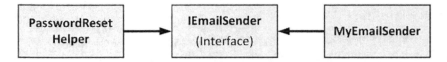

Figure 3-5. *Using interfaces to decouple components*

By introducing IEmailSender, I ensure that there is no direct dependency between PasswordResetHelper and MyEmailSender. I could replace MyEmailSender with another e-mail provider or even use a mock implementation for testing purposes without needing to make any changes to PasswordResetHelper. (I introduce mock implementations later in this chapter and return to them again in Chapter 6).

Using Dependency Injection

Interfaces help decouple components, but I still face a problem: C# doesn't provide a built-in way to easily create objects that implement interfaces, except to create an instance of the concrete component with the new keyword. I end up with code like this:

```
public class PasswordResetHelper {

    public void ResetPassword() {

        IEmailSender mySender = new MyEmailSender();

        //...call interface methods to configure e-mail details...

        mySender.SendEmail();
    }
}
```

This undermines my goal of being able to replace MyEmailSender without having to change PasswordReset helper and means that I am only part of the way to loosely coupled components. The PasswordResetHelper class is configuring and sending e-mails through the IEmailSender interface, but to create an object that implements that interface, it had to create an instance of MyEmailSender. In fact, I have made things worse for myself because PasswordResetHelper now depends on the MyEmailSender class *and* the IEmailSender interface, as shown in Figure 3-6.

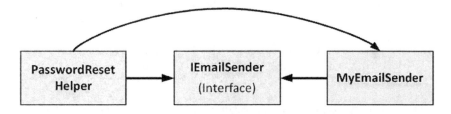

Figure 3-6. *Components which are tightly coupled after all*

What I need is a way to get objects that implement an interface *without* having to create the object directly. The solution to this problem is called *dependency injection* (DI), also known as *Inversion of Control* (IoC).

DI is a design pattern that completes the loose coupling process. As I describe DI, you might wonder what the fuss is about, but bear with me—this is an important concept that is central to effective MVC development and it can cause a lot of confusion.

Breaking and Declaring Dependencies

There are two parts to the DI pattern. The first is that I remove any dependencies on concrete classes from my component—in this case PasswordResetHelper. I do this by creating a class constructor that accepts implementations of the interfaces I need as arguments, like this:

```
public class PasswordResetHelper {
    private IEmailSender emailSender;

    public PasswordResetHelper(IEmailSender emailSenderParam) {
        emailSender = emailSenderParam;
    }

    public void ResetPassword() {
        // ...call interface methods to configure e-mail details...
        emailSender.SendEmail();
    }
}
```

The constructor for the PasswordResetHelper class is now said to *declare a dependency* on the IEmailSender interface, meaning that it can't be created and used unless it receives an object that implements the IEmailSender interface. In declaring its dependency, the PasswordResetHelper class no longer has any knowledge of MyEmailSender, it only depends on the IEmailSender interface. In short, the PassworsResetHelper no longer knows or cares how the IEmailSender interface is implemented.

Injecting Dependencies

The second part of the DI pattern is to *inject* the dependencies declared by the PasswordResetHelper class when I create instances of it, hence the term *dependency injection*.

All this really means is that I need to decide which class that implements the IEmailSender interface I am going to use, create an object from that class and then pass the object as an argument to the PasswordResetHelper constructor.

■ **Note** The PasswordResetHelper class declares its dependencies through its constructor. This is known as *constructor injection*. I could also declare dependencies to be injected through a public property, known as *setter injection*.

The dependencies are injected into the PasswordResetHelper at runtime; that is to say, an instance of some class that implements the IEmailSender interface will be created and passed to the PasswordResetHelper constructor during instantiation. There is no compile-time dependency between PasswordResetHelper and any class that implements the interfaces it depends on.

Because the dependencies are dealt with at runtime, I can decide which interface implementations are going to be used when I run the application. I can choose between different e-mail providers or inject a special mocked implementation for testing. Dependency injection lets me achieve the relationships I was aiming for in Figure 3-5.

Using a Dependency Injection Container

I have resolved my dependency issue, but how do I instantiate the concrete implementation of interfaces without creating dependencies somewhere else in the application? As it stands, I still have to have statements somewhere in the application like these:

```
...
IEmailSender sender = new MyEmailSender();
helper = new PasswordResetHelper(sender);
...
```

The answer is to use a *dependency injection container*, also known as an IoC container. This is a component that acts as a broker between the dependencies that a class like PasswordResetHelper declares and the classes that can be used to resolve those dependencies, such as MyEmailSender.

I register the set of interfaces or abstract types that my application uses with the DI container, and specify which implementation classes should be instantiated to satisfy dependencies. So, I would register the IEmailSender interface with the container and specify that an instance of MyEmailSender should be created whenever an implementation of IEmailSender is required.

When I want a PasswordResetHelper object in my application, I ask the DI container to create one for me. It knows that the PasswordResetHelper has declared a dependency on the IEmailSender interface and it knows that that I have specified that I want to use the MyEmailSender class as the implementation of that interface. The DI container puts these two pieces of information together, creates the MyEmailSender object and then uses it as an argument to create a PasswordResetHelper object, which I am then able to use in the application.

■ **Note**   It is important to note that I no longer create the objects in my application myself using the new keyword. Instead, I go to the DI container and request the objects I need. It can take a while to get used to this when you are new to DI, but as you'll see, the MVC Framework provides some features to make the process simpler.

I do not need to write my own DI container—there are some great open source and freely licensed implementations available. The one I like and use in my own projects is called Ninject and you can get details at www.ninject.org. I'll introduce you to using Ninject in Chapter 6 and show you how to install the package using NuGet.

■ **Tip**   Microsoft has created its own DI container, called Unity. I are going to use Ninject, however, because I like it and to demonstrate the ability to mix and match tools when using MVC. If you want more information about Unity, see unity.codeplex.com.

The role of a DI container may seem simple and trivial, but that is not the case. A good DI container, such as Ninject, has some clever features:

- *Dependency chain resolution*: If you request a component that has its own dependencies (e.g., constructor parameters), the container will satisfy those dependencies, too. So, if the constructor for the MyEmailSender class requires an implementation of the INetworkTransport interface, the DI container will instantiate the default implementation of that interface, pass it to the constructor of MyEmailSender and return the result as the default implementation of IEmailSender.

- *Object lifecycle management*: If you request a component more than once, should you get the same instance each time or a fresh new instance? A good DI container will let you configure the lifecycle of a component, allowing you to select from predefined options including *singleton* (the same instance each time), *transient* (a new instance each time), *instance-per-thread*, *instance-per-HTTP-request*, *instance-from-a-pool*, and many others.

- *Configuration of constructor parameter values*: If the constructor for my implementation of the `INetworkTransport` interface requires a string called `serverName`, for example, you should be able to set a value for it in your DI container configuration. It is a crude but simple configuration system that removes any need for your code to pass around connection strings, server addresses, and so forth.

Writing your own DI container is an excellent way to understand how C# and .NET handle types and reflection and I recommend it as a good project for a rainy weekend. But don't be tempted to deploy your code in a real project. Writing a reliable, robust and high-performance DI container is difficult and you should find a proven and tested package to use. I like Ninject, but there are plenty of others available and you are sure to find something that suits your development style.

Getting Started with Automated Testing

The ASP.NET MVC Framework is designed to make it as easy as possible to set up automated tests and use development methodologies such as test-driven development (TDD), which I explain later in this chapter. ASP.NET MVC provides an ideal platform for automated testing and Visual Studio has some solid testing features. Between them they make designing and running tests simple and easy.

In broad terms, Web application developers today focus on two kinds of automated testing. The first is *unit testing*, which is a way to specify and verify the behavior of individual classes (or other small units of code) in isolation from the rest of the application. The second type is *integration testing*, which is a way to specify and verify the behavior of multiple components working together, up to and including the entire Web application.

Both kinds of testing can be valuable in Web applications. Unit tests, which are simple to create and run, are brilliantly precise when you are working on algorithms, business logic, or other back-end infrastructure. The value of integration testing is that it can model how a user will interact with the UI, and can cover the entire technology stack that your application uses, including the Web server and database. Integration testing tends to be better at detecting new bugs that have arisen in old features; this is known as *regression testing*.

Understanding Unit Testing

In the .NET world, you create a separate test project in your Visual Studio solution to hold *test fixtures*. This project will be created when you first add a unit test, or can be set up automatically when you use an MVC project template. A *test fixture* is a C# class that defines a set of test methods: one method for each behavior you want to verify. A test project can contain multiple test fixture classes.

GETTING THE UNIT TEST FEVER

Being able to perform unit testing is one of the benefits of working with the MVC Framework, but it isn't for everyone and I have no intention of pretending otherwise. If you have not encountered unit testing before, then I encourage you to give it a try and see how it works out.

I like unit testing and I use it in my own projects, but not all of them and not as consistently as you might expect. I tend to focus on writing unit tests for features and functions that I know will be hard to write and that are likely to be the source of bugs in deployment. In these situations, unit testing helps me structure my thoughts about how to best implement what I need. I find that just thinking about what I test helps throw up ideas about potential problems—and that's before I start dealing with actual bugs and defects.

That said, unit testing is a tool and not a religion and only you know how much testing—and what kind of testing—you require. If you don't find unit testing useful or if you have a different methodology that suits you better, then don't feel you need to unit test just because it is fashionable. (Although if you *don't* have a better methodology and you are not testing at all, then you are probably letting users find your bugs and you are officially a *bad person*. You don't have to unit test, but you really should do *some* testing of *some* kind).

■ **Note**   I show you how to create a test project and populate it with unit tests in Chapter 6. The goal for this chapter is just to introduce the concept of unit testing and give you an idea of what a test fixture looks like and how it is used.

To get started, I have created a class from an imaginary application, as shown in Listing 3-1. The class is called AdminController and it defines the ChangeLoginName method, which allows my imaginary users to change their passwords.

Listing 3-1. The Definition of the AdminController Class

```
using System.Web.Mvc;

namespace TestingDemo {

    public class AdminController : Controller {
        private IUserRepository repository;

        public AdminController(IUserRepository repo) {
            repository = repo;
        }

        public ActionResult ChangeLoginName(string oldName, string newName) {
            User user = repository.FetchByLoginName(oldName);
            user.LoginName = newName;
            repository.SubmitChanges();
            // render some view to show the result
            return View();
        }
    }
}
```

■ **Tip**   I created the classes for this demonstration in a new Visual Studio project called TestingDemo. You don't need to recreate the examples in this section to follow along but I have included the project in the source code download available from apress.com.

The controller relies on some model classes and an interface, which you can see in Listing 3-2. Once again, these are not from a real project and I have simplified these classes to make demonstrating the test easier. I am not suggesting that you create user classes that have just a single string property, for example.

Listing 3-2. The Model Classes and Interface that the AdminController Relies On

```
namespace TestingDemo {

    public class User {
        public string LoginName { get; set; }
    }

    public interface IUserRepository {
        void Add(User newUser);
        User FetchByLoginName(string loginName);
        void SubmitChanges();
    }

    public class DefaultUserRepository : IUserRepository {

        public void Add(User newUser) {
            // implement me
        }

        public User FetchByLoginName(string loginName) {
            // implement me
            return new User() { LoginName = loginName };
        }

        public void SubmitChanges() {
            // implement me
        }
    }
}
```

The User class represents a user in my application. Users are created, managed and stored through a repository whose functionality is defined by the IUserRepository interface and there is a partially complete implementation of this interface in the DefaultUserRepository class.

My goal in this section is to write a unit test for the functionality provided by the ChangeLoginName method defined by the AdminController, as shown in Listing 3-3.

Listing 3-3. A Test Fixture for the AdminController.ChangeLoginName Method

```
using System.Collections.Generic;
using System.Linq;
using Microsoft.VisualStudio.TestTools.UnitTesting;

namespace TestingDemo.Tests {

    [TestClass]
    public class AdminControllerTests {

        [TestMethod]
        public void CanChangeLoginName() {
```

```
            // Arrange (set up a scenario)
            User user = new User() { LoginName = "Bob" };
            FakeRepository repositoryParam = new FakeRepository();
            repositoryParam.Add(user);
            AdminController target = new AdminController(repositoryParam);
            string oldLoginParam = user.LoginName;
            string newLoginParam = "Joe";

            // Act (attempt the operation)
            target.ChangeLoginName(oldLoginParam, newLoginParam);

            // Assert (verify the result)
            Assert.AreEqual(newLoginParam, user.LoginName);
            Assert.IsTrue(repositoryParam.DidSubmitChanges);
        }
    }

    class FakeRepository : IUserRepository {
        public List<User> Users = new List<User>();
        public bool DidSubmitChanges = false;

        public void Add(User user) {
            Users.Add(user);
        }

        public User FetchByLoginName(string loginName) {
            return Users.First(m => m.LoginName == loginName);
        }

        public void SubmitChanges() {
            DidSubmitChanges = true;
        }
    }
}
```

The test fixture is the CanChangeLoginName method. Notice that the method is decorated with the TestMethod attribute and that the class it belongs to—called AdminControllerTests—is decorated with the TestClass attribute. This is how Visual Studio finds the test fixture.

The CanChangeLoginName method follows a pattern known as *arrange/act/assert* (A/A/A). *Arrange* refers to setting up the conditions for the test, *act* refers to performing the test, and *assert* refers to verifying that the result was the one that was required. Being consistent about the structure of your unit test methods makes them easier to read, something you'll appreciate when your project contains hundreds of unit tests.

The test fixture uses a test-specific fake implementation of the IUserRepository interface to simulate a specific condition—in this case, when there is a single member, Bob, in the repository. Creating the fake repository and the User are done in the *arrange* section of the test.

Next, the method being tested—AdminController.ChangeLoginName—is called. This is the *act* section of the test. Finally, I check the results using a pair of Assert calls (this is the *assert* part of the test). The Assert method is provided by the Visual Studio test suite and lets me check for specific outcomes. I run the test from the Visual Studio Test menu and receive visual feedback about the tests as they are performed, as shown in Figure 3-7.

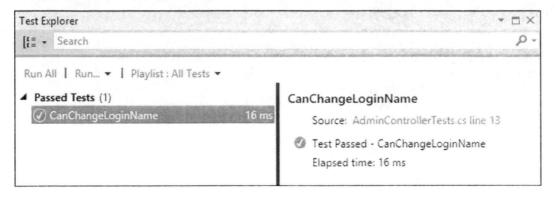

Figure 3-7. *Visual feedback on the progress of unit tests*

If the test runs without throwing any unhandled exceptions and all of the Assert statements pass without problems, the Test Explorer window shows a green light. If not, you get a red light and details of what went wrong.

■ **Note**   You can see how my use of DI has helped with unit testing. I was able to create a fake implementation of the repository and inject it into the controller to create a specific scenario. I am a big fan of DI and this is one of the reasons.

It might seem like I have gone to a lot of effort to test a simple method, but it wouldn't require much more code to test something far more complex. If you find yourself considering skipping small tests like this one, remember that test fixtures help to uncover bugs that can sometimes be hidden in more complex tests. One improvement I could have made to my test is to eliminate test-specific fake classes like FakeMembersRepository by using a *mocking tool*—I show you how to do this in Chapter 6.

Using TDD and the Red-Green-Refactor Workflow

With test-driven development (TDD), you use unit tests to help design your code. This can be an odd concept if you are used to testing after you have finished coding, but there is a lot of sense in this approach. The key concept is a development workflow called red-green-refactor. It works like this:

- Determine that you need to add a new feature or method to your application.

- Write the test that will validate the behavior of the new feature when it is written.

- Run the test and get a red light.

- Write the code that implements the new feature.

- Run the test again and correct the code until you get a green light.

- Refactor the code if required. For example, reorganize the statements, rename the variables, and so on.

- Run the test to confirm that your changes have not changed the behavior of your additions.

This workflow is repeated for every feature you add. TDD inverts the traditional development process: you start by writing tests for the perfect implementation of a feature, knowing that the tests will fail. You then implement the feature, creating each aspect of its behavior to pass one or more tests.

This cycle is the essence of TDD. There is a lot to recommend it as a development style, not least because it makes a programmer think about how a change or enhancement should behave *before* the coding starts. You always have a clear end-point in view and a way to check that you are there. And if you have unit tests that cover the rest of your application, you can be sure that your additions have not changed the behavior elsewhere.

TDD seems a little odd when you first try it, but it is strangely empowering, and writing the tests first make you consider what a perfect implementation should do before you become biased by the techniques that you use to write the code.

The drawback of TDD is that it requires discipline. As deadlines get closer, the temptation is always to discard TDD and just start writing code or, as I have witnessed several times on projects, sneakily discard problematic tests to make code appear in better shape than it really is. For these reasons, TDD should be used in established and mature development teams where there is generally a high level of skill and discipline or in teams where there the team leads can enforce good practice, even in the face of time constraints.

■ **Tip**   You can see a simple example of TDD in Chapter 6 when I demonstrate the testing tools built into Visual Studio.

Understanding Integration Testing

For Web applications, the most common approach to integration testing is *UI automation*, which means simulating or automating a Web browser to exercise the application's entire technology stack by reproducing the actions that a user would perform, such as pressing buttons, following links, and submitting forms. The two best-known open source browser automation options for .NET developers are

- *Selenium RC* (`http://seleniumhq.org/`), which consists of a Java "server" application that can send automation commands to Internet Explorer, Firefox, Safari, or Opera, plus clients for .NET, Python, Ruby, and multiple others so that you can write test scripts in the language of your choice. Selenium is powerful and mature; its only drawback is that you have to run its Java server.

- *WatiN* (`http://watin.org`), a .NET library that can send automation commands to Internet Explorer or Firefox. Its API isn't as powerful as Selenium, but it comfortably handles most common scenarios and is easy to set up. You need only reference a single DLL.

Integration testing is an ideal complement to unit testing. Although unit testing is well suited to validating the behavior of individual components at the server, integration testing lets you create tests that are client-focused, recreating the actions of a user. As a result, it can highlight problems that come from the interaction between components, hence the term *integration* testing. And because integration testing for a Web application is done through the browser, you can test that JavaScript behaviors work the way they are supposed to, something that is difficult with unit testing.

There are some drawbacks. Integration testing takes more time. It takes longer to create the tests and longer to perform them. And integration tests can be brittle. If you change the `id` attribute of an element that is checked in a test, for example, the test can (and usually will) fail.

As a consequence of the additional time and effort required, integration testing is often done at key project milestones, perhaps after a weekly source code check-in, or when major functional blocks are completed. Integration testing is every bit as useful as unit testing and it can highlight problems that unit testing cannot. The time required to set up and run integration testing is worthwhile, and I encourage you to add it to your development process.

I am not going to get into integration testing in this book. It is outside of my focus on the MVC Framework. Any web app can benefit from integration testing and there are no special features in the MVC Framework to support this activity. Integration testing is a separate art and what is true when performing integration testing on any Web application is also true for MVC.

Summary

In this chapter, I introduced you to the MVC architectural pattern and compared it to some other patterns you may have seen or heard of before. I discussed the significance of the domain model and introduced dependency injection, which allows us to decouple components to enforce a strict separation between the parts of an application. I demonstrated a simple unit test and you saw how decoupled components and dependency injection make unit testing simple and easy. In the next chapter, I describe the essential C# language features that are used in MVC Framework applications.

CHAPTER 4

■ ■ ■

Essential Language Features

C# is a feature-rich language and not all programmers are familiar with all of the features I rely on in this book. In this chapter, I describe the C# language features that a good MVC programmer needs to know and that I use in examples throughout this book.

I provide only a short summary of each feature. If you want more in-depth coverage of C# or LINQ, three of my books may be of interest. For a complete guide to C#, try *Introducing Visual C#;* for in-depth coverage of LINQ, check out *Pro LINQ in C#;* and for a detailed examination of the .NET support for asynchronous programming see *Pro .Net Parallel Programming in C#.* All of these books are published by Apress. Table 4-1 provides the summary for this chapter.

Table 4-1. *Chapter Summary*

Problem	Solution	Listing
Simplify C# properties	Use automatically implemented properties	1–7
Create an object and sets its properties in a single step	Use an object or collection initializer	8–10
Add functionality to a class which cannot be modified	Use an extension method	11–18
Simplify the use of delegates	Use a lambda expression	19–23
Use implicit typing	Use the var keyword	24
Create objects without defining a type	Use an anonymous type	25–26
Query collections of objects as though there were a database	Use LINQ	27–31
Simplify the use of asynchronous methods	Use the async and await keywords	32–33

Preparing the Example Project

To demonstrate the language features in this part of the book, I have created a new Visual Studio project called LanguageFeatures using the ASP.NET MVC Web Application template. I selected the Empty option for the initial content and checked the option for MVC folders and references, just as I did in Chapter 2. The language features that I describe in this chapter are not specific to MVC, but Visual Studio Express 2013 for Web doesn't support creating projects that can write to the console, so you will have to create an MVC app if you want to follow along with the examples. I need a simple controller to demonstrate these language features, so I created the HomeController.cs file in the Controllers folder–I did this by right-clicking on the Controllers folder in the Solution Explorer, selecting Add ➤ Controller from the pop-up menu, selecting MVC 5 Controller-Empty from the Add Scaffold menu, and clicking the Add button. I set the name to HomeController in the Add Controller dialog and clicked the Add button to create the controller class file, the edited contents of which you can see in Listing 4-1.

Listing 4-1. The Initial Content of the HomeController.cs File

```
using System;
using System.Web.Mvc;
using LanguageFeatures.Models;

namespace LanguageFeatures.Controllers {
    public class HomeController : Controller {

        public string Index() {
            return "Navigate to a URL to show an example";
        }
    }
}
```

I will create action methods for each example, so the result from the Index action method is a basic message to keep the project simple.

■ **Caution** The HomeController class won't compile at the moment because it imports the LanguageFeatures.Models namespace. This namespace won't create until I add a class to the Models folder, which I do as part of the first example in the next section.

To display the results from my action methods, I right-clicked the Index action method, selected Add View and created a new view called Result. You can see the contents of the view file in Listing 4-2. (It doesn't matter which options you select in the Add View dialog because you will replace the initial content of the file with the markup shown in the listing).

Listing 4-2. The Contents of the Result.cshtml File

```
@model String

@{
    Layout = null;
}

<!DOCTYPE html>

<html>
<head>
    <meta name="viewport" content="width=device-width" />
    <title>Result</title>
</head>
<body>
    <div>
        @Model
    </div>
</body>
</html>
```

You can see that this is a strongly typed view, where the model type is String-for the most part, the examples that follow are not complex examples and I can represent the results as a simple string.

Adding the System.Net.Http Assembly

Later in the chapter, I'll be using an example that relies on the System.Net.Http assembly, which isn't added to MVC projects by default. Select Add Reference from the Visual Studio Project menu to open the Reference Manager window. Ensure that the Assemblies section is selected on the left-hand side and locate and check the System.Net.Http item, as shown in Figure 4-1.

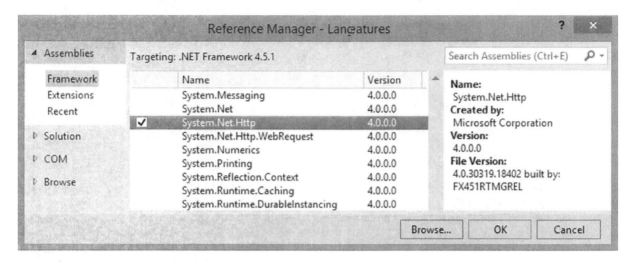

Figure 4-1. *Adding an assembly to the project*

Using Automatically Implemented Properties

The regular C# property feature lets you expose a piece of data from a class in a way that decouples the data from how it is set and retrieved. Listing 4-3 contains a simple example in a class called Product, which I added to the Models folder of the LanguageFeatures project in a class file called Product.cs

Listing 4-3. Defining a Property in the Product.cs File

```
namespace LanguageFeatures.Models {
    public class Product {
        private string name;

        public string Name {
            get { return name; }
            set { name = value; }
        }
    }
}
```

The property, called Name, is shown in bold. The statements in the get code block (known as the *getter*) are performed when the value of the property is read, and the statements in the set code block (known as the *setter*) are performed when a value is assigned to the property (the special variable value represents the assigned value). A property is consumed by other classes as though it were a field, as shown in Listing 4-4, which shows an AutoProperty action method I added to the Home controller.

Listing 4-4. Consuming a Property in the HomeController.cs File

```
using System;
using System.Web.Mvc;
using LanguageFeatures.Models;

namespace LanguageFeatures.Controllers {
    public class HomeController : Controller {

        public string Index() {
            return "Navigate to a URL to show an example";
        }

        public ViewResult AutoProperty() {
            // create a new Product object
            Product myProduct = new Product();

            // set the property value
            myProduct.Name = "Kayak";

            // get the property
            string productName = myProduct.Name;

            // generate the view
            return View("Result",
                (object)String.Format("Product name: {0}", productName));
        }
    }
}
```

You can see that the property value is read and set just like a regular field. Using properties is preferable to using fields because you can change the statements in the get and set blocks without needing to change the classes that depend on the property.

▨ **Tip**   You may notice that I cast the second argument to the View method to an object in Listing 4-4. This is because the View method has an overload that accepts two String arguments and which has a different meaning to the overload that accepts a String and an object. To avoid calling the wrong one, I explicitly cast the second argument. I return to the View method and its overloads in Chapter 20.

You can see the effect of this example by starting the project and navigating to /Home/AutoProperty (which targets the AutoProperty action method and will be the pattern for testing each example in this chapter). Because I pass a string from the action method to the view, I am going to show you the results as text, rather than a screen shot. Here is the result of targeting the action method in Listing 4-4:

```
Product name: Kayak
```

Properties are all well and good, but they become tedious when you have a class that has a lot of properties, all of which mediate access to a field, producing a class file that is needlessly verbose, as shown in Listing 4-5, which shows some additional properties I added to the Product class in the Product.cs file.

Listing 4-5. Verbose Property Definitions in the Product.cs File

```
namespace LanguageFeatures.Models {

    public class Product {
        private int productID;
        private string name;
        private string description;
        private decimal price;
        private string category;

        public int ProductID {
            get { return productID; }
            set { productID = value; }
        }

        public string Name {
            get { return name; }
            set { name = value; }
        }

        public string Description {
            get { return description; }
            set { description = value; }
        }

        //...and so on...
    }
}
```

What I want is the flexibility of properties without having to duplicate the getters and setters. The solution is an *automatically implemented property*, also known as an *automatic property*. With an automatic property, you can create the pattern of a field-backed property, without defining the field or specifying the code in the getter and setter, as Listing 4-6 shows.

Listing 4-6. Using Automatically Implemented Properties in the Product.cs File

```
namespace LanguageFeatures.Models {

    public class Product {
        public int ProductID { get; set; }
        public string Name { get; set; }
        public string Description { get; set; }
        public decimal Price { get; set; }
        public string Category { set; get; }
    }
}
```

Notice that I do not define the bodies of the getter and setter or the field that the property is backed by. Both of these are done for me by the C# compiler when the class is compiled. Using an automatic property is no different from using a regular property; the code in the action method in Listing 4-4 will work without any modification.

By using automatic properties, I save myself some typing, create code that is easier to read, but still preserve the flexibility that a property provides. If the day comes when I need to change the way a property is implemented, I can return to the regular property format. As a demonstration, Listing 4-7 shows what I would have to do if I needed to change the way the Name property is composed.

Listing 4-7. Reverting from an Automatic to a Regular Property in the Product.cs File

```
namespace LanguageFeatures.Models {

    public class Product {
        private string name;

        public int ProductID { get; set; }

        public string Name {
            get {
                return ProductID + name;
            }
            set {
                name = value;
            }
        }

        public string Description { get; set; }
        public decimal Price { get; set; }
        public string Category { set; get; }
    }
}
```

■ **Note**   Notice that I must implement both the getter and setter to return to a regular property. C# does not support mixing automatic- and regular-style getters and setters in a single property.

Using Object and Collection Initializers

Another tiresome programming task is constructing a new object and then assigning values to the properties, as illustrated by Listing 4-8, which shows the addition of a CreateProduct action method to the Home controller.

Listing 4-8. Constructing and Initializing an Object with Properties in the HomeController.cs File

```
using System;
using System.Web.Mvc;
using LanguageFeatures.Models;
```

```
namespace LanguageFeatures.Controllers {
    public class HomeController : Controller {

        public string Index() {
            return "Navigate to a URL to show an example";
        }

        public ViewResult AutoProperty() {
            // ...statements omitted for brevity...
        }

        public ViewResult CreateProduct() {

            // create a new Product object
            Product myProduct = new Product();

            // set the property values
            myProduct.ProductID = 100;
            myProduct.Name = "Kayak";
            myProduct.Description = "A boat for one person";
            myProduct.Price = 275M;
            myProduct.Category = "Watersports";

            return View("Result",
                (object)String.Format("Category: {0}", myProduct.Category));
        }
    }
}
```

I go through three stages to create a Product object and produce a result: create the object, set the parameter values, and then call the View method so I can display the result through the view. Fortunately, I can use the *object initializer* feature, which allows me to create and populate the Product instance in a single step, as shown in Listing 4-9.

Listing 4-9. Using the Object Initializer Feature in the HomeController.cs File

```
...
public ViewResult CreateProduct() {

    // create and populate a new Product object
    Product myProduct = new Product {
        ProductID = 100, Name = "Kayak",
        Description = "A boat for one person",
        Price = 275M, Category = "Watersports"
    };

    return View("Result",
        (object)String.Format("Category: {0}", myProduct.Category));
}
...
```

The braces ({}) after the call to the Product name form the *initializer*, which I use to supply values to the parameters as part of the construction process. The same feature let me initialize the contents of collections and arrays as part of the construction process, as demonstrated by Listing 4-10.

Listing 4-10. Initializing Collections and Arrays in the HomeController.cs File

```
using System;
using System.Collections.Generic;
using System.Web.Mvc;
using LanguageFeatures.Models;

namespace LanguageFeatures.Controllers {
    public class HomeController : Controller {

        public string Index() {
            return "Navigate to a URL to show an example";
        }

        // ...other action methods omitted for brevity...

        public ViewResult CreateCollection() {
            string[] stringArray = { "apple", "orange", "plum" };

            List<int> intList = new List<int> { 10, 20, 30, 40 };

            Dictionary<string, int> myDict = new Dictionary<string, int> {
                { "apple", 10 }, { "orange", 20 }, { "plum", 30 }
            };

            return View("Result", (object)stringArray[1]);
        }
    }
}
```

The listing demonstrates how to construct and initialize an array and two classes from the generic collection library. This feature is a syntax convenience—it just makes C# more pleasant to use but does not have any other impact or benefit.

Using Extension Methods

Extension methods are a convenient way of adding methods to classes that you do not own and cannot modify directly. Listing 4-11 shows a ShoppingCart class, which I added to the Models folder in a file called ShoppingCart.cs file and which represents a collection of Product objects.

Listing 4-11. The ShoppingCart Class in the ShoppingCart.cs File

```
using System.Collections.Generic;

namespace LanguageFeatures.Models {

    public class ShoppingCart {
        public List<Product> Products { get; set; }
    }
}
```

This is a simple class that acts as a wrapper around a `List` of `Product` objects (I only need a basic class for this example). Suppose I need to be able to determine the total value of the `Product` objects in the `ShoppingCart` class, but I cannot modify the class itself, perhaps because it comes from a third party and I do not have the source code. I can use an extension method to add the functionality I need. Listing 4-12 shows the `MyExtensionMethods` class that I added to the `Models` folder in the `MyExtensionMethods.cs` file.

Listing 4-12. Defining an Extension Method in the MyExtensionMethods.cs File

```
namespace LanguageFeatures.Models {

    public static class MyExtensionMethods {

        public static decimal TotalPrices(this ShoppingCart cartParam) {
            decimal total = 0;
            foreach (Product prod in cartParam.Products) {
                total += prod.Price;
            }
            return total;
        }
    }
}
```

The `this` keyword in front of the first parameter marks `TotalPrices` as an extension method. The first parameter tells .NET which class the extension method can be applied to—`ShoppingCart` in this case. I can refer to the instance of the `ShoppingCart` that the extension method has been applied to by using the `cartParam` parameter. My method enumerates the `Products` in the `ShoppingCart` and returns the sum of the `Product.Price` property. Listing 4-13 shows how I apply an extension method in a new action method called `UseExtension` I added to the `Home` controller.

Listing 4-13. Applying an Extension Method in the HomeController.cs File

```
using System;
using System.Collections.Generic;
using System.Web.Mvc;
using LanguageFeatures.Models;

namespace LanguageFeatures.Controllers {
    public class HomeController : Controller {

        public string Index() {
            return "Navigate to a URL to show an example";
        }

        // ...other action methods omitted for brevity...

        public ViewResult UseExtension() {
            // create and populate ShoppingCart
            ShoppingCart cart = new ShoppingCart {
                Products = new List<Product> {
                    new Product {Name = "Kayak", Price = 275M},
                    new Product {Name = "Lifejacket", Price = 48.95M},
                    new Product {Name = "Soccer ball", Price = 19.50M},
                    new Product {Name = "Corner flag", Price = 34.95M}
                }
            };
```

```
        // get the total value of the products in the cart
        decimal cartTotal = cart.TotalPrices();

        return View("Result",
            (object)String.Format("Total: {0:c}", cartTotal));
    }
  }
}
```

▨ **Note**   Extension methods do not let you break through the access rules that classes define for their methods, fields, and properties. You can extend the functionality of a class by using an extension method, but only using the class members that you had access to anyway.

The key statement is this one:

```
...
decimal cartTotal = cart.TotalPrices();
...
```

I call the TotalPrices method on a ShoppingCart object as though it were part of the ShoppingCart class, even though it is an extension method defined by a different class altogether. .NET will find extension classes if they are in the scope of the current class, meaning that they are part of the same namespace or in a namespace that is the subject of a using statement. Here is the result from the UseExtension action method, which you can see by starting the application and navigating to the /Home/UseExtension URL:

```
Total: $378.40
```

Applying Extension Methods to an Interface

I can also create extension methods that apply to an interface, which allows me to call the extension method on all of the classes that implement the interface. Listing 4-14 shows the ShoppingCart class updated to implement the IEnumerable<Product> interface.

Listing 4-14. Implementing an Interface in the ShoppingCart.cs File

```
using System.Collections;
using System.Collections.Generic;

namespace LanguageFeatures.Models {

    public class ShoppingCart: IEnumerable<Product> {

        public List<Product> Products { get; set; }
```

```
        public IEnumerator<Product> GetEnumerator() {
            return Products.GetEnumerator();
        }

        IEnumerator IEnumerable.GetEnumerator() {
            return GetEnumerator();
        }
    }
}
```

I can now update my extension method so that it deals with IEnumerable<Product>, as shown in Listing 4-15.

Listing 4-15. An Extension Method That Works on an Interface in the MyExtensionMethods.cs File

```
using System.Collections.Generic;

namespace LanguageFeatures.Models {

    public static class MyExtensionMethods {

        public static decimal TotalPrices(this IEnumerable<Product> productEnum) {
            decimal total = 0;
            foreach (Product prod in productEnum) {
                total += prod.Price;
            }
            return total;
        }
    }
}
```

The first parameter type has changed to IEnumerable<Product>, which means that the foreach loop in the method body works directly on Product objects. The switch to the interface means that I can calculate the total value of the Product objects enumerated by any IEnumerable<Product>, which includes instances of ShoppingCart but also arrays of Products, as shown in Listing 4-16.

Listing 4-16. Extension Methods Applies to Implementations of an Interface in the HomeController.cs File

```
using System;
using System.Collections.Generic;
using System.Web.Mvc;
using LanguageFeatures.Models;

namespace LanguageFeatures.Controllers {
    public class HomeController : Controller {

        public string Index() {
            return "Navigate to a URL to show an example";
        }
```

```
        // ...other action methods omitted for brevity...

    public ViewResult UseExtensionEnumerable() {

        IEnumerable<Product> products = new ShoppingCart {
            Products = new List<Product> {
                new Product {Name = "Kayak", Price = 275M},
                new Product {Name = "Lifejacket", Price = 48.95M},
                new Product {Name = "Soccer ball", Price = 19.50M},
                new Product {Name = "Corner flag", Price = 34.95M}
            }
        };

        // create and populate an array of Product objects
        Product[] productArray = {
            new Product {Name = "Kayak", Price = 275M},
            new Product {Name = "Lifejacket", Price = 48.95M},
            new Product {Name = "Soccer ball", Price = 19.50M},
            new Product {Name = "Corner flag", Price = 34.95M}
        };

        // get the total value of the products in the cart
        decimal cartTotal = products.TotalPrices();
        decimal arrayTotal = products.TotalPrices();

        return View("Result",
            (object)String.Format("Cart Total: {0}, Array Total: {1}",
                cartTotal, arrayTotal));
    }
  }
}
```

■ **Note** The way that C# arrays implement the IEnumerable<T> interface is a little unusual. You will not find it included in the list of implemented interfaces in the MSDN documentation. The support is handled by the compiler so that code for earlier versions C# will still compile. Odd, but true. I could have used another generic collection class in this example, but I wanted to show off my knowledge of the dark corners of the C# specification. Also odd, but true.

If you start the project and target the action method, you will see the following results, which demonstrate that I get the same result from the extension method, irrespective of how the Product objects are collected:

```
Cart Total: 378.40, Array Total: 378.40
```

Creating Filtering Extension Methods

The last thing I want to show you about extension methods is that they can be used to filter collections of objects. An extension method that operates on an IEnumerable<T> and that also returns an IEnumerable<T> can use the yield keyword to apply selection criteria to items in the source data to produce a reduced set of results. Listing 4-17 demonstrates such a method, which I have added to the MyExtensionMethods class.

Listing 4-17. A Filtering Extension Method in the MyExtensionMethods.cs File

```
using System.Collections.Generic;

namespace LanguageFeatures.Models {

    public static class MyExtensionMethods {

        public static decimal TotalPrices(this IEnumerable<Product> productEnum) {
            decimal total = 0;
            foreach (Product prod in productEnum) {
                total += prod.Price;
            }
            return total;
        }

        public static IEnumerable<Product> FilterByCategory(
                this IEnumerable<Product> productEnum, string categoryParam) {

            foreach (Product prod in productEnum) {
                if (prod.Category == categoryParam) {
                    yield return prod;
                }
            }
        }
    }
}
```

This extension method, called FilterByCategory, takes an additional parameter that allows me to inject a filter condition when I call the method. Those Product objects whose Category property matches the parameter are returned in the result IEnumerable<Product> and those that do not match are discarded. Listing 4-18 shows this method being used.

Listing 4-18. Using the Filtering Extension Method in the HomeController.cs File

```
using System;
using System.Collections.Generic;
using System.Web.Mvc;
using LanguageFeatures.Models;

namespace LanguageFeatures.Controllers {

    public class HomeController : Controller {

        public string Index() {
            return "Navigate to a URL to show an example";
        }
```

```csharp
// ... other action methods omitted for brevity...

public ViewResult UseFilterExtensionMethod() {

    IEnumerable<Product> products = new ShoppingCart {
        Products = new List<Product> {
            new Product {Name = "Kayak", Category = "Watersports", Price = 275M},
            new Product {Name = "Lifejacket", Category = "Watersports",
                Price = 48.95M},
            new Product {Name = "Soccer ball", Category = "Soccer",
                Price = 19.50M},
            new Product {Name = "Corner flag", Category = "Soccer",
                Price = 34.95M}
        }
    };

    decimal total = 0;
    foreach (Product prod in products.FilterByCategory("Soccer")) {
        total += prod.Price;
    }

    return View("Result", (object)String.Format("Total: {0}", total));
    }
    }
}
```

When I call the FilterByCategory method on the ShoppingCart, only those Products in the Soccer category are returned. If you start the project and target the UseFilterExtensionMethod action method, you will see the following result, which is the sum of the Soccer product prices:

```
Total: 54.45
```

Using Lambda Expressions

I can use a delegate to make my FilterByCategory method more general. That way, the delegate that will be invoked against each Product can filter the objects in any way I choose, as illustrated by Listing 4-19, which shows the Filter extension method I added to the MyExtensionMethods class.

Listing 4-19. Using a Delegate in an Extension Method in the MyExtensionMethods.cs File

```csharp
using System;
using System.Collections.Generic;

namespace LanguageFeatures.Models {

    public static class MyExtensionMethods {
```

```
    public static decimal TotalPrices(this IEnumerable<Product> productEnum) {
        decimal total = 0;
        foreach (Product prod in productEnum) {
            total += prod.Price;
        }
        return total;
    }

    public static IEnumerable<Product> FilterByCategory(
            this IEnumerable<Product> productEnum, string categoryParam) {

        foreach (Product prod in productEnum) {
            if (prod.Category == categoryParam) {
                yield return prod;
            }
        }
    }

    public static IEnumerable<Product> Filter(
            this IEnumerable<Product> productEnum, Func<Product, bool> selectorParam) {

        foreach (Product prod in productEnum) {
            if (selectorParam(prod)) {
                yield return prod;
            }
        }
    }
  }
}
```

I used a Func as the filtering parameter, which means that I do not need to define the delegate as a type. The delegate takes a Product parameter and returns a bool, which will be true if that Product should be included in the results. The other end of this arrangement is a little verbose, as illustrated by Listing 4-20, which shows the changes I made to the UseFilterExtensionMethod action method in the Home controller.

Listing 4-20. Using the Filtering Extension Method with a Func in the HomeController.cs File

```
...
public ViewResult UseFilterExtensionMethod() {

    // create and populate ShoppingCart
    IEnumerable<Product> products = new ShoppingCart {
        Products = new List<Product> {
            new Product {Name = "Kayak", Category = "Watersports", Price = 275M},
            new Product {Name = "Lifejacket", Category = "Watersports", Price = 48.95M},
            new Product {Name = "Soccer ball", Category = "Soccer", Price = 19.50M},
            new Product {Name = "Corner flag", Category = "Soccer", Price = 34.95M}
        }
    };
```

```
    Func<Product, bool> categoryFilter = delegate(Product prod) {
        return prod.Category == "Soccer";
    };

    decimal total = 0;

    foreach (Product prod in products.Filter(categoryFilter)) {
        total += prod.Price;
    }
    return View("Result", (object)String.Format("Total: {0}", total));
}
...
```

I have taken a step forward, in the sense that I can now filter the Product objects using any criteria specified in the delegate, but I must define a Func for each kind of filtering that I want, which is not ideal. The less verbose alternative is to use a *lambda expression*, which is a concise format for expressing a method body in a delegate. I can use it to replace my delegate definition in the action method, as shown in Listing 4-21.

Listing 4-21. Using a Lambda Expression to Replace a Delegate Definition in the HomeController.cs File

```
...
public ViewResult UseFilterExtensionMethod() {

    // create and populate ShoppingCart
    IEnumerable<Product> products = new ShoppingCart {
        Products = new List<Product> {
            new Product {Name = "Kayak", Category = "Watersports", Price = 275M},
            new Product {Name = "Lifejacket", Category = "Watersports", Price = 48.95M},
            new Product {Name = "Soccer ball", Category = "Soccer", Price = 19.50M},
            new Product {Name = "Corner flag", Category = "Soccer", Price = 34.95M}
        }
    };

    Func<Product, bool> categoryFilter = prod => prod.Category == "Soccer";

    decimal total = 0;

    foreach (Product prod in products.Filter(categoryFilter)) {
        total += prod.Price;
    }
    return View("Result", (object)String.Format("Total: {0}", total));
}
...
```

The lambda expression is shown in bold. The parameter is expressed without specifying a type, which will be inferred automatically. The => characters are read aloud as "goes to" and links the parameter to the result of the lambda expression. In my example, a Product parameter called prod goes to a bool result, which will be true if the Category parameter of prod is equal to Soccer. I can make my syntax even tighter by doing away with the Func entirely, as shown in Listing 4-22.

Listing 4-22. A Lambda Expression Without a Func in the HomeController.cs File

```
...
public ViewResult UseFilterExtensionMethod() {

    IEnumerable<Product> products = new ShoppingCart {
        Products = new List<Product> {
            new Product {Name = "Kayak", Category = "Watersports", Price = 275M},
            new Product {Name = "Lifejacket", Category = "Watersports", Price = 48.95M},
            new Product {Name = "Soccer ball", Category = "Soccer", Price = 19.50M},
            new Product {Name = "Corner flag", Category = "Soccer", Price = 34.95M}
        }
    };

    decimal total = 0;

    foreach (Product prod in products.Filter(prod => prod.Category == "Soccer")) {
        total += prod.Price;
    }
    return View("Result", (object)String.Format("Total: {0}", total));
}
...
```

In this example, I supplied the lambda expression as the parameter to the Filter method. This is a nice and natural way of expressing the filter I want to apply. I can combine multiple filters by extending the result part of the lambda expression, as shown in Listing 4-23.

Listing 4-23. Extending the Filtering Expressed by the Lambda Expression in the HomeController.cs File

```
...
public ViewResult UseFilterExtensionMethod() {

    IEnumerable<Product> products = new ShoppingCart {
        Products = new List<Product> {
            new Product {Name = "Kayak", Category = "Watersports", Price = 275M},
            new Product {Name = "Lifejacket", Category = "Watersports", Price = 48.95M},
            new Product {Name = "Soccer ball", Category = "Soccer", Price = 19.50M},
            new Product {Name = "Corner flag", Category = "Soccer", Price = 34.95M}
        }
    };

    decimal total = 0;

    foreach (Product prod in products
            .Filter(prod => prod.Category == "Soccer" || prod.Price > 20)) {
        total += prod.Price;
    }
    return View("Result", (object)String.Format("Total: {0}", total));
}
...
```

This revised lambda expression will match Product objects that are in the Soccer category or whose Price property is greater than 20.

OTHER FORMS FOR LAMBDA EXPRESSIONS

I don't need to express the logic of my delegate in the lambda expression. I can as easily call a method, like this:

```
prod => EvaluateProduct(prod)
```

If I need a lambda expression for a delegate that has multiple parameters, I must wrap the parameters in parentheses, like this:

```
(prod, count) => prod.Price > 20 && count > 0
```

And, finally, if I need logic in the lambda expression that requires more than one statement, I can do so by using braces ({}) and finishing with a `return` statement, like this:

```
(prod, count) => {
    //...multiple code statements
    return result;
}
```

You do not need to use lambda expressions in your code, but they are a neat way of expressing complex functions simply and in a manner that is readable and clear. I like them a lot, and you will see them used liberally throughout this book.

Using Automatic Type Inference

The C# var keyword allows you to define a local variable without explicitly specifying the variable type, as demonstrated by Listing 4-24. This is called *type inference*, or *implicit typing*.

Listing 4-24. Using Type Inference

```
..
var myVariable = new Product { Name = "Kayak", Category = "Watersports", Price = 275M };

string name = myVariable.Name;  // legal
int count = myVariable.Count;   // compiler error
...
```

It is not that myVariable does not have a type. It is just that I am asking the compiler to infer it from the code. You can see from the statements that follow that the compiler will allow only members of the inferred class—Product in this case—to be called.

Using Anonymous Types

By combining object initializers and type inference, I can create simple data-storage objects without needing to define the corresponding class or struct. Listing 4-25 shows an example.

Listing 4-25. Creating an Anonymous Type

```
...
var myAnonType = new {
    Name = "MVC",
    Category = "Pattern"
};

...
```

In this example, `myAnonType` is an anonymously typed object. This does not mean that it is dynamic in the sense that JavaScript variables are dynamic. It just means that the type definition will be created automatically by the compiler. Strong typing is still enforced. You can get and set only the properties that have been defined in the initializer, for example.

The C# compiler generates the class based on the name and type of the parameters in the initializer. Two anonymously typed objects that have the same property names and types will be assigned to the same automatically generated class. This means I can create arrays of anonymously typed objects, as demonstrated by Listing 4-26, which shows the `CreateAnonArray` action method I added to the Home controller.

Listing 4-26. Creating an Array of Anonymously Typed Objects in the HomeController.cs File

```
using System;
using System.Collections.Generic;
using System.Text;
using System.Web.Mvc;
using LanguageFeatures.Models;

namespace LanguageFeatures.Controllers {
    public class HomeController : Controller {

        public string Index() {
            return "Navigate to a URL to show an example";
        }

        // ...other action methods omitted for brevity...

        public ViewResult CreateAnonArray() {

            var oddsAndEnds = new[] {
                new { Name = "MVC", Category = "Pattern"},
                new { Name = "Hat", Category = "Clothing"},
                new { Name = "Apple", Category = "Fruit"}
            };

            StringBuilder result = new StringBuilder();
            foreach (var item in oddsAndEnds) {
                result.Append(item.Name).Append(" ");
            }

            return View("Result", (object)result.ToString());
        }
    }
}
```

Notice that I use var to declare the variable array. I must do this because I do not have a type to specify, as I would in a regularly typed array. Even though I have not defined a class for any of these objects, I can still enumerate the contents of the array and read the value of the Name property from each of them. This is important, because without this feature, I would not be able to create arrays of anonymously typed objects at all. Or, rather, I *could* create the arrays, but I would not be able to do anything useful with them. You will see the following results if you run the example and target the action method:

```
MVC Hat Apple
```

Performing Language Integrated Queries

All of the features I have described so far are put to good use in LINQ. I love LINQ. It is a wonderful and compelling addition to .NET. If you have never used LINQ, you have been missing out. LINQ is a SQL-like syntax for querying data in classes. Imagine that I have a collection of Product objects, and I want to find the three highest prices and pass them to the View method. Without LINQ, I would end up with something similar to Listing 4-27, which shows the FindProducts action method I added to the Home controller.

Listing 4-27. Querying Without LINQ in the HomeController.cs File

```
...
public ViewResult FindProducts() {

    Product[] products = {
        new Product {Name = "Kayak", Category = "Watersports", Price = 275M},
        new Product {Name = "Lifejacket", Category = "Watersports", Price = 48.95M},
        new Product {Name = "Soccer ball", Category = "Soccer", Price = 19.50M},
        new Product {Name = "Corner flag", Category = "Soccer", Price = 34.95M}
    };

    // define the array to hold the results
    Product[] foundProducts = new Product[3];
    // sort the contents of the array
    Array.Sort(products, (item1, item2) => {
        return Comparer<decimal>.Default.Compare(item1.Price, item2.Price);
    });
    // get the first three items in the array as the results
    Array.Copy(products, foundProducts, 3);

    // create the result
    StringBuilder result = new StringBuilder();
    foreach (Product p in foundProducts) {
        result.AppendFormat("Price: {0} ", p.Price);
    }

    return View("Result", (object)result.ToString());
}
...
```

With LINQ, I can significantly simplify the querying process, as demonstrated in Listing 4-28.

Listing 4-28. Using LINQ to Query Data in the HomeController.cs File

```
using System;
using System.Collections.Generic;
using System.Linq;
using System.Text;
using System.Web.Mvc;
using LanguageFeatures.Models;

namespace LanguageFeatures.Controllers {
    public class HomeController : Controller {

        public string Index() {
            return "Navigate to a URL to show an example";
        }

        // ...other action methods omitted for brevity...

        public ViewResult FindProducts() {

            Product[] products = {
             new Product {Name = "Kayak", Category = "Watersports", Price = 275M},
             new Product {Name = "Lifejacket", Category = "Watersports", Price = 48.95M},
             new Product {Name = "Soccer ball", Category = "Soccer", Price = 19.50M},
             new Product {Name = "Corner flag", Category = "Soccer", Price = 34.95M}
            };

            var foundProducts = from match in products
                                orderby match.Price descending
                                select new { match.Name, match.Price };

            // create the result
            int count = 0;
            StringBuilder result = new StringBuilder();
            foreach (var p in foundProducts) {
                result.AppendFormat("Price: {0} ", p.Price);
                if (++count == 3) {
                    break;
                }
            }

            return View("Result", (object)result.ToString());
        }
    }
}
```

This is a lot neater. You can see the SQL-like query shown in bold. I order the Product objects in descending order and use the select keyword to return an anonymous type that contains just the Name and Price properties. This style of LINQ is known as *query syntax,* and it is the kind that developers find most comfortable when they start using LINQ. The wrinkle in this query is that it returns one anonymously typed object for every Product in the array that I used in the source query, so I need to play around with the results to get the first three and print out the details.

However, if you are willing to forgo the simplicity of the query syntax, you can get a lot more power from LINQ. The alternative is the *dot-notation syntax*, or *dot notation*, which is based on extension methods. Listing 4-29 shows this alternative syntax used to process the Product objects.

Listing 4-29. Using LINQ Dot Notation in the HomeController.cs File

```
...
public ViewResult FindProducts() {

    Product[] products = {
        new Product {Name = "Kayak", Category = "Watersports", Price = 275M},
        new Product {Name = "Lifejacket", Category = "Watersports", Price = 48.95M},
        new Product {Name = "Soccer ball", Category = "Soccer", Price = 19.50M},
        new Product {Name = "Corner flag", Category = "Soccer", Price = 34.95M}
    };

    var foundProducts = products.OrderByDescending(e => e.Price)
                        .Take(3)
                        .Select(e => new { e.Name, e.Price });

    StringBuilder result = new StringBuilder();
    foreach (var p in foundProducts) {
        result.AppendFormat("Price: {0} ", p.Price);
    }

    return View("Result", (object)result.ToString());
}
...
```

This LINQ query, shown in bold, is not as nice to look at as the one expressed in query syntax, but not all LINQ features have corresponding C# keywords. For serious LINQ queries, I need to switch to using extension methods. Each of the LINQ extension methods in the listing is applied to an IEnumerable<T> and returns an IEnumerable<T> too, which allows me to chain the methods together to form complex queries.

■ **Note**   All of the LINQ extension methods are in the System.Linq namespace, which you must bring into scope with a using statement before you can make queries. Visual Studio adds the System.Linq namespace to controller classes automatically, but you may need to add it manually elsewhere in an MVC project.

The OrderByDescending method rearranges the items in the data source. In this case, the lambda expression returns the value I want used for comparisons. The Take method returns a specified number of items from the front of the results (this is what I couldn't do using query syntax). The Select method allows me to project my results, specifying the structure I want. In this case, I am projecting an anonymous object that contains the Name and Price properties.

■ **Tip**   Notice that I have not needed to specify the names of the properties in the anonymous type. C# has inferred this from the properties I picked in the Select method.

Table 4-2 describes the most useful LINQ extension methods. I use LINQ liberally throughout the rest of this book, and you may find it useful to return to this table when you see an extension method that you have not encountered before. All of the LINQ methods shown in the table operate on IEnumerable<T>.

Table 4-2. *Some Useful LINQ Extension Methods*

Extension Method	Description	Deferred
All	Returns true if all the items in the source data match the predicate	No
Any	Returns true if at least one of the items in the source data matches the predicate	No
Contains	Returns true if the data source contains a specific item or value	No
Count	Returns the number of items in the data source	No
First	Returns the first item from the data source	No
FirstOrDefault	Returns the first item from the data source or the default value if there are no items	No
Last	Returns the last item in the data source	No
LastOrDefault	Returns the last item in the data source or the default value if there are no items	No
Max Min	Returns the largest or smallest value specified by a lambda expression	No
OrderBy OrderByDescending	Sorts the source data based on the value returned by the lambda expression	Yes
Reverse	Reverses the order of the items in the data source	Yes
Select	Projects a result from a query	Yes
SelectMany	Projects each data item into a sequence of items and then concatenates all of those resulting sequences into a single sequence	Yes
Single	Returns the first item from the data source or throws an exception if there are multiple matches	No
SingleOrDefault	Returns the first item from the data source or the default value if there are no items, or throws an exception if there are multiple matches	No
Skip SkipWhile	Skips over a specified number of elements, or skips while the predicate matches	Yes
Sum	Totals the values selected by the predicate	No
Take TakeWhile	Selects a specified number of elements from the start of the data source or selects items while the predicate matches	Yes
ToArray ToDictionary ToList	Converts the data source to an array or other collection type	No
Where	Filters items from the data source that do not match the predicate	Yes

Understanding Deferred LINQ Queries

You will notice that Table 2 includes a Deferred column. There is an interesting variation in the way that the extension methods are executed in a LINQ query. A query that contains only deferred methods is not executed until the items in the result are enumerated, as demonstrated by Listing 4-30, which shows a simple change to the FindProducts action method.

Listing 4-30. Using Deferred LINQ Extension Methods in a Query in the HomeController.cs File

```
...
public ViewResult FindProducts() {

    Product[] products = {
        new Product {Name = "Kayak", Category = "Watersports", Price = 275M},
        new Product {Name = "Lifejacket", Category = "Watersports", Price = 48.95M},
        new Product {Name = "Soccer ball", Category = "Soccer", Price = 19.50M},
        new Product {Name = "Corner flag", Category = "Soccer", Price = 34.95M}
    };

    var foundProducts = products.OrderByDescending(e => e.Price)
                            .Take(3)
                            .Select(e => new {
                                e.Name,
                                e.Price
                            });

    products[2] = new Product { Name = "Stadium", Price = 79600M };

    StringBuilder result = new StringBuilder();
    foreach (var p in foundProducts) {
        result.AppendFormat("Price: {0} ", p.Price);
    }

    return View("Result", (object)result.ToString());
}
...
```

Between defining the LINQ query and enumerating the results, I changed one of the items in the products array. The output from this example is as follows:

```
Price: 79600 Price: 275 Price: 48.95
```

You can see that the query is not evaluated until the results are enumerated, and so the change I made—introducing Stadium into the Product array—is reflected in the output.

■ **Tip** One interesting feature that arises from deferred LINQ extension methods is that queries are evaluated from scratch every time the results are enumerated, meaning that you can perform the query repeatedly as the source data for the changes and get results that reflect the current state of the source data.

By contrast, using any of the non-deferred extension methods causes a LINQ query to be performed immediately. Listing 4-31 shows the SumProducts action method I added to the Home controller.

Listing 4-31. An Immediately Executed LINQ Query in the HomeController.cs File

```
...
public ViewResult SumProducts() {

    Product[] products = {
        new Product {Name = "Kayak", Category = "Watersports", Price = 275M},
        new Product {Name = "Lifejacket", Category = "Watersports", Price = 48.95M},
        new Product {Name = "Soccer ball", Category = "Soccer", Price = 19.50M},
        new Product {Name = "Corner flag", Category = "Soccer", Price = 34.95M}
    };

    var results = products.Sum(e => e.Price);

    products[2] = new Product { Name = "Stadium", Price = 79500M };

    return View("Result",
        (object)String.Format("Sum: {0:c}", results));
}
...
```

This example uses the Sum method, which is not deferred, and produces the following result:

```
Sum: $378.40
```

You can see that the Stadium item, with its much higher price, has not been included in the results—this is because the results from the Sum method are evaluated as soon as the method is called, rather than being deferred until the results are used.

Using Async Methods

One of the big recent additions to C# is improvements in the way that *asynchronous methods* are dealt with. Asynchronous methods go off and do work in the background and notify you when they are complete, allowing your code to take care of other business while the background work is performed. Asynchronous methods are an important tool in removing bottlenecks from code and allow applications to take advantage of multiple processors and processor cores to perform work in parallel.

C# and .NET have excellent support for asynchronous methods, but the code tends to be verbose and developers who are not used to parallel programming often get bogged down by the unusual syntax. As an example, Listing 4-32 shows an asynchronous method called GetPageLength, which I defined in a class called MyAsyncMethods and added to the Models folder in a class file called MyAsyncMethods.cs.

CHAPTER 4 ▪ ESSENTIAL LANGUAGE FEATURES

Listing 4-32. A Simple Asynchronous Method in the MyAsyncMethods.cs File

```
using System.Net.Http;
using System.Threading.Tasks;

namespace LanguageFeatures.Models {

    public class MyAsyncMethods {

        public static Task<long?> GetPageLength() {

            HttpClient client = new HttpClient();

            var httpTask = client.GetAsync("http://apress.com");

            // we could do other things here while we are waiting
            // for the HTTP request to complete

            return httpTask.ContinueWith((Task<HttpResponseMessage> antecedent) => {
                return antecedent.Result.Content.Headers.ContentLength;
            });
        }
    }
}
```

▪ **Caution**   This example requires the `System.Net.Http` assembly, which I added to the project at the start of the chapter.

This is a simple method that uses a `System.Net.Http.HttpClient` object to request the contents of the Apress home page and returns its length. I have highlighted the part of the method that tends to cause confusion, which is an example of a *task continuation*.

.NET represents work that will be done asynchronously as a `Task`. `Task` objects are strongly typed based on the result that the background work produces. So, when I call the `HttpClient.GetAsync` method, what I get back is a `Task<HttpResponseMessage>`. This tells me that the request will be performed in the background and that the result of the request will be an `HttpResponseMessage` object.

▪ **Tip**   When I use words like *background*, I am skipping over a lot of detail in order to make the key points that are important to the world of MVC. The .NET support for asynchronous methods and parallel programming in general is excellent and I encourage you to learn more about it if you want to create truly high-performing applications that can take advantage of multicore and multiprocessor hardware. I come back to asynchronous methods for MVC in Chapter 19.

The part that most programmers get bogged down with is the *continuation*, which is the mechanism by which you specify what you want to happen when the background task is complete. In the example, I have used the `ContinueWith` method to process the `HttpResponseMessage` object I get from the `HttpClient.GetAsync` method, which I do using a lambda expression that returns the value of a property that returns the length of the content I get from the Apress Web server. Notice that I use the return keyword twice:

```
...
return httpTask.ContinueWith((Task<HttpResponseMessage> antecedent) => {
    return antecedent.Result.Content.Headers.ContentLength;
});
...
```

This is the part that makes heads hurt. The first use of the return keyword specifies that I am returning a Task<HttpResponseMessage> object, which, when the task is complete, will return the length of the ContentLength header. The ContentLength header returns a long? result (a nullable long value) and this means that the result of my GetPageLength method is Task<long?>, like this:

```
...
public static Task<long?> GetPageLength() {
...
```

Do not worry if this does not make sense—you are not alone in your confusion. And this is a simple example—complex asynchronous operations can chain large numbers of tasks together using the ContinueWith method, which creates code that can be hard to read and harder to maintain.

Applying the async and await Keywords

Microsoft introduced two keywords to C# that are specifically intended to simplify using asynchronous methods like HttpClient.getAsync. The keywords are async and await and you can see how I have used them to simplify my example method in Listing 4-33.

Listing 4-33. Using the Async and Await Keywords in the MyAsyncMethods.cs File

```
using System.Net.Http;
using System.Threading.Tasks;

namespace LanguageFeatures.Models {

    public class MyAsyncMethods {

        public async static Task<long?> GetPageLength() {

            HttpClient client = new HttpClient();

            var httpMessage = await client.GetAsync("http://apress.com");

            // we could do other things here while we are waiting
            // for the HTTP request to complete
            return httpMessage.Content.Headers.ContentLength;
        }
    }
}
```

I used the await keyword when calling the asynchronous method. This tells the C# compiler that I want to wait for the result of the Task that the GetAsync method returns and then carry on executing other statements in the same method.

Applying the await keyword means I can treat the result from the GetAsync method as though it were a regular method and just assign the HttpResponseMessage object that it returns to a variable. And, even better, I can then use the return keyword in the normal way to produce a result from other method—in this case, the value of the ContentLength property. This is a much more natural technique and it means I do not have to worry about the ContinueWith method and multiple uses of the return keyword.

When you use the await keyword, you must also add the async keyword to the method signature, as I have done in the example. The method result type does not change—my example GetPageLength method still returns a Task<long?>. This is because the await and async are implemented using some clever compiler tricks, meaning that they allow a more natural syntax, but they do not change what is happening in the methods to which they are applied. Someone who is calling my GetPageLength method still has to deal with a Task<long?> result because there is still a background operation that produces a nullable long—although, of course, that programmer can also choose to use the await and async keywords as well.

▪ **Note**   You will have noticed that I did not provide an MVC example for you to test out the async and await keywords. This is because using asynchronous methods in MVC controllers requires a special technique, and I have a lot of information to present to you before I introduce it in Chapter 19.

Summary

In this chapter, I gave you an overview of the key C# language features that an effective MVC programmer needs to know. These features are combined in LINQ, which I use to query data throughout this book. As I said, I am a big fan of LINQ, and it plays an important role in MVC applications. I also showed you the async and await keywords, which make it easier to work with asynchronous methods—this is a topic that I return to in Chapter 19 when I show you an advanced technique for integrating asynchronous programming into your MVC controllers.

In the next chapter, I turn my attention to the Razor View Engine, which is the mechanism by which dynamic data is inserted into views.

CHAPTER 5

■ ■ ■

Working with Razor

A *view engine* procezses ASP.NET content and looks for instructions, typically to insert dynamic content into the output sent to a browser and *Razor* is the name of the MVC Framework view engine. There are no changes to Razor in MVC 5 and if you are already familiar with the syntax from earlier versions you can skip ahead.

In this chapter, I give you a quick tour of the Razor syntax so you can recognize Razor expressions when you see them. I am not going to supply an exhaustive Razor reference in this chapter; think of this more as a crash course in the syntax. I explore Razor in depth as I continue through the book, within the context of other MVC Framework features. Table 5-1 provides the summary for this chapter.

Table 5-1. *Chapter Summary*

Problem	Solution	Listing
Define and access the model type	Use the @model and @Model expressions	1–4, 15
Reduce duplication in views	Use a layout	5–7, 10–12
Specify a default layout	Use the view start view	8, 9
Pass data values to the view from the controller	Pass a view model object or the view bag	13, 14
Generate different content based on data values	Use Razor conditional statements	16, 17
Enumerate an array or a collection	Use a @foreach expression	18, 19
Add a namespace to a view	Use a @using expression	20

Preparing the Example Project

To demonstrate Razor, I created a new Visual Studio project called Razor using the ASP.NET MVC Web Application template. I selected the Empty option and checked the box to get the initial configuration for an MVC project.

Defining the Model

I am going to start with a simple domain model called Product, defined in a class file called Product.cs, which I added to the Models folder. You can see the contents of the new file in Listing 5-1.

Listing 5-1. The Contents of the Product.cs File

```
namespace Razor.Models {

    public class Product {

        public int ProductID { get; set; }
        public string Name { get; set; }
        public string Description { get; set; }
        public decimal Price { get; set; }
        public string Category { set; get; }
    }
}
```

Defining the Controller

I am going to follow the MVC Framework convention and define a controller called Home as the initial starting point for my project. Right-click the Controllers folder in the Solution Explorer, select Add ➤ Controller, select MVC 5 Controller-Empty, click Add and set the name to HomeController. When you click the second Add button, Visual Studio will create the Controllers/HomeController.cs file. Edit the contents to match those shown in Listing 5-2.

Listing 5-2. The Content of the HomeController.cs File

```
using System.Web.Mvc;
using Razor.Models;

namespace Razor.Controllers {

    public class HomeController : Controller {
        Product myProduct = new Product {
            ProductID = 1,
            Name = "Kayak",
            Description = "A boat for one person",
            Category = "Watersports",
            Price = 275M
        };

        public ActionResult Index() {
            return View(myProduct);
        }
    }
}
```

The controller defines an action method called Index, in which I create and populate the properties of a Product object. I pass the Product to the View method so that it is used as the model when the view is rendered. I do not specify the name of a view file when I call the View method, so the default view for the action method will be used.

Creating the View

Right-click on the Index method in the HomeController class and select Add View from the pop-up menu. Ensure that the name of the view is Index, change the Template to Empty and select Product for the model class. (If you don't see Product as an option for the model, compile the project and start over). Uncheck the View Option boxes and click Add to create the Index.cshtml file in the Views/Home folder. The initial contents of the new view are shown in Listing 5-3.

Listing 5-3. The Contents of the Index.cshtml File

```
@model Razor.Models.Product

@{
    Layout = null;
}

<!DOCTYPE html>

<html>
<head>
    <meta name="viewport" content="width=device-width" />
    <title>Index</title>
</head>
<body>
    <div>

    </div>
</body>
</html>
```

In the sections that follow, I go through the different parts of a Razor view and demonstrate some of the different things you can do with one. When learning about Razor, it is helpful to bear in mind that views exist to express one or more parts of the model to the user—and that means generating HTML that displays data that is retrieved from one or more objects. If you remember that I am always trying to build an HTML page that can be sent to the client, then everything that Razor does begins to make sense.

■ **Note** I repeat some information in the following sections that I already touched on in Chapter 2. I want to provide you with a single place in the reference that you can turn to when you need to look up a Razor feature and I thought that a small amount of duplication made this worthwhile.

Working with the Model Object

Let us start with the first line in the view:

```
...
@model Razor.Models.Product
...
```

Razor statements start with the @ character. In this case, the @model statement declares the type of the model object that I will pass to the view from the action method. This allows me to refer to the methods, fields, and properties of the view model object through @Model, as shown in Listing 5-4, which shows a simple addition to the Index view.

Listing 5-4. Referring to a View Model Object Property in the Index.cshtml File

```
@model Razor.Models.Product

@{
    Layout = null;
}

<!DOCTYPE html>

<html>
<head>
    <meta name="viewport" content="width=device-width" />
    <title>Index</title>
</head>
<body>
    <div>
        @Model.Name
    </div>
</body>
</html>
```

■ **Note**   Notice that I declare the view model object type using @model (lower case m) and access the Name property using @Model (upper case M). This is slightly confusing when you start working with Razor, but it becomes second nature pretty quickly.

If you start the project, you'll see the output shown in Figure 5-1.

Figure 5-1. *The Effect of Reading a Property Value in the View*

By using the @model expression, I tell MVC what kind of object I will be working with and Visual Studio takes advantage of this in a couple of ways. First, as you are writing your view, Visual Studio will pop up suggestions of member names when you type @Model followed by a period, as shown in Figure 5-2. This is similar to the way that autocomplete for lambda expressions passed to HTML helper methods works, which I described in Chapter 4.

Figure 5-2. *Visual Studio offering suggestions for member names based on the @Model expression*

Equally useful is that Visual Studio will flag errors when there are problems with the view model object members you are referring to. You can see an example of this in Figure 5-3, where I have tried to reference @Model.NotARealProperty. Visual Studio has realized that the Product class I specified at the model type does not have such a property and has highlighted an error in the editor.

```
    <meta name="viewport" content="width=device-width" />
    <title>Index</title>
</head>
<body>
    <div>
        @Model.NotARealProperty
    </div>
</body>
</html>
```

Figure 5-3. *Visual Studio reporting a problem with an @Model expression*

Working with Layouts

The other Razor expression in the Index.cshtml view file is this one:

```
...
@{
    Layout = null;
}
...
```

This is an example of a Razor *code block*, which allows me to include C# statements in a view. The code block is opened with @{ and closed with } and the statements it contains are evaluated when the view is rendered.

This code block sets the value of the Layout property to null. As I explain in detail in Chapter 20, Razor views are compiled into C# classes in an MVC application and the base class that is used defines the Layout property. I'll show you how this all works in Chapter 20, but the effect of setting the Layout property to null is to tell the MVC framework that the view is self-contained and will render all of the content required for the client.

Self-contained views are fine for simple example apps, but a real project can have dozens of views. Layouts are effectively templates that contain markup that you use to create consistency across your app—this could be to ensure that the right JavaScript libraries are included in the result or that a common look and feel is used throughout.

Creating the Layout

To create a layout, right-click on the Views folder in the Solution Explorer, click Add ➤ New Item from the Add menu and select the MVC 5 Layout Page (Razor) template, as shown in Figure 5-4.

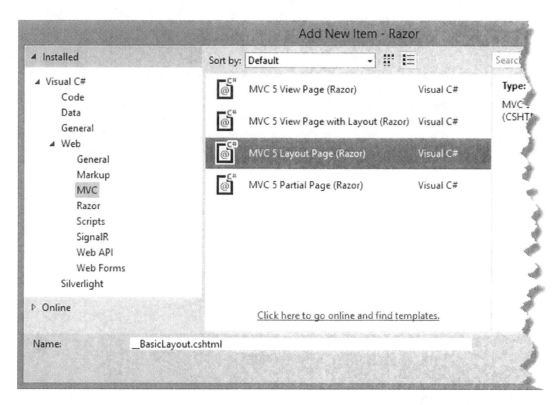

Figure 5-4. *Creating a new layout*

Set the name of the file to _BasicLayout.cshtml (notice the first character is an underscore) and click the Add button to create the file. Listing 5-5 shows the contents of the file as it is created by Visual Studio.

■ **Note**   Files in the Views folder whose names begin with an underscore (_) are not returned to the user, which allows the file name to differentiate between views that you want to render and the files that support them. Layouts, which are support files, are prefixed with an underscore.

Listing 5-5. The Initial Contents of the _BasicLayout.cshtml File

```
<!DOCTYPE html>

<html>
<head>
    <meta name="viewport" content="width=device-width" />
    <title>@ViewBag.Title</title>
</head>
<body>
    <div>
        @RenderBody()
    </div>
</body>
</html>
```

Layouts are a specialized form of view and I have highlighted the @ expressions in the listing. The call to the @RenderBody method inserts the contents of the view specified by the action method into the layout markup. The other Razor expression in the layout looks for a property called Title in the ViewBag in order to set the contents of the title element.

The elements in the layout will be applied to any view that uses the layout and this is why layouts are essentially templates. In Listing 5-6, I have added some simple markup to the layout to demonstrate how this works.

Listing 5-6. Adding Elements to the _BasicLayout.cshtml File

```
<!DOCTYPE html>

<html>
<head>
    <meta name="viewport" content="width=device-width" />
    <title>@ViewBag.Title</title>
</head>
<body>
    <h1>Product Information</h1>
    <div style="padding: 20px; border: solid medium black; font-size: 20pt">
        @RenderBody()
    </div>
    <h2>Visit <a href="http://apress.com">Apress</a></h2>
</body>
</html>
```

I have added a couple of header elements and applied some CSS styles to the div element which contains the @RenderBody expression, just to make it clear what content comes from the layout and what comes from the view.

Applying a Layout

To apply the layout to the view, I just need to set the value of the Layout property. The layout contains the HTML elements that define the structure of the response to the browser, so I can also remove those elements from the view. You can see how I have applied the layout in Listing 5-7, which shows a drastically simplified Index.cshtml file.

■ **Tip**   I also set a value for the ViewBag.Title property, which will be used as the contents of the title element in the HTML document sent back to the user—this is optional, but good practice. If there is no value for the property, the MVC framework will return an empty title element.

Listing 5-7. Using the Layout Property in the Index.cshtml File

```
@model Razor.Models.Product

@{
    ViewBag.Title = "Product Name";
    Layout = "~/Views/_BasicLayout.cshtml";
}

Product Name: @Model.Name
```

The transformation is dramatic, even for such a simple view. What I am left with is focused on presenting data from the view model object to the user, which is ideal–not only does it let me work with simpler markup, but it means that I don't have to duplicate common elements in every view that I create. To see the effect of the layout, run the example app. The results are shown in Figure 5-5.

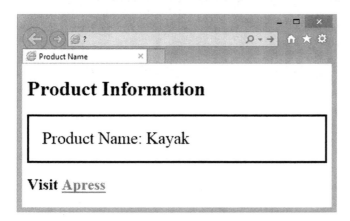

Figure 5-5. *The Effect of Applying a Simple Layout to a View*

Using a View Start File

I still have a tiny wrinkle to sort out, which is that I have to specify the layout file I want in every view. That means that if I need to rename the layout file, I am going to have to find every view that refers to it and make a change, which will be an error-prone process and counter to the general theme of easy maintenance that runs through the MVC framework.

I can resolve this by using a *view start file*. When it renders a view, the MVC framework will look for a file called _ViewStart.cshtml. The contents of this file will be treated as though they were contained in the view file itself and I can use this feature to automatically set a value for the Layout property.

To create a view start file, add a new layout file to the Views folder and set the name of the file to _ViewStart.cshtml (once again, notice the leading underscore). Edit the contents of the new file so that they match those shown in Listing 5-8.

Listing 5-8. The contents of the _ViewStart.cshtml File

```
@{
    Layout = "~/Views/_BasicLayout.cshtml";
}
```

My view start file contains a value for the Layout property, which means that I can remove the corresponding expression from the Index.cshtml file, as shown in Listing 5-9.

Listing 5-9. Updating the Index.cshtml File to Reflect the Use of a View Start File

```
@model Razor.Models.Product

@{
    ViewBag.Title = "Product Name";
}

Product Name: @Model.Name
```

I do not have to specify that I want to use the view start file. The MVC framework will locate the file and use its contents automatically. The values defined in the view file take precedence, which makes it easy to override the view start file.

■ **Caution**   It is important to understand the difference between omitting the Layout property from the view file and setting it to null. If your view is self-contained and you do not want to use a layout, then set the Layout property to null. If you omit the Layout property, then the MVC framework will assume that you *do* want a layout and that it should use the value it finds in the view start file.

Demonstrating Shared Layouts

As a quick and simple demonstration of how layouts are shared, I have added a new action method to the Home controller called NameAndPrice. You can see the definition of this method in Listing 5-10, which shows the changes I made to the HomeController.cs file.

Listing 5-10. Adding a New Action Method to the HomeController.cs File

```
using System.Web.Mvc;
using Razor.Models;

namespace Razor.Controllers {

    public class HomeController : Controller {
        Product myProduct = new Product {
```

```
            ProductID = 1,
            Name = "Kayak",
            Description = "A boat for one person",
            Category = "Watersports",
            Price = 275M
        };

        public ActionResult Index() {
            return View(myProduct);
        }

        public ActionResult NameAndPrice() {
            return View(myProduct);
        }
    }
}
```

The action method passes the myProduct object to the view method, just like the Index action method does—this is not something that you would do in a real project, but I am demonstrating Razor functionality and so a simple example suits my needs. Right-click on the NameAndPrice action method and select Add View from the pop-up menu. Fill in the Add View dialog to match Figure 5-6: set View Name to NameAndPrice; set Template to Empty and set the Model Class to Product.

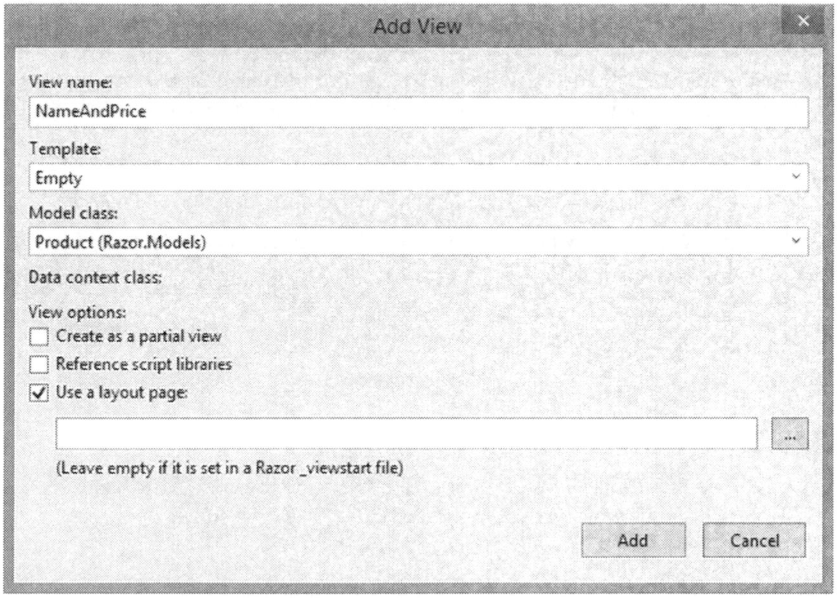

Figure 5-6. *Adding a view that relies on a layout*

Ensure that the Use a Layout Page box is checked–and notice the text beneath the text field. It says that you should leave the textbox empty if you have specified the view you want to use in a view start file. If you were to click the Add button at this point, the view would be created without a value for the Layout property.

I want to explicitly specify the view, so click on the button with an ellipsis label (...) that is to the right of the text field. Visual Studio will present you with a dialog that allows you to select a layout file, as shown in Figure 5-7.

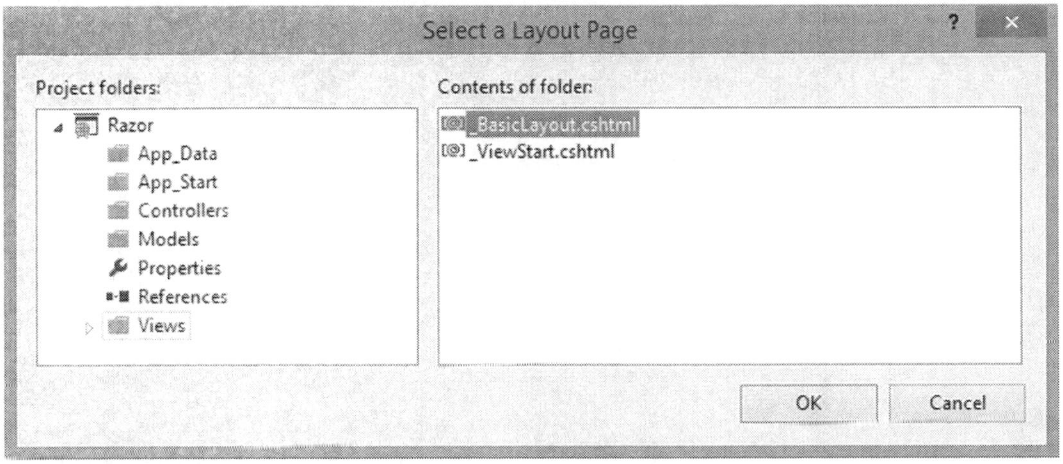

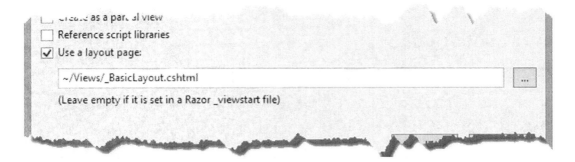

Figure 5-7. Selecting the layout file

The convention for an MVC project is to place layout files in the Views folder, but is only a convention, which is why the left-hand panel of the dialog lets you navigate around the project, just in case you have decided to put them somewhere else.

I have only defined one layout file, so select _BasicLayout.cshtml and click the OK button to return to the Add View dialog. You will see that the name of the layout file has been placed in the textbox, as shown in Figure 5-8.

Figure 5-8. Specifying a layout file when creating a view

Click the Add button to create the /Views/Home/NameAndPrice.cshtml file. You can see the contents of this file in Listing 5-11.

Listing 5-11. The Contents of the NameAndPrice.cshtml File

```
@model Razor.Models.Product

@{
    ViewBag.Title = "NameAndPrice";
    Layout = "~/Views/_BasicLayout.cshtml";
}

<h2>NameAndPrice</h2>
```

Visual Studio uses slightly different default content for view files when you specify a layout, but you can see that the result contains the same Razor expressions I used when I applied the layout to a view directly. To complete this example, Listing 5-12 shows a simple addition to the NameAndPrice.cshtml file that displays data values from the view model object.

Listing 5-12. Adding to the NameAndPrice.cshtml File

```
@model Razor.Models.Product

@{
    ViewBag.Title = "NameAndPrice";
    Layout = "~/Views/_BasicLayout.cshtml";
}

<h2>NameAndPrice</h2>
The product name is @Model.Name and it costs $@Model.Price
```

If you start the app and navigate to /Home/NameAndPrice, you will see the results illustrated by Figure 5-9. As you might have expected, the common elements and styles defined in the layout have been applied to the view, demonstrating how a layout can be used as a template to create a common look and feel (albeit a simple and unattractive one in this example).

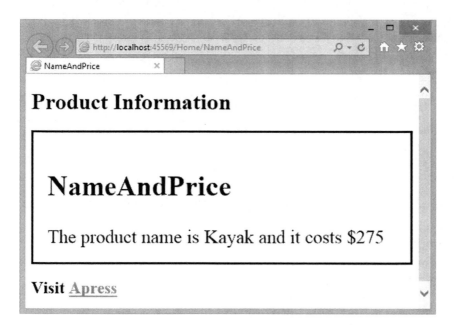

Figure 5-9. *The content in the layout file applied to the NameAndPrice view*

■ **Note**   I would have gotten the same result if I had left the text field in the Add View dialog empty and relied on the view start file. I specified the file explicitly only because I wanted to show you the Visual Studio feature which helps you make a selection.

Using Razor Expressions

Now that I have shown you the basics of views and layouts, I am going to turn to the different kinds of expressions that Razor supports and how you can use them to create view content. In a good MVC Framework application, there is a clear separation between the roles that the action method and view perform. The rules are simple and I have summarized them in Table 5-2.

Table 5-2. *The Roles Played by the Action Method and the View*

Component	Does Do	Doesn't Do
Action Method	Passa view model object to the view	Pass formatted data to the view
View	Use the view model object to present content to the user	Change any aspect of the view model object

I am going to come back to this theme throughout this book. To get the best from the MVC Framework, you need to respect and enforce the separation between the different parts of the app. As you will see, you can do quite a lot with Razor, including using C# statements—but you should not use Razor to perform business logic or manipulate your domain model objects in any way.

Equally, you should not format the data that your action method passed to the view. Instead, let the view figure out data it needs to display. You can see a simple example of this in the previous section of this chapter. I defined an action method called NameAndPrice, which displays the value of the Name and Price properties of a Product object. Even though I knew which properties I needed to display, I passed the complete Product object to the view model, like this:

```
...
public ActionResult NameAndPrice() {
    return View(myProduct);
}
...
```

I then used the Razor @Model expression in the view to get the value of the properties I was interested in, like this:

```
...
The product name is @Model.Name and it costs $@Model.Price
...
```

I could have created the string I wanted to display in the action method and passed it as the view model object to the view. It would have worked, but taking this approach undermines the benefit of the MVC pattern and reduces my ability to respond to changes in the future. As I said, I will return to this theme again, but you should remember that the MVC Framework does not enforce proper use of the MVC pattern and that you must remain aware of the effect of the design and coding decisions you make.

```
┌─────────────────────────────────────────────────────────────────────────────┐
│                    PROCESSING VERSUS FORMATTING DATA                          │
└─────────────────────────────────────────────────────────────────────────────┘
```

It is important to differentiate between *processing* data and *formatting* it. Views *format* data, which is why I passed the Product object in the previous section to the view, rather than formatting the object's properties into a display string. Processing data–including selecting the data objects to display–is the responsibility of the controller, which will call on the model to get and modify the data it requires. It can sometimes be hard to figure out where the line between processing and formatting is, but as a rule of thumb, I recommend erring on the side of caution and pushing anything but the most simple of expressions out of the view and into the controller.

Inserting Data Values

The simplest thing you can do with a Razor expression is to insert a data value into the markup. You can do this using the @Model expression to refer to properties and methods defined by the view model object or use the @ViewBag expression to refer to properties you have defined dynamically using the view bag feature (which I introduced in Chapter 2).

You have already seen examples of both these expressions, but for completeness, I have added a new action method to the Home controller called DemoExpressions that passes data to the view using a model object and the view bag. You can see the definition of the new action method in Listing 5-13.

Listing 5-13. The DemoExpression Action Method in the HomeController.cs File

```
using System.Web.Mvc;
using Razor.Models;

namespace Razor.Controllers {
    public class HomeController : Controller {
        Product myProduct = new Product {
            ProductID = 1,
            Name = "Kayak",
            Description = "A boat for one person",
            Category = "Watersports",
            Price = 275M
        };

        public ActionResult Index() {
            return View(myProduct);
        }

        public ActionResult NameAndPrice() {
            return View(myProduct);
        }

        public ActionResult DemoExpression() {

            ViewBag.ProductCount = 1;
            ViewBag.ExpressShip = true;
```

```
            ViewBag.ApplyDiscount = false;
            ViewBag.Supplier = null;

            return View(myProduct);
        }
    }
}
```

I have created a strongly typed view called DemoExpression.cshtml in the Views/Home folder to show these basic expressions and you can see the contents of the view file in Listing 5-14.

Listing 5-14. The Contents of the DemoExpression.cshtml File

```
@model Razor.Models.Product

@{
    ViewBag.Title = "DemoExpression";
}

<table>
    <thead>
        <tr><th>Property</th><th>Value</th></tr>
    </thead>
    <tbody>
        <tr><td>Name</td><td>@Model.Name</td></tr>
        <tr><td>Price</td><td>@Model.Price</td></tr>
        <tr><td>Stock Level</td><td>@ViewBag.ProductCount</td></tr>
    </tbody>
</table>
```

I created a simple HTML table and used the properties from the model object and the view bag to populate some of the cell values. You can see the result of starting the app and navigating to the /Home/DemoExpression URL, as shown in Figure 5-10. This is just a reconfirmation of the basic Razor expressions that I have been using in the examples so far.

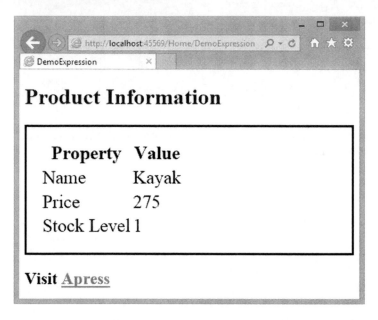

Figure 5-10. *Using basic Razor expressions to insert data values into the HTML markup*

The result is not pretty because I have not applied any CSS styles to the HTML elements that the view and the layout generate, but the example serves to reinforce the way in which the basic Razor expressions can be used to display the data passed from the action method to the view.

Setting Attribute Values

All of my examples so far have set the content of elements, but you can also use Razor expressions to set the value of element *attributes*. Listing 5-15 shows how I have changed the DemoExpression.cshtml view to use view bag properties to set attribute values.

Listing 5-15. Using a Razor Expression to Set an Attribute Value in the DemoExpression.cshtml File

```
@model Razor.Models.Product

@{
    ViewBag.Title = "DemoExpression";
    Layout = "~/Views/_BasicLayout.cshtml";
}

<table>
    <thead>
        <tr><th>Property</th><th>Value</th></tr>
    </thead>
    <tbody>
        <tr><td>Name</td><td>@Model.Name</td></tr>
        <tr><td>Price</td><td>@Model.Price</td></tr>
        <tr><td>Stock Level</td><td>@ViewBag.ProductCount</td></tr>
    </tbody>
</table>
```

```
<div data-discount="@ViewBag.ApplyDiscount" data-express="@ViewBag.ExpressShip"
    data-supplier="@ViewBag.Supplier">
    The containing element has data attributes
</div>

Discount:<input type="checkbox" checked="@ViewBag.ApplyDiscount" />
Express:<input type="checkbox" checked="@ViewBag.ExpressShip" />
Supplier:<input type="checkbox" checked="@ViewBag.Supplier" />
```

I used basic Razor expressions to set the value for some data attributes on a div element.

■ **Tip**   Data attributes, which are attributes whose names are prefixed by data-, have been an informal way of creating custom attributes for many years and have been made part of the formal standard as part of HTML5. I have used the values of the ApplyDiscount, ExpressShip and Supplier view bag properties to set the value of these attributes.

Start the example app, target the action method, and look at the HTML source that has been used to render the page. You will see that Razor has set the value of the attributes like this:

```
...
<div data-discount="False" data-express="True" data-supplier="">
    The containing element has data attributes
</div>
...
```

The False and True values correspond to the Boolean view bag values, but Razor has done something sensible for the property whose value is null, which is to render an empty string.

But things get interesting in the second set of additions to the view, which are a series of checkboxes whose checked attribute is set to the same view bag properties that I used for the data attributes. The HTML that Razor has rendered is as follows:

```
...
Discount: <input type="checkbox" />
Express:  <input type="checkbox" checked="checked" />
Supplier: <input type="checkbox" />
...
```

Razor is aware of the way that attributes such as checked are used, where the presence of the attribute rather than its value changes the configuration of the element (known as a *Boolean attribute* in the HTML specification). If Razor had inserted False or null or the empty string as the value of the checked attribute, then the checkbox that the browser displays would be checked. Instead, Razor has deleted the attribute from the element entirely when the value is false or null, creating an effect that is consistent with the view data, as shown in Figure 5-11.

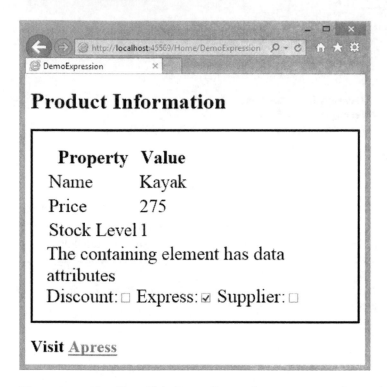

Figure 5-11. *The effect of deleting attributes whose presence configures their element*

Using Conditional Statements

Razor is able to process conditional statements, which means that I can tailor the output from a view based on values in the view data. This kind of technique is at the heart of Razor, and allows you to create complex and fluid layouts that are still reasonably simple to read and maintain. In Listing 5-16, I have updated the DemoExpression.cshtml view file to include a conditional statement.

Listing 5-16. Using a Conditional Razor Statement in the DemoExpression.cshtml File

```
@model Razor.Models.Product

@{
    ViewBag.Title = "DemoExpression";
    Layout = "~/Views/_BasicLayout.cshtml";
}

<table>
    <thead>
        <tr><th>Property</th><th>Value</th></tr>
    </thead>
    <tbody>
        <tr><td>Name</td><td>@Model.Name</td></tr>
        <tr><td>Price</td><td>@Model.Price</td></tr>
```

```
        <tr>
            <td>Stock Level</td>
            <td>
            @switch ((int)ViewBag.ProductCount) {
                case 0:
                    @: Out of Stock
                    break;
                case 1:
                    <b>Low Stock (@ViewBag.ProductCount)</b>
                    break;
                default:
                    @ViewBag.ProductCount
                    break;
            }
            </td>
        </tr>
    </tbody>
</table>
```

To start a conditional statement, you place an @ character in front of the C# conditional keyword, which is switch in this example. You terminate the code block with a close brace character (}) just as you would with a regular C# code block.

■ **Tip**   Notice that I had to cast the value of the `ViewBag.ProductCount` property to an `int` in order to use it with a `switch` statement. This is required because the Razor `switch` expression cannot evaluate a dynamic property–you must cast to a specific type so that it knows how to perform comparisons.

Inside of the Razor code block, you can include HTML elements and data values into the view output just by defining the HTML and Razor expressions, like this:

```
...
<b>Low Stock (@ViewBag.ProductCount)</b>
...
```

Or like this:

```
...
@ViewBag.ProductCount
...
```

I do not have to put the elements or expressions in quotes or denote them in any special way—the Razor engine will interpret these as output to be processed. However, if you want to insert literal text into the view when it is not contained in an HTML element, then you need to give Razor a helping hand and prefix the line like this:

```
...
@: Out of Stock
...
```

The @: characters prevent Razor from interpreting this as a C# statement, which is the default behavior when it encounters text. You can see the result of the conditional statement in Figure 5-12.

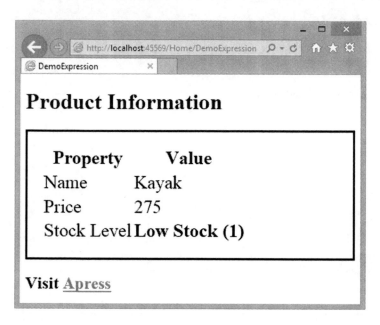

Figure 5-12. *Using a switch statement in a Razor view*

Conditional statements are important in Razor views because they allow content to be varied based on the data values that the view receives from the action method. As an additional demonstration, Listing 5-17 shows the addition of an if statement to the DemoExpression.cshtml view. As you might imagine, this is a commonly used conditional statement.

Listing 5-17. Using an if Statement in a Razor View in the DemoExpression.cshtml File

```
@model Razor.Models.Product

@{
    ViewBag.Title = "DemoExpression";
    Layout = "~/Views/_BasicLayout.cshtml";
}

<table>
    <thead>
        <tr><th>Property</th><th>Value</th></tr>
    </thead>
    <tbody>
        <tr><td>Name</td><td>@Model.Name</td></tr>
        <tr><td>Price</td><td>@Model.Price</td></tr>
        <tr>
            <td>Stock Level</td>
            <td>
                @if (ViewBag.ProductCount == 0) {
                    @:Out of Stock
```

```
        } else if (ViewBag.ProductCount == 1) {
            <b>Low Stock (@ViewBag.ProductCount)</b>
        } else {
            @ViewBag.ProductCount
        }
    </td>
</tr>
</tbody>
</table>
```

This conditional statement produces the same results as the switch statement, but I wanted to demonstrate how you can mesh C# conditional statements with Razor views. I explain how this all works in Chapter 20, when I explore views in depth.

Enumerating Arrays and Collections

When writing an MVC application, you will often want to enumerate the contents of an array or some other kind of collection of objects and generate content that details each one. To demonstrate how this is done, I have defined a new action method in the Home controller called DemoArray which you can see in Listing 5-18.

Listing 5-18. The DemoArray Action Method in the HomeController.cs File

```
using System.Web.Mvc;
using Razor.Models;

namespace Razor.Controllers {

    public class HomeController : Controller {

        Product myProduct = new Product {
            ProductID = 1,
            Name = "Kayak",
            Description = "A boat for one person",
            Category = "Watersports",
            Price = 275M
        };

        // ...other action methods omitted for brevity...

        public ActionResult DemoArray() {

            Product[] array = {
                new Product {Name = "Kayak", Price = 275M},
                new Product {Name = "Lifejacket", Price = 48.95M},
                new Product {Name = "Soccer ball", Price = 19.50M},
                new Product {Name = "Corner flag", Price = 34.95M}
            };
            return View(array);
        }
    }
}
```

This action method creates a Product[ ] object that contains simple data values and passes them to the View method so that the data is rendered using the default view. The Visual Studio scaffold feature won't let you specify an array as a model type. (I don't know why, since Razor itself happily supports array.) To create a view for an action method that passes an array, the best approach is to create a view without a model and then manually add the @model expression after the file has been created. In Listing 5-19, you can see the contents of the DemoArray.cshtml file that I created this way in the Views/Home folder and then edited.

Listing 5-19. The Contents of the DemoArray.cshtml File

```
@model Razor.Models.Product[]

@{
    ViewBag.Title = "DemoArray";
    Layout = "~/Views/_BasicLayout.cshtml";
}

@if (Model.Length > 0) {
    <table>
        <thead><tr><th>Product</th><th>Price</th></tr></thead>
        <tbody>
            @foreach (Razor.Models.Product p in Model) {
                <tr>
                    <td>@p.Name</td>
                    <td>$@p.Price</td>
                </tr>
            }
        </tbody>
    </table>
} else {
    <h2>No product data</h2>
}
```

I used an @if statement to vary the content based on the length of the array that I receive as the view model and a @foreach expression to enumerate the contents of the array and generate a row in an HTML table for each of them. You can see how these expressions match their C# counterpart. You can also see how I created a local variable called p in the foreach loop and then referred to its properties using the Razor expressions @p.Name and @p.Price.

The result is that I generate an h2 element if the array is empty and produce one row per array item in an HTML table otherwise. Because my data is static in this example, you will always see the same result, which I have shown in Figure 5-13.

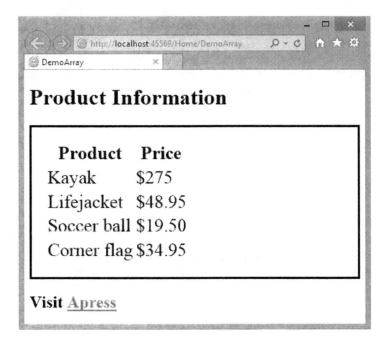

Figure 5-13. *Generating elements using a foreach statement*

Dealing with Namespaces

You will notice that I had to refer to the Product class by its fully qualified name in the foreach loop in the last example, like this:

```
...
@foreach (Razor.Models.Product p in Model) {
...
```

This can become annoying in a complex view, where you will have many references to view model and other classes. I can tidy up my views by applying the @using expression to bring a namespace into context for a view, just like I would in a regular C# class. Listing 5-20 shows how I have applied the @using expression to the DemoArray.cshtml view.

Listing 5-20. Applying the @using Expression in the DemoArray.cshtml File

```
@using Razor.Models
@model Product[]

@{
    ViewBag.Title = "DemoArray";
    Layout = "~/Views/_BasicLayout.cshtml";
}
```

```
@if (Model.Length > 0) {
    <table>
        <thead><tr><th>Product</th><th>Price</th></tr></thead>
        <tbody>
            @foreach (Product p in Model) {
                <tr>
                    <td>@p.Name</td>
                    <td>$@p.Price</td>
                </tr>
            }
        </tbody>
    </table>
} else {
    <h2>No product data</h2>
}
```

A view can contain multiple @using expressions. I have used the @using expression to import the Razor.Models namespace, which means that I can remove the namespace from the @model expression and from within the foreach loop.

Summary

In this chapter, I have given you an overview of the Razor view engine and how it can be used to generate HTML. I showed you how to refer to data passed from the controller via the view model object and the view bag, and how Razor expressions can be used to tailor responses to the user based on data values. You will see many different examples of how Razor can be used in the rest of the book and I describe how the MVC view mechanism works in detail in Chapter 20. In the next chapter, I describe the essential development and testing tools that underpin the MVC Framework and that help you to get the best from your projects.

CHAPTER 6

■ ■ ■

Essential Tools for MVC

In this chapter, I am going to look at three tools that should be part of every MVC programmer's arsenal: a dependency injection (DI) container, a unit test framework, and a mocking tool.

I have picked three specific implementations of these tools for this book, but there are many alternatives for each type of tool. If you cannot get along with the ones I use, do not worry. There are so many out there, that you are certain to find something that suits the way your mind and workflow operate.

As I noted in Chapter 3, Ninject is my preferred DI container. It is simple, elegant, and easy to use. There are more sophisticated alternatives, but I like the way that Ninject works with a minimum of configuration. If you do not like Ninject, I recommend trying Unity, which is an alternative from Microsoft.

For unit testing, I am going to be using the built-in Visual Studio testing tools. I used to use NUnit, which is a popular .NET unit-testing framework, but Microsoft has made a big push to improve the unit-testing support in Visual Studio and now includes it in the free Visual Studio editions. The result is a unit test framework that is tightly integrated into the rest of the IDE and which has actually become pretty good.

The third tool I selected is Moq, which is a mocking tool kit. I use Moq to create implementations of interfaces to use in unit tests. Programmers either love or hate Moq; there is nothing in the middle. Either you will find the syntax elegant and expressive, or you will be cursing every time you try to use it. If you just cannot get along with it, I suggest looking at Rhino Mocks, which is a nice alternative.

I introduce each of these tools and demonstrate their core features, but I do not provide exhaustive coverage of these tools. Each could easily fill a book in its own right. I have given you enough to get started and, critically, to follow the examples in the rest of the book. Table 6-1 provides the summary for this chapter.

Table 6-1. *Chapter Summary*

Problem	Solution	Listing
Decouple classes	Introduce interfaces and declare dependencies on them in the class constructor	1–9, 13–16
Automatically resolve dependencies expressed using interfaces	Use Ninject or another dependency injection container	10
Integrate Ninject into an MVC application	Create an implementation of the IDependencyResolver interface that calls the Ninject kernel and register it as a resolver by calling the System.Web.Mvc.DependencyResolver.SetResolver method	11, 12
Inject property and constructor values into newly created objects	Use the WithPropertyValue and WithConstructorArgument methods	17–20
Dynamically select an implementation class for an interface	Use an Ninject conditional binding	21, 22

(*continued*)

Table 6-1. (*continued*)

Problem	Solution	Listing
Control the lifecycle of the objects that Ninject creates	Set an object scope	23–25
Create a unit test	Add a unit test project to the solution and annotate a class file with `TestClass` and `TestMethod` attributes	26, 27, 29, 30
Check for expected outcomes in a unit test	Use the `Assert` class	28
Focus a unit test on a single feature of component	Isolate the test target using mock objects	31–34

░ **Note**   This chapter assumes that you want all of the benefits that come from the MVC Framework, including an architecture that supports lots of testing and an emphasis on creating applications that are easily modified and maintained. I love this stuff, but I know that some readers will just want to understand the features that the MVC Framework offers and not get into the development philosophy and methodology. I am not going to try to convert you. It is a personal decision and you know what you need to do to deliver your projects. I suggest that you at least have a quick skim through this chapter to see what is available, but if you are not the unit-testing type, then you can skip to the next chapter and see how to build a more realistic example MVC app.

Preparing the Example Project

I am going to start by creating a simple example project, called `EssentialTools`, which I will use throughout this chapter. I used the `ASP.NET MVC Web Application` template, selected the `Empty` option and checked the box to add the basic MVC project content.

Creating the Model Classes

I added a class file to the `Models` project folder called `Product.cs` and set the content as shown in Listing 6-1. This is the model class from in previous chapters and the only change is that the namespace matches that of the `EssentialTools` project.

Listing 6-1. The Contents of the Product.cs File

```
namespace EssentialTools.Models {

    public class Product {
        public int ProductID { get; set; }
        public string Name { get; set; }
        public string Description { get; set; }
        public decimal Price { get; set; }
        public string Category { set; get; }
    }
}
```

I also want to add a class that will calculate the total price of a collection of Product objects. I added a new class file to the Models folder called LinqValueCalculator.cs and set the contents to match Listing 6-2.

Listing 6-2. The Contents of the LinqValueCalculator.cs File

```
using System.Collections.Generic;
using System.Linq;

namespace EssentialTools.Models {

    public class LinqValueCalculator {

        public decimal ValueProducts(IEnumerable<Product> products) {
            return products.Sum(p => p.Price);
        }
    }
}
```

The LinqValueCalculator class defines a single method called ValueProducts, which uses the LINQ Sum method to add together the value of the Price property of each Product object in an enumerable passed to the method (a nice LINQ feature that I use often).

My final model class is ShoppingCart and it represents a collection of Product objects and uses a LinqValueCalculator to determine the total value. I created a new class file called ShoppingCart.cs and added the statements shown in Listing 6-3.

Listing 6-3. The contents of the ShoppingCart.cs File

```
using System.Collections.Generic;

namespace EssentialTools.Models {
    public class ShoppingCart {
        private LinqValueCalculator calc;

        public ShoppingCart(LinqValueCalculator calcParam) {
            calc = calcParam;
        }

        public IEnumerable<Product> Products { get; set; }

        public decimal CalculateProductTotal() {
            return calc.ValueProducts(Products);
        }
    }
}
```

Adding the Controller

I added a new controller to the Controllers folder called HomeController and set the content to match Listing 6-4. The Index action method creates an array of Product objects and uses a LinqValueCalculator object to produce the total value, which I then pass to the View method. I do not specify a view when I call the View method, so the MVC Framework will select the default view associated with the action method (the Views/Home/Index.cshtml file).

121

Listing 6-4. The Contents of the HomeController.cs File

```
using System.Web.Mvc;
using System.Linq;
using EssentialTools.Models;

namespace EssentialTools.Controllers {
    public class HomeController : Controller {
        private Product[] products = {
            new Product {Name = "Kayak", Category = "Watersports", Price = 275M},
            new Product {Name = "Lifejacket", Category = "Watersports", Price = 48.95M},
            new Product {Name = "Soccer ball", Category = "Soccer", Price = 19.50M},
            new Product {Name = "Corner flag", Category = "Soccer", Price = 34.95M}
        };

        public ActionResult Index() {

            LinqValueCalculator calc = new LinqValueCalculator();

            ShoppingCart cart = new ShoppingCart(calc) { Products = products };

            decimal totalValue = cart.CalculateProductTotal();

            return View(totalValue);
        }
    }
}
```

Adding the View

The last addition to the project is the view, called Index. It does not matter which options you check as you create the view as long as you set the contents to match those shown in Listing 6-5.

Listing 6-5. The Contents of the Index.cshtml File

```
@model decimal

@{
    Layout = null;
}

<!DOCTYPE html>

<html>
<head>
    <meta name="viewport" content="width=device-width" />
    <title>Value</title>
</head>
<body>
    <div>
        Total value is $@Model
    </div>
</body>
</html>
```

This view uses the @Model expression to display the value of the decimal passed from the action method. If you start the project, you will see the total value, as calculated by the LinqValueCalculator class, illustrated by Figure 6-1. This is a simple project, but it sets the scene for the different tools and techniques that I describe in this chapter.

Figure 6-1. *Testing the example app*

Using Ninject

I introduced dependency injection (DI) in Chapter 3. To recap, the idea is to decouple the components in an MVC application, with a combination of interfaces and DI container that creates instances of objects by creating implementations of the interfaces they depend on and injecting them into the constructor.

In the sections that follow, I explain a problem I deliberately created in the example for this chapter and show how to use Ninject–my preferred DI container–to solve it. Do not worry if you find that you cannot get along with Ninject–the basic principles are the same for all DI containers and there are many alternatives from which to choose.

Understanding the Problem

In the example app, I created an example of the basic problem that DI addresses: tightly coupled classes. The ShoppingCart class is tightly coupled to the LinqValueCalculator class and the HomeController class is tightly coupled to both ShoppingCart and LinqValueCalculator.

This means that if I want to replace the LinqValueCalculator class, I have to locate and the change the references in the classes that are tightly coupled to it. This is not a problem with such a simple project, but it becomes a tedious and error-prone process in a real project, especially if I want to switch between different calculator implementations (for testing, for example), rather than just replace one class with another.

Applying an Interface

I can solve part of the problem by using a C# interface to abstract the definition of the calculator functionality from its implementation. To demonstrate this, I have added the IValueCalculator.cs class file to the Models folder and created the interface shown in Listing 6-6.

Listing 6-6. The Contents of the IValueCalculator.cs File

```
using System.Collections.Generic;

namespace EssentialTools.Models {
    public interface IValueCalculator {

        decimal ValueProducts(IEnumerable<Product> products);
    }
}
```

I can then implement this interface in the LinqValueCalculator class, as shown in Listing 6-7.

Listing 6-7. Applying an Interface in the LinqValueCalculator.cs File

```
using System.Collections.Generic;
using System.Linq;

namespace EssentialTools.Models {

    public class LinqValueCalculator : IValueCalculator {

        public decimal ValueProducts(IEnumerable<Product> products) {
            return products.Sum(p => p.Price);
        }
    }
}
```

The interface allows me to break the tight coupling between the ShoppingCart and LinqValueCalculator class, as shown in Listing 6-8.

Listing 6-8. Applying the Interface in the ShoppingCart.cs File

```
using System.Collections.Generic;

namespace EssentialTools.Models {
    public class ShoppingCart {
        private IValueCalculator calc;

        public ShoppingCart(IValueCalculator calcParam) {
            calc = calcParam;
        }

        public IEnumerable<Product> Products { get; set; }

        public decimal CalculateProductTotal() {
            return calc.ValueProducts(Products);
        }
    }
}
```

I have made some progress, but C# requires me to specify the implementation class for an interface during instantiation, which is understandable because it needs to know *which* implementation class I want to use–but it means I still have a problem in the Home controller when I create the LinqValueCalculator object, as shown in Listing 6-9.

Listing 6-9. Applying the Interface to the HomeController.cs File

```
...
public ActionResult Index() {

    IValueCalculator calc = new LinqValueCalculator();

    ShoppingCart cart = new ShoppingCart(calc) { Products = products };

    decimal totalValue = cart.CalculateProductTotal();

    return View(totalValue);
}
...
```

My goal with Ninject is to reach the point where I specify that I want to instantiate an implementation of the IValueCalculator interface, but the details of which implementation is required are not part of the code in the Home controller.

This will mean telling Ninject that LinqValueCalculator is the implementation of the IValueCalculator interface that I want it to use and updating the HomeController class so that it obtains its objects via Ninject, rather than by using the new keyword.

Adding Ninject to the Visual Studio Project

The simplest way to add Ninject to an MVC project is to use the integrated Visual Studio support for *NuGet*, which makes it easy to install a wide range of packages and keep them up to date. I used NuGet in Chapter 2 to install the Bootstrap library, but there is a huge catalog of packages available, including Ninject.

Select Tools ➤ Library Package Manager ➤ Package Manager Console in Visual Studio to open the NuGet command line and enter the following commands:

```
Install-Package Ninject -version 3.0.1.10
Install-Package Ninject.Web.Common -version 3.0.0.7
Install-Package Ninject.MVC3 -Version 3.0.0.6
```

The first command installs the Ninject core package and the others install extensions to the core that makes Ninject work nicely with ASP.NET applications (as I explain shortly). Do not be put off by the reference to MVC3 in the last package name–it works just fine with MVC 5.

I have used the version argument to install specific versions of these packages. These are the latest versions as I write this. You should use the version argument to ensure that you get the right results in the examples for this chapter, but you can omit the argument and get the latest (and potentially more recent) releases for real projects.

Getting Started with Ninject

There are three stages to getting the basic Ninject functionality working, and you can see all of them in Listing 6-10, which shows changes I have made to the Home controller.

■ **Tip** I am going to go slowly in this section and the sections that follow. Dependency Injection can take a while to understand and I do not want to skip over anything that might help reduce confusion.

Listing 6-10. Adding the Basic Ninject Functionality to the Index Action Method in the HomeController.cs File

```
using System.Web.Mvc;
using EssentialTools.Models;
using Ninject;

namespace EssentialTools.Controllers {

    public class HomeController : Controller {

        private Product[] products = {
            new Product {Name = "Kayak", Category = "Watersports", Price = 275M},
            new Product {Name = "Lifejacket", Category = "Watersports", Price = 48.95M},
```

```
            new Product {Name = "Soccer ball", Category = "Soccer", Price = 19.50M},
            new Product {Name = "Corner flag", Category = "Soccer", Price = 34.95M}
        };

        public ActionResult Index() {

            IKernel ninjectKernel = new StandardKernel();
            ninjectKernel.Bind<IValueCalculator>().To<LinqValueCalculator>();

            IValueCalculator calc = ninjectKernel.Get<IValueCalculator>();

            ShoppingCart cart = new ShoppingCart(calc) { Products = products };

            decimal totalValue = cart.CalculateProductTotal();

            return View(totalValue);
        }
    }
}
```

The first stage is to prepare Ninject for use. To do this, I create an instance of a Ninject *kernel*, which is the object that is responsible for resolving dependencies and creating new objects. When I need an object, I will use the kernel instead of the new keyword. Here is the statement that creates the kernel from the listing:

```
...
IKernel ninjectKernel = new StandardKernel();
...
```

I need to create an implementation of the Ninject.IKernel interface, which I do by creating a new instance of the StandardKernel class. Ninject can be extended and customized to use different kinds of kernel, but I only need the built-in StandardKernel in this chapter. (In fact, I have been using Ninject for years and I have only ever needed the StandardKernel).

The second stage of the process is to configure the Ninject kernel so that it understands which implementation objects I want to use for each interface I am working with. Here is the statement from the listing that does that:

```
...
ninjectKernel.Bind<IValueCalculator>().To<LinqValueCalculator>();
...
```

Ninject uses C# type parameters to create a relationship: I set the interface I want to work with as the type parameter for the Bind method and call the To method on the result it returns. I set the implementation class I want instantiated as the type parameter for the To method. This statement tells Ninject that dependencies on the IValueCalculator interface should be resolved by creating an instance of the LinqValueCalculator class. The last step is to use Ninject to create an object, which I do through the kernel Get method, like this:

```
...
IValueCalculator calc = ninjectKernel.Get<IValueCalculator>();
...
```

The type parameter used for the Get method tells Ninject which interface I am interested in and the result from this method is an instance of the implementation type I specified with the To method a moment ago.

Setting up MVC Dependency Injection

The result of the three steps I showed you in the previous section is that the knowledge about the implementation class that should be instantiated to fulfill requests for the IValueCalculator interface has been set up in Ninject. Of course, I have not improved my application because that knowledge remains defined in the Home controller, meaning that the Home controller is still tightly coupled to the LinqValueCalculator class.

In the following sections, I will show you how to embed Ninject at the heart of the MVC application, which will allow me to simplify the controller, expand the influence Ninject has so that it works across the app, and move the configuration out of the controller.

Creating the Dependency Resolver

The first change I am going to make is to create a *custom dependency resolver*. The MVC Framework uses a dependency resolver to create instances of the classes it needs to service requests. By creating a custom resolver, I can ensure that the MVC Framework uses Ninject whenever it creates an object–including instances of controllers, for example.

To set up the resolver, I created a new folder called Infrastructure, which is the folder that I use to put classes that do not fit into the other folders in an MVC application. I added a new class file to the folder called NinjectDependencyResolver.cs, the contents of which you can see in Listing 6-11.

Listing 6-11. The Contents of the NinjectDependencyResolver.cs File

```
using System;
using System.Collections.Generic;
using System.Web.Mvc;
using EssentialTools.Models;
using Ninject;

namespace EssentialTools.Infrastructure {
    public class NinjectDependencyResolver : IDependencyResolver {
        private IKernel kernel;

        public NinjectDependencyResolver(IKernel kernelParam) {
            kernel = kernelParam;
            AddBindings();
        }

        public object GetService(Type serviceType) {
            return kernel.TryGet(serviceType);
        }

        public IEnumerable<object> GetServices(Type serviceType) {
            return kernel.GetAll(serviceType);
        }

        private void AddBindings() {
            kernel.Bind<IValueCalculator>().To<LinqValueCalculator>();
        }
    }
}
```

The NinjectDependencyResolver class implements the IDependencyResolver interface, which is part of the System.Mvc namespace and which the MVC Framework uses to get the objects it needs. The MVC Framework will call the GetService or GetServices methods when it needs an instance of a class to service an incoming request. The job of a dependency resolver is to create that instance, a task that I perform by calling the Ninject TryGet and GetAll methods. The TryGet method works like the Get method I used previously, but it returns null when there is no suitable binding rather than throwing an exception. The GetAll method supports multiple bindings for a single type, which is used when there are several different implementation objects available.

My dependency resolver class is also where I set up my Ninject binding. In the AddBindings method, I use the Bind and To methods to configure up the relationship between the IValueCalculator interface and the LinqValueCalculator class.

Register the Dependency Resolver

It is not enough to simply create an implementation of the IDependencyResolver interface–I also have to tell the MVC Framework that I want to use it. The Ninject packages I added with NuGet created a file called NinjectWebCommon.cs in the App_Start folder that defines methods called automatically when the application starts, in order to integrate into the ASP.NET request lifecycle. (This is to provide the *scopes* feature that I describe later in the chapter.) In the RegisterServices method of the NinjectWebCommon class, I add a statement that creates an instance of my NinjectDependencyResolver class and uses the static SetResolver method defined by the System.Web.Mvc.DependencyResolver class to register the resolver with the MVC Framework, as shown in Listing 6-12. Do not worry if this does not make complete sense. The effect of this statement is to create a bridge between Ninject and the MVC Framework support for DI.

Listing 6-12. Registering the Resolver in the NinjectWebCommon.cs File

```
...
private static void RegisterServices(IKernel kernel) {
    System.Web.Mvc.DependencyResolver.SetResolver(new
        EssentialTools.Infrastructure.NinjectDependencyResolver(kernel));
}
...
```

Refactoring the Home Controller

The final step is to refactor the Home controller so that it takes advantage of the facilities I set up in the previous sections. You can see the changes I made in Listing 6-13.

Listing 6-13. Refactoring the Controller in the HomeController.cs File

```
using System.Web.Mvc;
using EssentialTools.Models;

namespace EssentialTools.Controllers {

    public class HomeController : Controller {
        private IValueCalculator calc;
        private Product[] products = {
            new Product {Name = "Kayak", Category = "Watersports", Price = 275M},
            new Product {Name = "Lifejacket", Category = "Watersports", Price = 48.95M},
            new Product {Name = "Soccer ball", Category = "Soccer", Price = 19.50M},
            new Product {Name = "Corner flag", Category = "Soccer", Price = 34.95M}
        };
```

```
public HomeController(IValueCalculator calcParam) {
    calc = calcParam;
}

public ActionResult Index() {

    ShoppingCart cart = new ShoppingCart(calc) { Products = products };

    decimal totalValue = cart.CalculateProductTotal();

    return View(totalValue);
}
}
}
```

The main change I have made is to add a class constructor that accepts an implementation of the IValueCalculator interface, changing the HomeController class so that it declares a dependency. Ninject will provide an object that implements the IValueCalculator interface when it creates an instance of the controller, using the configuration I set up in the NinjectDependencyResolver class in Listing 6-10.

The other change I made is to remove any mention of Ninject or the LinqValueCalculator class from the controller. At last, I have broken the tight coupling between the HomeController and LinqValueCalculator class.

If you run the example, you will see the result shown in Figure 6-2. Of course, I got this same result when I was instantiating the LinqValueCalculator class directly in the controller.

Figure 6-2. *The effect of running the example app*

I have created an example of *constructor injection*, which is one form of dependency injection. Here is what happened when you ran the example app and Internet Explorer made the request for the root URL of the app:

1. The MVC Framework received the request and figured out that the request is intended for the Home controller. (I will explain how the MVC framework figures this out in Chapter 17).

2. The MVC Framework asked my custom dependency resolver class to create a new instance of the HomeController class, specifying the class using the Type parameter of the GetService method.

3. My dependency resolver asked Ninject to create a new HomeController class, passing on the Type object to the TryGet method.

4. Ninject inspected the HomeController constructor and found that it has declared a dependency on the IValueCalculator interface, for which it has a binding.

5.   Ninject creates an instance of the LinqValueCalculator class and uses it to create a new instance of the HomeController class.

6.   Ninject passes the HomeController instance to the custom dependency resolver, which returns it to the MVC Framework. The MVC Framework uses the controller instance to service the request.

I labored this slightly because DI can be a bit mind-bending when you see it used for the first time. One benefit of the approach I have taken here is that *any* controller in the application can declare a dependency and the MVC Framework will use Ninject to resolve it.

The best part is that I only have to modify my dependency resolver class when I want to replace the LinqValueCalculator with another implementation, because this is the only place where I have to specify the implementation used to satisfy dependencies on the IValueCalculator interface.

Creating Chains of Dependency

When you ask Ninject to create a type, it examines the dependencies that the type has declared. It also looks at those dependencies to see if they rely on other types–or, put another way, if they declare their own dependencies. If there *are* additional dependencies, Ninject automatically resolves them and creates instances of all of the classes that are required, working its way along the chain of dependencies so that it can ultimately create an instance of the type you asked for.

To demonstrate this feature, I have added a file called Discount.cs to the Models folder and used it to define a new interface and a class that implements it, as shown in Listing 6-14.

Listing 6-14. The Contents of the Discount.cs File

```
namespace EssentialTools.Models {

    public interface IDiscountHelper {
        decimal ApplyDiscount(decimal totalParam);
    }

    public class DefaultDiscountHelper : IDiscountHelper {

        public decimal ApplyDiscount(decimal totalParam) {
            return (totalParam - (10m / 100m * totalParam));
        }
    }
}
```

The IDiscountHelper defines the ApplyDiscount method, which will apply a discount to a decimal value. The DefaultDiscounterHelper class implements the IDiscountHelper interface and applies a fixed 10 percent discount. I have modified the LinqValueCalculator class so that it uses the IDiscountHelper interface when it performs calculations, as shown in Listing 6-15.

Listing 6-15. Adding a Dependency in the LinqValueCalculator.cs File

```
using System.Collections.Generic;
using System.Linq;

namespace EssentialTools.Models {
```

```
public class LinqValueCalculator: IValueCalculator {
    private IDiscountHelper discounter;

    public LinqValueCalculator(IDiscountHelper discountParam) {
        discounter = discountParam;
    }

    public decimal ValueProducts(IEnumerable<Product> products) {
        return discounter.ApplyDiscount(products.Sum(p => p.Price));
    }
}
}
```

The new constructor declares a dependency on the IDiscountHelper interface. I assign the implementation object that the constructor receives to a field and use it in the ValueProducts method to apply a discount to the cumulative value of the Product objects.

I bind the IDiscountHelper interface to the implementation class with the Ninject kernel in the NinjectDependencyResolver class, just as I did for IValueCalculator, as shown in Listing 6-6.

Listing 6-16. Binding Another Interface to Its Implementation in the NinjectDependencyResolver.cs File

```
...
private void AddBindings() {
    kernel.Bind<IValueCalculator>().To<LinqValueCalculator>();
    kernel.Bind<IDiscountHelper>().To<DefaultDiscountHelper>();
}
...
```

I have created a dependency chain. My Home controller depends on the IValueCalculator interface, which I have told Ninject to resolve using the LinqValueCalculator class. The LinqValueCalculator class depends on the IDiscountHelper interface, which I have told Ninject to resolve using the DefaultDiscountHelper class.

Ninject resolves the chain of dependencies seamlessly, creating the objects it needs to resolve every dependency and, ultimately in this example, create an instance of the HomeController class to service an HTTP request.

Specifying Property and Constructor Parameter Values

I can configure the objects that Ninject creates by providing details of values I want applied to properties when I bind the interface to its implementation. To demonstrate this feature, I have revised the DefaultDiscountHelper class so that it defines a DiscountSize property, which I use to calculate the discount amount, as shown in Listing 6-17.

Listing 6-17. Adding a Property in the Discount.cs File

```
namespace EssentialTools.Models {

    public interface IDiscountHelper {
        decimal ApplyDiscount(decimal totalParam);
    }

    public class DefaultDiscountHelper : IDiscountHelper {

        public decimal DiscountSize { get; set; }
```

```
        public decimal ApplyDiscount(decimal totalParam) {
            return (totalParam - (DiscountSize / 100m * totalParam));
        }
    }
}
```

When I tell Ninject which class to use for an interface, I can use the WithPropertyValue method to set the value for the DiscountSize property in the DefaultDiscountHelper class. You can see the change I made to the AddBindings method in the NinjectDependencyResolver class to set this up, as shown in Listing 6-18. Notice that I supply the name of the property to set as a string value.

Listing 6-18. Using the Ninject WithPropertyValue Method in the NinjectDependencyResolver.cs File

```
...
private void AddBindings() {
    kernel.Bind<IValueCalculator>().To<LinqValueCalculator>();
    kernel.Bind<IDiscountHelper>()
        .To<DefaultDiscountHelper>().WithPropertyValue("DiscountSize", 50M);
}
...
```

I do not need to change any other binding, nor change the way I use the Get method to obtain an instance of the ShoppingCart class. The property value is set following construction of the DefaultDiscountHelper class, and has the effect of halving the total value of the items. Figure 6-3 shows the result of this change.

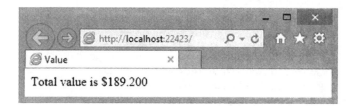

Figure 6-3. *The effect of applying a discount through a property when resolving the dependency chain*

If you have more than one property value you need to set, you can chain calls to the WithPropertyValue method to cover them all. I can do the same thing with constructor parameters. Listing 6-19 shows the DefaultDiscounterHelper class reworked so that the size of the discount is passed as a constructor parameter.

Listing 6-19. Using a Constructor Property in the Discount.cs File

```
namespace EssentialTools.Models {

    public interface IDiscountHelper {
        decimal ApplyDiscount(decimal totalParam);
    }

    public class DefaultDiscountHelper : IDiscountHelper {
        public decimal discountSize;
```

```
    public DefaultDiscountHelper(decimal discountParam) {
        discountSize = discountParam;
    }

    public decimal ApplyDiscount(decimal totalParam) {
        return (totalParam - (discountSize / 100m * totalParam));
    }
  }
}
```

To bind this class using Ninject, I specify the value of the constructor parameter using the WithConstructorArgument method in the AddBindings method, as shown in Listing 6-20.

Listing 6-20. Specifying a Constructor Parameter in the NinjectDependencyResolver.cs File

```
...
private void AddBindings() {
    kernel.Bind<IValueCalculator>().To<LinqValueCalculator>();
    kernel.Bind<IDiscountHelper>()
            .To<DefaultDiscountHelper>().WithConstructorArgument("discountParam", 50M);
}
...
```

Once again, I can chain these method calls together to supply multiple values and mix and match with dependencies. Ninject will figure out what I need and create it accordingly.

■ **Tip** Notice that I did not just change the WithPropertyValue call to WithConstructorArgument. I also changed the name of the member targeted so that it matches the C# convention for parameter names.

Using Conditional Binding

Ninject supports a number of conditional binding methods that allow me to specify which classes the kernel should use to respond to requests for particular interfaces. To demonstrate this feature, I have added a new file to the Models folder of the example project called FlexibleDiscountHelper.cs, the contents of which you can see in Listing 6-21.

Listing 6-21. The Contents of the FlexibleDiscountHelper.cs File

```
namespace EssentialTools.Models {
    public class FlexibleDiscountHelper : IDiscountHelper {

        public decimal ApplyDiscount(decimal totalParam) {
            decimal discount = totalParam > 100 ? 70 : 25;
            return (totalParam - (discount / 100m * totalParam));
        }
    }
}
```

The FlexibleDiscountHelper class applies different discounts based on the magnitude of the total. Now that I have a choice of classes that implement the IDiscountHelper interface, I can modify the AddBindings method of the NinjectDependencyResolver to tell Ninject when I want to use each of them, as shown in Listing 6-22.

Listing 6-22. Using Conditional Binding in the NinjectDependencyResolver.cs File

```
...
private void AddBindings() {
    kernel.Bind<IValueCalculator>().To<LinqValueCalculator>();
    kernel.Bind<IDiscountHelper>()
        .To<DefaultDiscountHelper>().WithConstructorArgument("discountParam", 50M);
    kernel.Bind<IDiscountHelper>().To<FlexibleDiscountHelper>()
        .WhenInjectedInto<LinqValueCalculator>();

}
...
```

The new binding specifies that the Ninject kernel should use the FlexibleDiscountHelper class as the implementation of the IDiscountHelper interface when it is creating a LinqValueCalculator object. Notice that I have left the original binding for IDiscountHelper in place. Ninject tries to find the best match and it helps to have a default binding for the same class or interface, so that Ninject has a fallback if the criteria for a conditional binding are not satisfied. Ninject supports a number of different conditional binding methods, the most useful of which I have listed in Table 6-2.

Table 6-2. *Ninject Conditional Binding Methods*

Method	Effect
When(predicate)	Binding is used when the predicate—a lambda expression—evaluates to true.
WhenClassHas<T>()	Binding is used when the class being injected is annotated with the attribute whose type is specified by T.
WhenInjectedInto<T>()	Binding is used when the class being injected into is of type T.

Setting the Object Scope

The last Ninject feature helps tailor the lifecycle of the objects that Ninject creates to match the needs of your application. By default, Ninject will create a new instance of every object needed to resolve every dependency each time you request an object.

To demonstrate what happens, I have modified the constructor for the LinqValueCalculator class so that it writes a message to the Visual Studio Output window when a new instance is created, as shown in Listing 6-23.

Listing 6-23. Adding a Constructor in the LinqValueCalculator.cs File

```
using System.Collections.Generic;
using System.Linq;

namespace EssentialTools.Models {

    public class LinqValueCalculator : IValueCalculator {
        private IDiscountHelper discounter;
        private static int counter = 0;

        public LinqValueCalculator(IDiscountHelper discountParam) {
            discounter = discountParam;
```

```
        System.Diagnostics.Debug.WriteLine(
            string.Format("Instance {0} created", ++counter));
    }

    public decimal ValueProducts(IEnumerable<Product> products) {
        return discounter.ApplyDiscount(products.Sum(p => p.Price));
    }
  }
}
```

The System.Diagnostics.Debug class contains a number of methods that can be used to write out debugging messages and I find them useful when following code through to see how it works. I am, sadly, old enough that debuggers were not sophisticated when I started writing code and I still find myself going back to basics when it comes to debugging.

In Listing 6-24, I have modified the Home controller so that it demands two implementations of the IValueCalculator interface from Ninject.

Listing 6-24. Using Multiple Instances of the Calculator Class in the HomeController.cs File

```
...
public HomeController(IValueCalculator calcParam, IValueCalculator calc2) {
    calc = calcParam;
}
...
```

I do not perform any useful task with the object that Ninject provides–what is important it that I asked for two implementations of the interface. If you run the example and look at the Visual Studio Output window, you will see messages that show Ninject created two instances of the LinqValueCalculator class:

```
Instance 1 created
Instance 2 created
```

The LinqValueCalculator can be instantiated repeatedly without any problems–but that is not true for all classes. For some classes, you will want to share a single instance throughout the entire application and for others, you will want to create a new instance for each HTTP request that the ASP.NET platform receives. Ninject lets you control the lifecycle of the objects you create using a feature called a *scope*, which is expressed using a method call when setting up the binding between an interface and its implementation type. In Listing 6-25, you can see how I applied the most useful scope for MVC Framework applications: the *request scope* to the LinqValueCalculator class in the NinjectDependencyResolver.

Listing 6-25. Using the Request Scope in the NinjectDependencyResolver.cs File

```
using System;
using System.Collections.Generic;
using System.Web.Mvc;
using EssentialTools.Models;
using Ninject;
using Ninject.Web.Common;
```

```
namespace EssentialTools.Infrastructure {
    public class NinjectDependencyResolver : IDependencyResolver {
        private IKernel kernel;

        public NinjectDependencyResolver(IKernel kernelParam) {
            kernel = kernelParam;
            AddBindings();
        }

        public object GetService(Type serviceType) {
            return kernel.TryGet(serviceType);
        }

        public IEnumerable<object> GetServices(Type serviceType) {
            return kernel.GetAll(serviceType);
        }

        private void AddBindings() {
            kernel.Bind<IValueCalculator>().To<LinqValueCalculator>().InRequestScope();
            kernel.Bind<IDiscountHelper>()
              .To<DefaultDiscountHelper>().WithConstructorArgument("discountParam", 50M);
            kernel.Bind<IDiscountHelper>().To<FlexibleDiscountHelper>()
              .WhenInjectedInto<LinqValueCalculator>();
        }
    }
}
```

The InRequestScope extension method, which is in the Ninject.Web.Common namespace, tells Ninject that it should only create one instance of the LinqValueCalculator class for each HTTP request that ASP.NET receives. Each request will get its own separate object, but multiple dependencies resolved within the same request will be resolved using a single instance of the class. You can see the effect of this change by starting the application and looking at the Visual Studio Output window, which will show that Ninject has created only one instance of the LinqValueCalculator class. If you reload the browser window without restarting the application, you will see Ninject create a second object. Ninject provides a range of different object scopes and I have summarized the most useful in Table 6-3.

Table 6-3. *Ninject Scope Methods*

Name	Effect
InTransientScope()	This is the same as not specifying a scope and creates a new object for each dependency that is resolved.
InSingletonScope() ToConstant(object)	Creates a single instance which is shared throughout the application. Ninject will create the instance if you use InSingletonScope or you can provide it with the ToConstant method.
InThreadScope()	Creates a single instance which is used to resolve dependencies for objects requested by a single thread.
InRequestScope()	Creates a single instance which is used to resolve dependencies for objects requested by a single HTTP request.

Unit Testing with Visual Studio

In this book, I use the built-in unit test support that comes with Visual Studio, but there are other .NET unit-test packages available. The most popular is probably NUnit, but all of the test packages do much the same thing. The reason I have selected the Visual Studio test tools is that I like the integration with the rest of the IDE.

To demonstrate the Visual Studio unit-test support, I added a new implementation of the IDiscountHelper interface to the example project. Create a new file in the Models folder called MinimumDiscountHelper.cs and ensure that the contents match those shown in Listing 6-26.

Listing 6-26. The Contents of the MinumumDiscountHelper.cs File

```
using System;

namespace EssentialTools.Models {
    public class MinimumDiscountHelper : IDiscountHelper {

        public decimal ApplyDiscount(decimal totalParam) {
            throw new NotImplementedException();
        }
    }
}
```

My objective in this example is to make the MinimumDiscountHelper demonstrate the following behaviors:

- If the total is greater than $100, the discount will be 10 percent.

- If the total is between $10 and $100 inclusive, the discount will be $5.

- No discount will be applied on totals less than $10.

- An ArgumentOutOfRangeException will be thrown for negative totals.

The MinimumDiscountHelper class does not implement any of these behaviors yet. I am going to follow the Test Driven Development (TDD) approach of writing the unit tests and only then implement the code, as described in Chapter 3.

Creating the Unit Test Project

The first step I take is to create the unit test project, which I do by right-clicking the top-level item in the Solution Explorer (which is labeled Solution 'EssentialTools' for my example app) and selecting Add ➤ New Project from the pop-up menu.

■ **Tip** You can choose to create a test project when you create a new MVC project: there is an Add Unit Tests option on the dialog where you choose the initial content for the project.

This will open the Add New Project dialog. Select Test from the Visual C# templates section in the left panel and ensure that Unit Test Project is selected in the middle panel, as shown in Figure 6-4.

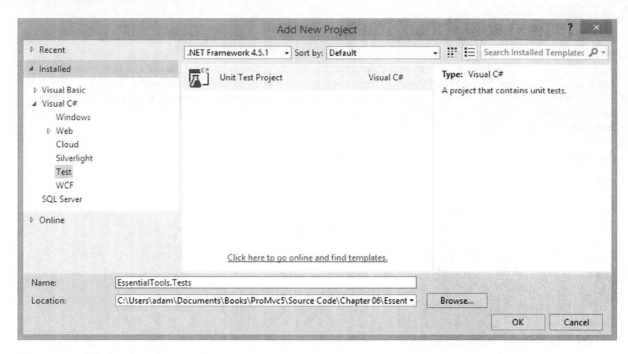

Figure 6-4. *Creating the unit test project*

Set the project name to EssentialTools.Tests and click the OK button to create the new project, which Visual Studio will add to the current solution alongside the MVC application project.

I need to give the test project a reference to the application project so that it can access the classes and perform tests upon them. Right-click the References item for the EssentialTools.Tests project in the Solution Explorer, and then select Add Reference from the pop-up menu. Click Solution in the left panel and check the box next to the EssentialTools item, as shown in Figure 6-5.

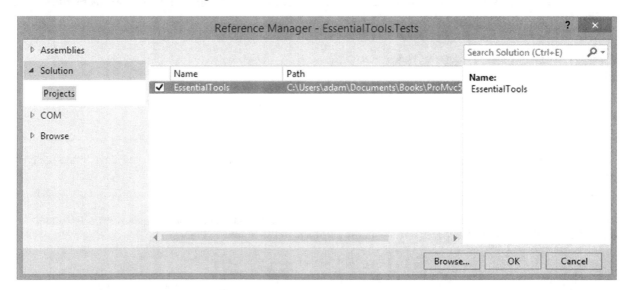

Figure 6-5. *Adding a reference to the MVC project*

Creating the Unit Tests

I will add my unit tests to the `UnitTest1.cs` file in the `EssentialTools.Tests` project. The paid-for Visual Studio editions have some nice features for automatically generating test methods for a class that are not available in the Express edition, but I can still create useful and meaningful tests. To get started, I made the changes shown in Listing 6-27.

Listing 6-27. Adding the Test Methods to the UnitTest1.cs File

```
using System;
using Microsoft.VisualStudio.TestTools.UnitTesting;
using EssentialTools.Models;

namespace EssentialTools.Tests {

    [TestClass]
    public class UnitTest1 {

        private IDiscountHelper getTestObject() {
            return new MinimumDiscountHelper();
        }

        [TestMethod]
        public void Discount_Above_100() {
            // arrange
            IDiscountHelper target = getTestObject();
            decimal total = 200;

            // act
            var discountedTotal = target.ApplyDiscount(total);

            // assert
            Assert.AreEqual(total * 0.9M, discountedTotal);
        }
    }
}
```

I have added a single unit test. A class that contains tests is annotated with the `TestClass` attribute and individual tests are methods annotated with the `TestMethod` attribute. Not all methods in a unit test class have to be unit tests. To demonstrate this, I have defined the `getTestObject` method, which I will use to arrange my tests. Because this method does not have a `TestMethod` attribute, Visual Studio will not treat it as a unit test.

■ **Tip**　Notice that I had to add a `using` statement to import the `EssentialTools.Models` namespace into the test class. Test classes are just regular C# classes and have no special knowledge about the MVC project. It is the `TestClass` and `TestMethod` attributes which add the testing magic to the project.

You can see that I have followed the arrange/act/assert (A/A/A) pattern in the unit test method that I described in Chapter 3. There are countless conventions about how to name unit tests, but my advice is simply that you use names that make it clear what the test is checking. My unit test method is called Discount_Above_100, which is clear and meaningful to me. But all that really matters is that you (and your team) understand whatever naming pattern you settle on, so you adopt a different naming scheme if you do not like mine.

I set up the test method by calling the getTestObject method, which creates an instance of the object I am going to test: the MinimumDiscountHelper class in this case. I also define the total value with which I am going to test. This is the *arrange* section of the unit test.

For the *act* section of the test, I call the MinimumDiscountHelper.ApplyDiscount method and assign the result to the discountedTotal variable. Finally, for the assert section of the test, I use the Assert.AreEqual method to check that the value I got back from the ApplyDiscount method is 90% of the total that I started with.

The Assert class has a range of static methods that you can use in your tests. The class is in the Microsoft. VisualStudio.TestTools.UnitTesting namespace along with some additional classes that can be useful for setting up and performing tests. You can learn more about classes in the namespace at http://msdn.microsoft.com/en-us/library/ms182530.aspx.

The Assert class is the one that I use the most and I have summarized the most important methods in Table 6-4.

Table 6-4. *Static Assert Methods*

Method	Description
AreEqual<T>(T, T) AreEqual<T>(T, T, string)	Asserts that two objects of type T have the same value.
AreNotEqual<T>(T, T) AreNotEqual<T>(T, T, string)	Asserts that two objects of type T do not have the same value.
AreSame<T>(T, T) AreSame<T>(T, T, string)	Asserts that two variables refer to the same object.
AreNotSame<T>(T, T) AreNotSame<T>(T, T, string)	Asserts that two variables refer to different objects.
Fail() Fail(string)	Fails an assertion: no conditions are checked.
Inconclusive() Inconclusive(string)	Indicates that the result of the unit test cannot be definitively established.
IsTrue(bool) IsTrue(bool, string)	Asserts that a bool value is true. Most often used to evaluate an expression that returns a bool result.
IsFalse(bool) IsFalse(bool, string)	Asserts that a bool value is false.
IsNull(object) IsNull(object, string)	Asserts that a variable is not assigned an object reference.
IsNotNull(object) IsNotNull(object, string)	Asserts that a variable is assigned an object reference.
IsInstanceOfType(object, Type) IsInstanceOfType(object, Type, string)	Asserts that an object is of the specified type or is derived from the specified type.
IsNotInstanceOfType(object, Type) IsNotInstanceOfType(object, Type, string)	Asserts that an object is not of the specified type.

Each of the static methods in the Assert class allows you to check some aspect of your unit test and the methods throw an exception if the check fails. All of the assertions have to succeed for the unit test to pass.

Each of the methods in the table has an overloaded version that takes a string parameter. The string is included as the message element of the exception if the assertion fails. The AreEqual and AreNotEqual methods have a number of overloads that cater to comparing specific types. For example, there is a version that allows strings to be compared without taking case into account.

▪ **Tip** One noteworthy member of the Microsoft.VisualStudio.TestTools.UnitTesting namespace is the ExpectedException attribute. This is an assertion that succeeds only if the unit test throws an exception of the type specified by the ExceptionType parameter. This is a neat way of ensuring that exceptions are thrown without needing to mess around with try...catch blocks in your unit test.

Now that I have shown you how to put together one unit test, I have added further tests to the test project to validate the other behaviors I want for my MinimumDiscountHelper class. You can see the additions in Listing 6-28, but these unit tests are so short and simple (which is generally a characteristic of unit tests) that I am not going to explain them in detail.

Listing 6-28. Defining the Remaining Tests in the UnitTest1.cs File

```
using System;
using Microsoft.VisualStudio.TestTools.UnitTesting;
using EssentialTools.Models;

namespace EssentialTools.Tests {

    [TestClass]
    public class UnitTest1 {

        private IDiscountHelper getTestObject() {
            return new MinimumDiscountHelper();
        }

        [TestMethod]
        public void Discount_Above_100() {
            // arrange
            IDiscountHelper target = getTestObject();
            decimal total = 200;

            // act
            var discountedTotal = target.ApplyDiscount(total);

            // assert
            Assert.AreEqual(total * 0.9M, discountedTotal);
        }

        [TestMethod]
        public void Discount_Between_10_And_100() {
            //arrange
            IDiscountHelper target = getTestObject();
```

```
        // act
        decimal TenDollarDiscount = target.ApplyDiscount(10);
        decimal HundredDollarDiscount = target.ApplyDiscount(100);
        decimal FiftyDollarDiscount = target.ApplyDiscount(50);

        // assert
        Assert.AreEqual(5, TenDollarDiscount, "$10 discount is wrong");
        Assert.AreEqual(95, HundredDollarDiscount, "$100 discount is wrong");
        Assert.AreEqual(45, FiftyDollarDiscount, "$50 discount is wrong");
    }

    [TestMethod]
    public void Discount_Less_Than_10() {
        //arrange
        IDiscountHelper target = getTestObject();

        // act
        decimal discount5 = target.ApplyDiscount(5);
        decimal discount0 = target.ApplyDiscount(0);

        // assert
        Assert.AreEqual(5, discount5);
        Assert.AreEqual(0, discount0);

    }

    [TestMethod]
    [ExpectedException(typeof(ArgumentOutOfRangeException))]
    public void Discount_Negative_Total() {
        //arrange
        IDiscountHelper target = getTestObject();

        // act
        target.ApplyDiscount(-1);
    }
  }
}
```

Running the Unit Tests (and Failing)

Visual Studio provides the Test Explorer window for managing and running tests. Select Windows ➤ Test Explorer from the Visual Studio Test menu to see the window and click the Run All button near the top-left corner. You will see results similar to the ones shown in Figure 6-6.

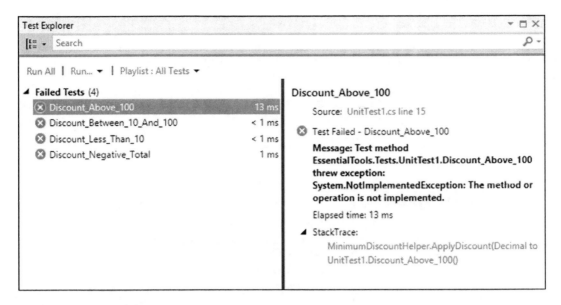

Figure 6-6. *Running the tests in the project*

You can see the list of tests I defined in the left-hand panel of the Test Explorer window. All of the tests have failed, of course, because I have yet to implement the method I am testing. You can click any of the tests in the window to see details of why it has failed. The Test Explorer window provides a range of different ways to select and filter unit tests and to choose which tests to run. For my simple example project, however, I will just run all of the tests by clicking Run All.

Implementing the Feature

I have reached the point where I can implement the feature, safe in the knowledge that I will be able to check that the code works as expected when I am finished. For all of my preparation, the implementation of the MinimumDiscountHelper class is simple, as shown by Listing 6-29.

Listing 6-29. The Contents of the MinimumDiscountHelper.cs File

```
using System;

namespace EssentialTools.Models {
    public class MinimumDiscountHelper : IDiscountHelper {

        public decimal ApplyDiscount(decimal totalParam) {
            if (totalParam < 0) {
                throw new ArgumentOutOfRangeException();
            } else if (totalParam > 100) {
                return totalParam * 0.9M;
            } else if (totalParam > 10 && totalParam <= 100) {
                return totalParam -5;
            } else {
                return totalParam;
            }
        }
    }
}
```

Testing and Fixing the Code

I have left a deliberate error in the code to demonstrate how iterative unit testing with Visual Studio works and you can see the effect of the error if you click the Run All button in the Test Explorer window. You can see the test results in Figure 6-7.

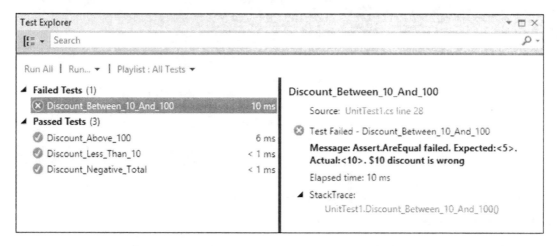

Figure 6-7. *The effect of implementing the feature with a bug*

Visual Studio always tries to promote the most useful information to the top of the Test Explorer window. In this situation, this means that it displays failed tests before passed tests.

You can see that I passed three of the unit tests, but I have a problem that the Discount_Between_10_And_100 test method detected. When I click the failed test, I can see that my test expected a result of 5, but actually got a value of 10.

At this point, I return to my code and see that I have not implemented my expected behaviors properly. Specifically, I do not handle the discounts for totals that are 10 or 100 properly. The problem is in this statement from the MinumumDiscountHelper class:

```
...
} else if (totalParam > 10 && totalParam < 100) {
...
```

The specification that I am working to implement sets out the behavior for values which are between $10 and $100 *inclusive*, but my implementation excludes those values and only checks for values which are greater than $10, excluding totals which are exactly $10. The solution is simple and is shown in Listing 6-30. Only a single character needs to be added to change the effect of the if statement.

Listing 6-30. Fixing the Feature Code in the MinimumDiscountHelper.cs File

```
using System;

namespace EssentialTools.Models {
    public class MinimumDiscountHelper : IDiscountHelper {

        public decimal ApplyDiscount(decimal totalParam) {
            if (totalParam < 0) {
                throw new ArgumentOutOfRangeException();
```

```
        } else if (totalParam > 100) {
            return totalParam * 0.9M;
        } else if (totalParam >= 10 && totalParam <= 100) {
            return totalParam -5;
        } else {
            return totalParam;
        }
    }
  }
}
```

When I click the Run All button in the Test Explorer window, the results show that I have fixed the problem and that my code passed all of the tests (see Figure 6-8).

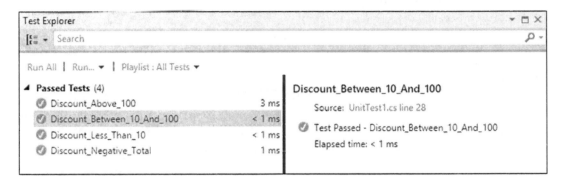

Figure 6-8. *Passing all of the unit tests*

This is just a quick introduction to unit testing, and I will further demonstrate unit tests in later chapters as well. The unit test support in Visual Studio is pretty good and I recommend you explore the unit testing documentation on MSDN, which you can find at http://msdn.microsoft.com/en-us/library/dd264975.aspx.

Using Moq

One of the reasons that I am able to keep my tests so simple in the previous section was because I am testing a single class that depends on no other class to function. Such objects exist in real projects, of course, but you will also need to test objects that cannot function in isolation. In these situations, you need to be able to focus on the class or method you are interested in, so that you are not implicitly testing the dependencies as well.

One useful approach is to use *mock objects*, which simulate the functionality of real objects from your project, but in a specific and controlled way. Mock objects let you narrow the focus of your tests so that you only examine the functionality in which you are interested.

The paid-for versions of Visual Studio include support for creating mock objects through a feature called *fakes*, but I prefer to use a library called Moq, which is simple, easy-to-use and you can use with all Visual Studio editions, including the free ones.

Understanding the Problem

Before I get into the using Moq, I want to demonstrate the problem that I am trying to fix. In this section, I am going to unit test the LinqValueCalculator class, which I defined in the Models folder of the example project. As a reminder, Listing 6-31 shows the definition of the LinqValueCalculator class.

Listing 6-31. The Contents of the LinqValueCalculator.cs File

```
using System.Collections.Generic;
using System.Linq;

namespace EssentialTools.Models {

    public class LinqValueCalculator : IValueCalculator {
        private IDiscountHelper discounter;
        private static int counter = 0;

        public LinqValueCalculator(IDiscountHelper discountParam) {
            discounter = discountParam;
            System.Diagnostics.Debug.WriteLine(
                string.Format("Instance {0} created", ++counter));
        }

        public decimal ValueProducts(IEnumerable<Product> products) {
            return discounter.ApplyDiscount(products.Sum(p => p.Price));
        }
    }
}
```

To test this class, I added a new unit test class to the test project. You do this by right-clicking the test project in the Solution Explorer and selecting Add ➤ Unit Test from the pop-up menu. If your Add menu does not have a Unit Test item, select New Item instead and use the Basic Unit Test template. You can see the changes I made to the new file, which Visual Studio names UnitTest2.cs by default, in Listing 6-32.

Listing 6-32. Adding a Unit Test for the ShoppingCart Class in the UnitTest2.cs File

```
using System;
using Microsoft.VisualStudio.TestTools.UnitTesting;
using EssentialTools.Models;
using System.Linq;

namespace EssentialTools.Tests {
    [TestClass]
    public class UnitTest2 {

        private Product[] products = {
            new Product {Name = "Kayak", Category = "Watersports", Price = 275M},
            new Product {Name = "Lifejacket", Category = "Watersports", Price = 48.95M},
            new Product {Name = "Soccer ball", Category = "Soccer", Price = 19.50M},
            new Product {Name = "Corner flag", Category = "Soccer", Price = 34.95M}
        };
```

```
[TestMethod]
public void Sum_Products_Correctly() {

    // arrange
    var discounter = new MinimumDiscountHelper();
    var target = new LinqValueCalculator(discounter);
    var goalTotal = products.Sum(e => e.Price);

    // act
    var result = target.ValueProducts(products);

    // assert
    Assert.AreEqual(goalTotal, result);
    }
  }
}
```

The problem I face is that the LinqValueCalculator class depends on an implementation of the IDiscountHelper interface to operate. In the example, I used the MinimumDiscountHelper class and this presents two different issues.

First, I have made my unit test complex and brittle. In order to create a unit test that works, I need to take into account the discount logic in the IDiscountHelper implementation to figure out the expected value from the ValueProducts method. The brittleness comes from the fact that my tests will fail if the discount logic in the implementation changes, even though the LinqValueCalculator class may well be working properly.

Second, and most troubling, I have extended the scope of my unit test so that it implicitly includes the MinimumDiscountHelper class. When my unit test fails, I will not know if the problem is in the LinqValueCalculator or MinimumDiscountHelper class.

The best unit tests are simple and focused, and my current setup does not allow for either of these characteristics. In the sections that follow, I show you how to add and apply Moq in your MVC project so that you can avoid these problems.

Adding Moq to the Visual Studio Project

Just like with Ninject earlier in the chapter, the easiest way to add Moq to an MVC project is to use the integrated Visual Studio support for *NuGet*. Open the NuGet console and enter the following command:

```
Install-Package Moq -version 4.1.1309.1617 -projectname EssentialTools.Tests
```

The projectname argument allows me to tell NuGet that I want the Moq package installed in my unit test project, rather than in the main application.

Adding a Mock Object to a Unit Test

Adding a mock object to a unit test means telling Moq what kind of object you want to work with, configuring its behavior and then applying the object to the test target. You can see how I added a mock object to my unit test for the LinqValueCalculator in Listing 6-33.

Listing 6-33. Using a Mock Object in a Unit Test in the UnitTest2.cs File

```
using EssentialTools.Models;
using Microsoft.VisualStudio.TestTools.UnitTesting;
using System.Linq;
using Moq;
```

```
namespace EssentialTools.Tests {
    [TestClass]
    public class UnitTest2 {

        private Product[] products = {
            new Product {Name = "Kayak", Category = "Watersports", Price = 275M},
            new Product {Name = "Lifejacket", Category = "Watersports", Price = 48.95M},
            new Product {Name = "Soccer ball", Category = "Soccer", Price = 19.50M},
            new Product {Name = "Corner flag", Category = "Soccer", Price = 34.95M}
        };

        [TestMethod]
        public void Sum_Products_Correctly() {
            // arrange
            Mock<IDiscountHelper> mock = new Mock<IDiscountHelper>();
            mock.Setup(m => m.ApplyDiscount(It.IsAny<decimal>()))
                .Returns<decimal>(total => total);
            var target = new LinqValueCalculator(mock.Object);

            // act
            var result = target.ValueProducts(products);

            // assert
            Assert.AreEqual(products.Sum(e => e.Price), result);
        }
    }
}
```

The syntax for using Moq is a little odd when you first see it, so I will walk through each stage of the process.

■ **Tip**   Bear in mind that there are a number of different mocking libraries available, so the chances are good that you can find an alternative to suit you if you do not like the way that Moq works, although Moq is actually an easy library to use. You can expect some of the other popular libraries to have manuals hundreds of pages long.

Creating a Mock Object

The first step is to tell Moq what kind of mock object you want to work with. Moq relies heavily on type parameters, and you can see this in the way that I tell Moq I want to create a mock IDiscountHelper implementation:

```
...
Mock<IDiscountHelper> mock = new Mock<IDiscountHelper>();
...
```

I create a strongly typed Mock<IDiscountHelper> object, which tells the Moq library the type it will be handling. This is the IDiscountHelper interface for my unit test, but it can be any type that you want to isolate to improve the focus of your unit tests.

Selecting a Method

In addition to creating the strongly typed Mock object, I also need to specify the way that it behaves. This is at the heart of the mocking process and it allows you to ensure that you establish a baseline behavior in the mock object, which you can use to test the functionality of your target object in the unit test. Here is the statement from the unit test that sets up the behavior I want:

```
...
mock.Setup(m => m.ApplyDiscount(It.IsAny<decimal>())).Returns<decimal>(total => total);
...
```

I use the Setup method to add a method to my mock object. Moq works using LINQ and lambda expressions. When I call the Setup method, Moq passes me the interface that I have asked it to implement, cleverly wrapped up in some LINQ magic that I am not going to get into here. This allows me to select the method I want to configure by using a lambda expression. For my unit test, I want to define the behavior of the ApplyDiscount method, which is the only method in the IDiscountHelper interface, and the method I need to test the LinqValueCalculator class.

I also have to tell Moq what parameter values I am interested in, which I do using the It class, which I have highlighted as follows:

```
...
mock.Setup(m => m.ApplyDiscount(It.IsAny<decimal>())).Returns<decimal>(total => total);
...
```

The It class defines a number of methods that are used with generic type parameters. In this case, I have called the IsAny method using decimal as the generic type. This tells Moq to apply the behavior I am defining whenever I call the ApplyDiscount method any decimal value. Table 6-5 shows the methods that the It class provides, all of which are static.

Table 6-5. *The Methods of the It Class*

Method	Description
Is<T>(predicate)	Specifies values of type T for which the predicate will return true. See Listing 6-34 for an example).
IsAny<T>()	Specifies any value of the type T.
IsInRange<T>(min, max, kind)	Matches if the parameter is between the defined values and of type T. The final parameter is a value from the Range enumeration and can be either Inclusive or Exclusive.
IsRegex(expr)	Matches a string parameter if it matches the specified regular expression.

I will show you a more complex example later that uses some other It methods, but for the moment I will stick with the IsAny<decimal> method which allows me to respond to any decimal value.

Defining the Result

The Returns method allows me to specify the result that Moq will return when I call my mocked method. I specify the type of the result using a type parameter and specify the result itself using a lambda expression. You can see how I have done this for the example:

```
...
mock.Setup(m => m.ApplyDiscount(It.IsAny<decimal>())).Returns<decimal>(total => total);
...
```

By calling Returns method with a decimal type parameter (i.e., Returns<decimal>), I tell Moq that I am going to return a decimal value. For the lambda expression, Moq passes me a value of the type I receive in the ApplyDiscount method. I create a *pass-through* method in the example, in which I return the value that is passed to the mock ApplyDiscount method without performing any operations on it. This is the simplest kind of mock method, but I will show you more sophisticated examples shortly.

Using the Mock Object

The last step is to use the mock object in the unit test, which I do by reading the value of the Object property of the Mock<IDiscountHelper> object:

```
...
var target = new LinqValueCalculator(mock.Object);
...
```

To summarize the example, the Object property returns an implementation of the IDiscountHelper interface where the ApplyDiscount method returns the value of the decimal parameter it is passed.

This makes it easy to perform my unit test because I can sum the prices of my test Product objects myself and check that I get the same value back from the LinqValueCalculator object:

```
...
Assert.AreEqual(products.Sum(e => e.Price), result);
...
```

The benefit of using Moq in this way is that my unit test only checks the behavior of the LinqValueCalculator object and does not depend on any of the real implementations of the IDiscountHelper interface in the Models folder. This means that when my tests fail, I know that the problem is either in the LinqValueCalculator implementation or in the way I set up mock object, and solving a problem from either of these sources is simpler and easier than dealing with a chain of real objects and the interactions between them.

Creating a More Complex Mock Object

I showed you a simple mock object in the last section, but part of the beauty of Moq is the ability to build up complex behaviors to test different situations. In Listing 6-34, I added a new unit test to the UnitTest2.cs file that mocks a more complex implementation of the IDiscountHelper interface. In fact, I used Moq to model the behavior of the MinimumDiscountHelper class.

Listing 6-34. Mocking the Behavior of the MinimumDiscountHelper Class in the UnitTest2.cs File

```
using EssentialTools.Models;
using Microsoft.VisualStudio.TestTools.UnitTesting;
using Moq;
using System.Linq;

namespace EssentialTools.Tests {
    [TestClass]
    public class UnitTest2 {

        private Product[] products = {
            new Product {Name = "Kayak", Category = "Watersports", Price = 275M},
            new Product {Name = "Lifejacket", Category = "Watersports", Price = 48.95M},
            new Product {Name = "Soccer ball", Category = "Soccer", Price = 19.50M},
            new Product {Name = "Corner flag", Category = "Soccer", Price = 34.95M}
        };

        [TestMethod]
        public void Sum_Products_Correctly() {
            // arrange
            Mock<IDiscountHelper> mock = new Mock<IDiscountHelper>();
            mock.Setup(m => m.ApplyDiscount(It.IsAny<decimal>()))
                .Returns<decimal>(total => total);
            var target = new LinqValueCalculator(mock.Object);

            // act
            var result = target.ValueProducts(products);

            // assert
            Assert.AreEqual(products.Sum(e => e.Price), result);
        }

        private Product[] createProduct(decimal value) {
            return new[] { new Product { Price = value } };
        }

        [TestMethod]
        [ExpectedException(typeof(System.ArgumentOutOfRangeException))]
        public void Pass_Through_Variable_Discounts() {
            // arrange
            Mock<IDiscountHelper> mock = new Mock<IDiscountHelper>();
            mock.Setup(m => m.ApplyDiscount(It.IsAny<decimal>()))
                .Returns<decimal>(total => total);
            mock.Setup(m => m.ApplyDiscount(It.Is<decimal>(v => v == 0)))
                .Throws<System.ArgumentOutOfRangeException>();
            mock.Setup(m => m.ApplyDiscount(It.Is<decimal>(v => v > 100)))
                .Returns<decimal>(total => (total * 0.9M));
            mock.Setup(m => m.ApplyDiscount(It.IsInRange<decimal>(10, 100,
                Range.Inclusive))).Returns<decimal>(total => total - 5);
            var target = new LinqValueCalculator(mock.Object);
```

```
        // act
        decimal FiveDollarDiscount = target.ValueProducts(createProduct(5));
        decimal TenDollarDiscount = target.ValueProducts(createProduct(10));
        decimal FiftyDollarDiscount = target.ValueProducts(createProduct(50));
        decimal HundredDollarDiscount = target.ValueProducts(createProduct(100));
        decimal FiveHundredDollarDiscount = target.ValueProducts(createProduct(500));

        // assert
        Assert.AreEqual(5, FiveDollarDiscount, "$5 Fail");
        Assert.AreEqual(5, TenDollarDiscount, "$10 Fail");
        Assert.AreEqual(45, FiftyDollarDiscount, "$50 Fail");
        Assert.AreEqual(95, HundredDollarDiscount, "$100 Fail");
        Assert.AreEqual(450, FiveHundredDollarDiscount, "$500 Fail");
        target.ValueProducts(createProduct(0));
    }
  }
}
```

In unit test terms, replicating the expected behavior of one of the other model classes would be an odd thing to do, but it is a perfect demonstration of some of the different Moq features.

I have defined four different behaviors for the ApplyDiscount method based on the value of the parameter that I receive. The simplest is the catch-all, which returns a value for any decimal value, like this:

```
...
mock.Setup(m => m.ApplyDiscount(It.IsAny<decimal>())).Returns<decimal>(total => total);
...
```

This is the same behavior used in the previous example, and I have included it here because the order in which you call the Setup method affects the behavior of the mock object. Moq evaluates the behaviors in reverse order, so that it considers the most recent calls to the Setup method first. This means that you have to take care to create your mock behaviors in order from the most general to the most specific. The It.IsAny<decimal> condition is the most general condition I define in this example and so I apply it first. If I reversed the order of my Setup calls, this behavior would capture all of the calls I make to the ApplyDiscount method and generate the wrong mock results.

Mocking For Specific Values (and Throwing an Exception)

For the second call to the Setup method, I have used the It.Is method:

```
...
mock.Setup(m => m.ApplyDiscount(It.Is<decimal>(v => v == 0)))
    .Throws<System.ArgumentOutOfRangeException>();
...
```

The predicate I have passed to the Is method returns true if the value passed to the ApplyDiscount method is 0. Rather than return a result, I used the Throws method, which causes Moq to throw a new instance of the exception I specify with the type parameter.

I also use the Is method to capture values that are greater than 100, like this:

```
...
mock.Setup(m => m.ApplyDiscount(It.Is<decimal>(v => v > 100)))
    .Returns<decimal>(total => (total * 0.9M));
...
```

The It.Is method is the most flexible way of setting up specific behaviors for different parameter values because you can use any predicate that returns true or false. This is the method I use most often when creating complex mock objects.

Mocking For a Range of Values

My final use of the It object is with the IsInRange method, which allows me to capture a range of parameter values:

```
...
mock.Setup(m => m.ApplyDiscount(It.IsInRange<decimal>(10, 100, Range.Inclusive)))
    .Returns<decimal>(total => total - 5);
...
```

I have included this for completeness, but in my own projects I tend to use the Is method and a predicate that does the same thing, like this:

```
...
mock.Setup(m => m.ApplyDiscount(It.Is<decimal>(v => v >= 10 && v <= 100)))
    .Returns<decimal>(total => total - 5);
...
```

The effect is the same, but I find the predicate approach more flexible. Moq has a range of extremely useful features and you can see how to apply them by reading the quick start provided at http://code.google.com/p/moq/wiki/QuickStart.

Summary

In this chapter, I looked at the three tools I find essential for effective MVC development: Ninject, the built-in Visual Studio support for unit testing, and Moq. There are many alternatives, both open source and commercial, for all three tools and you will not lack alternatives if you do not get along with the tools I like and use.

You may find that you do not like TDD or unit testing in general, or that you are happy performing DI and mocking manually. That, of course, is entirely your choice. However, I think there are some substantial benefits in using all three tools in the development cycle. If you are hesitant to adopt them because you have never tried them, I encourage you to suspend disbelief and give them a go, at least for the duration of this book.

CHAPTER 7

■ ■ ■

SportsStore: A Real Application

In the previous chapters, I built quick and simple MVC applications. I described the MVC pattern, the essential C# features and the kinds of tools that good MVC developers require. Now it is time to put everything together and build a simple but realistic e-commerce application.

My application, called *SportsStore*, will follow the classic approach taken by online stores everywhere. I will create an online product catalog that customers can browse by category and page, a shopping cart where users can add and remove products, and a checkout where customers can enter their shipping details. I will also create an administration area that includes create, read, update, and delete (CRUD) facilities for managing the catalog; and I will protect it so that only logged-in administrators can make changes.

My goal in this chapter and those that follow is to give you a sense of what real MVC Framework development is like by creating as realistic an example as possible. I want to focus on the MVC Framework, of course, and so I have simplified the integration with external systems, such as the database, and omitted others entirely, such as payment processing.

You might find the going a little slow as I build up the levels of infrastructure I need. Certainly, you *would* get the initial functionality built more quickly with Web Forms, just by dragging and dropping controls bound directly to a database. But the initial investment in an MVC application pays dividends, resulting in maintainable, extensible, well-structured code with excellent support for unit testing.

UNIT TESTING

I have made quite a big deal about the ease of unit testing in MVC, and about my belief that unit testing is an important part of the development process. You will see this demonstrated throughout this part of the book because I have included details of unit tests and techniques as they relate to key MVC features.

I know this is not a universal opinion. If you do not want to unit test, that is fine with me. To that end, when I have something to say that is purely about testing, I put it in a sidebar like this one. If you are not interested in unit testing, you can skip right over these sections, and the SportsStore application will work just fine. You do not need to do any kind of unit testing to get the technology benefits of ASP.NET MVC, although, of course, support for testing is a key reason for adopting the MVC Framework.

Most of the MVC features I use for the SportsStore application have their own chapters later in the book. Rather than duplicate everything here, I tell you just enough to make sense for the example application and point you to the other chapter for in-depth information.

I will call out each step needed to build the application, so that you can see how the MVC features fit together. You should pay particular attention when I create views. You will get some odd results if you do not follow the examples closely.

Getting Started

You will need to install Visual Studio if you are planning to code the SportsStore application on your own computer as you read through this part of the book. You can also download the SportsStore project as part of the code archive that accompanies this book (available from apress.com). You do not need to follow along, of course. I have tried to make the screenshots and code listings as easy to follow as possible, just in case you are reading this book on a train, in a coffee shop, or the like.

Creating the Visual Studio Solution and Projects

I am going to create a Visual Studio solution that contains three projects. One project will contain the domain model, one will be the MVC application, and the third will contain the unit tests. To get started, I created a new Visual Studio solution called SportsStore using the Blank Solution template, which you can find in the Other Project Types/Visual Studio Solutions section of the New Project dialog, as shown in Figure 7-1. Click the OK button to create the solution.

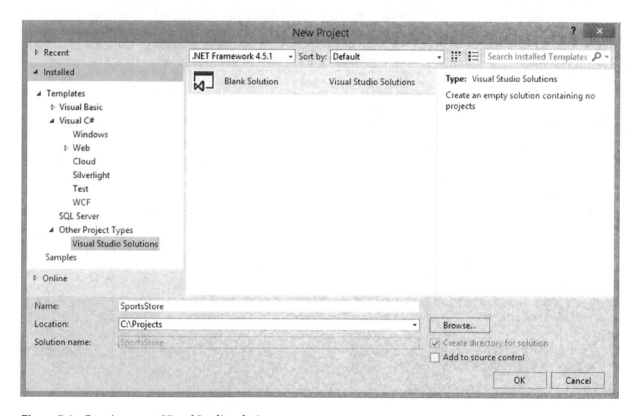

Figure 7-1. *Creating a new Visual Studio solution*

A Visual Studio solution is a container for one or more projects. I require three projects for my example app, which I have described in Table 7-1. You add a project by right-clicking the Solution entry in the Solution Explorer and selecting Add ➤ New Project from the pop-up menus.

Table 7-1. *The Three SportsStore Projects*

Project Name	Visual Studio Project Template	Purpose
SportsStore.Domain	Class Library	Holds the domain entities and logic; set up for persistence via a repository created with the Entity Framework.
SportsStore.WebUI	ASP.NET MVC Web Application (choose Empty when prompted to choose a project template and check the MVC option)	Holds the controllers and views; acts as the UI for the SportsStore application.
SportsStore.UnitTests	Unit Test Project	Holds the unit tests for the other two projects

I always use the Empty option for the ASP.NET MVC Web Application template. The other options add an initial setup to the project that includes JavaScript libraries, CSS style sheets, and C# classes that configure application features like security and routing. None of this is inherently bad–and some of the open-source libraries that Microsoft has recently "blessed" to be included in new projects are excellent–but you can manually set up all of the content and configuration and, in doing so, learn more about the workings of the MVC Framework.

When you have created the three projects, the Solution Explorer should look like Figure 7-2. I have deleted the Class1.cs file that Visual Studio adds to the SportsStore.Domain project. I will not be using it.

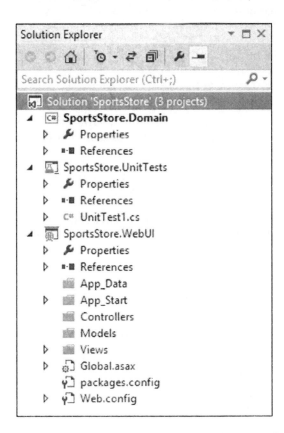

Figure 7-2. *The projects shown in the Solution Explorer window*

To make debugging easier, right-click the SportsStore.WebUI project and select Set as Startup Project from the pop-up menu (you will see the name turn bold). This means that when you select Start Debugging or Start without Debugging from the Debug menu, it is this project that will be started.

Visual Studio will try to navigate to individual view files if you are editing them when you start the debugger, so right-click the SportsStore.WebUI project in the Solution Explorer and select Properties from the pop-up menu. Click on Web to open the web-related properties and select the Specific Page option. There is no need to enter a value into the Specific Page text field. Just selecting the option is enough to stop Visual Studio from trying to guess the URL you want to view and ensure that the browser requests the root URL for the application when you start the debugger.

Installing the Tool Packages

I will be using Ninject and Moq in this chapter. Select Tools ➤ Library Package Manger ➤ Package Manager Console in Visual Studio to open the NuGet command line and enter the following commands:

```
Install-Package Ninject -version 3.0.1.10 -projectname SportsStore.WebUI
Install-Package Ninject.Web.Common -version 3.0.0.7 -projectname SportsStore.WebUI
Install-Package Ninject.MVC3 -Version 3.0.0.6 -projectname SportsStore.WebUI
Install-Package Ninject -version 3.0.1.10 -projectname SportsStore.UnitTests
Install-Package Ninject.Web.Common -version 3.0.0.7 -projectname SportsStore.UnitTests
Install-Package Ninject.MVC3 -Version 3.0.0.6 -projectname SportsStore.UnitTests
Install-Package Moq -version 4.1.1309.1617 -projectname SportsStore.WebUI
Install-Package Moq -version 4.1.1309.1617 -projectname SportsStore.UnitTests
Install-Package Microsoft.Aspnet.Mvc -version 5.0.0 -projectname SportsStore.Domain
Install-Package Microsoft.Aspnet.Mvc -version 5.0.0 -projectname SportsStore.UnitTests
```

There are many NuGet commands to enter because I am being selective about which packages NuGet installs into which projects and, as in previous chapters, I am specifying particular versions of the packages to download and install.

Adding References Between Projects

I need to set up dependencies between projects and to some of the Microsoft assemblies. Right-click each project in the Solution Explorer window, select Add Reference, and add the references shown in Table 7-2 from the Assemblies ➤ Framework, Assemblies ➤ Extensions or Solution sections.

Table 7-2. *Required Project Dependencies*

Project Name	Solution Dependencies	Assemblies References
SportsStore.Domain	None	System.ComponentModel.DataAnnotations
SportsStore.WebUI	SportsStore.Domain	None
SportsStore.UnitTests	SportsStore.Domain	System.Web
	SportsStore.WebUI	Microsoft.CSharp

■ **Caution** Take the time to set these relationships up properly. If you do not have the right libraries and project references, you will get into trouble when trying to build the project.

Setting Up the DI Container

In Chapter 6, I showed you how to use Ninject to create a custom dependency resolver that the MVC Framework will use to instantiate objects across the application. I am going to repeat that process, starting with adding an Infrastructure folder to the SportsStore.WebUI project and adding a class file called NinjectDependencyResolver.cs to it. You can see the contents of the new file in Listing 7-1.

Listing 7-1. The Contents of the NinjectDependencyResolver.cs File

```
using System;
using System.Collections.Generic;
using System.Web.Mvc;
using Ninject;

namespace SportsStore.WebUI.Infrastructure {

    public class NinjectDependencyResolver : IDependencyResolver {
        private IKernel kernel;

        public NinjectDependencyResolver(IKernel kernelParam) {
            kernel = kernelParam;
            AddBindings();
        }

        public object GetService(Type serviceType) {
            return kernel.TryGet(serviceType);
        }

        public IEnumerable<object> GetServices(Type serviceType) {
            return kernel.GetAll(serviceType);
        }

        private void AddBindings() {
            // put bindings here
        }
    }
}
```

As you may recall from Chapter 6, the next step is to create a bridge between the NinjectDependencyResolver class and the MVC support for dependency injection in the App_Start/NinjectWebCommon.cs file, which one of the Ninject NuGet packages added to the project, as shown in Listing 7-2.

Listing 7-2. Integrating Ninject in the NinjectWebCommon.cs File

```
...
private static void RegisterServices(IKernel kernel) {
    System.Web.Mvc.DependencyResolver.SetResolver(new
        SportsStore.WebUI.Infrastructure.NinjectDependencyResolver(kernel));
}
...
```

Running the Application

If you select Start Debugging from the Debug menu, you will see an error page as shown in Figure 7-3. This is because you have requested a URL associated with a non-existent controller.

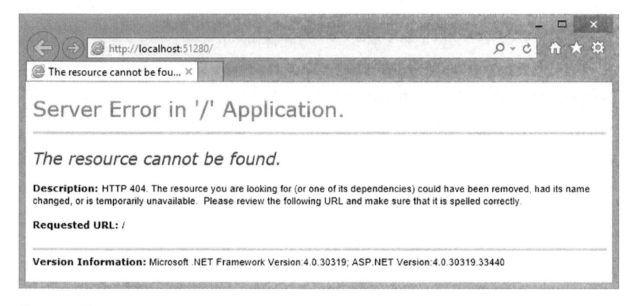

Figure 7-3. *The error page*

Starting the Domain Model

All MVC Framework projects start with the domain model because everything in an MVC Framework application revolves around it. Since this is an e-commerce application, the most obvious domain entity I need is a product. Create a new folder called Entities inside the SportsStore.Domain project and then a new C# class file called Product.cs within it. You can see the structure in Figure 7-4.

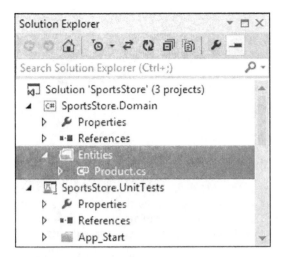

Figure 7-4. *Creating the Product class*

You are already familiar with the definition of the Product class, as I am going to use the one you saw in the previous chapters. Edit the Product.cs class file so that it matches Listing 7-3.

Listing 7-3. The Contents of the Product.cs File

```
namespace SportsStore.Domain.Entities {

    public class Product {
        public int ProductID { get; set; }
        public string Name { get; set; }
        public string Description { get; set; }
        public decimal Price { get; set; }
        public string Category { get; set; }
    }
}
```

I am following the technique of defining my domain model in a separate Visual Studio project, which means that the class must be marked as public. You do not need to follow this convention, but I find that it helps keep the model separate from the controllers, which is useful in large and complex projects.

Creating an Abstract Repository

I need some way of getting Product entities from a database. As I explained in Chapter 3, the model includes the persistence logic for storing and retrieving the data from the persistent data store, but even within the model, I want to keep a degree of separation between the data model entities and the storage and retrieval logic, which I achieve using the *repository pattern*. I will not worry about how I am going to implement data persistence for the moment, but I *will* start the process of defining an interface for it.

Create a new top-level folder inside the SportsStore.Domain project called Abstract and, within the new folder, a new interface file called IProductsRepository.cs, the contents of which Listing 7-4 shows. You can add a new interface by right-clicking the Abstract folder, selecting Add ➤ New Item, and selecting the Interface template.

Listing 7-4. The Contents of the IProductRepository.cs File

```
using System.Collections.Generic;
using SportsStore.Domain.Entities;

namespace SportsStore.Domain.Abstract {
    public interface IProductRepository {

        IEnumerable<Product> Products { get; }
    }
}
```

This interface uses IEnumerable<T> to allow a caller to obtain a sequence of Product objects, without saying how or where the data is stored or retrieved. A class that depends on the IProductRepository interface can obtain Product objects without needing to know anything about where they are coming from or how the implementation class will deliver them. This is the essence of the repository pattern. I will revisit the IProductRepository interface throughout the development process to add features.

Making a Mock Repository

Now that I have defined an abstract interface, I could implement the persistence mechanism and hook it up to a database, but I want to add some of the other parts of the application first. In order to do this, I am going to create a mock implementation of the IProductRepository interface that will stand in until I return to the topic of data storage.

I define the mock implementation and bind it to the IProductRepository interface in the AddBindings method of the NinjectDependencyResolver class in the SportsStore.WebUI project, as illustrated by Listing 7-5.

Listing 7-5. Adding the Mock IProductRepository Implementation in the NinjectDependencyResolver.cs File

```
using System;
using System.Collections.Generic;
using System.Linq;
using System.Web.Mvc;
using Moq;
using Ninject;
using SportsStore.Domain.Abstract;
using SportsStore.Domain.Entities;

namespace SportsStore.WebUI.Infrastructure {

    public class NinjectDependencyResolver : IDependencyResolver {
        private IKernel kernel;

        public NinjectDependencyResolver(IKernel kernelParam) {
            kernel = kernelParam;
            AddBindings();
        }

        public object GetService(Type serviceType) {
            return kernel.TryGet(serviceType);
        }
```

```
    public IEnumerable<object> GetServices(Type serviceType) {
        return kernel.GetAll(serviceType);
    }

    private void AddBindings() {
        Mock<IProductRepository> mock = new Mock<IProductRepository>();
        mock.Setup(m => m.Products).Returns(new List<Product> {
            new Product { Name = "Football", Price = 25 },
            new Product { Name = "Surf board", Price = 179 },
            new Product { Name = "Running shoes", Price = 95 }
        });

        kernel.Bind<IProductRepository>().ToConstant(mock.Object);
    }
  }
}
```

I had to add a number of namespaces to the file for this addition, but the process I used to create the mock repository implementation uses the same Moq techniques I introduced in Chapter 6. I want Ninject to return the same mock object whenever it gets a request for an implementation of the IProductRepository interface, which is why I used the ToConstant method to set the Ninject scope, like this:

```
...
kernel.Bind<IProductRepository>().ToConstant(mock.Object);
...
```

Rather than create a new instance of the implementation object each time, Ninject will always satisfy requests for the IProductRepository interface with the same mock object.

Displaying a List of Products

I could spend the rest of this chapter building out the domain model and the repository, and not touch the UI project at all. I think you would find that boring, though, so I am going to switch tracks and start using the MVC Framework in earnest. I will add model and repository features as I need them.

In this section, I am going to create a controller and an action method that can display details of the products in the repository. For the moment, this will be for only the data in the mock repository, but I will sort that out later. I will also set up an initial *routing configuration* so that MVC knows how to map requests for the application to the controller I create.

Adding a Controller

Right-click the Controllers folder in the SportsStore.WebUI project and select Add ➤ Controller from the pop-up menu. Select the MVC 5 Controller - Empty option, click the Add button and set the name to ProductController. Click the Add button and Visual Studio will create a new class file called ProductController.cs, which you should edit to match Listing 7-6.

Listing 7-6. The Initial Contents of the Product Controller.cs File

```
using System;
using System.Collections.Generic;
using System.Linq;
using System.Web;
using System.Web.Mvc;
using SportsStore.Domain.Abstract;
using SportsStore.Domain.Entities;

namespace SportsStore.WebUI.Controllers {

    public class ProductController : Controller {
        private IProductRepository repository;

        public ProductController(IProductRepository productRepository) {
            this.repository = productRepository;
        }
    }
}
```

In addition to removing the Index action method, I added a constructor that declares a dependency on the IProductRepository interface, which will lead Ninject to inject the dependency for the product repository when it instantiates the controller class. I also imported the SportsStore.Domain namespaces so that I can refer to the repository and model classes without having to qualify their names. Next, I have added an action method, called List, which will render a view showing the complete list of products, as shown in Listing 7-7.

Listing 7-7. Adding an Action Method to the ProductController.cs File

```
using System;
using System.Collections.Generic;
using System.Linq;
using System.Web;
using System.Web.Mvc;
using SportsStore.Domain.Abstract;
using SportsStore.Domain.Entities;

namespace SportsStore.WebUI.Controllers {

    public class ProductController : Controller {
        private IProductRepository repository;

        public ProductController(IProductRepository productRepository) {
            this.repository = productRepository;
        }

        public ViewResult List() {
            return View(repository.Products);
        }
    }
}
```

Calling the View method like this (without specifying a view name) tells the framework to render the default view for the action method. Passing a List of Product objects to the View method, provides the framework with the data with which to populate the Model object in a strongly typed view.

Adding the Layout, View Start File and View

Now I need to add the default view for the List action method. Right-click on the List action method in the HomeController class and select Add View from the pop-up menu. Set View Name to List, set Template to Empty, and select Product for the Model Class, as shown in Figure 7-5. Ensure that the Use A Layout Page box is checked and click the Add button to create the view.

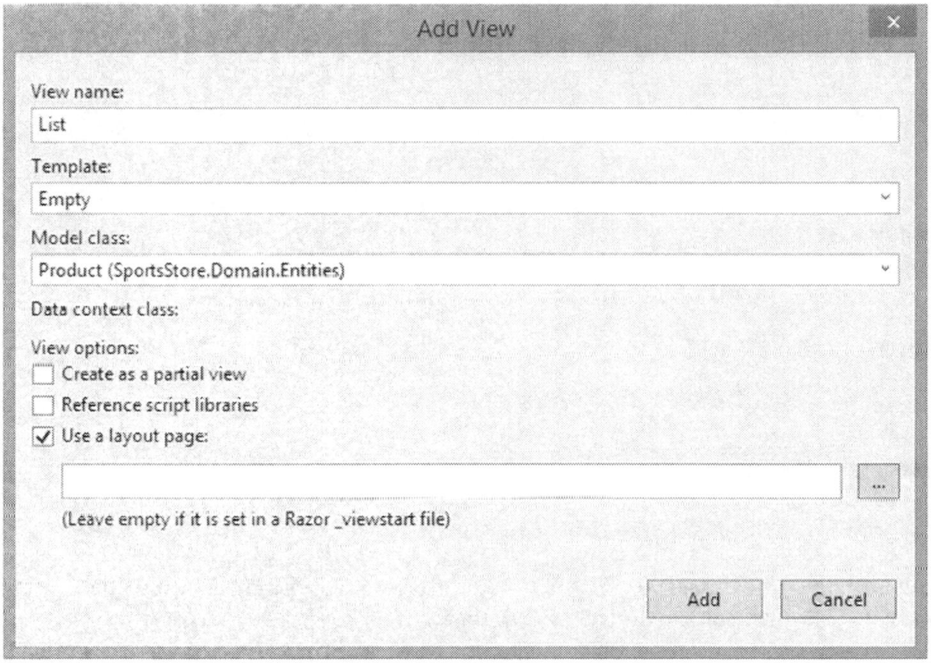

Figure 7-5. *Adding the Views/Product/List.cshtml view*

When you click the Add button, Visual Studio will create the List.cshtml file, but it will also create a _ViewStart.cshtml file and a Shared/_Layout.cshtml file. This is a helpful feature, but in keeping with the Microsoft approach to default content, the _Layout.cshtml file contains template content that I do not want or need. Edit the layout so that it matches the content shown in Listing 7-8.

Listing 7-8. Editing the _Layout.cshtml File

```
<!DOCTYPE html>
<html>
<head>
    <meta charset="utf-8" />
    <meta name="viewport" content="width=device-width, initial-scale=1.0">
    <title>@ViewBag.Title</title>
</head>
```

```
<body>
    <div>
        @RenderBody()
    </div>
</body>
</html>
```

Rendering the View Data

Although I set the model type of the view to be the Product class, I actually want to work with an IEnumerable<Product>, which is what the Product controller obtains from the repository and passes to the view. In Listing 7-9, you can see that I have edited the @model expression and added some HTML and Razor expressions to display details of the products.

Listing 7-9. Editing the List.cshtml File

```
@using SportsStore.Domain.Entities
@model IEnumerable<Product>

@{
    ViewBag.Title = "Products";
}


@foreach (var p in Model) {
    <div>
        <h3>@p.Name</h3>
        @p.Description
        <h4>@p.Price.ToString("c")</h4>
    </div>
}
```

I also changed the title of the page. Notice that I do not need to use the Razor @: expression to display the view data. This is because each of the content lines in the code body either is a Razor directive or starts with an HTML element.

■ **Tip** I converted the Price property to a string using the ToString("c") method, which renders numerical values as currency according to the culture settings that are in effect on your server. For example, if the server is set up as en-US, then (1002.3).ToString("c") will return $1,002.30, but if the server is set to en-GB, then the same method will return £1,002.30. You can change the culture setting for your server by adding a section to the <system.web> node in the Web.config file like this: <globalization culture="en-GB" uiCulture="en-GB" />.

Setting the Default Route

I need to tell the MVC Framework that it should send requests that arrive for the root URL of my application (http://mysite/) to the List action method in the ProductController class. I do this by editing the statement in the RegisterRoutes method in the App_Start/RouteConfig.cs file, as shown in Listing 7-10.

Listing 7-10. Adding the Default Route in the RouteConfig.cs File

```
using System;
using System.Collections.Generic;
using System.Linq;
using System.Web;
using System.Web.Mvc;
using System.Web.Routing;

namespace SportsStore.WebUI {
    public class RouteConfig {
        public static void RegisterRoutes(RouteCollection routes) {
            routes.IgnoreRoute("{resource}.axd/{*pathInfo}");

            routes.MapRoute(
                name: "Default",
                url: "{controller}/{action}/{id}",
                defaults: new { controller = "Product", action = "List",
                    id = UrlParameter.Optional }
            );
        }
    }
}
```

You can see the changes in bold. Change Home to Product and Index to List, as shown in the listing. I cover the ASP.NET routing feature in detail in Chapters 15 and 16. For now, it is enough to know that this change directs requests for the default URL to the List action method in the Product controller.

▪ **Tip** Notice that I have set the value of the controller in Listing 7-10 to be Product and not ProductController, which is the name of the class. This is part of the ASP.NET MVC naming scheme, in which controller classes *always* end in Controller but you omit this part of the name when referring to the class.

Running the Application

I have all the basics in place. I have a controller with an action method that the MVC Framework will call when the default URL is requested. That action method relies on a mock implementation of the repository interface, which generates some simple test data. The controller passes the test data to the view that I associated with the action method, and the view displays a simple list of the details for each product. You can see the result by running the application, as shown in Figure 7-6. If you don't get the result in the figure, check that you have navigated to the root URL and not one that targets another action.

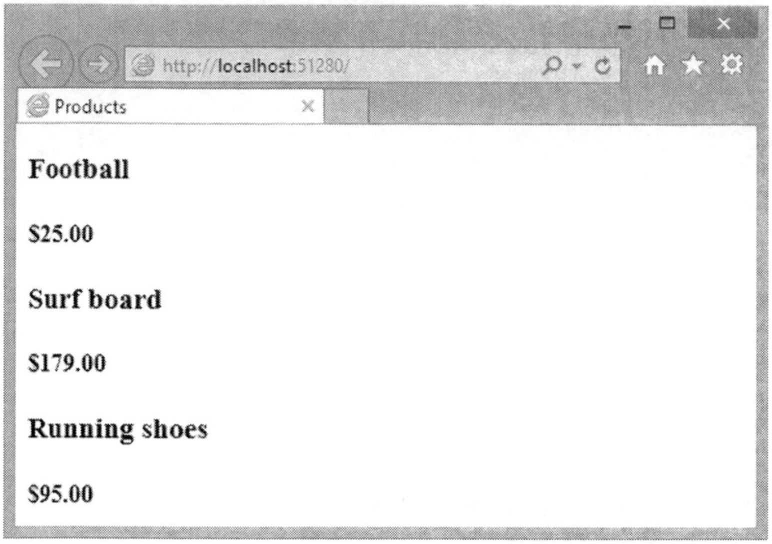

Figure 7-6. *Viewing the basic application functionality*

This is the typical pattern of development for the ASP.NET MVC Framework. An initial investment of time setting everything up is necessary, and then the basic features of the application snap together quickly.

EASIER DEBUGGING

When you run the project from the Debug menu, Visual Studio will create a new browser window to display the application, which can take a few seconds. There are some tricks that you can use to speed the process up.

If you are editing view files and not classes, then you can make changes in Visual Studio while the debugger is running. Reload the browser window when you want to see the effect of your changes. ASP.NET will recompile your views into classes and display the changes immediately. Visual Studio won't let you edit class files when the debugger is running or make some kinds of change to the project in the Solution Explorer, so this technique is most useful when you are tweaking the fit and finish of the HTML that your application generates.

Visual Studio 2013 includes a new feature called *browser link* that lets you have multiple browser windows open and to reload them from the Visual Studio menu bar. I demonstrate this feature in Chapter 14.

As a final alternative, you can keep your application open in a stand-alone browser window. To do this (assuming you have launched the debugger at least once already), right-click the IIS Express icon in the system tray and select the URL for your app from the pop-up menu. After you have made your changes, compile the solution in Visual Studio by pressing F6 or choosing Build ➤ Build Solution, and then switch to your browser window and reload the Web page.

Preparing a Database

I can already display simple views that contain details of the products, but I am displaying the test data that the mock IproductRepository returns. Before I can implement a real repository, I need to set up a database and populate it with some data.

I am going to use SQL Server as the database, and I will access the database using the Entity Framework (EF), which is the Microsoft.NET ORM framework. An ORM framework presents the tables, columns, and rows of a relational database through regular C# objects. I mentioned in Chapter 6 that LINQ can work with different sources of data, and one of these is the Entity Framework. You will see how this simplifies things in a little while.

■ **Note** This is an area where you can choose from a wide range of tools and technologies. Not only are there different relational databases available, but you can also work with object repositories, document stores, and some esoteric alternatives. There are other .NET ORM frameworks as well, each of which takes a slightly different approach: variations that may give you a better fit for your projects.

I am using the Entity Framework for a several reasons: it is simple and easy to get it up and working; the integration with LINQ is first rate (and I like using LINQ); and it is good. The earlier releases were a bit hit-and-miss, but the current versions are elegant and feature-rich.

Creating the Database

A nice feature of Visual Studio and SQL Server is the *LocalDB* feature, which is an administration-free implementation of the core SQL Server features specifically designed for developers. Using this feature, I can skip the process of setting up a database while I build my project and then deploy to a full SQL Server instance. Most MVC applications are deployed to hosted environments that are run by professional administrators and so the LocalDB feature means that database configuration can be left in the hands of DBAs and developers can get on with coding. The LocalDB feature is installed automatically with Visual Studio Express 2013 for Web, but you can download it directly from www.microsoft.com/sqlserver if you prefer.

The first step is to create the database connection in Visual Studio. Open the Server Explorer window from the View menu and click the Connect to Database button (it looks like a power cable with a green plus sign).

You will see the Choose Data Source dialog. Select the Microsoft SQL Server option, as shown in Figure 7-7, and click the Continue button. (Visual Studio remembers the selection you make, so you will not see this window if you already created a database connection in another project).

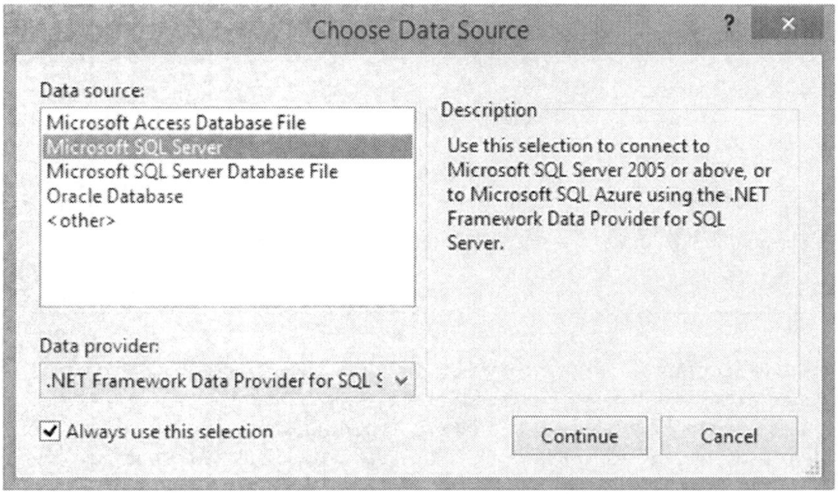

Figure 7-7. Selecting the Data Source

Next, you will see the Add Connection dialog. Set the server name to (localdb)\v11.0. This is a special name that indicates that you want to use the LocalDB feature. Check the Use Windows Authentication option and set the database name to SportsStore, as shown by Figure 7-8.

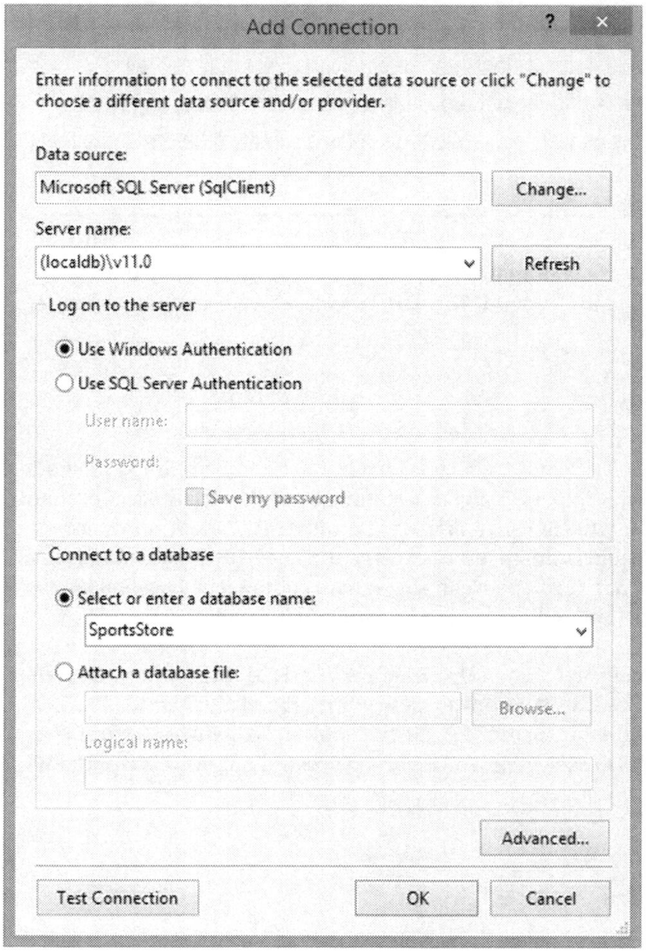

Figure 7-8. *Setting up the SportsStore database*

■ **Tip**   If you did not see the Choose Data Source dialog, you can click the Change button in the top right of the Add Connection dialog.

Click the OK button and Visual Studio will prompt you to create the new database: click the Yes to go ahead. A new item will appear in the Data Connections section of the Server Explorer window, which you can expand to see the different facets of the database, as shown in Figure 7-9. You should see something similar, but the name of the database connection will be different because it will include the local PC name (the name of my workstation is tiny).

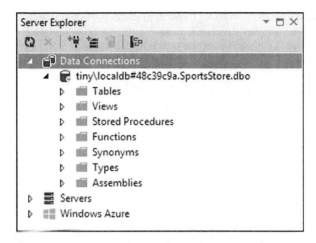

Figure 7-9. *The LocalDB database as shown in the Server Explorer window*

Defining the Database Schema

As I explained at the start of the chapter, my focus with the SportsStore application is to focus on the MVC Framework development process, and that means keeping the other components that the application relies on as simple as possible. I do not want to get into the topics of database design and the in-depth details of the Entity Framework, beyond what I need to demonstrate how to get data in and out of an application. These are topics in their own right and they are not part of ASP.NET or the MVC Framework.

With this in mind, I am going to use a database that contains only one table. This is not how real e-commerce sites would structure their data, of course, but the important lesson in this section is about the repository pattern and how I use it to store and retrieve data, not the structure of the database.

To create the database table, right-click the Tables item for the new SportsStore database in the Server Explorer window and select Add New Table, as shown in Figure 7-10.

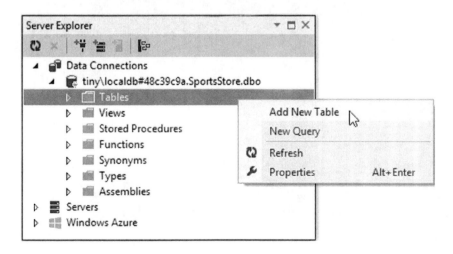

Figure 7-10. *Adding a new table*

Visual Studio will display a designer window for creating a new table. You can create new database tables using the visual part of the designer, but I am going to use the T-SQL section because it is a more concise and accurate way of describing the table specification I require in a book. Enter the SQL statement shown in Listing 7-11 and click the Update button in the top-left corner of the table design window.

Listing 7-11. The SQL Statement to Create the Table in the SportsStore Database

```
CREATE TABLE Products
(
    [ProductID] INT NOT NULL PRIMARY KEY IDENTITY,
    [Name] NVARCHAR(100) NOT NULL,
    [Description] NVARCHAR(500) NOT NULL,
    [Category] NVARCHAR(50) NOT NULL,
    [Price] DECIMAL(16, 2) NOT NULL
)
```

This statement creates a table called Products, which has columns for the different properties I defined in the Product model class earlier in the chapter.

■ **Tip**   Setting the IDENTITY property for the ProductID column means that SQL Server will generate a unique primary key value when I add data to this table. When using a database in a Web application, it can be difficult to generate unique primary keys because requests from users arrive concurrently. By enabling this feature, I can store new table rows and rely on SQL Server to sort out unique values.

When you click the Update button, Visual Studio will show a summary of the effect of the statement, as shown in Figure 7-11.

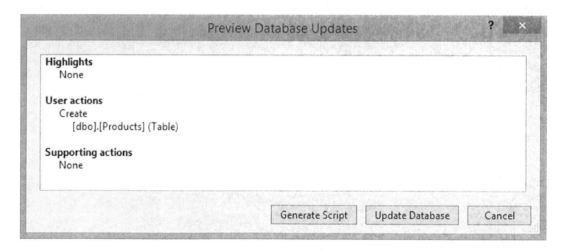

Figure 7-11. *The summary of the effect of the SQL statement*

Click the Update Database button to execute the SQL and create the Products table in the database. You will be able to see the effect the update has if you click the Refresh button in the Server Explorer window. The Tables section shows the new Product table and details of each of the rows.

■ **Tip** After you have updated the database, you can close the dbo.Products window. Visual Studio will offer you the chance to save the SQL script used to create the database. You do not need to save the script for this chapter, but it can be useful in real projects if you need to configure multiple databases.

Adding Data to the Database

I am going to add data to the database so that I have something to work with until I add the catalog administration features in Chapter 11.

In the Server Explorer window, expand the Tables item of the SportsStore database, right-click the Products table, and select Show Table Data. Enter the data shown in Figure 7-12. You can move from row to row by using the Tab key. At the end of each row, pressing tab will move to the next row and update the data in the database.

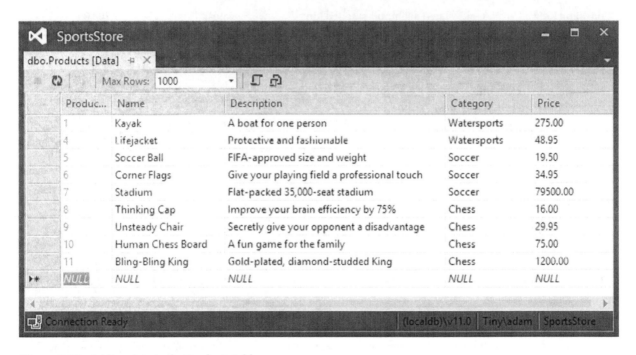

Figure 7-12. *Adding data to the Products table*

■ **Note** You must leave the ProductID column empty. It is an identity column, so SQL Server will generate a unique value when you tab to the next row.

I listed the product details in Table 7-3 in case you cannot make out the detail from the figure. It doesn't matter if you don't enter all of the details exactly as I have, although you'll see different results from the ones I show as you work through the process of creating the rest of the SportsStore application.

Table 7-3. *The Data for the Products Table*

Name	Description	Category	Price
Kayak	A boat for one person	Watersports	275.00
Lifejacket	Protective and fashionable	Watersports	48.95
Soccer Ball	FIFA-approved size and weight	Soccer	19.50
Corner Flags	Give your playing field a professional touch	Soccer	34.95
Stadium	Flat-packed, 35,000-seat stadium	Soccer	79,500.00
Thinking Cap	Improve your brain efficiency by 75%	Chess	16.00
Unsteady Chair	Secretly give your opponent a disadvantage	Chess	29.95
Human Chess Board	A fun game for the family	Chess	75.00
Bling-Bling King	Gold-plated, diamond-studded King	Chess	1,200.00

Creating the Entity Framework Context

Recent versions of the Entity Framework include a nice feature called *code-first*. The idea is that I can define classes in my model and then generate a database from those classes.

This is great for green-field development projects, but these are few and far between. Instead, I am going to show you a variation on code-first, where I associate the model classes with an existing database. Select Tools ➤ Library Package Manager ➤ Package Manager Console in Visual Studio to open the NuGet command line and enter the following command:

```
Install-Package EntityFramework -projectname SportsStore.Domain
Install-Package EntityFramework -projectname SportsStore.WebUI
```

■ **Tip**　You may see errors in the Package Manager Console telling you that *binding redirects* cannot be created. You can safely ignore these warnings.

This command adds the Entity Framework package to the solution. I need to install the same package in the Domain and WebUI projects so that I create the classes that will access the database in the Domain project and access the database in the WebUI project.

The next step is to create a *context* class that will associate the model with the database. Create a new folder in the SportsStore.Domain project called Concrete and add a new class file called EFDbContext.cs within it. Edit the contents of the class file so they match Listing 7-12.

Listing 7-12. The Content of the EFDbContext.cs File

```
using SportsStore.Domain.Entities;
using System.Data.Entity;

namespace SportsStore.Domain.Concrete {
```

```
    public class EFDbContext : DbContext {
        public DbSet<Product> Products { get; set; }
    }
}
```

To take advantage of the code-first feature, I need to create a class that is derived from System.Data.Entity. DbContext. This class then automatically defines a property for each table in the database that I want to work with.

The name of the property specifies the table, and the type parameter of the DbSet result specifies the model type that the Entity Framework should use to represent rows in that table. In this case, the property name is Products and the type parameter is Product, meaning that the Entity Framework should use the Product model type to represent rows in the Products table.

Next, I need to tell the Entity Framework how to connect to the database, which I do by adding a database connection string to the Web.config file in the SportsStore.WebUI project with the same name as the context class, as shown in Listing 7-13.

Listing 7-13. Adding a Database Connection in the Web.config File

```xml
<?xml version="1.0" encoding="utf-8"?>

<configuration>

  <connectionStrings>
    <add name="EFDbContext" connectionString="Data Source=(localdb)\v11.0;Initial
        Catalog=SportsStore;Integrated Security=True"
        providerName="System.Data.SqlClient"/>
  </connectionStrings>

  <appSettings>
    <add key="webpages:Version" value="3.0.0.0" />
    <add key="webpages:Enabled" value="false" />
     <add key="ClientValidationEnabled" value="true" />
    <add key="UnobtrusiveJavaScriptEnabled" value="true" />
  </appSettings>
  <system.web>
    <compilation debug="true" targetFramework="4.5.1" />
    <httpRuntime targetFramework="4.5.1" />
  </system.web>
</configuration>
```

▓ **Tip**   Notice that I have switched project here. I define the model and the repository logic in the SportsStore.Domain project, but the database connection information is put in the Web.config file in the SportsStore.WebUI project.

▓ **Caution**   I have had to split the value of the connectionString attribute across multiple lines to fit it on the page, but it is important to put everything on a single line in the Web.config file.

There will be another add element in the connectionsStrings section of the Web.config file. Visual Studio creates this element by default and you can either ignore it or, as I have, delete it from the Web.config file.

Creating the Product Repository

All that remains is to add a class file to the Concrete folder of the SportsStore.Domain project called EFProductRepository.cs. Edit your class file so it matches Listing 7-14.

Listing 7-14. The Contents of the EFProductRepostory.cs File

```
using SportsStore.Domain.Abstract;
using SportsStore.Domain.Entities;
using System.Collections.Generic;

namespace SportsStore.Domain.Concrete {

    public class EFProductRepository : IProductRepository {
        private EFDbContext context = new EFDbContext();

        public IEnumerable<Product> Products {
            get { return context.Products; }
        }
    }
}
```

This is the repository class. It implements the IProductRepository interface and uses an instance of EFDbContext to retrieve data from the database using the Entity Framework. You will see how I work with the Entity Framework (and how simple it is) as I add features to the repository.

To use the new repository class, I need to edit the Ninject bindings and replace the mock repository with a binding for the real one. Edit the NinjectDependencyResolver.cs class file in the SportsStore.WebUI project so that the AddBindings method looks like Listing 7-15.

Listing 7-15. Adding the Real Repository Binding in the NinjectDependencyResolver.cs File

```
using System;
using System.Collections.Generic;
using System.Linq;
using System.Web.Mvc;
using Moq;
using Ninject;
using SportsStore.Domain.Abstract;
using SportsStore.Domain.Concrete;
using SportsStore.Domain.Entities;

namespace SportsStore.WebUI.Infrastructure {

    public class NinjectDependencyResolver : IDependencyResolver {
        private IKernel kernel;

        public NinjectDependencyResolver(IKernel kernelParam) {
            kernel = kernelParam;
            AddBindings();
        }
```

```
public object GetService(Type serviceType) {
    return kernel.TryGet(serviceType);
}

public IEnumerable<object> GetServices(Type serviceType) {
    return kernel.GetAll(serviceType);
}

private void AddBindings() {
    kernel.Bind<IProductRepository>().To<EFProductRepository>();
}
    }
}
```

The new binding is in bold. It tells Ninject to create instances of the EFProductRepository class to service requests for the IProductRepository interface. All that remains now is to run the application again. Figure 7-13 shows the results, which demonstrate the application is getting its product data from the database, rather than the mock repository.

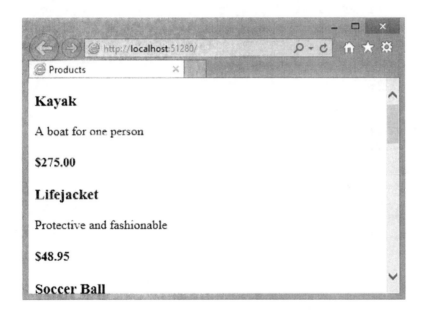

Figure 7-13. *The result of implementing the real repository*

■ **Tip** If you get a System.ArgumentException when you start the project, then you have split the details of the database connection over two lines in the Web.config file. See the previous section for details.

This approach to getting the Entity Framework to present a SQL Server database as a series of model objects is simple and easy to work with, and it allows me to keep my focus on the MVC Framework. Of course, I am skipping over a lot of the detail in how the Entity Framework operates and the huge number of configuration options that are available. I like the Entity Framework a lot and I recommend that you spend some time getting to know it in detail. A good place to start is the Microsoft site for the Entity Framework: http://msdn.microsoft.com/data/ef.

Adding Pagination

You can see from Figure 7-13 that the List.cshtml view displays all of the products in the database on a single page. In this section, I will add support for pagination so that the view displays a number of products on a page, and the user can move from page to page to view the overall catalog. To do this, I am going to add a parameter to the List method in the Product controller, as shown in Listing 7-16.

Listing 7-16. Adding Pagination Support to the List Action Method in the ProductController.cs File

```
using System;
using System.Collections.Generic;
using System.Linq;
using System.Web;
using System.Web.Mvc;
using SportsStore.Domain.Abstract;
using SportsStore.Domain.Entities;

namespace SportsStore.WebUI.Controllers {

    public class ProductController : Controller {
        private IProductRepository repository;
        public int PageSize = 4;

        public ProductController(IProductRepository productRepository) {
            this.repository = productRepository;
        }

        public ViewResult List(int page = 1) {
            return View(repository.Products
                .OrderBy(p => p.ProductID)
                .Skip((page - 1) * PageSize)
                .Take(PageSize));
        }
    }
}
```

The PageSize field specifies that I want four products per page. I will come back and replace this with a better mechanism later on. I have added an *optional parameter* to the List method. This means that if I call the method without a parameter (List()), my call is treated as though I had supplied the value specified in the parameter definition (List(1)). The effect is that the action method displays the first page of products when the MVC Framework invokes it without an argument. Within the body of the action method, I get the Product objects, order them by the primary key, skip over the products that occur before the start of the current page, and take the number of products specified by the PageSize field.

UNIT TEST: PAGINATION

I can unit test the pagination feature by creating a mock repository, injecting it into the constructor of the ProductController class, and then calling the List method to request a specific page. I can then compare the Product objects I get with what I would expect from the test data in the mock implementation. See Chapter 6 for details of how to set up unit tests. Here is the unit test I created for this purpose, in the UnitTest1.cs file of the SportsStore.UnitTests project:

```csharp
using System.Collections.Generic;
using System.Linq;
using Microsoft.VisualStudio.TestTools.UnitTesting;
using Moq;
using SportsStore.Domain.Abstract;
using SportsStore.Domain.Entities;
using SportsStore.WebUI.Controllers;

namespace SportsStore.UnitTests {

    [TestClass]
    public class UnitTest1 {

        [TestMethod]
        public void Can_Paginate() {

            // Arrange
            Mock<IProductRepository> mock = new Mock<IProductRepository>();
            mock.Setup(m => m.Products).Returns(new Product[] {
                new Product {ProductID = 1, Name = "P1"},
                new Product {ProductID = 2, Name = "P2"},
                new Product {ProductID = 3, Name = "P3"},
                new Product {ProductID = 4, Name = "P4"},
                new Product {ProductID = 5, Name = "P5"}
            });

            ProductController controller = new ProductController(mock.Object);
            controller.PageSize = 3;

            // Act
            IEnumerable<Product> result =
                (IEnumerable<Product>)controller.List(2).Model;

            // Assert
            Product[] prodArray = result.ToArray();
            Assert.IsTrue(prodArray.Length == 2);
            Assert.AreEqual(prodArray[0].Name, "P4");
            Assert.AreEqual(prodArray[1].Name, "P5");
        }
    }
}
```

Notice how easy it is to get the data that returned from a controller method. I call the `Model` property on the result to get the `IEnumerable<Product>` sequence generated in the `List` method. I then check that the data is what I expect. In this case, I converted the sequence to an array using the LINQ `ToArray` extension method and checked the length and the values of the individual objects.

Displaying Page Links

If you run the application, you will see that there are only four items shown on the page. If you want to view another page, you can append query string parameters to the end of the URL, like this:

```
http://localhost:51280/?page=2
```

You will need to change the port part of the URL to match whatever port your ASP.NET development server is running on. Using these query strings, you can navigate through the catalog of products.

Of course, there is no way for customers to figure out that these query string parameters exist, and even if there were, they are not going to want to navigate this way. Instead, I need to render some page links at the bottom of the each list of products so that customers can navigate between pages. To do this, I am going to implement a reusable HTML helper method, similar to the `Html.TextBoxFor` and `Html.BeginForm` methods I used in Chapter 2. The helper will generate the HTML markup for the navigation links I require.

Adding the View Model

To support the HTML helper, I am going to pass information to the view about the number of pages available, the current page, and the total number of products in the repository. The easiest way to do this is to create a view model, which I introduced briefly in Chapter 3. Add the class shown in Listing 7-17, called `PagingInfo`, to the `Models` folder in the `SportsStore.WebUI` project.

Listing 7-17. The Contents of the PagingInfo.cs File

```
using System;

namespace SportsStore.WebUI.Models {

    public class PagingInfo {
        public int TotalItems { get; set; }
        public int ItemsPerPage { get; set; }
        public int CurrentPage { get; set; }

        public int TotalPages {
            get { return (int)Math.Ceiling((decimal)TotalItems / ItemsPerPage); }
        }
    }
}
```

A view model is not part of the domain model. It is just a convenient class for passing data between the controller and the view. To emphasize this, I put this class in the `SportsStore.WebUI` project to keep it separate from the domain model classes.

Adding the HTML Helper Method

Now that I have a view model, I can implement the HTML helper method, which I am going to call PageLinks. Create a new folder in the SportsStore.WebUI project called HtmlHelpers and add a new class file called PagingHelpers.cs, the contents of which Listing 7-18 shows.

Listing 7-18. The Contents of the PagingHelpers.cs Class File

```csharp
using System;
using System.Text;
using System.Web.Mvc;
using SportsStore.WebUI.Models;

namespace SportsStore.WebUI.HtmlHelpers {

    public static class PagingHelpers {

        public static MvcHtmlString PageLinks(this HtmlHelper html,
                                              PagingInfo pagingInfo,
                                              Func<int, string> pageUrl) {

            StringBuilder result = new StringBuilder();
            for (int i = 1; i <= pagingInfo.TotalPages; i++) {
                TagBuilder tag = new TagBuilder("a");
                tag.MergeAttribute("href", pageUrl(i));
                tag.InnerHtml = i.ToString();
                if (i == pagingInfo.CurrentPage) {
                    tag.AddCssClass("selected");
                    tag.AddCssClass("btn-primary");
                }
                tag.AddCssClass("btn btn-default");
                result.Append(tag.ToString());
            }
            return MvcHtmlString.Create(result.ToString());
        }
    }
}
```

The PageLinks extension method generates the HTML for a set of page links using the information provided in a PagingInfo object. The Func parameter accepts a delegate that it uses to generate the links to view other pages.

UNIT TEST: CREATING PAGE LINKS

To test the PageLinks helper method, I call the method with test data and compare the results to the expected HTML. The unit test method is as follows:

```csharp
using System;
using System.Collections.Generic;
using System.Linq;
using System.Web.Mvc;
using Microsoft.VisualStudio.TestTools.UnitTesting;
using Moq;
using SportsStore.Domain.Abstract;
using SportsStore.Domain.Entities;
using SportsStore.WebUI.Controllers;
using SportsStore.WebUI.Models;
using SportsStore.WebUI.HtmlHelpers;

namespace SportsStore.UnitTests {
    [TestClass]
    public class UnitTest1 {

        [TestMethod]
        public void Can_Paginate() {
            // ...statements removed for brevity...
        }

        [TestMethod]
        public void Can_Generate_Page_Links() {

            // Arrange - define an HTML helper - we need to do this
            // in order to apply the extension method
            HtmlHelper myHelper = null;

            // Arrange - create PagingInfo data
            PagingInfo pagingInfo = new PagingInfo {
                CurrentPage = 2,
                TotalItems = 28,
                ItemsPerPage = 10
            };

            // Arrange - set up the delegate using a lambda expression
            Func<int, string> pageUrlDelegate = i => "Page" + i;

            // Act
            MvcHtmlString result = myHelper.PageLinks(pagingInfo, pageUrlDelegate);
```

```
        // Assert
        Assert.AreEqual(@"<a class=""btn btn-default"" href=""Page1"">1</a>"
    + @"<a class=""btn btn-default btn-primary selected"" href=""Page2"">2</a>"
        + @"<a class=""btn btn-default"" href=""Page3"">3</a>",
        result.ToString());
    }
    }
}
```

This test verifies the helper method output by using a literal string value that contains double quotes. C# is perfectly capable of working with such strings, as long as the string is prefixed with @ and use two sets of double quotes ("") in place of one set of double quotes. You must remember not to break the literal string into separate lines, unless the string you are comparing to is similarly broken. For example, the literal I use in the test method has wrapped onto two lines because the width of a printed page is narrow. I have not added a newline character; if I did, the test would fail.

An extension method is available for use only when the namespace that contains it is in scope. In a code file, this is done with a using statement; but for a Razor view, you must add a configuration entry to the Web.config file, or add a @using statement to the view itself. There are, confusingly, two Web.config files in a Razor MVC project: the main one, which resides in the root directory of the application project, and the view-specific one, which is in the Views folder. The change I want to make is to the Views/web.config file as shown in Listing 7-19.

Listing 7-19. Adding the HTML Helper Method Namespace to the Views/web.config File

```
...
  <system.web.webPages.razor>
    <host factoryType="System.Web.Mvc.MvcWebRazorHostFactory, System.Web.Mvc, Version=5.0.0.0,
Culture=neutral, PublicKeyToken=31BF3856AD364E35" />
    <pages pageBaseType="System.Web.Mvc.WebViewPage">
      <namespaces>
        <add namespace="System.Web.Mvc" />
        <add namespace="System.Web.Mvc.Ajax" />
        <add namespace="System.Web.Mvc.Html" />
        <add namespace="System.Web.Routing" />
        <add namespace="SportsStore.WebUI" />
        <add namespace="SportsStore.WebUI.HtmlHelpers"/>
      </namespaces>
    </pages>
  </system.web.webPages.razor>
...
```

Every namespace that I refer to in a Razor view needs to be used explicitly, declared in the web.config file or applied with a @using expression.

Adding the View Model Data

I am not quite ready to use the HTML helper method. I have yet to provide an instance of the PagingInfo view model class to the view. I could do this using the view bag feature, but I would rather wrap all of the data I am going to send from the controller to the view in a single view model class. To do this, I added a class file called

ProductsListViewModel.cs to the Models folder of the SportsStore.WebUI project. Listing 7-20 shows the contents of the new file.

Listing 7-20. The Contents of the ProductsListViewModel.cs File

```
using System.Collections.Generic;
using SportsStore.Domain.Entities;

namespace SportsStore.WebUI.Models {
    public class ProductsListViewModel {

        public IEnumerable<Product> Products { get; set; }
        public PagingInfo PagingInfo { get; set; }
    }
}
```

I can update the List action method in the ProductController class to use the ProductsListViewModel class to provide the view with details of the products to display on the page and details of the pagination, as shown in Listing 7-21.

Listing 7-21. Updating the List Method in the ProductController.cs File

```
using System;
using System.Collections.Generic;
using System.Linq;
using System.Web;
using System.Web.Mvc;
using SportsStore.Domain.Abstract;
using SportsStore.Domain.Entities;
using SportsStore.WebUI.Models;

namespace SportsStore.WebUI.Controllers {

    public class ProductController : Controller {
        private IProductRepository repository;
        public int PageSize = 4;

        public ProductController(IProductRepository productRepository) {
            this.repository = productRepository;
        }

        public ViewResult List(int page = 1) {
            ProductsListViewModel model = new ProductsListViewModel {
                Products = repository.Products
                .OrderBy(p => p.ProductID)
                .Skip((page - 1) * PageSize)
                .Take(PageSize),
```

```
            PagingInfo = new PagingInfo {
                CurrentPage = page,
                ItemsPerPage = PageSize,
                TotalItems = repository.Products.Count()
            }
        };
        return View(model);
    }
}
}
```

These changes pass a ProductsListViewModel object as the model data to the view.

UNIT TEST: PAGE MODEL VIEW DATA

I need to ensure that the controller sends the correct pagination data to the view. Here is the unit test I added to the test project to test this:

```
...
[TestMethod]
public void Can_Send_Pagination_View_Model() {

    // Arrange
    Mock<IProductRepository> mock = new Mock<IProductRepository>();
    mock.Setup(m => m.Products).Returns(new Product[] {
        new Product {ProductID = 1, Name = "P1"},
        new Product {ProductID = 2, Name = "P2"},
        new Product {ProductID = 3, Name = "P3"},
        new Product {ProductID = 4, Name = "P4"},
        new Product {ProductID = 5, Name = "P5"}
    });

    // Arrange
    ProductController controller = new ProductController(mock.Object);
    controller.PageSize = 3;

    // Act
    ProductsListViewModel result = (ProductsListViewModel)controller.List(2).Model;

    // Assert
    PagingInfo pageInfo = result.PagingInfo;
    Assert.AreEqual(pageInfo.CurrentPage, 2);
    Assert.AreEqual(pageInfo.ItemsPerPage, 3);
    Assert.AreEqual(pageInfo.TotalItems, 5);
    Assert.AreEqual(pageInfo.TotalPages, 2);
}
...
```

I also need to modify the earlier pagination unit test, contained in the Can_Paginate method. It relies on the List action method returning a ViewResult whose Model property is a sequence of Product objects, but I have wrapped that data inside another view model type. Here is the revised test:

```
...
[TestMethod]
public void Can_Paginate() {

    // Arrange
    Mock<IProductRepository> mock = new Mock<IProductRepository>();
    mock.Setup(m => m.Products).Returns(new Product[] {
        new Product {ProductID = 1, Name = "P1"},
        new Product {ProductID = 2, Name = "P2"},
        new Product {ProductID = 3, Name = "P3"},
        new Product {ProductID = 4, Name = "P4"},
        new Product {ProductID = 5, Name = "P5"}
    });

    ProductController controller = new ProductController(mock.Object);
    controller.PageSize = 3;

    // Act
    ProductsListViewModel result = (ProductsListViewModel)controller.List(2).Model;

    // Assert
    Product[] prodArray = result.Products.ToArray();
    Assert.IsTrue(prodArray.Length == 2);
    Assert.AreEqual(prodArray[0].Name, "P4");
    Assert.AreEqual(prodArray[1].Name, "P5");
}
...
```

I would usually create a common setup method, given the degree of duplication between these two test methods. However, since I am delivering the unit tests in individual sidebars like this one, I am going to keep everything separate so you can see each test on its own.

The view is currently expecting a sequence of Product objects, so I need to update the List.cshtml file, as shown in Listing 7-22, to deal with the new view model type.

Listing 7-22. Updating the List.cshtml File

```
@model SportsStore.WebUI.Models.ProductsListViewModel

@{
    ViewBag.Title = "Products";
}
```

```
@foreach (var p in Model.Products) {
    <div>
        <h3>@p.Name</h3>
        @p.Description
        <h4>@p.Price.ToString("c")</h4>
    </div>
}
```

I have changed the @model directive to tell Razor that I am now working with a different data type. I updated the foreach loop so that the data source is the Products property of the model data.

Displaying the Page Links

I have everything in place to add the page links to the List view. I created the view model that contains the paging information, updated the controller so that it passes this information to the view, and changed the @model directive to match the new model view type. All that remains is to call the HTML helper method from the view, which you can see in Listing 7-23.

Listing 7-23. Calling the HTML Helper Method in the List.cshtml File

```
@model SportsStore.WebUI.Models.ProductsListViewModel

@{
    ViewBag.Title = "Products";
}

@foreach (var p in Model.Products) {
    <div>
        <h3>@p.Name</h3>
        @p.Description
        <h4>@p.Price.ToString("c")</h4>
    </div>
}

<div>
    @Html.PageLinks(Model.PagingInfo, x => Url.Action("List", new { page = x }))
</div>
```

If you run the application, you will see the new page links, as illustrated in Figure 7-14. The style is still basic, which I will fix later in the chapter. What is important for the moment is that the links take the user from page to page in the catalog and let him explore the products for sale.

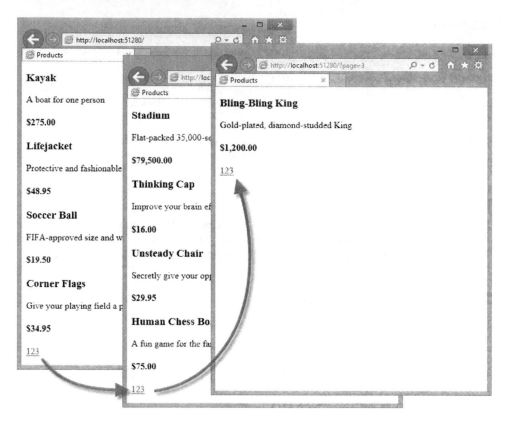

Figure 7-14. *Displaying page navigation links*

WHY NOT JUST USE A GRIDVIEW?

If you have worked with ASP.NET before, you might think that was a lot of work for an unimpressive result. It has taken me pages and pages just to get a page list. If I were using Web Forms, I could have done the same thing using the ASP.NET Web Forms GridView or ListView controls, right out of the box, by hooking it up directly to the Products database table.

What I have accomplished in this chapter may not look like much, but it is different from dragging a control onto a design surface. First, I am building an application with a sound and maintainable architecture that involves proper separation of concerns. Unlike the simplest use of the ListView control, I have not directly coupled the UI and the database: an approach that gives quick results but that causes pain and misery over time. Second, I have been creating unit tests as I go, and these allow me to validate the behavior of the application in a natural way that is nearly impossible with a complex Web Forms control. Finally, bear in mind that I have given over a lot of this chapter to creating the underlying infrastructure on which I am building the application. I need to define and implement the repository only once, for example, and now that I have, I will be able to build and test new features quickly and easily, as the following chapters will demonstrate.

None of this detracts from the immediate results that Web Forms can deliver, of course, but as I explained in Chapter 3, that immediacy comes with a cost that can be expensive and painful in large and complex projects.

Improving the URLs

I have the page links working, but they still use the query string to pass page information to the server, like this:

```
http://localhost/?page=2
```

I create URLs that are more appealing by creating a scheme that follows the pattern of *composable URLs*. A composable URL is one that makes sense to the user, like this one:

```
http://localhost/Page2
```

MVC makes it easy to change the URL scheme in application because it uses the ASP.NET *routing* feature. All I need do is add a new route to the RegisterRoutes method in the RouteConfig.cs file, which you will find in the App_Start folder of the SportsStore.WebUI project. You can see the change I made to this file in Listing 7-24.

Listing 7-24. Adding a New Route to the RouteConfig.cs File

```
using System;
using System.Collections.Generic;
using System.Linq;
using System.Web;
using System.Web.Mvc;
using System.Web.Routing;

namespace SportsStore.WebUI {
    public class RouteConfig {
        public static void RegisterRoutes(RouteCollection routes) {
            routes.IgnoreRoute("{resource}.axd/{*pathInfo}");

            routes.MapRoute(
                name: null,
                url: "Page{page}",
                defaults: new { Controller = "Product", action = "List" }
            );

            routes.MapRoute(
                name: "Default",
                url: "{controller}/{action}/{id}",
                defaults: new { controller = "Product", action = "List",
                    id = UrlParameter.Optional }
            );
        }
    }
}
```

It is important that you add this route before the Default one that is already in the file. As you will see in Chapter 15, the routing system processes routes in the order they are listed, and I need the new route to take precedence over the existing one.

This is the only alteration required to change the URL scheme for product pagination. The MVC Framework and the routing function are tightly integrated, and so the application automatically reflects a change like this in the result produced by the Url.Action method (which is what I used in the List.cshtml view to generate the page links). Do not worry if routing does not make sense to you now. I explain it in detail in Chapters 15 and 16.

If you run the application and navigate to a page, you will see the new URL scheme in action, as illustrated in Figure 7-15.

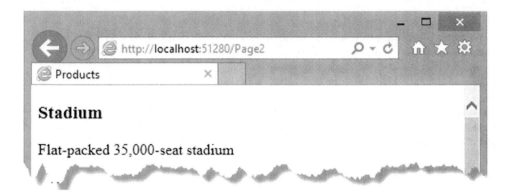

Figure 7-15. *The new URL scheme displayed in the browser*

Styling the Content

I have built a great deal of infrastructure and the application is really starting to come together, but I have not paid any attention to its appearance. Even though this book is not about design or CSS, the SportsStore application design is so miserably plain that it undermines its technical strengths. In this section, I will put some of that right. I am going to implement a classic two-column layout with a header, as shown in Figure 7-16.

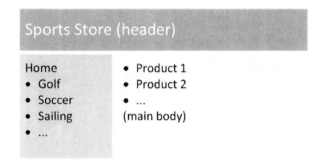

Figure 7-16. *The design goal for the SportsStore application*

Installing the Bootstrap Package

I am going to use the Bootstrap package to provide the CSS styles I will apply to the application. To install the Bootstrap package, select Library Package Manager ➤ Package Manager Console from the Visual Studio Tools menu. Visual Studio will open the NuGet command line. Enter the following command and hit return:

```
Install-Package -version 3.0.0 bootstrap –projectname SportsStore.WebUI
```

This is the same basic NuGet command I used in Chapter 2, with the addition of the projectname argument to ensure NuGet adds the files to the right project.

■ **Note**   Once again, I am going to use Bootstrap without going into the details of the features that the package provides. For full details of Bootstrap and the other client-side libraries that Microsoft has blessed for use with the MVC Framework, see my Pro ASP.NET MVC 5 Client book, published by Apress in 2014.

Applying Bootstrap Styles to the Layout

In Chapter 5, I explained how Razor layouts work and how you apply them. When I created the List.cshtml view for the Product controller, I asked you to check the option to use a layout, but leave the box that specifies a layout blank. This has the effect of using the layout specified by the Views/_ViewStart.cshtml file, which Visual Studio created automatically along the view. You can see the contents of the view start file in Listing 7-25.

Listing 7-25. The Contents of the _ViewStart.cshtml File

```
@{
    Layout = "~/Views/Shared/_Layout.cshtml";
}
```

The value of the Layout property specifies that views will use the Views/Shared/_Layout.cshtml file as a layout, unless they explicitly specify an alternative. I reset the content of the _Layout.cshtml file earlier in the chapter to remove the template content that Visual Studio adds and in Listing 7-26 you can see how I have returned to this file to add the Bootstrap CSS file and apply some of the CSS styles it defines.

Listing 7-26. Applying Bootstrap CSS to the _Layout.cshtml File

```
<!DOCTYPE html>
<html>
<head>
    <meta charset="utf-8" />
    <meta name="viewport" content="width=device-width, initial-scale=1.0">
    <link href="~/Content/bootstrap.css" rel="stylesheet" />
    <link href="~/Content/bootstrap-theme.css" rel="stylesheet" />
    <title>@ViewBag.Title</title>
</head>
<body>
    <div class="navbar navbar-inverse" role="navigation">
        <a class="navbar-brand" href="#">SPORTS STORE</a>
    </div>
    <div class="row panel">
        <div id="categories" class="col-xs-3">
            Put something useful here later
        </div>
        <div class="col-xs-8">
            @RenderBody()
        </div>
    </div>
</body>
</html>
```

I have added the bootstrap.css and bootstrap-theme.css files to the layout using link elements and applied various Bootstrap classes to create a simple layout. I also need to change the List.cshtml file, as shown in Listing 7-27.

Listing 7-27. Applying Bootstrap to Style the List.cshtml File

```
@model SportsStore.WebUI.Models.ProductsListViewModel

@{
    ViewBag.Title = "Products";
}

@foreach (var p in Model.Products) {
    <div class="well">
        <h3>
            <strong>@p.Name</strong>
            <span class="pull-right label label-primary">@p.Price.ToString("c")</span>
        </h3>
        <span class="lead"> @p.Description</span>
    </div>
}

<div class="btn-group pull-right">
    @Html.PageLinks(Model.PagingInfo, x => Url.Action("List", new { page = x }))
</div>
```

THE PROBLEM WITH STYLING ELEMENTS

The HTML elements generated by an MVC application come from a variety of sources (static content, Razor expressions, HTML helper methods, etc.), so the style classes become diffused throughout the project. If this makes you feel slightly uncomfortable, then you are not alone. Mixing the CSS styles in with element generation is not a great idea and runs counter to the idea of separating out unrelated functionality that pervades MVC. You can improve on this situation by assigning non-Bootstrap classes to elements based on their role in the application and then use a library like jQuery or LESS to map between your custom classes and the Bootstrap ones.

I am going to keep things simple for this application and accept that I have embedded the Bootstrap classes throughout the application, even though it complicates the process of changing styles in the future. I would not do this in a real project, but I know this example application is not going to enter into a maintenance phase.

If you run the application, you will see that I have improved the appearance—at least a little, anyway—as illustrated by Figure 7-17.

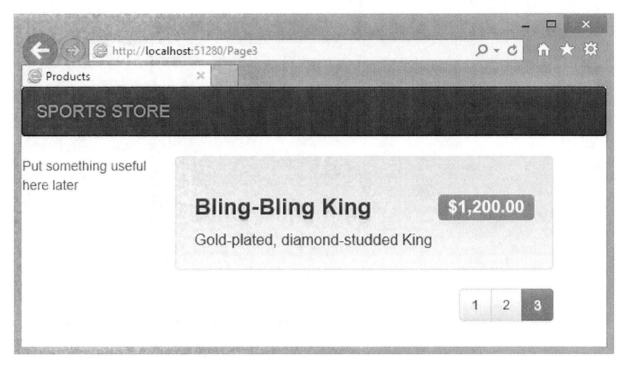

Figure 7-17. *The design-enhanced SportsStore application*

Creating a Partial View

As a finishing trick for this chapter, I am going to refactor the application to simplify the List.cshtml view. I am going to create a *partial view*, which is a fragment of content that you can embed into another view, rather like a template. Partial views are contained within their own files and are reusable across multiple views, which can help reduce duplication if you need to render the same kind of data in several places in your application.

To add the partial view, right-click the /Views/Shared folder in the SportsStore.WebUI project and select Add ➤ View from the pop-up menu. Set View Name to ProductSummary, set Template to Empty, select Product from the Model Class drop-down list and check the Create As A Partial View box, as shown in Figure 7-18.

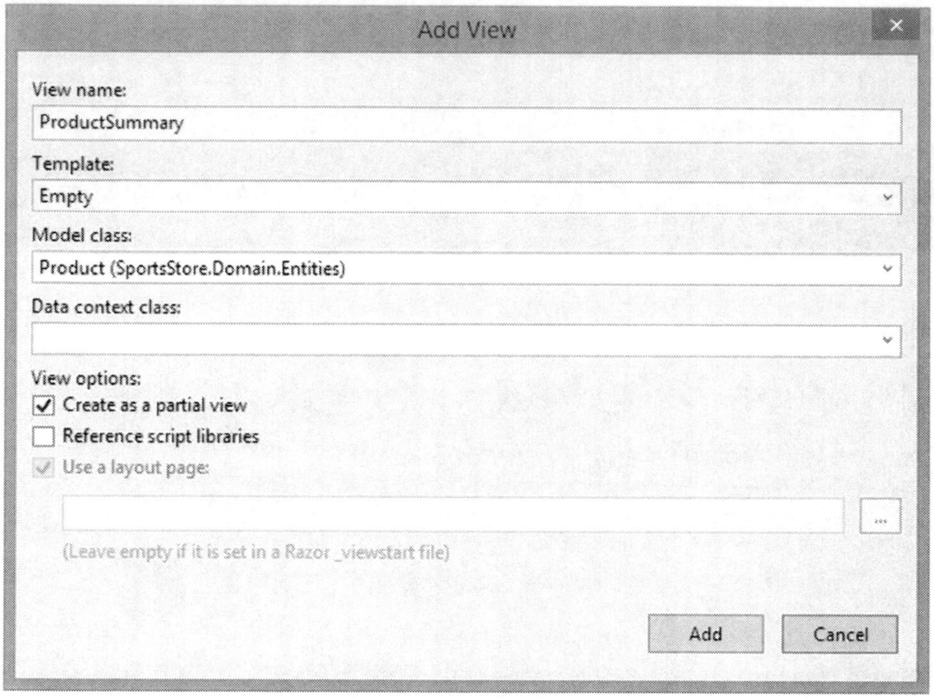

Figure 7-18. *Creating a partial view*

Click the Add button, and Visual Studio will create a partial view file called Views/Shared/ProductSummary.cshtml. A partial view is similar to a regular view, except that it produces a fragment of HTML, rather than a full HTML document. If you open the ProductSummary view, you will see that it contains only the model view directive, which is set to the Product domain model class. Apply the changes shown in Listing 7-28.

Listing 7-28. Adding Markup to the ProductSummary.cshtml File

```
@model SportsStore.Domain.Entities.Product

<div class="well">
    <h3>
        <strong>@Model.Name</strong>
        <span class="pull-right label label-primary">@Model.Price.ToString("c")</span>
    </h3>
    <span class="lead"> @Model.Description</span>
</div>
```

Now I need to update Views/Products/List.cshtml so that it uses the partial view. You can see the change in Listing 7-29.

Listing 7-29. Using a Partial View in the List.cshtml File

```
@model SportsStore.WebUI.Models.ProductsListViewModel

@{
    ViewBag.Title = "Products";
}

@foreach (var p in Model.Products) {
    @Html.Partial("ProductSummary", p)
}

<div class="pager">
   @Html.PageLinks(Model.PagingInfo, x => Url.Action("List", new {page = x}))
</div>
```

I have taken the markup that was previously in the foreach loop in the List.cshtml view and moved it to the new partial view. I call the partial view using the Html.Partial helper method. The parameters are the name of the view and the view model object. Switching to a partial view like this is good practice, but it does not change the appearance of the application, as Figure 7-19 shows.

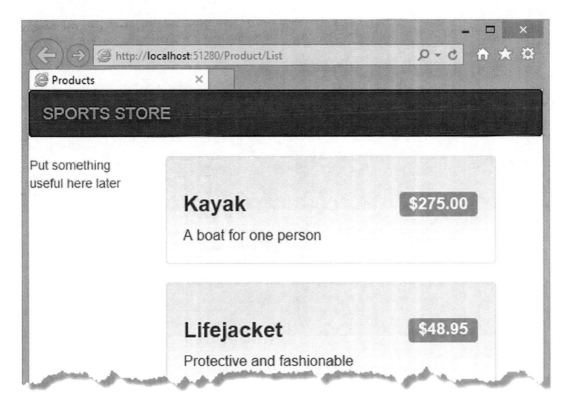

Figure 7-19. *Applying a partial view*

Summary

In this chapter, I built most of the core infrastructure for the SportsStore application. It does not have many features that you could demonstrate to a client at this point, but behind the scenes, there are the beginnings of a domain model with a product repository backed by SQL Server and the Entity Framework. There is a single controller, ProductController, that can produce paginated lists of products, and I have set up DI and defined a clean and friendly URL scheme.

If this chapter felt like a lot of setup for little benefit, then the next chapter will balance the equation. Now that the fundamental structure is in place, we can forge ahead and add all of the customer-facing features: navigation by category, a shopping cart, and a checkout process.

SportsStore: Navigation

In the previous chapter, I set up the core infrastructure of the SportsStore application. Now I will use that infrastructure to add features to the application and you will start to see how the investment in the basic plumbing pays off. I will be able to add important customer-facing features simply and easily and, along the way, you will see some additional functionality that the MVC Framework provides.

Adding Navigation Controls

The SportsStore application will be more usable if customers can navigate products by category. I will do this in three phases:

- Enhance the List action model in the ProductController class so that it is able to filter the Product objects in the repository.

- Revisit and enhance the URL scheme and revise the routing strategy.

- Create a category list that will go into the sidebar of the site, highlighting the current category and linking to others.

Filtering the Product List

I am going to start by enhancing the view model class, ProductsListViewModel, which I added to the SportsStore. WebUI project in the last chapter. I need to communicate the current category to the view in order to render the sidebar, and this is as good a place to start as any. Listing 8-1 shows the changes I made to the ProductsListView.cs file.

Listing 8-1. Enhancing the ProductsListView .cs File

```
using System.Collections.Generic;
using SportsStore.Domain.Entities;

namespace SportsStore.WebUI.Models {
    public class ProductsListViewModel {

        public IEnumerable<Product> Products { get; set; }
        public PagingInfo PagingInfo { get; set; }
        public string CurrentCategory { get; set; }
    }
}
```

I added a property called CurrentCategory. The next step is to update the Product controller so that the List action method will filter Product objects by category and use the new property I added to the view model to indicate which category has been selected. The changes are shown in Listing 8-2.

Listing 8-2. Adding Category Support to the List Action Method in the ProductController.cs File

```csharp
using System;
using System.Collections.Generic;
using System.Linq;
using System.Web;
using System.Web.Mvc;
using SportsStore.Domain.Abstract;
using SportsStore.Domain.Entities;
using SportsStore.WebUI.Models;

namespace SportsStore.WebUI.Controllers {

    public class ProductController : Controller {
        private IProductRepository repository;
        public int PageSize = 4;

        public ProductController(IProductRepository productRepository) {
            this.repository = productRepository;
        }

        public ViewResult List(string category, int page = 1) {
            ProductsListViewModel model = new ProductsListViewModel {
                Products = repository.Products
                    .Where(p => category == null || p.Category == category)
                    .OrderBy(p => p.ProductID)
                    .Skip((page - 1) * PageSize)
                    .Take(PageSize),
                PagingInfo = new PagingInfo {
                    CurrentPage = page,
                    ItemsPerPage = PageSize,
                    TotalItems = repository.Products.Count()
                },
                CurrentCategory = category
            };
            return View(model);
        }
    }
}
```

I made three changes to the action method. First, I added a parameter called category. This category parameter is used by the second change in the listing, which is an enhancement to the LINQ query. If category is not null, only those Product objects with a matching Category property are selected. The last change is to set the value of the CurrentCategory property I added to the ProductsListViewModel class. However, these changes mean that the value of PagingInfo.TotalItems is incorrectly calculated. I will fix this in a while.

UNIT TEST: UPDATING EXISTING UNIT TESTS

I changed the signature of the List action method, which will prevent some of the existing unit test methods from compiling. To address this, I need to pass null as the first parameter to the List method in those unit tests that work with the controller. For example, in the Can_Paginate test, the action section of the unit test becomes as follows:

```
...
[TestMethod]
public void Can_Paginate() {

    // Arrange
    Mock<IProductRepository> mock = new Mock<IProductRepository>();
    mock.Setup(m => m.Products).Returns(new Product[] {
        new Product {ProductID = 1, Name = "P1"},
        new Product {ProductID = 2, Name = "P2"},
        new Product {ProductID = 3, Name = "P3"},
        new Product {ProductID = 4, Name = "P4"},
        new Product {ProductID = 5, Name = "P5"}
    });

    // create a controller and make the page size 3 items
    ProductController controller = new ProductController(mock.Object);
    controller.PageSize = 3;

    // Act
    ProductsListViewModel result
        = (ProductsListViewModel)controller.List(null, 2).Model;

    // Assert
    Product[] prodArray = result.Products.ToArray();
    Assert.IsTrue(prodArray.Length == 2);
    Assert.AreEqual(prodArray[0].Name, "P4");
    Assert.AreEqual(prodArray[1].Name, "P5");
}
...
```

By using null, I receive all of the Product objects that the controller gets from the repository, which is the same situation I had before adding the new parameter. I need to make the same kind of change to the Can_Send_Pagination_View_Model test as well:

```
...
[TestMethod]
public void Can_Send_Pagination_View_Model() {
```

```
// Arrange
Mock<IProductRepository> mock = new Mock<IProductRepository>();
mock.Setup(m => m.Products).Returns(new Product[] {
    new Product {ProductID = 1, Name = "P1"},
    new Product {ProductID = 2, Name = "P2"},
    new Product {ProductID = 3, Name = "P3"},
    new Product {ProductID = 4, Name = "P4"},
    new Product {ProductID = 5, Name = "P5"}
});

// Arrange
ProductController controller = new ProductController(mock.Object);
controller.PageSize = 3;

// Act
ProductsListViewModel result
    = (ProductsListViewModel)controller.List(null, 2).Model;

// Assert
PagingInfo pageInfo = result.PagingInfo;
Assert.AreEqual(pageInfo.CurrentPage, 2);
Assert.AreEqual(pageInfo.ItemsPerPage, 3);
Assert.AreEqual(pageInfo.TotalItems, 5);
Assert.AreEqual(pageInfo.TotalPages, 2);
}
...
```

Keeping your unit tests synchronized with your code changes quickly becomes second nature when you get into the testing mind-set.

The effect of the category filtering is evident, even with these small changes. Start the application and select a category using the follow query string, changing the port to match the one that Visual Studio assigned for your project:

```
http://localhost:51280/?category=Soccer
```

You will see only the products in the Soccer category, as shown in Figure 8-1.

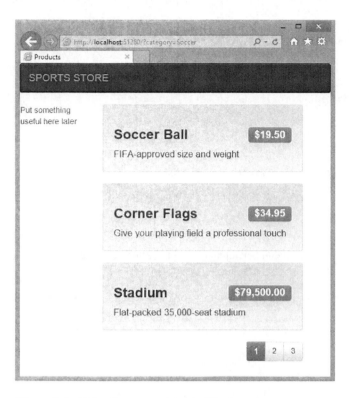

Figure 8-1. *Using the query string to filter by category*

Obviously, users won't want to navigate to categories using URLs, but you can see how small changes can have a big impact in an MVC Framework application once the basic structure is in place.

UNIT TEST: CATEGORY FILTERING

I need a unit test to properly test the category filtering function, to ensure that the filter can correctly generate products in a specified category. Here is the test:

```
...
[TestMethod]
public void Can_Filter_Products() {

    // Arrange
    // - create the mock repository
    Mock<IProductRepository> mock = new Mock<IProductRepository>();
    mock.Setup(m => m.Products).Returns(new Product[] {
        new Product {ProductID = 1, Name = "P1", Category = "Cat1"},
        new Product {ProductID = 2, Name = "P2", Category = "Cat2"},
        new Product {ProductID = 3, Name = "P3", Category = "Cat1"},
        new Product {ProductID = 4, Name = "P4", Category = "Cat2"},
        new Product {ProductID = 5, Name = "P5", Category = "Cat3"}
    });
```

```
    // Arrange - create a controller and make the page size 3 items
    ProductController controller = new ProductController(mock.Object);
    controller.PageSize = 3;

    // Action
    Product[] result = ((ProductsListViewModel)controller.List("Cat2", 1).Model)
        .Products.ToArray();

    // Assert
    Assert.AreEqual(result.Length, 2);
    Assert.IsTrue(result[0].Name == "P2" && result[0].Category == "Cat2");
    Assert.IsTrue(result[1].Name == "P4" && result[1].Category == "Cat2");
}
...
```

This test creates a mock repository containing Product objects that belong to a range of categories. One specific category is requested using the Action method, and the results are checked to ensure that the results are the right objects in the right order.

Refining the URL Scheme

No one wants to see or use ugly URLs such as /?category=Soccer. To address this, I am going to revisit the routing scheme to create an approach to URLs that better suits me and my customers. To implement the new scheme, I changed the RegisterRoutes method in the App_Start/RouteConfig.cs file, as shown in Listing 8-3.

Listing 8-3. The New URL Scheme in the RouteConfig.cs File

```
using System;
using System.Collections.Generic;
using System.Linq;
using System.Web;
using System.Web.Mvc;
using System.Web.Routing;

namespace SportsStore.WebUI {

    public class RouteConfig {

        public static void RegisterRoutes(RouteCollection routes) {
            routes.IgnoreRoute("{resource}.axd/{*pathInfo}");

            routes.MapRoute(null,
                "",
                new {
                    controller = "Product", action = "List",
                    category = (string)null, page = 1
                }
            );
```

```
        routes.MapRoute(null,
            "Page{page}",
            new { controller = "Product", action = "List", category = (string)null },
            new { page = @"\d+" }
        );

        routes.MapRoute(null,
            "{category}",
            new { controller = "Product", action = "List", page = 1 }
        );

        routes.MapRoute(null,
            "{category}/Page{page}",
            new { controller = "Product", action = "List" },
            new { page = @"\d+" }
        );

        routes.MapRoute(null, "{controller}/{action}");
    }
  }
}
```

■ **Caution** It is important to add the new routes in Listing 8-3 in the order they are shown. Routes are applied in the order in which they are defined, and you will get some odd effects if you change the order.

Table 8-1 describes the URL scheme that these routes represent. I explain the routing system in detail in Chapters 15 and 16.

Table 8-1. *Route Summary*

URL	Leads To
/	Lists the first page of products from all categories
/Page2	Lists the specified page (in this case, page 2), showing items from all categories
/Soccer	Shows the first page of items from a specific category (in this case, the Soccer category)
/Soccer/Page2	Shows the specified page (in this case, page 2) of items from the specified category (in this case, Soccer)

The ASP.NET routing system is used by MVC to handle *incoming* requests from clients, but it also generates *outgoing* URLs that conform to the URL scheme and that can be embedded in Web pages. By using the routing system to handle incoming requests and generate outgoing URLs, I can ensure that all of the URLs in the application are consistent.

■ **Note** I show you how to unit test routing configurations in Chapter 15.

The Url.Action method is the most convenient way of generating outgoing links. In the previous chapter, I used this helper method in the List view in order to display the page links. Now that I have added support for category filtering, I need to go back and pass this information to the helper method, as shown in Listing 8-4.

Listing 8-4. Adding Category Information to the Pagination Links in the List.cshtml File

```
@model SportsStore.WebUI.Models.ProductsListViewModel

@{
    ViewBag.Title = "Products";
}

@foreach (var p in Model.Products) {
    @Html.Partial("ProductSummary", p)
}

<div class="btn-group pull-right">
    @Html.PageLinks(Model.PagingInfo, x => Url.Action("List",
        new { page = x, category = Model.CurrentCategory }))
</div>
```

Prior to this change, the links generated for the pagination links were like this:

```
http://<myserver>:<port>/Page1
```

If the user clicked a page link like this, the category filter he applied would be lost, and he would be presented with a page containing products from all categories. By adding the current category, taken from the view model, I generate URLs like this instead:

```
http://<myserver>:<port>/Chess/Page1
```

When the user clicks this kind of link, the current category will be passed to the List action method, and the filtering will be preserved. After you have made this change, you can visit a URL such as /Chess or /Soccer, and you will see that the page link at the bottom of the page correctly includes the category.

Building a Category Navigation Menu

I need to provide customers with a way to select a category that does not involve typing in URLs. This means presenting them with a list of the categories available and indicating which, if any, is currently selected. As I build out the application, I will use this list of categories in more than one controller, so I need something that is self-contained and reusable.

The ASP.NET MVC Framework has the concept of *child actions*, which are perfect for creating items such as a reusable navigation control. A child action relies on the HTML helper method called Html.Action, which lets you include the output from an arbitrary action method in the current view. In this case, I can create a new controller (I will call it NavController) with an action method (which I will call Menu) that renders a navigation menu. I will then use the Html.Action helper method to inject the output from that method into the layout.

This approach gives me a real controller that can contain whatever application logic I need and that can be unit tested like any other controller. It is a nice way of creating smaller segments of an application while preserving the overall MVC Framework approach.

Creating the Navigation Controller

Right-click the `Controllers` folder in the `SportsStore.WebUI` project and select Add ➤ Controller from the pop-up menu. Select `MVC 5 Controller - Empty` from the list, click the Add button, set the controller name to `NavController` and click the Add button to create the `NavController.cs` class file. Remove the Index method that Visual Studio adds to new controllers by default and add a new action method called `Menu`, as shown in Listing 8-5.

Listing 8-5. Adding The Menu Action Method to the NavController.cs File

```
using System.Web.Mvc;

namespace SportsStore.WebUI.Controllers {
    public class NavController : Controller {

        public string Menu() {
            return "Hello from NavController";
        }
    }
}
```

This method returns a static message string but it is enough to get me started while I integrate the child action into the rest of the application. I want the category list to appear on all pages, so I am going to render the child action in the layout, rather than in a specific view. Edit the `Views/Shared/_Layout.cshtml` file so that it calls the `Html.Action` helper method, as shown in Listing 8-6.

Listing 8-6. Adding the RenderAction Call to the _Layout.cshtml File

```
<!DOCTYPE html>
<html>
<head>
    <meta charset="utf-8" />
    <meta name="viewport" content="width=device-width, initial-scale=1.0">
    <link href="~/Content/bootstrap.css" rel="stylesheet" />
    <link href="~/Content/bootstrap-theme.css" rel="stylesheet" />
    <title>@ViewBag.Title</title>
</head>
<body>
    <div class="navbar navbar-inverse" role="navigation">
        <a class="navbar-brand" href="#">SPORTS STORE</a>
    </div>
    <div class="row panel">
        <div id="categories" class="col-xs-3">
            @Html.Action("Menu", "Nav")
        </div>
        <div class="col-xs-8">
            @RenderBody()
        </div>
    </div>
</body>
</html>
```

I removed the placeholder text and replaced it with a call to the Html.Action method. The parameters to this method are the name of the action method I want to call (Menu) and the controller that contains it (Nav). If you run the application, you will see that the output of the Menu action method is included in the response sent to the browser, as shown in Figure 8-2.

Figure 8-2. *Displaying the output from the Menu action method*

Generating Category Lists

I can now return to the Nav controller and generate a real set of categories. I do not want to generate the category URLs in the controller. Instead, I am going to use a helper method in the view to do that. All I am going to do in the Menu action method is create the list of categories, which I have done in Listing 8-7.

Listing 8-7. Implementing the Menu Method in the NavController.cs File

```
using System.Collections.Generic;
using System.Web.Mvc;
using SportsStore.Domain.Abstract;
using System.Linq;

namespace SportsStore.WebUI.Controllers {

    public class NavController : Controller {
        private IProductRepository repository;

        public NavController(IProductRepository repo) {
            repository = repo;
        }

        public PartialViewResult Menu() {
            IEnumerable<string> categories = repository.Products
                                    .Select(x => x.Category)
                                    .Distinct()
                                    .OrderBy(x => x);
```

```
        return PartialView(categories);
    }
  }
}
```

The first change is to add a constructor that accepts an `IProductRepository` implementation as its argument. This has the effect of declaring a dependency that Ninject will resolve when it creates instances of the `NavController` class. The second change is to the `Menu` action method, which now uses a LINQ query to obtain a list of categories from the repository and passes them to the view. Notice that, since I am working with a partial view in this controller, I call the `PartialView` method in the action method and that the result is a `PartialViewResult` object.

UNIT TEST: GENERATING THE CATEGORY LIST

The unit test for my ability to produce a category list is relatively simple. My goal is to create a list that is sorted in alphabetical order and contains no duplicates. The simplest way to do this is to supply some test data that *does* have duplicate categories and that is *not* in order, pass this to the `NavController`, and assert that the data has been properly cleaned up. Here is the unit test:

```
...
[TestMethod]
public void Can_Create_Categories() {

    // Arrange
    // - create the mock repository
    Mock<IProductRepository> mock = new Mock<IProductRepository>();
    mock.Setup(m => m.Products).Returns(new Product[] {
        new Product {ProductID = 1, Name = "P1", Category = "Apples"},
        new Product {ProductID = 2, Name = "P2", Category = "Apples"},
        new Product {ProductID = 3, Name = "P3", Category = "Plums"},
        new Product {ProductID = 4, Name = "P4", Category = "Oranges"},
    });

    // Arrange - create the controller
    NavController target = new NavController(mock.Object);

    // Act = get the set of categories
    string[] results = ((IEnumerable<string>)target.Menu().Model).ToArray();

    // Assert
    Assert.AreEqual(results.Length, 3);
    Assert.AreEqual(results[0], "Apples");
    Assert.AreEqual(results[1], "Oranges");
    Assert.AreEqual(results[2], "Plums");
}
...
```

I created a mock repository implementation that contains repeating categories and categories that are not in order. I assert that the duplicates are removed and that alphabetical ordering is imposed.

Creating the View

To create the view for the Menu action method, right-click on the Views/Nav folder and select Add ➤ MVC 5 View Page (Razor) from the pop-up menu. Set the name to Menu and click the OK button to create the Menu.cshtml file. Remove the contents that Visual Studio adds to new views and set the content to match Listing 8-8.

Listing 8-8. The Contents of the Menu.cshtml File

```
@model IEnumerable<string>

@Html.ActionLink("Home", "List", "Product", null,
    new { @class = "btn btn-block btn-default btn-lg" })

@foreach (var link in Model) {
    @Html.RouteLink(link, new {
        controller = "Product",
        action = "List",
        category = link,
        page = 1
    }, new {
        @class = "btn btn-block btn-default btn-lg"
    })
}
```

I added a link called Home that will appear at the top of the category list and will list all of the products with no category filter. I did this using the ActionLink helper method, which generates an HTML anchor element using the routing information configured earlier.

I then enumerated the category names and created links for each of them using the RouteLink method. This is similar to ActionLink, but it lets me supply a set of name/value pairs that are taken into account when generating the URL from the routing configuration. Do not worry if all this talk of routing does not make sense yet. I explain everything in depth in Chapters 15 and 16.

The links I generate will look pretty ugly by default, so I have supplied an object to both the ActionLink and RouteLink helper methods that specifies values for attributes on the elements that are created. The objects I created define the class attribute (prefixed with a @ because class is a reserved C# keyword) and apply Bootstrap classes to style the links as large buttons.

You can see the category links if you run the application, as shown in Figure 8-3. If you click a category, the list of items is updated to show only items from the selected category.

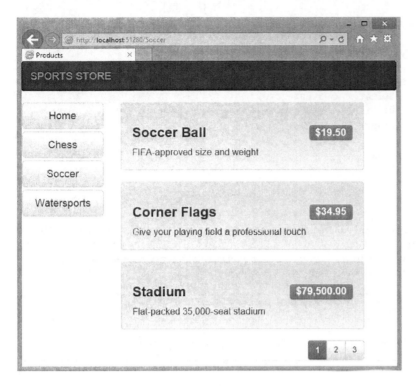

Figure 8-3. *The category links*

Highlighting the Current Category

At present, I do not indicate to users which category they are viewing. It might be something that the customer could infer from the items in the list, but I would prefer to provide solid visual feedback. I could do this by creating a view model that contains the list of categories and the selected category, and in fact, this is exactly what I would usually do. But for variety I am going to use the view bag feature I introduced in Chapter 2. This feature allows me to pass data from the controller to the view without using a view model. Listing 8-9 shows the changes to the Menu action method in the Nav controller.

Listing 8-9. Using the View Bag Feature in the NavController.cs File

```
using System.Collections.Generic;
using System.Web.Mvc;
using SportsStore.Domain.Abstract;
using System.Linq;

namespace SportsStore.WebUI.Controllers {

    public class NavController : Controller {
        private IProductRepository repository;

        public NavController(IProductRepository repo) {
            repository = repo;
        }
```

```
        public PartialViewResult Menu(string category = null) {

            ViewBag.SelectedCategory = category;

            IEnumerable<string> categories = repository.Products
                                .Select(x => x.Category)
                                .Distinct()
                                .OrderBy(x => x);

            return PartialView(categories);
        }
    }
}
```

I added a parameter to the Menu action method called category. The value for this parameter will be provided automatically by the routing configuration. Inside the method body, I have dynamically assigned a SelectedCategory property to the ViewBag object and set its value to be the current category. As I explained in Chapter 2, the ViewBag is a dynamic object and I create new properties simply by setting values for them.

UNIT TEST: REPORTING THE SELECTED CATEGORY

I can test that the Menu action method correctly adds details of the selected category by reading the value of the ViewBag property in a unit test, which is available through the ViewResult class. Here is the test:

```
...
[TestMethod]
public void Indicates_Selected_Category() {

    // Arrange
    // - create the mock repository
    Mock<IProductRepository> mock = new Mock<IProductRepository>();
    mock.Setup(m => m.Products).Returns(new Product[] {
        new Product {ProductID = 1, Name = "P1", Category = "Apples"},
        new Product {ProductID = 4, Name = "P2", Category = "Oranges"},
    });

    // Arrange - create the controller
    NavController target = new NavController(mock.Object);

    // Arrange - define the category to selected
    string categoryToSelect = "Apples";

    // Action
    string result = target.Menu(categoryToSelect).ViewBag.SelectedCategory;

    // Assert
    Assert.AreEqual(categoryToSelect, result);
}
...
```

This unit test will not compile unless you add a reference to the Microsoft.CSharp assembly, as described in the previous chapter.

Now that I am providing information about which category is selected, I can update the view to take advantage of this, and add a CSS class to the HTML anchor element that represents the selected category. Listing 8-10 shows the changes to the Menu.cshtml file.

Listing 8-10. Highlighting the Selected Category in the Menu.cshtml File

```
@model IEnumerable<string>

@Html.ActionLink("Home", "List", "Product", null,
    new { @class = "btn btn-block btn-default btn-lg" })

@foreach (var link in Model) {
    @Html.RouteLink(link, new {
        controller = "Product",
        action = "List",
        category = link,
        page = 1
    }, new {
        @class = "btn btn-block btn-default btn-lg"
            + (link == ViewBag.SelectedCategory ? " btn-primary" : "")
    })
}
```

The change is simple. If the current link value matches the SelectedCategory value, then I add the element I am creating to another Bootstrap class, which will cause the button to be highlighted. Running the application shows the effect of the category highlighting, which you can also see in Figure 8-4.

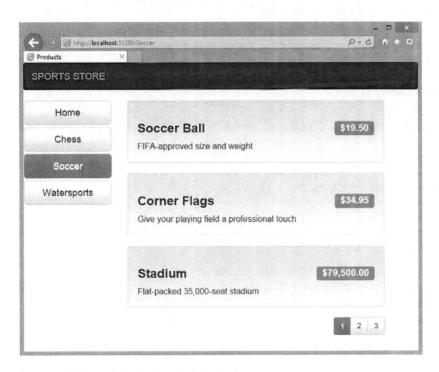

Figure 8-4. *Highlighting the selected category*

Correcting the Page Count

I need to correct the page links so that they work correctly when a category is selected. Currently, the number of page links is determined by the total number of products in the repository and not the number of products in the selected category. This means that the customer can click the link for page 2 of the Chess category and end up with an empty page because there are not enough chess products to fill two pages. You can see the problem in Figure 8-5.

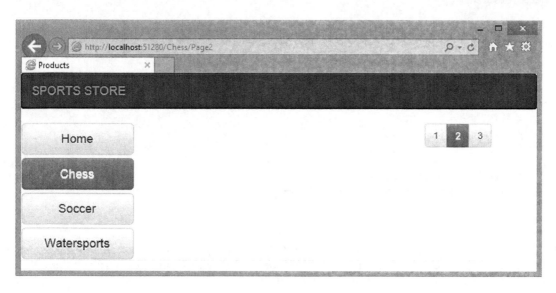

Figure 8-5. *Displaying the wrong page links when a category is selected*

I can fix this by updating the List action method in the Product controller so that the pagination information takes the categories into account. You can see the required changes in Listing 8-11.

Listing 8-11. Creating Category-Aware Pagination Data in the ProductController.cs File

```
...
public ViewResult List(string category, int page = 1) {

    ProductsListViewModel viewModel = new ProductsListViewModel {
        Products = repository.Products
            .Where(p => category == null || p.Category == category)
            .OrderBy(p => p.ProductID)
            .Skip((page - 1) * PageSize)
            .Take(PageSize),
        PagingInfo = new PagingInfo {
            CurrentPage = page,
            ItemsPerPage = PageSize,
            TotalItems = category == null ?
                repository.Products.Count() :
                repository.Products.Where(e => e.Category == category).Count()
        },
        CurrentCategory = category
    };
```

```
    return View(viewModel);
}
...
```

If a category has been selected, I return the number of items in that category; if not, I return the total number of products. Now when I view a category, the links at the bottom of the page correctly reflect the number of products in the category, as shown in Figure 8-6.

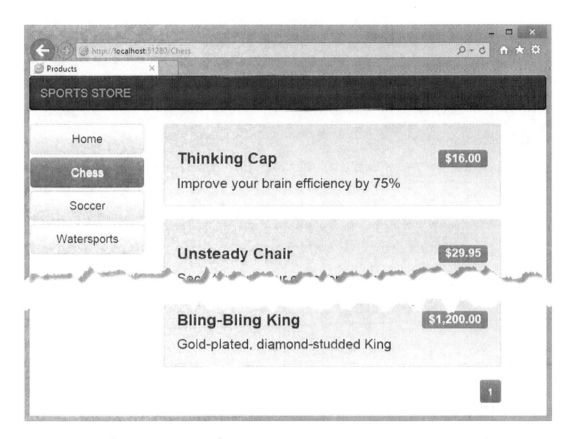

Figure 8-6. *Displaying category-specific page counts*

UNIT TEST: CATEGORY-SPECIFIC PRODUCT COUNTS

Testing that I am able to generate the current product count for different categories is simple. I create a mock repository that contains known data in a range of categories and then call the List action method requesting each category in turn. Here is the unit test:

```
...
[TestMethod]
public void Generate_Category_Specific_Product_Count() {
    // Arrange
    // - create the mock repository
    Mock<IProductRepository> mock = new Mock<IProductRepository>();
```

```
mock.Setup(m => m.Products).Returns(new Product[] {
    new Product {ProductID = 1, Name = "P1", Category = "Cat1"},
    new Product {ProductID = 2, Name = "P2", Category = "Cat2"},
    new Product {ProductID = 3, Name = "P3", Category = "Cat1"},
    new Product {ProductID = 4, Name = "P4", Category = "Cat2"},
    new Product {ProductID = 5, Name = "P5", Category = "Cat3"}
});

// Arrange - create a controller and make the page size 3 items
ProductController target = new ProductController(mock.Object);
target.PageSize = 3;

// Action - test the product counts for different categories
int res1 = ((ProductsListViewModel)target
    .List("Cat1").Model).PagingInfo.TotalItems;
int res2 = ((ProductsListViewModel)target
    .List("Cat2").Model).PagingInfo.TotalItems;
int res3 = ((ProductsListViewModel)target
    .List("Cat3").Model).PagingInfo.TotalItems;
int resAll = ((ProductsListViewModel)target
    .List(null).Model).PagingInfo.TotalItems;

// Assert
Assert.AreEqual(res1, 2);
Assert.AreEqual(res2, 2);
Assert.AreEqual(res3, 1);
Assert.AreEqual(resAll, 5);
}
...
```

Notice that I also call the List method, specifying no category, to make sure I get the right total count as well.

Building the Shopping Cart

The application is progressing nicely, but I cannot sell any products until I implement a shopping cart. In this section, I will create the shopping cart experience shown in Figure 8-7. This will be familiar to anyone who has ever made a purchase online.

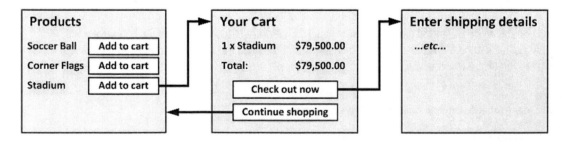

Figure 8-7. *The basic shopping cart flow*

An Add to Cart button will be displayed alongside each of the products in the catalog. Clicking this button will show a summary of the products the customer has selected so far, including the total cost. At this point, the user can click the Continue Shopping button to return to the product catalog, or click the Checkout Now button to complete the order and finish the shopping session.

Defining the Cart Entity

A shopping cart is part of the business domain, so it makes sense to represent a cart by creating an entity in the domain model. Add a class file called Cart.cs to the Entities folder in the SportsStore.Domain project and use it to define the classes shown in Listing 8-12.

Listing 8-12. The Cart and CartLine Classes in the Cart.cs File

```
using System.Collections.Generic;
using System.Linq;

namespace SportsStore.Domain.Entities {

    public class Cart {
        private List<CartLine> lineCollection = new List<CartLine>();

        public void AddItem(Product product, int quantity) {
            CartLine line = lineCollection
                .Where(p => p.Product.ProductID == product.ProductID)
                .FirstOrDefault();

            if (line == null) {
                lineCollection.Add(new CartLine { Product = product,
                    Quantity = quantity });
            } else {
                line.Quantity += quantity;
            }
        }

        public void RemoveLine(Product product) {
            lineCollection.RemoveAll(l => l.Product.ProductID == product.ProductID);
        }

        public decimal ComputeTotalValue() {
            return lineCollection.Sum(e => e.Product.Price * e.Quantity);

        }
        public void Clear() {
            lineCollection.Clear();
        }

        public IEnumerable<CartLine> Lines {
            get { return lineCollection; }
        }
    }
```

```
    public class CartLine {
        public Product Product { get; set; }
        public int Quantity { get; set; }
    }
}
```

The Cart class uses the CartLine class, defined in the same file, to represent a product selected by the customer and the quantity the user wants to buy. I defined methods to add an item to the cart, remove a previously added item from the cart, calculate the total cost of the items in the cart, and reset the cart by removing all of the items. I also provided a property that gives access to the contents of the cart using an IEnumerable<CartLine>. This is all straightforward stuff, easily implemented in C# with the help of a little LINQ.

UNIT TEST: TESTING THE CART

The Cart class is relatively simple, but it has a range of important behaviors that must work properly. A poorly functioning cart would undermine the entire SportsStore application. I have broken down the features and tested them individually. I created a new unit test file in the SportsStore.UnitTests project called CartTests.cs to contain these tests.

The first behavior relates to when I add an item to the cart. If this is the first time that a given Product has been added to the cart, I want a new CartLine to be added. Here is the test, including the unit test class definition:

```
using System. Linq;
using Microsoft.VisualStudio.TestTools.UnitTesting;
using SportsStore.Domain.Entities;

namespace SportsStore.UnitTests {
    [TestClass]
    public class CartTests {

        [TestMethod]
        public void Can_Add_New_Lines() {

            // Arrange - create some test products
            Product p1 = new Product { ProductID = 1, Name = "P1" };
            Product p2 = new Product { ProductID = 2, Name = "P2" };

            // Arrange - create a new cart
            Cart target = new Cart();

            // Act
            target.AddItem(p1, 1);
            target.AddItem(p2, 1);
            CartLine[] results = target.Lines.ToArray();

            // Assert
            Assert.AreEqual(results.Length, 2);
            Assert.AreEqual(results[0].Product, p1);
            Assert.AreEqual(results[1].Product, p2);
        }

    }
}
```

However, if the customer has already added a `Product` to the cart, I want to increment the quantity of the corresponding `CartLine` and not create a new one. Here is the test:

```
..
[TestMethod]
public void Can_Add_Quantity_For_Existing_Lines() {

    // Arrange - create some test products
    Product p1 = new Product { ProductID = 1, Name = "P1" };
    Product p2 = new Product { ProductID = 2, Name = "P2" };

    // Arrange - create a new cart
    Cart target = new Cart();

    // Act
    target.AddItem(p1, 1);
    target.AddItem(p2, 1);
    target.AddItem(p1, 10);
    CartLine[] results = target.Lines.OrderBy(c => c.Product.ProductID).ToArray();

    // Assert
    Assert.AreEqual(results.Length, 2);
    Assert.AreEqual(results[0].Quantity, 11);
    Assert.AreEqual(results[1].Quantity, 1);
}
...
```

I also need to check that users can change their mind and remove products from the cart. This feature is implemented by the `RemoveLine` method. Here is the test:

```
...
[TestMethod]
public void Can_Remove_Line() {

    // Arrange - create some test products
    Product p1 = new Product { ProductID = 1, Name = "P1" };
    Product p2 = new Product { ProductID = 2, Name = "P2" };
    Product p3 = new Product { ProductID = 3, Name = "P3" };

    // Arrange - create a new cart
    Cart target = new Cart();
    // Arrange - add some products to the cart
    target.AddItem(p1, 1);
    target.AddItem(p2, 3);
    target.AddItem(p3, 5);
    target.AddItem(p2, 1);
```

```
    // Act
    target.RemoveLine(p2);

    // Assert
    Assert.AreEqual(target.Lines.Where(c => c.Product == p2).Count(), 0);
    Assert.AreEqual(target.Lines.Count(), 2);
}
...
```

The next behavior I want to test is the ability to calculate the total cost of the items in the cart. Here's the test for this behavior:

```
...
[TestMethod]
public void Calculate_Cart_Total() {

    // Arrange - create some test products
    Product p1 = new Product { ProductID = 1, Name = "P1", Price = 100M};
    Product p2 = new Product { ProductID = 2, Name = "P2" , Price = 50M};

    // Arrange - create a new cart
    Cart target = new Cart();

    // Act
    target.AddItem(p1, 1);
    target.AddItem(p2, 1);
    target.AddItem(p1, 3);
    decimal result = target.ComputeTotalValue();

    // Assert
    Assert.AreEqual(result, 450M);
}
...
```

The final test is simple. I want to ensure that the contents of the cart are properly removed when reset. Here is the test:

```
...
[TestMethod]
public void Can_Clear_Contents() {

    // Arrange - create some test products
    Product p1 = new Product { ProductID = 1, Name = "P1", Price = 100M };
    Product p2 = new Product { ProductID = 2, Name = "P2", Price = 50M };

    // Arrange - create a new cart
    Cart target = new Cart();

    // Arrange - add some items
    target.AddItem(p1, 1);
    target.AddItem(p2, 1);
```

```
    // Act - reset the cart
    target.Clear();

    // Assert
    Assert.AreEqual(target.Lines.Count(), 0);
}
...
```

Sometimes, as in this case, the code required to test the functionality of a type is longer and more complex than the type itself. Do not let that put you off writing the unit tests. Defects in simple classes can have huge impacts, especially ones that play such an important role as Cart does in the example application.

Adding the Add to Cart Buttons

I need to edit the Views/Shared/ProductSummary.cshtml view to add the buttons to the product listings. The changes are shown in Listing 8-13.

Listing 8-13. Adding the Buttons to the Product Summary.cshtml File View

```
@model SportsStore.Domain.Entities.Product

<div class="well">
    <h3>
        <strong>@Model.Name</strong>
        <span class="pull-right label label-primary">@Model.Price.ToString("c")</span>
    </h3>

    @using (Html.BeginForm("AddToCart", "Cart")) {
        <div class="pull-right">
            @Html.HiddenFor(x => x.ProductID)
            @Html.Hidden("returnUrl", Request.Url.PathAndQuery)
            <input type="submit" class="btn btn-success" value="Add to cart" />
        </div>
    }

    <span class="lead"> @Model.Description</span>
</div>
```

I added a Razor block that creates a small HTML form for each product in the listing. When this form is submitted, it will invoke the AddToCart action method in the Cart controller (which I will implement in just a moment).

■ **Note**   By default, the BeginForm helper method creates a form that uses the HTTP POST method. You can change this so that forms use the GET method, but you should think carefully about doing so. The HTTP specification requires that GET requests must be *idempotent*, meaning that they must not cause changes, and adding a product to a cart is definitely a change. I have more to say on this topic in Chapter 16, including an explanation of what can happen if you ignore the need for idempotent GET requests.

> # CREATING MULTIPLE HTML FORMS IN A PAGE
>
> Using the `Html.BeginForm` helper in each product listing means that every `Add to cart` button is rendered in its own separate HTML `form` element. This may be surprising if you have been developing with ASP.NET Web Forms, which imposes a limit of one form per page if you want to use the view state feature or complex controls (which tend to rely on view state). Since ASP.NET MVC does not use view state, there is no limit the number of forms you can create.
>
> Equally, there is no requirement to create a form for each button. However, since each form will post back to the same controller method, but with a different set of parameter values, it is a nice and simple way to deal with the button presses.

Implementing the Cart Controller

I need a controller to handle the `Add to cart` button presses. Create a new controller called `CartController` in the `SportsStore.WebUI` project and edit the content so that it matches Listing 8-14.

Listing 8-14. The Contents of the CartController.cs File

```
using System.Linq;
using System.Web.Mvc;
using SportsStore.Domain.Abstract;
using SportsStore.Domain.Entities;

namespace SportsStore.WebUI.Controllers {

    public class CartController : Controller {
        private IProductRepository repository;

        public CartController(IProductRepository repo) {
            repository = repo;
        }

        public RedirectToRouteResult AddToCart(int productId, string returnUrl) {
            Product product = repository.Products
                .FirstOrDefault(p => p.ProductID == productId);

            if (product != null) {
                GetCart().AddItem(product, 1);
            }
            return RedirectToAction("Index", new { returnUrl });
        }

        public RedirectToRouteResult RemoveFromCart(int productId, string returnUrl) {
            Product product = repository.Products
                .FirstOrDefault(p => p.ProductID == productId);

            if (product != null) {
                GetCart().RemoveLine(product);
            }
```

```
            return RedirectToAction("Index", new { returnUrl });
        }

        private Cart GetCart() {

            Cart cart = (Cart)Session["Cart"];
            if (cart == null) {
                cart = new Cart();
                Session["Cart"] = cart;
            }
            return cart;
        }
    }
}
```

There are a few points to note about this controller. The first is that I use the ASP.NET session state feature to store and retrieve Cart objects. This is the purpose of the GetCart method. ASP.NET has a nice session feature that uses cookies or URL rewriting to associate multiple requests from a user together to form a single browsing session. A related feature is session state, which associates data with a session. This is an ideal fit for the Cart class. I want each user to have their own cart, and I want the cart to be persistent between requests. Data associated with a session is deleted when a session expires (typically because a user has not made a request for a while), which means that I do not need to manage the storage or life cycle of the Cart objects. To add an object to the session state, I set the value for a key on the Session object, like this:

```
...
Session["Cart"] = cart;
...
```

To retrieve an object again, I simply read the same key, like this:

```
...
Cart cart = (Cart)Session["Cart"];
...
```

■ **Tip** Session state objects are stored in the memory of the ASP.NET server by default, but you can configure a range of different storage approaches, including using a SQL database. See my book, *Pro ASP.NET MVC 5 Platform*, published by Apress in 2014, for details.

For the AddToCart and RemoveFromCart methods, I have used parameter names that match the input elements in the HTML forms created in the ProductSummary.cshtml view. This allows the MVC Framework to associate incoming form POST variables with those parameters, meaning I do not need to process the form myself.

Displaying the Contents of the Cart

The final point to note about the Cart controller is that both the AddToCart and RemoveFromCart methods call the RedirectToAction method. This has the effect of sending an HTTP redirect instruction to the client browser, asking the browser to request a new URL. In this case, I have asked the browser to request a URL that will call the Index action method of the Cart controller.

I am going to implement the Index method and use it to display the contents of the Cart. If you refer back to Figure 8-7, you will see that this is the workflow when the user clicks the Add to cart button.

I need to pass two pieces of information to the view that will display the contents of the cart: the Cart object and the URL to display if the user clicks the Continue shopping button. I created a new class file called CartIndexViewModel.cs in the Models folder of the SportsStore.WebUI project. The contents of this file are shown in Listing 8-15.

Listing 8-15. The Contents of the CartIndexViewModel.cs File

```
using SportsStore.Domain.Entities;

namespace SportsStore.WebUI.Models {
    public class CartIndexViewModel {
        public Cart Cart { get; set; }
        public string ReturnUrl { get; set; }
    }
}
```

Now that I have the view model, I can implement the Index action method in the Cart controller class, as shown in Listing 8-16.

Listing 8-16. The Index Action Method in the CartController.cs File

```
using System.Linq;
using System.Web.Mvc;
using SportsStore.Domain.Abstract;
using SportsStore.Domain.Entities;
using SportsStore.WebUI.Models;

namespace SportsStore.WebUI.Controllers {

    public class CartController : Controller {
        private IProductRepository repository;

        public CartController(IProductRepository repo) {
            repository = repo;
        }

        public ViewResult Index(string returnUrl) {
            return View(new CartIndexViewModel {
                Cart = GetCart(),
                ReturnUrl = returnUrl
            });
        }
```

```
            // ...other action methods omitted for brevity...
        }

}
```

The last step to display the contents of the cart is to create the new view. Right-click on the Index action method and select Add View from the pop-up menu. Set the name to Index and click the OK button to create the Index.cshtml view file. Edit the view to match the contents shown in Listing 8-17.

Listing 8-17. The Contents of the Index.cshtml File

```
@model SportsStore.WebUI.Models.CartIndexViewModel

@{
    ViewBag.Title = "Sports Store: Your Cart";
}

<h2>Your cart</h2>
<table class="table">
    <thead>
        <tr>
            <th>Quantity</th>
            <th>Item</th>
            <th class="text-right">Price</th>
            <th class="text-right">Subtotal</th>
        </tr>
    </thead>
    <tbody>
        @foreach (var line in Model.Cart.Lines) {
            <tr>
                <td class="text-center">@line.Quantity</td>
                <td class="text-left">@line.Product.Name</td>
                <td class="text-right">@line.Product.Price.ToString("c")</td>
                <td class="text-right">
                    @((line.Quantity * line.Product.Price).ToString("c"))
                </td>
            </tr>
        }
    </tbody>
    <tfoot>
        <tr>
            <td colspan="3" class="text-right">Total:</td>
            <td class="text-right">
                @Model.Cart.ComputeTotalValue().ToString("c")
            </td>
        </tr>
    </tfoot>
</table>

<div class="text-center">
    <a class="btn btn-primary" href="@Model.ReturnUrl">Continue shopping</a>
</div>
```

The view enumerates the lines in the cart and adds rows for each of them to an HTML table, along with the total cost per line and the total cost for the cart. The classes I have assigned the elements to correspond to Bootstrap styles for tables and text alignment. I now have the basic functions of the shopping cart in place. First, products are listed along with a button to add them to the cart, as shown in Figure 8-8.

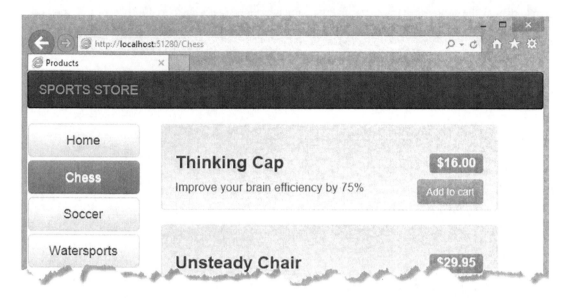

Figure 8-8. *The Add to cart button*

And second, when the user clicks the Add to cart button, the appropriate product is added to their cart and a summary of the cart is displayed, as shown in Figure 8-9. And clicking the Continue shopping button returns the user to the product page they came from.

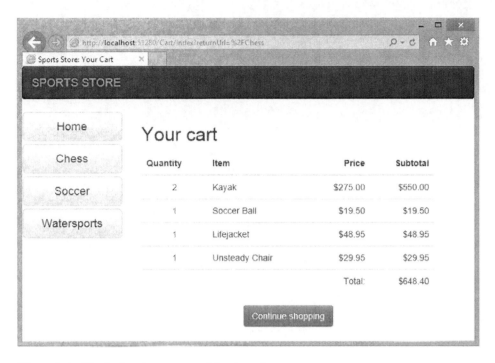

Figure 8-9. *Displaying the contents of the shopping cart*

Summary

In this chapter, I started to flesh out the customer-facing parts of the SportsStore app. I provided the means by which the user can navigate by category and put the basic building blocks in place for adding items to a shopping cart. I have more work to do and I continue the development of the application in the next chapter.

CHAPTER 9

■ ■ ■

SportsStore: Completing the Cart

In this chapter, I continue to build out the SportsStore example app. In the previous chapter, I added the basic support for a shopping cart and now I am going to improve on and complete that functionality.

Using Model Binding

The MVC Framework uses a system called *model binding* to create C# objects from HTTP requests in order to pass them as parameter values to action methods. This is how the MVC framework processes forms, for example: it looks at the parameters of the action method that has been targeted and uses a *model binder* to get the form values sent by the browser and convert them to the type of the parameter with the same name before passing them to the action method.

Model binders can create C# types from any information that is available in the request. This is one of the central features of the MVC Framework. I am going to create a custom model binder to improve the CartController class.

I like using the session state feature in the Cart controller to store and manage the Cart objects that I set up in Chapter 8, but I do not like the way I have to go about it. It does not fit the rest of the application model, which is based around action method parameters. I cannot properly unit test the CartController class unless I mock the Session parameter of the base class, and that means mocking a whole bunch of other stuff I would rather not deal with.

To solve this problem, I am going to create a custom model binder that obtains the Cart object contained in the session data. The MVC Framework will then be able to create Cart objects and pass them as parameters to the action methods in the CartController class. The model binding feature is powerful and flexible. I go into a lot more depth about this feature in Chapter 24, but this is a nice example to get started with.

Creating a Custom Model Binder

I create a custom model binder by implementing the System.Web.Mvc.IModelBinder interface. To create this implementation, I added a new folder in the SportsStore.WebUI project called Infrastructure/Binders and created a CartModelBinder.cs class file inside it. Listing 9-1 shows the contents of the new file.

Listing 9-1. The Contents of the CartModelBinder.cs File

```
using System.Web.Mvc;
using SportsStore.Domain.Entities;

namespace SportsStore.WebUI.Infrastructure.Binders {

    public class CartModelBinder : IModelBinder {
        private const string sessionKey = "Cart";
```

227

```
        public object BindModel(ControllerContext controllerContext,
            ModelBindingContext bindingContext) {

            // get the Cart from the session

            Cart cart = null;
            if (controllerContext.HttpContext.Session != null) {
                cart = (Cart)controllerContext.HttpContext.Session[sessionKey];
            }
            // create the Cart if there wasn't one in the session data
            if (cart == null) {
                cart = new Cart();
                if (controllerContext.HttpContext.Session != null) {
                    controllerContext.HttpContext.Session[sessionKey] = cart;
                }
            }
            // return the cart
            return cart;
        }
    }
}
```

The IModelBinder interface defines one method: BindModel. The two parameters are provided to make creating the domain model object possible. The ControllerContext provides access to all the information that the controller class has, which includes details of the request from the client. The ModelBindingContext gives you information about the model object you are being asked to build and some tools for making the binding process easier.

For my purposes, the ControllerContext class is the one I am interested in. It has an HttpContext property, which in turn has a Session property that lets me get and set session data. I can obtain the Cart object associated with the user's session by reading a value from the session data, and create a Cart if there is not one there already.

I need to tell the MVC Framework that it can use the CartModelBinder class to create instances of Cart. I do this in the Application_Start method of Global.asax, as shown in Listing 9-2.

Listing 9-2. Registering the CartModelBinder Class in the Global.asax.cs File

```
using System;
using System.Collections.Generic;
using System.Linq;
using System.Web;
using System.Web.Mvc;
using System.Web.Routing;
using SportsStore.Domain.Entities;
using SportsStore.WebUI.Infrastructure.Binders;

namespace SportsStore.WebUI {

    public class MvcApplication : System.Web.HttpApplication {

        protected void Application_Start() {
            AreaRegistration.RegisterAllAreas();
            RouteConfig.RegisterRoutes(RouteTable.Routes);
```

```
        ModelBinders.Binders.Add(typeof(Cart), new CartModelBinder());
    }
  }
}
```

I can now update the Cart controller to remove the GetCart method and rely on the model binder to provide the controller with Cart objects. Listing 9-3 shows the changes.

Listing 9-3. Relying on the Model Binder in the CartController.cs File

```
using System.Linq;
using System.Web.Mvc;
using SportsStore.Domain.Abstract;
using SportsStore.Domain.Entities;
using SportsStore.WebUI.Models;

namespace SportsStore.WebUI.Controllers {

    public class CartController : Controller {
        private IProductRepository repository;

        public CartController(IProductRepository repo) {
            repository = repo;
        }

        public ViewResult Index(Cart cart, string returnUrl) {
            return View(new CartIndexViewModel {
                ReturnUrl = returnUrl,
                Cart = cart
            });
        }

        public RedirectToRouteResult AddToCart(Cart cart, int productId,
                string returnUrl) {
            Product product = repository.Products
                .FirstOrDefault(p => p.ProductID == productId);

            if (product != null) {
                cart.AddItem(product, 1);
            }
            return RedirectToAction("Index", new { returnUrl });
        }

        public RedirectToRouteResult RemoveFromCart(Cart cart, int productId,
                string returnUrl) {
            Product product = repository.Products
                .FirstOrDefault(p => p.ProductID == productId);

            if (product != null) {
                cart.RemoveLine(product);
            }
```

```
            return RedirectToAction("Index", new { returnUrl });
        }
    }
}
```

I have removed the GetCart method and added a Cart parameter to each of the action methods. When the MVC Framework receives a request that requires, say, the AddToCart method to be invoked, it begins by looking at the parameters for the action method. It looks at the list of binders available and tries to find one that can create instances of each parameter type. The custom binder is asked to create a Cart object, and it does so by working with the session state feature. Between the custom binder and the default binder, the MVC Framework is able to create the set of parameters required to call the action method, allowing me to refactor the controller so that it has no knowledge of how Cart objects are created when requests are received.

There are several benefits to using a custom model binder like this. The first is that I have separated the logic used to create a Cart from that of the controller, which allows me to change the way I store Cart objects without needing to change the controller. The second benefit is that any controller class that works with Cart objects can simply declare them as action method parameters and take advantage of the custom model binder. The third benefit, and the one I think is most important, is that I can now unit test the Cart controller without needing to mock a lot of ASP.NET plumbing.

UNIT TEST: THE CART CONTROLLER

I can unit test the CartController class by creating Cart objects and passing them to the action methods. I want to test three different aspects of this controller:

- The AddToCart method should add the selected product to the customer's cart.

- After adding a product to the cart, the user should be redirected to the Index view.

- The URL that the user can follow to return to the catalog should be correctly passed to the Index action method.

Here are the unit tests I added to the CartTests.cs file in the SportsStore.UnitTests project:

```
using System;
using Microsoft.VisualStudio.TestTools.UnitTesting;
using SportsStore.Domain.Entities;
using System.Linq;
using Moq;
using SportsStore.Domain.Abstract;
using SportsStore.WebUI.Controllers;
using System.Web.Mvc;
using SportsStore.WebUI.Models;

namespace SportsStore.UnitTests {
    [TestClass]
    public class CartTests {

        //...existing test methods omitted for brevity...

        [TestMethod]
        public void Can_Add_To_Cart() {
```

```
    // Arrange - create the mock repository
    Mock<IProductRepository> mock = new Mock<IProductRepository>();
    mock.Setup(m => m.Products).Returns(new Product[] {
        new Product {ProductID = 1, Name = "P1", Category = "Apples"},
    }.AsQueryable());

    // Arrange - create a Cart
    Cart cart = new Cart();

    // Arrange - create the controller
    CartController target = new CartController(mock.Object);

    // Act - add a product to the cart
    target.AddToCart(cart, 1, null);

    // Assert
    Assert.AreEqual(cart.Lines.Count(), 1);
    Assert.AreEqual(cart.Lines.ToArray()[0].Product.ProductID, 1);
}

[TestMethod]
public void Adding_Product_To_Cart_Goes_To_Cart_Screen() {
    // Arrange - create the mock repository
    Mock<IProductRepository> mock = new Mock<IProductRepository>();
    mock.Setup(m => m.Products).Returns(new Product[] {
        new Product {ProductID = 1, Name = "P1", Category = "Apples"},
    }.AsQueryable());

    // Arrange - create a Cart
    Cart cart = new Cart();

    // Arrange - create the controller
    CartController target = new CartController(mock.Object);

    // Act - add a product to the cart
    RedirectToRouteResult result = target.AddToCart(cart, 2, "myUrl");

    // Assert
    Assert.AreEqual(result.RouteValues["action"], "Index");
    Assert.AreEqual(result.RouteValues["returnUrl"], "myUrl");
}

[TestMethod]
public void Can_View_Cart_Contents() {
    // Arrange - create a Cart
    Cart cart = new Cart();

    // Arrange - create the controller
    CartController target = new CartController(null);
```

```
            // Act - call the Index action method
            CartIndexViewModel result
                = (CartIndexViewModel)target.Index(cart, "myUrl").ViewData.Model;

            // Assert
            Assert.AreSame(result.Cart, cart);
            Assert.AreEqual(result.ReturnUrl, "myUrl");
        }

    }
}
```

Completing the Cart

Now that I have introduced the custom model binder, it is time to complete the cart functionality by adding two new features. The first will allow the customer to remove an item from the cart. The second feature will display a summary of the cart at the top of the page.

Removing Items from the Cart

I already defined and tested the RemoveFromCart action method in the controller, so letting the customer remove items is just a matter of exposing this method in a view, which I are going to do by adding a Remove button in each row of the cart summary. The changes to Views/Cart/Index.cshtml are shown in Listing 9-4.

Listing 9-4. Introducing a Remove Button to the Index.cshtml File

```
@model SportsStore.WebUI.Models.CartIndexViewModel

@{
    ViewBag.Title = "Sports Store: Your Cart";
}

<style>
    #cartTable td { vertical-align: middle; }
</style>

<h2>Your cart</h2>
<table id="cartTable" class="table">
    <thead>
        <tr>
            <th>Quantity</th>
            <th>Item</th>
            <th class="text-right">Price</th>
            <th class="text-right">Subtotal</th>
        </tr>
    </thead>
```

```
    <tbody>
        @foreach (var line in Model.Cart.Lines) {
            <tr>
                <td class="text-center">@line.Quantity</td>
                <td class="text-left">@line.Product.Name</td>
                <td class="text-right">@line.Product.Price.ToString("c")</td>
                <td class="text-right">
                    @((line.Quantity * line.Product.Price).ToString("c"))
                </td>
                <td>
                    @using (Html.BeginForm("RemoveFromCart", "Cart")) {
                        @Html.Hidden("ProductId", line.Product.ProductID)
                        @Html.HiddenFor(x => x.ReturnUrl)
                        <input class="btn btn-sm btn-warning"
                            type="submit" value="Remove" />
                    }
                </td>
            </tr>
        }
    </tbody>
    <tfoot>
        <tr>
            <td colspan="3" class="text-right">Total:</td>
            <td class="text-right">
                @Model.Cart.ComputeTotalValue().ToString("c")
            </td>
        </tr>
    </tfoot>
</table>

<div class="text-center">
    <a class="btn btn-primary" href="@Model.ReturnUrl">Continue shopping</a>
</div>
```

I added a new column to each row of the table that contains a form with an input element. I styled the input element as a button with Bootstrap and added a style element and an id to the table element to ensure that the button and the content of the other columns are properly aligned.

■ **Note**   I used the strongly typed Html.HiddenFor helper method to create a hidden field for the ReturnUrl model property, but I had to use the string-based Html.Hidden helper to do the same for the ProductId field. If I had written Html.HiddenFor(x => line.Product.ProductID), the helper would render a hidden field with the name line. Product.ProductID. The name of the field would not match the names of the parameters for the CartController. RemoveFromCart action method, which would prevent the default model binders from working, so the MVC Framework would not be able to call the method.

You can see the Remove buttons at work by running the application and adding items to the shopping cart. Remember that the cart already contains the functionality to remove it, which you can test by clicking one of the new buttons, as shown in Figure 9-1.

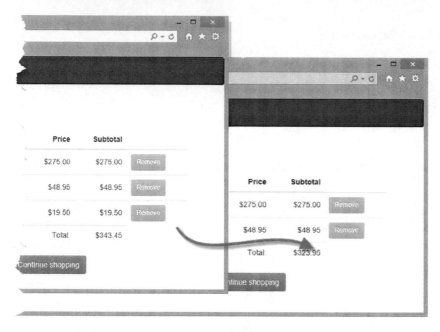

Figure 9-1. *Removing an item from the shopping cart*

Adding the Cart Summary

I may have a functioning cart, but there is an issue with the way it is integrated into the interface. Customers can tell what is in their cart only by viewing the cart summary screen. And they can view the cart summary screen only by adding a new a new item to the cart.

To solve this problem, I am going to add a widget that summarizes the contents of the cart and that can be clicked to display the cart contents throughout the application. I will do this in much the same way that I added the navigation widget—as an action whose output I will inject into the Razor layout. To start, I need to add the simple method, shown in Listing 9-5, to the CartController class.

Listing 9-5. Adding the Summary Method to the CartController.cs File

```
using System.Linq;
using System.Web.Mvc;
using SportsStore.Domain.Abstract;
using SportsStore.Domain.Entities;
using SportsStore.WebUI.Models;

namespace SportsStore.WebUI.Controllers {

    public class CartController : Controller {
        private IProductRepository repository;

        public CartController(IProductRepository repo) {
            repository = repo;
        }

        // ...other action methods omitted for brevity...
```

```
    public PartialViewResult Summary(Cart cart) {
        return PartialView(cart);
    }
  }
}
```

This simple method needs to render a view, supplying the current Cart (which will be obtained using the custom model binder) as view data. To create the view, right-click the Summary action method and select Add View from the pop-up menu. Set the name of the view to Summary and click the OK button to create the Views/Cart/Summary.cshtml file. Edit the view so that it matches Listing 9-6.

Listing 9-6. The Contents of the Summary.cshtml File

```
@model SportsStore.Domain.Entities.Cart

<div class="navbar-right">
    @Html.ActionLink("Checkout", "Index", "Cart",
        new { returnUrl = Request.Url.PathAndQuery },
        new { @class = "btn btn-default navbar-btn" })
</div>

<div class="navbar-text navbar-right">
    <b>Your cart:</b>
    @Model.Lines.Sum(x => x.Quantity) item(s),
    @Model.ComputeTotalValue().ToString("c")
</div>
```

The view displays the number of items in the cart, the total cost of those items, and a link that shows the details of the cart to the user (and, as you will have expected by now, I have assigned the elements that the view contains to classes defined by Bootstrap). Now that I have created the view that is returned by the Summary action method, I can call the Summary action method in the _Layout.cshtml file to display the cart summary, as shown in Listing 9-7.

Listing 9-7. Adding the Summary Partial View to the _Layout.cshtml File

```
<!DOCTYPE html>
<html>
<head>
    <meta charset="utf-8" />
    <meta name="viewport" content="width=device-width, initial-scale=1.0">
    <link href="~/Content/bootstrap.css" rel="stylesheet" />
    <link href="~/Content/bootstrap-theme.css" rel="stylesheet" />
    <title>@ViewBag.Title</title>
</head>
<body>
    <div class="navbar navbar-inverse" role="navigation">
        <a class="navbar-brand" href="#">SPORTS STORE</a>
        @Html.Action("Summary", "Cart")
    </div>
    <div class="row panel">
        <div id="categories" class="col-xs-3">
            @Html.Action("Menu", "Nav")
        </div>
```

```
        <div class="col-xs-8">
            @RenderBody()
        </div>
    </div>
</body>
</html>
```

You can see the cart summary by running the application. The item count and total increase as you add items to the cart, as shown by Figure 9-2.

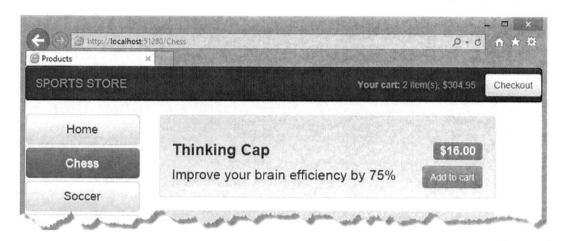

Figure 9-2. *The cart summary widget*

With this addition, customers know what is in their cart and have an obvious way to check out from the store. You can see, once again, how easy it is to use the Html.Action helper method to incorporate the output from an action method in another view. This is a nice technique for breaking down the functionality of an application into distinct, reusable blocks.

Submitting Orders

I have now reached the final customer feature in SportsStore: the ability to check out and complete an order. In the following sections, I will extend the domain model to provide support for capturing the shipping details from a user and add the application support to process those details.

Extending the Domain Model

Add a class file called ShippingDetails.cs to the Entities folder of the SportsStore.Domain project and edit it to match the contents shown in Listing 9-8. This is the class I will use to represent the shipping details for a customer.

Listing 9-8. The Contents of the ShippingDetails.cs File

```
using System.ComponentModel.DataAnnotations;

namespace SportsStore.Domain.Entities {
```

```
public class ShippingDetails {
    [Required(ErrorMessage = "Please enter a name")]
    public string Name { get; set; }

    [Required(ErrorMessage = "Please enter the first address line")]
    public string Line1 { get; set; }
    public string Line2 { get; set; }
    public string Line3 { get; set; }

    [Required(ErrorMessage = "Please enter a city name")]
    public string City { get; set; }

    [Required(ErrorMessage = "Please enter a state name")]
    public string State { get; set; }

    public string Zip { get; set; }

    [Required(ErrorMessage = "Please enter a country name")]
    public string Country { get; set; }

    public bool GiftWrap { get; set; }
    }
}
```

You can see that I am using the validation attributes from the `System.ComponentModel.DataAnnotations` namespace, just as I did in Chapter 2. I explore validation further in Chapter 25.

■ **Note**   The `ShippingDetails` class does not have any functionality, so there is nothing that that can be sensibly unit tested.

Adding the Checkout Process

The goal is to reach the point where users are able to enter their shipping details and submit their order. To start this off, I need to add a Checkout now button to the cart summary view. Listing 9-9 shows the change I applied to the `Views/Cart/Index.cshtml` file.

Listing 9-9. Adding the Checkout Now Button to the Index.cshtml File

```
. . .
<div class="text-center">
    <a class="btn btn-primary" href="@Model.ReturnUrl">Continue shopping</a>
    @Html.ActionLink("Checkout now", "Checkout", null, new { @class = "btn btn-primary"})
</div>
. . .
```

This change generates a link that I have styled as a button and that, when clicked, calls the Checkout action method of the Cart controller. You can see how this button appears in Figure 9-3.

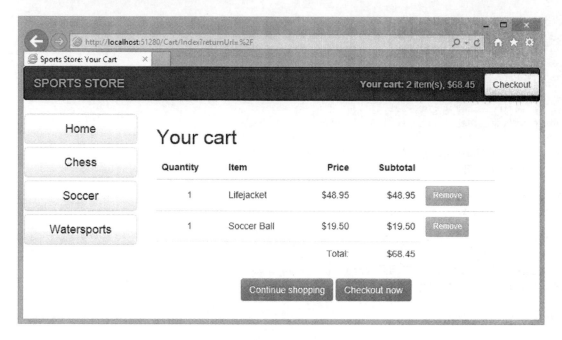

Figure 9-3. *The Checkout now button*

As you might expect, I now need to define the Checkout method in the CartController class, as shown in Listing 9-10.

Listing 9-10. The Checkout Action Method in the CartController.cs File

```
using System.Linq;
using System.Web.Mvc;
using SportsStore.Domain.Abstract;
using SportsStore.Domain.Entities;
using SportsStore.WebUI.Models;

namespace SportsStore.WebUI.Controllers {

    public class CartController : Controller {
        private IProductRepository repository;

        public CartController(IProductRepository repo) {
            repository = repo;
        }

        //...other action methods omitted for brevity...

        public ViewResult Checkout() {
            return View(new ShippingDetails());
        }
    }
}
```

The Checkout method returns the default view and passes a new ShippingDetails object as the view model. To create the view for the action method, right-click on the Checkout action method and select Add View from the pop-up menu. Set the name to Checkout and click the OK button. Visual Studio will create the Views/Cart/Checkout. cshtml file, which you should edit to match Listing 9-11.

Listing 9-11. The Contents of the Checkout.cshtml File

```
@model SportsStore.Domain.Entities.ShippingDetails

@{
    ViewBag.Title = "SportStore: Checkout";
}

<h2>Check out now</h2>
<p>Please enter your details, and we'll ship your goods right away!</p>

@using (Html.BeginForm()) {

    <h3>Ship to</h3>
    <div class="form-group">
        <label>Name:</label>
        @Html.TextBoxFor(x => x.Name, new {@class = "form-control"})
    </div>

    <h3>Address</h3>

    <div class="form-group">
        <label>Line 1:</label>
        @Html.TextBoxFor(x => x.Line1, new {@class = "form-control"})
    </div>
    <div class="form-group">
        <label>Line 2:</label>
        @Html.TextBoxFor(x => x.Line2, new {@class = "form-control"})
    </div>
    <div class="form-group">
        <label>Line 3:</label>
        @Html.TextBoxFor(x => x.Line3, new {@class = "form-control"})
    </div>
    <div class="form-group">
        <label>City:</label>
        @Html.TextBoxFor(x => x.City, new {@class = "form-control"})
    </div>
    <div class="form-group">
        <label>State:</label>
        @Html.TextBoxFor(x => x.State, new {@class = "form-control"})
    </div>
    <div class="form-group">
        <label>Zip:</label>
        @Html.TextBoxFor(x => x.Zip, new {@class = "form-control"})
    </div>
```

```
    <div class="form-group">
        <label>Country:</label>
        @Html.TextBoxFor(x => x.Country, new {@class = "form-control"})
    </div>

    <h3>Options</h3>
    <div class="checkbox">
        <label>
            @Html.EditorFor(x => x.GiftWrap)
            Gift wrap these items
        </label>
    </div>

    <div class="text-center">
        <input class="btn btn-primary" type="submit" value="Complete order" />
    </div>
}
```

For each of the properties in the model, I have created a label and input element formatted with Bootstrap to capture the user input. You can see the effect I have created by starting the application and clicking the Checkout button at the top of the page and then clicking Checkout now, as shown by Figure 9-4. (You can also reach this view by navigating to the /Cart/Checkout URL).

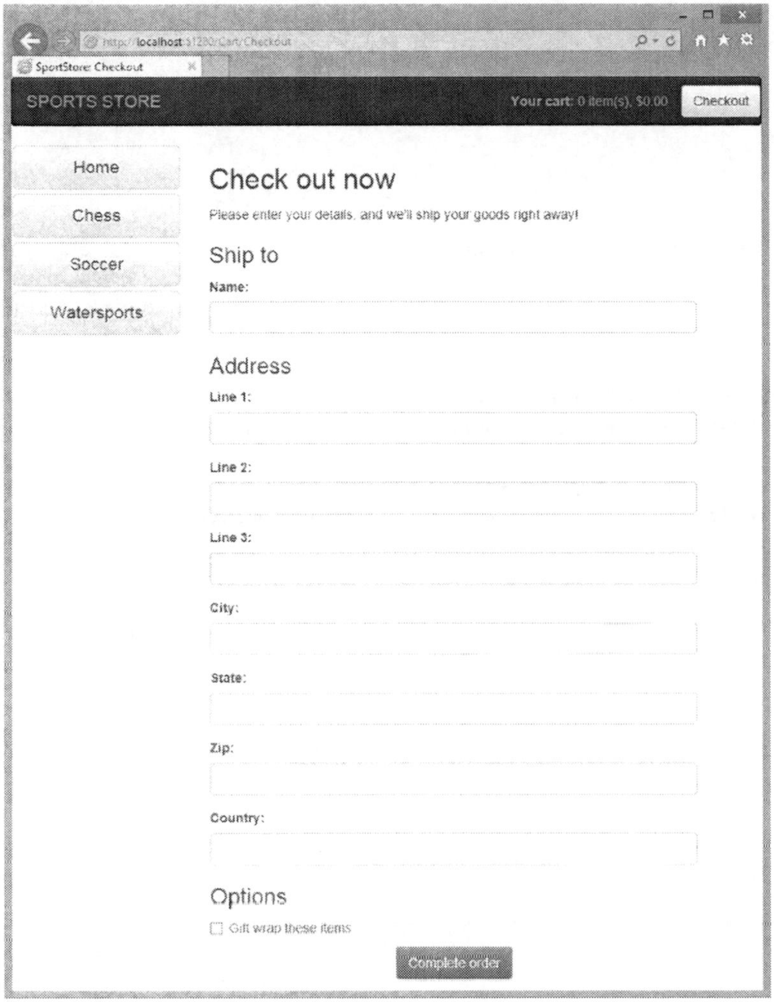

Figure 9-4. *The shipping details form*

The problem with this view is that it contains a lot of repeated markup. There are MVC Framework HTML helpers that could reduce the duplication, but they make it hard to structure and style the content in the way that I want. Instead, I am going to use a handy feature to get metadata about the view model object and combine it with a mix of C# and Razor expressions. You can see what I have done in Listing 9-12.

Listing 9-12. Reducing Duplication in the Checkout.cshtml File

```
@model SportsStore.Domain.Entities.ShippingDetails

@{
    ViewBag.Title = "SportStore: Checkout";
}
```

```
<h2>Check out now</h2>
<p>Please enter your details, and we'll ship your goods right away!</p>

@using (Html.BeginForm()) {

    <h3>Ship to</h3>
    <div class="form-group">
        <label>Name</label>
        @Html.TextBoxFor(x => x.Name, new {@class = "form-control"})
    </div>

    <h3>Address</h3>

    foreach (var property in ViewData.ModelMetadata.Properties) {
        if (property.PropertyName != "Name" && property.PropertyName != "GiftWrap") {
            <div class="form-group">
                <label>@(property.DisplayName ?? property.PropertyName)</label>
                @Html.TextBox(property.PropertyName, null, new {@class = "form-control"})
            </div>
        }
    }

    <h3>Options</h3>
    <div class="checkbox">
        <label>
            @Html.EditorFor(x => x.GiftWrap)
            Gift wrap these items
        </label>
    </div>

    <div class="text-center">
        <input class="btn btn-primary" type="submit" value="Complete order" />
    </div>
}
```

The static `ViewData.ModelMetadata` property returns a `System.Web.Mvc.ModelMetaData` object that provides information about the model type for the view. The `Properties` property I use in the `foreach` loop returns a collection of `ModelMetaData` objects, each of which represents a property defined by the model type. I use the `PropertyName` property to ensure that I don't generate content for the `Name` or `GiftWrap` properties (which I deal with elsewhere in the view) and generate a set of elements, complete with Bootstrap classes, for all of the other properties.

■ **Tip** The `for` and `if` keywords I have used are within the scope of a Razor expression (the `@using` expression that creates the form) and so I don't need to prefix them with the @ character. In fact, were I to do so, Razor would report an error. It can take a little while to get used to when the @ character is required with Razor, but it becomes second nature for most programmers. For those that can't quite get it right first time (which includes me), the Razor error message displayed in the browser provides specific instructions to correct any mistakes.

I am not quite done, however. If you run the example and look at the output generated by the view, you will see that some of the labels are not quite correct, as Figure 9-5 illustrates.

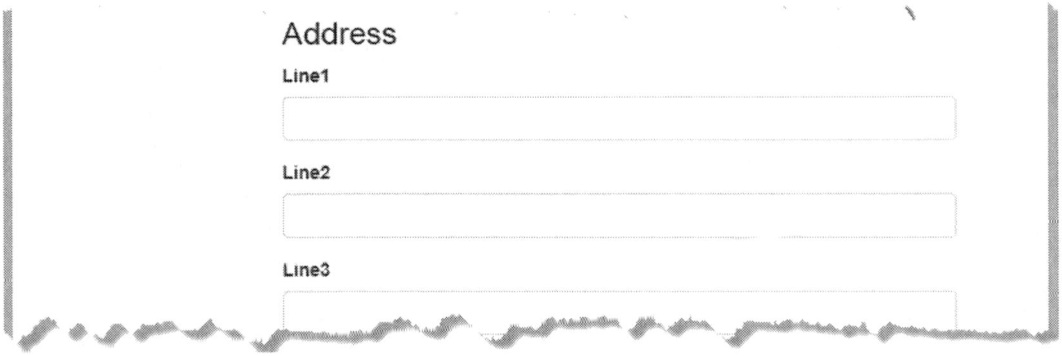

Figure 9-5. *The problem with generating labels from property names*

The issue is that the property names don't always make for good labels. This is why I check to see if there is a DisplayName value available when I generate the form elements, like this:

```
. . .
<label>@(property.DisplayName ?? property.PropertyName)</label>
. . .
```

To take advantage of the DisplayName property, I need to apply the Display attribute to the model class, as shown in Listing 9-13.

Listing 9-13. Applying th e Display attribute to the ShippingDetails.cs File

```
using System.ComponentModel.DataAnnotations;

namespace SportsStore.Domain.Entities {

    public class ShippingDetails {
        [Required(ErrorMessage = "Please enter a name")]
        public string Name { get; set; }

        [Required(ErrorMessage = "Please enter the first address line")]
        [Display(Name="Line 1")]
        public string Line1 { get; set; }
        [Display(Name = "Line 2")]
        public string Line2 { get; set; }
        [Display(Name = "Line 3")]
        public string Line3 { get; set; }

        [Required(ErrorMessage = "Please enter a city name")]
        public string City { get; set; }

        [Required(ErrorMessage = "Please enter a state name")]
        public string State { get; set; }
```

```
        public string Zip { get; set; }

        [Required(ErrorMessage = "Please enter a country name")]
        public string Country { get; set; }

        public bool GiftWrap { get; set; }
    }
}
```

Setting the Name value for the Display attribute allows me to set up a value that will be read by the DisplayName property in the view. You can see the effect by starting the application and viewing the checkout page, as shown in Figure 9-6.

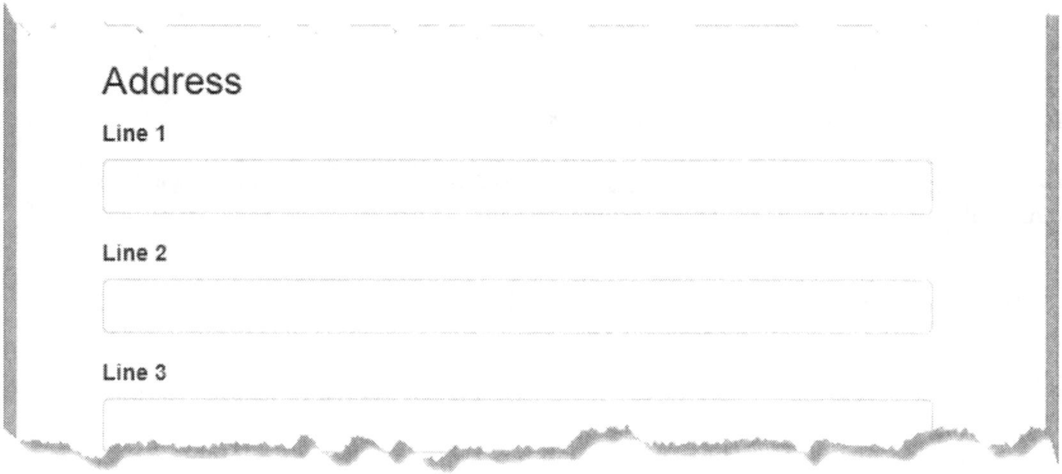

Address

Line 1

Line 2

Line 3

Figure 9-6. *The effect of the Display attribute on the model type*

This example shows two different aspects of working with the MVC Framework. The first is that you can work around any situation to simplify your markup or code. The second is that even though the role that views play in the MVC pattern is restricted to displaying data and markup, the tools that Razor and C# provide for this task are rich and flexible, even to the extent of working with type metadata.

Implementing the Order Processor

I need a component in the application to which I can hand details of an order for processing. In keeping with the principles of the MVC model, I am going to define an interface for this functionality, write an implementation of the interface, and then associate the two using the DI container, Ninject.

Defining the Interface

Add a new interface called IOrderProcessor to the Abstract folder of the SportsStore.Domain project and edit the contents so that they match Listing 9-14.

Listing 9-14. The Contents of the IOrderProcessor.cs File

```
using SportsStore.Domain.Entities;

namespace SportsStore.Domain.Abstract {

    public interface IOrderProcessor {

        void ProcessOrder(Cart cart, ShippingDetails shippingDetails);
    }
}
```

Implementing the Interface

The implementation of IOrderProcessor is going to deal with orders by e-mailing them to the site administrator. I am simplifying the sales process, of course. Most e-commerce sites would not simply e-mail an order, and I have not provided support for processing credit cards or other forms of payment. But I want to keep things focused on MVC, and so e-mail it is.

Create a new class file called EmailOrderProcessor.cs in the Concrete folder of the SportsStore.Domain project and edit the contents so that they match Listing 9-15. This class uses the built-in SMTP support included in the .NET Framework library to send an e-mail.

Listing 9-15. The Contents of the EmailOrderProcessor.cs File

```
using System.Net;
using System.Net.Mail;
using System.Text;
using SportsStore.Domain.Abstract;
using SportsStore.Domain.Entities;

namespace SportsStore.Domain.Concrete {

    public class EmailSettings {
        public string MailToAddress = "orders@example.com";
        public string MailFromAddress = "sportsstore@example.com";
        public bool UseSsl = true;
        public string Username = "MySmtpUsername";
        public string Password = "MySmtpPassword";
        public string ServerName = "smtp.example.com";
        public int ServerPort = 587;
        public bool WriteAsFile = false;
        public string FileLocation = @"c:\sports_store_emails";
    }

    public class EmailOrderProcessor :IOrderProcessor {
        private EmailSettings emailSettings;

        public EmailOrderProcessor(EmailSettings settings) {
            emailSettings = settings;
        }
```

```
public void ProcessOrder(Cart cart, ShippingDetails shippingInfo) {

    using (var smtpClient = new SmtpClient()) {

        smtpClient.EnableSsl = emailSettings.UseSsl;
        smtpClient.Host = emailSettings.ServerName;
        smtpClient.Port = emailSettings.ServerPort;
        smtpClient.UseDefaultCredentials = false;
        smtpClient.Credentials
            = new NetworkCredential(emailSettings.Username,
                  emailSettings.Password);

        if (emailSettings.WriteAsFile) {
            smtpClient.DeliveryMethod
                = SmtpDeliveryMethod.SpecifiedPickupDirectory;
            smtpClient.PickupDirectoryLocation = emailSettings.FileLocation;
            smtpClient.EnableSsl = false;
        }

        StringBuilder body = new StringBuilder()
            .AppendLine("A new order has been submitted")
            .AppendLine("---")
            .AppendLine("Items:");

        foreach (var line in cart.Lines) {
            var subtotal = line.Product.Price * line.Quantity;
            body.AppendFormat("{0} x {1} (subtotal: {2:c}", line.Quantity,
                              line.Product.Name,
                              subtotal);
        }

        body.AppendFormat("Total order value: {0:c}", cart.ComputeTotalValue())
            .AppendLine("---")
            .AppendLine("Ship to:")
            .AppendLine(shippingInfo.Name)
            .AppendLine(shippingInfo.Line1)
            .AppendLine(shippingInfo.Line2 ?? "")
            .AppendLine(shippingInfo.Line3 ?? "")
            .AppendLine(shippingInfo.City)
            .AppendLine(shippingInfo.State ?? "")
            .AppendLine(shippingInfo.Country)
            .AppendLine(shippingInfo.Zip)
            .AppendLine("---")
            .AppendFormat("Gift wrap: {0}",
                shippingInfo.GiftWrap ? "Yes" : "No");

        MailMessage mailMessage = new MailMessage(
                              emailSettings.MailFromAddress,    // From
                              emailSettings.MailToAddress,      // To
                              "New order submitted!",           // Subject
                              body.ToString());                 // Body
```

```
            if (emailSettings.WriteAsFile) {
                mailMessage.BodyEncoding = Encoding.ASCII;
            }

            smtpClient.Send(mailMessage);
        }
    }
}
```

To make things simpler, I have defined the EmailSettings class in Listing 9-15 as well. An instance of this class is demanded by the EmailOrderProcessor constructor and contains all the settings that are required to configure the .NET e-mail classes.

■ **Tip**   Do not worry if you do not have an SMTP server available. If you set the EmailSettings.WriteAsFile property to true, the e-mail messages will be written as files to the directory specified by the FileLocation property. This directory must exist and be writable. The files will be written with the .eml extension, but they can be read with any text editor. The location I have set in the listing is c:\sports_store_emails.

Registering the Implementation

Now that I have an implementation of the IOrderProcessor interface and the means to configure it, I can use Ninject to create instances of it. Edit the NinjectDependencyResolver.cs file in the Infrastructure folder of the SportsStore.WebUI project and make the changes shown in Listing 9-16 to the AddBindings method.

Listing 9-16. Adding Ninject Bindings for IOrderProcessor to the NinjectDependencyResolver.cs File

```
using System;
using System.Collections.Generic;
using System.Configuration;
using System.Web.Mvc;
using Moq;
using Ninject;
using SportsStore.Domain.Abstract;
using SportsStore.Domain.Concrete;
using SportsStore.Domain.Entities;

namespace SportsStore.WebUI.Infrastructure {

    public class NinjectDependencyResolver : IDependencyResolver {
        private IKernel kernel;

        public NinjectDependencyResolver(IKernel kernelParam) {
            kernel = kernelParam;
            AddBindings();
        }

        public object GetService(Type serviceType) {
            return kernel.TryGet(serviceType);
        }
```

```
        public IEnumerable<object> GetServices(Type serviceType) {
            return kernel.GetAll(serviceType);
        }

        private void AddBindings() {
            kernel.Bind<IProductRepository>().To<EFProductRepository>();

            EmailSettings emailSettings = new EmailSettings {
                WriteAsFile = bool.Parse(ConfigurationManager
                    .AppSettings["Email.WriteAsFile"] ?? "false")
            };

            kernel.Bind<IOrderProcessor>().To<EmailOrderProcessor>()
                .WithConstructorArgument("settings", emailSettings);
        }
    }
}
```

I created an EmailSettings object, which I use with the Ninject WithConstructorArgument method so that
I can inject it into the EmailOrderProcessor constructor when new instances are created to service requests for
the IOrderProcessor interface. In Listing 9-16, I specified a value for only one of the EmailSettings properties:
WriteAsFile. I read the value of this property using the ConfigurationManager.AppSettings property, which
provides access to application settings defined in the Web.config file (the one in the root project folder), which are
shown in Listing 9-17.

Listing 9-17. Application Settings in the Web.config File

```
...
<appSettings>
  <add key="webpages:Version" value="3.0.0.0" />
  <add key="webpages:Enabled" value="false" />
  <add key="ClientValidationEnabled" value="true" />
  <add key="UnobtrusiveJavaScriptEnabled" value="true" />
  <add key="Email.WriteAsFile" value="true"/>
</appSettings>
...
```

Completing the Cart Controller

To complete the CartController class, I need to modify the constructor so that it demands an implementation of the
IOrderProcessor interface and add a new action method that will handle the HTTP form POST request when the user
clicks the Complete order button. Listing 9-18 shows both changes.

Listing 9-18. Completing the Controller in the CartController.cs File

```
using System.Linq;
using System.Web.Mvc;
using SportsStore.Domain.Abstract;
using SportsStore.Domain.Entities;
using SportsStore.WebUI.Models;
```

```
namespace SportsStore.WebUI.Controllers {

    public class CartController : Controller {
        private IProductRepository repository;
        private IOrderProcessor orderProcessor;

        public CartController(IProductRepository repo, IOrderProcessor proc) {
            repository = repo;
            orderProcessor = proc;
        }

        //...other action methods omitted for brevity...

        public ViewResult Checkout() {
            return View(new ShippingDetails());
        }

        [HttpPost]
        public ViewResult Checkout(Cart cart, ShippingDetails shippingDetails) {
            if (cart.Lines.Count() == 0) {
                ModelState.AddModelError("", "Sorry, your cart is empty!");
            }

            if (ModelState.IsValid) {
                orderProcessor.ProcessOrder(cart, shippingDetails);
                cart.Clear();
                return View("Completed");
            } else {
                return View(shippingDetails);
            }
        }
    }
}
```

You can see that the Checkout action method I added is decorated with the HttpPost attribute, which means that it will be invoked for a POST request—in this case, when the user submits the form. Once again, I am relying on the model binder system, both for the ShippingDetails parameter (which is created automatically using the HTTP form data) and the Cart parameter (which is created using the custom binder).

■ **Note**   The change in constructor forces me to update the unit tests I created for the CartController class. Passing null for the new constructor parameter will let the unit tests compile.

The MVC Framework checks the validation constraints that I applied to ShippingDetails using the data annotation attributes, and any validation problems violations are passed to the action method through the ModelState property. I can see if there are any problems by checking the ModelState.IsValid property. Notice that I call the ModelState.AddModelError method to register an error message if there are no items in the cart. I will explain how to display such errors shortly, and I have much more to say about model binding and validation in Chapters 24 and 25.

UNIT TEST: ORDER PROCESSING

To complete the unit testing for the CartController class, I need to test the behavior of the new overloaded version of the Checkout method. Although the method looks short and simple, the use of MVC Framework model binding means that there is a lot going on behind the scenes that needs to be tested.

I want to process an order only if there are items in the cart *and* the customer has provided valid shipping details. Under all other circumstances, the customer should be shown an error. Here is the first test method:

```
...
[TestMethod]
public void Cannot_Checkout_Empty_Cart() {

    // Arrange - create a mock order processor
    Mock<IOrderProcessor> mock = new Mock<IOrderProcessor>();
    // Arrange - create an empty cart
    Cart cart = new Cart();
    // Arrange - create shipping details
    ShippingDetails shippingDetails = new ShippingDetails();
    // Arrange - create an instance of the controller
    CartController target = new CartController(null, mock.Object);

    // Act
    ViewResult result = target.Checkout(cart, shippingDetails);

    // Assert - check that the order hasn't been passed on to the processor
    mock.Verify(m => m.ProcessOrder(It.IsAny<Cart>(), It.IsAny<ShippingDetails>()),
        Times.Never());
    // Assert - check that the method is returning the default view
    Assert.AreEqual("", result.ViewName);
    // Assert - check that I am passing an invalid model to the view
    Assert.AreEqual(false, result.ViewData.ModelState.IsValid);
}
...
```

This test ensures that I cannot check out with an empty cart. I check this by ensuring that the ProcessOrder of the mock IOrderProcessor implementation is never called, that the view that the method returns is the default view (which will redisplay the data entered by customers and give them a chance to correct it), and that the model state being passed to the view has been marked as invalid. This may seem like a belt-and-braces set of assertions, but I need all three to be sure that I have the right behavior. The next test method works in much the same way, but injects an error into the view model to simulate a problem reported by the model binder (which would happen in production when the customer enters invalid shipping data):

```
...
[TestMethod]
public void Cannot_Checkout_Invalid_ShippingDetails() {

    // Arrange - create a mock order processor
    Mock<IOrderProcessor> mock = new Mock<IOrderProcessor>();
```

```
    // Arrange - create a cart with an item
    Cart cart = new Cart();
    cart.AddItem(new Product(), 1);

    // Arrange - create an instance of the controller
    CartController target = new CartController(null, mock.Object);
    // Arrange - add an error to the model
    target.ModelState.AddModelError("error", "error");

    // Act - try to checkout
    ViewResult result = target.Checkout(cart, new ShippingDetails());

    // Assert - check that the order hasn't been passed on to the processor
    mock.Verify(m => m.ProcessOrder(It.IsAny<Cart>(), It.IsAny<ShippingDetails>()),
        Times.Never());
    // Assert - check that the method is returning the default view
    Assert.AreEqual("", result.ViewName);
    // Assert - check that I am passing an invalid model to the view
    Assert.AreEqual(false, result.ViewData.ModelState.IsValid);
}
...
```

Having established that an empty cart or invalid details will prevent an order from being processed, I need to ensure that I process orders when appropriate. Here is the test:

```
...
[TestMethod]
public void Can_Checkout_And_Submit_Order() {
    // Arrange - create a mock order processor
    Mock<IOrderProcessor> mock = new Mock<IOrderProcessor>();
    // Arrange - create a cart with an item
    Cart cart = new Cart();
    cart.AddItem(new Product(), 1);
    // Arrange - create an instance of the controller
    CartController target = new CartController(null, mock.Object);

    // Act - try to checkout
    ViewResult result = target.Checkout(cart, new ShippingDetails());

    // Assert - check that the order has been passed on to the processor
    mock.Verify(m => m.ProcessOrder(It.IsAny<Cart>(), It.IsAny<ShippingDetails>()),
        Times.Once());
    // Assert - check that the method is returning the Completed view
    Assert.AreEqual("Completed", result.ViewName);
    // Assert - check that I am passing a valid model to the view
    Assert.AreEqual(true, result.ViewData.ModelState.IsValid);
}
...
```

Notice that I did not need to test that I can identify valid shipping details. This is handled for me automatically by the model binder using the attributes applied to the properties of the ShippingDetails class.

Displaying Validation Errors

The MVC Framework will use the validation attributes applied to the `ShippingDetails` class to validate user data. However, I need to make a couple of changes to display any problems to the user. The first issue is that I need to provide a summary of any problems to the user. This is especially important when dealing with problems that are not related to specific fields, such as when the user tries to check out with no items in the cart.

To display a useful summary of the validation errors, I can use the `Html.ValidationSummary` helper method, just as I did in Chapter 2. Listing 9-19 shows the addition to `Checkout.cshtml` view.

Listing 9-19. Adding a Validation Summary to the Checkout.cshtml File

```
. . .
@using (Html.BeginForm()) {

    @Html.ValidationSummary()
    <h3>Ship to</h3>
    <div class="form-group">
        <label>Name</label>
        @Html.TextBoxFor(x => x.Name, new {@class = "form-control"})
    </div>

    <h3>Address</h3>
. . .
```

The next step is to create some CSS styles that target the classes used by the validation summary and those to which the MVC Framework adds invalid elements. I created a new `Style Sheet` called `ErrorStyles.css` in the `Content` folder of the `SportsStore.WebUI` project and defined the styles shown in Listing 9-20. This is the same set of styles that I used in Chapter 2.

Listing 9-20. The Contents of the ErrorStyles.css File

```
.field-validation-error    {color: #f00;}
.field-validation-valid    { display: none;}
.input-validation-error    { border: 1px solid #f00; background-color: #fee; }
.validation-summary-errors { font-weight: bold; color: #f00;}
.validation-summary-valid  { display: none;}
```

In order to use apply the styles, I updated the `_Layout.cshtml` file to add a link element for the `ErrorStyles.css` file, as shown in Listing 9-21.

Listing 9-21. Adding a Link Element in the _Layout.cshtml File

```
. . .
<head>
    <meta charset="utf-8" />
    <meta name="viewport" content="width=device-width, initial-scale=1.0">
    <link href="~/Content/bootstrap.css" rel="stylesheet" />
    <link href="~/Content/bootstrap-theme.css" rel="stylesheet" />
    <link href="~/Content/ErrorStyles.css" rel="stylesheet" />
    <title>@ViewBag.Title</title>
</head>
. . .
```

With these changes, validation errors are reported through highlighting problematic fields and by showing a summary of problems, as Figure 9-7 illustrates.

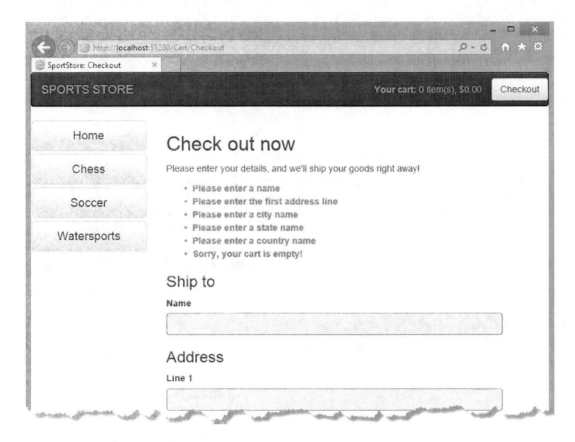

Figure 9-7. *Displaying validation messages*

■ **Tip**   The data submitted by the user is sent to the server before it is validated, which is known as server-side validation and for which the MVC Framework has excellent support. The problem with server-side validation is that the user isn't told about errors until after the data has been sent to the server, processed and the result page generated—something that can take a few seconds on a busy server. For this reason, server-side validation is usually complemented by client-side validation, where JavaScript is used to check the values that the user has entered before the form data is sent to the server. I describe client-side validation in Chapter 25.

Displaying a Summary Page

To complete the checkout process, I will show customers a page that confirms the order has been processed and thanks them for their business. Create a new view called `Completed.cshtml` in the `Views/Cart` folder and edit the content to match Listing 9-22.

Listing 9-22. The Contents of the Completed.cshtml File

```
@{
    ViewBag.Title = "SportsStore: Order Submitted";
}

<h2>Thanks!</h2>
Thanks for placing your order. We'll ship your goods as soon as possible.
```

I don't need to make any code changes to integrate this view into the application because I already added the required statements when I defined the `Checkout` action method back in Listing 9-18. Now customers can go through the entire process, from selecting products to checking out. If they provide valid shipping details (and have items in their cart), they will see the summary page when they click the `Complete` order button, as shown in Figure 9-8.

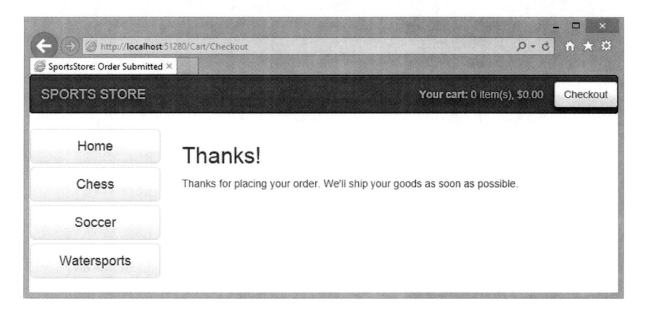

Figure 9-8. The thank-you page

Summary

I have completed all the major parts of the customer-facing portion of SportsStore. It might not be enough to worry Amazon, but I have a product catalog that can be browsed by category and page, a neat shopping cart, and a simple checkout process.

The well-separated architecture means I can easily change the behavior of any piece of the application without worrying about causing problems or inconsistencies elsewhere. For example, I could process orders by storing them in a database, and it would not have any impact on the shopping cart, the product catalog, or any other area of the application. In the next chapter, I use two different techniques to create a mobile version of the SportsStore application.

■ ■ ■

CHAPTER 10

SportsStore: Mobile

There is no escaping the popularity of devices such as smartphones and tablets, and if you want to deliver your application to the widest possible audience, you will have to embrace the world of mobile web browsers. If I sound less than enthusiastic, it is because the phrase *mobile web browsers* runs the gamut from fast, capable, and modern browsers that can rival a decent desktop browser right through to the slow, inconsistent, and outdated.

The bottom line is that delivering a good experience to mobile users is *hard*—much harder than delivering content just to desktops. It takes careful planning, design and an enormous amount of testing—and even then it is easy to be caught out by a new smartphone or tablet.

Putting Mobile Web Development in Context

The MVC Framework does have some features that can help with mobile development. But the MVC Framework is a server-side framework that receives HTTP requests and generates HTML responses and there is a limited amount it can do to deal with the wide variation in capabilities that you will encounter when targeting mobile clients. The degree to which The MVC Framework can help depends on the mobile strategy that you have adopted. There are three basic mobile web strategies you can follow, which I describe the following sections.

■ **Tip**   There is a fourth option, which is to create a native application, but I don't discuss that here since it doesn't directly involve the MVC Framework or, for that matter, web applications.

Doing Nothing (Or As Little As Possible)

It may seem like an odd idea to do nothing, but some mobile devices are capable of handling content that has been developed for desktop clients. Many—admittedly the most recent—have high-resolution, high-density displays with plenty of memory and browsers that can render HTML and run JavaScript quickly. If your app isn't too demanding, you may find that many mobile devices won't encounter any problems at all displaying your application content. As an example, Figure 10-1 shows how an iPad displays the SportsStore application without any modifications.

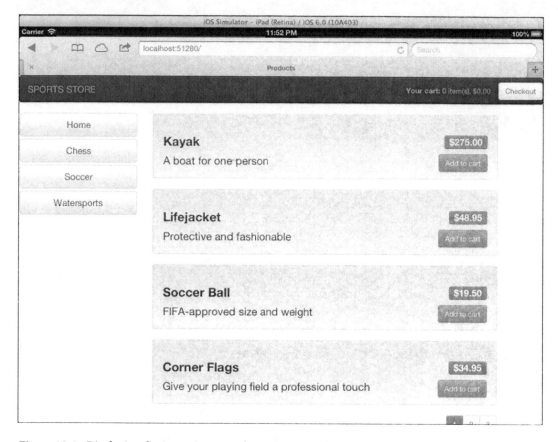

Figure 10-1. *Displaying the SportsStore application on a tablet*

It does pretty well. The only issue is that the pagination links are off the bottom of the page, which is easily adjusted by changing the page layout or changing the number of products that are displayed on a page.

■ **Note** The screenshots I show in this chapter are all obtained using browserstack.com, which is the cross-platform browser testing service I use for my own projects. It isn't a perfect service. It is often slow to use at peak times, can be fragile from outside of the US, and the mobile devices are emulated. I use it mainly for the desktop browser support, which is more robust, but I get decent results and I don't have to maintain my own set of emulators. You can get a free trial to follow the examples in this chapter and there are plenty of competitors out there if you want to go elsewhere. Note that I don't have any relationship with Browser Stack other than as a regular customer, for which I pay full price and receive no special treatment.

Using Responsive Design

The next strategy is to create content that adapts to the capabilities of the device on which it is being displayed, known as *responsive design*. The CSS standard has features that let you change the styling applied to elements based on the capabilities of the device, a technique that is most frequently used to alter the layout of content based on screen width.

Responsive design is something that is handled by the client using CSS and not directly managed by the MVC Framework. I go into the topic of responsive design in depth in my *Pro ASP.NET MVC 5 Client* book, but to give a demonstration how the technique can be applied (and some considerations that *do* touch on the MVC Framework), I am going to use some responsive features that are included in the Bootstrap library, which I have been using to style the SportsStore application (and which has become one of the libraries Microsoft includes in the MVC 5 project templates for Visual Studio 2013).

My goal will be to adjust the layout of the main part of the application so that it is visible on an iPhone. My "do nothing" strategy doesn't pay off for this kind of device because it has a narrow screen, as Figure 10-2 shows.

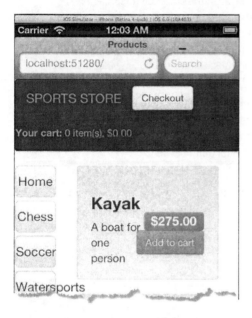

Figure 10-2. *Displaying the SportsStore application on a smartphone*

I am going to tackle this problem in sections, focusing on different aspects of the layout. My goal is to preserve all of the functionality of the application, but presented in a different way.

░ **Note**   The MVC Framework isn't an active participant in the responsive design. It sends all browsers the same content and lets them figure out which bits they need to display. This means that there is no sensible way to add unit tests for responsive design to a Visual Studio project. It is a technique that requires careful testing in the client and is difficult to automate.

Creating a Responsive Header

I am going to start with the page header, which contains the SportsStore name, the cart summary, and the Checkout button. Although the simplest solution would be to remove the SportsStore name and free up enough space for the rest of the content, I am going to keep it there (see the *Accepting the Realities of Branding* sidebar) and rearrange everything across two lines.

ACCEPTING THE REALITIES OF BRANDING

One of the easiest ways to free up screen real-estate is to remove your branding from the application. I am only displaying the SportsStore name as text, but you can see how much of the screen it occupies. What was a modest degree of branding on the desktop becomes a space hog on a smart phone.

Removing branding is difficult, however. Not for technical reasons, but because most branding teams are obsessed with slathering branding on everything. It is the reason that there are company-branded pens in the boardroom, company-branded cups in the break room, and why you get business cards with new logos every 18 months. Companies rebrand so often because people who work in branding know, deep down, that they don't have real jobs and the constant emphasis on logos and color schemes creates a frenzy of activity that distracts them from the creeping existential dread that haunts their every waking moment.

My advice is to accept that a certain amount of screen space will always be given over to branding, even on the smallest and least capable device. You might try to fight against the idea, but the branding team is usually part of the marketing department, marketing usually reports to the VP of Sales, and the VP of Sales has a hot line to the CEO because revenue is all that the board cares about. Some arguments just can't be won.

In Listing 10-1, you can see how I have adjusted the content of the header in the `_Layout.cshtml` file in the `SportsStore.WebUI` project.

Listing 10-1. Adding Responsive Content to the _Layout.cshtml File

```
<!DOCTYPE html>
<html>
<head>
    <meta charset="utf-8" />
    <meta name="viewport" content="width=device-width, initial-scale=1.0">
    <link href="~/Content/bootstrap.css" rel="stylesheet" />
    <link href="~/Content/bootstrap-theme.css" rel="stylesheet" />
    <link href="~/Content/ErrorStyles.css" rel="stylesheet" />
    <title>@ViewBag.Title</title>
    <style>
        .navbar-right {
            float: right !important;
            margin-right: 15px; margin-left: 15px;
        }
    </style>
</head>
<body>
    <div class="navbar navbar-inverse">
        <a class="navbar-brand" href="#">
            <span class="hidden-xs">SPORTS STORE</span>
```

```
            <div class="visible-xs">SPORTS</div>
            <div class="visible-xs">STORE</div>
        </a>
        @Html.Action("Summary", "Cart")
    </div>
    <div class="row panel">
        <div id="categories" class="col-xs-3">
            @Html.Action("Menu", "Nav")
        </div>
        <div class="col-xs-8">
            @RenderBody()
        </div>
    </div>
</body>
</html>
```

Bootstrap defines a set of classes that can be used to show or hide elements based on the width of the device screen. This is something you can do manually using CSS *media queries*, but the Bootstrap classes are integrated into the other styles.

For the SportsStore branding, I have used the visible-xs and hidden-xs classes to switch to text on two lines that will be shown vertically when the window size is below 768 pixels. Bootstrap provides pairs of classes that show and hide elements at different browser window sizes, the names of which start with visible- or hidden-. The *-xs classes (i.e., visible-xs and hidden-xs) are the ones I used in the example. The *-sm classes work on windows wider than 768 pixels, the *-md classes work on windows wider than 992 pixels, and the *-lg classes work on windows wider than 1200 pixels.

■ **Caution**   Responsive CSS features like the ones that Bootstrap provide are based on the size of the browser window, not the device screen. Mobile device browsers are usually displayed full-screen, which means that the window size and the screen size are the same, but you can't always rely on this being the case. As ever, you need to test against the devices you are targeting to ensure that you have not made assumptions that catch you out.

You can see the effect of these changes by starting the application and viewing the product listing in a regular desktop browser, which has the advantage of letting you change the size of the window. Make the window smaller (less than 786 pixels), and you will see the SportsStore text break into two lines, as illustrated by Figure 10-3.

Figure 10-3. *Using Bootstrap responsive design features to adjust the application branding*

This may seem like a small change but it has a big impact on smaller screens, especially when combined with the changes I made to the Views/Cart/Summary.cshtml file, which is the view that provides the summary of the cart and its contents. You can see the changes I made in Listing 10-2.

Listing 10-2. Adding Responsive Content to the Summary.cshtml File

```
@model SportsStore.Domain.Entities.Cart

<div class="navbar-right hidden-xs">
    @Html.ActionLink("Checkout", "Index", "Cart",
    new { returnUrl = Request.Url.PathAndQuery },
    new { @class = "btn btn-default navbar-btn" })
</div>

<div class="navbar-right visible-xs">
    <a href=@Url.Action("Index", "Cart", new { returnUrl = Request.Url.PathAndQuery })
        class="btn btn-default navbar-btn">
        <span class="glyphicon glyphicon-shopping-cart"></span>
    </a>
</div>

<div class="navbar-text navbar-right">
    <b class="hidden-xs">Your cart:</b>
    @Model.Lines.Sum(x => x.Quantity) item(s),
    @Model.ComputeTotalValue().ToString("c")
</div>
```

This is the same technique that I applied to the _Layout.cshtml file, where I selectively show and hide content. In this case, however, I hide the standard Checkout now button on small screens and replace it with an icon button, using one of the icons that is included in the Bootstrap package.

The Bootstrap icons are applied through a span element, which means that I can't use the Html.ActionLink helper method because it doesn't present me with the ability to set the contents of the element it creates. Instead, I define the a element directly and use the Url.Action helper method (which I describe properly in Chapter 23) to generate a URL for the href attribute. The result is an a element with the same attributes that would be created by the Html.ActionLink method, but that contains a span element. You can see the effect of the changes I made to both files in Figure 10-4, which shows the header content displayed on the iPhone.

Figure 10-4. The modified SportsStore header displayed on an iPhone simulator

---

MOBILE FIRST VERSUS DESKTOP FIRST

Most web application projects start with desktop clients and then add support for mobile clients, just as I am doing in this book. This is known as *desktop first* design/development and a common problem is that the server-side development has largely finished before work on the mobile client begins, resulting in an awkward mobile experience which is hacked out of features designed for more capable desktop clients.

There is an alternative philosophy called *mobile first* design/development which, as the name suggests, starts with the mobile client as the foundation for the application and adds features to take advantage of more capable desktop browsers.

Or to put it another way, desktop first tends to start with a full set of features and degrade gracefully for less capable devices, while mobile first tends to start with a smaller set of features that are gracefully enhanced for more capable devices.

Both approaches have their merits and I tend to favor desktop first development because it is easy to get desktop browsers to load content from a local development workstation, something that can be surprisingly hard when working with real mobile hardware. I tend to work on a tight cycle of write-compile-check (which means reloading URLs into the browser frequently), and I get frustrated with the hoops one has to go through to get the same cycle going on a mobile device.

The danger in putting any group of users first is that you create a substandard experience for another group, just moving the pain around. Proponents of mobile first design often argue that this can't happen when you start with the basic features and then scale up, but that has not been my experience.

It is important to have a solid plan for what functionality and layout you are going to deliver to *all* devices *before* you start developing for *any* of them. When you have such a plan, it doesn't matter what kind of device you begin with and, critically, the server-side parts of the application will be built from the ground up to support a full range of clients.

Creating a Responsive Product List

To complete my responsive adaptations, I need a product list that will display on narrow devices. The biggest problem that I have is caused by the horizontal space that is taken up by the category buttons. I am going to move the buttons out of the way, giving individual product descriptions the whole width of the display. In Listing 10-3, you can see that I have further modified the _Layout.cshtml file.

Listing 10-3. Creating a Responsive Product List in the _Layout.cshtml File

```
<!DOCTYPE html>
<html>
<head>
    <meta charset="utf-8" />
    <meta name="viewport" content="width=device-width, initial-scale=1.0">
    <link href="~/Content/bootstrap.css" rel="stylesheet" />
    <link href="~/Content/bootstrap-theme.css" rel="stylesheet" />
    <link href="~/Content/ErrorStyles.css" rel="stylesheet" />
    <title>@ViewBag.Title</title>
    <style>
```

```
            .navbar-right {
                float: right !important;
                margin-right: 15px; margin-left: 15px;
            }
        </style>
</head>
<body>
    <div class="navbar navbar-inverse">
        <a class="navbar-brand" href="#">
            <span class="hidden-xs">SPORTS STORE</span>
            <div class="visible-xs">SPORTS</div>
            <div class="visible-xs">STORE</div>
        </a>
        @Html.Action("Summary", "Cart")
    </div>
    <div class="row panel">
        <div class="col-sm-3 hidden-xs">
            @Html.Action("Menu", "Nav")
        </div>
        <div class="col-xs-12 col-sm-8">
            @RenderBody()
        </div>
    </div>
</body>
</html>
```

There can only be one call to the RenderBody method in a layout. I get into the details of layouts in Chapter 20, but the effect of this limit is that I can't have duplicate sets of elements that I show and hide, each containing a RenderBody call. Instead, I need to change the layout of the grid that contains the RenderBody method call so that the elements in the layout adapt around the content from the view.

One of the reasons that I used the Bootstrap grid to structure the content in the _Layout.cshtml file in Chapter 7 is that it includes some responsive design features that let me work around the RenderBody limitation. The Bootstrap grid layout supports 12 columns and you specify how many an element will occupy by applying a class, like this, which is how I applied the Bootstrap classes in Chapter 7:

```
...
<div class="col-xs-8">
    @RenderBody()
</div>
...
```

Much like the hidden-* and visible-* classes that I described earlier, Bootstrap provides a set of classes that set the number of columns that an element occupies in the grid based on the width of the window.

The col-xs-* classes are fixed and don't change based on the width of the screen. My use of the col-xs-8 class tells Bootstrap that the div element should span 8 of the 12 available columns and that the visibility of the element should not change based on the width of the window. The col-sm-* classes set the columns when the window is 768 pixels or wider, the col-md-* classes work on windows that are 992 pixels or wider and, finally, the col-lg-*

classes work on windows that are 1200 pixels or wider. With this in mind, here are the classes that I applied to the `div` element that surrounds the RenderBody method call from Listing 10-3:

```
...
<div class="col-xs-12 col-sm-8">
    @RenderBody()
</div>
...
```

The effect of applying both classes is that the `div` element will occupy all 12 columns in the grid by default and 8 columns when the screen is 768 pixels or wider. The other columns in the grid contain the category buttons, as follows:

```
...
<div class="col-sm-3 hidden-xs">
    @Html.Action("Menu", "Nav")
</div>
...
```

This element will occupy 3 columns when the screen is wider than 768 pixels and be hidden otherwise. Combined with the other classes I applied, the effect is that the product descriptions fill small windows and share the available space with the category buttons for larger windows. You can see both layouts in Figure 10-5. I used a desktop browser to for this figure because I am able to easily vary the width of the window.

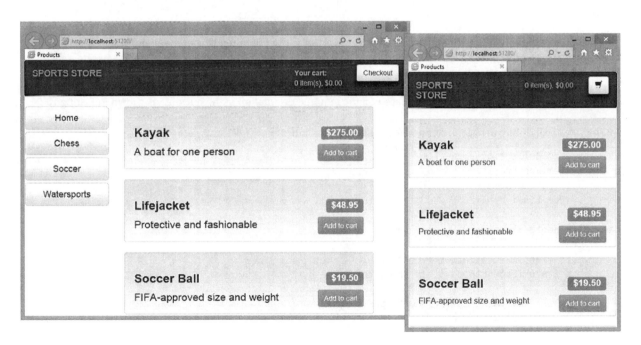

Figure 10-5. Using a responsive grid in the product layout

Helping the Controller Select a View

I don't want to leave mobile users without the ability to filter products, which means that I need to present the categories in a different way. To do this, I created a new view called MenuHorizontal.cshtml in the Views/Nav folder with the content shown in Listing 10-4.

Listing 10-4. The Contents of the MenuHorizontal.cshtml File

```
@model IEnumerable<string>

<div class="btn-group btn-group-sm btn-group-justified">
    @Html.ActionLink("Home", "List", "Product", new { @class = "btn btn-default btn-sm" })

    @foreach (var link in Model) {
        @Html.RouteLink(link, new {
            controller = "Product",
            action = "List",
            category = link,
            page = 1
        }, new {
            @class = "btn btn-default btn-sm"
                + (link == ViewBag.SelectedCategory ? " btn-primary" : ""))
        })
    }
</div>
```

This is a variation on the original Menu.cshtml layout, but with a container div element and some Bootstrap classes to create a horizontal layout of the buttons. The basic functionality, however, is the same. I generate a set of links which will filter the products by category.

The set of category buttons is generated through the Menu action method of the Nav controller, which I need to update so that it selects the right view file based on the required orientation of the buttons, as shown in Listing 10-5.

Listing 10-5. Updating the Menu Action Method in the NavController.cs File

```
using System.Collections.Generic;
using System.Web.Mvc;
using SportsStore.Domain.Abstract;
using System.Linq;

namespace SportsStore.WebUI.Controllers {

    public class NavController : Controller {
        private IProductRepository repository;

        public NavController(IProductRepository repo) {
            repository = repo;
        }

        public PartialViewResult Menu(string category = null,
            bool horizontalLayout = false) {

            ViewBag.SelectedCategory = category;
```

```
            IEnumerable<string> categories = repository.Products
                            .Select(x => x.Category)
                            .Distinct()
                            .OrderBy(x => x);

        string viewName = horizontalLayout ? "MenuHorizontal" : "Menu";
        return PartialView(viewName, categories);
        }
    }
}
```

I have defined a new parameter for the action method that specifies the orientation, which I use to select the name of the view file passed to the PartialView method. To set the value of this parameter, I need to return to the _Layout.cshtml file, as shown in Listing 10-6.

Listing 10-6. Updating the _Layout.cshtml File to Include the Horizontal Buttons

```
...
<body>
    <div class="navbar navbar-inverse">
        <a class="navbar-brand" href="#">
            <span class="hidden-xs">SPORTS STORE</span>
            <div class="visible-xs">SPORTS</div>
            <div class="visible-xs">STORE</div>
        </a>
        @Html.Action("Summary", "Cart")
    </div>
    <div class="visible-xs">
        @Html.Action("Menu", "Nav", new { horizontalLayout = true })
    </div>
    <div class="row panel">
        <div class="col-sm-3 hidden-xs">
            @Html.Action("Menu", "Nav")
        </div>
        <div class="col-xs-12 col-sm-8">
            @RenderBody()
            </div>
    </div>
</body>
...
```

The optional third argument to the Html.Action method is an object that lets me set values for the routing system, which I explain in Chapters 15 and 16. I use this feature to signal which view the controller should select. The overall effect of these changes is shown in Figure 10-6.

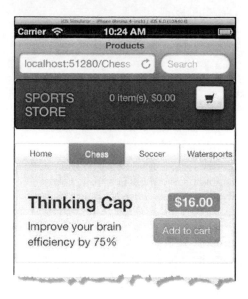

Figure 10-6. *The revised product listing for small screens*

You can see that moving the buttons to the top of the product listing creates enough space for each product to be displayed properly. I could continue improving the fit and finish of the views, but you get the idea. Aside from a brief demonstration of how responsive CSS classes can be used, I wanted to touch upon some of the limitations that the MVC Framework imposes (such as the RenderBody method limit) and some of the facilities it can provide to assist generating content in different ways (such as passing data from a view to a controller via the routing system and the Html.Action helper method).

■ **Tip**   I have focused on one orientation for the iPhone, but don't forget that most mobile devices allow for multiple orientations and that you will have to cater for them all in a real project.

Removing View Duplication

In the previous example, I wanted to show you how you can have a controller select a view based on routing information passed by a call to the Html.Action helper method. It is an important and useful feature, but I would not have used it in a real project because it leaves me with two views, Menu.cshtml and MenuHorizontal.cshtml, that contain largely similar markup and Razor expressions. This is a maintenance risk because any changes that I require to the category filter buttons will have to be applied in two places. To resolve this I am going to consolidate the views. I created a new view file called FlexMenu.cshtml in the Views/Nav folder with the content shown in Listing 10-7.

Listing 10-7. The Contents of the FlexMenu.cshtml File

```
@model IEnumerable<string>

@{
bool horizontal = ((bool)(ViewContext.RouteData.Values["horizontalLayout"] ?? false));
string wrapperClasses = horizontal ? "btn-group btn-group-sm btn-group-justified" : null;
}
```

```
<div class="@wrapperClasses">

    @Html.ActionLink("Home", "List", "Product",
    new { @class =  horizontal ? "btn btn-default btn-sm" :
        "btn btn-block btn-default btn-lg"
     })

    @foreach (var link in Model) {
        @Html.RouteLink(link, new {
            controller = "Product",
            action = "List",
            category = link,
            page = 1
        }, new {
            @class = (horizontal ? "btn btn-default btn-sm"
                : "btn btn-block btn-default btn-lg" )
                + (link == ViewBag.SelectedCategory ? " btn-primary" : "")
        })
    }

</div>
```

The cost of removing duplication is a more complex view that can generate both orientations of buttons and it is a matter of personal preference as to which approach you take. If you are like me and prefer to avoid duplication, then this listing shows several useful features you can apply to views.

The first is the ability to access routing information directly from the view. The ViewContext property provides information about the current state of the request that is being processed, including details of the routing information, as follows:

```
...
bool horizontal = ((bool)(ViewContext.RouteData.Values["horizontalLayout"] ?? false));
...
```

The second feature is the ability to create local variables within a view. This is possible because of the way that Razor views are compiled into classes (which I describe in Chapter 20), and I have created a local variable called horizontal that means I don't have to check the route data throughout the listing to figure out which orientation the view is being used for.

■ **Caution** Local variables should be used sparingly because it is the slippery slope into creating views that are hard to maintain and hard to test, but I sometimes use them in situations like this where I see them as an acceptable cost of simplifying a view.

A related feature is the way that Razor will conditionally set attributes based on variables. I defined a string of class names as a local variable in the view like this:

```
...
string wrapperClasses = horizontal ? "btn-group btn-group-sm btn-group-justified" : null;
...
```

The value of the `wrapperClasses` variable is either the string of class names that I used for horizontal layouts or `null`. I apply this variable to the class attribute like this:

```
...
<div class="@wrapperClasses">
...
```

When the variable is `null`, Razor is smart enough to remove the `class` attribute from the `div` element entirely, generating an element like this:

```
<div>
```

When the variable is not `null`, Razor will insert the value and leave the `class` attribute intact, producing a result like this:

```
<div class="btn-group btn-group-sm btn-group-justified">
```

This is a nice way of matching the characteristics of the C# with the semantics of HTML and is a feature that is endlessly useful when writing complex views because it won't insert `null` values into attributes and it won't generate empty attributes, which can cause problems with CSS selectors (and JavaScript libraries that use attributes to select elements, such as jQuery).

■ **Tip** Conditional attributes will work on any variable, not just the ones you have defined in the view. This means that you can apply this feature to model properties and the view bag.

To use my consolidate view, I need to revise the `Menu` action method in the `Nav` controller, as shown in Listing 10-8.

Listing 10-8. Updating the Menu Action in the NavController.cs File

```
...
public PartialViewResult Menu(string category = null) {

    ViewBag.SelectedCategory = category;

    IEnumerable<string> categories = repository.Products
                    .Select(x => x.Category)
                    .Distinct()
                    .OrderBy(x => x);

    return PartialView("FlexMenu", categories);
}
...
```

I removed the parameter that receives the orientation and changed the call to the `PartialView` method so that the FlexMenu view is always selected. The result of these changes doesn't alter the layout of the content or the effect of the responsive design, but it does remove the duplication in the views and means that you can delete the `Menu.cshtml` and `MenuHorizontal.cshtml` views from the Visual Studio project. Both orientations of category filter button are now produced by the `FlexMenu.cshtml` view.

THE LIMITATIONS OF RESPONSIVE DESIGN

There are some problems with responsive design as a way to support mobile clients. The first is that you end up duplicating a lot of content and sending it to the server so that it can be displayed in different scenarios. You saw this in the previous section when the HTML generated by the layout contained multiple sets of elements for the page header and the category filter buttons. The extra elements don't amount to much on a per-request basis, but the overall effect for a busy application is a sharp increase in the amount of bandwidth you will need to provision, with the corresponding increase in running costs.

The second problem is that responsive design can be fiddly and it requires endless testing to get right. Not all devices handle the underlying CSS features that enable responsive design (known as *media queries*) properly and, unless you are thorough and careful, you will end up with an application that delivers an adequate experience on every device without excelling on any of them, a kind of blandness that comes from averaging out all of the device quirks.

Responsive design can be useful when applied thoughtfully, but it can easily result in an application that is riddled with compromises that don't deliver a good experience for any of your target users.

Creating Mobile Specific Content

Responsive design delivers the same content to all devices and uses CSS to figure out how that content should be presented, a process that doesn't involve the server-side part of the application and which assumes that you want to treat all devices as being variations on the same basic theme. An alternative approach is to use the server to assess the capabilities of the client browser and send different HTML to different kinds of client. This works well if you want to present a completely different aspect of the application on the desktop to, say, a tablet.

■ **Tip**   You don't have to choose between responsive design and mobile-specific content and, in most projects, you'll need to use both to get a good result on the devices you target. As an example, you may decide to create content specifically for tablets and use responsive design to create the horizontal and vertical orientations that most tablets support.

The MVC Framework supports a feature called *display modes*, which allows you to create different views that are delivered based on the client that has made the request, a feature provided by the ASP.NET Framework. I explain how you can create and manage display modes in depth in my *Pro ASP.NET MVC 5 Platform* book, but for the SportsStore application, I am going to use the simplest form of display modes, which is to treat all mobile devices as being the same. My goal will be to deliver an experience to mobile devices using the popular jQuery Mobile library, while keeping the existing content for desktop devices.

■ **Tip**   I am not going to go into any detail about jQuery Mobile in this book, other than to demonstrate how it can be used to deliver mobile-specific content. For full details of jQuery Mobile, see my *Pro jQuery 2.0* book, published by Apress.

Creating a Mobile Layout

All I have to do to create mobile-specific content is to create views and layouts that have a `.Mobile.cshtml` suffix. I created a new layout called `_Layout.Mobile.cshtml` in the Views/Shared folder with the content shown in Listing 10-9.

■ **Tip** Because the name of the view contains an additional period, you will need to create the view by right-clicking the Shared folder and selecting Add ➤ MVC 5 Layout Page (Razor) from the pop-up menu.

Listing 10-9. The Contents of the _Layout.Mobile.cshtml File

```
<!DOCTYPE html>
<html>
<head>
    <meta charset="utf-8" />
    <meta name="viewport" content="width=device-width, initial-scale=1.0">
    <link rel="stylesheet"
        href="http://code.jquery.com/mobile/1.3.2/jquery.mobile-1.3.2.min.css" />
    <script src="http://code.jquery.com/jquery-1.9.1.min.js"></script>
    <script
        src="http://code.jquery.com/mobile/1.3.2/jquery.mobile-1.3.2.min.js"></script>
    <title>@ViewBag.Title</title>
</head>
<body>
    <div data-role="page" id="page1">
        <div data-theme="a" data-role="header" data-position="fixed">
            <h3>SportsStore</h3>
            @Html.Action("Menu", "Nav")
        </div>
        <div data-role="content">
            <ul data-role="listview" data-divider-theme="b" data-inset="false">
                @RenderBody()
            </ul>
        </div>
    </div>
</body>
</html>
```

This layout uses jQuery Mobile, which I obtain using a content delivery network (CDN) so that I don't have to install a NuGet package for the JavaScript and CSS files I need.

■ **Tip** I am just scratching the surface by creating mobile-specific views, because I am using the same controllers and action methods that are used for desktop clients. Having separate views allows you to introduce different controllers, which are particular to a set of clients, and this can be used to create totally different features and functionality for different types of client.

The MVC Framework will automatically identify mobile clients and use the _Layout.Mobile.cshtml file when it is rendering views, seamlessly replacing the _Layout.cshtml file which is used for other clients. You can see the impact of the change in Figure 10-7.

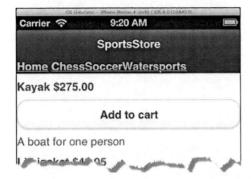

Figure 10-7. *The effect of creating a mobile layout in the SportsStore application*

You can see that the layout is different, but the overall effect is a mess, and that's because I need to create mobile versions of the main view that is handling the request and the partial view that is used for the category filtering buttons.

Creating the Mobile Views

I am going to start with the category filtering, which means creating a view called FlexMenu.Mobile.cshtml in the Views/Nav folder with the content shown in Listing 10-10.

Listing 10-10. The Contents of the FlexMenu.Mobile.html File

```
@model IEnumerable<string>

<div data-role="navbar">
    <ul>
        @foreach (var link in Model) {
            <li>
                @Html.RouteLink(link, new {
                    controller = "Product",
                    action = "List",
                    category = link,
                    page = 1
                }, new {
                    data_transition = "fade",
                    @class = (link == ViewBag.SelectedCategory
                        ? "ui-btn-active" : null)
                })
            </li>
        }
    </ul>
</div>
```

This view uses a Razor foreach expression to generate li elements for the product categories, producing elements that are organized in the way that jQuery Mobile expects for a navigation bar at the top of the page. You can see the effect in Figure 10-8.

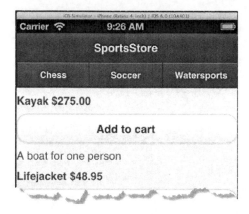

Figure 10-8. *The effect of creating a mobile-specific view*

■ **Tip** jQuery Mobile relies on the use of data attributes to format elements. Data attributes are prefixed with data- and were an unofficial way of defining custom attributes for years before becoming an official part of the HTML5 standard. In the listing, I needed to add a data-transition attribute to the li elements, but I can't use data-transition as the property name for the anonymous object because this would be a C# expression. The problem is the hyphen and Razor works around this by translating underscores in the property names to hyphens in attribute names, such that I was able to use data_transition in the listing and get a data-transition attribute on the elements I generate.

The product information is still a mess, but the category buttons are now being generated by the new mobile-specific view. It is worth taking a moment to reflect on what the MVC Framework is doing to render the content in Figure 10-8.

The HTTP request from the browser targets the List action method in the Product controller, which tells the MVC Framework to render the List.cshtml view file. The MVC Framework knows that the request came from a mobile browser and so it starts looking for mobile-specific views. There is no List.Mobile.cshtml, and so the List.cshtml file is processed instead. This view relies on the _Layout.cshtml file, but the MVC Framework notices that there is a mobile-specific version available and so it uses _Layout.Mobile.cshtml instead. The layout requires the FlexMobile.cshtml file but there is a mobile version of that as well, and so on.

The result is that the response to the browser is generated from a mix of mobile-specific and general views, with the MVC Framework using the most specific view file available, but seamlessly falling back when needed.

THE TWO PROBLEMS IN THE EXAMPLE

The example in this chapter is intended to demonstrate the way that the MVC Framework can deliver mobile-specific content, but I would be remiss if I didn't point out two potentially serious problems that this example introduces to the SportsStore application.

The first is that I have provided less functionality in my mobile views than in the desktop ones. There is no cart summary in the page header, for example. I left some features out to simplify the changes I had to make, but I recommend against delivering reduced functionality to *any* device unless there is a technical limitation that prevents the device from being able to support it. Mobile devices are increasingly capable and many users will only access your application with a mobile browser. The days when you could assume that mobile access was a supplement to desktop use have passed.

The second problem is that I have not offered the user the chance to switch back to the desktop layout. Don't underestimate the number of users that would prefer to have the desktop layout on a mobile device, even though it might be a little awkward and require some zooming and scrolling on smaller screens. Some mobile devices allow larger monitors to be connected, for example, and this is rarely detected by the mechanism that the ASP.NET Framework uses to identify mobile devices. You should always give mobile users the choice about which layout they receive.

Neither of these issues prevents me from deploying my application, but they are the kind of frustration that plagues mobile web application users. Mobile devices will be a big part of any modern web application and you should take every precaution to deliver a good user experience to this important category of users.

My last change is to create a mobile-specific version of the view that generates the product summary. I created a view file called `ProductSummary.Mobile.cshtml` in the `Views/Shared` folder with the contents shown in Listing 10-11.

Listing 10-11. The Contents of the ProductSummary.Mobile.cshtml File

```
@model SportsStore.Domain.Entities.Product

<div data-role="collapsible" data-collapsed="false" data-content-theme="c">
    <h2>
        @Model.Name
    </h2>
    <div class="ui-grid-b">
        <div class="ui-block-a">
            @Model.Description
        </div>
        <div class="ui-block-b">
            <strong>(@Model.Price.ToString("c"))</strong>
        </div>
        <div class="ui-block-c">
            @using (Html.BeginForm("AddToCart", "Cart")) {
                @Html.HiddenFor(x => x.ProductID)
                @Html.Hidden("returnUrl", Request.Url.PathAndQuery)
                <input type="submit" data-inline="true"
                        data-mini="true" value="Add to cart" />
            }
        </div>
    </div>
</div>
```

This view uses a jQuery Mobile widget that allows users to open and collapse regions of content. It isn't an ideal way of presenting product information, but it is simple and my emphasis in this section is on mobile-specific content rather than the jQuery Mobile library. You can see the effect of this new view in Figure 10-9.

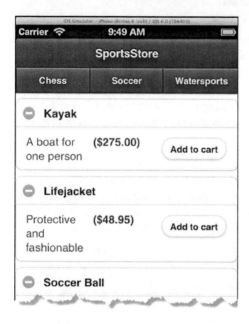

Figure 10-9. *The effect of mobile-specific views*

In a real project, I would carry on, of course, and create mobile-specific versions of the views that display the pagination links, the shopping cart and the checkout form. I am not going to because you have already seen how the MVC Framework lets you target mobile devices.

Summary

In this chapter I have shown you two techniques for handling mobile devices: responsive design and mobile-specific content. Responsive design isn't directly related to the MVC Framework, which sends the same content to all browsers and lets them figure out what to do with it. But as I demonstrated, there are some limitations in the way that views work that require careful thought and some nice Razor features that can ease the overall process.

Creating mobile-specific content is something that the MVC Framework does actively participate in by automatically applying mobile-specific views and layouts if they are available and blending them seamlessly into the process that renders HTML for the clients. In the next chapter, I add the basic features required to administer the SportsStore product catalog.

CHAPTER 11

■ ■ ■

SportsStore: Administration

In this chapter, I continue to build the SportsStore application in order to give the site administrator a way of managing the product catalog. I will add support for creating, editing, and removing items from the product repository, as well as for uploading and displaying images alongside products in the catalog.

Adding Catalog Management

The convention for managing collections of items is to present the user with two types of pages: a *list* page and an *edit* page, as shown in Figure 11-1.

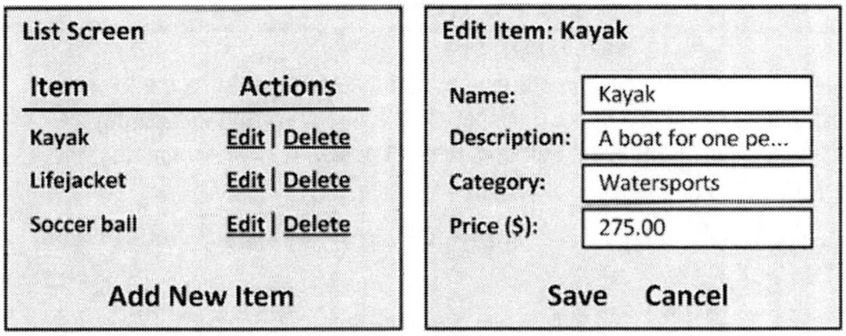

Figure 11-1. *Sketch of a CRUD UI for the product catalog*

Together, these pages allow a user to create, read, update, and delete items in the collection. Collectively, these actions are known as *CRUD*. Developers need to implement CRUD so often that Visual Studio tries to help by offering to generate MVC controllers that have action methods for CRUD operations and view templates that support them. But like all of the Visual Studio templates, I think it is better to learn how to use the features of the MVC Framework directly.

Creating a CRUD Controller

I am going to create a new controller for the SportsStore administration features. Right-click on the Controllers folder for the SportsStore.WebUI project in the Solution Explorer and select Add ➤ Controller from the pop-up menu. Select MVC 5 Controller - Empty from the list of options, click the Add button, set the name to AdminController and click the Add button to create the Controllers/AdminController.cs file. Edit the contents of the controller class to match Listing 11-1.

Listing 11-1. *The Contents of the AdminController.cs File*

```
using System.Web.Mvc;
using SportsStore.Domain.Abstract;

namespace SportsStore.WebUI.Controllers {

    public class AdminController : Controller {
        private IProductRepository repository;

        public AdminController(IProductRepository repo) {
            repository = repo;
        }

        public ViewResult Index() {
            return View(repository.Products);
        }
    }
}
```

The controller constructor declares a dependency on the IProductRepository interface, which Ninject will resolve when instances are created. The controller defines a single action method, Index, that calls the View method to select the default view for the action, passing the set of products in the database as the view model.

UNIT TEST: THE INDEX ACTION

The behavior that I care about for the Index method of the Admin controller is that it correctly returns the Product objects that are in the repository. I can test this by creating a mock repository implementation and comparing the test data with the data returned by the action method. Here is the unit test, which I placed into a new unit test file called AdminTests.cs in the SportsStore.UnitTests project:

```
using Microsoft.VisualStudio.TestTools.UnitTesting;
using Moq;
using SportsStore.Domain.Abstract;
using SportsStore.Domain.Entities;
using SportsStore.WebUI.Controllers;
using System;
using System.Collections.Generic;
using System.Linq;
using System.Web.Mvc;

namespace SportsStore.UnitTests {
    [TestClass]
    public class AdminTests {

        [TestMethod]
        public void Index_Contains_All_Products() {
            // Arrange - create the mock repository
            Mock<IProductRepository> mock = new Mock<IProductRepository>();
            mock.Setup(m => m.Products).Returns(new Product[] {
```

```
                new Product {ProductID = 1, Name = "P1"},
                new Product {ProductID = 2, Name = "P2"},
                new Product {ProductID = 3, Name = "P3"},
            });

            // Arrange - create a controller
            AdminController target = new AdminController(mock.Object);

            // Action
            Product[] result = ((IEnumerable<Product>)target.Index().
                ViewData.Model).ToArray();

            // Assert
            Assert.AreEqual(result.Length, 3);
            Assert.AreEqual("P1", result[0].Name);
            Assert.AreEqual("P2", result[1].Name);
            Assert.AreEqual("P3", result[2].Name);
        }
    }
}
```

Creating a New Layout

I am going to create a new layout to use with the SportsStore administration views. It will be a simple layout that provides a single point where I can apply changes to all the administration views.

Create the new layout, by right-clicking the Views/Shared folder in the SportsStore.WebUI project and select Add > MVC 5 Layout Page (Razor) from the pop-up menu. Set the name to _AdminLayout.cshtml (don't forget the underscore) and click the OK button to create the Views/Shared/_AdminLayout.cshtml file. Set the contents of the new view to match Listing 11-2.

■ **Note** As I explained previously, the convention is to start the layout name with an underscore (_). Razor is also used by another Microsoft technology called WebMatrix, which uses the underscore to prevent layout pages from being served to browsers. MVC does not need this protection, but the convention for naming layouts is carried over to MVC applications anyway.

Listing 11-2. The Contents of the _AdminLayout.cshtml File

```
@{
    Layout = null;
}

<!DOCTYPE html>

<html>
<head>
```

```
    <meta name="viewport" content="width=device-width" />
    <link href="~/Content/bootstrap.css" rel="stylesheet" />
    <link href="~/Content/bootstrap-theme.css" rel="stylesheet" />
    <link href="~/Content/ErrorStyles.css" rel="stylesheet" />
    <title></title>
</head>
<body>
    <div>
        @RenderBody()
    </div>
</body>
</html>
```

I have added a call to the RenderBody method, so that the contents of the view that the layout is being used for will be inserted into the response to the server. (I would not have had to do this if I had used the Add ➤ New Item menu option and used the Visual Studio layout template, but I took a shortcut to create the view directly, which meant I had to edit the new file to get the content I require.) I also added link elements for the Bootstrap files and for the CSS file that contains the styles I created to highlight validation errors to the user.

Implementing the List View

Now that I have the new layout, I can add a view to the project for the Index action method of the Admin controller. Even though I am not a fan of the Visual Studio scaffold and template features, I am going to create the view for the Index method using the scaffold system so you can see how it works. Just because I don't like pre-cut code, doesn't mean that you shouldn't use it.

Right-click on the Views/Admin folder in the SportsStore.WebUI project and select Add ➤ View from the menu. Set View Name to Index, select the List for the Template option (this is where I usually select one of the Empty options), select Product as the Model Class, check the option to use a layout page, and select the _AdminLayout. cshtml file from the Views/Shared folder. You can see all of the configuration options in Figure 11-2.

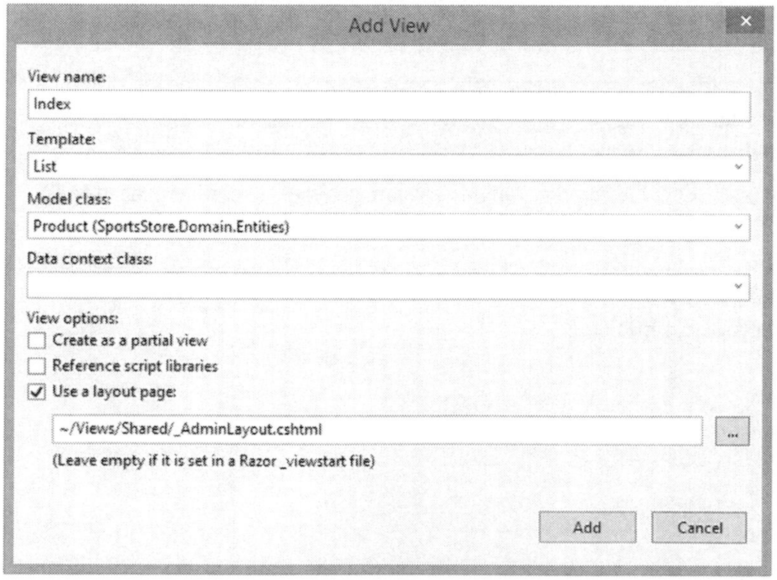

Figure 11-2. Configuring a scaffold view

■ **Note**   When using the List scaffold, Visual Studio assumes you are working with an IEnumerable sequence of the model view type, so you can just select the singular form of the class from the list.

Click the Add button to create the new view, which will have the contents shown in Listing 11-3. (I have formatted the markup so that it doesn't require so much space on the page.)

Listing 11-3. The Contents of the Views/Admin/Index.cshtml File

```
@model IEnumerable<SportsStore.Domain.Entities.Product>

@{
    ViewBag.Title = "Index";
    Layout = "~/Views/Shared/_AdminLayout.cshtml";
}

<h2>Index</h2>
<p>
    @Html.ActionLink("Create New", "Create")
</p>
<table class="table">
    <tr>
        <th>@Html.DisplayNameFor(model => model.Name)</th>
        <th>@Html.DisplayNameFor(model => model.Description)</th>
        <th>@Html.DisplayNameFor(model => model.Price)</th>
        <th>@Html.DisplayNameFor(model => model.Category)</th>
        <th></th>
    </tr>

@foreach (var item in Model) {
    <tr>
        <td>@Html.DisplayFor(modelItem => item.Name)</td>
        <td>@Html.DisplayFor(modelItem => item.Description)</td>
        <td>@Html.DisplayFor(modelItem => item.Price)</td>
        <td>@Html.DisplayFor(modelItem => item.Category)</td>
        <td>
            @Html.ActionLink("Edit", "Edit", new { id=item.ProductID }) |
            @Html.ActionLink("Details", "Details", new { id=item.ProductID }) |
            @Html.ActionLink("Delete", "Delete", new { id=item.ProductID })
        </td>
    </tr>
}

</table>
```

Visual Studio looks at the type of view model object and generates elements in a table that correspond to the properties defined by the model type. You can see how this view is rendered by starting the application and navigating to the /Admin/Index URL. Figure 11-3 shows the results.

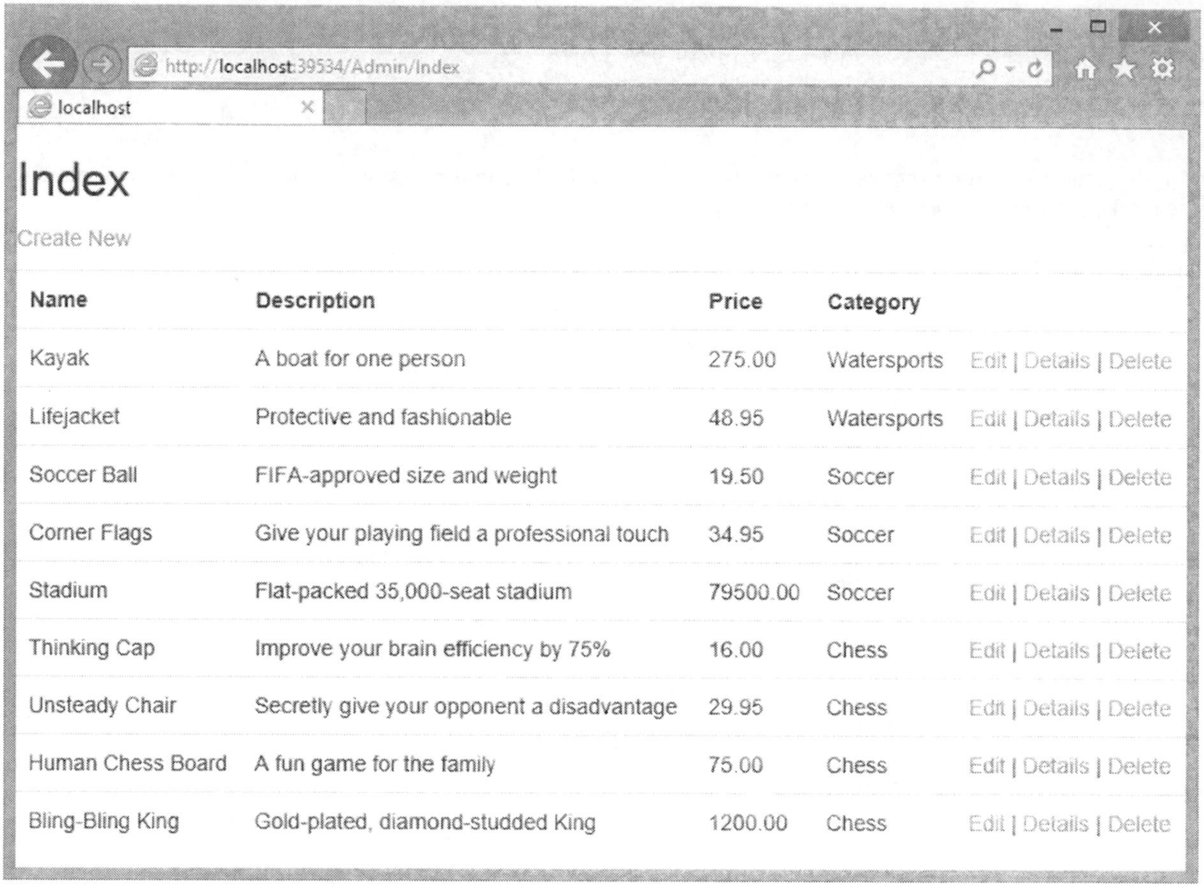

Figure 11-3. *Rendering the scaffold List view*

The scaffold view makes a reasonable attempt at setting up a sensible baseline for the view. I have columns for each of the properties in the `Product` class and links for the other CRUD operations that target action methods in the `Admin` controller (although, since I created that controller without using scaffolding, the action methods do not exist).

The scaffolding is clever, but the views that it generates are bland and so general as to be worthless in a project of any complexity. My advice is to start with empty controllers, views and layouts and add the functionality you need as and when you need it.

Returning to the do-it-yourself approach, edit the `Index.cshtml` file so that it corresponds to Listing 11-4.

Listing 11-4. Modifying the Index.cshtml View

```
@model IEnumerable<SportsStore.Domain.Entities.Product>

@{
    ViewBag.Title = "Admin: All Products";
    Layout = "~/Views/Shared/_AdminLayout.cshtml";
}
```

```
<div class="panel panel-default">

    <div class="panel-heading">
        <h3>All Products</h3>
    </div>
    <div class="panel-body">
        <table class="table table-striped table-condensed table-bordered">
            <tr>
                <th class="text-right">ID</th>
                <th>Name</th>
                <th class="text-right">Price</th>
                <th class="text-center">Actions</th>
            </tr>
            @foreach (var item in Model) {
                <tr>
                    <td class="text-right">@item.ProductID</td>
                    <td>@Html.ActionLink(item.Name, "Edit", new { item.ProductID })</td>
                    <td class="text-right">@item.Price.ToString("c")</td>
                    <td class="text-center">
                        @using (Html.BeginForm("Delete", "Admin")) {
                            @Html.Hidden("ProductID", item.ProductID)
                            <input type="submit"
                                    class="btn btn-default btn-xs"
                                    value="Delete" />
                        }
                    </td>
                </tr>
            }
        </table>
    </div>
    <div class="panel-footer">
        @Html.ActionLink("Add a new product", "Create", null,
            new { @class = "btn btn-default" })
    </div>
</div>
```

This view presents the information in a more compact form, omitting some of the properties from the Product class and using Bootstrap to apply styling. You can see how this view renders in Figure 11-4.

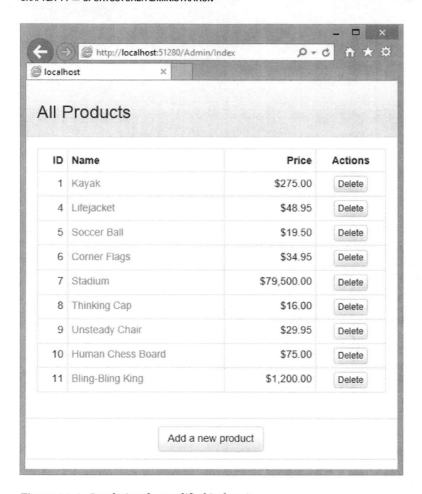

Figure 11-4. *Rendering the modified Index view*

Now I have a nice list page. The administrator can see the products in the catalog and there are links or buttons to add, delete, and inspect items. In the following sections, I will add the functionality to support each of these actions.

Editing Products

To provide create and update features, I will add a product-editing page similar to the one shown in Figure 11-1. There are two parts to this job:

- Display a page that will allow the administrator to change values for the properties of a product

- Add an action method that can process those changes when they are submitted

Creating the Edit Action Method

Listing 11-5 shows the Edit method I added to the Admin controller. This is the action method I specified in the calls to the Html.ActionLink helper method in the Index view.

Listing 11-5. Adding the Edit Action Method in the AdminController.cs File

```
using System.Linq;
using System.Web.Mvc;
using SportsStore.Domain.Abstract;
using SportsStore.Domain.Entities;

namespace SportsStore.WebUI.Controllers {

    public class AdminController : Controller {
        private IProductRepository repository;

        public AdminController(IProductRepository repo) {
            repository = repo;
        }

        public ViewResult Index() {
            return View(repository.Products);
        }

        public ViewResult Edit(int productId) {
            Product product = repository.Products
                .FirstOrDefault(p => p.ProductID == productId);
            return View(product);
        }
    }
}
```

This simple method finds the product with the ID that corresponds to the productId parameter and passes it as a view model object to the View method.

UNIT TEST: THE EDIT ACTION METHOD

I want to test for two behaviors in the Edit action method. The first is that I get the product I ask for when I provide a valid ID value. Obviously, I want to make sure that I am editing the product I expected. The second behavior is that I do not get any product at all when I request an ID value that is not in the repository. Here are the test methods I added to the AdminTests.cs unit test file:

```
...
[TestMethod]
public void Can_Edit_Product() {

    // Arrange - create the mock repository
    Mock<IProductRepository> mock = new Mock<IProductRepository>();
    mock.Setup(m => m.Products).Returns(new Product[] {
        new Product {ProductID = 1, Name = "P1"},
        new Product {ProductID = 2, Name = "P2"},
        new Product {ProductID = 3, Name = "P3"},
    });
```

```
        // Arrange - create the controller
        AdminController target = new AdminController(mock.Object);

        // Act
        Product p1 = target.Edit(1).ViewData.Model as Product;
        Product p2 = target.Edit(2).ViewData.Model as Product;
        Product p3 = target.Edit(3).ViewData.Model as Product;

        // Assert
        Assert.AreEqual(1, p1.ProductID);
        Assert.AreEqual(2, p2.ProductID);
        Assert.AreEqual(3, p3.ProductID);
    }

    [TestMethod]
    public void Cannot_Edit_Nonexistent_Product() {

        // Arrange - create the mock repository
        Mock<IProductRepository> mock = new Mock<IProductRepository>();
        mock.Setup(m => m.Products).Returns(new Product[] {
            new Product {ProductID = 1, Name = "P1"},
            new Product {ProductID = 2, Name = "P2"},
            new Product {ProductID = 3, Name = "P3"},
        });

        // Arrange - create the controller
        AdminController target = new AdminController(mock.Object);

        // Act
        Product result = (Product)target.Edit(4).ViewData.Model;

        // Assert
        Assert.IsNull(result);
    }
    ...
```

Creating the Edit View

Now that I have an action method, I can create a view for it to render. Right-click on the Views/Admin folder in the Solution Explorer and select Add ➤ MVC 5 View Page (Razor) from the menu. Set the name to Edit.cshtml, click the button to create the file and edit the contents to match Listing 11-6.

Listing 11-6. The Contents of the Edit .cshtml File

```
@model SportsStore.Domain.Entities.Product

@{
    ViewBag.Title = "Admin: Edit " + @Model.Name;
    Layout = "~/Views/Shared/_AdminLayout.cshtml";
}
```

```
<h1>Edit @Model.Name</h1>

@using (Html.BeginForm()) {
    @Html.EditorForModel()
    <input type="submit" value="Save" />
    @Html.ActionLink("Cancel and return to List", "Index")
}
```

Instead of writing out markup for each of the labels and inputs by hand, I have called the `Html.EditorForModel` helper method. This method asks the MVC Framework to create the editing interface for me, which it does by inspecting the model type—in this case, the `Product` class. To see the page that is generated from the `Edit` view, run the application and navigate to `/Admin/Index`. Click one of the product name links, and you will see the page shown in Figure 11-5.

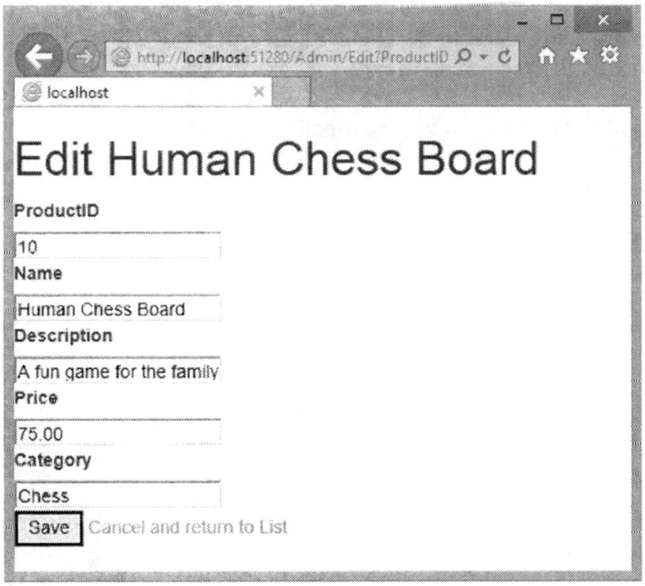

Figure 11-5. *The page generated using the EditorForModel helper method*

Let's be honest: the `EditorForModel` method is convenient, but it does not produce the most attractive results. In addition, I do not want the administrator to be able to see or edit the `ProductID` attribute, and the text box for the `Description` property is far too small.

I can give the MVC Framework directions about how to create editors for properties by using *model metadata*. This allows me to apply attributes to the properties of the new model class to influence the output of the `Html.EditorForModel` method. Listing 11-7 shows how to use metadata on the `Product` class in the `SportsStore.Domain` project.

Listing 11-7. Using Model Metadata in the Product.cs File

```
using System.ComponentModel.DataAnnotations;
using System.Web.Mvc;

namespace SportsStore.Domain.Entities {
```

```
    public class Product {

        [HiddenInput(DisplayValue = false)]
        public int ProductID { get; set; }
        public string Name { get; set; }

        [DataType(DataType.MultilineText)]
        public string Description { get; set; }
        public decimal Price { get; set; }
        public string Category { get; set; }
    }
}
```

The HiddenInput attribute tells the MVC Framework to render the property as a hidden form element, and the DataType attribute allows me to specify how a value is presented and edited. In this case, I have selected the MultilineText option. The HiddenInput attribute is part of the System.Web.Mvc namespace and the DataType attribute is part of the System.ComponentModel.DataAnnotations namespace, which is why I had you add references to the assemblies for these namespace to the SportsStore.Domain project in Chapter 7.

Figure 11-6 shows the Edit page once the metadata has been applied. You can no longer see or edit the ProductId property, and there is a multiline text box for entering the description. However, the overall appearance is poor.

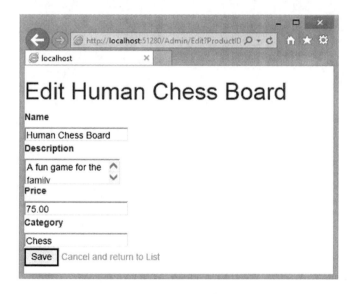

Figure 11-6. *The effect of applying metadata*

The problem is that the Html.EditorForModel helper doesn't know anything about the Product class and generates some basic and safe HTML. There are three ways we can deal with this. The first is to define CSS styles for the content that the helper generates, which is made easier by the classes that are automatically added to the HTML elements by the MVC Framework.

If you look at the source for the page shown in Figure 11-6, you will see that the textarea element that has been created for the product description has been assigned to the text-box-multi-line CSS class:

```
<textarea class="text-box-multi-line" id="Description" name="Description">
```

Other HTML elements are assigned similar classes and you can create CSS styles for each of them. This approach works well when you are creating custom styles, but doesn't make it easy to apply predefined classes like the ones that Bootstrap defines.

The second approach is to provide the helper with templates that it can use to generate the elements, including the styling that we require. I show you how to do this in Chapter 22.

The third approach is to create the elements needed directly, without using the model-level helper method. I like the idea of the model helper, but I rarely use it, preferring to create the HTML myself and use helpers on the individual properties, as shown in Listing 11-8.

Listing 11-8. Updating the Edit.cshtml File

```
@model SportsStore.Domain.Entities.Product

@{
    ViewBag.Title = "Admin: Edit " + @Model.Name;
    Layout = "~/Views/Shared/_AdminLayout.cshtml";
}

<div class="panel">
    <div class="panel-heading">
        <h3>Edit @Model.Name</h3>
    </div>

    @using (Html.BeginForm()) {
        <div class="panel-body">
        @Html.HiddenFor(m => m.ProductID)
        @foreach (var property in ViewData.ModelMetadata.Properties) {
            if (property.PropertyName != "ProductID") {
                <div class="form-group">
                    <label>@(property.DisplayName ?? property.PropertyName)</label>
                    @if (property.PropertyName == "Description") {
                        @Html.TextArea(property.PropertyName, null,
                                new { @class = "form-control", rows = 5 })
                    } else {
                        @Html.TextBox(property.PropertyName, null,
                                new { @class = "form-control" })
                    }
                </div>
            }
        }
        </div>

        <div class="panel-footer">
            <input type="submit" value="Save" class="btn btn-primary"/>
            @Html.ActionLink("Cancel and return to List", "Index", null, new {
                @class = "btn btn-default"
            })
        </div>
    }
</div>
```

This is a variation on the metadata technique that I used in Chapter 9 and it is something that I find myself using often, even though I could achieve similar results through the HTML helper methods with the customization techniques I describe in Chapter 22. There is something pleasing about this approach that gels with my development style but, as ever with the MVC Framework, there are different approaches you can use if processing metadata doesn't do it for you. You can see how this view is displayed in the browser in Figure 11-7.

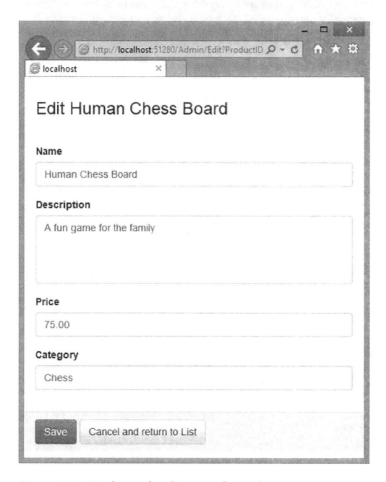

Figure 11-7. *Displaying the editor page for products*

Updating the Product Repository

Before I can process edits, I need to enhance the product repository so that it is able to save changes. First, I will add a new method to the IProductRepository interface, as shown in Listing 11-9. (As a reminder, you will find this interface in the Abstract folder of the SportsStore.Domain project.)

Listing 11-9. Adding a Method to the IProductRespository.cs File

```
using System.Collections.Generic;
using SportsStore.Domain.Entities;
```

```
namespace SportsStore.Domain.Abstract {
    public interface IProductRepository {

        IEnumerable<Product> Products { get; }

        void SaveProduct(Product product);
    }
}
```

I can then add the new method to the Entity Framework implementation of the repository, defined in the Concrete/EFProductRepository.cs file, as shown in Listing 11-10.

Listing 11-10. Implementing the SaveProduct Method in the EFProductRepository.cs File

```
using SportsStore.Domain.Abstract;
using SportsStore.Domain.Entities;
using System.Collections.Generic;

namespace SportsStore.Domain.Concrete {

    public class EFProductRepository : IProductRepository {
        private EFDbContext context = new EFDbContext();

        public IEnumerable<Product> Products {
            get { return context.Products; }
        }

        public void SaveProduct(Product product) {

            if (product.ProductID == 0) {
                context.Products.Add(product);
            } else {
                Product dbEntry = context.Products.Find(product.ProductID);
                if (dbEntry != null) {
                    dbEntry.Name = product.Name;
                    dbEntry.Description = product.Description;
                    dbEntry.Price = product.Price;
                    dbEntry.Category = product.Category;
                }
            }
            context.SaveChanges();
        }
    }
}
```

The implementation of the SaveChanges method adds a product to the repository if the ProductID is 0; otherwise, it applies any changes to the existing entry in the database.

I do not want to go into details of the Entity Framework because, as I explained earlier, it is a topic in itself and not part of the MVC Framework. But there is something in the SaveProduct method that has a bearing on the design of the MVC application.

I know I need to perform an update when I receive a Product parameter that has a ProductID that is not zero. I do this by getting a Product object from the repository with the same ProductID and updating each of the properties so they match the parameter object.

I can do this because the Entity Framework keeps track of the objects that it creates from the database. The object passed to the SaveChanges method is created by the MVC Framework using the default model binder, which means that the Entity Framework does not know anything about the parameter object and will not apply an update to the database. There are lots of ways of resolving this issue and I have taken the simplest one, which is to locate the corresponding object that the Entity Framework *does* know about and update it explicitly.

An alternative approach would be to create a custom model binder that only obtains objects from the repository. This may seem like a more elegant approach, but it would require me to add a find capability to the repository interface so I could locate Product objects by ProductID values.

Handling Edit POST Requests

At this point, I am ready to implement an overload of the Edit action method in the Admin controller that will handle POST requests when the administrator clicks the Save button. The new method is shown in Listing 11-11.

Listing 11-11. Adding the POST-Handling Edit Action Method in the AdminController.cs File

```
using System.Linq;
using System.Web.Mvc;
using SportsStore.Domain.Abstract;
using SportsStore.Domain.Entities;

namespace SportsStore.WebUI.Controllers {

    public class AdminController : Controller {
        private IProductRepository repository;

        public AdminController(IProductRepository repo) {
            repository = repo;
        }

        public ViewResult Index() {
            return View(repository.Products);
        }

        public ViewResult Edit(int productId) {
            Product product = repository.Products
                .FirstOrDefault(p => p.ProductID == productId);
            return View(product);
        }

        [HttpPost]
        public ActionResult Edit(Product product) {
            if (ModelState.IsValid) {
                repository.SaveProduct(product);
                TempData["message"] = string.Format("{0} has been saved", product.Name);
                return RedirectToAction("Index");
            } else {
```

```
        // there is something wrong with the data values
        return View(product);
    }
}
    }
}
```

I check that the model binder has been able to validate the data submitted to the user by reading the value of the ModelState.IsValid property. If everything is OK, I save the changes to the repository, and invoke the Index action method to return the user to the list of products. If there is a problem with the data, I render the Edit view again so that the user can make corrections.

After I have saved the changes in the repository, I store a message using the *TempData* feature. This is a key/value dictionary similar to the session data and view bag features I used previously. The key difference from session data is that temp data is deleted at the end of the HTTP request.

Notice that I return the ActionResult type from the Edit method. I have been using the ViewResult type until now. ViewResult is derived from ActionResult, and it is used when you want the framework to render a view. However, other types of ActionResults are available, and one of them is returned by the RedirectToAction method, which redirects the browser so that the Index action method is invoked. I describe the set of action results in Chapter 17.

I cannot use ViewBag in this situation because the user is being redirected. ViewBag passes data between the controller and view, and it cannot hold data for longer than the current HTTP request. I could have used the session data feature, but then the message would be persistent until I explicitly removed it, which I would rather not have to do. So, the TempData feature is the perfect fit. The data is restricted to a single user's session (so that users do not see each other's TempData) and will persist long enough for me to read it. I will read the data in the view rendered by the action method to which I have redirected the user, which I define in the next section.

UNIT TEST: EDIT SUBMISSIONS

For the POST-processing Edit action method, I need to make sure that valid updates to the Product object that the model binder has created are passed to the product repository to be saved. I also want to check that invalid updates (where a model error exists) are not passed to the repository. Here are the test methods:

```
...
[TestMethod]
public void Can_Save_Valid_Changes() {

    // Arrange - create mock repository
    Mock<IProductRepository> mock = new Mock<IProductRepository>();
    // Arrange - create the controller
    AdminController target = new AdminController(mock.Object);
    // Arrange - create a product
    Product product = new Product {Name = "Test"};

    // Act - try to save the product
    ActionResult result = target.Edit(product);

    // Assert - check that the repository was called
    mock.Verify(m => m.SaveProduct(product));
    // Assert - check the method result type
    Assert.IsNotInstanceOfType(result, typeof(ViewResult));
}
```

```
[TestMethod]
public void Cannot_Save_Invalid_Changes() {

    // Arrange - create mock repository
    Mock<IProductRepository> mock = new Mock<IProductRepository>();
    // Arrange - create the controller
    AdminController target = new AdminController(mock.Object);
    // Arrange - create a product
    Product product = new Product { Name = "Test" };
    // Arrange - add an error to the model state
    target.ModelState.AddModelError("error", "error");

    // Act - try to save the product
    ActionResult result = target.Edit(product);

    // Assert - check that the repository was not called
    mock.Verify(m => m.SaveProduct(It.IsAny<Product>()), Times.Never());
    // Assert - check the method result type
    Assert.IsInstanceOfType(result, typeof(ViewResult));
}
...
```

Displaying a Confirmation Message

I am going to deal with the message I stored using TempData in the _AdminLayout.cshtml layout file. By handling
the message in the template, I can create messages in any view that uses the template without needing to create
additional Razor blocks. Listing 11-12 shows the change to the file.

Listing 11-12. Handling the ViewBag Message in the _AdminLayout.cshtml File

```
@{
    Layout = null;
}

<!DOCTYPE html>

<html>
<head>
    <meta name="viewport" content="width=device-width" />
    <link href="~/Content/bootstrap.css" rel="stylesheet" />
    <link href="~/Content/bootstrap-theme.css" rel="stylesheet" />
    <link href="~/Content/ErrorStyles.css" rel="stylesheet" />
    <title></title>
</head>
<body>
    <div>
        @if (TempData["message"] != null) {
            <div class="alert alert-success">@TempData["message"]</div>
        }
```

```
        @RenderBody()
    </div>
</body>
</html>
```

Tip   The benefit of dealing with the message in the template like this is that users will see it displayed on whatever page is rendered after they have saved a change. At the moment, I return them to the list of products, but I could change the workflow to render some other view, and the users will still see the message (as long as the next view also uses the same layout).

I now have all the pieces in place to edit products. To see how it all works, start the application, navigate to the Admin/Index URL, and make some edits. Click the Save button. You will be returned to the list view, and the TempData message will be displayed, as shown in Figure 11-8.

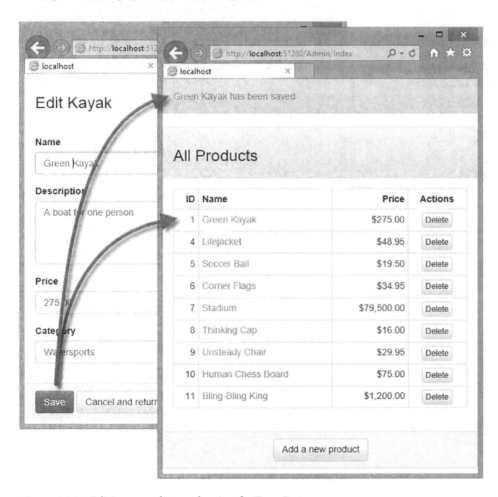

Figure 11-8. *Editing a product and seeing the TempData message*

The message will disappear if you reload the product list screen, because TempData is deleted when it is read. That is convenient, since I do not want old messages hanging around.

Adding Model Validation

As is the case for most projects, I need to add validation rules to the model entity. At the moment, the administrator could enter negative prices or blank descriptions, and SportsStore would happily try and store that data in the database. Whether or not the bad data would be stored would depend on whether it conformed to the constraints in the table definition I used to create the database in Chapter 7. Listing 11-13 shows how I have applied data annotations to the Product class, just as I did for the ShippingDetails class in the last chapter.

Listing 11-13. Applying Validation Attributes to the Product.cs File

```
using System.ComponentModel.DataAnnotations;
using System.Web.Mvc;

namespace SportsStore.Domain.Entities {

    public class Product {

        [HiddenInput(DisplayValue = false)]
        public int ProductID { get; set; }

        [Required(ErrorMessage = "Please enter a product name")]
        public string Name { get; set; }
        [DataType(DataType.MultilineText)]

        [Required(ErrorMessage = "Please enter a description")]
        public string Description { get; set; }

        [Required]
        [Range(0.01, double.MaxValue, ErrorMessage = "Please enter a positive price")]
        public decimal Price { get; set; }

        [Required(ErrorMessage = "Please specify a category")]
        public string Category { get; set; }
    }
}
```

The Html.TextBox and Html.TextArea helper methods that I used in the Edit.cshtml view to create the input and textarea elements will be used by the MVC Framework to signal validation problems. These signals are sent using classes for which I defined styles in the Content/ErrorStyles.css file, which have the effect of highlighting problems. I need to provide the user with details of any problems and you can see how I have done this in Listing 11-14.

Listing 11-14. Adding Validation Messages to the Edit.cshtml File

```
...
<div class="panel-body">
@foreach (var property in ViewData.ModelMetadata.Properties) {
    if (property.PropertyName != "ProductID") {
        <div class="form-group">
            <label>@(property.DisplayName ?? property.PropertyName)</label>
```

```
            @if (property.PropertyName == "Description") {
                @Html.TextArea(property.PropertyName, null,
                        new { @class = "form-control", rows = 5 })
            } else {
                @Html.TextBox(property.PropertyName, null,
                        new { @class = "form-control" })
            }
            @Html.ValidationMessage(property.PropertyName)
        </div>
    }
}
</div>
...
```

In Chapter 9, I used the Html.ValidationSummary helper method to create a consolidated list of all of the validation problems in the form. In this listing, I used the Html.ValidationMessage helper, which displays a message for a single model property. You can put the Html.ValidationMessage helper anywhere in a view, but it is conventional (and sensible) to put it somewhere near the element that has the validation issue to give the user some context. Figure 11-9 shows how the validation messages appear when you edit a product and enter data that breaks the rules applied to the Product class.

Figure 11-9. *Data validation when editing products*

Enabling Client-Side Validation

At present, data validation is applied only when the administration user submits edits to the server, but most users expect immediate feedback if there are problems with the data they have entered. This is why developers often want to perform *client-side validation,* where the data is checked in the browser using JavaScript. The MVC Framework can perform client-side validation based on the data annotations I applied to the domain model class.

This feature is enabled by default, but it has not been working because I have not added links to the required JavaScript libraries. Microsoft provides support for client-side validation based on the jQuery library and a popular jQuery plug-in called, obviously enough, jQuery Validation. Microsoft extends these tools to add support for validation attributes.

The first step is to install the validation package. Select Tools ➤ Library Package Manager ➤ Package Manager Console in Visual Studio to open the NuGet command line and enter the following command:

```
Install-Package Microsoft.jQuery.Unobtrusive.Validation -version 3.0.0
   -projectname SportsStore.WebUI
```

■ **Tip**   Do not worry if you see a message telling you that the package is already installed. Visual Studio will silently add this package to the project if you accidentally checked the Reference Script Libraries option when using the scaffolding feature to create a view.

Next, I need to add script elements to bring the JavaScript files in the package into the application HTML. The simplest place to add these links is in the _AdminLayout.cshtml file, so that client validation can work on any page that uses this layout. You can see the changes I made in Listing 11-15. (The order of the script elements is important.)

Listing 11-15. Importing JavaScript Files for Client-Side Validation into the _AdminLayout.cshtml File

```
@{
    Layout = null;
}

<!DOCTYPE html>

<html>
<head>
    <meta name="viewport" content="width=device-width" />
    <link href="~/Content/bootstrap.css" rel="stylesheet" />
    <link href="~/Content/bootstrap-theme.css" rel="stylesheet" />
    <link href="~/Content/ErrorStyles.css" rel="stylesheet" />
    <script src="~/Scripts/jquery-1.9.1.js"></script>
    <script src="~/Scripts/jquery.validate.js"></script>
    <script src="~/Scripts/jquery.validate.unobtrusive.js"></script>
    <title></title>
</head>
<body>
    <div>
        @if (TempData["message"] != null) {
            <div class="alert alert-success">@TempData["message"]</div>
        }
```

```
        @RenderBody()
    </div>
</body>
</html>
```

These additions to the layout enable the client-side validation feature, providing feedback to the user about the values they are entering before they submit the form. The appearance of error messages to the user is the same because the CSS classes that are used by the server validation are also used by the client-side validation, but the response is immediate and does not require a request to be sent to the server. In most situations, client-side validation is a useful feature, but if for some reason you do not want to validate at the client, you need to add the following statements to the view:

```
...
@{
    ViewBag.Title = "Admin: Edit " ı @Model.Name;
    Layout = "~/Views/Shared/_AdminLayout.cshtml";
    HtmlHelper.ClientValidationEnabled = false;
    HtmlHelper.UnobtrusiveJavaScriptEnabled = false;
}
...
```

These statements disable client-side validation for the view to which they are added. You can disable client-side validation for the entire application by setting values in the Web.config file, like this:

```
...
<configuration>
    <appSettings>
        <add key="ClientValidationEnabled" value="false"/>
        <add key="UnobtrusiveJavaScriptEnabled" value="false"/>
    </appSettings>
</configuration>
...
```

Creating New Products

Next, I will implement the Create action method, which is the one specified by the Add a new product link in the product list page. This will allow the administrator to add new items to the product catalog. Adding the ability to create new products will require one small addition and one small change to the application. This is a great example of the power and flexibility of a well-structured MVC application. First, add the Create method, shown in Listing 11-16, to the Admin controller.

Listing 11-16. Adding the Create Action Method to the AdminController.cs File

```
using System.Linq;
using System.Web.Mvc;
using SportsStore.Domain.Abstract;
using SportsStore.Domain.Entities;
```

```
namespace SportsStore.WebUI.Controllers {

    public class AdminController : Controller {
        private IProductRepository repository;

        public AdminController(IProductRepository repo) {
            repository = repo;
        }

        // ...other action methods omitted for brevity...

        public ViewResult Create() {
            return View("Edit", new Product());
        }
    }
}
```

The Create method does not render its default view. Instead, it specifies that the Edit view should be used. It is perfectly acceptable for one action method to use a view that is usually associated with another view. In this case, I inject a new Product object as the view model so that the Edit view is populated with empty fields.

■ **Note** I have not added a unit test for this action method. Doing so would only be testing the MVC Framework ability to process the ViewResult I return as the action method result, which is something we can take for granted. (One does not usually write tests for underlying frameworks unless there is a suspicion of a problem.)

This leads to the modification. I would usually expect a form to post back to the action that rendered it, and this is what the Html.BeginForm assumes by default when it generates an HTML form. However, this does not work for the Create method, because I want the form to be posted back to the Edit action so that I can save the newly created product data. To address this, I can use an overloaded version of the Html.BeginForm helper method to specify that the target of the form generated in the Edit view is the Edit action method of the Admin controller, as shown in Listing 11-17, which illustrates the change I have made to the Views/Admin/Edit.cshtml view file.

Listing 11-17. Explicitly Specifying an Action Method and Controller for a Form in the Edit.cshtml File

```
@model SportsStore.Domain.Entities.Product

@{
    ViewBag.Title = "Admin: Edit " + @Model.Name;
    Layout = "~/Views/Shared/_AdminLayout.cshtml";
}

<div class="panel">
    <div class="panel-heading">
        <h3>Edit @Model.Name</h3>
    </div>

    @using (Html.BeginForm("Edit", "Admin")) {
        <div class="panel-body">
        @foreach (var property in ViewData.ModelMetadata.Properties) {
            if (property.PropertyName != "ProductID") {
                <div class="form-group">
```

```
            <label>@(property.DisplayName ?? property.PropertyName)</label>
            @if (property.PropertyName == "Description") {
                @Html.TextArea(property.PropertyName, null,
                        new { @class = "form-control", rows = 5 })
            } else {
                @Html.TextBox(property.PropertyName, null,
                        new { @class = "form-control" })
            }
            @Html.ValidationMessage(property.PropertyName)
        </div>
        }
    }
    </div>

    <div class="panel-footer">
        <input type="submit" value="Save" class="btn btn-primary"/>
        @Html.ActionLink("Cancel and return to List", "Index", null, new {
            @class = "btn btn-default"
        })
    </div>
    }
</div>
```

Now the form will always be posted to the Edit action, regardless of which action rendered it. I can now create products by clicking the Add a new product link and filling in the details, as shown in Figure 11-10.

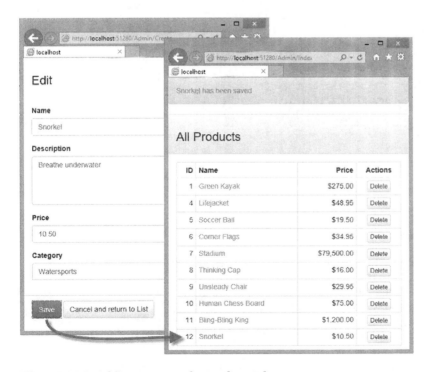

Figure 11-10. *Adding a new product to the catalog*

Deleting Products

Adding support for deleting items is also simple. First, I add a new method to the IProductRepository interface, as shown in Listing 11-18.

Listing 11-18. Adding a Method to Delete Products to the IProductRepository.cs File

```
using System.Collections.Generic;
using SportsStore.Domain.Entities;

namespace SportsStore.Domain.Abstract {
    public interface IProductRepository {

        IEnumerable<Product> Products { get; }

        void SaveProduct(Product product);

        Product DeleteProduct(int productID);
    }
}
```

Next, I implement this method in the Entity Framework repository class, EFProductRepository, as shown in Listing 11-19.

Listing 11-19. Implementing Deletion Support in the EFProductRepository.cs File

```
using SportsStore.Domain.Abstract;
using SportsStore.Domain.Entities;
using System.Collections.Generic;

namespace SportsStore.Domain.Concrete {

    public class EFProductRepository : IProductRepository {
        private EFDbContext context = new EFDbContext();

        public IEnumerable<Product> Products {
            get { return context.Products; }
        }

        public void SaveProduct(Product product) {

            if (product.ProductID == 0) {
                context.Products.Add(product);
            } else {
                Product dbEntry = context.Products.Find(product.ProductID);
                if (dbEntry != null) {
                    dbEntry.Name = product.Name;
                    dbEntry.Description = product.Description;
                    dbEntry.Price = product.Price;
                    dbEntry.Category = product.Category;
                }
            }
```

```
            context.SaveChanges();
        }

        public Product DeleteProduct(int productID) {
            Product dbEntry = context.Products.Find(productID);
            if (dbEntry != null) {
                context.Products.Remove(dbEntry);
                context.SaveChanges();
            }
            return dbEntry;
        }
    }
}
```

The final step is to implement a Delete action method in the Admin controller. This action method should support only POST requests, because deleting objects is not an idempotent operation. As I will explain in Chapter 16, browsers and caches are free to make GET requests without the user's explicit consent, and so I must be careful to avoid making changes as a consequence of GET requests. Listing 11-20 shows the new action method.

Listing 11-20. The Delete Action Method in the AdminController.cs File

```
using System.Linq;
using System.Web.Mvc;
using SportsStore.Domain.Abstract;
using SportsStore.Domain.Entities;

namespace SportsStore.WebUI.Controllers {

    public class AdminController : Controller {
        private IProductRepository repository;

        public AdminController(IProductRepository repo) {
            repository = repo;
        }

        // ...other action methods omitted for brevity...

        [HttpPost]
        public ActionResult Delete(int productId) {
            Product deletedProduct = repository.DeleteProduct(productId);
            if (deletedProduct != null) {
                TempData["message"] = string.Format("{0} was deleted",
                    deletedProduct.Name);
            }
            return RedirectToAction("Index");
        }
    }
}
```

UNIT TEST: DELETING PRODUCTS

I want to test the basic behavior of the Delete action method, which is that when a valid ProductID is passed as a parameter, the action method calls the DeleteProduct method of the repository and passes the correct ProductID value to be deleted. Here is the test:

```
...
[TestMethod]
public void Can_Delete_Valid_Products() {

    // Arrange - create a Product
    Product prod = new Product { ProductID = 2, Name = "Test" };

    // Arrange - create the mock repository
    Mock<IProductRepository> mock = new Mock<IProductRepository>();
    mock.Setup(m => m.Products).Returns(new Product[] {
        new Product {ProductID = 1, Name = "P1"},
        prod,
        new Product {ProductID = 3, Name = "P3"},
    });

    // Arrange - create the controller
    AdminController target = new AdminController(mock.Object);

    // Act - delete the product
    target.Delete(prod.ProductID);

    // Assert - ensure that the repository delete method was
    // called with the correct Product
    mock.Verify(m => m.DeleteProduct(prod.ProductID));
}
...
```

You can see the delete feature by clicking one of the Delete buttons in the product list page, as shown in Figure 11-11. As shown in the figure, I have taken advantage of the TempData variable to display a message when a product is deleted from the catalog.

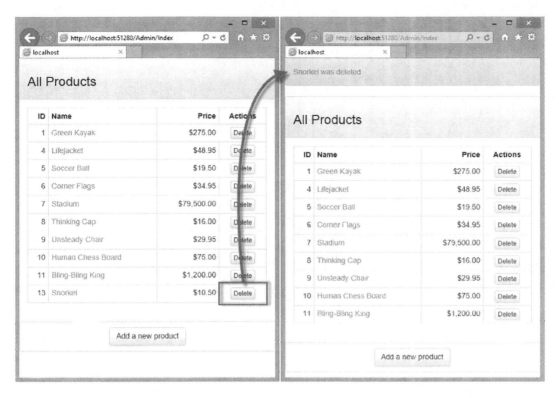

Figure 11-11. *Deleting a product from the catalog*

Summary

In this chapter, I introduced the administration capability and showed you how to implement CRUD operations that allow the administrator to create, read, update, and delete products from the repository. In the next chapter, I show you how to secure the administration functions so that they are not available to all users, and I add the finishing touches to complete the SportsStore functionality.

CHAPTER 12

▩ ▩ ▩

SportsStore: Security & Finishing Touches

In the previous chapter, I added support for administering the SportsStore application, and it will not have escaped your attention that anyone could modify the product catalog if I deployed the application as it is. All they would need to know is that the administration features are available using the Admin/Index URL. In this chapter, I am going to show you how to prevent random people from using the administration functions by password-protecting access to the entire Admin controller. Once I have the security in place, I will complete the SportsStore app by adding support for product images. This may seem like a simple feature, but it requires some interesting MVC techniques.

Securing the Administration Controller

Because ASP.NET MVC is built on the core ASP.NET platform, I have access to the ASP.NET authentication and authorization features, which are packaged as a general-purpose system for keeping track of who is logged in.

DIGGING INTO THE ASP.NET SECURITY FEATURES

In this chapter, I only touch on the security features that are available. In part, this is because these features are part of the ASP.NET platform rather than the MVC Framework and in part because there are several different approaches available. I cover all the authentication and authorization features in detail in my *Pro ASP.NET MVC 5 Platform* book, which Apress will publish in 2014. But I don't want you have to buy a second book to learn about something as fundamental as web application security, and so Apress has kindly agreed to package up the key security chapters from the *Platform* book and distribute them for free from apress.com. They won't be available until I have written the book, of course, but it is the next project on my slate and it shouldn't be too far into 2014 before they are available for download.

Creating a Basic Security Policy

I am going to start by configuring *forms authentication*, which is one of the ways in which users can be authenticated in an ASP.NET application. In Listing 12-1, you can see the additions I have made to the Web.config file in the SportsStore.WebUI project (the one in the root of the project and not the one in the views folder).

Listing 12-1. Configuring Forms Authentication in the Web.config File

```xml
<?xml version="1.0" encoding="utf-8"?>
<configuration>
  <configSections>
  </configSections>

  <connectionStrings>
    <add name="EFDbContext" connectionString="Data Source=(localdb)\v11.0;Initial
        Catalog=SportsStore;Integrated Security=True"
            providerName="System.Data.SqlClient" />
  </connectionStrings>

  <appSettings>
    <add key="webpages:Version" value="3.0.0.0" />
    <add key="webpages:Enabled" value="false" />
     <add key="ClientValidationEnabled" value="true" />
    <add key="UnobtrusiveJavaScriptEnabled" value="true" />
    <add key="Email.WriteAsFile" value="true"/>
  </appSettings>
  <system.web>
    <compilation debug="true" targetFramework="4.5.1" />
    <httpRuntime targetFramework="4.5.1" />
    <globalization uiCulture="en-US" culture="en-US" />
    <authentication mode="Forms">
      <forms loginUrl="~/Account/Login" timeout="2880" />
    </authentication>
  </system.web>
</configuration>
```

Authentication is set up using the `authentication` element and I have used the `mode` attribute to specify that I want forms authentication, which is the kind most often used for Internet-facing web applications. In ASP.NET 4.5.1, Microsoft has added support for a wider range of Internet-suitable authentication options, which I describe in the *Pro ASP.NET MVC 5 Platform* book, as noted earlier in the chapter. I am going to stick with forms authentication because it works with local user credentials and is simple to set up and manage.

■ **Note** The main alternatives to forms authentication are *Windows authentication*, where the operating system credentials are used to identify users and *Organizational authentication*, where the user is authenticated using a cloud service such as Windows Azure. I am not going to get into either of these options because they are not widely used in Internet-facing applications.

The `loginUrl` attribute tells ASP.NET where to redirect users when they need to authenticate themselves (in this case the `~/Account/Login URL`) and the `timeout` attribute specifies how long a user remains authenticated once they have successfully logged in, expressed in minutes (2,880 minutes is 48 hours).

The next step is to tell ASP.NET where it will get details of the application users. I have broken this into a separate step because I am about to do something that should never, ever, be done in a real project: I am going to define a username and password in the `Web.config` file. You can see the changes in Listing 12-2.

Listing 12-2. Defining a Username and Password in the Web.config File

```
...
<authentication mode="Forms">
  <forms loginUrl="~/Account/Login" timeout="2880">
    <credentials passwordFormat="Clear">
      <user name="admin" password="secret" />
    </credentials>
  </forms>
</authentication>
...
```

I want to keep the example simple and focus on the way that the MVC Framework allows you to apply authentication and authorization to a web application. But putting credentials in the Web.config file is a recipe for disaster, especially if you set the passwordFormat attribute on the credentials element to Clear, meaning that passwords are stored as plain text.

■ **Caution**   Don't store user credentials in the Web.config file and don't store passwords as plain text. See the free chapters excepted from my *Pro ASP.NET MVC 5 Platform* book (as described at the start of the section) for details of managing users via a database.

Despite being unsuitable for real projects, using the Web.config file to store credentials lets me focus on MVC features without getting sidetracked into aspects of the core ASP.NET platform. The result of the additions to the Web.config file is that I have a hard-coded username (admin) and password (secret).

Applying Authorization with Filters

The MVC Framework has a powerful feature called *filters*. These are .NET attributes that you can apply to an action method or a controller class and they introduce additional logic when a request is processed to change the behavior of the MVC Framework.

There are different kinds of filters available and you can create your own custom filters, as I explain in Chapter 18. The filter that interests me at the moment is the default *authorization filter*, Authorize. In Listing 12-3, you can see how I have applied this filter to the Admin controller.

Listing 12-3. Adding the Authorize Attribute in the AdminController.cs File

```
using System.Linq;
using System.Web.Mvc;
using SportsStore.Domain.Abstract;
using SportsStore.Domain.Entities;

namespace SportsStore.WebUI.Controllers {

    [Authorize]
    public class AdminController : Controller {
        private IProductRepository repository;
```

```
    public AdminController(IProductRepository repo) {
        repository = repo;
    }

    // ...action methods omitted for brevity...
    }
}
```

When applied without parameters, the Authorize attribute grants access to the controller action methods to all authenticated users. This means that if you are authenticated, you are automatically authorized to use the administration features. This is fine for SportsStore, where there is only one set of restricted action methods and only one user.

▪ **Note**   You can apply filters to an individual action method or to a controller. When you apply a filter to a controller, it works as though you had applied it to every action method in the controller class. In Listing 12-3, I applied the Authorize filter to the class, so all of the action methods in the Admin controller are available only to authenticated users.

You can see the effect that the Authorize filter has by running the application and navigating to the /Admin/Index URL. You will see an error similar to the one shown in Figure 12-1.

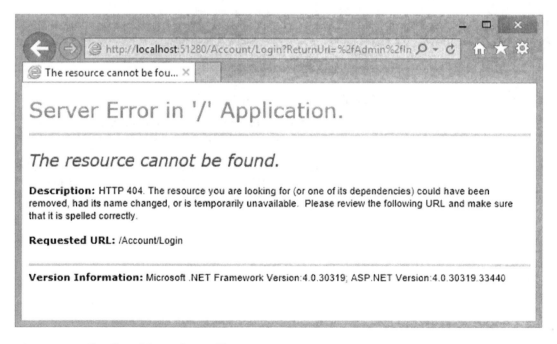

Figure 12-1. *The effect of the Authorize filter*

When you try to access the Index action method of the Admin controller, the MVC Framework detects the Authorize filter. Because you have not been authenticated, you are redirected to the URL specified in the Web.config forms authentication section: /Account/Login. I have not created the Account controller yet (which is what causes the error shown in the figure), but the fact that the MVC Framework has tried to redirect the request shows that the Authorize filter is working.

Creating the Authentication Provider

Using the forms authentication feature requires calls to two static methods of the System.Web.Security. FormsAuthentication class:

- The Authenticate method validates credentials supplied by the user.

- The SetAuthCookie method adds a cookie to the response to the browser, so that users do not need to authenticate every time they make a request.

The problem with calling static methods from within action methods is that it makes unit testing the controller difficult: mocking frameworks typically mock only instance members. The classes that comprise the MVC Framework have been designed with unit testing in mind, but the FormsAuthentication class predates the unit testing-friendly design of MVC.

The best way to address the problem is to decouple the controller from the static methods using an interface, which offers the additional benefit that this fits in with the broader MVC design pattern and makes it easier to switch to a different authentication system later.

I start by defining the authentication provider interface. Create a new folder called Abstract in the Infrastructure folder of the SportsStore.WebUI project and add a new interface called IAuthProvider. The contents of this interface are shown in Listing 12-4.

Listing 12-4. The Contents of the IAuthProvider.cs File

```
namespace SportsStore.WebUI.Infrastructure.Abstract {

    public interface IAuthProvider {
        bool Authenticate(string username, string password);
    }
}
```

I can now create an implementation of this interface that acts as a wrapper around the static methods of the FormsAuthentication class. Create another new folder in Infrastructure—this time called Concrete—and create a new class called FormsAuthProvider. The contents of this class are shown in Listing 12-5.

Listing 12-5. The Contents of the FormsAuthProvider.cs File

```
using System.Web.Security;
using SportsStore.WebUI.Infrastructure.Abstract;

namespace SportsStore.WebUI.Infrastructure.Concrete {

    public class FormsAuthProvider : IAuthProvider {

        public bool Authenticate(string username, string password) {
```

```
            bool result = FormsAuthentication.Authenticate(username, password);
            if (result) {
                FormsAuthentication.SetAuthCookie(username, false);
            }
            return result;
        }
    }
}
```

■ **Note**　You will see a warning from Visual Studio that the FormsAuthentication.Authenticate method has been deprecated. This is part of Microsoft's ongoing efforts to rationalize user security, which is a thorny area for any web application framework. For this chapter, the deprecated method will suffice and allow me to perform authentication using the static details I added to the Web.config file.

The implementation of the Authenticate method calls the static FormsAuthentication methods that I wanted to keep out of the controller. The final step is to register the FormsAuthProvider in the AddBindings method of the NinjectDependencyResolver class, as shown in Listing 12-6.

Listing 12-6. Registering the Authentication Provider in the NinjectDependencyResolver.cs File

```
using System;
using System.Collections.Generic;
using System.Configuration;
using System.Web.Mvc;
using Moq;
using Ninject;
using SportsStore.Domain.Abstract;
using SportsStore.Domain.Concrete;
using SportsStore.Domain.Entities;
using SportsStore.WebUI.Infrastructure.Abstract;
using SportsStore.WebUI.Infrastructure.Concrete;

namespace SportsStore.WebUI.Infrastructure {

    public class NinjectDependencyResolver : IDependencyResolver {
        private IKernel kernel;

        public NinjectDependencyResolver(IKernel kernelParam) {
            kernel = kernelParam;
            AddBindings();
        }

        public object GetService(Type serviceType) {
            return kernel.TryGet(serviceType);
        }

        public IEnumerable<object> GetServices(Type serviceType) {
            return kernel.GetAll(serviceType);
        }
```

```
        private void AddBindings() {
            kernel.Bind<IProductRepository>().To<EFProductRepository>();

            EmailSettings emailSettings = new EmailSettings {
                WriteAsFile = bool.Parse(ConfigurationManager
                    .AppSettings["Email.WriteAsFile"] ?? "false")
            };

            kernel.Bind<IOrderProcessor>().To<EmailOrderProcessor>()
                .WithConstructorArgument("settings", emailSettings);

            kernel.Bind<IAuthProvider>().To<FormsAuthProvider>();
        }
    }
}
```

Creating the Account Controller

The next task is to create the Account controller and the Login action method referred to in the Web.config file. In fact, I will create two versions of the Login method. The first will render a view that contains a login prompt, and the other will handle the POST request when users submit their credentials.

To get started, I created a view model class that I will pass between the controller and the view. Add a new class file called LoginViewModel.cs to the Models folder of the SportsStore.WebUI project and edit the content so that it matches Listing 12-7.

Listing 12-7. The Contents of the LoginViewModel.cs File

```
using System.ComponentModel.DataAnnotations;

namespace SportsStore.WebUI.Models {

    public class LoginViewModel {
        [Required]
        public string UserName { get; set; }

        [Required]
        public string Password { get; set; }
    }
}
```

This class contains properties for the username and password, and uses data annotation attributes to specify that values for both are required. Given that there are only two properties, you might be tempted to do without a view model and rely on the ViewBag to pass data to the view. However, it is good practice to define view models so that the data passed from the controller to the view and from the model binder to the action method is typed consistently.

Next, I create the Account controller that will handle authentication. Create a new class file called AccountController.cs in the Controllers folder and edit the file contents to match Listing 12-8.

Listing 12-8. The the Contents of the AccountController.cs File

```
using System.Web.Mvc;
using SportsStore.WebUI.Infrastructure.Abstract;
using SportsStore.WebUI.Models;
```

```
namespace SportsStore.WebUI.Controllers {

    public class AccountController : Controller {
        IAuthProvider authProvider;

        public AccountController(IAuthProvider auth) {
            authProvider = auth;
        }

        public ViewResult Login() {
            return View();
        }

        [HttpPost]
        public ActionResult Login(LoginViewModel model, string returnUrl) {

            if (ModelState.IsValid) {
                if (authProvider.Authenticate(model.UserName, model.Password)) {
                    return Redirect(returnUrl ?? Url.Action("Index", "Admin"));
                } else {
                    ModelState.AddModelError("", "Incorrect username or password");
                    return View();
                }
            } else {
                return View();
            }
        }
    }
}
```

Creating the View

To create the view that will ask the users for their credentials, create the Views/Account folder in the SportsStore. WebUI folder. Right-click on the new folder, select Add ➤ MVC 5 View Page (Razor) from the menu, set the name to Login and click OK to create the Login.cshtml file. Edit the contents of the new file to match Listing 12-9.

Listing 12-9. The Contents of the Login.cshtml File

```
@model SportsStore.WebUI.Models.LoginViewModel

@{
    ViewBag.Title = "Admin: Log In";
    Layout = "~/Views/Shared/_AdminLayout.cshtml";
}

<div class="panel">
    <div class="panel-heading">
        <h3> Log In</h3>
    </div>
    <div class="panel-body">
        <p class="lead">Please log in to access the administration area:</p>
```

```
    @using (Html.BeginForm()) {
        @Html.ValidationSummary()
        <div class="form-group">
            <label>User Name:</label>
            @Html.TextBoxFor(m => m.UserName, new { @class = "form-control" })
        </div>
        <div class="form-group">
            <label>Password:</label>
            @Html.PasswordFor(m => m.Password, new { @class = "form-control" })
        </div>
        <input type="submit" value="Log in"  class="btn btn-primary"/>
    }
</div>
</div>
```

This view uses the _AdminLayout.cshtml layout and Bootstrap classes to style the content. There are no new techniques in this view, other than the use of the Html.PasswordFor helper method, which generates an input element whose type attribute is set to password. I describe the complete set of HTML helper methods in Chapter 21. You can see how the view appears by starting the app and navigating to the /Admin/Index URL, as shown in Figure 12-2.

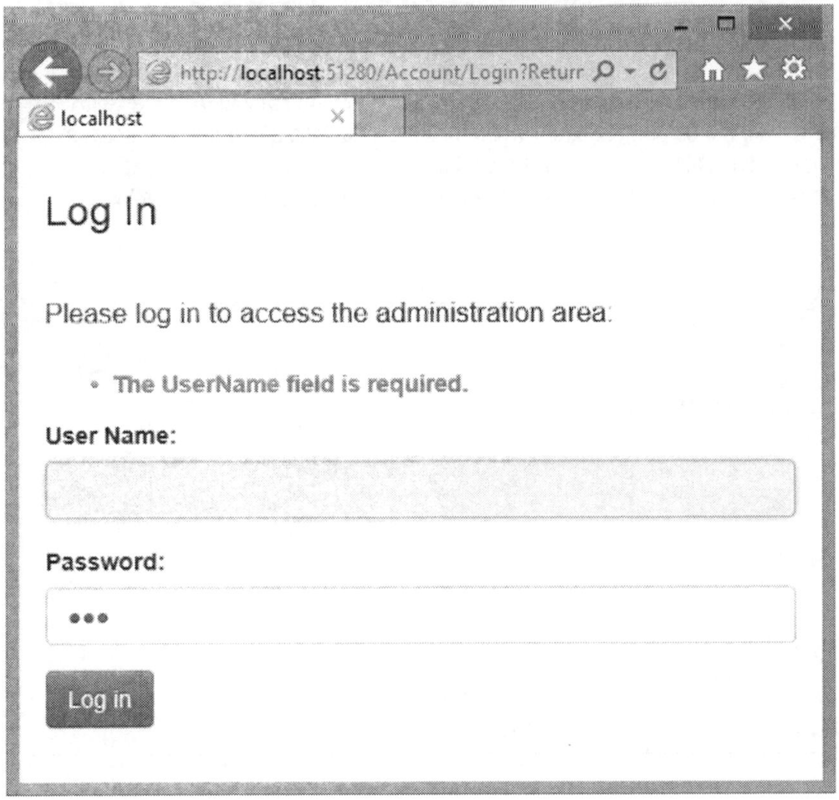

Figure 12-2. *The Login view*

The Required attributes that I applied to the properties of the view model are enforced using client-side validation. (Remember that the required JavaScript libraries are included in the _AdminLayout.cshtml layout created in the previous chapter.) Users can submit the form only after they have provided both a username and password, and the authentication is performed at the server when I call the FormsAuthentication.Authenticate method.

■ **Caution**   In general, using client-side data validation is a good idea. It offloads some of the work from your server and gives users immediate feedback about the data they are providing. However, you should not be tempted to perform authentication at the client, as this would typically involve sending valid credentials to the client so they can be used to check the username and password that the user has entered, or at least trusting the client's report of whether they have successfully authenticated. Authentication must always be done at the server.

When I receive bad credentials, I add an error to the ModelState and re-render the view. This causes a message to be displayed in the validation summary area, which I created by calling the Html.ValidationSummary helper method in the view. This takes care of protecting the SportsStore administration functions. Users will be allowed to access these features only after they have supplied valid credentials and received a cookie, which will be attached to subsequent requests.

UNIT TEST: AUTHENTICATION

Testing the Account controller requires me to check two behaviors: a user should be authenticated when valid credentials are supplied, and a user should *not* be authenticated when invalid credentials are supplied. I perform these tests by creating mock implementations of the IAuthProvider interface and checking the type and nature of the result of the controller Login method. I created the following tests in a new unit test file called AdminSecurityTests.cs:

```
using System.Web.Mvc;
using Microsoft.VisualStudio.TestTools.UnitTesting;
using Moq;
using SportsStore.WebUI.Controllers;
using SportsStore.WebUI.Infrastructure.Abstract;
using SportsStore.WebUI.Models;

namespace SportsStore.UnitTests {
    [TestClass]
    public class AdminSecurityTests {

        [TestMethod]
        public void Can_Login_With_Valid_Credentials() {

            // Arrange - create a mock authentication provider
            Mock<IAuthProvider> mock = new Mock<IAuthProvider>();
            mock.Setup(m => m.Authenticate("admin", "secret")).Returns(true);

            // Arrange - create the view model
            LoginViewModel model = new LoginViewModel {
```

```
            UserName = "admin",
            Password = "secret"
        };

        // Arrange - create the controller
        AccountController target = new AccountController(mock.Object);

        // Act - authenticate using valid credentials
        ActionResult result = target.Login(model, "/MyURL");

        // Assert
        Assert.IsInstanceOfType(result, typeof(RedirectResult));
        Assert.AreEqual("/MyURL", ((RedirectResult)result).Url);
    }

    [TestMethod]
    public void Cannot_Login_With_Invalid_Credentials() {

        // Arrange - create a mock authentication provider
        Mock<IAuthProvider> mock = new Mock<IAuthProvider>();
        mock.Setup(m => m.Authenticate("badUser", "badPass")).Returns(false);

        // Arrange - create the view model
        LoginViewModel model = new LoginViewModel {
            UserName - "badUser",
            Password = "badPass"
        };

        // Arrange - create the controller
        AccountController target = new AccountController(mock.Object);

        // Act - authenticate using valid credentials
        ActionResult result = target.Login(model, "/MyURL");

        // Assert
        Assert.IsInstanceOfType(result, typeof(ViewResult));
        Assert.IsFalse(((ViewResult)result).ViewData.ModelState.IsValid);
    }
  }
}
```

Image Uploads

I am going to complete the SportsStore user experience with something a little more sophisticated: I will add the ability for the administrator to upload product images and store them in the database so that they are displayed in the product catalog. This isn't something that is especially interesting or useful in its own right, but it does allow me to demonstrate some important MVC Framework features.

Extending the Database

Open the Visual Studio Server Explorer window and navigate to the Products table in the database created in Chapter 7. The name of the data connection may have changed to be EFDbContext, which is the name assigned to the connection in the Web.config file. Visual Studio is a little bit inconsistent about when it renames the connection, so you might also see the original name that was shown when the connection was created. Right-click on the Products table and select New Query from the pop-up menu and enter the following SQL into the text area:

```
ALTER TABLE [dbo].[Products]
    ADD [ImageData]     VARBINARY (MAX) NULL,
        [ImageMimeType] VARCHAR (50)    NULL;
```

Click the Execute button (which is marked with an arrow) in the top-left cover of the window and Visual Studio will update the database, adding two new columns to the table. To test the update, right-click on the Products table in the Server Explorer window and select Open Table Definition from the menu. You will see that there are now columns called ImageData and ImageMimeType, as shown in Figure 12-3.

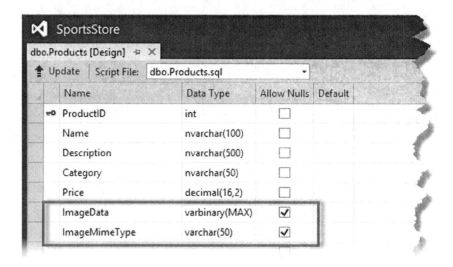

Figure 12-3. Adding columns to the database

■ **Tip**   If the columns are not visible, close the design window, right-click on the data connection in the Server Explorer window and select Refresh from the menu. The new columns should now be visible when you select the Open Table Definition menu item again.

Enhancing the Domain Model

I need to add two new fields to the Products class in the SportsStore.Domain project that correspond to the new database columns, as shown in Listing 12-10.

Listing 12-10. Adding Properties in the Product.cs File

```
using System.ComponentModel.DataAnnotations;
using System.Web.Mvc;

namespace SportsStore.Domain.Entities {

    public class Product {

        [HiddenInput(DisplayValue = false)]
        public int ProductID { get; set; }

        [Required(ErrorMessage = "Please enter a product name")]
        public string Name { get; set; }
        [DataType(DataType.MultilineText)]

        [Required(ErrorMessage = "Please enter a description")]
        public string Description { get; set; }

        [Required]
        [Range(0.01, double.MaxValue, ErrorMessage = "Please enter a positive price")]
        public decimal Price { get; set; }

        [Required(ErrorMessage = "Please specify a category")]
        public string Category { get; set; }

        public byte[] ImageData { get; set; }
        public string ImageMimeType { get; set; }
    }
}
```

▓ **Caution**   Make sure that the names of the properties that you add to the Product class exactly match the names you gave to the new columns in the database.

Creating the Upload User Interface Elements

The next step is to add support for handling file uploads. This involves creating a UI that the administrator can use to upload an image. Modify the Views/Admin/Edit.cshtml view so that it matches Listing 12-11.

Listing 12-11. Adding Support for Images in the Edit.cshtml File

```
@model SportsStore.Domain.Entities.Product

@{
    ViewBag.Title = "Admin: Edit " + @Model.Name;
    Layout = "~/Views/Shared/_AdminLayout.cshtml";
}
```

```
<div class="panel">
    <div class="panel-heading">
        <h3>Edit @Model.Name</h3>
    </div>

@using (Html.BeginForm("Edit", "Admin",
        FormMethod.Post, new { enctype = "multipart/form-data" })) {

    <div class="panel-body">
        @Html.HiddenFor(m => m.ProductID)
        @foreach (var property in ViewData.ModelMetadata.Properties) {
            switch (property.PropertyName) {
                case "ProductID":
                case "ImageData":
                case "ImageMimeType":
                    // do nothing
                    break;
                default:
                    <div class="form-group">
                        <label>@(property.DisplayName ?? property.PropertyName)</label>
                        @if (property.PropertyName == "Description") {
                            @Html.TextArea(property.PropertyName, null,
                                new { @class = "form-control", rows = 5 })
                        } else {
                            @Html.TextBox(property.PropertyName, null,
                                new { @class = "form-control" })
                        }
                        @Html.ValidationMessage(property.PropertyName)
                    </div>
                    break;
            }
        }

        <div class="form-group">
            <div style="position:relative;">
                <label>Image</label>
                <a class='btn' href='javascript:;'>
                    Choose File...
                    <input type="file" name="Image" size="40"
                        style="position:absolute;z-index:2;top:0;
                            left:0;filter: alpha(opacity=0); opacity:0;
                            background-color:transparent;color:transparent;"
                        onchange='$("#upload-file-info").html($(this).val());'>
                </a>
                <span class='label label-info' id="upload-file-info"></span>
            </div>
            @if (Model.ImageData == null) {
                <div class="form-control-static">No Image</div>
```

```
        } else {
            <img class="img-thumbnail" width="150" height="150"
                    src="@Url.Action("GetImage", "Product",
                    new { Model.ProductID })" />
        }
    </div>
</div>

<div class="panel-footer">
    <input type="submit" value="Save" class="btn btn-primary" />
    @Html.ActionLink("Cancel and return to List", "Index", null, new {
    @class = "btn btn-default"
})
    </div>
}
</div>
```

You may already be aware that Web browsers will upload files properly only when the HTML form element defines an enctype value of multipart/form-data. In other words, for a successful upload, the form element must look like this:

```
...
<form action="/Admin/Edit" enctype="multipart/form-data" method="post">
...
```

Without the enctype attribute, the browser will transmit only the name of the file and not its content, which is no use at all. To ensure that the enctype attribute appears, I must use an overload of the Html.BeginForm helper method that lets me specify HTML attributes, like this:

```
...
@using (Html.BeginForm("Edit", "Admin",
    FormMethod.Post, new { enctype = "multipart/form-data" })) {
...
```

There are two other changes in the view. The first is that I have replaced the Razor if expression I used when generating input elements with a switch statement. The effect is the same, but it allows me to specify the model properties I want to skip more concisely, and I don't want to display the image-related properties directly to the user.

Instead, I have made the remaining change, which is to add an input element whose type is file to allow file upload, along with an img element to display the image associated with a product, if there is one in the database.

The horrific mess of inline CSS and JavaScript addresses a shortcoming in the Bootstrap library: it does not properly style file input elements. There are a number of extensions that add the missing functionality, but I have chosen the magic incantation shown in the listing because it is self-contained and is reliable. It doesn't change the way that the MVC Framework works, just the way in which the elements in the Edit.cshtml file are styled.

Saving Images to the Database

I need to enhance the POST version of the Edit action method in the Admin controller so that I take the image data that has been uploaded and save it in the database. Listing 12-12 shows the changes that are required.

Listing 12-12. Handling Image Data in the AdminController.cs File

```
using System.Linq;
using System.Web;
using System.Web.Mvc;
using SportsStore.Domain.Abstract;
using SportsStore.Domain.Entities;

namespace SportsStore.WebUI.Controllers {

    [Authorize]
    public class AdminController : Controller {
        private IProductRepository repository;

        public AdminController(IProductRepository repo) {
            repository = repo;
        }

        public ViewResult Index() {
            return View(repository.Products);
        }

        public ViewResult Edit(int productId) {
            Product product = repository.Products
                .FirstOrDefault(p => p.ProductID == productId);
            return View(product);
        }

        [HttpPost]
        public ActionResult Edit(Product product, HttpPostedFileBase image = null) {
            if (ModelState.IsValid) {
                if (image != null) {
                    product.ImageMimeType = image.ContentType;
                    product.ImageData = new byte[image.ContentLength];
                    image.InputStream.Read(product.ImageData, 0, image.ContentLength);
                }
                repository.SaveProduct(product);
                TempData["message"] = string.Format("{0} has been saved", product.Name);
                return RedirectToAction("Index");
            } else {
                // there is something wrong with the data values
                return View(product);
            }
        }

        public ViewResult Create() {
            return View("Edit", new Product());
        }

        [HttpPost]
        public ActionResult Delete(int productId) {
            Product deletedProduct = repository.DeleteProduct(productId);
```

```
            if (deletedProduct != null) {
                TempData["message"] = string.Format("{0} was deleted",
                    deletedProduct.Name);
            }
            return RedirectToAction("Index");
        }
    }
}
```

I have added a new parameter to the Edit method, which the MVC Framework uses to pass the uploaded file data to the action method. I check to see if the parameter value is null; if it is not, I copy the data and the MIME type from the parameter to the Product object so that it is saved to the database. I must also update the EFProductRepository class in the SportsStore.Domain project to ensure that the values assigned to the ImageData and ImageMimeType properties are stored in the database. Listing 12-13 shows the required changes to the SaveProduct method.

Listing 12-13. Ensuring That the Image Values Are Stored in the Database in the EFProductRepository.cs File

```
...
public void SaveProduct(Product product) {

    if (product.ProductID == 0) {
        context.Products.Add(product);
    } else {
        Product dbEntry = context.Products.Find(product.ProductID);
        if (dbEntry != null) {
            dbEntry.Name = product.Name;
            dbEntry.Description = product.Description;
            dbEntry.Price = product.Price;
            dbEntry.Category = product.Category;
            dbEntry.ImageData = product.ImageData;
            dbEntry.ImageMimeType = product.ImageMimeType;
        }
    }
    context.SaveChanges();
}
...
```

Implementing the GetImage Action Method

In Listing 12-11, I added an img element whose content was obtained through a GetImage action method on the Product controller. I am going to implement this action method so that I can display images contained in the database. Listing 12-14 shows the definition of the action method.

Listing 12-14. The GetImage Action Method in the ProductController.cs File

```
using System;
using System.Collections.Generic;
using System.Linq;
using System.Web;
using System.Web.Mvc;
using SportsStore.Domain.Abstract;
```

```
using SportsStore.Domain.Entities;
using SportsStore.WebUI.Models;

namespace SportsStore.WebUI.Controllers {

    public class ProductController : Controller {
        private IProductRepository repository;
        public int PageSize = 4;

        public ProductController(IProductRepository productRepository) {
            this.repository = productRepository;
        }

        public ViewResult List(string category, int page = 1) {
            ProductsListViewModel model = new ProductsListViewModel {
                Products = repository.Products
                    .Where(p => category == null || p.Category == category)
                    .OrderBy(p => p.ProductID)
                    .Skip((page - 1) * PageSize)
                    .Take(PageSize),
                PagingInfo = new PagingInfo {
                    CurrentPage = page,
                    ItemsPerPage = PageSize,
                    TotalItems = category == null ?
                        repository.Products.Count() :
                        repository.Products.Where(e => e.Category == category).Count()
                },
                CurrentCategory = category
            };
            return View(model);
        }

        public FileContentResult GetImage(int productId) {
            Product prod = repository.Products
                .FirstOrDefault(p => p.ProductID == productId);
            if (prod != null) {
                return File(prod.ImageData, prod.ImageMimeType);
            } else {
                return null;
            }
        }
    }
}
```

This method tries to find a product that matches the ID specified by the parameter. The FileContentResult class is used as the result from an action method when you want to return a file to the client browser, and instances are created using the File method of the base controller class. I discuss the different types of results you can return from action methods in Chapter 17.

UNIT TEST: RETRIEVING IMAGES

I want to make sure that the GetImage method returns the correct MIME type from the repository and make sure that no data is returned when I request a product ID that doesn't exist. Here are the test methods I created, which I defined in a new unit test file called ImageTests.cs:

```csharp
using Microsoft.VisualStudio.TestTools.UnitTesting;
using Moq;
using SportsStore.Domain.Abstract;
using SportsStore.Domain.Entities;
using SportsStore.WebUI.Controllers;
using System.Linq;
using System.Web.Mvc;

namespace SportsStore.UnitTests {
    [TestClass]
    public class ImageTests {

        [TestMethod]
        public void Can_Retrieve_Image_Data() {

            // Arrange - create a Product with image data
            Product prod = new Product {
                ProductID = 2,
                Name = "Test",
                ImageData = new byte[] { },
                ImageMimeType = "image/png"
            };

            // Arrange - create the mock repository
            Mock<IProductRepository> mock = new Mock<IProductRepository>();
            mock.Setup(m => m.Products).Returns(new Product[] {
                new Product {ProductID = 1, Name = "P1"},
                prod,
                new Product {ProductID = 3, Name = "P3"}
            }.AsQueryable());

            // Arrange - create the controller
            ProductController target = new ProductController(mock.Object);

            // Act - call the GetImage action method
            ActionResult result = target.GetImage(2);

            // Assert
            Assert.IsNotNull(result);
            Assert.IsInstanceOfType(result, typeof(FileResult));
            Assert.AreEqual(prod.ImageMimeType, ((FileResult)result).ContentType);
        }
```

```
[TestMethod]
public void Cannot_Retrieve_Image_Data_For_Invalid_ID() {

    // Arrange - create the mock repository
    Mock<IProductRepository> mock = new Mock<IProductRepository>();
    mock.Setup(m => m.Products).Returns(new Product[] {
        new Product {ProductID = 1, Name = "P1"},
        new Product {ProductID = 2, Name = "P2"}
    }.AsQueryable());

    // Arrange - create the controller
    ProductController target = new ProductController(mock.Object);

    // Act - call the GetImage action method
    ActionResult result = target.GetImage(100);

    // Assert
    Assert.IsNull(result);
    }
  }
}
```

When dealing with a valid product ID, I check that I get a `FileResult` result from the action method and that the content type matches the type in the mock data. The `FileResult` class does not let me access the binary contents of the file, so I must be satisfied with a less than perfect test. When I request an invalid product ID, I check to ensure that the result is `null`.

The administrator can now upload images for products. You can try this yourself by starting the application, navigating to the /Admin/Index URL and editing one of the products. Figure 12-4 shows an example.

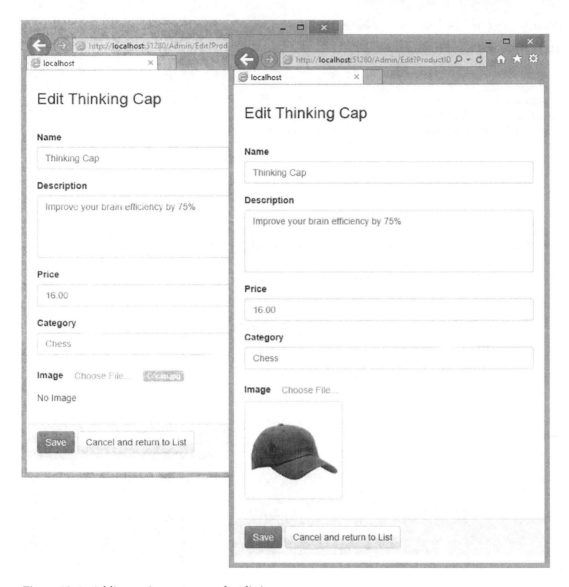

Figure 12-4. *Adding an image to a product listing*

Displaying Product Images

All that remains is to display the images alongside the product description in the product catalog. Edit the Views/
Shared/ProductSummary.cshtml view to reflect the changes shown in bold in Listing 12-15.

Listing 12-15. Displaying Images in the ProductSummary.cshtml File

```
@model SportsStore.Domain.Entities.Product

<div class="well">

    @if (Model.ImageData != null) {
        <div class="pull-left" style="margin-right: 10px">
            <img class="img-thumbnail" width="75" height="75"
                src="@Url.Action("GetImage", "Product",
                 new { Model.ProductID })" />
        </div>
    }

    <h3>
        <strong>@Model.Name</strong>
        <span class="pull-right label label-primary">@Model.Price.ToString("c")</span>
    </h3>
    @using (Html.BeginForm("AddToCart", "Cart")) {
        <div class="pull-right">
            @Html.HiddenFor(x => x.ProductID)
            @Html.Hidden("returnUrl", Request.Url.PathAndQuery)
            <input type="submit" class="btn btn-success" value="Add to cart" />
        </div>
    }
    <span class="lead"> @Model.Description</span>
</div>
```

With these changes in place, the customers will see images displayed as part of the product description when they browse the catalog, as shown in Figure 12-5.

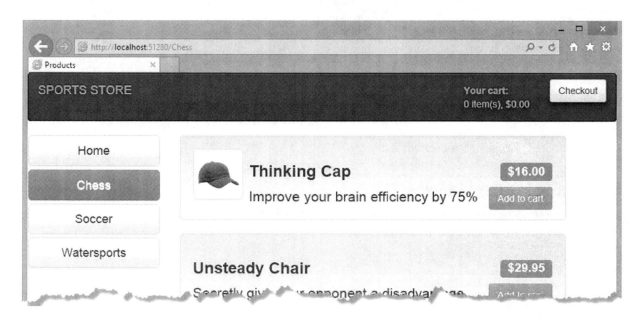

Figure 12-5. *Displaying product images*

Summary

In this and previous chapters, I have demonstrated how the ASP.NET MVC Framework can be used to create a realistic e-commerce application. This extended example has introduced many of the framework's key features: controllers, action methods, routing, views, model binding, metadata, validation, layouts, authentication, and more. You have also seen how some of the key technologies related to MVC can be used. These included the Entity Framework, Ninject, Moq, and the Visual Studio support for unit testing. The result is an application that has a clean, component-oriented architecture that separates out the various concerns, and a code base that will be easy to extend and maintain. In the next chapter, I show you how to deploy the SportsStore application into production.

CHAPTER 13

▨ ▨ ▨

Deployment

The final, and critical, step in application development is deployment: making your application available for the world to use. In this chapter, I'll show you how to prepare and deploy the SportsStore application.

There are lots of different ways to deploy MVC Framework applications and a wide range of deployment targets. You can deploy to a Windows Server machine running Internet Information Services (IIS) which you run and manage locally; you can deploy to a remote hosting service that manages servers for you; or, increasingly, you can deploy to a cloud infrastructure platform that provisions and scales your application to seamlessly meet demand.

I thought long and hard about how to create a useful example deployment in this chapter. I ruled out showing you how to deploy directly to IIS because the server configuration process is long and complicated, and most MVC Framework developers that are targeting local servers rely on an IT operations group to perform configuration and deployment tasks. I also ruled out demonstrating deployment to a managed hosting company because each has its own custom deployment processes and no one company sets the standard for hosting.

So, somewhat by default, I settled on demonstrating a deployment to Windows Azure, which is Microsoft's cloud platform and which has some nice support for MVC applications. I am not suggesting that Azure is suitable for all deployments, but I like the way it works and using it in this chapter allows me to demonstrate the deployment process rather than getting bogged down in IIS and Windows configuring issues. There is a free 90-day trial available on Azure as I write this (and MSDN subscriptions include Azure), which means that you should be able to follow the example in this chapter, even if you don't intend to use Azure to host your application.

■ **Caution**   I recommend that you practice deployment using a test application and server before attempting to deploy a real application into a production environment. Like every other aspect of the software development life cycle, the deployment process benefits from testing. I have a stock of horror stories of project teams who have destroyed operational applications through overly hasty and poorly tested deployment procedures. It is not that the ASP.NET deployment features are especially dangerous—they are not—but rather, any interaction that involves a running application with real user data deserves careful thought and planning.

Deploying a web application used to be a tedious and error-prone process, but Microsoft has put a lot of effort into improving the deployment tools in Visual Studio. So even if you need to deploy to a different kind of infrastructure, you will find that Visual Studio is able to do a lot of the heavy lifting for you.

Preparing Windows Azure

You have to create an account before you can use Azure, which you can do by going to www.windowsazure.com. At the time of writing, Microsoft is offering free trial accounts, and MSDN packages include Azure services. Once you have created your account, you can manage your Azure services by going to http://manage.windowsazure.com to provide your credentials. When you start, you will see the summary view shown in Figure 13-1.

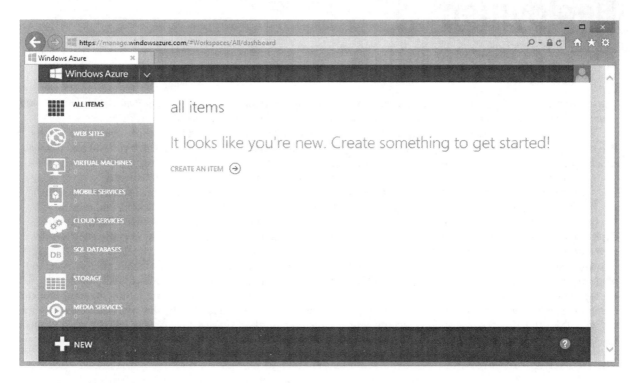

Figure 13-1. *The Azure portal*

Creating the Web Site and Database

I start by creating a new web site and database service, which are two of the cloud services offered by Azure. Click the large plus sign in the bottom-left corner of the portal window and select Compute ➤ Web Site ➤ Custom Create. You will see the form illustrated in Figure 13-2.

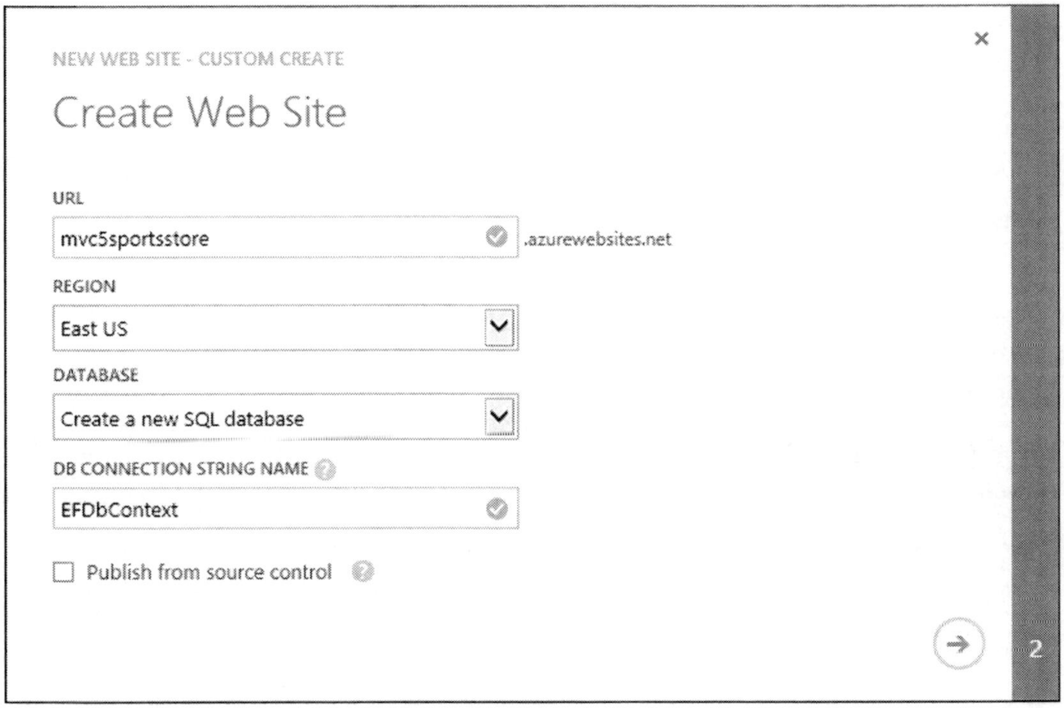

Figure 13-2. *Creating a new web site and database*

I need to select a URL for my application. For the free Azure services, I am restricted to names in the azurewebsites.net domain. I have chosen the name mvc5sportsstore, but you will have to choose your own name since each Azure web site requires a unique name.

Select the region that you want your application deployed to and ensure that the Create a new SQL database option is selected for the Database field. (Azure can use MySql, which the SportsStore application is not set up to use, so I want the option that gives me a SQL Server database.)

Set the DB Connection String Name field to EFDbContext. This is the name the SportsStore application uses to get a database connection from the Web.config file, and by using this name in the Azure service, I ensure that the application code works in deployment without modification.

When you have filled out the form, click the arrow button to proceed to the form shown in Figure 13-3.

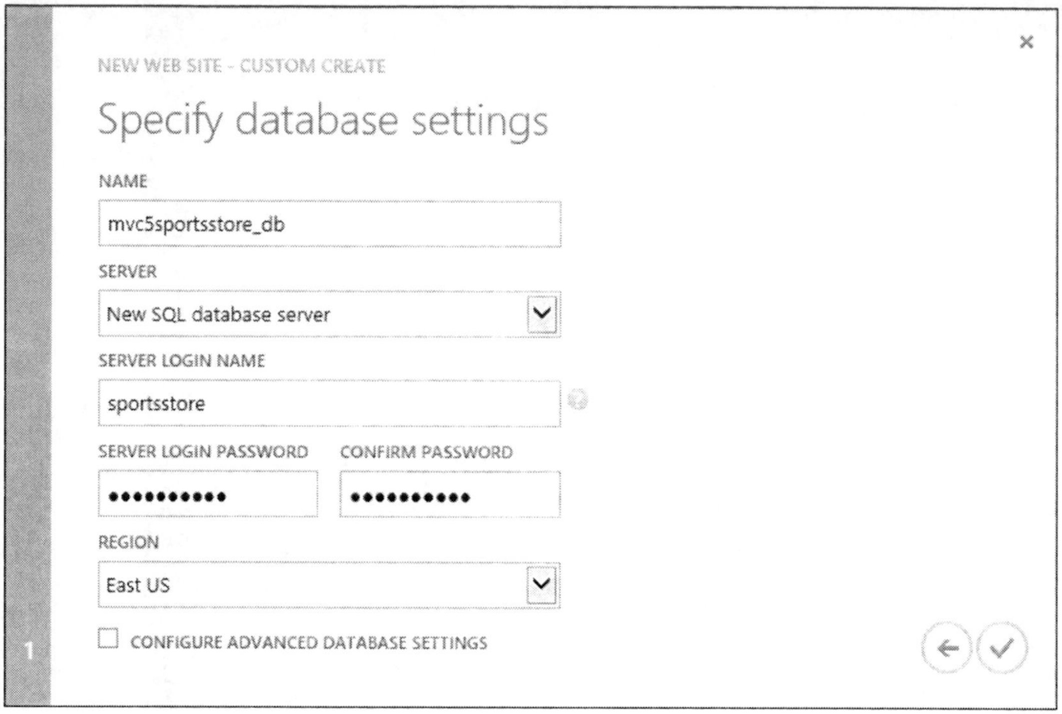

Figure 13-3. *Configuring the database*

Set a name for the database. I have used mvc5sportsstore_db so that it is obvious which application the database relates to. Select the New SQL Data Server option for the Server field and enter a login name and password. I specified a name of sportsstore and followed the guidance provided by the form to select a password containing mixed-case letters and numbers. Make a note of the username and password you use because you will need them in the next section. Click the check mark button to complete the setup process. Azure will create new web site and database services, which can take a few minutes. You will be returned to the overview when setup is complete and you will see that the Web Sites and SQL Databases categories each report one item, as shown in Figure 13-4.

Figure 13-4. *The effect of creating a web site with a database*

Preparing the Database for Remote Administration

The next step is to configure the Azure database so that it contains the same schema and data that I used in Chapter 7. Click the SQL Databases link in the Azure summary page and then click the entry that appears in the SQL Databases table. (If you are following my example, the database will be called mvc5sportsstore_db.)

The portal will show you details of the database and various options for configuring and managing it. Click the Set up Windows Azure firewall rules for this address link, which you will find in the Design Your Database section of the page. You will see a message that tells you that your current IP address (which is to say the IP address of your workstation) is not in the firewall rules. Click the Yes button as shown in Figure 13-5.

Figure 13-5. *Adding the workstation IP address to the Azure firewall rules*

▪ **Caution**   Visual Studio has support for deploying the database along with the application. I recommend against using this feature since it is trivially easy to wipe out your real application data with a careless menu selection. Always update your database separately and test thoroughly before doing so.

Creating the Schema

The next step is to create the schema for the database. Click the Design your SQL database link in the Connect to your Database section. Enter the database name (mvc5sportsstore_db), username (sportsstore), and the password that you defined when creating the database, and click the Log On button, as shown in Figure 13-6.

Figure 13-6. *Connecting to the database*

■ **Tip** Managing the database requires Silverlight, which you may need to install in your browser before you can continue.

At the top of the window you will see a New Query button. Click the button and a text area will enter into which you can type SQL commands. This is where I am going to provide the SQL commands that will create the database table I need.

Getting the Schema Command

I can get the SQL statements I need from Visual Studio. Open the Server Explorer window and expand the items it contains until you reach the entry for the Products table in the development SportsStore application. Right-click the Products table and select Open Table Definition. The editor for the table schema will be opened. In the T-SQL tab, you will see the SQL shown in Listing 13-1.

Listing 13-1. The Statement to Create the Products Table

```
CREATE TABLE [dbo].[Products] (
    [ProductID]     INT             IDENTITY (1, 1) NOT NULL,
    [Name]          NVARCHAR (100)  NOT NULL,
    [Description]   NVARCHAR (500)  NOT NULL,
    [Category]      NVARCHAR (50)   NOT NULL,
    [Price]         DECIMAL (16, 2) NOT NULL,
    [ImageData]     VARBINARY (MAX) NULL,
    [ImageMimeType] VARCHAR (50)    NULL,
    PRIMARY KEY CLUSTERED ([ProductID] ASC)
);
```

Copy the SQL from Visual Studio, paste it into the text area in the browser, and click the Run button at the top of the browser window. After a second, you will see the message Command(s) completed successfully, which indicates that the Azure database contains a Product database using the same schema as I defined in the SportsStore application.

Adding the Table Data

Now that I have created the table, I can populate it with the product data that I used in Chapter 7. Return to the Products entry in the Database Explorer window, right-click, and select Show Table Data from the pop-up menu. You will find a Script button at the top of the window that is opened, as shown in Figure 13-7.

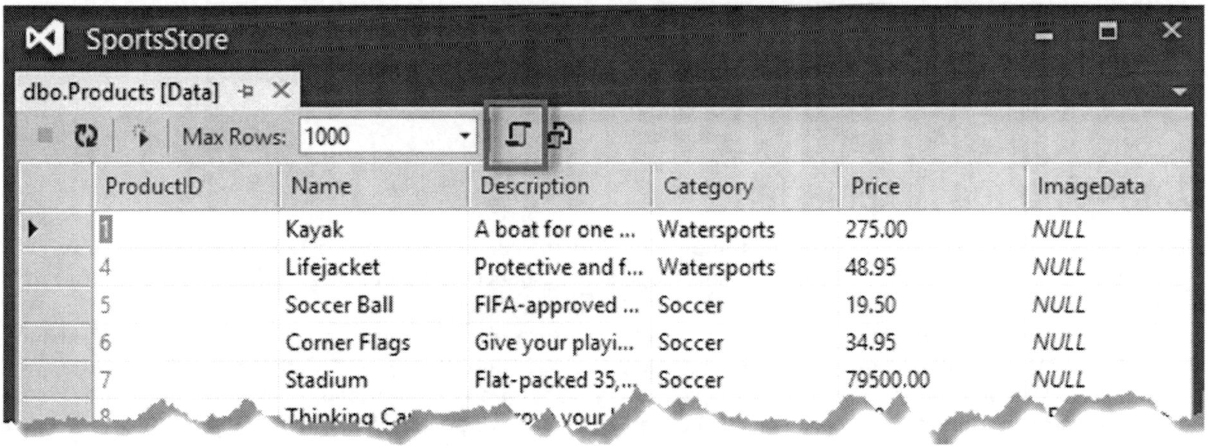

Figure 13-7. *The script button in the table data display*

A new window will open containing another SQL statement, which I have shown in Listing 13-2.

Listing 13-2. The SQL Statement to Add Data to the Products Table

```
SET IDENTITY_INSERT [dbo].[Products] ON
INSERT INTO [dbo].[Products] ([ProductID], [Name], [Description], [Category], [Price],
[ImageMimeType]) VALUES (1, N'Kayak', N'A boat for one person', N'Watersports', CAST(275.00 AS
Decimal(16, 2)), NULL)
INSERT INTO [dbo].[Products] ([ProductID], [Name], [Description], [Category], [Price],
[ImageMimeType]) VALUES (4, N'Lifejacket', N'Protective and fashionable', N'Watersports', CAST(48.95
AS Decimal(16, 2)), NULL)
INSERT INTO [dbo].[Products] ([ProductID], [Name], [Description], [Category], [Price],
[ImageMimeType]) VALUES (5, N'Soccer Ball', N'FIFA-approved size and weight', N'Soccer', CAST(19.50
AS Decimal(16, 2)), NULL)
INSERT INTO [dbo].[Products] ([ProductID], [Name], [Description], [Category], [Price],
[ImageMimeType]) VALUES (6, N'Corner Flags', N'Give your playing field a professional touch',
N'Soccer', CAST(34.95 AS Decimal(16, 2)), NULL)
INSERT INTO [dbo].[Products] ([ProductID], [Name], [Description], [Category], [Price],
[ImageMimeType]) VALUES (7, N'Stadium', N'Flat-packed 35,000-seat stadium', N'Soccer', CAST(79500.00
AS Decimal(16, 2)), NULL)
INSERT INTO [dbo].[Products] ([ProductID], [Name], [Description], [Category], [Price],
[ImageMimeType]) VALUES (8, N'Thinking Cap', N'Improve your brain efficiency by 75%', N'Chess',
CAST(16.00 AS Decimal(16, 2)), N'image/jpeg')
INSERT INTO [dbo].[Products] ([ProductID], [Name], [Description], [Category], [Price],
[ImageMimeType]) VALUES (9, N'Unsteady Chair', N'Secretly give your opponent a disadvantage',
N'Chess', CAST(29.95 AS Decimal(16, 2)), NULL)
INSERT INTO [dbo].[Products] ([ProductID], [Name], [Description], [Category], [Price],
[ImageMimeType]) VALUES (10, N'Human Chess Board', N'A fun game for the family', N'Chess',
CAST(75.00 AS Decimal(16, 2)), NULL)
INSERT INTO [dbo].[Products] ([ProductID], [Name], [Description], [Category], [Price],
[ImageMimeType]) VALUES (11, N'Bling-Bling King', N'Gold-plated, diamond-studded King', N'Chess',
CAST(1200.00 AS Decimal(16, 2)), NULL)
SET IDENTITY_INSERT [dbo].[Products] OFF
```

Clear the text area in the Azure browser window and paste the SQL shown in the listing in its place. Click the Run button. The script will be executed and add the data to the table.

Deploying the Application

Now that the setup is complete, deploying the application is simple. Return to the main Azure portal and click the Web Sites button. Click the mvc5sportsstore web site to open the dashboard page and click the Download the publish profile link in the Publish your app section. Save this file in a prominent location.

For my Azure service, the file is called mvc5sportsstore.azurewebsites.net.PublishSettings and I saved it to the desktop. This file contains the details that Visual Studio needs to publish your app to the Azure infrastructure.

Return to Visual Studio and right-click the SportsStore.WebUI project in the Solution Explorer and select Publish from the pop-up menu. You will see the Publish Web dialog window, as illustrated by Figure 13-8.

Figure 13-8. *The Publish Web dialog*

Click the Import button and locate the file that you downloaded from the Azure portal. Visual Studio will process the file and display the details of your Azure service configuration, as shown in Figure 13-9. Your details will reflect the name you selected for your web site.

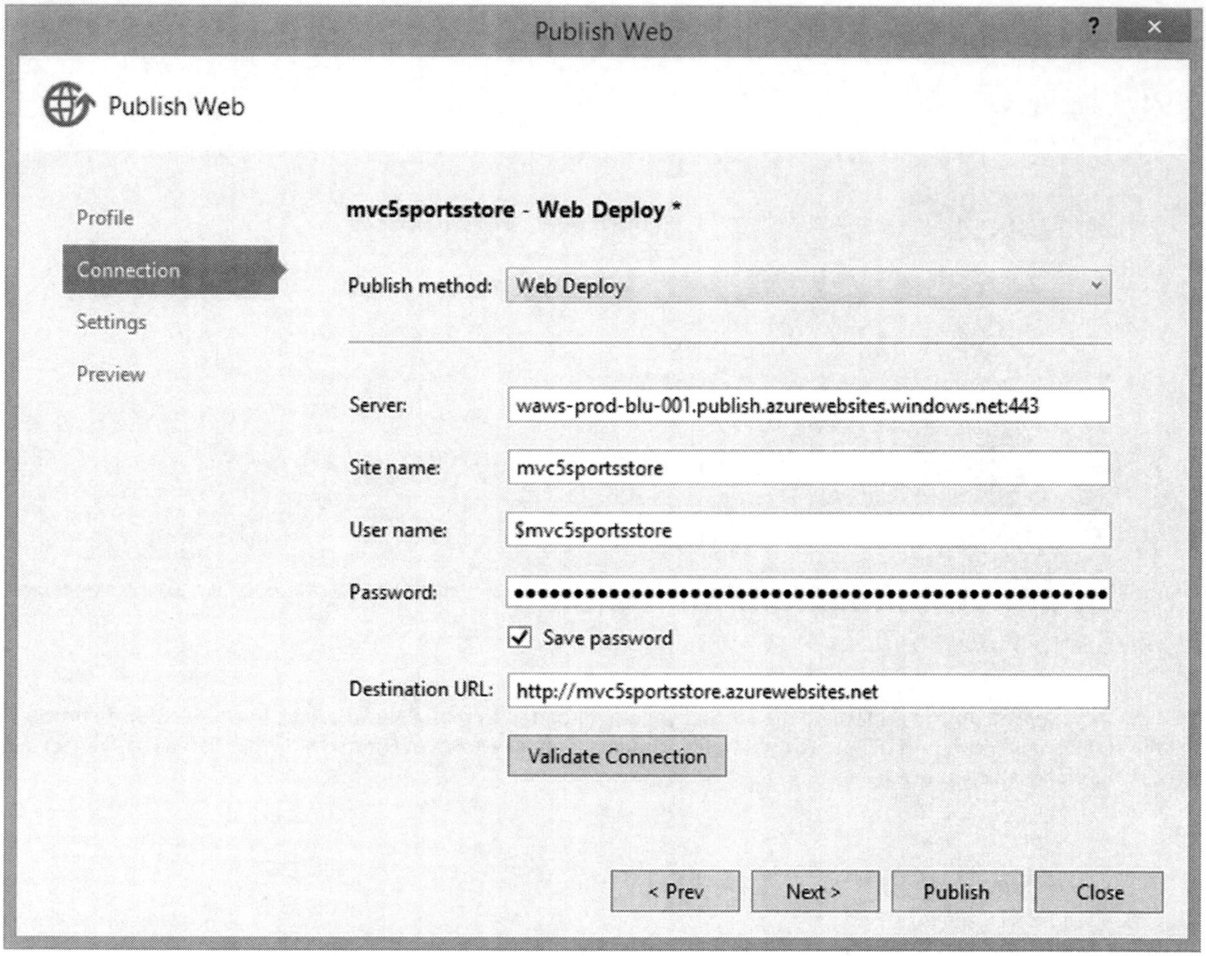

Figure 13-9. *Details of the Azure service that the application will be deployed to*

There is no need to change any of the values that are displayed. Click the Next button to move to the next stage of the deployment process, which you can see in Figure 13-10.

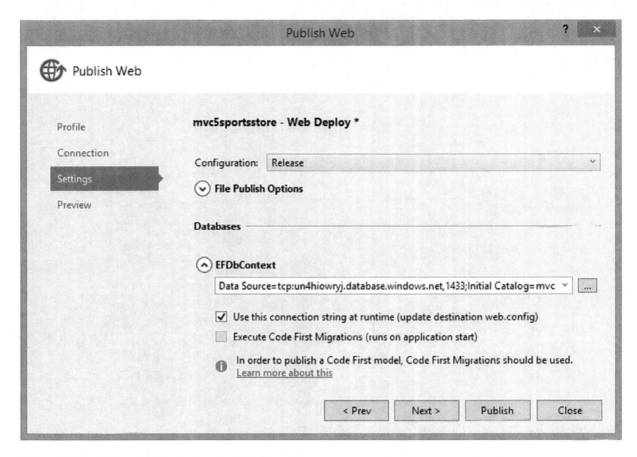

Figure 13-10. *Settings for the deployed application*

You can choose the configuration that will be used in deployment. This will usually be Release, but you can select Debug if you intend to test your application on the Azure infrastructure and want the debug settings for the compiler and your application bundles.

The other part of this process is configuring database connections. Visual Studio gives you the opportunity to create mappings between the database connections defined in your project and the databases that are associated with your Azure web site. My Web.config file contains only one set of details, and since I only created one Azure database, there is only one entry to pick from the drop-down list. If you have multiple databases in your application, you should take care to ensure that the right Azure database is selected.

Click the Next button to preview the effect of your deployment, as shown in Figure 13-11. When you click the Start Preview button, Visual Studio walks through the deployment process, but does not actually send the files to the server. If you are upgrading an application that is already deployed, this can be a useful check to ensure that you are only replacing the files that you expect.

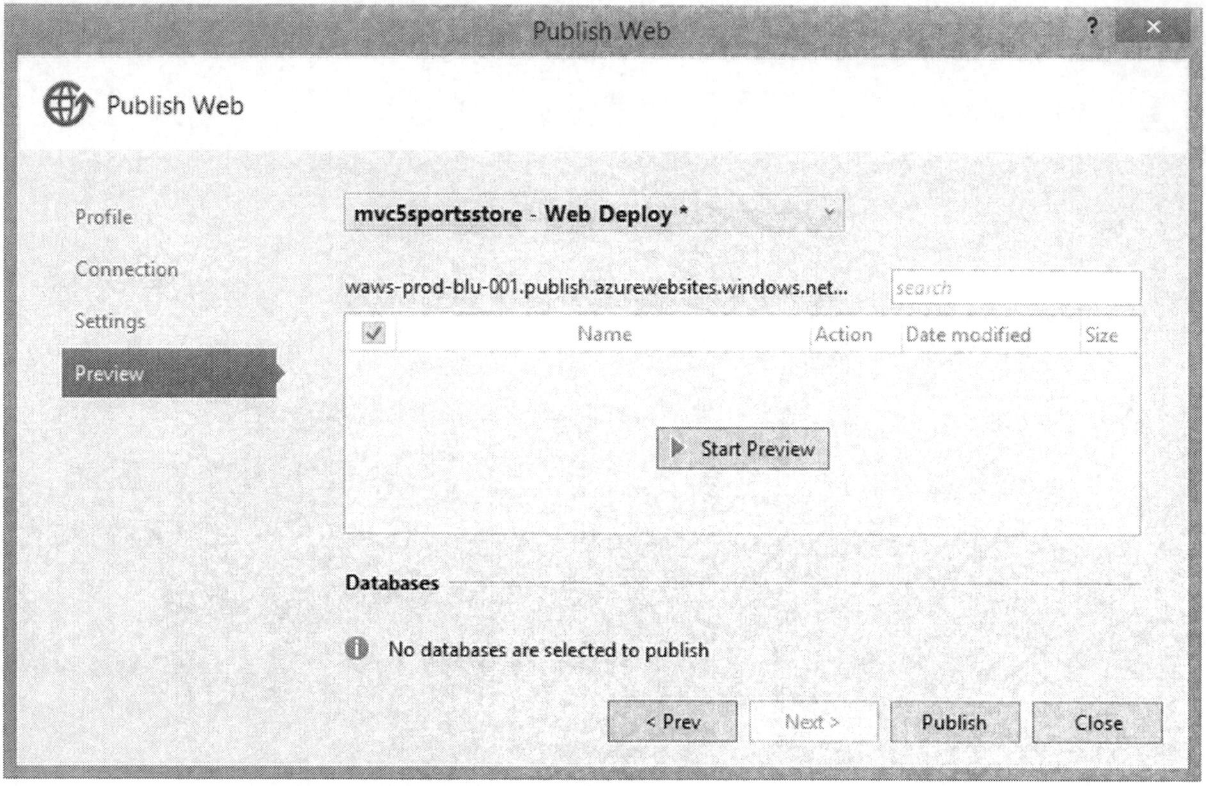

Figure 13-11. *The Preview section of the Publish Web dialog*

This is the first time that I have deployed this application, so all the files in the project will appear in the preview window, as shown in Figure 13-12. Notice that each file has a check box next to it. You can prevent individual files from being deployed, although you should be careful when doing this. I am pretty conservative in this regard and I would rather deploy files that I do not need rather than forget to deploy one that I do.

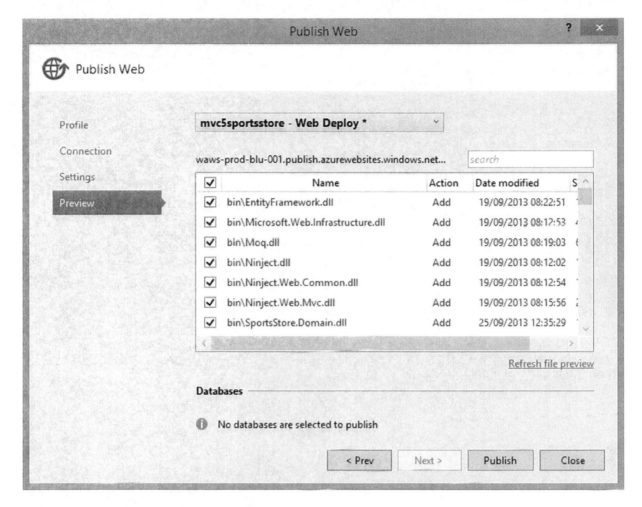

Figure 13-12. *Previewing the deployment changes*

Click the Publish button to deploy your application to the Azure platform. The Publish Web dialog window will close and you will be able to see details of the deployment progress in the Visual Studio Output window, as shown in Figure 13-13.

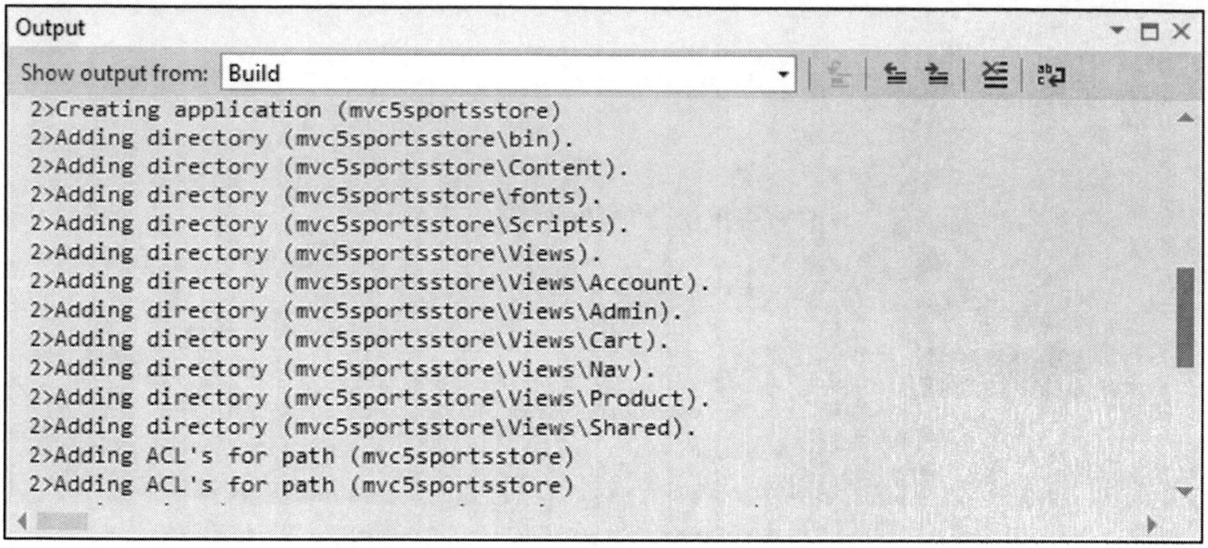

Figure 13-13. *Deploying an application to the Azure platform*

It can take a few minutes to deploy an application, but then the process is complete. Visual Studio will open a browser window that navigates to the URL of your Azure web site. For me, this URL is http://mvc5sportsstore. azurewebsites.net, as shown in Figure 13-14.

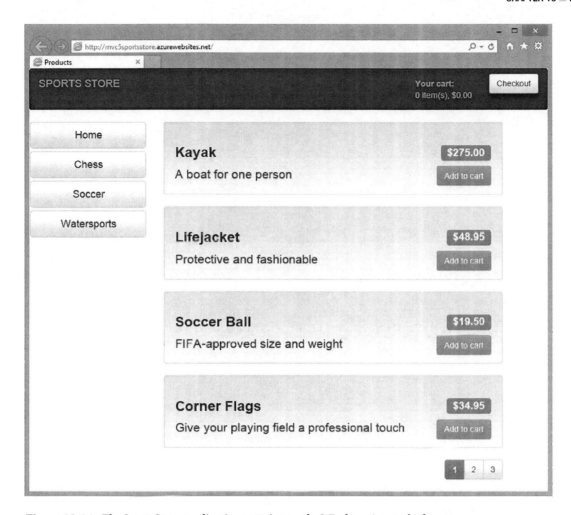

Figure 13-14. *The SportsStore application running on the Windows Azure platform*

Summary

In this chapter, I have shown you how to deploy an MVC Framework to the Windows Azure platform. There are many different ways to deploy applications and many different platforms that you can target, but the process I have shown you in this chapter is representative of what you can expect, even if you don't use Azure.

And that's the end of the SportsStore application and this part of the book. In Part 2, I begin the process of digging into the detail and showing you how the features I used to create the application work in depth.

■ ■ ■

CHAPTER 14

Overview of MVC Projects

I am going to provide some additional context before diving into MVC Framework features. This chapter gives an overview of the structure and nature of an ASP.NET MVC application, including the default project structure and naming conventions, some of which are optional and some of which are hard-coded into the way that the MVC Framework operates.

Working with Visual Studio MVC Projects

When you create a new ASP.NET project, Visual Studio gives you a number of choices as to the initial content you want in the project. The idea is to ease the learning process for new developers and apply some time-saving best practices for common features and tasks. This support continues with templates used to create controllers and views that are created with template code for listing data objects, editing model properties and so on.

With Visual Studio 2013 and MVC 5, Microsoft has updated the templates and *scaffolding*, as it is known, to blur the boundaries between different kinds of ASP.NET project and to provide a wider range of project templates and code configurations.

Part 1 of this book will have left you in no doubt that I am not a fan of this kind of approach to cookie cutter project or code. The intent is good, but the execution is always underwhelming. One of the characteristics I like most about ASP.NET and the MVC Framework is just how much flexibility I have in tailoring the platform to suit my development style, and the projects, classes and views that Visual Studio creates and populates make me feel constrained to work in someone else's style. I also find the content and configuration too generic and too bland to be useful. In Chapter 10, I mentioned that one of the dangers of using responsive design to target mobile devices is a kind of averaging that ends up compromising the experience for all devices, and something similar has happened to the Visual Studio templates. Microsoft can't possibly know what kind of application you need to create and so they cover all the bases, but in such a drab and generalized way that I end up just ripping out the default content anyway.

My advice (given to anyone who makes the mistake of asking) is to start with an empty project and add the folders, files, and packages that you need. Not only will you learn more about the way that the MVC Framework works, but you will have complete control over what your application contains.

But my preferences should not color your development experience. You may find the templates and scaffolding more useful than I do, especially if you are new to ASP.NET development and you have not yet developed a distinctive personal development style that suits you. You may also find the project templates a useful resource and a source of ideas, although you should be cautious about adding any functionality to an application before you completely understand how it works.

Creating the Project

When you first create a new MVC Framework project, you have two basic starting points to choose from: the Empty template and the MVC template. The names are a little misleading, because you can add the basic folders and assemblies required for the MVC Framework to any project template by checking the MVC option in the Add Folders and Core References section of the New ASP.NET Project dialog window, as shown in Figure 14-1. For the MVC option, this option is checked for you.

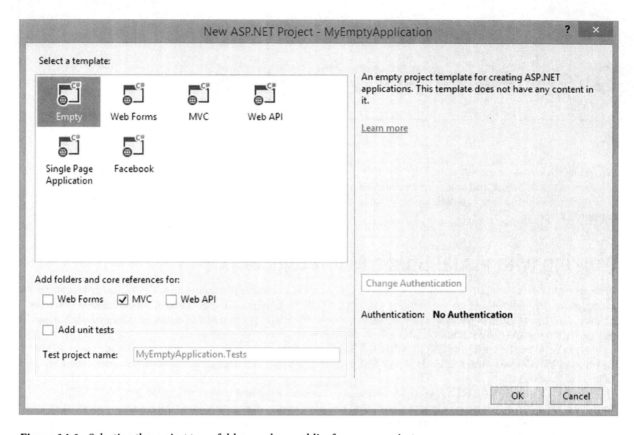

Figure 14-1. *Selecting the project type, folders and assemblies for a new project*

The real difference is the additional content that the MVC project template adds to new projects, which provides a ready-made starting point that includes some default controllers and views, a security configuration, some popular JavaScript and CSS packages (such as jQuery and Bootstrap) and a layout that uses Bootstrap to provide a theme for the application content. The Empty project option just contains the basic references required for an MVC framework and the barebones folder structure. There is a fair amount of content added by the MVC template and you can see the differences in Figure 14-2, which shows the contents of two newly created projects. The one on the left was created with the Empty template with the MVC folders and references option checked. The others show the content of a project that was created with the MVC template, and to be able to show the files on the page, I had to focus the Solution Explorer on different folders because a single listing was too long for a printed page.

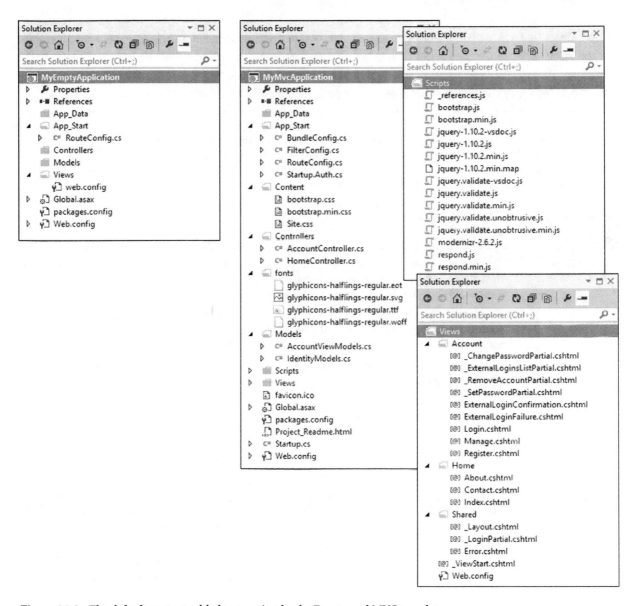

Figure 14-2. *The default content added to a project by the Empty and MVC templates*

The extra files that the MVC project adds look worse than they really are. Some are related to authentication and others are JavaScript and CSS files for which there are regular and minified versions. (I describe how these can be used in Chapter 26.)

■ **Tip** Visual Studio assembles a project created with the MVC template using NuGet packages, which means that you can see which packages are used by selecting `Manage NuGet Packages for Solution` from the `Visual Studio Tools` ➤ `Library Package Manager` menu. It also means that you can add the same packages to any project, including one created with the `Empty` template (and this is what I was doing for the examples in Part 1 of this book).

Whichever template you choose, you will notice that the resulting projects have similar folder structures. Some of the items in an MVC project have special roles, which are hard-coded into ASP.NET or the MVC Framework. Others are subject to naming conventions. I have described each of the core files and folders in Table 14-1, some of which are not present in projects by default but which I introduce in later chapters.

Table 14-1. *Summary of MVC Project Items*

Folder or File	Description	Notes
/App_Data	This folder is where you put private data, such as XML files or databases if you are using SQL Server Express, SQLite, or other file-based repositories.	IIS will not serve the contents of this folder.
/App_Start	This folder contains some core configuration settings for your project, including the definition of routes and filters and content bundles.	I describe routes in Chapters 15 and 16, filters in Chapter 18 and content bundles in Chapter 26.
/Areas	Areas are a way of partitioning a large application into smaller pieces.	I describe areas in Chapter 15.
/bin	The compiled assembly for your MVC application is placed here, along with any referenced assemblies that are not in the GAC.	You won't see the bin directory in the Solution Explorer window unless you click the Show All Files button. Since these are binary files generated on compilation, you should not normally store them in source control.
/Content	This is where you put static content such as CSS files and images.	This is a convention but not required. You can put your static content anywhere that suits you.
/Controllers	This is where you put your controller classes.	This is a convention. You can put your controller classes anywhere you like, because they are all compiled into the same assembly.
/Models	This is where you put your view model and domain model classes, although all but the simplest applications benefit from defining the domain model in a dedicated project, as I demonstrated for SportsStore.	This is a convention. You can define your model classes anywhere in the project or in a separate project.
/Scripts	This directory is intended to hold the JavaScript libraries for your application.	This is a convention. You can put script files in any location, as they are just another type of static content. See Chapter 26 for more information about managing script files.

(continued)

Table 14-1. (*continued*)

Folder or File	Description	Notes
/Views	This directory holds views and partial views, usually grouped together in folders named after the controller with which they are associated.	The /Views/web.config file prevents IIS from serving the content of these directories. Views must be rendered through an action method.
/Views/Shared	This directory holds layouts and views which are not specific to a single controller.	
/Views/Web.config	This is *not* the configuration file for your application. It contains the configuration required to make views work with ASP.NET and prevents views from being served by IIS and the namespaces imported into views by default.	
/Global.asax	This is the global ASP.NET application class. Its code-behind class (Global.asax.cs) is the place to register routing configuration, as well as set up any code to run on application initialization or shutdown, or when unhandled exceptions occur.	The Global.asax file has the same role in an MVC application as it does in a Web Forms application.
/Web.config	This is the configuration file for your application.	The Web.config file has the same role in an MVC application as it does in a Web Forms application.

Understanding MVC Conventions

There are two kinds of conventions in an MVC project. The first kind is just suggestions as to how you might like to structure your project. For example, it is conventional to put your JavaScript files in the Scripts folder. This is where other MVC developers would expect to find them, and where NuGet packages will install them. But you are free to rename the Scripts folder, or remove it entirely and put your scripts somewhere else. That would not prevent the MVC Framework from running your application as long as the script elements in your views refer to the location you settle on.

The other kind of convention arises from the principle of *convention over configuration*, which was one of the main selling points that made Ruby on Rails so popular. Convention over configuration means that you don't need to explicitly configure associations between controllers and their views, for example. You just follow a certain naming convention for your files, and everything just works. There is less flexibility in changing your project structure when dealing with this kind of convention. The following sections explain the conventions that are used in place of configuration.

■ **Tip** All of the conventions can be changed if you are using a custom view engine (which I cover in Chapter 20), but this is not a step to be taken lightly and, for the most part, these are the conventions you will be dealing with in MVC projects.

Following Conventions for Controller Classes

Controller classes must have names that end with `Controller`, such as `ProductController`, `AdminController`, and `HomeController`. When referencing a controller from elsewhere in the project, such as when using an HTML helper method, you specify the first part of the name (such as `Product`), and the MVC Framework automatically appends `Controller` to the name and starts looking for the controller class.

■ **Tip**   You can change this behavior by creating your own implementation of the `IControllerFactory` interface, which I describe in Chapter 19.

Following Conventions for Views

Views and partial views go into the folder `/Views/Controllername`. For example, a view associated with the `ProductController` class would go in the `/Views/Product` folder.

■ **Tip**   Notice that I omit the `Controller` part of the class from the `Views` folder: `/Views/Product`, *not* `/Views/ProductController`. This may seem counterintuitive at first, but it quickly becomes second nature.

The MVC Framework expects that the default view for an action method should be named after that method. For example, the default view associated with an action method called `List` should be called `List.cshtml`. Thus, for the `List` action method in the `ProductController` class, the default view is expected to be `/Views/Product/List.cshtml`. The default view is used when you return the result of calling the `View` method in an action method, like this:

```
...
return View();
...
```

You can specify a different view by name, like this:

```
...
return View("MyOtherView");
...
```

Notice that I do not include the file name extension or the path to the view. When looking for a view, the MVC Framework looks in the folder named after the controller and then in the `/Views/Shared` folder. This means that I can put views that will be used by more than one controller in the `/Views/Shared` folder and the framework will find them.

Following Conventions for Layouts

The naming convention for layouts is to prefix the file with an underscore (_) character, and layout files are placed in the /Views/Shared folder. This layout is applied to all views by default through the /Views/_ViewStart.cshtml file. If you do not want the default layout applied to views, you can change the settings in _ViewStart.cshtml (or delete the file entirely) to specify another layout in the view, like this:

```
@{
    Layout = "~/Views/Shared/_MyLayout.cshtml";
}
```

Or you can disable any layout for a given view, like this:

```
@{
    Layout = null;
}
```

Debugging MVC Applications

You debug an ASP.NET MVC application in exactly the same way as you debug an ASP.NET Web Forms application. The Visual Studio debugger is a powerful and flexible tool, with many features and uses. I can only scratch the surface in this book, but in the sections that follow I show you how to set up the debugger and perform different debugging activities on your MVC project.

Preparing the Example Project

To demonstrate using the debugger, I have created a new MVC project using the MVC project template, just so you can see how the default content and configuration is set up and the effect of the default theme that is applied to views. I called the new project DebuggingDemo, as shown in Figure 14-3. I have chosen the Individual User Accounts authentication option, which sets up a basic user security system.

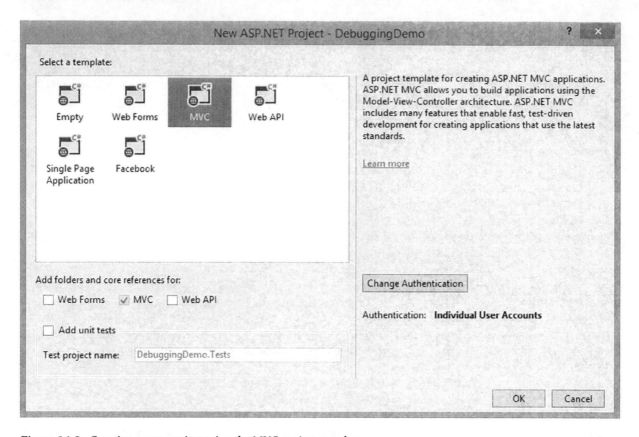

Figure 14-3. Creating a new project using the MVC project template

Click the OK button and Visual Studio will create the project and add the default packages, files, and folders that the MVC template includes. You can see how the files and settings added to the project are applied by starting the application, as shown in Figure 14-4.

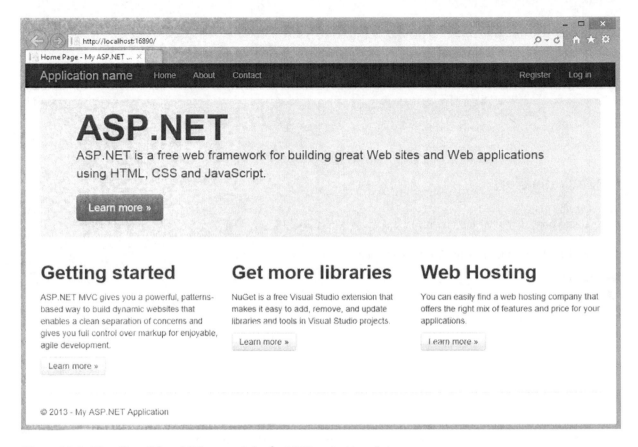

Figure 14-4. *The effect of the additions made by the MVC project template*

There are some placeholder elements for the name of the application and branding, and some pointers to the MVC documents, NuGet, and some hosting options. The navigation bar at the top of the screen is the same kind I used for the SportsStore application and the layout has some responsive features. Change the width of the window to see the effect.

Creating the Controller

Visual Studio creates a Home controller as part of the initial project content, but I am going to replace the code that Visual Studio added with that shown in Listing 14-1.

Listing 14-1. The Contents of the HomeController.cs File

```
using System.Web.Mvc;

namespace DebuggingDemo.Controllers {
    public class HomeController : Controller {

        public ActionResult Index() {
            int firstVal = 10;
```

```
            int secondVal = 5;
            int result = firstVal / secondVal;

            ViewBag.Message = "Welcome to ASP.NET MVC!";

            return View(result);
        }
    }
}
```

Creating the View

Visual Studio also created the Views/Home/Index.cshtml view file as part of the project setup. I don't need the default content and have to replace it with the markup shown in Listing 14-2.

Listing 14-2. The Contents of the Index.cshtml File

```
@model int

@{
    Layout = null;
}

<!DOCTYPE html>

<html>
<head>
    <meta name="viewport" content="width=device-width" />
    <link href="~/Content/Site.css" rel="stylesheet" type="text/css" />
    <title>Index</title>
</head>
<body>
    <h2 class="message">@ViewData["Message"]</h2>
    <p>
        The calculation result value is: @Model
    </p>
</body>
</html>
```

The last preparatory step I need to take is to add a style to the /Content/Site.css file and change one of the existing ones, as shown in Listing 14-3. The Site.css file is created by Visual Studio as part of the MVC project template and is the default location for application CSS styles. (I added a link element to the view in Listing 14-2 that imports this file into the Index.cshtml view.)

Listing 14-3. Adding a Style to the /Content/Site.css File

```
body { padding-top: 5px; padding-bottom: 5px; }
.field-validation-error { color: #b94a48; }
.field-validation-valid { display: none; }
input.input-validation-error { border: 1px solid #b94a48; }
input[type="checkbox"].input-validation-error { border: 0 none; }
```

```
.validation-summary-errors { color: #b94a48; }
.validation-summary-valid { display: none; }
.no-color { background-color: white; border-style:none; }
.message { font-size: 20pt; text-decoration: underline;}
```

Launching the Visual Studio Debugger

Visual Studio prepares new projects for debugging automatically, but it is useful to understand how to change the configuration. The important setting is in the Web.config file in the root project folder and can be found in the system.web element, as shown in Listing 14-4.

Listing 14-4. The Debug Attribute in the Web.config File

```
...
<system.web>
    <compilation debug="true" targetFramework="4.5.1" />
    <httpRuntime targetFramework="4.5.1" />
</system.web>
...
```

A lot of compilation in an MVC Framework project is done when the application is running in IIS, and so you need to ensure that the debug attribute on the compilation attribute is set to true during the development process. This ensures that the debugger is able to operate on the classes files produced through on-demand compilation

---

■ **Caution**   Do not deploy your application to a production server without setting the debug value to false. If you are using Visual Studio to deploy your application (as I did in Chapter 13), then the setting will be changed automatically when you select the Release configuration for the project.

In addition to the Web.config file, I want to ensure that Visual Studio includes debugging information in the class files that it creates. This isn't critical, but it can cause problems if the different debug settings are not in sync. Ensure that the Debug configuration is selected in the Visual Studio toolbar, as shown in Figure 14-5.

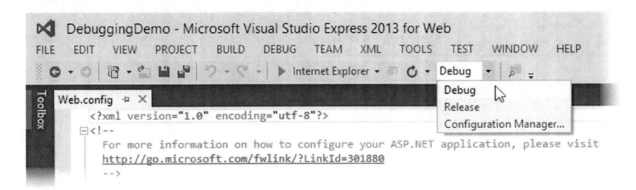

Figure 14-5. *Selecting the Debug configuration*

To debug an MVC Framework application, select Start Debugging from the Visual Studio Debug menu or click on the green arrow in the Visual Studio toolbar (which you can see in Figure 14-5, next to the name of the browser that will be used to display the app—Internet Explorer in this case).

If the debug attribute in the Web.config file is set to false when you start the debugger, then Visual Studio will display the dialog shown in Figure 14-6. Select the option which allows Visual Studio to edit the Web.config file and click the OK button and the debugger will start.

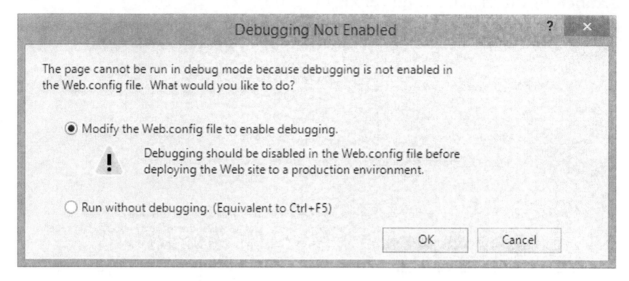

Figure 14-6. *The dialog that Visual Studio displays when the Web.config File disables debugging*

At this point, your application will be displayed in a new browser window, as shown in Figure 14-7.

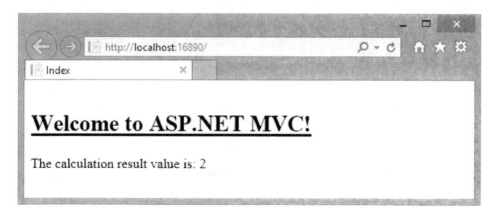

Figure 14-7. *Running the debugger*

The debugger will be attached to your application, but you will not notice any difference until the debugger breaks. (I explain what this means in the next section.) To stop the debugger, select Stop Debugging from the Visual Studio Debug menu or close the browser window.

Causing the Visual Studio Debugger to Break

An application that is running with the debugger attached will behave normally until a *break* occurs, at which point the execution of the application is halted and control is turned over to the debugger. While in this state, you can inspect and control the state of the application. Breaks occur for two main reasons: when a breakpoint is reached and when an unhandled exception arises. You will see examples of both in the following sections.

Using Breakpoints

A *breakpoint* is an instruction that tells the debugger to halt execution of the application and hand control to the programmer. You can inspect the state of the application and see what is happening and, optionally, resume execution again.

To create a breakpoint, right-click a code statement and select Breakpoint ➤ Insert Breakpoint from the pop-up menu. As a demonstration, apply a breakpoint to the first statement in the Index action method of the Home controller and you will see a red dot appear in the margin of the text editor, as shown in Figure 14-8.

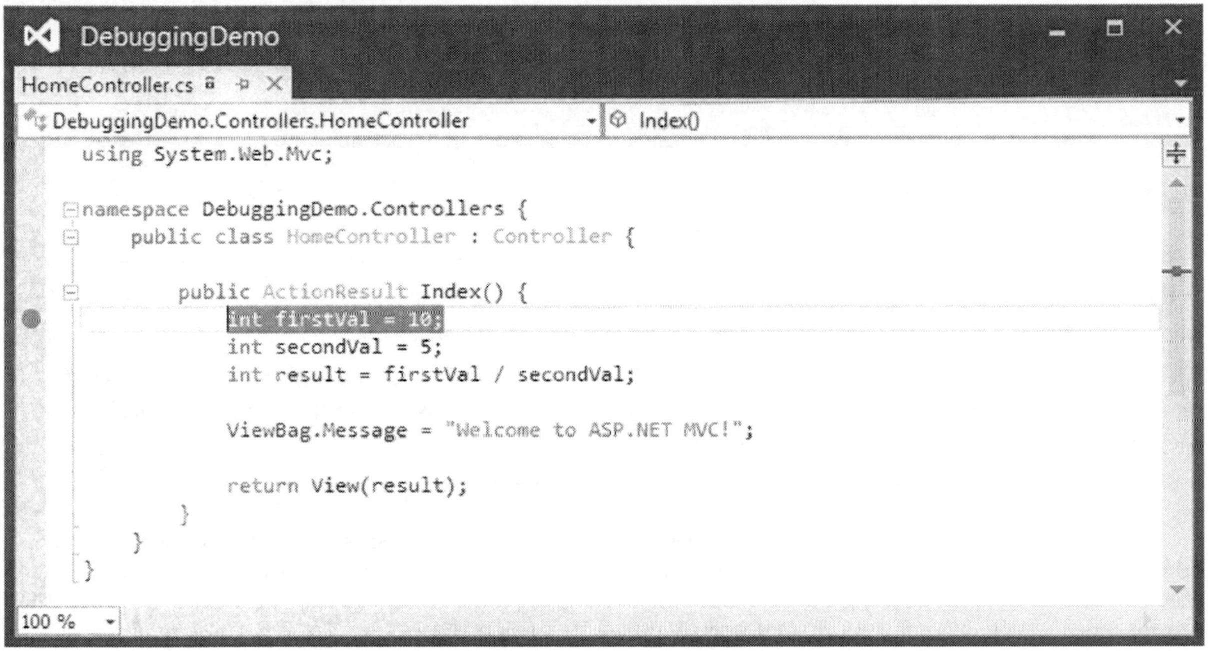

Figure 14-8. Applying a breakpoint to the first statement in the Index action method

To see the effect of the breakpoint, start the debugger by selecting Start Debugging from the Visual Studio Debug menu. The application will run until the statement to which the breakpoint has been applied is reached, at which point the debugger will break, halting execution of the application and transferring control. Visual Studio highlights the point at which the execution has been stopped with yellow highlights, as shown in Figure 14-9.

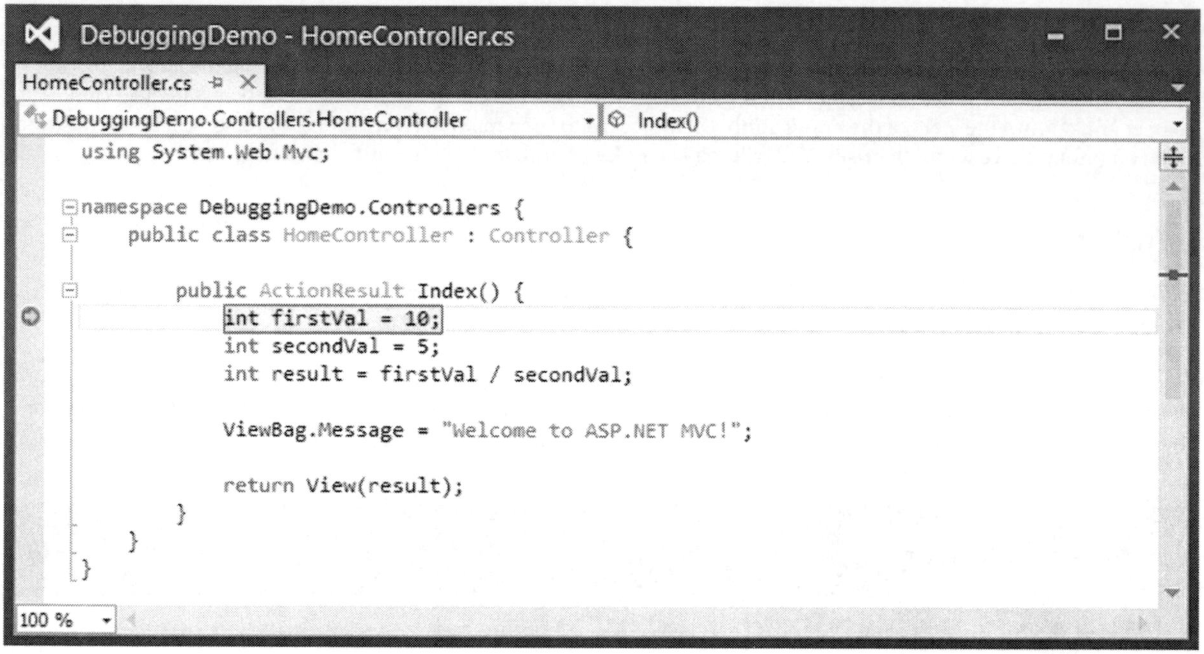

```
DebuggingDemo - HomeController.cs                                    —  □  ✕

HomeController.cs  ⌗  ✕

DebuggingDemo.Controllers.HomeController        ▾   ⊕  Index()                  ▾

    using System.Web.Mvc;

  ⊟namespace DebuggingDemo.Controllers {
    ⊟    public class HomeController : Controller {

      ⊟        public ActionResult Index() {
○                  int firstVal = 10;
                   int secondVal = 5;
                   int result = firstVal / secondVal;

                   ViewBag.Message = "Welcome to ASP.NET MVC!";

                   return View(result);
               }
           }
    }

100 %  ▾  ◁
```

Figure 14-9. Hitting a breakpoint

■ **Note**   A breakpoint is triggered only when the statement it is associated with is executed. My example breakpoint was reached as soon as the application was started because it is inside the action method that is called when a request for the default URL is received. If you place a breakpoint inside another action method, you must use the browser to request a URL associated with that method. This can mean working with the application in the way a user would or navigating directly to the URL in the browser window.

Once you have control of the application's execution, you can move to the next statement, follow execution into other methods and generally explore the state of your application. You can do this using the toolbar buttons or using the items in the Visual Studio Debug menu. In addition to giving you control of the execution of the app, Visual Studio provides you with a lot of useful information about the state of your app. In fact, there is so much information that I only have room to show you the basics.

Viewing Data Values in the Code Editor

The most common use for breakpoints is to track down bugs in your code. Before you can fix a bug, you have to figure out what is going on and one of the most useful features that Visual Studio provides is the ability to view and monitor the values of variables right in the code editor.

As an example, start the app using the debugger and wait until the breakpoint I added in the previous section is reached. When the debugger breaks, move the mouse pointer over the statement that defines the result variable. You will see a small pop-up which shows you the current value, as illustrated by Figure 14-10. It can be hard to make out the pop-up, so I have shown a magnified version in the figure.

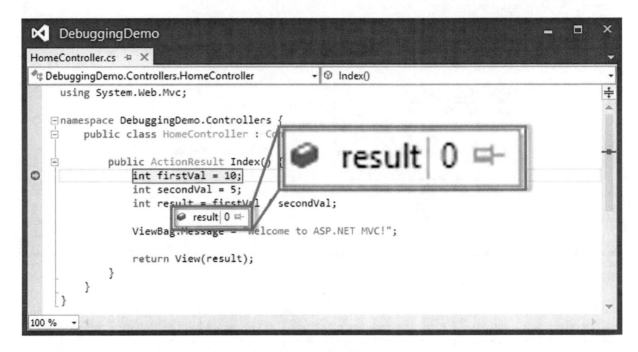

Figure 14-10. *Displaying the value of a variable in the Visual Studio code editor*

The execution of the statements in the Index action method has not reached the point where a value has been assigned to the result variable, so Visual Studio shows the default value, which is 0 for the int type. Select the Step Over menu item in the Visual Studio Debug menu (or press F10) to advance the point of execution to the statement which defines the ViewBag.Message property and hold your mouse over the result variable again. The debugger executed the statement that assigns a value to the result variable, and you can see the effect in Figure 14-11.

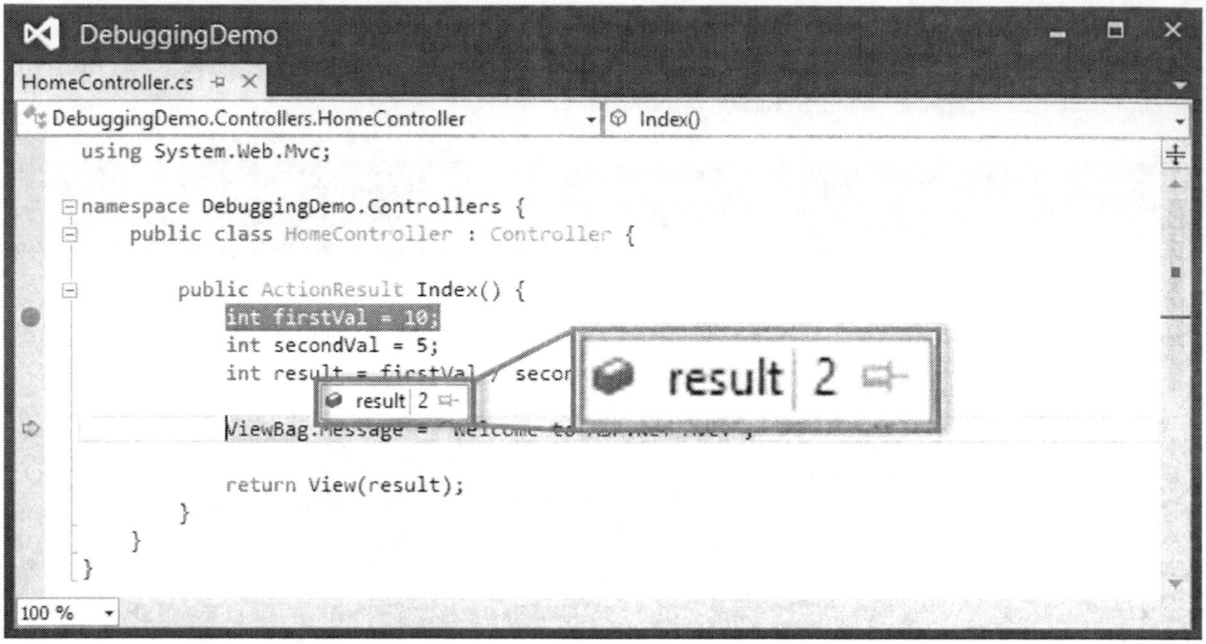

Figure 14-11. The effect of assigning a value of a variable

I use this feature when I start the process of tracking down a bug because it gives an immediate insight into what is going on inside the app. I find it especially useful for spotting null values, which indicate that a variable has not been assigned a value (a cause of many bugs early in the development process, in my experience).

You will notice that there is a pushpin icon to the right of the value in the pop-up. If you click on this, the pop-up becomes permanent and will indicate when the value of the variable changes. This allows you to monitor one or more variables and see when they change and what their new values are.

Viewing Application State in the Debugger Windows

Visual Studio provides a number of different windows that you can use to get information about your app while the execution has been halted following a breakpoint. A complete list of the windows available is shown on the Debug ➤ Windows menu, but two of the most useful are the Locals and Call Stack windows. The Locals window automatically displays the value of all of the variables in the current scope, as Figure 14-12 illustrates. This gives you an all-in-one view of the variables, which are likely to be of interest.

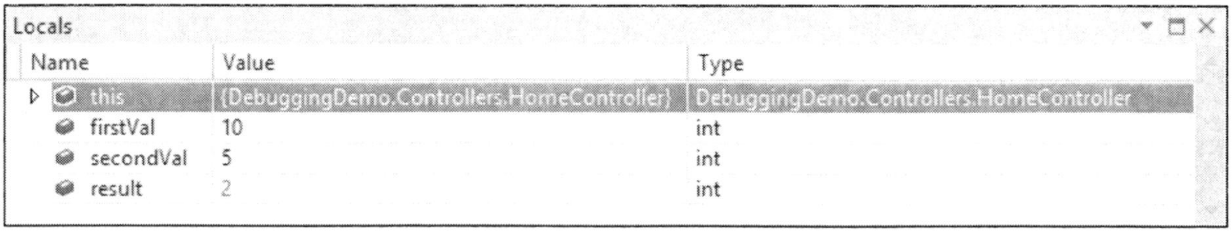

Figure 14-12. The Locals window

Variables whose values were changed by the previously executed statement are shown in red. In the figure, the `result` variable is red because I just executed the statement that assigns a value.

■ **Tip**   The set of variables shown in the `Locals` window changes as you navigate through the application, but if you want to keep an eye on a variable globally, then right-click on one of the items shown in the `Locals` window and select the `Add Watch` option. The items in the `Watch` window don't change as you execute statements in the app, providing you with a fixed point of reference.

The `Call Stack` window shows you the sequence of calls that have led to the current statement being executed. This can be helpful if you are trying to figure out odd behavior because you can unwind the call stack and explore the circumstances that led to the breakpoint being triggered. (I have not shown you the `Call Stack` window in a figure because the example app doesn't have enough call depth to provide a useful insight. But I recommend you explore this and the other Visual Studio windows to get more of an idea of what information the debugger is able to provide.)

■ **Tip**   You can add breakpoints to views. This can be helpful for inspecting the values of view model properties, for example. You add a breakpoint to a view just as I did in the code file: right-click the Razor statement that you are interested in and select `Breakpoint` ➤ `Insert Breakpoint`.

Breaking on Exceptions

Unhandled exceptions are a fact of development. One of the reasons that I unit and integration test my projects is to minimize the likelihood that such an exception will occur in production. As an aid to finding and fixing unhandled exceptions, the Visual Studio debugger will break automatically when it encounters one.

■ **Note**   Only *unhandled* exceptions cause the debugger to break. An exception becomes *handled* if you catch and handle it in a `try...catch` block. Handled exceptions can be a useful programming tool. They are used to represent the scenario where a method was unable to complete its task and needs to notify its caller. Unhandled exceptions are bad, because they represent an *unforeseen* condition and because they generally drop the user into an error page.

To demonstrate breaking on an exception, I have made a small change to the `Index` action method in the `Home` controller, as shown in Listing 14-5.

Listing 14-5. Adding a Statement That Will Cause an Exception in the HomeController.cs File

```
using System.Web.Mvc;

namespace DebuggingDemo.Controllers {
    public class HomeController : Controller {

        public ActionResult Index() {
            int firstVal = 10;
```

```
        int secondVal = 0;
        int result = firstVal / secondVal;

        ViewBag.Message = "Welcome to ASP.NET MVC!";

        return View(result);
        }
    }
}
```

I changed the value of the secondVal variable to be 0, which will cause an exception in the statement that divides firstVal by secondVal.

■ **Note** I also removed the breakpoint from the Index action method by right-clicking on the breakpoint icon in the margin and selecting Delete Breakpoint from the pop-up menu.

When you start the debugger, the application will run until the exception is thrown, at which point the exception helper pop-up will appear, as shown in Figure 14-13.

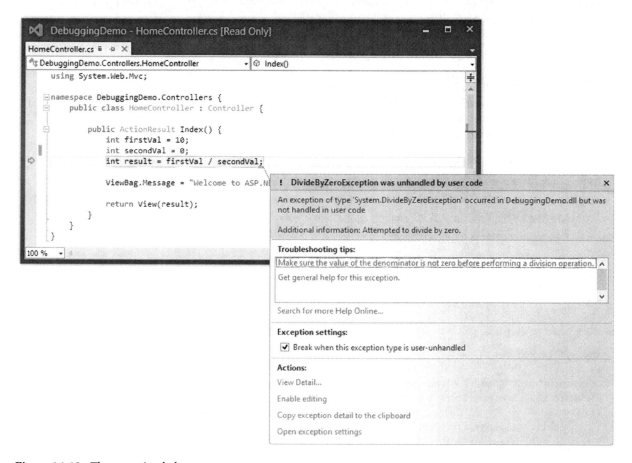

Figure 14-13. The exception helper

The exception helper gives you details of the exception. When the debugger breaks on an exception, you can inspect the application state and control execution, just as when a breakpoint is hit.

Using Edit and Continue

An interesting Visual Studio debugging feature is called *Edit and Continue*. When the debugger breaks, you can edit your code and then continue debugging. Visual Studio recompiles your application and re-creates the state of your application at the moment of the debugger break.

Enabling Edit and Continue

I need to make sure that Edit and Continue is enabled in two places:

- In the `Edit and Continue` section of the `Debugging` options (select `Options` from the Visual Studio Tools menu), make sure that `Enable Edit and Continue` is checked, as shown in Figure 14-14.

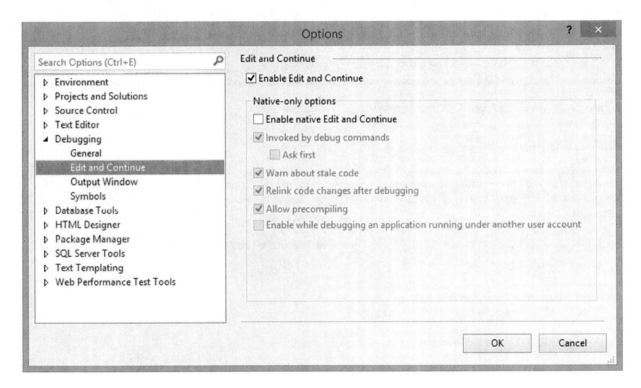

Figure 14-14. *Enabling Edit and Continue in the Options dialog box*

- In the project properties (select `DebuggingDemo Properties` from the Visual Studio `Project` menu), click the `Web` section and ensure that `Enable Edit and Continue` is checked, as shown in Figure 14-15.

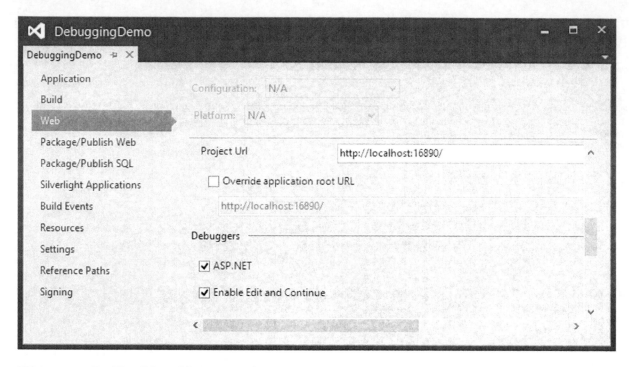

Figure 14-15. Enabling Edit and Continue in the project properties

Modifying the Project

The Edit and Continue feature is somewhat picky. There are some conditions under which it cannot work. One such condition is present in the Index action method of the HomeController class: the use of dynamic objects. To work around this, I have commented out the line that uses the view bag in the HomeController.cs class, as shown in Listing 14-6.

Listing 14-6. Removing the ViewBag Call from the Index Method in the HomeController.cs File

```
using System.Web.Mvc;

namespace DebuggingDemo.Controllers {
    public class HomeController : Controller {

        public ActionResult Index() {
            int firstVal = 10;
            int secondVal = 0;
            int result = firstVal / secondVal;

            // This statement has been commented out
            //ViewBag.Message = "Welcome to ASP.NET MVC!";

            return View(result);
        }
    }
}
```

I need to make a corresponding change in the Index.cshtml view, as shown in Listing 14-7.

Listing 14-7. Removing the ViewBag Call from the Index.cshtml File

```
@model int

@{
    Layout = null;
}

<!DOCTYPE html>

<html>
<head>
    <meta name="viewport" content="width=device-width" />
    <link href="~/Content/Site.css" rel="stylesheet" type="text/css" />
    <title>Index</title>
</head>
<body>
    <!-- This element has been commented out -->
    <!--<h2 class="message">@ViewData["Message"]</h2>-->
    <p>
        The calculation result value is: @Model
    </p>
</body>
</html>
```

Editing and Continuing

I am now ready for a demonstration of the Edit and Continue feature. Begin by selecting Start Debugging from the Visual Studio Debug menu. The application will be started with the debugger attached and run until it reaches the line where I perform the calculation in the Index method. The value of the second parameter is zero, which causes an exception to be thrown. At this point, the debugger halts execution, and the exception helper pops up (just like the one shown in Figure 14-13).

Click the Enable editing link in the exception helper window. In the code editor, change the expression that calculates the value for the result variable, as follows:

```
...
int result = firstVal / 2;
...
```

I have removed the reference to the secondVal variable and replaced it with a numeric literal value of 2. Now select Continue from the Visual Studio Debug menu to resume execution of the application. The new value is used to generate the value for the result variable, producing the output shown in Figure 14-16.

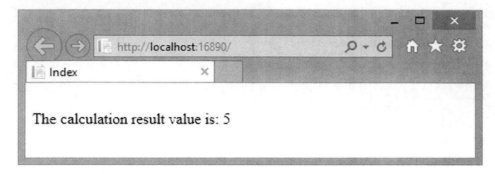

Figure 14-16. *The effect of correcting a bug using the Edit and Continue feature*

Take a moment to reflect on what happened here. I started the application with a bug in it: an attempt to divide a value by zero. The debugger detected the exception and stopped executing the program. I edited the code and then told the debugger to continue the execution. At this point, Visual Studio recompiled the application, restored its state and continued execution as normal using the new value. The browser received the rendered result, which reflected the new data value. Without Edit and Continue, I would have needed to stop the application, make a change, compile the application, and restart the debugger. I would then use the browser to repeat the steps that I took up to the moment of the debugger break. It is avoiding this last step that can be the most important. Complex bugs may require many steps through the application to re-create, and the ability to test potential fixes without needing to repeat those steps over and over can save the programmer's time and sanity.

Using Browser Link

Visual Studio 2013 includes a feature called *browser link* that allows you to view the application in multiple browsers simultaneously and have them all reload when you make a change. This feature is most useful once an application has stabilized and you are doing fit and finish work on the HTML and CSS that your views generate. (I'll explain why shortly.)

To use browser link, click on the small down arrow next to the selected browser on the Visual Studio toolbar and select Browse With from the menu, as shown in Figure 14-17.

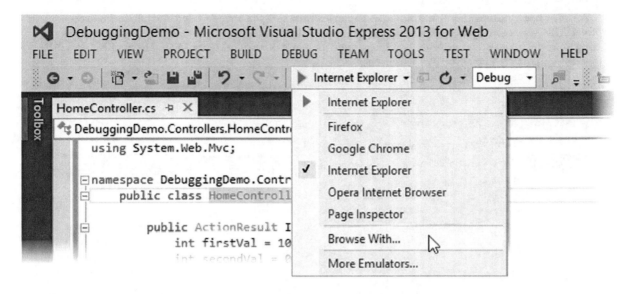

Figure 14-17. *Preparing to select the browsers used for the browser link feature*

The Browse With dialog window will appear. Hold the control key and select the browsers that you want to use. In Figure 14-18, you can see that I have chosen Internet Explorer and Chrome. You can also use this dialog to add new browsers (although Visual Studio is pretty good at detecting most of the mainstream ones).

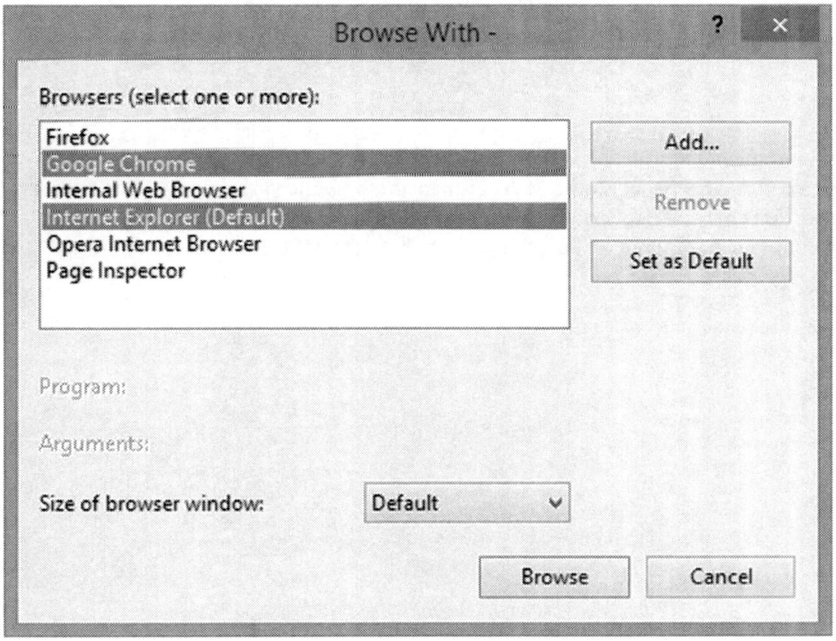

Figure 14-18. *Selecting multiple browsers*

Click the Browse button and Visual Studio will open the browsers you have selected and have each of them load the project URL. You can edit the code and views in the application and then update all of the browser windows by selecting Refresh Linked Browsers from the Visual Studio toolbar, as shown in Figure 14-19. The application will be compiled automatically so that you can see changes.

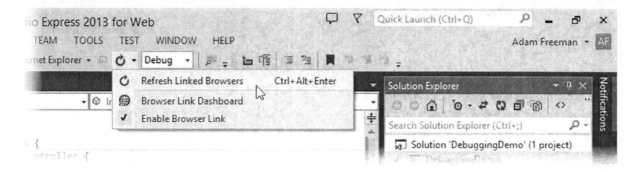

Figure 14-19. *Refreshing linked browsers*

This feature works by including some JavaScript in the HTML sent to the browser and it can be a nice way of developing iteratively. The reason that I recommend it only for working on views is that they are less likely to cause IIS to send HTTP error messages to the browser, which is what happens when there is an error in the code. The JavaScript code isn't added to error responses, which means that the link between Visual Studio and the browsers is lost. You have to start over using the Browse With menu. The browser link feature is a good idea, but the use of JavaScript is a problem. I use a similar tool called LiveReload (http://livereload.com) for my non-ASP.NET development and it provides a better approach because it uses browser plugins that are not affected by HTTP error messages. The value of Visual Studio browser link will be limited until Microsoft takes a similar approach.

Summary

In this chapter, I have shown you the structure of a Visual Studio MVC project and how the various parts fit together. I also touched on one of the most important characteristics of the MVC Framework: convention. These are topics that I will return to again and again in the chapters that follow, as I dig deeper into how the MVC Framework operates.

CHAPTER 15

■ ■ ■

URL Routing

Before the introduction of the MVC Framework, ASP.NET assumed that there was a direct relationship between requested URLs and the files on the server hard disk. The job of the server was to receive the request from the browser and deliver the output from the corresponding file.

This approach works just fine for Web Forms, where each ASPX page is both a file and a self-contained response to a request. It *doesn't* make sense for an MVC application, where requests are processed by action methods in controller classes and there is no one-to-one correlation to the files on the disk.

To handle MVC URLs, the ASP.NET platform uses the *routing system*. In this chapter, I will show you how to use the routing system to create powerful and flexible URL handling for your projects. As you will see, the routing system lets you create any pattern of URLs you desire and express them in a clear and concise manner. The routing system has two functions:

- Examine an *incoming URL* and figure out for which controller and action the request is intended.

- Generate *outgoing URLs*. These are the URLs that appear in the HTML rendered from views so that a specific action will be invoked when the user clicks the link (at which point, it has become an incoming URL again).

In this chapter, I will focus on defining routes and using them to process incoming URLs so that the user can reach your controllers and actions. There are two ways to create routes in an MVC Framework application: *convention-based routing* and *attribute routing*. You will be familiar with convention-based routing if you have used earlier versions of the MVC Framework, but attribute routing is new to MVC 5. I explain both approaches in this chapter.

Then, in the next chapter, I will show you how to use those same routes to generate the outgoing URLs you will need to include in your views, as well as show you how to customize the routing system and use a related feature called *areas*. Table 15-1 provides the summary for this chapter.

Table 15-1. *Chapter Summary*

Problem	Solution	Listing
Map between URLs and action methods	Define a route	1–8
Allow URL segments to be omitted	Define default values for segment variables	9, 10
Match URL segments that don't have corresponding routing variables	Use static segments	11–14
Pass URL segments to action methods	Define custom segment variables	15–18
Allow URL segments for which there is no default value to be omitted	Define optional segments	19–22
Define routes that match any number of URL segments	Use a catchall segment	23
Avoid controller name confusion	Specify priority namespaces in a route	24–27
Limit the URLs that a route can match	Apply a route constraint	28–34
Enable attribute routing	Call the MapMvcAttributeRoutes method	35
Define a route within a controller	Apply the Route attribute to the action methods	36, 37
Constrain an attribute route	Apply a constraint to the segment variable in the route pattern	38, 39
Define a common prefix for all of the attribute routes in a controller	Apply the RoutePrefix attribute to the controller class	40

Preparing the Example Project

To demonstrate the routing system, I need a project to which I can add routes. I created a new MVC application using the Empty template, and I called the project UrlsAndRoutes. I added a test project to the Visual Studio solution called UrlsAndRoutes.Tests by checking the Add Unit Tests option, as shown in Figure 15-1.

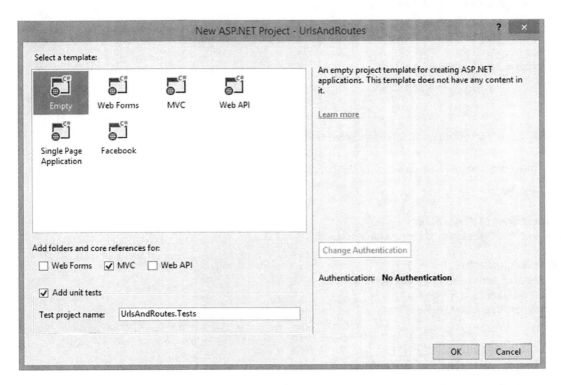

Figure 15-1. *Creating an Empty MVC application project with unit tests*

I showed you how to create the unit tests manually for the SportsStore chapter, but this produces the same result and handles the references between projects automatically. You will still need to add Moq, however, and so enter the following command in the NuGet console:

```
Install-Package Moq -version 4.1.1309.1617 -projectname UrlsAndRoutes.Tests
```

Creating the Example Controllers

To demonstrate the routing feature, I am going to add some simple controllers to the example application. I only care about the way in which URLs are interpreted in order to call action methods, so the view models I use are string values in the view bag which report the controller and action method name. First, create a Home controller and set its contents to match those in Listing 15-1.

Listing 15-1. The Contents of the HomeController.cs File

```
using System.Web.Mvc;

namespace UrlsAndRoutes.Controllers {
    public class HomeController : Controller {
```

```
        public ActionResult Index() {
            ViewBag.Controller = "Home";
            ViewBag.Action = "Index";
            return View("ActionName");
        }
    }
}
```

Create a Customer controller and set its contents to match Listing 15-2.

Listing 15-2. The Contents of the CustomerController.cs File

```
using System.Web.Mvc;

namespace UrlsAndRoutes.Controllers {
    public class CustomerController : Controller {

        public ActionResult Index() {
            ViewBag.Controller = "Customer";
            ViewBag.Action = "Index";
            return View("ActionName");
        }

        public ActionResult List() {
            ViewBag.Controller = "Customer";
            ViewBag.Action = "List";
            return View("ActionName");
        }
    }
}
```

Create an Admin controller and edit its contents to match the code shown in Listing 15-3.

Listing 15-3. The Contents of the AdminController.cs File

```
using System.Web.Mvc;

namespace UrlsAndRoutes.Controllers {
    public class AdminController : Controller {

        public ActionResult Index() {
            ViewBag.Controller = "Admin";
            ViewBag.Action = "Index";
            return View("ActionName");
        }
    }
}
```

Creating the View

I specified the ActionName view in all of the action methods in these controllers, which allows me to define one view and use it throughout the example application. Create a folder called Shared in the Views folder and add a new view called ActionName.cshtml to it, setting the contents of the view to match Listing 15-4.

Listing 15-4. The Contents of the ActionName.cshtml File

```
@{
    Layout = null;
}

<!DOCTYPE html>

<html>
<head>
    <meta name="viewport" content="width=device-width" />
    <title>ActionName</title>
</head>
<body>
    <div>The controller is: @ViewBag.Controller</div>
    <div>The action is: @ViewBag.Action</div>
</body>
</html>
```

Setting the Start URL and Testing the Application

As I explained in Part 1 of this book, Visual Studio will try to figure out the URL you want the browser to request based on the file you are editing when you start the debugger. This is a good idea that quickly becomes annoying and is a feature that I always disable. Select UrlsAndRoutes Properties from the Visual Studio Project menu, switch to the Web tab and check the Specific Page option in the Start Action section. You don't have to provide a value—just checking the option is enough. If you start the example app, you will see the response shown in Figure 15-2.

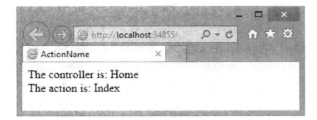

Figure 15-2. Running the example app

Introducing URL Patterns

The routing system works its magic using a set of *routes*. These routes collectively comprise the URL *schema* or *scheme* for an application, which is the set of URLs that your application will recognize and respond to.

I do not need to manually type out all of the individual URLs I am willing to support in my applications. Instead, each route contains a *URL pattern*, which is compared to incoming URLs. If a URL matches the pattern, then it is used by the routing system to process that URL. Let's start with a URL for the example application:

```
http://mysite.com/Admin/Index
```

CHAPTER 15 ■ URL ROUTING

URLs can be broken down into *segments*. These are the parts of the URL, excluding the hostname and query string, that are separated by the / character. In the example URL, there are two segments, as shown in Figure 15-3.

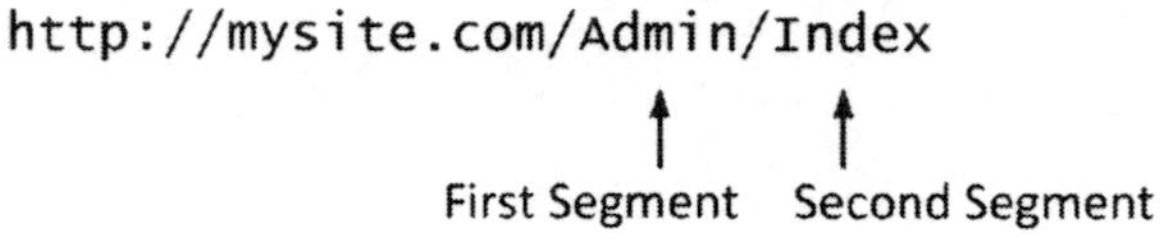

```
http://mysite.com/Admin/Index
```

Figure 15-3. The segments in an example URL

The first segment contains the word Admin, and the second segment contains the word Index. To the human eye, it is obvious that the first segment relates to the controller and the second segment relates to the action. But, of course, I need to express this relationship in a way that the routing system can understand. Here is a URL pattern that does this:

```
{controller}/{action}
```

When processing an incoming request, the job of the routing system is to match the URL that has been requested to a pattern and extract values from the URL for the *segment variables* defined in the pattern. The segment variables are expressed using braces (the { and } characters). The example pattern has two segment variables with the names controller and action, and so the value of the controller segment variable will be Admin and the value of the action segment variable will be Index.

I say match to *a* pattern, because an MVC application will usually have several routes and the routing system will compare the incoming URL to the URL pattern of each route until it finds a match.

■ **Note** The routing system does not have any special knowledge of controllers and actions. It just extracts values for the segment variables. It is later in the request handling process, when the request reaches the MVC Framework proper, that meaning is assigned to the controller and action variables. This is why the routing system can be used with Web Forms and the Web API. (I introduce the Web API in Chapter 27 and I describe the ASP.NET request handling process in detail in my *Pro ASP.NET MVC 5 Platform* book.)

By default, a URL pattern will match any URL that has the correct number of segments. For example, the pattern {controller}/{action} will match any URL that has two segments, as illustrated by Table 15-2.

Table 15-2. Matching URLs

Request URL	Segment Variables
http://mysite.com/**Admin/Index**	controller = Adminaction = Index
http://mysite.com/**Index/Admin**	controller = Indexaction = Admin
http://mysite.com/**Apples/Oranges**	controller = Applesaction = Oranges
http://mysite.com/**Admin**	No match—too few segments
http://mysite.com/**Admin/Index/Soccer**	No match—too many segments

Table 15-2 highlights two key behaviors of URL patterns:

- URL patterns are *conservative*, and will match only URLs that have the same number of segments as the pattern. You can see this in the fourth and fifth examples in the table.

- URL patterns are *liberal*. If a URL *does* have the correct number of segments, the pattern will extract the value for the segment variable, whatever it might be.

These are the default behaviors, which are the keys to understanding how URL patterns function. I show you how to change the defaults later in this chapter.

As already mentioned, the routing system does not know anything about an MVC application, and so URL patterns will match even when there is no controller or action that corresponds to the values extracted from a URL. You can see this demonstrated in the second example in Table 15-2. I transposed the Admin and Index segments in the URL, and so the values extracted from the URL have also been transposed, even though there is no Index controller in the example project.

Creating and Registering a Simple Route

Once you have a URL pattern in mind, you can use it to define a route. Routes are defined in the RouteConfig.cs file, which is in the App_Start project folder. You can see the initial content that Visual Studio defines for this file in Listing 15-5.

Listing 15-5. The Default Contents of the RouteConfig.cs File

```
using System;
using System.Collections.Generic;
using System.Linq;
using System.Web;
using System.Web.Mvc;
using System.Web.Routing;

namespace UrlsAndRoutes {
    public class RouteConfig {

        public static void RegisterRoutes(RouteCollection routes) {
            routes.IgnoreRoute("{resource}.axd/{*pathInfo}");

            routes.MapRoute(
                name: "Default",
                url: "{controller}/{action}/{id}",
                defaults: new { controller = "Home", action = "Index",
                    id = UrlParameter.Optional }
            );
        }
    }
}
```

The static RegisterRoutes method that is defined in the RouteConfig.cs file is called from the Global.asax.cs file, which sets up some of the core MVC features when the application is started. You can see the default contents of the Global.asax.cs file in Listing 15-6, and I have highlighted the call to the RouteConfig.RegisterRoutes method, which is made from the Application_Start method.

Listing 15-6. The Default Contents of the Global.asax.cs File

```
using System;
using System.Collections.Generic;
using System.Linq;
using System.Web;
using System.Web.Mvc;
using System.Web.Routing;

namespace UrlsAndRoutes {

    public class MvcApplication : System.Web.HttpApplication {
        protected void Application_Start() {
            AreaRegistration.RegisterAllAreas();
            RouteConfig.RegisterRoutes(RouteTable.Routes);
        }
    }
}
```

The Application_Start method is called by the underlying ASP.NET platform when the MVC application is first started, which leads to the RouteConfig.RegisterRoutes method being called. The parameter to this method is the value of the static RouteTable.Routes property, which is an instance of the RouteCollection class, which I describe shortly.

■ **Tip**   The other call made in the Application_Start method sets up a related feature called *areas*, which I describe in the next chapter.

Listing 15-7 shows how to create a route using the example URL pattern from the previous section in the RegisterRoutes method of the RouteConfig.cs file. (I have removed the other statements in the method so I can focus on the example.)

Listing 15-7. Registering a Route in the RouteConfig.cs File

```
using System;
using System.Collections.Generic;
using System.Linq;
using System.Web;
using System.Web.Mvc;
using System.Web.Routing;

namespace UrlsAndRoutes {
    public class RouteConfig {
        public static void RegisterRoutes(RouteCollection routes) {
            Route myRoute = new Route("{controller}/{action}", new MvcRouteHandler());
            routes.Add("MyRoute", myRoute);
        }
    }
}
```

I created a new Route using a URL pattern as a constructor parameter, which I express as a string. I also pass an instance of MvcRouteHandler to the constructor. Different ASP.NET technologies provide different classes to tailor the routing behavior, and this is the class used for ASP.NET MVC applications. Once I have created the route, I add it to the RouteCollection object using the Add method, passing in the name I want the route to be known by and the route itself.

■ **Tip**   Naming your routes is optional, and there is a philosophical argument that doing so sacrifices some of the clean separation of concerns that otherwise comes from routing. I am relaxed about naming, but I explain why this can be a problem in the "Generating a URL from a Specific Route" section in Chapter 16.

A more convenient way of registering routes is to use the MapRoute method defined by the RouteCollection class. Listing 15-8 shows how I can use this method to register a route, which has the same effect as the previous example, but has a cleaner syntax.

Listing 15-8. Registering a Route Using the MapRoute Method in the RouteConfig.cs File

```
using System;
using System.Collections.Generic;
using System.Linq;
using System.Web;
using System.Web.Mvc;
using System.Web.Routing;

namespace UrlsAndRoutes {
    public class RouteConfig {
        public static void RegisterRoutes(RouteCollection routes) {
            routes.MapRoute("MyRoute", "{controller}/{action}");
        }
    }
}
```

This approach is more compact, mainly because I do not need to create an instance of the MvcRouteHandler class (it is done for me, behind the scenes). The MapRoute method is solely for use with MVC applications. ASP.NET Web Forms applications can use the MapPageRoute method, also defined in the RouteCollection class.

Using the Simple Route

You can see the effect of the changes I made to the routing by starting the example application. You will see an error when the browser tries to navigate to the root URL for the application, but if you navigate to a route that matches the {controller}/{action} pattern, you will see a result like the one shown in Figure 15-4, which illustrates the effect of navigating to /Admin/Index.

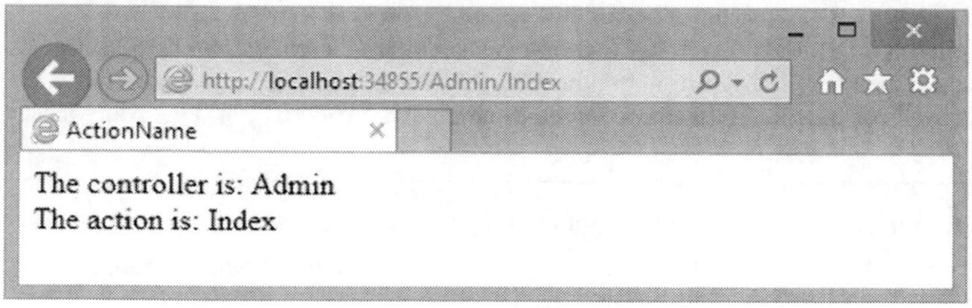

Figure 15-4. *Navigating using a simple route*

My simple route in Listing 15-8 does not tell the MVC Framework how to respond to requests for the root URL and only supports a single, specific, URL pattern. I have temporarily taken a step back from the functionality that Visual Studio adds to the RouteConfig.cs file when it creates the project, but I will show you how to build more complex patterns and routes throughout the rest of this chapter.

UNIT TEST: TESTING INCOMING URLS

I recommend that you unit test your routes to make sure they process incoming URLs as expected, even if you choose not to unit test the rest of your application. URL schemas can get pretty complex in large applications, and it is easy to create something that has unexpected results.

In previous chapters, I avoided creating common helper methods to be shared among tests in order to keep each unit test description self-contained. For this chapter, I am taking a different approach. Testing the routing schema for an application is most readily done when you can batch several tests in a single method, and this becomes much easier with some helper methods.

To test routes, I need to mock three classes from the MVC Framework: HttpRequestBase, HttpContextBase, and HttpResponseBase. (This last class is required for testing outgoing URLs, which I cover in the next chapter.) Together, these classes recreate enough of the MVC infrastructure to support the routing system. I added a new Unit Tests file called RouteTests.cs to the UrlsAndRoutes.Tests unit test project and my first addition is the helper method that creates the mock HttpContextBase objects, as follows:

```
using Microsoft.VisualStudio.TestTools.UnitTesting;
using Moq;
using System;
using System.Reflection;
using System.Web;
using System.Web.Routing;

namespace UrlsAndRoutes.Tests {
    [TestClass]
    public class RouteTests {

        private HttpContextBase CreateHttpContext(string targetUrl = null,
                                                  string httpMethod = "GET") {
            // create the mock request
            Mock<HttpRequestBase> mockRequest = new Mock<HttpRequestBase>();
```

```
        mockRequest.Setup(m => m.AppRelativeCurrentExecutionFilePath)
            .Returns(targetUrl);
        mockRequest.Setup(m => m.HttpMethod).Returns(httpMethod);

        // create the mock response
        Mock<HttpResponseBase> mockResponse = new Mock<HttpResponseBase>();
        mockResponse.Setup(m => m.ApplyAppPathModifier(
            It.IsAny<string>())).Returns<string>(s => s);

        // create the mock context, using the request and response
        Mock<HttpContextBase> mockContext = new Mock<HttpContextBase>();
        mockContext.Setup(m => m.Request).Returns(mockRequest.Object);
        mockContext.Setup(m => m.Response).Returns(mockResponse.Object);

        // return the mocked context
        return mockContext.Object;
    }
    }
}
```

The setup here is simpler than it looks. I expose the URL I want to test through the
AppRelativeCurrentExecutionFilePath property of the HttpRequestBase class, and expose the
HttpRequestBase through the Request property of the mock HttpContextBase class. My next helper method
lets me test a route:

```
...
private void TestRouteMatch(string url, string controller, string action,
    object routeProperties = null, string httpMethod = "GET") {

    // Arrange
    RouteCollection routes = new RouteCollection();
    RouteConfig.RegisterRoutes(routes);
    // Act - process the route
    RouteData result
        = routes.GetRouteData(CreateHttpContext(url, httpMethod));
    // Assert
    Assert.IsNotNull(result);
    Assert.IsTrue(TestIncomingRouteResult(result, controller,
        action, routeProperties));
}
...
```

The parameters of this method let me specify the URL to test, the expected values for the controller and
action segment variables, and an object that contains the expected values for any additional variables I have
defined. I will show you how to create such variables later in the chapter and in the next chapter. I also defined a
parameter for the HTTP method, which I will explain in the "Constraining Routes" section.

The TestRouteMatch method relies on another method, TestIncomingRouteResult, to compare the result obtained from the routing system with the segment variable values I expect. This method uses .NET reflection so that I can use an anonymous type to express any additional segment variables. Do not worry if this method doesn't make sense, as this is just to make testing more convenient; it is not a requirement for understanding MVC. Here is the TestIncomingRouteResult method:

```
...
private bool TestIncomingRouteResult(RouteData routeResult,
    string controller, string action, object propertySet = null) {

    Func<object, object, bool> valCompare = (v1, v2) => {
        return StringComparer.InvariantCultureIgnoreCase
            .Compare(v1, v2) == 0;
    };

    bool result = valCompare(routeResult.Values["controller"], controller)
        && valCompare(routeResult.Values["action"], action);

    if (propertySet != null) {
        PropertyInfo[] propInfo = propertySet.GetType().GetProperties();
        foreach (PropertyInfo pi in propInfo) {
            if (!(routeResult.Values.ContainsKey(pi.Name)
                    && valCompare(routeResult.Values[pi.Name],
                    pi.GetValue(propertySet, null)))) {

                result = false;
                break;
            }
        }
    }
    return result;
}
...
```

I also need a method to check that a URL does not work. As you will see, this can be an important part of defining a URL schema.

```
...
private void TestRouteFail(string url) {
    // Arrange
    RouteCollection routes = new RouteCollection();
    RouteConfig.RegisterRoutes(routes);
    // Act - process the route
    RouteData result = routes.GetRouteData(CreateHttpContext(url));
    // Assert
    Assert.IsTrue(result == null || result.Route == null);
}
...
```

TestRouteMatch and TestRouteFail contain calls to the Assert method, which throws an exception if the assertion fails. Because C# exceptions are propagated up the call stack, I can create simple test methods that test a set of URLs and get the test behavior I require. Here is a test method that tests the route I defined in Listing 15-8:

```
...
[TestMethod]
public void TestIncomingRoutes() {

    // check for the URL that is hoped for
    TestRouteMatch("~/Admin/Index", "Admin", "Index");
    // check that the values are being obtained from the segments
    TestRouteMatch("~/One/Two", "One", "Two");

    // ensure that too many or too few segments fails to match
    TestRouteFail("~/Admin/Index/Segment");
    TestRouteFail("~/Admin");
}
...
```

This test uses the TestRouteMatch method to check the URL I am expecting and also checks a URL in the same format to make sure that the controller and action values are being obtained properly using the URL segments. I use the TestRouteFail method to make sure that the application won't accept URLs that have a different number of segments. When testing, I must prefix the URL with the tilde (~) character, because this is how the ASP.NET Framework presents the URL to the routing system.

Notice that I didn't need to define the routes in the test methods. This is because I am loading them directly using the RegisterRoutes method in the RouteConfig class.

Defining Default Values

The reason that I got an error when I requested the default URL for the application is that it didn't match the route I had defined. The default URL is expressed as ~/ to the routing system and there are no segments in this string that can be matched to the controller and action variables defined by the simple route pattern.

I explained earlier that URL patterns are conservative, in that they will match only URLs with the specified number of segments. I also said that this was the default behavior and one way to change this behavior is to use *default values*. A default value is applied when the URL doesn't contain a segment that can be matched to the value. Listing 15-9 provides an example of a route that contains a default value.

Listing 15-9. Providing a Default Value in the RouteConfig.cs File

```
using System;
using System.Collections.Generic;
using System.Linq;
using System.Web;
using System.Web.Mvc;
using System.Web.Routing;
```

```
namespace UrlsAndRoutes {
    public class RouteConfig {
        public static void RegisterRoutes(RouteCollection routes) {
            routes.MapRoute("MyRoute", "{controller}/{action}",
                new { action = "Index" });
        }
    }
}
```

Default values are supplied as properties in an anonymous type. In Listing 15-9, I provided a default value of Index for the action variable. This route will match all two-segment URLs, as it did previously. For example, if the URL http://mydomain.com/Home/Index is requested, the route will extract Home as the value for the controller and Index as the value for the action.

Now that I have provided a default value for the action segment, the route will *also* match single-segment URLs as well. When processing a single-segment URL, the routing system will extract the controller value from the sole URL segment, and use the default value for the action variable. In this way, I can request the URL http://mydomain.com/Home and invoke the Index action method on the Home controller.

I can go further and define URLs that do not contain any segment variables at all, relying on just the default values to identify the action and controller. And as an example, Listing 15-10 shows how I have mapped the root URL for the application by providing default values for both segments.

Listing 15-10. Providing Action and Controller Default Values in the RouteConfig.cs File

```
using System;
using System.Collections.Generic;
using System.Linq;
using System.Web;
using System.Web.Mvc;
using System.Web.Routing;

namespace UrlsAndRoutes {
    public class RouteConfig {
        public static void RegisterRoutes(RouteCollection routes) {
            routes.MapRoute("MyRoute", "{controller}/{action}",
                new { controller = "Home", action = "Index" });
        }
    }
}
```

By providing default values for both the controller and action variables, I have created a route that will match URLs that have zero, one, or two segments, as shown in Table 15-3.

Table 15-3. *Matching URLs*

Number of Segments	Example	Maps To
0	mydomain.com	controller = Home action = Index
1	mydomain.com/**Customer**	controller = Customer action = Index
2	mydomain.com/**Customer/List**	controller = Customer action = List
3	mydomain.com/**Customer/List/All**	No match—too many segments

The fewer segments I receive in the incoming URL, the more I rely on the default values, up until the point I receive a URL with no segments and only default values are used. You can see the effect of the default values by starting the example app again. This time, when the browser requests the root URL for the application, the default values for the controller and action segment variables will be used, which will lead the MVC Framework to invoke the Index action method on the Home controller, as shown in Figure 15-5.

Figure 15-5. *Using default values to broaden the scope of a route*

UNIT TESTING: DEFAULT VALUES

I do not need to take any special actions to use the helper methods to test routes that define default values. Here are the revisions I made to the TestIncomingRoutes test method in the RouteTests.cs file for the route I defined in Listing 15-10:

```
...
[TestMethod]
public void TestIncomingRoutes() {
    TestRouteMatch("~/", "Home", "Index");
    TestRouteMatch("~/Customer", "Customer", "Index");
    TestRouteMatch("~/Customer/List", "Customer", "List");
    TestRouteFail("~/Customer/List/All");
}
...
```

The only point of note is that I must specify the default URL as ~/, as this is how ASP.NET presents the URL to the routing system. If I specify the empty string ("") that I used to define the route or /, the routing system will throw an exception, and the test will fail.

Using Static URL Segments

Not all of the segments in a URL pattern need to be variables. You can also create patterns that have *static segments*. Suppose that I want to match a URL like this to support URLs that are prefixed with Public:

```
http://mydomain.com/Public/Home/Index
```

I can do so by using a pattern like the one shown in Listing 15-11.

Listing 15-11. A URL Pattern with Static Segments in the RouteConfig.cs File

```
using System;
using System.Collections.Generic;
using System.Linq;
using System.Web;
using System.Web.Mvc;
using System.Web.Routing;

namespace UrlsAndRoutes {
    public class RouteConfig {
        public static void RegisterRoutes(RouteCollection routes) {

            routes.MapRoute("MyRoute", "{controller}/{action}",
                new { controller = "Home", action = "Index" });

            routes.MapRoute("", "Public/{controller}/{action}",
                new { controller = "Home", action = "Index" });
        }
    }
}
```

This new pattern will match only URLs that contain three segments, the first of which *must* be Public. The other two segments can contain any value, and will be used for the controller and action variables. If the last two segments are omitted, then the default values will be used.

I can also create URL patterns that have segments containing both static and variable elements, such as the one shown in Listing 15-12.

Listing 15-12. A URL Pattern with a Mixed Segment in the RouteConfig.cs File

```
using System;
using System.Collections.Generic;
using System.Linq;
using System.Web;
using System.Web.Mvc;
using System.Web.Routing;

namespace UrlsAndRoutes {
    public class RouteConfig {
        public static void RegisterRoutes(RouteCollection routes) {

            routes.MapRoute("", "X{controller}/{action}");

            routes.MapRoute("MyRoute", "{controller}/{action}",
                new { controller = "Home", action = "Index" });

            routes.MapRoute("", "Public/{controller}/{action}",
                new { controller = "Home", action = "Index" });
        }
    }
}
```

The pattern in this route matches any two-segment URL where the first segment starts with the letter X. The value for `controller` is taken from the first segment, excluding the X. The `action` value is taken from the second segment. You can see the effect of this route if you start the application and navigate to /XHome/Index, the result of which is illustrated by Figure 15-6.

Figure 15-6. *Mixing static and variable elements in a single segment*

ROUTE ORDERING

In Listing 15-12, I defined a new route and placed it before all of the others in the `RegisterRoutes` method. I did this because routes are applied in the order in which they appear in the `RouteCollection` object. The `MapRoute` method adds a route to the end of the collection, which means that routes are generally applied in the order in which they are defined. I say "generally" because there are methods that insert routes in specific locations. I tend not to use these methods, because having routes applied in the order in which they are defined makes understanding the routing for an application simpler.

The route system tries to match an incoming URL against the URL pattern of the route that was defined first, and proceeds to the next route only if there is no match. The routes are tried in sequence until a match is found or the set of routes has been exhausted. The result of this is that the most specific routes must be defined first. The route I added in Listing 15-12 is more specific than the route that follows. Suppose that I reversed the order of the routes, like this:

```
...
routes.MapRoute("MyRoute", "{controller}/{action}",
    new { controller = "Home", action = "Index" });

routes.MapRoute("", "X{controller}/{action}");
...
```

Then the first route, which matches *any* URL with zero, one, or two segments, will be the one that is used. The more specific route, which is now second in the list, will never be reached. The new route excludes the leading X of a URL, but this won't be done by the older route. Therefore, a URL such as this:

```
http://mydomain.com/XHome/Index
```

will be targeted to a controller called XHome, which does not exist, and so will lead to a 404–Not Found error being sent to the user.

I can combine static URL segments and default values to create an alias for a specific URL. This can be useful if you have published your URL schema publicly and it has formed a contract with your user. If you refactor an application in this situation, you need to preserve the previous URL format so that any URL favorites, macros or scripts the user has created continue to work. Imagine that I used to have a controller called Shop, which has now been replaced by the Home controller. Listing 15-13 shows how I can create a route to preserve the old URL schema.

Listing 15-13. Mixing Static URL Segments and Default Values in the RouteConfig.cs File

```
using System;
using System.Collections.Generic;
using System.Linq;
using System.Web;
using System.Web.Mvc;
using System.Web.Routing;

namespace UrlsAndRoutes {
    public class RouteConfig {
        public static void RegisterRoutes(RouteCollection routes) {

            routes.MapRoute("ShopSchema", "Shop/{action}",
                new { controller = "Home" });

            routes.MapRoute("", "X{controller}/{action}");

            routes.MapRoute("MyRoute", "{controller}/{action}",
                new { controller = "Home", action = "Index" });

            routes.MapRoute("", "Public/{controller}/{action}",
                new { controller = "Home", action = "Index" });
        }
    }
}
```

The route I added matches any two-segment URL where the first segment is Shop. The action value is taken from the second URL segment. The URL pattern doesn't contain a variable segment for controller, so the default value I have supplied is used. This means that a request for an action on the Shop controller is translated to a request for the Home controller. You can see the effect of this route by starting the app and navigating to the /Shop/Index URL. As Figure 15-7 shows, the new route causes the MVC Framework to target the Index action method in the Home controller.

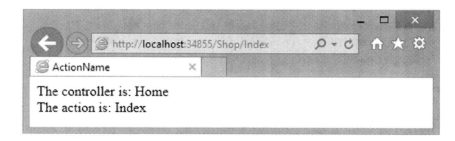

Figure 15-7. Creating an alias to preserve URL schemas

I can go one step further and create aliases for action methods that have been refactored away as well and are no longer present in the controller. To do this, I create a static URL and provide the controller and action values as defaults, as shown in Listing 15-14.

Listing 15-14. Aliasing a Controller and an Action in the RouteConfig.cs File

```
using System;
using System.Collections.Generic;
using System.Linq;
using System.Web;
using System.Web.Mvc;
using System.Web.Routing;

namespace UrlsAndRoutes {
    public class RouteConfig {
        public static void RegisterRoutes(RouteCollection routes) {

            routes.MapRoute("ShopSchema2", "Shop/OldAction",
                new { controller = "Home", action = "Index" });

            routes.MapRoute("ShopSchema", "Shop/{action}",
                new { controller = "Home" });

            routes.MapRoute("", "X{controller}/{action}");

            routes.MapRoute("MyRoute", "{controller}/{action}",
                new { controller = "Home", action = "Index" });

            routes.MapRoute("", "Public/{controller}/{action}",
                new { controller = "Home", action = "Index" });
        }
    }
}
```

Notice that, once again, I have placed the new route so that it is defined first. This is because it is more specific than the routes that follow. If a request for Shop/OldAction were processed by the next defined route, for example, I would get a different result from the one I want. The request would be dealt with using a 404–Not Found error, rather than being translated in order to preserve a contract with my clients.

UNIT TEST: TESTING STATIC SEGMENTS

Once again, I can use my helper methods to routes whose URL patterns contain static segments. Here is the addition I made to the TestIncomingRoutes unit test method to test the route added in Listing 15-14:

```
...
[TestMethod]
public void TestIncomingRoutes() {
    TestRouteMatch("~/", "Home", "Index");
    TestRouteMatch("~/Customer", "Customer", "Index");
    TestRouteMatch("~/Customer/List", "Customer", "List");
```

```
        TestRouteFail("~/Customer/List/All");
        TestRouteMatch("~/Shop/Index", "Home", "Index");
    }
    ...
```

Defining Custom Segment Variables

The `controller` and `action` segment variables have special meaning to the MVC Framework and, obviously, they correspond to the controller and action method that will be used to service the request. But these are only the built-in segment variables. I can also define my own variables, as shown in Listing 15-15. (I have removed the existing routes from the previous section so I can start over.)

Listing 15-15. Defining Additional Variables in a URL Pattern in the RouteConfig.cs File

```
using System;
using System.Collections.Generic;
using System.Linq;
using System.Web;
using System.Web.Mvc;
using System.Web.Routing;

namespace UrlsAndRoutes {
    public class RouteConfig {
        public static void RegisterRoutes(RouteCollection routes) {
            routes.MapRoute("MyRoute", "{controller}/{action}/{id}",
                new { controller = "Home", action = "Index",
                    id = "DefaultId" });
        }
    }
}
```

The route's URL pattern defines the standard `controller` and `action` variables, as well as a custom variable called `id`. This route will match any zero-to-three-segment URL. The contents of the third segment will be assigned to the `id` variable, and if there is no third segment, the default value will be used.

■ **Caution**   Some names are reserved and not available for custom segment variable names. These are `controller`, `action`, and `area`. The meaning of the first two is obvious, and I will explain *areas* in the next chapter.

I can access any of the segment variables in an action method by using the `RouteData.Values` property. To demonstrate this, I have added an action method to the `Home` controller called `CustomVariable`, as shown in Listing 15-16.

Listing 15-16. Accessing a Custom Segment Variable in an Action Method in the HomeController.cs File

```
using System.Web.Mvc;

namespace UrlsAndRoutes.Controllers {
    public class HomeController : Controller {
```

```
        public ActionResult Index() {
            ViewBag.Controller = "Home";
            ViewBag.Action = "Index";
            return View("ActionName");
        }

        public ActionResult CustomVariable() {
            ViewBag.Controller = "Home";
            ViewBag.Action = "CustomVariable";
            ViewBag.CustomVariable = RouteData.Values["id"];
            return View();
        }
    }
}
```

This method obtains the value of the custom variable in the route URL pattern and passes it to the view using the ViewBag. To create the view for the action method, create the Views/Home folder, right-click on it, select Add ➤ MVC 5 View Page (Razor) from the pop-up menu and set the name to CustomVariable.cshtml. Click the OK button to create the view and edit the contents to match Listing 15-17.

Listing 15-17. The Contents of the CustomVariable.cshtml File

```
@{
    Layout = null;
}

<!DOCTYPE html>

<html>
<head>
    <meta name="viewport" content="width=device-width" />
    <title>Custom Variable</title>
</head>
<body>
    <div>The controller is: @ViewBag.Controller</div>
    <div>The action is: @ViewBag.Action</div>
    <div>The custom variable is: @ViewBag.CustomVariable</div>
</body>
</html>
```

To see the effect of the custom segment variable, start the application and navigate to the URL /Home/CustomVariable/Hello. The CustomVariable action method in the Home controller is called, and the value of the custom segment variable is retrieved from the ViewBag and passed to the view. You can see the results in Figure 15-8.

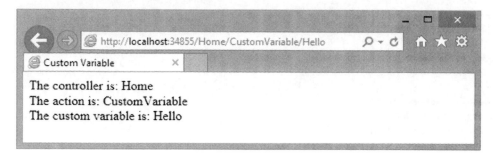

Figure 15-8. *Displaying the value of a custom segment variable*

I have provided a default value for the id segment variable in the route, which means that you will see the results shown in Figure 15-9 if you navigate to /Home/CustomVariable.

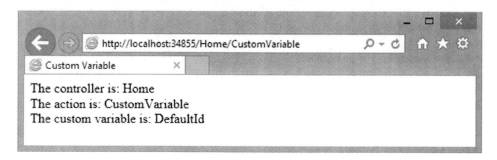

Figure 15-9. *The default value for a custom segment variable*

UNIT TEST: TESTING CUSTOM SEGMENT VARIABLES

I included support for testing custom segment variables in the test helper methods. The TestRouteMatch method has an optional parameter that accepts an anonymous type containing the names of the properties I want to test for and the values I expect. Here are the changes I made to the TestIncomingRoutes test method to test the route defined in Listing 15-15:

```
...
[TestMethod]
public void TestIncomingRoutes() {
    TestRouteMatch("~/", "Home", "Index", new { id = "DefaultId" });
    TestRouteMatch("~/Customer", "Customer", "index", new { id = "DefaultId" });
    TestRouteMatch("~/Customer/List", "Customer", "List",
        new { id = "DefaultId" });
    TestRouteMatch("~/Customer/List/All", "Customer", "List", new { id = "All" });
    TestRouteFail("~/Customer/List/All/Delete");
}
...
```

Using Custom Variables as Action Method Parameters

Using the RouteData.Values property is only one way to access custom route variables. The other way is much more elegant. If I define parameters to the action method with names that match the URL pattern variables, the MVC Framework will pass the values obtained from the URL as parameters to the action method. For example, the custom variable I defined in the route in Listing 15-15 is called id. I can modify the CustomVariable action method in the Home controller so that it has a matching parameter, as shown in Listing 15-18.

Listing 15-18. Adding an Action Method Parameter in the HomeController.cs File

```
using System;
using System.Collections.Generic;
using System.Linq;
using System.Web;
using System.Web.Mvc;

namespace UrlsAndRoutes.Controllers {
    public class HomeController : Controller {

        public ActionResult Index() {
            ViewBag.Controller = "Home";
            ViewBag.Action = "Index";
            return View("ActionName");
        }

        public ActionResult CustomVariable(string id) {
            ViewBag.Controller = "Home";
            ViewBag.Action = "CustomVariable";
            ViewBag.CustomVariable = id;
            return View();
        }
    }
}
```

When the routing system matches a URL against the route defined in Listing 15-18, the value of the third segment in the URL is assigned to the custom variable id. The MVC Framework compares the list of segment variables with the list of action method parameters, and if the names match, passes the values from the URL to the method.

I have defined the id parameter as a string, but the MVC Framework will try to convert the URL value to whatever parameter type I define. If I declared the id parameter as an int or a DateTime, then I would receive the value from the URL parsed to an instance of that type. This is an elegant and useful feature that removes the need for me to handle the conversion myself.

■ **Note** The MVC Framework uses the *model binding* feature to convert the values contained in the URL to .NET types and can handle much more complex situations than shown in this example. I cover model binding in Chapter 24.

Defining Optional URL Segments

An *optional* URL segment is one that the user does not need to specify, but for which no default value is specified. Listing 15-19 shows an example, and you can see that I specify that a segment variable is optional by setting the default value to UrlParameter.Optional.

Listing 15-19. Specifying an Optional URL Segment in the RouteConfig.cs File

```
using System;
using System.Collections.Generic;
using System.Linq;
using System.Web;
using System.Web.Mvc;
using System.Web.Routing;

namespace UrlsAndRoutes {
    public class RouteConfig {
        public static void RegisterRoutes(RouteCollection routes) {

            routes.MapRoute("MyRoute", "{controller}/{action}/{id}",
                new { controller = "Home", action = "Index",
                    id = UrlParameter.Optional });
        }
    }
}
```

This route will match URLs whether or not the id segment has been supplied. Table 15-4 shows how this works for different URLs.

Table 15-4. *Matching URLs with an Optional Segment Variable*

Segments	Example URL	Maps To
0	mydomain.com	controller = Home action = Index
1	mydomain.com/Customer	controller = Customer action = Index
2	mydomain.com/Customer/List	controller = Customer action = List
3	mydomain.com/Customer/List/All	controller = Customer action = List id = All
4	mydomain.com/Customer/List/All/Delete	No match—too many segments

As you can see from the table, the id variable is added to the set of variables only when there is a corresponding segment in the incoming URL. This feature is useful if you need to know whether the user supplied a value for a segment variable. When no value has been supplied for an optional segment variable, the value of the corresponding parameter will be null. I have updated the controller to respond when no value is provided for the id segment variable in Listing 15-20.

Listing 15-20. Checking for an Optional Segment Variable in the HomeController.cs File

```
using System.Web.Mvc;

namespace UrlsAndRoutes.Controllers {
    public class HomeController : Controller {

        public ActionResult Index() {
            ViewBag.Controller = "Home";
            ViewBag.Action = "Index";
            return View("ActionName");
        }
```

```
    public ActionResult CustomVariable(string id) {
        ViewBag.Controller = "Home";
        ViewBag.Action = "CustomVariable";
        ViewBag.CustomVariable = id ?? "<no value>";
        return View();
    }

  }
}
```

You can see the result of starting the application and navigating to the /Home/CustomVariable controller URL (which doesn't define a value for the id segment variable) in Figure 15-10.

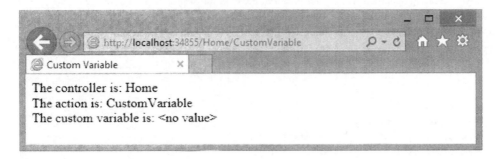

Figure 15-10. *Detecting when a URL doesn't contain a value for an optional segment variable*

Using Optional URL Segments to Enforce Separation of Concerns

Some developers who are focused on the separation of concerns in the MVC pattern do not like putting the default values for segment variables into the routes for an application. If this is an issue, you can use C# optional parameters along with an optional segment variable in the route to define the default values for action method parameters. As an example, Listing 15-21 shows the CustomVariable action method to define a default value for the id parameter that will be used if the URL doesn't contain a value.

Listing 15-21. Defining a Default Value for an Action Method Parameter in the HomeController.cs File

```
...
public ActionResult CustomVariable(string id = "DefaultId") {
    ViewBag.Controller = "Home";
    ViewBag.Action = "CustomVariable";
    ViewBag.CustomVariable = id;
    return View();
}
...
```

There will always be a value for the id parameter (either one from the URL or the default), so I am able to remove the code which deals with the null value. This action method combined with the route I defined in Listing 15-21 is the functional equivalent to the route shown in Listing 15-22:

Listing 15-22. An Equivalent Route

```
...
routes.MapRoute("MyRoute", "{controller}/{action}/{id}",
    new { controller = "Home", action = "Index", id = "DefaultId" });
...
```

The difference is that the default value for the id segment variable is defined in the controller code and not in the routing definition.

UNIT TESTING: OPTIONAL URL SEGMENTS

The issue to be aware of when testing optional URL segments is that the segment variable will not be added to the RouteData.Values collection unless a value was found in the URL. This means that you should not include the variable in the anonymous type unless you are testing a URL that contains the optional segment. Here are the changes to the TestIncomingRoutes unit test method for the route defined in Listing 15-22.

```
...
[TestMethod]
public void TestIncomingRoutes() {
    TestRouteMatch("~/", "Home", "Index");
    TestRouteMatch("~/Customer", "Customer", "index");
    TestRouteMatch("~/Customer/List", "Customer", "List");
    TestRouteMatch("~/Customer/List/All", "Customer", "List", new { id = "All" });
    TestRouteFail("~/Customer/List/All/Delete");
}
...
```

Defining Variable-Length Routes

Another way of changing the default conservatism of URL patterns is to accept a variable number of URL segments. This allows you to route URLs of arbitrary lengths in a single route. You define support for variable segments by designating one of the segment variables as a *catchall*, done by prefixing it with an asterisk (*), as shown in Listing 15-23.

Listing 15-23. Designating a Catchall Variable in the RouteConfig.cs File

```
using System;
using System.Collections.Generic;
using System.Linq;
using System.Web;
using System.Web.Mvc;
using System.Web.Routing;

namespace UrlsAndRoutes {
    public class RouteConfig {
        public static void RegisterRoutes(RouteCollection routes) {

            routes.MapRoute("MyRoute", "{controller}/{action}/{id}/{*catchall}",
                new { controller = "Home", action = "Index",
```

```
                                id = UrlParameter.Optional });
            }
        }
    }
```

I have extended the route from the previous example to add a catchall segment variable, which I imaginatively called catchall. This route will now match *any* URL, irrespective of the number of segments it contains or the value of any of those segments. The first three segments are used to set values for the controller, action, and id variables, respectively. If the URL contains additional segments, they are all assigned to the catchall variable, as shown in Table 15-5.

Table 15-5. *Matching URLs with a Catchall Segment Variable*

Segments	Example URL	Maps To
0	/	controller = Homeaction = Index
1	/Customer	controller = Customeraction = Index
2	/Customer/List	controller = Customeraction = List
3	/Customer/List/All	controller = Customeraction = Listid = All
4	/Customer/List/All/Delete	controller = Customeraction = Listid = Allcatchall = Delete
5	/Customer/List/All/Delete/Perm	controller = Customeraction = Listid = Allcatchall = Delete/Perm

There is no upper limit to the number of segments that the URL pattern in this route will match. Notice that the segments captured by the catchall are presented in the form *segment/segment/segment*. I am responsible for processing the string to break out the individual segments.

UNIT TEST: TESTING CATCHALL SEGMENT VARIABLES

I can treat a catchall variable just like a custom variable. The only difference is that I must expect multiple segments to be concatenated in a single value, such as *segment/segment/segment*. Notice that I will not receive the leading or trailing / character. Here are the changes to the TestIncomingRoutes method that demonstrate testing for a catchall segment, using the route defined in Listing 15-23 and the URLs shown in Table 15-5:

```
...
[TestMethod]
public void TestIncomingRoutes() {
    TestRouteMatch("~/", "Home", "Index");
    TestRouteMatch("~/Customer", "Customer", "Index");
    TestRouteMatch("~/Customer/List", "Customer", "List");
    TestRouteMatch("~/Customer/List/All", "Customer", "List", new { id = "All" });
    TestRouteMatch("~/Customer/List/All/Delete", "Customer", "List",
        new { id = "All", catchall = "Delete" });
    TestRouteMatch("~/Customer/List/All/Delete/Perm", "Customer", "List",
        new { id = "All", catchall = "Delete/Perm" });
}
...
```

Prioritizing Controllers by Namespaces

When an incoming URL matches a route, the MVC Framework takes the value of the controller variable and looks for the appropriate name. For example, when the value of the controller variable is Home, then the MVC Framework looks for a controller called HomeController. This is an *unqualified* class name, which means that the MVC Framework doesn't know what to do if there are two or more classes called HomeController in different namespaces.

To demonstrate the problem, create a new folder in the root of the example project called AdditionalControllers and add a new Home controller, setting the contents to match those in Listing 15-24.

Listing 15-24. The Contents of the AdditionalControllers/HomeController.cs File

```
using System.Web.Mvc;

namespace UrlsAndRoutes.AdditionalControllers {
    public class HomeController : Controller {

        public ActionResult Index() {
            ViewBag.Controller = "Additional Controllers - Home";
            ViewBag.Action = "Index";
            return View("ActionName");
        }
    }
}
```

When you start the app, you will see the error shown in Figure 15-11.

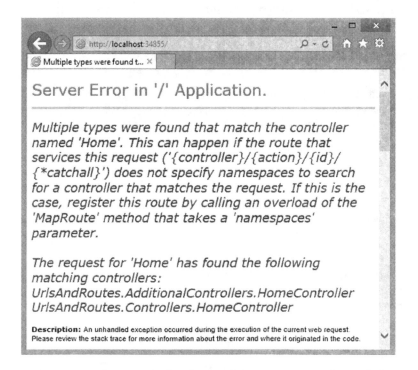

Figure 15-11. *The error displayed when there are two controllers with the same name*

The MVC Framework searched for a class called HomeController and found two: one in the original RoutesAndUrls.Controllers namespace and one in the new RoutesAndUrls.AdditionalControllers namespace. If you read the text of the error shown in Figure 15-11, you can see that the MVC Framework helpfully reports which classes it has found.

This problem arises more often than you might expect, especially if you are working on a large MVC project that uses libraries of controllers from other development teams or third-party suppliers. It is natural to name a controller relating to user accounts AccountController, for example, and it is only a matter of time before you encounter a naming clash.

To address this problem, I can tell the MVC Framework to give preference to certain namespaces when attempting to resolve the name of a controller class, as demonstrated in Listing 15-25.

Listing 15-25. Specifying Namespace Resolution Order in the RouteConfig.cs File

```
using System;
using System.Collections.Generic;
using System.Linq;
using System.Web;
using System.Web.Mvc;
using System.Web.Routing;

namespace UrlsAndRoutes {
    public class RouteConfig {
        public static void RegisterRoutes(RouteCollection routes) {

            routes.MapRoute("MyRoute", "{controller}/{action}/{id}/{*catchall}",
                new { controller = "Home", action = "Index",
                    id = UrlParameter.Optional
                }, new[] { "URLsAndRoutes.AdditionalControllers" });
        }
    }
}
```

I express the namespaces as an array of strings and in the listing I have told the MVC Framework to look in the URLsAndRoutes.AdditionalControllers namespace before looking anywhere else.

If a suitable controller cannot be found in that namespace, then the MVC Framework will default to its regular behavior and look in all of the available namespaces. If you start the app once you have made this addition to the route, you will see the result shown in Figure 15-12, which shows that the request for the root URL, which is translated in to a request for the Index action method in the Home controller, has been sent to the controller in the AdditionalControllers namespace.

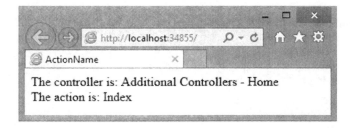

Figure 15-12. *Giving priority to controllers in a specified namespaces*

The namespaces added to a route are given equal priority. The MVC Framework does not check the first namespace before moving on to the second and so forth. For example, suppose that I added both of the project namespaces to the route, like this:

```
...
routes.MapRoute("MyRoute", "{controller}/{action}/{id}/{*catchall}",
    new { controller = "Home", action = "Index", id = UrlParameter.Optional },
    new[] { "URLsAndRoutes.AdditionalControllers", "UrlsAndRoutes.Controllers" });
...
```

I would see the same error as shown in Figure 15-11, because the MVC Framework is trying to resolve the controller class name in *all* of the namespaces added to the route. If I want to give preference to a single controller in one namespace, but have all other controllers resolved in another namespace, I need to create multiple routes, as shown in Listing 15-26.

Listing 15-26. Using Multiple Routes to Control Namespace Resolution in the RouteConfig.cs File

```
using System;
using System.Collections.Generic;
using System.Linq;
using System.Web;
using System.Web.Mvc;
using System.Web.Routing;

namespace UrlsAndRoutes {
    public class RouteConfig {
        public static void RegisterRoutes(RouteCollection routes) {

            routes.MapRoute("AddContollerRoute", "Home/{action}/{id}/{*catchall}",
                new { controller = "Home", action = "Index",
                    id = UrlParameter.Optional },
                new[] { "URLsAndRoutes.AdditionalControllers" });

            routes.MapRoute("MyRoute", "{controller}/{action}/{id}/{*catchall}",
                new { controller = "Home", action = "Index",
                    id = UrlParameter.Optional },
                new[] { "URLsAndRoutes.Controllers" });
        }
    }
}
```

The first route applies when the user explicitly requests a URL whose first segment is Home and will target the Home controller in the AdditionalControllers folder. All other requests, including those where no first segment is specified, will be handled by controllers in the Controllers folder.

I can tell the MVC Framework to look *only* in the namespaces that I specify. If a matching controller cannot be found, then the framework will not search elsewhere. Listing 15-27 shows how this feature is used.

Listing 15-27. Disabling Fallback Namespaces in the RouteConfig.cs File

```
using System;
using System.Collections.Generic;
using System.Linq;
```

```
using System.Web;
using System.Web.Mvc;
using System.Web.Routing;

namespace UrlsAndRoutes {
    public class RouteConfig {
        public static void RegisterRoutes(RouteCollection routes) {

            Route myRoute = routes.MapRoute("AddContollerRoute",
                    "Home/{action}/{id}/{*catchall}",
                new { controller = "Home", action = "Index",
                    id = UrlParameter.Optional },
                new[] { "URLsAndRoutes.AdditionalControllers" });

            myRoute.DataTokens["UseNamespaceFallback"] = false;
        }
    }
}
```

The MapRoute method returns a Route object. I have been ignoring this in previous examples, because I didn't need to make any adjustments to the routes that were created. To disable searching for controllers in other namespaces, I take the Route object and set the UseNamespaceFallback key in the DataTokens collection property to false.

This setting will be passed along to the component responsible for finding controllers, which is known as the *controller factory* and which I discuss in detail in Chapter 19. The effect of this addition is that requests that cannot be satisfied by the Home controller in the AdditionalControllers folder will fail.

Constraining Routes

At the start of the chapter, I described how URL patterns are conservative in how they match segments and liberal in how they match the content of segments. The previous few sections have explained different techniques for controlling the degree of conservatism: making a route match more or fewer segments using default values, optional variables, and so on.

It is now time to look at how to control the liberalism in matching the content of URL segments: how to restrict the set of URLs that a route will match against. Once I have control over both of these aspects of the behavior of a route, I can create URL schemas that are expressed with laser-like precision.

Constraining a Route Using a Regular Expression

The first technique is constraining a route using regular expressions. Listing 15-28 contains an example.

Listing 15-28. Using a Regular Expression to Constrain a Route in the RouteConfig.cs File

```
using System;
using System.Collections.Generic;
using System.Linq;
using System.Web;
using System.Web.Mvc;
using System.Web.Routing;
```

```
namespace UrlsAndRoutes {
    public class RouteConfig {
        public static void RegisterRoutes(RouteCollection routes) {

            routes.MapRoute("MyRoute", "{controller}/{action}/{id}/{*catchall}",
                new { controller = "Home", action = "Index", id = UrlParameter.Optional },
                new { controller = "^H.*" },
                new[] { "URLsAndRoutes.Controllers" });
        }
    }
}
```

Constraints are defined by passing them as a parameter to the MapRoute method. Like default values, constraints are expressed as an anonymous type, where the properties of the type correspond to the names of the segment variables they constrain. In this example, I have used a constraint with a regular expression that matches URLs only where the value of the controller variable begins with the letter H.

■ **Note**   Default values are applied before constraints are checked. So, for example, if I request the URL /, the default value for controller, which is Home, is applied. The constraints are then checked, and since the controller value begins with H, the default URL will match the route.

Constraining a Route to a Set of Specific Values

Regular expressions can constrain a route so that only specific values for a URL segment will cause a match. I do this using the bar (|) character, as shown in Listing 15-29.

Listing 15-29. Constraining a Route to a Specific Set of Segment Variable Values in the RouteConfig.cs File

```
using System;
using System.Collections.Generic;
using System.Linq;
using System.Web;
using System.Web.Mvc;
using System.Web.Routing;

namespace UrlsAndRoutes {
    public class RouteConfig {
        public static void RegisterRoutes(RouteCollection routes) {

            routes.MapRoute("MyRoute", "{controller}/{action}/{id}/{*catchall}",
                new { controller = "Home", action = "Index", id = UrlParameter.Optional },
                new { controller = "^H.*", action = "^Index$|^About$" },
                new[] { "URLsAndRoutes.Controllers" });
        }
    }
}
```

This constraint will allow the route to match only URLs where the value of the action segment is Index or About. Constraints are applied together, so the restrictions imposed on the value of the action variable are combined with those imposed on the controller variable. This means that the route in Listing 15-29 will match URLs only when the controller variable begins with the letter H and the action variable is Index or About. So now you can see what I mean about creating precise routes.

Constraining a Route Using HTTP Methods

Routes can be constrained so that they match a URL only when it is requested using a specific HTTP method, as demonstrated in Listing 15-30.

Listing 15-30. Constraining a Route Based on an HTTP Method in the RouteConfig.cs File

```
using System;
using System.Collections.Generic;
using System.Linq;
using System.Web;
using System.Web.Mvc;
using System.Web.Routing;

namespace UrlsAndRoutes {
    public class RouteConfig {
        public static void RegisterRoutes(RouteCollection routes) {

            routes.MapRoute("MyRoute", "{controller}/{action}/{id}/{*catchall}",
                new { controller = "Home", action = "Index", id = UrlParameter.Optional },
                new {
                    controller = "^H.*", action = "Index|About",
                    httpMethod = new HttpMethodConstraint("GET")
                },
                new[] { "URLsAndRoutes.Controllers" });
        }
    }
}
```

The format for specifying an HTTP method constraint is slightly odd. It does not matter what name is given to the property, as long as it is assigned to an instance of the HttpMethodConstraint class. In the listing, I called the constraint property httpMethod to help distinguish it from the value-based constraints I defined previously.

■ **Note** The ability to constrain routes by HTTP method is unrelated to the ability to restrict action methods using attributes such as HttpGet and HttpPost. The route constraints are processed much earlier in the request pipeline, and they determine the name of the controller and action required to process a request. The action method attributes are used to determine which specific action method will be used to service a request by the controller. I provide details of how to handle different kinds of HTTP methods (including the more unusual ones such as PUT and DELETE) in Chapter 16.

I pass the names of the HTTP methods I want to support as string parameters to the constructor of the HttpMethodConstraint class. In the listing, I limited the route to GET requests, but I could have easily added support for other methods, like this:

```
...
httpMethod = new HttpMethodConstraint("GET", "POST") },
...
```

UNIT TESTING: ROUTE CONSTRAINTS

When testing constrained routes, it is important to test for both the URLs that will match and the URLs you are trying to exclude, which you can do by using the helper methods introduced at the start of the chapter. Here are the changes to the TestIncomingRoutes test method that I used to test the route defined in Listing 15-30:

```
...
[TestMethod]
public void TestIncomingRoutes() {

    TestRouteMatch("~/", "Home", "Index");
    TestRouteMatch("~/Home", "Home", "Index");
    TestRouteMatch("~/Home/Index", "Home", "Index");

    TestRouteMatch("~/Home/About", "Home", "About");
    TestRouteMatch("~/Home/About/MyId", "Home", "About", new { id = "MyId" });
    TestRouteMatch("~/Home/About/MyId/More/Segments", "Home", "About",
        new {
            id = "MyId",
            catchall = "More/Segments"
});

    TestRouteFail("~/Home/OtherAction");
    TestRouteFail("~/Account/Index");
    TestRouteFail("~/Account/About");
}
...
```

Using Type and Value Constraints

The MVC Framework contains a number of built-in constraints that can be used to restrict the URLs that a route matches based on the type and value of segment variables. In Listing 15-31, you can see how I have applied one of these constraints to the routing configuration of the example application.

Listing 15-31. Using a Built-in Type/Value Constraint in the RouteConfig.cs File

```
using System;
using System.Collections.Generic;
using System.Linq;
using System.Web;
using System.Web.Mvc;
using System.Web.Routing;
using System.Web.Mvc.Routing.Constraints;

namespace UrlsAndRoutes {
    public class RouteConfig {

        public static void RegisterRoutes(RouteCollection routes) {

            routes.MapRoute("MyRoute", "{controller}/{action}/{id}/{*catchall}",
                new { controller = "Home", action = "Index", id = UrlParameter.Optional },
                new {
                    controller = "^H.*", action = "Index|About",
                    httpMethod = new HttpMethodConstraint("GET"),
                    id = new RangeRouteConstraint(10, 20)
                },
                new[] { "URLsAndRoutes.Controllers" });
        }
    }
}
```

In the constraint classes, which are in the System.Web.Mvc.Routing.Constraints namespace, check to see if segment variables are values for different C# types and can perform basic checks. In the listing, I have used the RangeRouteConstraint class, which checks that the value provided for a segment variable is a valid int value that falls between two bounds – , in this case 10 and 20. Table 15-6 describes the complete set of constraint classes. Not all of them accept arguments and so I have shown the class names as they would be used to configure routes. Ignore the *Attribute Constraint* column for the moment. I'll refer back to it when I introduce the attribute routing feature later in this chapter.

Table 15-6. *The route constraint classes*

Name	Description	Attribute Constraint
AlphaRouteConstraint()	Matches alphabet characters, irrespective of case (A–Z, a–z)	alpha
BoolRouteConstraint()	Matches a value that can be parsed into a bool	bool
DateTimeRouteConstraint()	Matches a value that can be parsed into a DateTime	datetime
DecimalRouteConstraint()	Matches a value that can be parsed into a decimal	decimal
DoubleRouteConstraint()	Matches a value that can be parsed into a double	double
FloatRouteConstraint()	Matches a value that can be parsed into a float	float
IntRouteConstraint()	Matches a value that can be parsed into an int	int

(continued)

Table 15-6. (*continued*)

Name	Description	Attribute Constraint
LengthRouteConstraint(len) LengthRouteConstraint(min, max)	Matches a value with the specified number of characters or that is between min and max characters in length.	length(len) length(min, max)
LongRouteConstraint()	Matches a value that can be parsed into a long	long
MaxRouteConstraint(val)	Matches an int value if the value is less than val	max(val)
MaxLengthRouteConstraint(len)	Matches a string with no more than len characters	maxlength(len)
MinRouteConstraint(val)	Matches an int value if the value is more than val	min(val)
MinLengthRouteConstraint(len)	Matches a string with at least len characters	minlength(len)
RangeRouteConstraint(min, max)	Matches an int value if the value is between min and max	range(min, max)

You can combine different constraints for a single segment variable by using the CompoundRouteConstraint class, which accepts an array of constraints as its constructor argument. In Listing 15-32, you can see how I have used this feature to apply both the AlphaRouteConstraint and the MinLengthRouteConstraint to the id segment variable to ensure that the route will only match string values that contain solely alphabetic characters and have at least six characters.

Listing 15-32. Combining Route Constraints in the RouteConfig.cs File

```
using System;
using System.Collections.Generic;
using System.Linq;
using System.Web;
using System.Web.Mvc;
using System.Web.Routing;
using System.Web.Mvc.Routing.Constraints;

namespace UrlsAndRoutes {
    public class RouteConfig {

        public static void RegisterRoutes(RouteCollection routes) {

            routes.MapRoute("MyRoute", "{controller}/{action}/{id}/{*catchall}",
                new { controller = "Home", action = "Index", id = UrlParameter.Optional },
                new {
                    controller = "^H.*", action = "Index|About",
                    httpMethod = new HttpMethodConstraint("GET"),
                    id = new CompoundRouteConstraint(new IRouteConstraint[] {
                        new AlphaRouteConstraint(),
                        new MinLengthRouteConstraint(6)
                    })
                },
                new[] { "URLsAndRoutes.Controllers" });
        }
    }
}
```

Defining a Custom Constraint

If the standard constraints are not sufficient for your needs, you can define your own custom constraints by implementing the IRouteConstraint interface. To demonstrate this feature, I added an Infrastructure folder to the example project and created a new class file called UserAgentConstraint.cs, the contents of which are shown in Listing 15-33.

Listing 15-33. The Contents of the UserAgentConstraint.cs File

```
using System.Web;
using System.Web.Routing;

namespace UrlsAndRoutes.Infrastructure {

    public class UserAgentConstraint : IRouteConstraint {

        private string requiredUserAgent;

        public UserAgentConstraint(string agentParam) {
            requiredUserAgent = agentParam;
        }

        public bool Match(HttpContextBase httpContext, Route route, string parameterName,
                        RouteValueDictionary values, RouteDirection routeDirection) {

            return httpContext.Request.UserAgent != null &&
                httpContext.Request.UserAgent.Contains(requiredUserAgent);
        }
    }
}
```

The IRouteConstraint interface defines the Match method, which an implementation can use to indicate to the routing system if its constraint has been satisfied. The parameters for the Match method provide access to the request from the client, the route that is being evaluated, the parameter name of the constraint, the segment variables extracted from the URL, and details of whether the request is to check an incoming or outgoing URL. For the example, I check the value of the UserAgent property of the client request to see if it contains a value that was passed to the constructor. Listing 15-34 shows the custom constraint used in a route.

Listing 15-34. Applying a Custom Constraint in a Route in the RouteConfig.cs File

```
using System;
using System.Collections.Generic;
using System.Linq;
using System.Web;
using System.Web.Mvc;
using System.Web.Routing;
```

```
using System.Web.Mvc.Routing.Constraints;
using UrlsAndRoutes.Infrastructure;

namespace UrlsAndRoutes {
    public class RouteConfig {

        public static void RegisterRoutes(RouteCollection routes) {

            routes.MapRoute("ChromeRoute", "{*catchall}",
                new { controller = "Home", action = "Index" },
                new { customConstraint = new UserAgentConstraint("Chrome") },
                new[] { "UrlsAndRoutes.AdditionalControllers" });

            routes.MapRoute("MyRoute", "{controller}/{action}/{id}/{*catchall}",
                new { controller = "Home", action = "Index", id = UrlParameter.Optional },
                new {
                    controller = "^H.*", action = "Index|About",
                    httpMethod = new HttpMethodConstraint("GET"),
                    id = new CompoundRouteConstraint(new IRouteConstraint[] {
                        new AlphaRouteConstraint(),
                        new MinLengthRouteConstraint(6)
                    })
                },
                new[] { "URLsAndRoutes.Controllers" });
        }
    }
}
```

In the listing, I have constrained the first route so that it will match only requests made from browsers whose user-agent string contains Chrome. If the route matches, then the request will be sent to the Index action method in the Home controller defined in the AdditionalControllers folder, irrespective of the structure and content of the URL that has been requested. The URL pattern consists of just a catchall segment variable, which means that the values for the controller and action segment variables will always be taken from the defaults and not the URL itself.

The second route will match all other requests and target controllers in the Controllers folder, subject to the type and value constraints I applied in the previous section. The effect of these routes is that one kind of browser always ends up at the same place in the application. You can see this in Figure 15-13, which shows the effect of navigating to the app using Google Chrome.

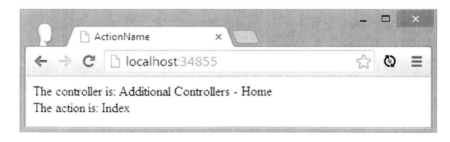

Figure 15-13. *Navigating to the app using the Google Chrome browser*

Figure 15-14 shows the result of navigating to the example application using Internet Explorer. (Notice that I have to add a third segment that contains six or more alpha characters to make the second route match the URL because of the constraints I applied in the last section.)

Figure 15-14. *Navigating to the app using Internet Explorer*

■ **Note** To be clear, because this is the kind of thing I get angry letters about, I am not suggesting that you restrict your application so that it supports only one kind of browser. I used user-agent strings solely to demonstrate custom route constraints and believe in equal opportunities for all browsers. I really hate Web sites that try to force their preference for browsers on users.

Using Attribute Routing

All of the examples so far in this chapter have been defined using a technique known as *convention-based routing*. MVC 5 adds support for a new technique known as *attribute routing*, in which routes are defined by C# attributes that are applied directly to the controller classes. In the sections that follow, I'll show you how to create and configure routes using attributes, which can be mixed freely with the standard convention-based routes.

CONVENTION VERSUS ATTRIBUTE ROUTING

Attribute routing is one of the major additions to MVC 5, but I must admit that I am not a fan. One of the main goals of the MVC pattern is, as I described in Chapter 3, to separate out different parts of the application to make them easier to write, test and maintain. I prefer convention-based routing because the controllers have no knowledge or dependency on the routing configuration of the application. By contrast, I find attribute routing muddies the waters and blurs the lines between two important components of an application.

That said, attribute routing is supported as part of the MVC Framework as of MVC 5 and you should read the following sections and make up your own mind. The fact that I don't like a feature shouldn't deter you from giving it due consideration for use in your projects.

The good news is that both approaches to creating routes use the same underlying infrastructure and that means, as you'll see in the sections that follow, that you can use both approaches in a single project with no ill effects.

Enabling and Applying Attribute Routing

Attribute routing is disabled by default and is enabled by the MapMvcAttributeRoutes extension method, which is called on the RouteCollection object passed as the argument to the static RegisterRoutes method. I have added this method call to the RouteConfig.cs file in Listing 15-35, as well as simplifying the routes in the application so that I can focus on using attributes.

Listing 15-35. Enabling Attribute Routing in the RouteConfig.cs File

```
using System;
using System.Collections.Generic;
using System.Linq;
using System.Web;
using System.Web.Mvc;
using System.Web.Routing;
using UrlsAndRoutes.Infrastructure;

namespace UrlsAndRoutes {
    public class RouteConfig {

        public static void RegisterRoutes(RouteCollection routes) {

            routes.MapMvcAttributeRoutes();

            routes.MapRoute("Default", "{controller}/{action}/{id}",
                new { controller = "Home", action = "Index",
                    id = UrlParameter.Optional },
                new[] { "UrlsAndRoutes.Controllers" });
        }
    }
}
```

Calling the MapMvcAttributeRoutes method causes the routing system to inspect the controller classes in the application and look for attributes that configure routes. The most important attribute is called Route and you can see how I have applied it to the Customer controller in Listing 15-36.

Listing 15-36. Applying the Route Attribute in the CustomerController.cs File

```
using System.Web.Mvc;

namespace UrlsAndRoutes.Controllers {
    public class CustomerController : Controller {

        [Route("Test")]
        public ActionResult Index() {
            ViewBag.Controller = "Customer";
            ViewBag.Action = "Index";
            return View("ActionName");
        }
```

```
        public ActionResult List() {
            ViewBag.Controller = "Customer";
            ViewBag.Action = "List";
            return View("ActionName");
        }
    }
}
```

This is the basic use of the Route attribute, which is to define a static route for an action method. The Route defines two properties, as described in Table 15-7.

Table 15-7. *The Parameters Supported by the Route Attribute*

Name	Description
Name	Assigns a name to the route, used for generating outgoing URLs from a specific route
Template	Defines the pattern that will be used to match URLs that target the action method

If you supply just one value when applying the Route attribute—as I did in the listing—then the value is assumed to be the pattern that will be used to match routes. Patterns for the Route attribute follow the same structure as for convention-based routing, although there are some differences when it comes to constraining route matching (which I describe in the *Applying Route Constraints* section, later in the chapter). In this example, I used the Route attribute to specify that the Index action on the Customer controller can be accessed through the URL /Test. You can see the result in Figure 15-15. I show you how to use the Name property in Chapter 16.

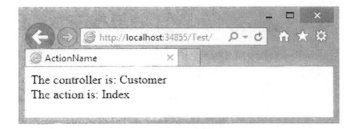

Figure 15-15. *The effect of applying the Route attribute to create a static route*

When an action method is decorated with the Route attribute, it can no longer be accessed through the convention-based routes defined in the RouteConfig.cs file. For my example, this means that the Index action of Customer controller can no longer be reached through the /Customer/Index URL.

■ **Caution** The Route attribute stops convention-based routes from targeting an action method even if attribute routing is disabled. Take care to call the MapMvcAttributeRoutes method in the RouteConfig.cs file or you will create unreachable action methods.

The Route attribute only affects the methods that it is applied to, which means that although the Index action method in the Customer controller is reachable via the /Test URL, the List action must still be targeted using the /Customer/List URL.

■ **Tip** You can apply the Route attribute to the same action method multiple times and each instance will create a new route.

Creating Routes with Segment Variables

The attribute routing feature supports all of the same features as convention-based routing, albeit expressed through attributes. This includes creating routes that contain segment variables and you can see an example of such a route in Listing 15-37.

Listing 15-37. Creating an Attribute Route with a Segment Variable in the CustomerController.cs File

```
using System.Web.Mvc;

namespace UrlsAndRoutes.Controllers {
    public class CustomerController : Controller {

        [Route("Test")]
        public ActionResult Index() {
            ViewBag.Controller = "Customer";
            ViewBag.Action = "Index";
            return View("ActionName");
        }

        [Route("Users/Add/{user}/{id}")]
        public string Create(string user, int id) {
            return string.Format("User: {0}, ID: {1}", user, id);
        }

        public ActionResult List() {
            ViewBag.Controller = "Customer";
            ViewBag.Action = "List";
            return View("ActionName");
        }
    }
}
```

I have added an action method called Create that takes string and int arguments. For simplicity, I return a string result from the method so that I don't have to create a view. The route I defined with the Route attribute mixes a static prefix (Users/Add) with user and id segment variables that correspond to the method arguments. The MVC Framework uses the model binding feature, which I describe in Chapter 25, to convert the segment variable values to the correct types in order to invoke the Create method. Figure 15-16 shows the effect of navigating to the URL /Users/Add/Adam/100.

Figure 15-16. *Navigating to a URL with segment variables*

Notice that each instance of the Route attribute operates independently, and that means that I am able to create entirely different routes to target each of the action methods in the controller, as described in Table 15-8.

Table 15-8. *The Actions in the Customer Controller and the Routes that Target Them*

Action	URL
Index	/Test
Create	/Users/Add/Adam/100 (or any values for the last two segments)
List	/Customer/List (through the route defined in the RouteConfig.cs file)

Applying Route Constraints

Routes defined using attributes can be constrained just like those defined in the RouteConfig.cs file, although the technique is more direct. To demonstrate how this works, I have added an additional action method to the Customer controller, as shown in Listing 15-38.

Listing 15-38. Adding an Action Method and Route to the CustomerController.cs File

```csharp
using System.Web.Mvc;

namespace UrlsAndRoutes.Controllers {
    public class CustomerController : Controller {

        [Route("Test")]
        public ActionResult Index() {
            ViewBag.Controller = "Customer";
            ViewBag.Action = "Index";
            return View("ActionName");
        }

        [Route("Users/Add/{user}/{id:int}")]
        public string Create(string user, int id) {
            return string.Format("Create Method - User: {0}, ID: {1}", user, id);
        }
```

411

```
[Route("Users/Add/{user}/{password}")]
public string ChangePass(string user, string password) {
    return string.Format("ChangePass Method - User: {0}, Pass: {1}",
        user, password);
}

public ActionResult List() {
    ViewBag.Controller = "Customer";
    ViewBag.Action = "List";
    return View("ActionName");
    }
  }
}
```

The new action method, called ChangePass, takes two string arguments. But I have used the Route attribute to associate the action with the same URL pattern as for the Create action method: a static prefix of /Users/Add, followed by two segment variables. To differentiate between the actions, I applied a constraint to the Route attribute for the Create method, as follows:

```
...
[Route("Users/Add/{user}/{id:int}")]
...
```

I followed the name of the segment variable—id—with a colon and then int. This tells the routing system that the Create action method should only be targeted by requests where the value provided for the id segment is a valid int value. The int constraint corresponds to the IntRouteConstraint constraint class and Table 15-6 includes the set of constraint names you can use to access the built-in type and value constraints.

You can see the effect of my constraints by starting the application and requesting the /Users/Add/Adam/100 and /Users/Add/Adam/Secret URLs. The final segment of the first URL is a valid int and is directed to the Create method. The final segment of the second URL isn't an int value and so is directed to the ChangePass method, as shown in Figure 15-17.

Figure 15-17. *The effect of applying a constraint through the Route attribute*

Combining Constraints

You can apply multiple constraints to a segment variable to further restrict the range of values that the route will match. In Listing 15-39, you can see how I have combined the alpha and length constraints on the route for the ChangePass method.

Listing 15-39. Applying Multiple Constraints to a Route in the CustomerController.cs File

```
...
[Route("Users/Add/{user}/{password:alpha:length(6)}")]
public string ChangePass(string user, string password) {
    return string.Format("ChangePass Method - User: {0}, Pass: {1}",
        user, password);
}
...
```

Multiple constraints are chained together using the same format as for a single constraint: a colon followed by the name of the constraint and, if required, a value in parentheses. The route created by the attribute in this example will only match alphabetic strings that have exactly six characters.

■ **Caution** Be careful when applying constraints. The routes defined by the Route attribute work in just the same way as those defined in the RouteConfig.cs file and a 404–Not Found result will be sent to the browser for URLs that can't be matched to an action method. Always define a fallback route that will match irrespective of the values that the URL contains.

Using a Route Prefix

You can use the RoutePrefix attribute to define a common prefix that will be applied to all of the routes defined in a controller, which can be useful when you have multiple action methods that should be targeted using the same URL root. You can see how I have applied the RoutePrefix attribute to the CustomerController in Listing 15-40.

Listing 15-40. Setting a Common Route Prefix in the CustomerController.cs File

```
using System.Web.Mvc;

namespace UrlsAndRoutes.Controllers {
    [RoutePrefix("Users")]
    public class CustomerController : Controller {

        [Route("~/Test")]
        public ActionResult Index() {
            ViewBag.Controller = "Customer";
            ViewBag.Action = "Index";
            return View("ActionName");
        }

        [Route("Add/{user}/{id:int}")]
        public string Create(string user, int id) {
            return string.Format("Create Method - User: {0}, ID: {1}", user, id);
        }
```

```
    [Route("Add/{user}/{password}")]
    public string ChangePass(string user, string password) {
        return string.Format("ChangePass Method - User: {0}, Pass: {1}",
            user, password);
    }

    public ActionResult List() {
        ViewBag.Controller = "Customer";
        ViewBag.Action = "List";
        return View("ActionName");
    }
  }
}
```

I used the RoutePrefix attribute to specify that the routes for the action method should be prefixed with Users. With the prefix defined, I am able to update the Route attribute for the Create and ChangePass action methods to remove the prefix. The MVC Framework will combine the prefix with the URL pattern automatically when the routes are created.

Notice that I have also changed the URL pattern for the Route attribute applied to the Index action method, as follows:

```
...
[Route("~/Test")]
...
```

Prefixing the URL with ~/ tells the MVC Framework that I don't want the RoutePrefix attribute applied to the Index action method, which means that it will still be accessible through the URL /Test.

Summary

In this chapter, I took an in-depth look at the routing system. You have seen how routes are defined by convention or with attributes. You have seen how incoming URLs are matched and handled, how to customize routes by changing the way that they match URL segments and by using default values and optional segments. I also showed you how to constrain routes to narrow the range of requests that they will match, using both built-in constraints and using custom constraint classes.

In the next chapter, I show you how to generate outgoing URLs from routes in your views and how to use the MVC Framework *areas* feature, which relies on the routing system and which can be used to manage large and complex MVC Framework applications.

CHAPTER 16

■ ■ ■

Advanced Routing Features

In the previous chapter, I showed you how to use the routing system to handle incoming URLs, but this is only part of the story. You also need to be able use your URL schema to generate *outgoing URLs* you can embed in your views, so that users can click links and submit forms back to your application in a way that will target the correct controller and action. In this chapter, I will show you different techniques for generating outgoing URLs, show you how to customize the routing system by replacing the standard MVC routing implementation classes and use the MVC Framework *areas* feature, which allows you to break a large and complex MVC application into manageable chucks. I finish this chapter with some best-practice advice about URL schemas in MVC Framework applications. Table 16-1 provides the summary for this chapter.

Table 16-1. *Chapter Summary*

Problem	Solution	Listing
Generate an a element with an outgoing URL	Use the `Html.ActionLink` helper method	1–5, 9
Provide values for segment variables	Pass an anonymous object to the `ActionLink` helper whose properties correspond to the segment variable names.	6, 7
Define attributes for the a element	Pass an anonymous object to the `ActionLink` helper whose properties correspond to the attribute names	8
Generate an outgoing URL without the a element	Use the `Url.Action` helper method	10–13
Generate a URL from a specific route	Specify the route name when calling the helper	14, 15
Create a custom URL matching and generation policy	Derive from the `RouteBase` class	16–21
Create a custom mapping between URLs and action methods	Implement the `IRouteHandler` interface	22, 23
Break an application into sections	Create areas or apply the `RouteArea` attribute	24–27, 30
Resolve controller name ambiguity in areas	Give priority to a controller namespace	28, 29
Prevent IIS and ASP.NET processing requests for static files before they are passed to the routing system	Use the `RouteExistingFiles` property	31–33
Prevent the routing system from processing a request	Use the `IgnoreRoute` method	34

Preparing the Example Project

I am going to continue to use the UrlsAndRoutes project from the previous chapter, but I need to make a couple of changes. First, I deleted the AdditionalControllers folder and HomeController.cs file that it contains. To perform the deletion, right-click on the AdditionalControllers folder and select Delete from the pop-up menu.

Simplifying the Routes

I need to simplify the routes in the application. Edit your App_Start/RouteConfig.cs file so that it matches the content shown in Listing 16-1.

Listing 16-1. Simplifying the Example Routes in the RouteConfig.cs File

```
using System.Web.Mvc;
using System.Web.Routing;

namespace UrlsAndRoutes {
    public class RouteConfig {

        public static void RegisterRoutes(RouteCollection routes) {

            routes.MapMvcAttributeRoutes();

            routes.MapRoute("MyRoute", "{controller}/{action}/{id}",
                new {
                    controller = "Home", action = "Index",
                    id = UrlParameter.Optional
                });
        }
    }
}
```

Adding the Optimization Package

Later in the chapter I describe the *areas* feature, which requires a new package be installed into the project. Enter the following command into the NuGet console:

```
Install-Package Microsoft.AspNet.Web.Optimization -version 1.1.0
    -projectname UrlsAndRoutes
```

This package contains functionality for optimizing the JavaScript and CSS files in the project, which I describe in Chapter 26. I won't be using this feature directly in this chapter, but the areas feature has a dependency on it.

Updating the Unit Test Project

I need to make two changes to the unit test project. The first is to delete the TestIncomingRoutes method, which I won't be using since this chapter is about generating outgoing routes. To avoid failed tests, simply remove the method from the RouteTests.cs file.

The second change is to add a reference to the `System.Web.Mvc` namespace, which I do by installing the MVC NuGet package into the unit test project. Enter the following command into the NuGet console:

```
Install-Package Microsoft.Aspnet.Mvc -version 5.0.0 -projectname UrlsAndRoutes.Tests
```

I need to add the MVC 5 package so that I can use some helper methods to generate outgoing URLs. I didn't need to do this in the last chapter because the support for dealing with incoming URLs is in the `System.Web` and `System.Web.Routing` namespaces.

Generating Outgoing URLs in Views

In almost every MVC Framework application, you will want to allow the user to navigate from one view to another, which will usually rely on including a link in the first view that targets the action method that generates the second view.

It is tempting to just add a static a element whose href attribute targets the action method, like this:

```
<a href="/Home/CustomVariable">This is an outgoing URL</a>
```

With the standard routing configuration, the HTML element creates a link that will target the `CustomVariable` action method on the Home controller. Manually defined URLs like this one are quick and simple to create. They are also extremely dangerous and you will break all of the URLs you have hard-coded when you change the URL schema for your application. You then must trawl through all of the views in your application and update all of the references to your controllers and action methods, a process that is tedious, error-prone, and difficult to test. A better alternative is to use the routing system to generate outgoing URLs, which ensures that the URLs scheme is used to produce the URLs dynamically and in a way that is guaranteed to reflect the URL schema of the application.

Using the Routing System to Generate an Outgoing URL

The simplest way to generate an outgoing URL in a view is to call the `Html.ActionLink` helper method within as illustrated by Listing 16-2, which shows an addition I made to the `/Views/Shared/ActionName.cshtml` view.

Listing 16-2. Using the Html.ActionLink Helper Method in the ActionName.cshtml File

```
@{
    Layout = null;
}

<!DOCTYPE html>

<html>
<head>
    <meta name="viewport" content="width=device-width" />
    <title>ActionName</title>
</head>
<body>
    <div>The controller is: @ViewBag.Controller</div>
    <div>The action is: @ViewBag.Action</div>
```

```
    <div>
        @Html.ActionLink("This is an outgoing URL", "CustomVariable")
    </div>
</body>
</html>
```

The parameters to the ActionLink method are the text for the link and the name of the action method that the link should target. You can see the result of this addition by starting the app and allowing the browser to navigate to the root URL, as illustrated by Figure 16-1.

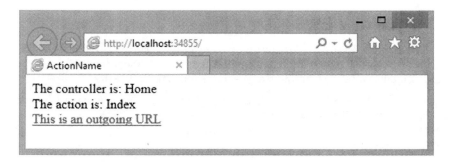

Figure 16-1. *Adding an outgoing URL to a view*

The HTML that the ActionLink method generates is based on the current routing configuration. For example, using the schema defined in Listing 16-1 (and assuming that the view is being rendered by a request to the Home controller) generates this HTML:

```
<a href="/Home/CustomVariable">This is an outgoing URL</a>
```

Now, this may seem like a long path to recreate the manually defined URL I showed you earlier, but the benefit of this approach is that it automatically responds to changes in the routing configuration. As a demonstration, I have changed the route defined and added a new route to the RouteConfig.cs file, as shown in Listing 16-3.

Listing 16-3. *Adding a Route to the RouteConfig.cs File*

```
...
public static void RegisterRoutes(RouteCollection routes) {

    routes.MapMvcAttributeRoutes();

    routes.MapRoute("NewRoute", "App/Do{action}",
        new { controller = "Home" });

    routes.MapRoute("MyRoute", "{controller}/{action}/{id}",
        new { controller = "Home", action = "Index",
            id = UrlParameter.Optional });
}
...
```

The new route changes the URL schema for requests that target the Home controller. If you start the app, you will see that this change is reflected in the HTML that is generated by the ActionLink HTML helper method, as follows:

```
<a href="/App/DoCustomVariable">This is an outgoing URL</a>
```

You can see how generating links in this way addresses the issue of maintenance. I am able to change the routing schema and have the outgoing links in the views reflect the change automatically. And, of course an outgoing URL becomes a regular request when you click on the link, and so the routing system is used again to target the action method correctly, as shown in Figure 16-2.

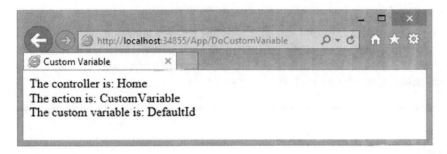

Figure 16-2. *The effect of clicking on a link is to make an outgoing URL into an incoming request*

UNDERSTANDING OUTBOUND URL ROUTE MATCHING

You have seen how changing the routes that define your URL schema changes the way that outgoing URLs are generated. Applications will usually define several routes, and it is important to understand just how routes are selected for URL generation. The routing system processes the routes in the order that they were added to the RouteCollection object passed to the RegisterRoutes method. Each route is inspected to see if it is a match, which requires three conditions to be met:

- A value must be available for every segment variable defined in the URL pattern. To find values for each segment variable, the routing system looks first at the values you have provided (using the properties of an anonymous type), then the variable values for the current request, and finally at the default values defined in the route. (I return to the second source of these values later in this chapter.)

- None of the values provided for the segment variables may disagree with the default-only variables defined in the route. These are variables for which default values have been provided, but which do not occur in the URL pattern. For example, in this route definition, myVar is a default-only variable:

```
routes.MapRoute("MyRoute", "{controller}/{action}",
    new { myVar = "true" });
```

For this route to be a match, I must take care to not supply a value for myVar or to make sure that the value I do supply matches the default value.

- The values for all of the segment variables must satisfy the route constraints. See the "Constraining Routes" section in the previous chapter for examples of different kinds of constraints.

To be clear: the routing system doesn't try to find the route that provides the *best* matching route. It finds only the *first* match, at which point it uses the route to generate the URL; any subsequent routes are ignored. For this reason, you should define your most specific routes first. It is important to test your outbound URL generation. If you try to generate a URL for which no matching route can be found, you will create a link that contains an empty href attribute, like this:

```
<a href="">About this application</a>
```

The link will render in the view properly, but won't function as intended when the user clicks it. If you are generating just the URL (which I show you how to do later in the chapter), then the result will be null, which renders as the empty string in views. You can exert some control over route matching by using named routes. See the "Generating a URL from a Specific Route" section later in this chapter for details.

The first Route object meeting these criteria will produce a non-null URL, and that will terminate the URL-generating process. The chosen parameter values will be substituted for each segment parameter, with any trailing sequence of default values omitted. If you have supplied explicit parameters that do not correspond to segment parameters or default parameters, then the method will append them as a set of query string name/value pairs.

Targeting Other Controllers

The default version of the ActionLink method assumes that you want to target an action method in the same controller that has caused the view to be rendered. To create an outgoing URL that targets a *different* controller, you can use an overload that allows you to specify the controller name, as illustrated by Listing 16-4.

Listing 16-4. Targeting a Different Controller in the ActionName.cshtml File

```
@{
    Layout = null;
}

<!DOCTYPE html>

<html>
<head>
    <meta name="viewport" content="width=device-width" />
    <title>ActionName</title>
</head>
<body>
    <div>The controller is: @ViewBag.Controller</div>
    <div>The action is: @ViewBag.Action</div>
    <div>
        @Html.ActionLink("This is an outgoing URL", "CustomVariable")
    </div>
    <div>
        @Html.ActionLink("This targets another controller", "Index", "Admin")
    </div>
</body>
</html>
```

■ **Caution** The routing system has no more knowledge of the application when generating outgoing URLs than when processing incoming requests. This means that the values you supply for action methods and controllers are not validated, and you must take care not to specify nonexistent targets.

When you render the view, you will see the following HTML generated:

```
<a href="/Admin">This targets another controller</a>
```

My call for a URL that targets the Index action method on the Admin controller has been expressed as /Admin by the ActionLink method. The routing system is pretty clever and it knows that the route defined in the application will use the Index action method by default, allowing it to omit unneeded segments.

The routing system includes routes that have been defined using the Route attribute when determining how to target a given action method. In Listing 16-5, you can see how I have changed the controller name in the ActionLink call so that it targets the Index action in the Customer controller.

Listing 16-5. Targeting an Action Decorated with the Route Attribute in the ActionName.cshtml File

```
@{
    Layout = null;
}

<!DOCTYPE html>

<html>
<head>
    <meta name="viewport" content="width=device-width" />
    <title>ActionName</title>
</head>
<body>
    <div>The controller is: @ViewBag.Controller</div>
    <div>The action is: @ViewBag.Action</div>
    <div>
        @Html.ActionLink("This is an outgoing URL", "CustomVariable")
    </div>
    <div>
        @Html.ActionLink("This targets another controller", "Index", "Customer")
    </div>
</body>
</html>
```

The link that is generated is as follows:

```
<a href="/Test">This targets another controller</a>
```

This corresponds to the Route attribute I applied to the Index action method in the Customer controller in Chapter 15:

```
...
[Route("~/Test")]
public ActionResult Index() {
    ViewBag.Controller = "Customer";
    ViewBag.Action = "Index";
    return View("ActionName");
}
...
```

Passing Extra Values

You can pass values for segment variables using an anonymous type, with properties representing the segments. Listing 16-6 provides an example, which I added to the ActionName.cshtml view file.

Listing 16-6. Supplying Values for Segment Variables in the ActionName.cshtml File

```
@{
    Layout = null;
}

<!DOCTYPE html>

<html>
<head>
    <meta name="viewport" content="width=device-width" />
    <title>ActionName</title>
</head>
<body>
    <div>The controller is: @ViewBag.Controller</div>
    <div>The action is: @ViewBag.Action</div>
    <div>
        @Html.ActionLink("This is an outgoing URL",
            "CustomVariable", new { id = "Hello" })
    </div>
</body>
</html>
```

I have supplied a value for a segment variable called id. If the application uses the route shown in Listing 16-3, then the following HTML will be rendered in the view:

```
<a href="/App/DoCustomVariable?id=Hello">This is an outgoing URL</a>
```

Notice that the value I supplied has been added as part of the query string to fit into the URL pattern described by the route. This is because there is no segment variable that corresponds to id in that route. In Listing 16-7, I have edited the routes in the RouteConfig.cs file to leave only a route that *does* have an id segment.

Listing 16-7. Editing the Routes in the RouteConfig.cs File

```
...
public static void RegisterRoutes(RouteCollection routes) {

    routes.MapMvcAttributeRoutes();

    routes.MapRoute("MyRoute", "{controller}/{action}/{id}",
        new {
            controller = "Home", action = "Index",
            id = UrlParameter.Optional
        });
}
...
```

Start the application again and you will see that the call to the `ActionLink` helper method in the `ActionName.cshtml` view produces the following HTML element:

```
<a href="/Home/CustomVariable/Hello">This is an outgoing URL</a>
```

This time, the value I assigned to the `id` property is included as a URL segment, in keeping with the active route in the application configuration.

UNDERSTANDING SEGMENT VARIABLE REUSE

When I described the way that routes are matched for outbound URLs, I explained that when trying to find values for each of the segment variables in a route's URL pattern, the routing system will look at the values from the current request. This is a behavior that confuses many programmers and can lead to a lengthy debugging session.

Imagine the application has a single route, as follows:

```
...
routes.MapRoute("MyRoute", "{controller}/{action}/{color}/{page}");
...
```

Now imagine that a user is currently at the URL /Catalog/List/Purple/123, and I render a link as follows:

```
...
@Html.ActionLink("Click me", "List", "Catalog", new {page=789}, null)
...
```

You might expect that the routing system would be unable to match the route, because I have not supplied a value for the color segment variable, and there is no default value defined. You would, however, be wrong. The routing system *will* match against the route I defined. It will generate the following HTML:

```
<a href="/Catalog/List/Purple/789">Click me</a>
```

The routing system is keen to make a match against a route, to the extent that it will reuse segment variable values from the incoming URL. In this case, I end up with the value Purple for the color variable, because of the URL from which my imaginary user started.

This is *not* a behavior of last resort. The routing system will apply this technique as part of its regular assessment of routes, even if there is a subsequent route that would match without requiring values from the current request to be reused. The routing system will reuse values only for segment variables that occur earlier in the URL pattern rather than any parameters that are supplied to the Html.ActionLink method. Suppose I tried to create a link like this:

```
...
@Html.ActionLink("Click me", "List", "Catalog", new {color="Aqua"}, null)
...
```

I have supplied a value for color, but not for page. But color appears before page in the URL pattern, and so the routing system *won't* reuse the values from the incoming URL, and the route will not match.

The best way to deal with this behavior is to prevent it from happening. I strongly recommend that you do not rely on this behavior, and that you supply values for all of the segment variables in a URL pattern. Relying on this behavior will not only make your code harder to read, but you end up making assumptions about the order in which your users make requests, which is something that will ultimately bite you as your application enters maintenance.

Specifying HTML Attributes

I have focused on the URL that the ActionLink helper method generates, but remember that the method generates a complete HTML anchor (a) element. I can set attributes for this element by providing an anonymous type whose properties correspond to the attributes I require. Listing 16-8 shows how I modified the ActionName.cshtml view to set an id attribute and assign a class to the HTML a element.

Listing 16-8. Generating an Anchor Element with Attributes in the ActionName.cshtml File

```
@{
    Layout = null;
}

<!DOCTYPE html>

<html>
<head>
    <meta name="viewport" content="width=device-width" />
    <title>ActionName</title>
</head>
<body>
    <div>The controller is: @ViewBag.Controller</div>
    <div>The action is: @ViewBag.Action</div>
    <div>
        @Html.ActionLink("This is an outgoing URL",
            "Index", "Home", null, new {
                id = "myAnchorID",
```

```
        @class = "myCSSClass"
    })
</div>
</body>
</html>
```

I created a new anonymous type that has id and class properties, and passed it as a parameter to the ActionLink method. I passed null for the additional segment variable values, indicating that I do not have any values to supply.

■ **Tip** Notice that I prepended the class property with a @ character. This is a C# language feature that lets reserved keywords be used as the names for class members. This is the technique that I used to assign elements to Bootstrap classes in the SportsStore application in Part 1 of this book.

When this call to ActionLink is rendered, I get the following HTML:

```
<a class="myCSSClass" href="/" id="myAnchorID">This is an outgoing URL</a>
```

Generating Fully Qualified URLs in Links

All of the links that I have generated so far have contained relative URLs, but I can also use the ActionLink helper method to generate fully qualified URLs, as shown in Listing 16-9.

Listing 16-9. Generating a Fully Qualified URL in the ActionNane.cshtml File

```
@{
    Layout = null;
}

<!DOCTYPE html>

<html>
<head>
    <meta name="viewport" content="width=device-width" />
    <title>ActionName</title>
</head>
<body>
    <div>The controller is: @ViewBag.Controller</div>
    <div>The action is: @ViewBag.Action</div>
    <div>
        @Html.ActionLink("This is an outgoing URL", "Index", "Home",
            "https", "myserver.mydomain.com", " myFragmentName",
            new { id = "MyId" },
            new { id = "myAnchorID", @class = "myCSSClass" })
    </div>
</body>
</html>
```

This is the ActionLink overload with the most parameters, and accepts values for the protocol (https, in the listing), the name of the target server (myserver.mydomain.com), and the URL fragment (myFragmentName), as well as all of the other options you saw previously. When rendered in a view, the ActionLink helper generates the following HTML:

```
<a class="myCSSClass"
    href="https://myserver.mydomain.com/Home/Index/MyId#myFragmentName"
    id="myAnchorID">This is an outgoing URL</a>
```

I recommend using relative URLs wherever possible. Fully qualified URLs create dependencies on the way that your application infrastructure is presented to your users. I have seen large applications that relied on absolute URLs broken by uncoordinated changes to the network infrastructure or domain name policy, which are often outside the control of the programmers.

Generating URLs (and Not Links)

The Html.ActionLink helper method generates complete HTML `<a>` elements, which is usually what is required when creating views, but there will be times when you want just a URL, without the surrounding HTML. In these circumstances, the Url.Action method can be used to generate just the URL and not the surrounding HTML. Listing 16-10 shows the changes I made to the ActionName.cshtml file to create a URL with the Url.Action helper.

Listing 16-10. Generating a URL Without the Surrounding HTML in the ActionName.cshtml File

```
@{
    Layout = null;
}

<!DOCTYPE html>

<html>
<head>
    <meta name="viewport" content="width=device-width" />
    <title>ActionName</title>
</head>
<body>
    <div>The controller is: @ViewBag.Controller</div>
    <div>The action is: @ViewBag.Action</div>
    <div>
        This is a URL:
        @Url.Action("Index", "Home", new { id = "MyId" })
    </div>
</body>
</html>
```

The Url.Action method works in the same way as the Html.ActionLink method, except that it generates only the URL. The overloaded versions of the method and the parameters they accept are the same for both methods, and you can do all of the things with Url.Action that I demonstrated with Html.ActionLink in the previous sections. You can see how the URL in Listing 16-10 is rendered in the view in Figure 16-3.

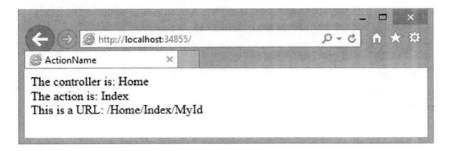

Figure 16-3. *Rendering a URL (as opposed to a link) in a view*

Generating Outgoing URLs in Action Methods

Mostly, you will need to generate outgoing URLs in views, but there are times when you may need to do something similar inside an action method. This can be achieved using the same helper method used in the view, as illustrated by Listing 16-11, which shows a new action method I added to the Home controller.

Listing 16-11. Generating an Outgoing URL in the HomeController.cs File

```
using System.Web.Mvc;

namespace UrlsAndRoutes.Controllers {
    public class HomeController : Controller {

        public ActionResult Index() {
            ViewBag.Controller = "Home";
            ViewBag.Action = "Index";
            return View("ActionName");
        }

        public ActionResult CustomVariable(string id = "DefaultId") {
            ViewBag.Controller = "Home";
            ViewBag.Action = "CustomVariable";
            ViewBag.CustomVariable = id;
            return View();
        }

        public ViewResult MyActionMethod() {
            string myActionUrl = Url.Action("Index", new { id = "MyID" });
            string myRouteUrl = Url.RouteUrl(new { controller = "Home",
                action = "Index" });
            //... do something with URLs...
            return View();
        }
    }
}
```

For the routing in the example app, the myActionUrl variable would be set to /Home/Index/MyID and the myRouteUrl variable would be set to /, which is consistent with the results that calling these helpers in a view would produce.

A more common requirement is to redirect the client browser to another URL, which can be achieved by returning the result of calling the RedirectToAction method, as shown in Listing 16-12.

Listing 16-12. Redirecting to Another Action in the HomeController.cs File

```
...
public RedirectToRouteResult MyActionMethod() {
    return RedirectToAction("Index");
}
...
```

The result of the RedirectToAction method is a RedirectToRouteResult, which instructs the MVC Framework to issue a redirect instruction to a URL that will invoke the specified action. There are the usual overloaded versions of the RedirectToAction method that specify the controller and values for the segment variables in the generated URL.

If you want to send a redirect using a URL generated from just object properties, you can use the RedirectToRoute method, as shown in Listing 16-13. This method also returns a RedirectToRouteResult object and has exactly the same effect as calling the RedirectToAction method.

Listing 16-13. Redirecting to a URL in the HomeController.cs File

```
...
public RedirectToRouteResult MyActionMethod() {
    return RedirectToRoute(new { controller = "Home", action = "Index", id = "MyID" });
}
...
```

Generating a URL from a Specific Route

In the previous examples, I left the routing system to select the route which will be used to generate a URL or a link. In this section, I will show you how to control this process and select specific routes. In Listing 16-14, I have changed the routing information in the RouteConfig.cs file to better demonstrate this feature.

Listing 16-14. Changing the Routing Configuration in the RouteConfig.cs File

```
...
public static void RegisterRoutes(RouteCollection routes) {
    routes.MapMvcAttributeRoutes();
    routes.MapRoute("MyRoute", "{controller}/{action}");
    routes.MapRoute("MyOtherRoute", "App/{action}", new { controller = "Home" });
}
...
```

There are two routes in this configuration and I have specified names for both of these routes: MyRoute and MyOtherRoute. There are two reasons for naming your routes:

- As a reminder of the purpose of the route

- So that you can select a specific route to be used to generate an outgoing URL

I have arranged the routes so that the least specific appears first in the list. This means that if I were to generate a link using the ActionLink method like this:

```
...
@Html.ActionLink("Click me", "Index", "Customer")
...
```

The outgoing link would always be generated using MyRoute, as follows:

```
<a href="/Customer/Index">Click me</a>
```

You can override the default route matching behavior by using the Html.RouteLink method, which lets you specify which route you want to use, as follows:

```
...
@Html.RouteLink("Click me", "MyOtherRoute","Index", "Customer")
...
```

The result is that the link generated by the helper looks like this:

```
<a Length="8" href="/App/Index?Length-5">Click me</a>
```

In this case, the controller I specified, Customer, is overridden by the route and the link targets the Home controller instead.

You can also give names to the routes you define with the Route attribute. In Listing 16-15, you can see how I have given a name to such a route in the Customer controller.

Listing 16-15. Naming a Route in the CustomerController.cs File

```
...
[Route("Add/{user}/{id:int}", Name="AddRoute")]
public string Create(string user, int id) {
    return string.Format("Create Method - User: {0}, ID: {1}", user, id);
}
...
```

The addition in this example sets a value for the Name property that I described in Chapter 15. In this example, I assigned the name AddRoute to the route that the attribute creates, which allows me to generate routes by name.

THE CASE AGAINST NAMED ROUTES

The problem with relying on route names to generate outgoing URLs is that doing so breaks through the separation of concerns that is so central to the MVC design pattern. When generating a link or a URL in a view or action method, I want to focus on the action and controller that the user will be directed to, not the format of the URL that will be used. By bringing knowledge of the different routes into the views or controllers, I am creating dependencies that I would prefer to avoid. I tend to avoid naming my routes (by specifying null for the route name parameter) and prefer to use code comments to remind myself of what each route is intended to do.

Customizing the Routing System

You have seen how flexible and configurable the routing system is, but if it does not meet your requirements, you can customize the behavior. In this section, I will show you the two ways to do this.

Creating a Custom RouteBase Implementation

If you do not like the way that standard Route objects match URLs, or want to implement something unusual, you can derive an alternative class from RouteBase. This gives you control over how URLs are matched, how parameters are extracted, and how outgoing URLs are generated. To derive a class from RouteBase, you need to implement two methods:

- GetRouteData(HttpContextBase httpContext): This is the mechanism by which *inbound URL matching* works. The framework calls this method on each RouteTable.Routes entry in turn, until one of them returns a non-null value.

- GetVirtualPath(RequestContext requestContext, RouteValueDictionary values): This is the mechanism by which *outbound URL generation* works. The framework calls this method on each RouteTable.Routes entry in turn, until one of them returns a non-null value.

To demonstrate this kind of customization, I am going to create a RouteBase class that will handle legacy URL requests. Imagine that I have migrated an existing application to the MVC Framework, but some users have bookmarked the pre-MVC URLs or hard-coded them into scripts. I still want to support those old URLs. I could handle this using the regular routing system, but this problem provides a nice example for this section.

To begin, I need to create a controller that will receive the legacy requests. I have called the controller LegacyController, and its contents are shown in Listing 16-16.

Listing 16-16. The Contents of the LegacyController.cs File

```
using System.Web.Mvc;

namespace UrlsAndRoutes.Controllers {

    public class LegacyController : Controller {

        public ActionResult GetLegacyURL(string legacyURL) {
            return View((object)legacyURL);
        }
    }
}
```

In this simple controller, the GetLegacyURL action method takes the parameter and passes it as a view model to the view. If I were implementing this controller in a real project, I would use this method to retrieve the files that were requested. But as it is, I am simply going to display the URL in a view.

■ **Tip**   Notice that I cast the parameter to the View method in Listing 16-16 to object. One of the overloaded versions of the View method takes a string specifying the name of the view to render and, without the cast, this would be the overload that the C# compiler thinks I want. To avoid this, I cast to object so that I unambiguously call the overload that passes a view model and uses the default view. I could also have solved this by using the overload that takes both the view name and the view model, but I prefer not to make explicit associations between action methods and views if I can help it.

Create a view called GetLegacyURL.cshtml within the Views/Legacy folder and set the content of the new file to match Listing 16-17.

Listing 16-17. The Contents of the GetLegacyURL.cshtml File

```
@model string

@{
    ViewBag.Title = "GetLegacyURL";
    Layout = null;
}

<h2>GetLegacyURL</h2>

The URL requested was: @Model
```

I want to demonstrate the custom route behavior, so I am not going to spend any time creating complicated actions and views and I just display the model value. I have now reached the point where I can create a custom derivation of the RouteBase class.

Routing Incoming URLs

I added a class file called LegacyRoute.cs to the Infrastructure folder (which is where I like to put support classes that do not really belong anywhere else). The contents of this file are shown in Listing 16-18.

Listing 16-18. The Contents of the LegacyRoute.cs File

```
using System;
using System.Linq;
using System.Web;
using System.Web.Mvc;
using System.Web.Routing;

namespace UrlsAndRoutes.Infrastructure {

    public class LegacyRoute : RouteBase {
        private string[] urls;

        public LegacyRoute(params string[] targetUrls) {
            urls = targetUrls;
        }

        public override RouteData GetRouteData(HttpContextBase httpContext) {
            RouteData result = null;

            string requestedURL =
                httpContext.Request.AppRelativeCurrentExecutionFilePath;
            if (urls.Contains(requestedURL, StringComparer.OrdinalIgnoreCase)) {
                result = new RouteData(this, new MvcRouteHandler());
                result.Values.Add("controller", "Legacy");
```

```
                result.Values.Add("action", "GetLegacyURL");
                result.Values.Add("legacyURL", requestedURL);
            }
            return result;
        }

        public override VirtualPathData GetVirtualPath(RequestContext requestContext,
            RouteValueDictionary values) {

            return null;
        }
    }
}
```

The constructor of this class takes a string array that represents the individual URLs that this routing class will support. I will specify these when I register the route later. Of note in this class is the GetRouteData method, which is what the routing system calls to see if the LegacyRoute class can match an incoming URL.

If the class cannot match the request, then I just return null, and the routing system will move on to the next route in the list and repeat the process. If the class *can* match the request, I return an instance of the RouteData class containing the values for the controller and action variables, and anything else I want to pass along to the action method.

When I create the RouteData object, I need to pass in the handler that I want to deal with the values that generated. I use the standard MvcRouteHandler class, which is what assigns meaning to the controller and action values:

```
...
result = new RouteData(this, new MvcRouteHandler());
...
```

For the vast majority of MVC applications, this is the class that you will require, as it connects the routing system to the controller/action model of an MVC application. But you can implement a replacement for MvcRouteHandler, as I will demonstrate in the Creating a Custom Route Handler section later in the chapter.

In this custom RouteBase implementation, I am willing to match any request for the URLs that were passed to the constructor. When I get such a URL, I add hard-coded values for the controller and action method to the RouteValues object. I also pass along the requested URL as the legacyURL property. Notice that the name of this property matches the name of the parameter of the action method in the Legacy controller, ensuring that the value I generate will be passed to the action method via the parameter.

The last step is to register a new route that uses the custom RouteBase class. You can see how to do this in Listing 16-19, which shows the addition to the RouteConfig.cs file.

Listing 16-19. Registering the Custom RouteBase Implementation in the RouteConfig.cs File

```
using System.Web.Mvc;
using System.Web.Routing;
using UrlsAndRoutes.Infrastructure;

namespace UrlsAndRoutes {
    public class RouteConfig {

        public static void RegisterRoutes(RouteCollection routes) {
            routes.MapMvcAttributeRoutes();
```

```
        routes.Add(new LegacyRoute(
                "~/articles/Windows_3.1_Overview.html",
                "~/old/.NET_1.0_Class_Library"));

        routes.MapRoute("MyRoute", "{controller}/{action}");
        routes.MapRoute("MyOtherRoute", "App/{action}", new { controller = "Home" });
    }

  }
}
```

I create a new instance of the LegacyRoute class and pass in the URLs I want it to route. I then add the object to the RouteCollection using the Add method. Now when I start the application and request one of the legacy URLs I defined, the request is routed by the LegacyRoute class and directed toward the Legacy controller, as shown in Figure 16-4.

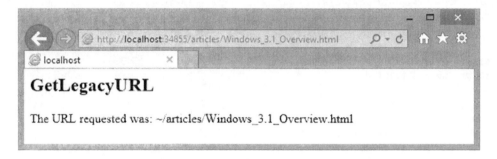

Figure 16-4. *Routing requests using a custom RouteBase implementation*

Generating Outgoing URLs

To support outgoing URL generation, I need to implement the GetVirtualPath method in the LegacyRoute class. If the class is unable to generate a specific URL, I let the routing system know by returning null. Otherwise, I return an instance of the VirtualPathData class. Listing 16-20 shows the implementation of this method.

Listing 16-20. Implementing the GetVirtualPath Method in the LegacyRoute.cs File

```
...
public override VirtualPathData GetVirtualPath(RequestContext requestContext,
        RouteValueDictionary values) {

    VirtualPathData result = null;

    if (values.ContainsKey("legacyURL") &&
        urls.Contains((string)values["legacyURL"], StringComparer.OrdinalIgnoreCase)) {
        result = new VirtualPathData(this,
            new UrlHelper(requestContext)
                .Content((string)values["legacyURL"]).Substring(1));
    }
    return result;
}
...
```

I have been passing segment variables and other details around in earlier chapters using anonymous types. But behind the scenes, the routing system has been converting these into `RouteValueDictionary` objects so they can be processed by `RouteBase` implementations. Listing 16-21 shows an addition to the `ActionName.cshtml` view file that generates an outgoing URL using the custom routing class.

Listing 16-21. Generating an Outgoing URL via a Custom Route in the ActionName.cshtml File

```
@{
    Layout = null;
}

<!DOCTYPE html>

<html>
<head>
    <meta name="viewport" content="width=device-width" />
    <title>ActionName</title>
</head>
<body>
    <div>The controller is: @ViewBag.Controller</div>
    <div>The action is: @ViewBag.Action</div>
    <div>
        This is a URL:
        @Html.ActionLink("Click me", "GetLegacyURL",
            new { legacyURL = "~/articles/Windows_3.1_Overview.html" })
    </div>
</body>
</html>
```

When this view is rendered the `ActionLink` helper generates the following HTML if you request a URL such as /Home/Index, just as you would expect:

```
<a href="/articles/Windows_3.1_Overview.html">Click me</a>
```

The anonymous type created with the `legacyURL` property is converted into a `RouteValueDictionary` class that contains a key of the same name. In this example, I decide I am able to deal with a request for an outbound URL if there is a key named `legacyURL` and if its value is one of the URLs passed to the constructor. I could be more specific and check for `controller` and `action` values, but for a simple example, this is sufficient.

If I get a match, I create a new instance of `VirtualPathData`, passing in a reference to the current object and the outbound URL. I have used the `Content` method of the `UrlHelper` class to convert the application-relative URL to one that can be passed to browsers. The routing system prepends an additional / to the URL, so I must take care to remove the leading character from the generated URL.

Creating a Custom Route Handler

I have relied on the `MvcRouteHandler` in my routes because it connects the routing system to the MVC Framework, the focus of this book. Even so, the routing system lets me define my own route handler by implementing the `IRouteHandler` interface. Listing 16-22 shows the content of the `CustomRouteHandler.cs` class file that I added to the `Infrastructure` folder in the example project.

Listing 16-22. Implementing the IRouteHandler Interface in the CustomRouteHandler.cs File

```
using System.Web;
using System.Web.Routing;

namespace UrlsAndRoutes.Infrastructure {

    public class CustomRouteHandler : IRouteHandler {
        public IHttpHandler GetHttpHandler(RequestContext requestContext) {
            return new CustomHttpHandler();
        }
    }

    public class CustomHttpHandler : IHttpHandler {
        public bool IsReusable {
            get { return false; }
        }

        public void ProcessRequest(HttpContext context) {
            context.Response.Write("Hello");
        }
    }
}
```

The purpose of the IRouteHandler interface is to provide a means to generate implementations of the IHttpHandler interface, which is responsible for processing requests. In the MVC implementation of these interfaces, controllers are found, action methods are invoked, views are rendered, and the results are written to the response. My implementation is a little simpler: it just writes the word Hello to the client (not an HTML document containing that word, but just the text).

■ **Note** The IHttpHandler interface is defined by the ASP.NET platform and is part of the standard request handling system, which I describe in my *Pro ASP.NET MVC 5 Platform* book, published by Apress in 2014. You don't need to understand the way that ASP.NET handles requests to write an MVC Framework application, but there are facilities to customize and extend the process that can be useful for advanced or complex applications.

I register the custom route handler in the RouteConfig.cs file when I define a route, as shown in Listing 16-23.

Listing 16-23. Using a Custom Routing Handler in the RouteConfig.cs File

```
...
public static void RegisterRoutes(RouteCollection routes) {
    routes.MapMvcAttributeRoutes();

    routes.Add(new Route("SayHello", new CustomRouteHandler()));

    routes.Add(new LegacyRoute(
            "~/articles/Windows_3.1_Overview.html",
            "~/old/.NET_1.0_Class_Library"));
```

```
    routes.MapRoute("MyRoute", "{controller}/{action}");
    routes.MapRoute("MyOtherRoute", "App/{action}", new { controller = "Home" });
}
...
```

When I request the URL /SayHello, the custom route handler is used to process the request. Figure 16-5 shows the result.

Figure 16-5. *Using a custom request handler*

Implementing custom route handling means taking on responsibility for functions that are usually handled for you, such as controller and action resolution. But it does give you incredible freedom: you can co-opt some parts of the MVC Framework and ignore others, or even implement an entirely new architectural pattern.

Working with Areas

The MVC Framework supports organizing a Web application into *areas*, where each area represents a functional segment of the application, such as administration, billing, customer support, and so on. This is useful in a large project, where having a single set of folders for all of the controllers, views, and models, and it can become difficult to manage.

Each MVC area has its own folder structure, allowing you to keep everything separate. This makes it more obvious which project elements relate to each functional area of the application, helping multiple developers to work on the project without colliding with one another. Areas are supported largely through the routing system, which is why I have chosen to cover this feature alongside URLs and routes. In this section, I will show you how to set up and use areas in your MVC projects.

Creating an Area

To add an area to the example MVC application, right-click the UrlsAndRoutes project item in the Solution Explorer window and select Add ➤ Area from the pop-up menu. Visual Studio will prompt you for the name of the area, as shown in Figure 16-6. In this case, I have specified an area called Admin. This is a pretty common area to create, because many Web applications need to separate the customer-facing and administration functions. Click the Add button to create the area.

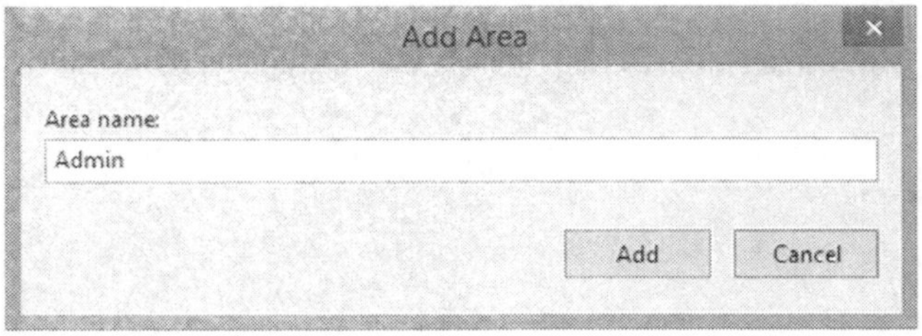

Figure 16-6. *Adding an area to an MVC application*

After you click Add, Visual Studio will add an Areas folder to the project. This contains a folder called Admin, which represents the area that I just created. If I were to create additional areas, other folders would be created here.

Inside the Areas/Admin folder, you will see a mini-MVC project. There are folders called Controllers, Models, and Views. The first two are empty, but the Views folder contains a Shared folder (and a web.config file that configures the view engine, but I am not interested in the view engine until Chapter 20).

The Areas folder also contains a file called AdminAreaRegistration.cs, which defines the AdminAreaRegistration class, as shown in Listing 16-24.

Listing 16-24. The Contents of the AdminAreaRegistration.cs File

```
using System.Web.Mvc;

namespace UrlsAndRoutes.Areas.Admin {
    public class AdminAreaRegistration : AreaRegistration {

        public override string AreaName {
            get {
                return "Admin";
            }
        }

        public override void RegisterArea(AreaRegistrationContext context) {
            context.MapRoute(
                "Admin_default",
                "Admin/{controller}/{action}/{id}",
                new { action = "Index", id = UrlParameter.Optional }
            );
        }
    }
}
```

The interesting part of this class is the RegisterArea method. As you can see from the listing, this method registers a route with the URL pattern Admin/{controller}/{action}/{id}. I can define additional routes in this method, which will be unique to this area.

■ **Caution** If you assign names to your routes, you must ensure that they are unique across the entire application and not just the area for which they are intended.

I do not need to take any action to make sure that this registration method is called. Visual Studio added a statement to the Global.asax file that takes care of setting up areas when it created the project, which you can see in Listing 16-25.

Listing 16-25. Area Registration Setup in the Global.asax File

```
using System;
using System.Collections.Generic;
using System.Linq;
using System.Web;
using System.Web.Mvc;
using System.Web.Routing;

namespace UrlsAndRoutes {
    public class MvcApplication : System.Web.HttpApplication {
        protected void Application_Start() {
            AreaRegistration.RegisterAllAreas();
            RouteConfig.RegisterRoutes(RouteTable.Routes);
        }
    }
}
```

The call to the static AreaRegistration.RegisterAllAreas method causes the MVC Framework to go through all of the classes in the application, find those that are derived from the AreaRegistration class and call the RegisterArea method on each of them.

■ **Caution**   Do not change the order of the statements related to routing in the Application_Start method. If you call RegisterRoutes before AreaRegistration.RegisterAllAreas is called, then your routes will be defined before the area routes. Given that routes are evaluated in order, this will mean that requests for area controllers are likely to be matched against the wrong routes.

The AreaRegistrationContext class that is passed to each area's RegisterArea method exposes a set of MapRoute methods that the area can use to register routes in the same way as your main application does in the RegisterRoutes method of Global.asax.

■ **Note**   The MapRoute methods in the AreaRegistrationContext class automatically limit the routes you register to the namespace that contains the controllers for the area. This means that when you create a controller in an area, you must leave it in its default namespace; otherwise, the routing system will not be able to find it.

Populating an Area

You can create controllers, views, and models in an area just as you have seen in previous examples. To create a controller, right-click the Controllers folder within the Admin area and select Add ➤ Controller from the pop-up menu. Select MVC 5 Controller - Empty from the list of options, click the Add button, set the controller name and click the Add button to create the new controller class.

To demonstrate the way that areas isolate sections of the application, I added a Home controller to the Admin area. You can see the contents of the Areas/Admin/Controllers/HomeController.cs file in Listing 16-26.

Listing 16-26. The Contents of the Areas/Admin/Controllers/HomeController.cs File

```
using System;
using System.Collections.Generic;
using System.Linq;
using System.Web;
using System.Web.Mvc;

namespace UrlsAndRoutes.Areas.Admin.Controllers {
    public class HomeController : Controller {
        public ActionResult Index() {
            return View();
        }
    }
}
```

I am not going to change the controller code. Just rendering the default view associated with the Index action method will be enough for this sample. Create the Areas/Admin/Views/Home folder, right-click it in the Solution Explorer and select Add ➤ MVC 5 View Page (Razor) from the menu. Set the name to Index.cshtml, click OK to create the file and edit the content to match those shown in Listing 16-27.

Listing 16-27. The Contents of the Areas/Admin/Views/Home/Index.cshtml File

```
@{
    ViewBag.Title = "Index";
    Layout = null;
}

<!DOCTYPE html>

<html>
<head>
    <meta name="viewport" content="width=device-width" />
    <title>Index</title>
</head>
<body>
    <div>
        <h2>Admin Area Index</h2>
    </div>
</body>
</html>
```

The point of all of this is to show that working inside an area is just the same as working in the main part of an MVC project. If you start the application and navigate to /Admin/Home/Index, you will see the view that was added to the Admin area, as shown in Figure 16-7.

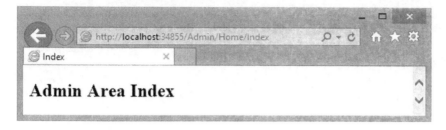

Figure 16-7. Rendering an area view

Resolving the Ambiguous Controller Issue

Okay, so I lied slightly: areas are not quite as self-contained as they might be. If you navigate to the /Home/Index URL, you will see the error shown in Figure 16-8.

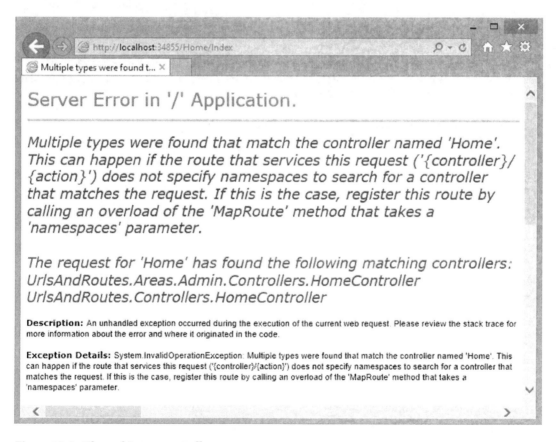

Figure 16-8. The ambiguous controller error

When an area is registered, any routes that it defines are limited to the namespace associated with the area. This is how I was able to request /Admin/Home/Index and get the HomeController class in the UrlsAndRuutes.Areas.Admin.Controllers namespace.

However, routes defined in the RegisterRoutes method of RouteConfig.cs are not similarly restricted. In Listing 16-28, as a reminder, I have listed the current routing configuration of the example app.

Listing 16-28. The Routing Configuration for the Example MVC App in the RouteConfig.cs File

```
...
public static void RegisterRoutes(RouteCollection routes) {

    routes.MapMvcAttributeRoutes();

    routes.Add(new Route("SayHello", new CustomRouteHandler()));

    routes.Add(new LegacyRoute(
        "~/articles/Windows_3.1_Overview.html",
        "~/old/.NET_1.0_Class_Library"));

    routes.MapRoute("MyRoute", "{controller}/{action}");
    routes.MapRoute("MyOtherRoute", "App/{action}", new { controller = "Home" });
}
...
```

The route named MyRoute translates the incoming URL from the browser to the Index action on the Home controller. At that point, I get an error, because there are no namespace restrictions in place for this route and the MVC Framework can see two HomeController classes. To resolve this, I need to prioritize the main controller namespace in all of the routes which might lead to a conflict, as shown in Listing 16-29.

Listing 16-29. Resolving the Area Namespace Conflict in the RouteConfig.cs File

```
...
public static void RegisterRoutes(RouteCollection routes) {

    routes.MapMvcAttributeRoutes();

    routes.Add(new Route("SayHello", new CustomRouteHandler()));

    routes.Add(new LegacyRoute(
            "~/articles/Windows_3.1_Overview.html",
            "~/old/.NET_1.0_Class_Library"));

    routes.MapRoute("MyRoute", "{controller}/{action}", null,
        new[] {"UrlsAndRoutes.Controllers"});
    routes.MapRoute("MyOtherRoute", "App/{action}", new { controller = "Home" },
        new[] { "UrlsAndRoutes.Controllers" });
}
...
```

This change ensures that the controllers in the main project are given priority in resolving requests. Of course, if you want to give preference to the controllers in an area, you can do that instead.

Creating Areas with Attributes

You can also create areas by applying the RouteArea attribute to controller classes. You can see how I have assigned the action methods in the Customer controller to a new area called Services in Listing 16-30.

Listing 16-30. Creating an Area Using an Attribute in the CustomerController.cs File

```
using System.Web.Mvc;

namespace UrlsAndRoutes.Controllers {
    [RouteArea("Services")]
    [RoutePrefix("Users")]
    public class CustomerController : Controller {

        [Route("~/Test")]
        public ActionResult Index() {
            ViewBag.Controller = "Customer";
            ViewBag.Action = "Index";
            return View("ActionName");
        }

        [Route("Add/{user}/{id:int}", Name="AddRoute")]
        public string Create(string user, int id) {
            return string.Format("Create Method - User: {0}, ID: {1}", user, id);
        }

        [Route("Add/{user}/{password}")]
        public string ChangePass(string user, string password) {
            return string.Format("ChangePass Method - User: {0}, Pass: {1}",
                user, password);
        }

        public ActionResult List() {
            ViewBag.Controller = "Customer";
            ViewBag.Action = "List";
            return View("ActionName");
        }
    }
}
```

The RouteArea attribute moves all of the routes defined by the Route attribute into the specified area. The effect of this attribute combined with the RoutePrefix attribute means that to reach the Create action method, for example, I have to create a URL like this:

```
http://localhost:34855/Services/Users/Add/Adam/100
```

The RouteArea attribute doesn't affect routes that are defined by the Route attribute but that start with ~/. This means, for example, that I continue to reach the Index action method with this URL:

```
http://localhost:34855/Test/
```

The `RouteArea` has no effect on action methods to which the `Route` attribute has not been defined, which means that the routing for the `List` action method is determined by the `RouteConfig.cs` file and not attribute-based routing.

Generating Links to Actions in Areas

You do not need to take any special steps to create links that refer to actions in the same MVC area that the current request relates to. The MVC Framework detects that a request relates to a particular area and ensures that outbound URL generation will find a match only among routes defined for that area. For example, adding a call to the `Html.ActionLink` helper from a view in the `Admin` area like this:

```
...
@Html.ActionLink("Click me", "About")
...
```

will generate the following HTML:

```
<a href="/Admin/Home/About">Click me</a>
```

To create a link to an action in a *different* area, or no area at all, you must create a variable called `area` and use it to specify the name of the area you want, like this:

```
...
@Html.ActionLink("Click me to go to another area", "Index", new { area = "Support" })
...
```

It is for this reason that `area` is reserved from use as a segment variable name. The HTML generated by this call is as follows (assuming that you created an area called `Support` that has a suitable route defined):

```
<a href="/Support/Home">Click me to go to another area</a>
```

If you want to link to an action on one of the top-level controllers (a controller in the `/Controllers` folder), then you should specify the area as an empty string, like this:

```
...
@Html.ActionLink("Click me to go to another area", "Index", new { area = "" })
...
```

Routing Requests for Disk Files

Not all of the requests for an MVC application are for controllers and actions. Most applications need a way to serve content such as images, static HTML files, JavaScript libraries, and so on. As a demonstration, I created a `Content` folder and added a file called `StaticContent.html` to it using the `HTML Page` item template. Listing 16-31 shows the contents of the HTML file.

Listing 16-31. The Contents of the StaticContent.html File

```
<!DOCTYPE html>
<html xmlns="http://www.w3.org/1999/xhtml">
    <head><title>Static HTML Content</title></head>
    <body>
        This is the static html file (~/Content/StaticContent.html)
    </body>
</html>
```

The routing system provides integrated support for serving such content. If you start the application and request the URL /Content/StaticContent.html, you will see the contents of this simple HTML file displayed in the browser, as shown in Figure 16-9.

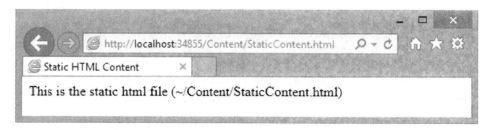

Figure 16-9. *Requesting the static content file*

By default, the routing system checks to see if a URL matches a disk file *before* evaluating the application's routes, which is why I didn't have to add a route to get the result shown in Figure 16-9.

If there is a match between the requested URL and a disk on the file, then the disk file is served and the routes defined by the application are never used. This behavior can be reversed so that the routes are evaluated before disk files are checked by setting the RouteExistingFiles property of the RouteCollection to true, as shown in Listing 16-32.

Listing 16-32. Enabling Route Evaluation Before File-Checking in the RouteConfig.cs File

```
using System.Web.Mvc;
using System.Web.Routing;
using UrlsAndRoutes.Infrastructure;

namespace UrlsAndRoutes {
    public class RouteConfig {

        public static void RegisterRoutes(RouteCollection routes) {

            routes.RouteExistingFiles = true;

            routes.MapMvcAttributeRoutes();

            routes.Add(new Route("SayHello", new CustomRouteHandler()));

            routes.Add(new LegacyRoute(
                    "~/articles/Windows_3.1_Overview.html",
                    "~/old/.NET_1.0_Class_Library"));
```

```
        routes.MapRoute("MyRoute", "{controller}/{action}", null,
            new[] { "UrlsAndRoutes.Controllers" });
        routes.MapRoute("MyOtherRoute", "App/{action}", new { controller = "Home" },
            new[] { "UrlsAndRoutes.Controllers" });
    }
  }
}
```

The convention is to place this statement close to the top of the RegisterRoutes method, although it will take effect even if you set it after you have defined your routes.

Configuring the Application Server

Visual Studio uses IIS Express as the application server for MVC application projects. Not only do I have to set the RouteExistingFiles property to true in the RegisterRoutes method, I also have to tell IIS Express not to intercept requests for disk files before they are passed to the MVC routing system.

First of all, start IIS Express. The easiest way to do this is to start the MVC application from Visual Studio, which will cause the IIS Express icon to appear on the task bar. Right-click on the icon and select Show All Applications from the pop-up menu. Click on UrlsAndRoutes in the Site Name column to display the IIS configuration information, as shown in Figure 16-10.

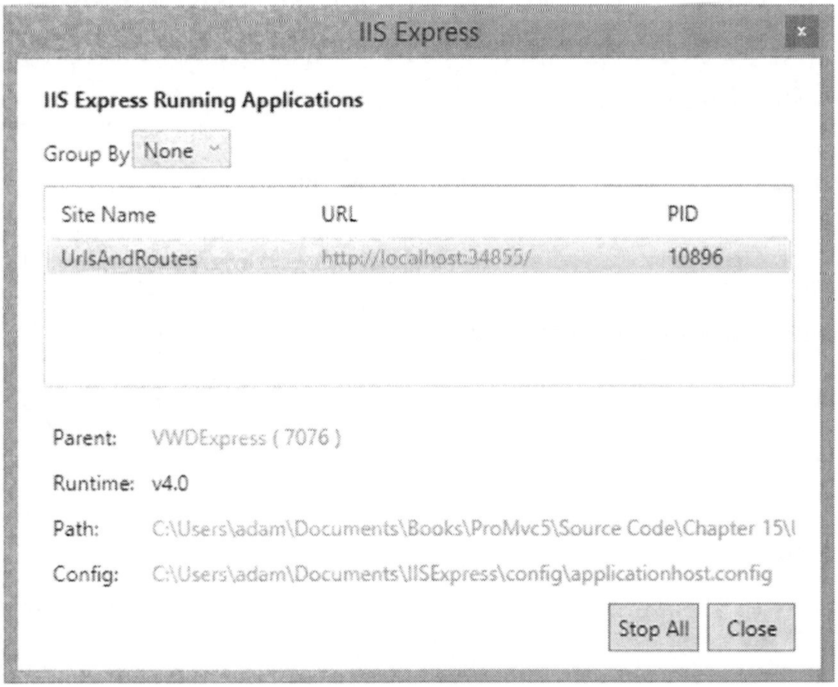

Figure 16-10. *The IIS Express configuration information*

Click on the Config link at the bottom of the window to open the IIS Express configuration file in Visual Studio. Now type Control+F and search for UrlRoutingModule-4.0. There will be an entry found in the modules section of the configuration file and you will need to set the preCondition attribute to the empty string, like this:

```
...
<add name="UrlRoutingModule-4.0" type="System.Web.Routing.UrlRoutingModule"
    preCondition="" />
...
```

Now restart the application in Visual Studio to let the modified settings take effect and navigate to the /Content/StaticContent.html URL. Rather than see the contents of the file, you will see the error message shown in Figure 16-11. This error occurs because the request for the HTML file has been passed to the MVC routing system but the route that matches the URL directs the request to the Content controller, which does not exist.

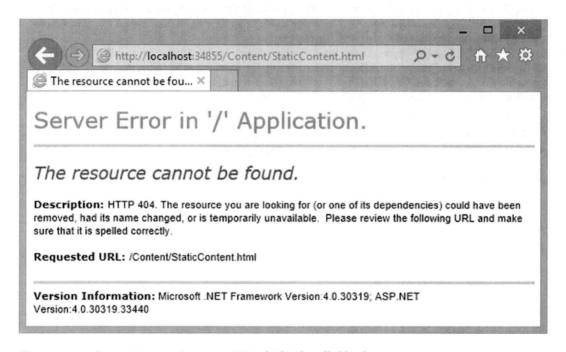

Figure 16-11. *Requesting a static content URL which is handled by the routing system*

Defining Routes for Disk Files

Once the property has been set to true, I can define routes that match URLs that correspond to disk files, such as the one shown in Listing 16-33.

Listing 16-33. A Route Whose URL Pattern Corresponds to a Disk File in the RouteConfig.cs File

```
using System.Web.Mvc;
using System.Web.Routing;
using UrlsAndRoutes.Infrastructure;
```

```
namespace UrlsAndRoutes {
    public class RouteConfig {

        public static void RegisterRoutes(RouteCollection routes) {

            routes.RouteExistingFiles = true;

            routes.MapMvcAttributeRoutes();

            routes.MapRoute("DiskFile", "Content/StaticContent.html",
                new {
                    controller = "Customer",
                    action = "List",
                });

            routes.Add(new Route("SayHello", new CustomRouteHandler()));

            routes.Add(new LegacyRoute(
                    "~/articles/Windows_3.1_Overview.html",
                    "~/old/.NET_1.0_Class_Library"));

            routes.MapRoute("MyRoute", "{controller}/{action}", null,
                new[] { "UrlsAndRoutes.Controllers" });
            routes.MapRoute("MyOtherRoute", "App/{action}", new { controller = "Home" },
                new[] { "UrlsAndRoutes.Controllers" });
        }
    }
}
```

This route maps requests for the URL Content/StaticContent.html to the List action of the Customer controller. You can see the URL mapping at work in Figure 16-12, which I created by starting the app and navigating to the /Content/StaticContent.html URL again.

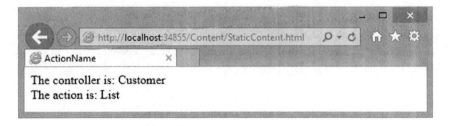

***Figure 16-12.** Intercepting a request for a disk file using a route*

■ **Tip**   Your browser may cache the old response, especially if you are using the browser link feature I described in Chapter 14. If this happens, reload the web page and you should see the response shown in the figure.

Routing requests intended for disk files requires careful thought, not least because URL patterns will match these kinds of URL as eagerly as any other. For example, as you saw in the previous section, a request for /Content/StaticContent.html will be matched by a URL pattern such as {controller}/{action}. Unless you are careful, you can end up with some exceptionally strange results and reduced performance. So, enabling this option is a last resort.

Bypassing the Routing System

Setting the RouteExistingFiles property, which I demonstrated in the previous section, makes the routing system more inclusive. Requests that would normally bypass the routing system are now evaluated against the routes the application defines.

The counterpart to this feature is the ability to make the routing system *less* inclusive and prevent URLs from being evaluated against routes. This is done using the IgnoreRoute method of the RouteCollection class, as shown in Listing 16-34.

Listing 16-34. Using the IgnoreRoute Method in the RouteConfig.cs File

```
using System.Web.Mvc;
using System.Web.Routing;
using UrlsAndRoutes.Infrastructure;

namespace UrlsAndRoutes {
    public class RouteConfig {

        public static void RegisterRoutes(RouteCollection routes) {

            routes.RouteExistingFiles = true;

            routes.MapMvcAttributeRoutes();

            routes.IgnoreRoute("Content/{filename}.html");

            routes.Add(new Route("SayHello", new CustomRouteHandler()));

            routes.Add(new LegacyRoute(
                    "~/articles/Windows_3.1_Overview.html",
                    "~/old/.NET_1.0_Class_Library"));

            routes.MapRoute("MyRoute", "{controller}/{action}", null,
                new[] { "UrlsAndRoutes.Controllers" });
            routes.MapRoute("MyOtherRoute", "App/{action}", new { controller = "Home" },
                new[] { "UrlsAndRoutes.Controllers" });
        }
    }
}
```

You can use segment variables like {filename} to match a range of URLs. In this case, the URL pattern will match any two-segment URL where the first segment is Content and the second content has the .html extension.

The IgnoreRoute method creates an entry in the RouteCollection where the route handler is an instance of the StopRoutingHandler class, rather than MvcRouteHandler. The routing system is hard-coded to recognize this handler. If the URL pattern passed to the IgnoreRoute method matches, then no subsequent routes will be evaluated, just as when a regular route is matched. It follows, therefore, that the location of the call to the IgnoreRoute method is significant. If you start the app and navigate to the /Content/StaticContent.html URL again, you will see the contents of the HTML file because the StopRoutingHandler object is processed before any other route which might have matched the URL.

URL Schema Best Practices

After all of this, you may be left wondering where to start in designing your own URL schema. You could just accept the default schema that Visual Studio generates for you, but there are benefits in giving your schema some thought. In recent years, the design of an application's URLs have been taken increasingly seriously and a few important design principles have emerged. If you follow these design patterns, you will improve the usability, compatibility, and search-engine rankings of your applications.

Make Your URLs Clean and Human-Friendly

Users notice the URLs in your applications. If you do not agree, then just think back to the last time you tried to send someone an Amazon URL. Here is the URL for an earlier edition of this book:

```
http://www.amazon.com/Pro-ASP-NET-MVC-Professional-
Apress/dp/1430242361/ref=la_B001IU0SNK_1_5?ie=UTF8&qid=1349978167&sr=1-5
```

It is bad enough sending someone such a URL by e-mail, but try reading this over the phone. When I needed to do this recently, I ended up quoting the ISBN number and asking the caller to look it up for himself. It would be nice if I could access the book with a URL like this:

```
http://www.amazon.com/books/pro-aspnet-mvc5-framework
```

That is the kind of URL that I *could* read out over the phone and that doesn't look like I dropped something on the keyboard while composing an e-mail message.

■ **Note** To be clear, I have only the highest respect for Amazon, who sells more of my books than everyone else combined. I know for a fact that each and every member of the Amazon team is a strikingly intelligent and beautiful person. Not one of them would be so petty as to stop selling my books over something so minor as criticism of their URL format. I love Amazon. I adore Amazon. I just wish they would fix their URLs.

Here are some simple guidelines to make friendly URLs:

- Design URLs to describe their content, not the implementation details of your application. Use /Articles/AnnualReport rather than /Website_v2/CachedContentServer/FromCache/AnnualReport.

- Prefer content titles over ID numbers. Use /Articles/AnnualReport rather than /Articles/2392. If you must use an ID number (to distinguish items with identical titles, or to avoid the extra database query needed to find an item by its title), then use both (/Articles/2392/AnnualReport). It takes longer to type, but it makes more sense to a human and improves search-engine rankings. Your application can just ignore the title and display the item matching that ID.

- Do *not* use file name extensions for HTML pages (for example, .aspx or .mvc), but *do* use them for specialized file types (such as .jpg, .pdf, and .zip). Web browsers do not care about file name extensions if you set the MIME type appropriately, but humans still expect PDF files to end with .pdf.

- Create a sense of hierarchy (for example, /Products/Menswear/Shirts/Red), so your visitor can guess the parent category's URL.

- Be case-insensitive. (Someone might want to type in the URL from a printed page.) The ASP.NET routing system is case-insensitive by default.

- Avoid symbols, codes, and character sequences. If you want a word separator, use a dash (as in /my-great-article). Underscores are unfriendly, and URL-encoded spaces are bizarre (/my+great+article) or disgusting (/my%20great%20article).

- Do not change URLs. Broken links equal lost business. When you do change URLs, continue to support the old URL schema for as long as possible via permanent (301) redirections.

- Be consistent. Adopt one URL format across your entire application.

URLs should be short, easy to type, hackable (human-editable), and persistent, and they should visualize site structure. Jakob Nielsen, usability guru, expands on this topic at http://www.useit.com/alertbox/990321.html. Tim Berners-Lee, inventor of the Web, offers similar advice. (See http://www.w3.org/Provider/Style/URI.)

GET and POST: Pick the Right One

The rule of thumb is that GET requests should be used for all read-only information retrieval, while POST requests should be used for any operation that changes the application state. In standards-compliance terms, GET requests are for *safe* interactions (having no side effects besides information retrieval), and POST requests are for *unsafe* interactions (making a decision or changing something). These conventions are set by the World Wide Web Consortium (W3C), at http://www.w3.org/Protocols/rfc2616/rfc2616-sec9.html.

GET requests are *addressable*: all the information is contained in the URL, so it's possible to bookmark and link to these addresses.

Do not use GET requests for operations that change state. Many Web developers learned this the hard way in 2005, when Google Web Accelerator was released to the public. This application pre-fetched all the content linked from each page, which is legal within the HTTP because GET requests should be safe. Unfortunately, many Web developers had ignored the HTTP conventions and placed simple links to "delete item" or "add to shopping cart" in their applications. Chaos ensued.

One company believed their content management system was the target of repeated hostile attacks, because all their content kept getting deleted. They later discovered that a search-engine crawler had hit upon the URL of an administrative page and was crawling all the delete links. Authentication might protect you from this, but it wouldn't protect you from Web accelerators.

Summary

In this chapter, I have shown you the advanced features of the MVC Framework routing system, showing you how to generate outgoing links and URLs, and how to customize the routing system. Along the way, I introduced the concept of areas and set out my views on how to create a useful and meaningful URL schema. In the next chapter, I turn to controllers and actions, which are the heart of the MVC Framework. I explain how these work in detail and show you how to use them to get the best results in your application.

CHAPTER 17

■ ■ ■

Controllers and Actions

Every request that comes to your application is handled by a controller. The controller is free to handle the request any way it sees fit, as long as it doesn't stray into the areas of responsibility that belong to the model and view. This means that controllers do not contain or store data, nor do they generate user interfaces.

In the ASP.NET MVC Framework, controllers are .NET classes that contain the logic required to handle a request. In Chapter 3, I explained that the role of the controller is to encapsulate your application logic. This means that controllers are responsible for processing incoming requests, performing operations on the domain model, and selecting views to render to the user. In this chapter, I show you how controllers are implemented and the different ways that you can use controllers to receive and generate output. Table 17-1 provides the summary for this chapter.

Table 17-1. *Chapter Summary*

Problem	Solution	Listing
Create a controller	Implement the `IController` interface or derive from the `Controller` class	1–4
Get information about a request	Use the context objects and properties or define action method parameters	5, 6
Generate a response from controller that directly implements the `IController` interface	Use the `HttpResponse` context object	7–8
Generate a response from a controller derived from the `Controller` class	Use an action result	9–12
Tell the MVC Framework to render a view	Use a `ViewResult`	13, 14
Pass data from the controller to the view	Use a view model object or the view bag	15–19
Redirect the browser to a new URL	Use the `Redirect` or `RedirectPermanent` methods	20–21
Redirect the browser to a URL generated by a route	Use the `RedirectToRoute` or `RedirectToRoutePermanent` methods	22
Redirect the browser to another action method	Use the `RedirectToAction` method	23
Send an HTTP result code to the browser	Return an `HttpStatusCodeResult` object or use one of the convenience methods such as `HttpNotFound`.	24–26

Preparing the Example Project

To prepare for this chapter, I created a new project called ControllersAndActions using the Empty template, checking the option for the MVC folders and references to create a unit test project called ControllersAndActions.Tests. The unit tests that I create in this chapter don't need mock implementations and so I don't need to install the Moq package, but I do need to install the MVC package so that my tests have access to the base controller classes. Enter the following command into the Visual Studio NuGet Package Manager Console:

```
Install-Package Microsoft.Aspnet.Mvc -version 5.0.0 -projectname
    ControllersAndActions.Tests
```

Setting the Start URL

Once you have created the project, select ControllersAndActions Properties from the Visual Studio Project menu, switch to the Web tab and check the Specific Page option in the Start Action section. You don't have to provide a value, just check the option.

Introducing the Controller

You have seen the use of controllers in almost all of the chapters so far. Now it is time to take a step back and look behind the scenes.

Creating a Controller with IController

In the MVC Framework, controller classes must implement the IController interface from the System.Web.Mvc namespace, which I have shown in Listing 17-1.

Listing 17-1. The System.Web.Mvc.IController Interface

```
public interface IController {
    void Execute(RequestContext requestContext);
}
```

■ **Tip** I got the definition of this interface by downloading the MVC Framework source code, which is endlessly useful for figuring out how things work behind the curtain. You can download the source code from http://aspnet.codeplex.com.

This is a simple interface. The sole method, Execute, is invoked when a request is targeted at the controller class. The MVC Framework knows which controller class has been targeted in a request by reading the value of the controller property generated by the routing data, or through your custom routing classes as described in the Chapters 15 and 16.

You can create controller classes by implementing IController, but it is a low-level interface and you must do a lot of work to get anything useful done. That said, the IController interface makes for a useful demonstration of how controllers operate and, to that end, I created a new class file called BasicController.cs in the Controllers folder with the content shown in Listing 17-2.

Listing 17-2. The Contents of the BasicController.cs File

```
using System.Web.Mvc;
using System.Web.Routing;

namespace ControllersAndActions.Controllers {

    public class BasicController : IController {

        public void Execute(RequestContext requestContext) {

            string controller = (string)requestContext.RouteData.Values["controller"];
            string action = (string)requestContext.RouteData.Values["action"];

                requestContext.HttpContext.Response.Write(
                string.Format("Controller: {0}, Action: {1}", controller, action));
        }
    }
}
```

The Execute method of the IController interface is passed to a System.Web.Routing.RequestContext object that provides information about the current request and the route that matched it (and led to this controller being invoked to process that request). The RequestContext class defines two properties, which I have described in Table 17-2.

Table 17-2. *The Properties Defined by the RequestContext Class*

Name	Description
HttpContext	Returns an HttpContextBase object that describes the current request
RouteData	Returns a RouteData object that describes the route that matched the request

The HttpContextBase object provides access to a set of objects that describe the current request, known as the *context objects*, and which I'll come back to later in the chapter. The RouteData object describes the route. I have described the important RouteData properties in Table 17-3.

Table 17-3. *The Properties Defined by the RouteData Class*

Name	Description
Route	Returns the RouteBase implementation that matched the route
RouteHandler	Returns the IRouteHandler that handled the route
Values	Returns a collection of segment values, indexed by name

---

CLASS NAMES THAT END WITH BASE

The MVC Framework relies on the ASP.NET platform to process requests, which makes a lot of sense because it is proven, feature-rich and integrates well into the IIS application server. One problem is that the classes that the ASP.NET platform uses to provide information about requests are not well-suited to unit testing, a key benefit of using the MVC Framework. Microsoft needed to introduce testability while maintaining compatibility with existing ASP.NET Web Forms applications and so introduced the *Base classes*, so-called because they have the same names as core ASP.NET platform classes followed by the word Base. So, for example, the ASP.NET platform provides context information about the current request and some key application services through an HttpContext object. The Base class counterpart is HttpContextBase, an instance of which is passed to the Execute method defined by the IController interface (and you'll see other Base classes in the examples that follow). The original and the Base classes define the same properties and methods, but the Base classes are always abstract, which means that they can easily be used for unit testing.

Sometime you will receive an instance of one of the original ASP.NET classes, such as HttpContext but need to create an MVC-friendly Base class, such as HttpContextBase. You can do this using one of the Wrapper classes, which have the same name as the original classes plus the word Wrapper, such as HttpContextWrapper. The wrapper classes are derived from the Base classes and have constructors that accept an instance of the original class, like this:

```
...
HttpContext myContext = getOriginalObjectFromSomewhere();
HttpContextBase myBase = new HttpContextWrapper(myContext);
...
```

There are original, Base and Wrapper classes throughout the System.Web namespace so that ASP.NET can support the MVC Framework and older Web Forms applications seamlessly.

I showed you how to use the RouteBase and IRouteHandler types to customize the routing system in Chapter 16. In this example, I use the Values property to get the values of the controller and action segment variables and write them to the response.

■ **Note** Part of the problem when creating custom controllers is that you don't have access to features like views. This means that you have to work at a lower level and is the reason that I write my content directly to the client. The HttpContextBase.Response property returns an HttpResponseBase object that allows you to configure and add to the response that will be sent to the client. This is another touch-point between the ASP.NET platform and the MVC Framework and one that I describe in depth in the *Pro ASP.NET MVC 5 Framework Platform* book, which will be published by Apress in 2014.

If you run the application and navigate to /Basic/Index, you can see the output generated by the custom controller, as shown in Figure 17-1.

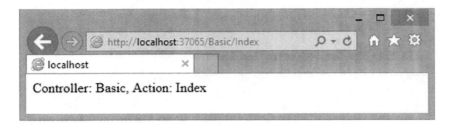

Figure 17-1. *A result generated from the BasicController class*

Implementing the IController interface allows you to create a class that the MVC Framework recognizes as a controller and sends requests to, without any limitation on how the request is processed and responded to. This is a nice example because it shows you how extensible the MVC Framework is, even for key building blocks like controllers, but it would be hard to write a complex application this way.

Creating a Controller by Deriving from the Controller Class

As the previous example suggested, the MVC Framework is endlessly customizable and extensible. You can implement the IController interface to create any kind of request handling and result generation you require. Don't like action methods? Don't care for rendered views? Then you can just take matters in your own hands and write a better, faster, and more elegant way of handling requests. Or you can build on the features that the Microsoft MVC Framework team has provided, which is achieved by deriving your controllers from the System.Web.Mvc.Controller class.

System.Web.Mvc.Controller is the class that provides the request handling support that most MVC developers will be familiar with. It is the class I have been using in all of the examples in previous chapters. The Controller class provides three key features:

- *Action methods*: A controller's behavior is partitioned into multiple methods (instead of having just one single Execute() method). Each action method is exposed on a different URL and is invoked with parameters extracted from the incoming request.

- *Action results*: You can return an object describing the result of an action (for example, rendering a view, or redirecting to a different URL or action method), which is then carried out on your behalf. The separation between *specifying results* and *executing them* simplifies unit testing.

- *Filters*: You can encapsulate reusable behaviors (for example, authentication, as you saw in Chapter 12) as filters, and then tag each behavior onto one or more controllers or action methods by putting an attribute in your source code.

Unless you have a specific requirement in mind, the best way to create controllers is to derive from the Controller class and, as you might hope, this is what Visual Studio does when it creates a new controller in response to the Add ➤ Scaffold menu item. Listing 17-3 shows a simple controller created this way, called DerivedController, generated using the MVC 5 Controller - Empty option, with some simple changesto set a ViewBag property and select a view.

Listing 17-3. The ontents of the DerivedController.cs File

```
using System;
using System.Collections.Generic;
using System.Linq;
using System.Web;
using System.Web.Mvc;
```

```
namespace ControllersAndActions.Controllers {
    public class DerivedController : Controller {
        public ActionResult Index() {
            ViewBag.Message = "Hello from the DerivedController Index method";
            return View("MyView");
        }
    }
}
```

The Controller class is also the link to the Razor view system. In the listing, I return the result of the View method, passing in the name of the view I want rendered to the client as a parameter. To create this view, create the Views/Derived folder, right-click on it and select Add ➤ MVC 5 View Page (Razor) from the menu. Set the name to MyView.cshtml and click the OK button to create the view file. Set the content of the view file to match Listing 17-4.

Listing 17-4. The Contents of the MyView.cshtml File

```
@{
    ViewBag.Title = "MyView";
}

<h2>MyView</h2>

Message: @ViewBag.Message
```

If you start the application and navigate to /Derived/Index, the action method will be invoked and the view I named will be rendered, as shown in Figure 17-2.

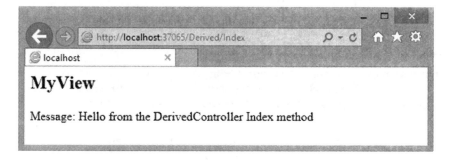

Figure 17-2. *A result generated from the DerivedController class*

The job of a derivation of the Controller class is to implement action methods, obtain whatever input is needed to process a request, and generate a suitable response. The myriad of ways to do this are covered in the rest of this chapter.

Receiving Request Data

Controllers frequently need to access data from the incoming request, such as query string values, form values, and parameters parsed from the URL by the routing system. There are three main ways to access that data:

- Extract it from a set of *context objects*.
- Have the data passed as *parameters* to your action method.
- Explicitly invoke the framework's *model binding* feature.

Here, I look at the approaches for getting input for your action methods, focusing on using context objects and action method parameters. In Chapter 24, I cover model binding in depth.

Getting Data from Context Objects

When you create a controller by deriving from the `Controller` base class, you get access to a set of convenience properties to access information about the request. These properties include `Request`, `Response`, `RouteData`, `HttpContext`, and `Server`. Each provides information about a different aspect of the request. I refer to these as *convenience properties*, because they each retrieve different types of data from the request's `ControllerContext` instance (which can be accessed through the `Controller.ControllerContext` property). I have described some of the most commonly used context objects and properties in Table 17-4.

Table 17-4. *Commonly Used Context Objects and Properties*

Property	Type	Description
Request.QueryString	NameValueCollection	GET variables sent with this request
Request.Form	NameValueCollection	POST variables sent with this request
Request.Cookies	HttpCookieCollection	Cookies sent by the browser with this request
Request.HttpMethod	string	The HTTP method (verb, such as GET or POST) used for this request
Request.Headers	NameValueCollection	The full set of HTTP headers sent with this request
Request.Url	Uri	The URL requested
Request.UserHostAddress	string	The IP address of the user making this request
RouteData.Route	RouteBase	The chosen RouteTable.Routes entry for this request
RouteData.Values	RouteValueDictionary	Active route parameters (either extracted from the URL or default values)
HttpContext.Application	HttpApplicationStateBase	Application state store
HttpContext.Cache	Cache	Application cache store
HttpContext.Items	IDictionary	State store for the current request
HttpContext.Session	HttpSessionStateBase	State store for the visitor's session
User	IPrincipal	Authentication information about the logged-in user
TempData	TempDataDictionary	Temporary data items stored for the current user

The individual properties that I refer to here—`Request`, `HttpContext`, and so on—provide *context objects*. I am not going to go into them in detail in this book (because they are part of the ASP.NET platform), but they provide access to some useful information and features and are worth exploring. An action method can use any of these context objects to get information about the request, as Listing 17-5 demonstrates in the form of a hypothetical action method.

Listing 17-5. *An Action Method Using Context Objects to Get Information About a Request*

```
...
public ActionResult RenameProduct() {
    // Access various properties from context objects
    string userName = User.Identity.Name;
    string serverName = Server.MachineName;
    string clientIP = Request.UserHostAddress;
    DateTime dateStamp = HttpContext.Timestamp;
    AuditRequest(userName, serverName, clientIP, dateStamp, "Renaming product");

    // Retrieve posted data from Request.Form
    string oldProductName = Request.Form["OldName"];
    string newProductName = Request.Form["NewName"];
    bool result = AttemptProductRename(oldProductName, newProductName);

    ViewData["RenameResult"] = result;
    return View("ProductRenamed");
}
...
```

You can explore the vast range of available request context information using IntelliSense (in an action method, type this. and browse the pop-up), and the Microsoft Developer Network (look up System.Web.Mvc.Controller and its base classes, or System.Web.Mvc.ControllerContext).

Using Action Method Parameters

As you've seen in previous chapters, action methods can take parameters. This is a neater way to receive incoming data than extracting it manually from context objects, and it makes your action methods easier to read. For example, suppose I have an action method that uses context objects like this:

```
...
public ActionResult ShowWeatherForecast() {
    string city = (string)RouteData.Values["city"];
    DateTime forDate = DateTime.Parse(Request.Form["forDate"]);
    // ... implement weather forecast here ...
    return View();
}
...
```

I can rewrite it to use parameters, like this:

```
...
public ActionResult ShowWeatherForecast(string city, DateTime forDate) {
    // ... implement weather forecast here ...
    return View();
}
...
```

Not only is this easier to read, but it also helps with unit testing. I can test the action method without needing to mock the convenience properties of the controller class.

■ **Tip**   It is worth noting that action methods aren't allowed to have out or ref parameters. It wouldn't make any sense if they did and the MVC Framework will simply throw an exception if it sees such a parameter.

The MVC Framework will provide values for action method parameters by checking the context objects and properties automatically, including Request.QueryString, Request.Form, and RouteData.Values. The names of the parameters are treated case-insensitively, so that an action method parameter called city can be populated by a value from Request.Form["City"], for example.

Understanding How Parameters Objects Are Instantiated

The base Controller class obtains values for action method parameters using MVC Framework components called *value providers* and *model binders*. Value providers represent the set of data items available to your controller. There are built-in value providers that fetch items from Request.Form, Request.QueryString, Request.Files, and RouteData.Values. The values are then passed to model binders that try to map them to the types that your action methods require as parameters.

The default model binders can create and populate objects of any .NET type, including collections and project-specific custom types. You saw an example of this in Chapter 11 when form posts from administrators were presented to an action method as a single Product object, even though the individual values were dispersed among the elements of the HTML form. I cover value providers and model binders in depth in Chapter 24.

Understanding Optional and Compulsory Parameters

If the MVC Framework cannot find a value for a reference type parameter (such as a string or object), the action method will still be called, but using a null value for that parameter. If a value cannot be found for a value type parameter (such as int or double), then an exception will be thrown, and the action method will *not* be called. Here is another way to think about it:

- Value-type parameters are compulsory. To make them optional, either specify a default value (see the next section) or change the parameter type to a nullable type (such as int? or DateTime?), so the MVC Framework can pass null if no value is available.

- Reference-type parameters are optional. To make them compulsory (to ensure that a non-null value is passed), add some code to the top of the action method to reject null values. For example, if the value equals null, throw an ArgumentNullException.

Specifying Default Parameter Values

If you want to process requests that do not contain values for action method parameters, but you would rather not check for null values in your code or have exceptions thrown, you can use the C# optional parameter feature instead. Listing 17-6 provides a demonstration.

Listing 17-6. Using the C# Optional Parameter Feature in an Action Method

```
...
public ActionResult Search(string query= "all", int page = 1) {
    // ...process request...
    return View();
}
...
```

You mark parameters as optional by assigning values when you define them. In the listing, I have provided default values for the query and page parameters. The MVC Framework will try to obtain values from the request for these parameters, but if there are no values available, the defaults I have specified will be used instead.

For the string parameter, query, this means that I do not need to check for null values. If the request I am processing didn't specify a query, then the action method will be called with the string all. For the int parameter, I do not need to worry about requests resulting in errors when there is no page value: the method will be called with the default value of 1. Optional parameters can be used for *literal types*, which are types that you can define without using the new keyword, including string, int, and double.

■ **Caution**   If a request *does* contain a value for a parameter but it cannot be converted to the correct type (for example, if the user gives a nonnumeric string for an int parameter), then the framework will pass the default value for that parameter type (for example, 0 for an int parameter), and will register the attempted value as a validation error in a special context object called ModelState. Unless you check for validation errors in ModelState, you can get into odd situations where the user has entered bad data into a form, but the request is processed as though the user had not entered any data or had entered the default value. See Chapter 25 for details of validation and ModelState, which can be used to avoid such problems.

Producing Output

After a controller has finished processing a request, it usually needs to generate a response. When I created the bare-metal controller by implementing the IController interface directly, I needed to take responsibility for every aspect of processing a request, including generating the response to the client. If I want to send an HTML response, for example, then I must create and assemble the HTML data and send it to the client using the Response.Write method. Similarly, if I want to redirect the user's browser to another URL, I need to call the Response.Redirect method and pass the URL I am interested in directly. Both of these approaches are shown in Listing 17-7, which shows enhancements to the BasicController class.

Listing 17-7. Generating Results in the BasicController.cs File

```
using System.Web.Mvc;
using System.Web.Routing;

namespace ControllersAndActions.Controllers {

    public class BasicController : IController {

        public void Execute(RequestContext requestContext) {

            string controller = (string)requestContext.RouteData.Values["controller"];
            string action = (string)requestContext.RouteData.Values["action"];

            if (action.ToLower() == "redirect") {
                requestContext.HttpContext.Response.Redirect("/Derived/Index");
```

```
        } else {
            requestContext.HttpContext.Response.Write(
                string.Format("Controller: {0}, Action: {1}",
                controller, action));
        }
    }
}
}
```

You can use the same approach when you have derived your controller from the Controller class. The HttpResponseBase class that is returned when you read the requestContext.HttpContext.Response property in your Execute method is available through the Controller.Response property, as shown in Listing 17-8, which shows enhancements to the DerivedController class.

Listing 17-8. Using the Response Property to Generate Output in the DerivedController.cs File

```
using System.Web.Mvc;

namespace ControllersAndActions.Controllers {

    public class DerivedController : Controller {

        public ActionResult Index() {
            ViewBag.Message = "Hello from the DerivedController Index method";
            return View("MyView");
        }

        public void ProduceOutput() {
            if (Server.MachineName == "TINY") {
                Response.Redirect("/Basic/Index");
            } else {
                Response.Write("Controller: Derived, Action: ProduceOutput");
            }
        }
    }
}
```

The ProduceOutput method uses the value of the Server.MachineName property to decide what response to send to the client. (TINY is the name of one of my development machines.) This approach works, but it has a few problems:

- The controller classes must contain details of HTML or URL structure, which makes the classes harder to read and maintain.

- It is hard to unit test a controller that generates its response directly to the output. You need to create mock implementations of the Response object, and then be able to process the output you receive from the controller in order to determine what the output represents. This can mean parsing HTML for keywords, for example, which is a drawn-out and painful process.

- Handling the fine detail of every response this way is tedious and error-prone. Some programmers will like the absolute control that building a raw controller gives, but normal people get frustrated pretty quickly.

Fortunately, the MVC Framework has a nice feature that addresses all of these issues, called *action results*. The following sections introduce the action result concept and show you the different ways that it can be used to generate responses from controllers.

Understanding Action Results

The MVC Framework uses action results to separate *stating intentions* from *executing intentions*. The concept is simple once you have mastered it, but it takes a while to get your head around the approach at first because there is a little bit of indirection going on.

Instead of working directly with the Response object, action methods return an object derived from the ActionResult class that describes what the response from controller will be, such as rendering a view or redirecting to another URL or action method. But—and this is where the indirection comes in—you don't generate the response directly. Instead, you create an ActionResult object that the MVC Framework processes to produce the result for you, after the action method has been invoked.

■ **Note** The system of action results is an example of the *command pattern*. This pattern describes scenarios where you store and pass around objects that describe operations to be performed. See http://en.wikipedia.org/wiki/Command_pattern for more details.

When the MVC Framework receives an ActionResult object from an action method, it calls the ExecuteResult method defined by that object. The action result implementation then deals with the Response object for you, generating the output that corresponds to your intention. To demonstrate how this works, I created an Infrastructure folder and added a new class file called CustomRedirectResult.cs to it, which I then used to define the custom ActionResult implementation shown in Listing 17-9.

Listing 17-9. The Contents of the CustomRedirectResult.cs File

```
using System.Web.Mvc;

namespace ControllersAndActions.Infrastructure {
    public class CustomRedirectResult : ActionResult {

        public string Url { get; set; }

        public override void ExecuteResult(ControllerContext context) {
            string fullUrl = UrlHelper.GenerateContentUrl(Url, context.HttpContext);
            context.HttpContext.Response.Redirect(fullUrl);
        }
    }
}
```

I based this class on the way that the System.Web.Mvc.RedirectResult class works. One of the benefits of the MVC Framework being open source is that you can see how things work behind the scenes. The CustomRedirectResult class is a lot simpler than the MVC equivalent, but is enough for my purposes in this chapter.

When I create an instance of the RedirectResult class, I pass in the URL I want to redirect the user to. The ExecuteResult method, which will be executed by the MVC Framework when the action method has finished, gets the Response object for the query through the ControllerContext object that the framework provides, and calls the Redirect method, which is exactly what I was doing in the bare-bones IController implementation in Listing 17-7. You can see how I have used the CustomRedirectResult class in the Derived controller in Listing 17-10.

Listing 17-10. Using the CustomRedirectResult Class in the DerivedController.cs File

```
using System;
using System.Collections.Generic;
using System.Linq;
using System.Web;
using System.Web.Mvc;
using ControllersAndActions.Infrastructure;

namespace ControllersAndActions.Controllers {
    public class DerivedController : Controller {
        public ActionResult Index() {
            ViewBag.Message = "Hello from the DerivedController Index method";
            return View("MyView");
        }

        public ActionResult ProduceOutput() {
            if (Server.MachineName == "TINY") {
                return new CustomRedirectResult { Url = "/Basic/Index" };
            } else {
                Response.Write("Controller: Derived, Action: ProduceOutput");
                return null;
            }
        }
    }
}
```

Notice that I have had to change the result of the action method to return an ActionResult. I return null if I do not want the MVC Framework to do anything after the action method has been executed, which is what I have done when I do not return a CustomRedirectResult instance.

UNIT TESTING CONTROLLERS AND ACTIONS

Many parts of the MVC Framework are designed to facilitate unit testing, and this is especially true for actions and controllers. There are a few reasons for this support:

- You can test actions and controllers outside a web server. The context objects are accessed through their base classes (such as HttpRequestBase), which are easy to mock.

- You do not need to parse any HTML to test the result of an action method. You can inspect the ActionResult object that is returned to ensure that you received the expected result.

- You do not need to simulate client requests. The MVC Framework model binding system allows you to write action methods that receive input as method parameters. To test an action method, you simply call the action method directly and provide the parameter values that interest you.

I will show you how to create unit tests for the different kinds of action results throughout this chapter.

Do not forget that unit testing isn't the complete story. Complex behaviors in an application arise when action methods are called in sequence. Unit testing is best combined with other testing approaches.

Now that you have seen how a custom redirection action result works, I can switch to the equivalent one provided by the MVC Framework, which has more features and has been thoroughly tested by Microsoft. Listing 17-11 shows the change to the Derived controller.

Listing 17-11. Using the Built-in RedirectResult Object in the DerivedController.cs File

```
...
public ActionResult ProduceOutput() {
    return new RedirectResult("/Basic/Index");
}
...
```

I have removed the conditional statement from the action method, which means that if you start the application and navigate to the /Derived/ProduceOutput method, your browser will be redirected to the /Basic/Index URL.

To make action method code simpler, the Controller class includes convenience methods for generating different kinds of ActionResult objects. So, as an example, I can achieve the effect in Listing 17-11 by returning the result of the Redirect method, as shown in Listing 17-12.

Listing 17-12. Using a Controller Convenience Method in the DerivedController.cs File

```
...
public ActionResult ProduceOutput() {
    return Redirect("/Basic/Index");
}
...
```

There is nothing in the action result system that is especially complex, but it helps you create with simpler, cleaner and more consistent code, which is easier to read and easier to unit test.

In the case of a redirection, for example, you can simply check that the action method returns an instance of RedirectResult and that the Url property contains the target you expect.

The MVC Framework contains a number of built-in action result types, which are shown in Table 17-5. All of these types are derived from ActionResult, and many of them have convenient helper methods in the Controller class. In the following sections, I will show you how to use the most important of these result types.

Table 17-5. Built-in ActionResult Types

Type	Description	Helper Methods
ViewResult	Renders the specified or default view template	View
PartialViewResult	Renders the specified or default partial view template	PartialView
RedirectToRouteResult	Issues an HTTP 301 or 302 redirection to an action method or specific route entry, generating a URL according to your routing configuration	RedirectToAction RedirectToActionPermanent RedirectToRoute RedirectToRoutePermanent
RedirectResult	Issues an HTTP 301 or 302 redirection to a specific URL	Redirect RedirectPermanent
ContentResult	Returns raw textual data to the browser, optionally setting a content-type header	Content

(continued)

Table 17-5. (*continued*)

Type	Description	Helper Methods
FileResult	Transmits binary data (such as a file from disk or a byte array in memory) directly to the browser	File
JsonResult	Serializes a .NET object in JSON format and sends it as the response. This kind of response is more typically generated using the Web API feature, which I describe in Chapter 27, but you can see this action type used in Chapter 23.	Json
JavaScriptResult	Sends a snippet of JavaScript source code that should be executed by the browser	JavaScript
HttpUnauthorizedResult	Sets the response HTTP status code to 401 (meaning "not authorized"), which causes the active authentication mechanism (forms authentication or Windows authentication) to ask the visitor to log in	None
HttpNotFoundResult	Returns a HTTP 404–Not found error	HttpNotFound
HttpStatusCodeResult	Returns a specified HTTP code	None
EmptyResult	Does nothing	None

Returning HTML by Rendering a View

The most common kind of response from an action method is to generate HTML and send it to the browser. To demonstrate how to render views, I added a controller called Example to the project. You can see the contents of the ExampleController.cs class file in Listing 17-13.

Listing 17-13. The Contents of the ExampleController.cs File

```
using System.Web.Mvc;

namespace ControllersAndActions.Controllers {

    public class ExampleController : Controller {

        public ViewResult Index() {
            return View("Homepage");
        }
    }
}
```

When using the action result system, you specify the view that you want the MVC Framework to render using an instance of the ViewResult class. The simplest way to do this is to call the controller's View method, passing the name of the view as an argument. In the listing, I called the View method with an argument of Homepage, which specifies that I want the HomePage.cshtml view to be used.

■ **Note**   Notice that that the return type for the action method in the listing is ViewResult. The method would compile and work just as well if I had specified the more general ActionResult type. In fact, some MVC programmers will define the result of every action method as ActionResult, even when they know it will always return a more specific type.

When the MVC Framework calls the ExecuteResult method of the ViewResult object, a search will begin for the view that you have specified. If you are using areas in your project, then the framework will look in the following locations:

- /Areas/*<AreaName>*/Views/*<ControllerName>*/*<ViewName>*.aspx

- /Areas/*<AreaName>*/Views/*<ControllerName>*/*<ViewName>*.ascx

- /Areas/*<AreaName>*/Views/Shared/*<ViewName>*.aspx

- /Areas/*<AreaName>*/Views/Shared/*<ViewName>*.ascx

- /Areas/*<AreaName>*/Views/*<ControllerName>*/*<ViewName>*.cshtml

- /Areas/*<AreaName>*/Views/*<ControllerName>*/*<ViewName>*.vbhtml

- /Areas/*<AreaName>*/Views/Shared/<ViewName>.cshtml

- /Areas/*<AreaName>*/Views/Shared/*<ViewName>*.vbhtml

You can see from the list that the framework looks for views that have been created for the legacy ASPX view engine (the .aspx and .ascx file extensions), even though the MVC Framework uses Razor. This is to preserve compatibility with early versions of the MVC Framework that used the rendering features from ASP.NET Web Forms.

The framework also looks for C# and Visual Basic .NET Razor templates. (The .cshtml files are the C# ones and .vbhtml files are Visual Basic. The Razor syntax is the same in these files, but the code fragments are, as the names suggest, in different languages.) The MVC Framework checks to see if each of these files exists in turn. As soon as it locates a match, it uses that view to render the result of the action method.

If you are not using areas, or you are using areas but none of the files in the preceding list have been found, then the framework continues its search, using the following locations:

- /Views/*<ControllerName>*/*<ViewName>*.aspx

- /Views/<ControllerName>/<ViewName>.ascx

- /Views/Shared/*<ViewName>*.aspx

- /Views/Shared/*<ViewName>*.ascx

- /Views/*<ControllerName>*/*<ViewName>*.cshtml

- /Views/*<ControllerName>*/*<ViewName>*.vbhtml

- /Views/Shared/*<ViewName>*.cshtml

- /Views/Shared/*<ViewName>*.vbhtml

Once again, as soon as the MVC Framework tests a location and finds a file, then the search stops, and the view that has been found is used to render the response to the client.

I am not using areas in the example application, so the first place that the framework will look will be /Views/Example/Index.aspx. Notice that the Controller part of the class name is omitted, so that creating a ViewResult in ExampleController leads to a search for a directory called Example.

UNIT TEST: RENDERING A VIEW

To test the view that an action method renders, you can inspect the `ViewResult` object that it returns. This is not quite the same thing (after all, you are not following the process through to check the final HTML that is generated) but it is close enough, as long as you have reasonable confidence that the MVC Framework view system works properly. I added a new unit test file called `ActionTests.cs` to the test project to hold the unit tests for this chapter.

The first situation I want to test is when an action method selects a specific view, like this:

```
...
public ViewResult Index() {
    return View("Homepage");
}
...
```

You can determine which view has been selected by reading the `ViewName` property of the `ViewResult` object, as shown in this test method.

```
using System.Web.Mvc;
using ControllersAndActions.Controllers;
using Microsoft.VisualStudio.TestTools.UnitTesting;

namespace ControllersAndActions.Tests {
    [TestClass]
    public class ActionTests {

        [TestMethod]
        public void ControllerTest() {

            // Arrange - create the controller
            ExampleController target = new ExampleController();

            // Act - call the action method
            ViewResult result = target.Index();

            // Assert - check the result
            Assert.AreEqual("Homepage", result.ViewName);
        }
    }
}
```

A slight variation arises when you are testing an action method that selects the default view, like this:

```
...
public ViewResult Index() {
    return View();
}
...
```

In such situations, you need to accept the empty string ("") for the view name, like this:

```
...
Assert.AreEqual("", result.ViewName);
...
```

The empty string is how the `ViewResult` object signals to the Razor view engine that the default view associated with the action method has been selected.

The sequence of directories that the MVC Framework searches for a view is another example of convention over configuration. You do not need to register your view files with the framework. You just put them in one of a set of known locations, and the framework will find them. I can take the convention a step further by omitting the name of the view I want rendered when calling the `View` method, as shown in Listing 17-14.

Listing 17-14. Creating a ViewResult Without Specifying a View in the ExampleController.cs File

```
using System.Web.Mvc;
using System;

namespace ControllersAndActions.Controllers {

    public class ExampleController : Controller {

        public ViewResult Index() {
            return View();
        }
    }
}
```

The MVC Framework assumes that I want to render a view that has the same name as the action method. This means that the call to the `View` method in Listing 17-14 starts a search for a view called `Index`.

■ **Note**   The MVC Framework actually gets the name of the action method from the `RouteData.Values["action"]` value, which I explained as part of the routing system in Chapters 15 and 16. The action method name and the routing value will be the same if you are using the built-in routing classes, but this may not be the case if you have implemented custom routing classes which do not follow the MVC Framework conventions.

There are a number of overridden versions of the `View` method. They correspond to setting different properties on the `ViewResult` object that is created. For example, you can override the layout used by a view by explicitly naming an alternative, like this:

```
...
public ViewResult Index() {
    return View("Index", "_AlternateLayoutPage");
}
...
```

SPECIFYING A VIEW BY ITS PATH

The naming convention approach is convenient and simple, but it does limit the views you can render. If you want to render a specific view, you can do so by providing an explicit path and bypass the search phase. Here is an example:

```
using System.Web.Mvc;

namespace ControllersAndActions.Controllers {

    public class ExampleController : Controller {

        public ViewResult Index() {
            return View("~/Views/Other/Index.cshtml");
        }
    }
}
```

When you specify a view like this, the path must begin with / or ~/ and include the file name extension (such as .cshtml for Razor views containing C# code).

If you find yourself using this feature, I suggest that you take a moment and ask yourself what you are trying to achieve. If you are attempting to render a view that belongs to another controller, then you might be better off redirecting the user to an action method in that controller (see the "Redirecting to an Action Method" section later in this chapter for an example). If you are trying to work around the naming scheme because it doesn't suit the way you have organized your project, then see Chapter 20, which explains how to implement a custom search sequence.

Passing Data from an Action Method to a View

The MVC Framework provides a number of different ways to pass data from an action method to a view, which I describe in the following sections. I touch on the topic of views, which I cover in depth in Chapter 20. In this chapter, I discuss only enough view functionality to demonstrate the controller features of interest.

Providing a View Model Object

You can send an object to the view by passing it as a parameter to the View method as shown in Listing 17-15.

Listing 17-15. Specifying a View Model Object in the ExampleController.cs File

```
using System;
using System.Web.Mvc;

namespace ControllersAndActions.Controllers {

    public class ExampleController : Controller {
```

```
        public ViewResult Index() {
            DateTime date = DateTime.Now;
            return View(date);
        }
    }
}
```

I passed a DateTime object as the view model and I can access the object in the view using the Razor Model keyword. To demonstrate the Model keyword, I added a view called Index.cshtml in the Views/Example folder, with the contents shown in Listing 17-16.

Listing 17-16. Accessing a View Model in the Index.cshtml File

```
@{
    ViewBag.Title = "Index";
}

<h2>Index</h2>

The day is: @(((DateTime)Model).DayOfWeek)
```

This is an *untyped* or *weakly typed* view. The view does not know anything about the view model object, and treats it as an instance of object. To get the value of the DayOfWeek property, I need to cast the object to an instance of DateTime. This works, but produces messy views. I can tidy this up by creating *strongly typed views*, in which the view includes details of the type of the view model object, as demonstrated in Listing 17-17.

Listing 17-17. Adding Strong Typing to the Index.cshtml File

```
@model DateTime
@{
    ViewBag.Title = "Index";
}

<h2>Index</h2>

The day is: @Model.DayOfWeek
```

I specified the view model type using the Razor model keyword. Notice that I use a lowercase m when specifying the model type and an uppercase M when reading the value. Not only does this help tidy up the view, but Visual Studio supports IntelliSense for strongly typed views, as shown in Figure 17-3.

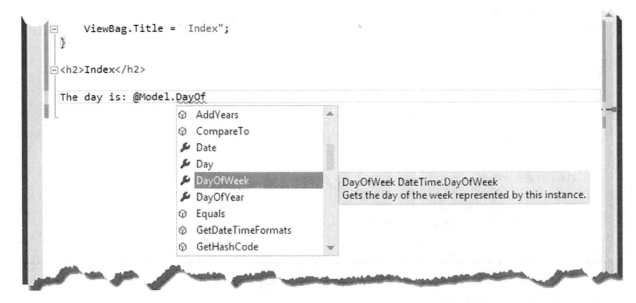

Figure 17-3. *IntelliSense support for strongly typed views*

UNIT TEST: VIEW MODEL OBJECTS

You can access the view model object passed from the action method to the view through the ViewResult. ViewData.Model property. Here is the test for the action method in Listing 17-17. You can see that I have used the Assert.IsInstanceOfType method to check that the view model object is an instance of DateTime:

```
...
[TestMethod]
public void ViewSelectionTest() {

    // Arrange - create the controller
    ExampleController target = new ExampleController();

    // Act - call the action method
    ViewResult result = target.Index();

    // Assert - check the result
    Assert.AreEqual("", result.ViewName);
    Assert.IsInstanceOfType(result.ViewData.Model, typeof(System.DateTime));
}
...
```

I had to change the name of the view that I check for to reflect the changes in the action method since the last unit test I showed you, as follows:

```
...
[TestMethod]
public void ControllerTest() {

    // Arrange - create the controller
    ExampleController target = new ExampleController();

    // Act - call the action method
    ViewResult result = target.Index();

    // Assert - check the result
    Assert.AreEqual("", result.ViewName);
}
...
```

Passing Data with the View Bag

I introduced the View Bag feature in Chapter 2. This feature allows you to define properties on a dynamic object and access them in a view. The dynamic object is accessed through the Controller.ViewBag property, as demonstrated in Listing 17-18.

Listing 17-18. Using the View Bag Feature in the ExampleController.cs File

```
using System;
using System.Web.Mvc;

namespace ControllersAndActions.Controllers {

    public class ExampleController : Controller {

        public ViewResult Index() {
            ViewBag.Message = "Hello";
            ViewBag.Date = DateTime.Now;
            return View();
        }
    }
}
```

I have defined View Bag properties called Message and Date simply by assigning values to them. Before this point, no such properties existed, and I made no preparations to create them. To read the data back in the view, I simply get the same properties that I set in the action method, as Listing 17-19 shows.

Listing 17-19. Reading Data from the ViewBag in the Index.cshtml File

```
@{
    ViewBag.Title = "Index";
}

<h2>Index</h2>

The day is: @ViewBag.Date.DayOfWeek
<p />
The message is: @ViewBag.Message
```

The ViewBag has an advantage over using a view model object in that it is easy to send multiple objects to the view. If I were restricted to using view models, then I would need to create a new type that had `string` and `DateTime` members in order to get the same effect.

When working with dynamic objects, you can enter any sequence of method and property calls in the view, like this:

```
...
The day is: @ViewBag.Date.DayOfWeek.Blah.Blah.Blah
...
```

Visual Studio cannot provide IntelliSense support for any dynamic objects, including the `ViewBag`, and errors such as this won't be revealed until the view is rendered.

UNIT TEST: VIEWBAG

You can read values from the `ViewBag` through the `ViewResult.ViewBag` property. The following test method is for the action method in Listing 17-18:

```
...
[TestMethod]
public void ControllerTest() {

    // Arrange - create the controller
    ExampleController target = new ExampleController();

    // Act - call the action method
    ViewResult result = target.Index();

    // Assert - check the result
    Assert.AreEqual("Hello", result.ViewBag.Message);
}
...
```

Performing Redirections

A common result from an action method is not to produce any output directly, but to redirect the user's browser to another URL. Most of the time, this URL is another action method in the application that generates the output you want the users to see.

THE POST/REDIRECT/GET PATTERN

The most frequent use of a redirect is in action methods that process HTTP POST requests. As I mentioned in the previous chapter, POST requests are used when you want to change the state of an application. If you just return HTML following the processing of a request, you run the risk that the user will click the browser's reload button and resubmit the form a second time, causing unexpected and undesirable results.

To avoid this problem, you can follow the pattern called Post/Redirect/Get. In this pattern, you receive a POST request, process it, and then redirect the browser so that a GET request is made by the browser for another URL. GET requests should not modify the state of your application, so any inadvertent resubmissions of this request won't cause any problems.

When you perform a redirect, you send one of two HTTP codes to the browser:

- Send the HTTP code 302, which is a *temporary* redirection. This is the most frequently used type of redirection and when using the Post/Redirect/Get pattern, this is the code that you want to send.

- Send the HTTP code 301, which indicates a permanent redirection. This should be used with caution, because it instructs the recipient of the HTTP code not to request the original URL ever again and to use the new URL that is included alongside the redirection code. If you are in doubt, use temporary redirections; that is, send code 302.

Redirecting to a Literal URL

The most basic way to redirect a browser is to call the Redirect method, which returns an instance of the RedirectResult class, as shown in Listing 17-20.

Listing 17-20. Redirecting to a Literal URL in the ExampleController.cs File

```
using System;
using System.Web.Mvc;

namespace ControllersAndActions.Controllers {

    public class ExampleController : Controller {

        public ViewResult Index() {
            ViewBag.Message = "Hello";
            ViewBag.Date = DateTime.Now;
            return View();
        }
```

```
        public RedirectResult Redirect() {
            return Redirect("/Example/Index");
        }
    }
}
```

The URL you want to redirect to is expressed as a string and passed as a parameter to the Redirect method. The Redirect method sends a temporary redirection. You can send a permanent redirection using the RedirectPermanent method, as shown in Listing 17-21.

Listing 17-21. Permanently Redirecting to a Literal URL in the ExampleController.cs File

```
...
public RedirectResult Redirect() {
    return RedirectPermanent("/Example/Index");
}
...
```

■ **Tip** If you prefer, you can use the overloaded version of the Redirect method, which takes a bool parameter that specifies whether or not a redirection is permanent.

UNIT TEST: LITERAL REDIRECTIONS

Literal redirections are easy to test. You can read the URL and test whether the redirection is permanent or temporary using the Url and Permanent properties of the RedirectResult class. The following is a test method for the redirection shown in Listing 17-21:

```
...
[TestMethod]
public void ControllerTest() {
    // Arrange - create the controller
    ExampleController target = new ExampleController();

    // Act - call the action method
    RedirectResult result = target.Redirect();

    // Assert - check the result
    Assert.IsTrue(result.Permanent);
    Assert.AreEqual("/Example/Index", result.Url);
}
...
```

Notice that I have updated the test to receive a RedirectResult when I call the action method.

Redirecting to a Routing System URL

If you are redirecting the user to a different part of your application, you need to make sure that the URL you send is valid within your URL schema. The problem with using literal URLs for redirection is that any change in your routing schema means that you need to go through your code and update the URLs. Fortunately, you can use the routing system to generate valid URLs with the RedirectToRoute method, which creates an instance of the RedirectToRouteResult, as shown in Listing 17-22.

Listing 17-22. Redirecting to a Routing System URL in the ExampleController.cs File

```
using System;
using System.Web.Mvc;

namespace ControllersAndActions.Controllers {

    public class ExampleController : Controller {

        public ViewResult Index() {

            ViewBag.Message = "Hello";
            ViewBag.Date = DateTime.Now;

            return View();
        }

        public RedirectToRouteResult Redirect() {
            return RedirectToRoute(new {
                controller = "Example",
                action = "Index",
                ID = "MyID"
            });
        }
    }
}
```

The RedirectToRoute method issues a temporary redirection. Use the RedirectToRoutePermanent method for permanent redirections. Both methods take an anonymous type whose properties are then passed to the routing system to generate a URL. For more details of this process, see the Chapters 15 and 16.

■ **Tip**   Notice that the RedirectToRoute method returns a RedirectToRouteResult object and that I have updated the action method to return this type.

UNIT TESTING: ROUTED REDIRECTIONS

Here is the unit test for the action method in Listing 17-22:

```
...
[TestMethod]
public void ControllerTest() {

    // Arrange - create the controller
    ExampleController target = new ExampleController();

    // Act - call the action method
    RedirectToRouteResult result = target.Redirect();

    // Assert - check the result
    Assert.IsFalse(result.Permanent);
    Assert.AreEqual("Example", result.RouteValues["controller"]);
    Assert.AreEqual("Index", result.RouteValues["action"]);
    Assert.AreEqual("MyID", result.RouteValues["ID"]);
}
...
```

You can see that I have tested the result indirectly by looking at the routing information provided by the RedirectToRouteResult object, which means that I don't have to parse a URL.

Redirecting to an Action Method

You can redirect to an action method more elegantly by using the RedirectToAction method (for temporary redirections) or the RedirectToActionPermanent (for permanent redirections). These are just wrappers around the RedirectToRoute method that lets you specify values for the action method and the controller without needing to create an anonymous type, as shown in Listing 17-23.

Listing 17-23. Redirecting Using the RedirectToAction Method in the ExampleController.cs File

```
...
public RedirectToRouteResult Redirect() {
    return RedirectToAction("Index");
}
...
```

If you just specify an action method, then it is assumed that you are referring to an action method in the current controller. If you want to redirect to another controller, you need to provide the name as a parameter, like this:

```
...
public RedirectToRouteResult Redirect() {
    return RedirectToAction("Index", "Basic");
}
...
```

There are other overloaded versions that you can use to provide additional values for the URL generation. These are expressed using an anonymous type, which does tend to undermine the purpose of the convenience method, but can still make your code easier to read.

■ **Note**   The values that you provide for the action method and controller are not verified before they are passed to the routing system. You are responsible for making sure that the targets you specify actually exist.

PRESERVING DATA ACROSS A REDIRECTION

A redirection causes the browser to submit an entirely new HTTP request, which means that you do not have access to the details of the original request. If you want to pass data from one request to the next, you can use the Temp Data feature.

TempData is similar to Session data, except that TempData values are marked for deletion when they are read, and they are removed when the request has been processed. This is an ideal arrangement for short-lived data that you want to persist across a redirection. Here is a simple example in an action method that uses the RedirectToAction method:

```
...
public RedirectToRouteResult RedirectToRoute() {
    TempData["Message"] = "Hello";
    TempData["Date"] = DateTime.Now;
    return RedirectToAction("Index");
}
...
```

When this method processes a request, it sets values in the TempData collection, and then redirects the user's browser to the Index action method in same controller. You can read the TempData values back in the target action method, and then pass them to the view, like this:

```
...
public ViewResult Index() {
    ViewBag.Message = TempData["Message"];
    ViewBag.Date = TempData["Date"];
    return View();
}
...
```

A more direct approach would be to read these values in the view, like this:

```
@{
    ViewBag.Title = "Index";
}

<h2>Index</h2>
```

```
The day is: @(((DateTime)TempData["Date"]).DayOfWeek)
<p />
The message is: @TempData["Message"]
```

Reading the values in the view means that you do not need to use the View Bag feature in the action method. However, you must cast the `TempData` results to an appropriate type.

You can get a value from `TempData` without marking it for removal by using the `Peek` method, like this:

```
...
DateTime time = (DateTime)TempData.Peek("Date");
...
```

You can preserve a value that would otherwise be deleted by using the `Keep` method, like this:

```
...
TempData.Keep("Date");
...
```

The `Keep` method doesn't protect a value forever. If the value is read again, it will be marked for removal once more. If you want to store items so that they won't be removed when the request is processed then use session data instead.

Returning Errors and HTTP Codes

The last of the built-in `ActionResult` classes that I will look at can be used to send specific error messages and HTTP result codes to the client. Most applications do not require these features because the MVC Framework will automatically generate these kinds of results. However, they can be useful if you need to take more direct control over the responses sent to the client.

Sending a Specific HTTP Result Code

You can send a specific HTTP status code to the browser using the `HttpStatusCodeResult` class. There is no controller helper method for this, so you must instantiate the class directly, as shown in Listing 17-24.

Listing 17-24. Sending a Specific Status Code in the ExampleController.cs File

```
using System;
using System.Web.Mvc;

namespace ControllersAndActions.Controllers {

    public class ExampleController : Controller {

        public ViewResult Index() {
            ViewBag.Message = "Hello";
            ViewBag.Date = DateTime.Now;
            return View();
        }
```

```
        public RedirectToRouteResult Redirect() {
            return RedirectToAction("Index");
        }

        public HttpStatusCodeResult StatusCode() {
            return new HttpStatusCodeResult(404, "URL cannot be serviced");
        }
    }
}
```

The constructor parameters for HttpStatusCodeResult are the numeric status code and an optional descriptive message. In the listing, I returned code 404, which signifies that the requested resource does not exist.

Sending a 404 Result

I can achieve the same effect as Listing 17-24 using the more convenient HttpNotFoundResult class, which is derived from HttpStatusCodeResult and can be created using the controller HttpNotFound convenience method, as shown in Listing 17-25.

Listing 17-25. Generating a 404 Result in the ExampleController.cs File

```
...
public HttpStatusCodeResult StatusCode() {
    return HttpNotFound();
}
...
```

Sending a 401 Result

Another wrapper class for a specific HTTP status code is the HttpUnauthorizedResult, which returns the 401 code, used to indicate that a request is unauthorized. Listing 17-26 provides a demonstration.

Listing 17-26. Generating a 401 Result in the ExampleController.cs File

```
...
public HttpStatusCodeResult StatusCode() {
    return new HttpUnauthorizedResult();
}
...
```

There is no helper method in the Controller class to create instances of HttpUnauthorizedResult, so you must do so directly. The effect of returning an instance of this class is usually to redirect the user to the authentication page, as you saw in Chapter 12.

UNIT TEST: HTTP STATUS CODES

The HttpStatusCodeResult class follows the pattern you have seen for the other result types, and makes its state available through a set of properties. In this case, the StatusCode property returns the numeric HTTP status code, and the StatusDescription property returns the associated descriptive string. The following test method is for the action method in Listing 17-26:

```
...
[TestMethod]
public void ControllerTest() {

    // Arrange - create the controller
    ExampleController target = new ExampleController();

    // Act - call the action method
    HttpStatusCodeResult result = target.StatusCode();

    // Assert - check the result
    Assert.AreEqual(401, result.StatusCode);
}
...
```

Summary

Controllers are one of the key building blocks in the MVC design pattern. In this chapter, you have seen how to create "raw" controllers by implementing the IController interface and more convenient controllers by deriving from the Controller class. You saw the role that action methods play in MVC Framework controllers and how they ease unit testing. I showed you the different ways that you can receive input and generate output from an action method and demonstrated the different kinds of ActionResult that make this a simple and flexible process. In the next chapter, I go deeper into the controller infrastructure to show you the *filters* feature, which changes how requests are processed.

CHAPTER 18

■ ■ ■

Filters

Filters inject extra logic into MVC Framework request processing. They provide a simple and elegant way to implement *cross-cutting concerns*. This term refers to functionality that is used all over an application and doesn't fit neatly into any one place, where it would break the separation of concerns pattern. Classic examples of cross-cutting concerns are logging, authorization, and caching. In this chapter, I show you the different categories of filters that the MVC Framework supports, how to create and use custom filters, and how to control their execution. Table 18-1 provides the summary for this chapter.

Table 18-1. *Chapter Summary*

Problem	Solution	Listing
Inject extra logic into request processing	Apply filters to the controller or its action methods	1–8
Restrict action methods to specific users and groups	Use authorization filters	9–12
Authenticate requests	Use authentication filters	13–19
Process errors when executing requests	Use exception filters	20–30
Inject general-purpose logic into the request handling process	Use action filters	31–35
Inspect or alter the results generated by action methods	Use result filters	36–41
Use filters without attributes	Use the built-in controller methods	42
Define filters that apply to all action methods in the application	Define global filters	43–46
Control the order in which filters are executed	Use the Order parameter	47–49
Override global and controller filters for an action method	Use an override filter	50–54

Preparing the Example Project

For this chapter I created a new MVC project called Filters using the Empty template, checking the option to add the core MVC folders and references. I created a Home controller which has the action method shown in Listing 18-1. I am only focused on controllers in this chapter, so I return string values from the action methods, rather than ActionResult objects. This has the effect of causing the MVC Framework to send the string value directly to the browser, by passing the Razor view engine.

Listing 18-1. The Contents of the HomeController.cs File

```
using System.Web.Mvc;

namespace Filters.Controllers {
    public class HomeController : Controller {

        public string Index() {
            return "This is the Index action on the Home controller";
        }
    }
}
```

Later in the chapter, I'll be demonstrating how you can use a new MVC feature called *authentication filters*, and for that I need to be able to perform some simple user authentication. As I explained in Chapter 12, I don't cover the security features of the underling ASP.NET platform in this book, but Apress will freely distribute the security chapters from my forthcoming *Pro ASP.NET MVC 5 Platform* book when it is published in 2014. So, in order to demonstrate the authentication filters feature, which is part of the MVC Framework, I am going to use the same approach I adopted in Chapter 12 and define static user credentials in the Web.config file, as shown in Listing 18-2.

Listing 18-2. Defining User Credentials in the Web.config File

```
...
<system.web>
  <compilation debug="true" targetFramework="4.5.1" />
  <httpRuntime targetFramework="4.5.1" />
  <authentication mode="Forms">
    <forms loginUrl="~/Account/Login" timeout="2880">
      <credentials passwordFormat="Clear">
        <user name="user"  password="secret"/>
        <user name="admin" password="secret" />
      </credentials>
    </forms>
  </authentication>
</system.web>
...
```

I have defined two users, user and admin, and assigned them the same password, secret, to keep things simple. I am using forms authentication once again and I have used the loginUrl attribute to specify that unauthenticated requests should be redirected to the /Account/Login URL. In Listing 18-3, you can see the contents of the Account controller I added to the project and whose Login action will be targeted by the default routing configuration.

Listing 18-3. The Contents of the AccountController.cs File

```
using System.Web.Mvc;
using System.Web.Security;

namespace Filters.Controllers {
    public class AccountController : Controller {

        public ActionResult Login() {
            return View();
        }
```

```
        [HttpPost]
        public ActionResult Login(string username, string password, string returnUrl) {
            bool result = FormsAuthentication.Authenticate(username, password);
            if (result) {
                FormsAuthentication.SetAuthCookie(username, false);
                return Redirect(returnUrl ?? Url.Action("Index", "Admin"));
            } else {
                ModelState.AddModelError("", "Incorrect username or password");
                return View();
            }
        }
    }
}
```

To create the view that will gather candidate credentials from the user, create a Views/Shared folder and right-click it. Select Add ➤ MVC 5 View Page (Razor), set the name Login.cshtml and click the OK button to create the view. Edit the new view to match the content shown in Listing 18-4.

> ■ **Note**   I am creating a shared view because I'll be adding a second authentication controller later in the chapter and I want to reuse the view.

Listing 18-4. The Contents of the Login.cshtml File

```
@{
    Layout = null;
}

<!DOCTYPE html>

<html>
<head>
    <meta name="viewport" content="width=device-width" />
    <title></title>
</head>
<body>
    @using (Html.BeginForm()) {
        @Html.ValidationSummary()
        <p><label>Username:</label><input name="username" /></p>
        <p><label>Password:</label><input name="password" type="password"/></p>
        <input type="submit" value="Log in" />
    }
</body>
</html>
```

Setting the Start URL and Testing the Application

As with all of the example projects, I want Visual Studio to start with the root URL for the application rather than guess the URL based on the file that is being edited. Select Filters Properties from the Visual Studio Project menu, switch to the Web tab and check the Specific Page option in the Start Action section. You don't have to provide a value. Just checking the option is enough. If you start the example app, you will get the response shown in Figure 18-1.

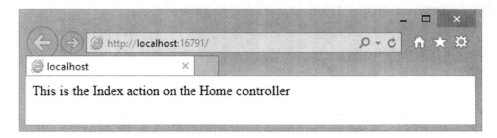

Figure 18-1. *Running the example application*

Using Filters

You have already seen an example of a filter in Chapter 12, when I applied authorization to the action methods of the SportsStore administration controller. I wanted the action method to be used only by users who had authenticated themselves, which presented me with a choice of approaches. I could have checked the authorization status of the request in each and every action method, as shown in Listing 18-5.

Listing 18-5. Explicitly Checking Authorization in Action Methods

```
namespace SportsStore.WebUI.Controllers {

    public class AdminController : Controller {

        // ... instance variables and constructor

        public ViewResult Index() {
            if (!Request.IsAuthenticated) {
                FormsAuthentication.RedirectToLoginPage();
            }
            // ...rest of action method
        }

        public ViewResult Create() {
            if (!Request.IsAuthenticated) {
                FormsAuthentication.RedirectToLoginPage();
            }
            // ...rest of action method
        }
```

```
    public ViewResult Edit(int productId) {
        if (!Request.IsAuthenticated) {
            FormsAuthentication.RedirectToLoginPage();
        }
        // ...rest of action method
    }

    // ... other action methods
    }
}
```

You can see that there is a lot of repetition in this approach, which is why I decided to use a filter instead, as shown in Listing 18-6.

Listing 18-6. Applying a Filter

```
namespace SportsStore.WebUI.Controllers {

    [Authorize]
    public class AdminController : Controller {

        // ... instance variables and constructor

        public ViewResult Index() {
            // ...rest of action method
        }

        public ViewResult Create() {
            // ...rest of action method
        }

        public ViewResult Edit(int productId) {
            // ...rest of action method
        }

        // ... other action methods
    }
}
```

Filters are .NET attributes that add extra steps to the request processing pipeline. I used the Authorize filter in Listing 18-6, which has the same effect as all of the duplicated checks in Listing 18-5.

Introducing the Filter Types

The MVC Framework supports five different types of filters. Each allows you to introduce logic at different points during request processing. The filter types are described in Table 18-2.

Table 18-2. *MVC Framework Filter Types*

Filter Type	Interface	Default Implementation	Description
Authentication	IAuthenticationFilter	N/A	Runs first, before any other filters or the action method, but can be run again after the authorization filters
Authorization	IAuthorizationFilter	AuthorizeAttribute	Runs second, after authentication, but before any other filters or the action method
Action	IActionFilter	ActionFilterAttribute	Runs before and after the action method
Result	IResultFilter	ActionFilterAttribute	Runs before and after the action result is executed
Exception	IExceptionFilter	HandleErrorAttribute	Runs only if another filter, the action method, or the action result throws an exception

Before the MVC Framework invokes an action, it inspects the method definition to see if it has attributes that implement the interfaces listed in Table 18-2. If so, then at the appropriate point in the request handling process, the methods defined by these interfaces are invoked. The framework includes default attribute classes that implement the filter interfaces. I will show you how to use these default classes later in this chapter.

■ **Tip**   MVC 5 introduces a new interface, IoverrideFilter, which I describe in the Overriding Filters section later in the chapter.

The ActionFilterAttribute class implements both the IActionFilter and IResultFilter interfaces. This class is abstract, which forces you to provide an implementation. The AuthorizeAttribute and HandleErrorAttribute classes contain useful features and can be used without creating a derived class.

Applying Filters to Controllers and Action Methods

Filters can be applied to individual action methods or to an entire controller. In Listing 18-6, I applied the Authorize filter to the AdminController class, which has the same effect as applying it to each action method in the controller, as shown in Listing 18-7.

Listing 18-7. *Applying a Filter to Action Methods Individually*

```
namespace SportsStore.WebUI.Controllers {

    public class AdminController : Controller {

        // ... instance variables and constructor
        [Authorize]
        public ViewResult Index() {
            // ...rest of action method
        }
```

```
[Authorize]
public ViewResult Create() {
    // ...rest of action method
}

// ... other action methods
}
}
```

You can apply multiple filters, and mix and match the levels at which they are applied, that is, whether they are applied to the controller or an individual action method. Listing 18-8 shows three different filters in use.

Listing 18-8. Applying Multiple Filters in a Controller Class

```
[Authorize(Roles="trader")] // applies to all actions
public class ExampleController : Controller {

    [ShowMessage]                 // applies to just this action
    [OutputCache(Duration=60)]    // applies to just this action
    public ActionResult Index() {
        // ... action method body
    }
}
```

Some of the filters in this listing take parameters. I will show you how these work as I describe the different kinds of filters.

■ **Note**   If you have defined a custom base class for your controllers, any filters applied to the base class will affect the derived classes.

Using Authorization Filters

Authorization filters are run after the authentication filters, before action filters and before the action method is invoked. As the name suggests, these filters enforce your authorization policy, ensuring that action methods can be invoked only by approved users.

There is a somewhat involved relationship between the authentication and authorization filters which is easier to explain once you understand how authorization filters work. I explain this relationship in the *Using Authentication Filters* section later in the chapter. Authorization filters implement the IAuthorizationFilter interface, which is shown in Listing 18-9.

Listing 18-9. The IAuthorizationFilter Interface

```
namespace System.Web.Mvc {

    public interface IAuthorizationFilter {
        void OnAuthorization(AuthorizationContext filterContext);
    }
}
```

You can, if you are so minded, create a class that implements the IAuthorizationFilter interface and create your own security logic. See the sidebar on why this is a really bad idea.

WARNING: WRITING SECURITY CODE IS DANGEROUS

Programming history is littered with the wreckage of applications whose programmers thought they knew how to write good security code. That's actually a skill that few people possess. There is usually some forgotten wrinkle or untested corner case that leaves a gaping hole in the application's security. If you do not believe me, just Google the term `security bug` and start reading through the top results.

Wherever possible, I like to use security code that is widely tested and proven. In this case, the MVC Framework has provided a full-featured authorization filter, which can be derived to implement custom authorization policies. I try to use this whenever I can, and I recommend that you do the same. At the least, you can pass some of the blame to Microsoft when your secret application data is spread far and wide on the Internet.

A much safer approach is to create a subclass of the AuthorizeAttribute class which takes care of all of the tricky stuff and makes it easy to write custom authorization code. The best way to demonstrate this is to create a custom filter and, to this end, I have added an Infrastructure folder to the example project and created a new class file within it called CustomAuthAttribute.cs. You can see the content of this file in Listing 18-10.

Listing 18-10. The Contents of the CustomAuthAttribute.cs File

```
using System.Web;
using System.Web.Mvc;

namespace Filters.Infrastructure {
    public class CustomAuthAttribute : AuthorizeAttribute {
        private bool localAllowed;

        public CustomAuthAttribute(bool allowedParam) {
            localAllowed = allowedParam;
        }

        protected override bool AuthorizeCore(HttpContextBase httpContext) {
            if (httpContext.Request.IsLocal) {
                return localAllowed;
            } else {
                return true;
            }
        }
    }
}
```

This is a simple authorization filter. It allows you to prevent access to local requests (a local request is one where the browser and the application server are running on the same device, such as your development PC).

I have used the simplest approach to creating an authorization filter, which is to subclass the AuthorizeAttribute class and then override the AuthorizeCore method. This ensures that I benefit from the features built in to AuthorizeAttribute. The constructor for the filter takes a bool value, indicating whether local requests are permitted.

The interesting part of the filter class is the implementation of the AuthorizeCore method, which is how the MVC Framework checks to see if the filter will authorize access for a request. The argument to this method is an HttpContextBase object, through which I can get information about the request being processed. By taking advantage of the built-in features of the AuthorizeAttribute base class, I only have to focus on the authorization logic and return true from the AuthorizeCore method if I want to authorize a request and return false if I do not.

KEEPING AUTHORIZATION ATTRIBUTES SIMPLE

The AuthorizeCore method is passed an HttpContextBase object, which provides access to information about the request, but not about the controller or action method that the authorization attribute has been applied to. The main reason that developers implement the IAuthorizationFilter interface directly is to get access to the AuthorizationContext passed to the OnAuthorization method, through which a much wider range of information can be obtained, including routing details and the current controller and action method.

I do not recommend this approach, and not just because I think writing your own security code is dangerous. Although authorization is a cross-cutting concern, building logic into your authorization attributes which is tightly coupled to the structure of your controllers undermines the separation of concerns and causes testing and maintenance problems. Keep your authorization attributes simple and focused on authorization based on the request. Let the context of what is being authorized come from where the attribute is applied.

Applying the Custom Authorization Filter

To use the custom authorization filter, I simply apply an attribute to the action methods or controllers that I want to protect, as illustrated by Listing 18-11, which demonstrates the application of the filter to the Index action method in the Home controller.

Listing 18-11. Applying a Custom Authorization Filter in the HomeController.cs File

```
using System.Web.Mvc;
using Filters.Infrastructure;

namespace Filters.Controllers {
    public class HomeController : Controller {

        [CustomAuth(false)]
        public string Index() {
            return "This is the Index action on the Home controller";
        }
    }
}
```

I have set the constructor argument for the filter to false, which means that local requests will be denied access to the Index action method. You can test this by starting the application. The routing configuration will target the Index action method when the root URL is requested by the browser. If the browser making the request is on the machine running Visual Studio, then you will see the result in Figure 18-2. The filter has denied authorization for the request and the MVC Framework has responded in the only way it knows how: by prompting the user for credentials. Of course, a username or password won't change the fact that the request is coming from the local machine and there is nothing you can do at this point to get past the authentication challenge.

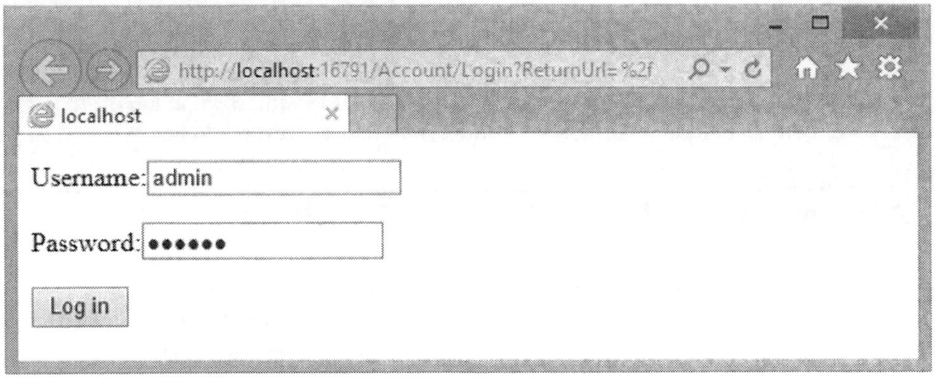

Figure 18-2. *Re-prompting for credentials for a local request by the custom authorization filter*

However, the filter will authorize the request if you change the constructor argument for the filter to `true` and restart the application. (You can't test by making a request from another machine because IIS Express, which runs the application, is configured to reject any connections that are not local.)

Using the Built-in Authorization Filter

Although I used the `AuthorizeAttribute` class as the base for the custom filter, it has its own implementation of the `AuthorizeCore` method which is useful for performing general purpose authorization tasks. When using the `AuthorizeAttribute` directly, I can specify an authorization policy using two public properties of this class, as shown in Table 18-3.

Table 18-3. *AuthorizeAttribute Properties*

Name	Type	Description
Users	string	A comma-separated list of usernames that are allowed to access the action method.
Roles	string	A comma-separated list of role names. To access the action method, users must be in at least one of these roles.

Listing 18-12 shows how I can use the built-in filter to protect an action method with one of these properties.

Listing 18-12. Using the Built-in Authorization Filter

```
using System.Web.Mvc;
using Filters.Infrastructure;

namespace Filters.Controllers {
    public class HomeController : Controller {

        [Authorize(Users = "admin")]
        public string Index() {
            return "This is the Index action on the Home controller";
        }
    }
}
```

I have specified that the admin user is authorized to invoke the Index action method, but there is an implicit condition as well: the request is authenticated. If I do not specify any users or roles, then any authenticated user can use the action method. For most applications, the authorization policy that AuthorizeAttribute provides is sufficient. If you want to implement something special, you can derive from this class as just I did earlier in the chapter or supplement your configuration with authentication filters, which I describe the next section.

Using Authentication Filters

Authentication filters are new in MVC version 5 and provide the means to provide fine-grain control over how users are authenticated for controllers and actions in an application.

Authentication filters have a relatively complex lifecycle. They are run before any other filter, which lets you define an authentication policy that will be applied before any other type of filter is used. Authentication filters can also be combined with authorization filters to provide authentication challenges for requests that don't comply to the authorization policy. Authentication filters are also run after an action method has been executed but before the ActionResult is processed. I explain how all of this works and provide some examples along the way.

Understanding the IAuthenticationFilter Interface

Authentication filters implement the IAuthenticationFilter interface, which is shown in Listing 18-13.

Listing 18-13. The IAuthenticationFilter Interface

```
namespace System.Web.Mvc.Filters {

    public interface IAuthenticationFilter {
        void OnAuthentication(AuthenticationContext context);
        void OnAuthenticationChallenge(AuthenticationChallengeContext context);
    }
}
```

The OnAuthenticationChallenge method is called by the MVC Framework whenever a request has failed the authentication or authorization policies for an action method. The OnAuthenticationChallenge method is passed an AuthenticationChallengeContext object, which is derived from the ControllerContext class I described in Chapter 17 and which defines the additional properties shown in Table 18-4.

Table 18-4. The properties defined by the AuthenticationChallengeContext class

Name	Description
ActionDescriptor	Returns an ActionDescriptor that describes the action method to which the filter has been applied
Result	Sets an ActionResult that expresses the result of the authentication challenge

The most important property is Result, because it allows the authentication filter to pass an ActionResult to the MVC Framework, a process known as *short-circuiting* that I will describe shortly. The best way of explaining how an authentication filter works is through an example. To my mind, the most interesting aspect of authentication filters is that they allow a single controller to define action methods that are authenticated in different ways, so my first step is to add a new controller that simulates Google logins. In Listing 18-14, you can see the definition of the GoogleAccountController.

Listing 18-14. The Contents of the GoogleAccountController.cs File

```
using System.Web.Mvc;
using System.Web.Security;

namespace Filters.Controllers {
    public class GoogleAccountController : Controller {

        public ActionResult Login() {
            return View();
        }

        [HttpPost]
        public ActionResult Login(string username, string password, string returnUrl) {
            if (username.EndsWith("@google.com") && password == "secret") {
                FormsAuthentication.SetAuthCookie(username, false);
                return Redirect(returnUrl ?? Url.Action("Index", "Home"));
            } else {
                ModelState.AddModelError("", "Incorrect username or password");
                return View();
            }
        }
    }
}
```

I don't want to implement real Google logins because it means delving into the dark world of third-party authentication, which is a topic in its own right. Instead, I have created a terrible hack that will authenticate any user name that ends with @google.com as long as it is provided with the password secret.

At the moment, my Google authentication controller isn't hooked up to the application, and that's where the authentication filter comes in. I created a new class file called GoogleAuthAttribute.cs, shown in Listing 18-15, in the Infrastructure folder. The FilterAttribute class, from which my GoogleAuth filter is derived, is the base for all filter classes.

Listing 18-15. The Contents of the GoogleAuthAttribute.cs File

```
using System;
using System.Web.Mvc;
using System.Web.Mvc.Filters;
using System.Web.Routing;

namespace Filters.Infrastructure {

    public class GoogleAuthAttribute : FilterAttribute, IAuthenticationFilter {

        public void OnAuthentication(AuthenticationContext context) {
            // not implemented
        }
```

```
        public void OnAuthenticationChallenge(AuthenticationChallengeContext context) {
            if (context.Result == null) {
                context.Result = new RedirectToRouteResult(new RouteValueDictionary {
                    {"controller", "GoogleAccount"},
                    {"action",    "Login"},
                    {"returnUrl", context.HttpContext.Request.RawUrl}
                });
            }
        }
    }
}
```

My implementation of the OnAuthenticationChallenge method checks to see if the Result property of the AuthenticationChallengeContext argument has been set. This allows me to avoid challenging the user when the filter is run after the action method has executed. Do not worry about that now. I explain why this is important in the *Handling the Final Challenge Request* section later in this chapter.

What's important for this section is that I use the OnAuthenticationChallenge method to challenge the user for credentials by redirecting their browser to my GoogleAccount controller with a RedirectToRouteResult. Authentication filters can use all of the ActionResult types that I described in Chapter 17, but the Controller convenience methods for creating them are not available, which is why I had to use a RouteValueDictionary object to specify the segment values so that a route to the challenge action method can be generated.

Implementing the Authentication Check

My authentication filter is ready to challenge users for their fake Google credentials, and now I can wire up the remaining behavior. The controller will call the OnAuthentication method before running any other kind of filter, providing an opportunity to perform a broad authentication check. You don't have to implement the OnAuthentication method, but I am going to do so in order to check that I am dealing with a Google account.

The OnAuthentication method is passed an AuthenticationContext object that, like the AuthenticationChallengeContext class, is derived from ControllerContext and provides access to all of the information I described in Chapter 17. The AuthenticationContext class also defines the properties shown in Table 18-5.

Table 18-5. *The properties defined by the AuthenticationContext class*

Name	Description
ActionDescriptor	Returns an ActionDescriptor that describes the action method to which the filter has been applied
Principal	Returns an IPrincipal implementation that identifies the current user, if they have already been authenticated.
Result	Sets an ActionResult that expresses the result of the authentication check

If the OnAuthentication sets a value for the Result property of the context object, then the MVC Framework will call the OnAuthenticationChallenge method. If the OnAuthenticationChallenge method doesn't set a value for the Result property on its context object, then the one from the OnAuthentication method will be executed.

I use the OnAuthentication method to create a result that reports an authentication error to the user, which can then be overridden by the OnAuthenticationChallenge method to challenge the user for credentials instead. This allows me to be sure that they see a meaningful response, even if no challenge can be issued (although I must admit that I have yet to encounter a situation where this has happened). In Listing 18-16, you can see how I have implemented the OnAuthentication method so that it checks that the request has been authenticated by using any Google credentials.

Listing 18-16. Implementing the OnAuthentication Method in the GoogleAuthAttribute.cs File

```
using System;
using System.Security.Principal;
using System.Web.Mvc;
using System.Web.Mvc.Filters;
using System.Web.Routing;

namespace Filters.Infrastructure {

    public class GoogleAuthAttribute : FilterAttribute, IAuthenticationFilter {

        public void OnAuthentication(AuthenticationContext context) {
            IIdentity ident = context.Principal.Identity;
            if (!ident.IsAuthenticated || !ident.Name.EndsWith("@google.com")) {
                context.Result = new HttpUnauthorizedResult();
            }
        }

        public void OnAuthenticationChallenge(AuthenticationChallengeContext context) {
            if (context.Result == null || context.Result is HttpUnauthorizedResult) {
                context.Result = new RedirectToRouteResult(new RouteValueDictionary {
                    {"controller", "GoogleAccount"},
                    {"action",   "Login"},
                    {"returnUrl", context.HttpContext.Request.RawUrl}
                });
            }
        }
    }
}
```

My implementation of the OnAuthentication method checks to see if the request has been authenticated using a username that ends with @google.com. If the request is not authenticated or the request is authenticated using a different kind of credential, then I set the Result property of the AuthenticationContext object to a new HttpUnauthorizedResult.

The HttpUnauthorizedResult is set as the Result value for the AuthenticationChallengeContext object that is passed to the OnAuthenticationChallenge method and you can see that I have updated this method to challenge the user when this happens, coordinating the actions of the two methods in the filter. The next step is to apply the filter to the controller, which you can see in Listing 18-17.

Listing 18-17. Applying the Authentication Filter in the HomeController.cs File

```
using System.Web.Mvc;
using Filters.Infrastructure;

namespace Filters.Controllers {
    public class HomeController : Controller {

        [Authorize(Users = "admin")]
        public string Index() {
            return "This is the Index action on the Home controller";
        }
```

```
    [GoogleAuth]
    public string List() {
        return "This is the List action on the Home controller";
    }
  }
}
```

I have defined a new action method called List, which I decorated with the GoogleAuth filter. The result is that access to the Index method is secured through the built-in support for forms authentication but that access to the List action method is secured through my custom fake Google authentication system.

You can see the effect by starting the application. By default the browser will target the Index action method, which will trigger the standard authentication and require you to log in using one of the usernames that I defined in the Web.config file. If you then request the /Home/List URL, then your existing credentials will be rejected and you will have to authenticate using a Google username.

Combining Authentication and Authorization Filters

You can combine authentication and authorization filters on the same action methods to narrow the scope of your security policy. The MVC Framework will call the OnAuthentication method of the authentication filter, just as in the previous example, and move on to run the authorization filter if the request passes the authentication check. If the request doesn't pass the authorization filter, then the OnAuthenticationChallenge method of the authentication filter will be called so that you can challenge the user for the required credentials. In Listing 18-18, you can see how I have combined the GoogleAuth and Authorize filters to restrict access to the List action in the Home controller.

Listing 18-18. Combining Authentication and Authorization Filters in the HomeController.cs File

```
using System.Web.Mvc;
using Filters.Infrastructure;

namespace Filters.Controllers {
    public class HomeController : Controller {

        [Authorize(Users = "admin")]
        public string Index() {
            return "This is the Index action on the Home controller";
        }

        [GoogleAuth]
        [Authorize(Users = "bob@google.com")]
        public string List() {
            return "This is the List action on the Home controller";
        }
    }
}
```

The Authorize filter restricts access to the bob@google.com account. If the action method is targeted by another Google account, then the authentication filter OnAuthenticationChallenge method will be passed an AuthenticationChallengeContext object whose Result property is set to an instance of the HttpUnauthorizedResult class (which is why I used the same class in the OnAuthentication method).

The filters in the Home controller restrict access to the Index method to the user admin, who is authenticated using the AccountController, and restrict access to the List method to the bob@google.com user, who is authenticated through the GoogleAccount controller.

Handling the Final Challenge Request

The MVC Framework calls the OnAuthenticationChallenge method one final time after the action method has been executed, but before the ActionResult is returned and executed. This provides authentication filters an opportunity to respond to the fact that the action has completed or even alter the result (something that is also possible with result filters, which I describe later in the chapter).

It is for this reason that I check the Result property of the AuthenticationChallengeContext object in the OnAuthenticationChallenge method. If I did not, I end up challenging the user for credentials once again, which makes little sense given that the action method has already been executed by this point.

The only reason I have found for responding to this last method call is to clear the authentication for the request, which can be useful when important action methods require temporarily elevated credentials that you want entered each and every time the action is to be executed. In Listing 18-19, you can see how I have implemented this feature.

Listing 18-19. Handling the Final Challenge Call in the GoogleAuthAttribute.cs File

```
using System;
using System.Security.Principal;
using System.Web.Mvc;
using System.Web.Mvc.Filters;
using System.Web.Routing;
using System.Web.Security;

namespace Filters.Infrastructure {

    public class GoogleAuthAttribute : FilterAttribute, IAuthenticationFilter {

        public void OnAuthentication(AuthenticationContext context) {
            IIdentity ident = context.Principal.Identity;
            if (!ident.IsAuthenticated || !ident.Name.EndsWith("@google.com")) {
                context.Result = new HttpUnauthorizedResult();
            }
        }

        public void OnAuthenticationChallenge(AuthenticationChallengeContext context) {
            if (context.Result == null || context.Result is HttpUnauthorizedResult) {
                context.Result = new RedirectToRouteResult(new RouteValueDictionary {
                    {"controller", "GoogleAccount"},
                    {"action",   "Login"},
                    {"returnUrl", context.HttpContext.Request.RawUrl}
                });
            } else {
                FormsAuthentication.SignOut();
            }
        }
    }
}
```

You can see the effect by starting the application and requesting the Home/List URL. You will be prompted to provide credentials and you will be able to execute the action method if you authenticate as bob@google.com. But you will be prompted for credentials again if you reload the browser, essentially targeting the List method a second time.

Using Exception Filters

Exception filters are run only if an unhandled exception has been thrown when invoking an action method. The exception can come from the following locations:

- Another kind of filter (authorization, action, or result filter)

- The action method itself

- When the action result is executed (see Chapter 17 for details on action results)

Creating an Exception Filter

Exception filters implement the IExceptionFilter interface, which is shown in Listing 18-20.

Listing 18-20. The IExceptionFilter Interface

```
namespace System.Web.Mvc {

    public interface IExceptionFilter {
        void OnException(ExceptionContext filterContext);
    }
}
```

The OnException method is called when an unhandled exception arises. The parameter for this method is an ExceptionContext object, which is derived from ControllerContext and provides a number of useful properties that you can use to get information about the request, as shown in Table 18-6.

Table 18-6. *Useful ControllerContext Properties*

Name	Type	Description
Controller	ControllerBase	Returns the controller object for this request
HttpContext	HttpContextBase	Provides access to details of the request and access to the response
IsChildAction	bool	Returns true if this is a child action (see Chapter 20)
RequestContext	RequestContext	Provides access to the HttpContext and the routing data, both of which are available through other properties
RouteData	RouteData	Returns the routing data for this request

In addition to the properties inherited from the ControllerContext class, the ExceptionContext class defines some additional properties which are useful with dealing with exceptions, as shown in Table 18-7.

Table 18-7. Additional ExceptionContext Properties

Name	Type	Description
ActionDescriptor	ActionDescriptor	Provides details of the action method
Result	ActionResult	The result for the action method; a filter can cancel the request by setting this property to a non-null value
Exception	Exception	The unhandled exception
ExceptionHandled	bool	Returns true if another filter has marked the exception as handled

The exception that has been thrown is available through the Exception property. An exception filter can report that it has handled the exception by setting the ExceptionHandled property to true. All of the exception filters applied to an action are invoked even if this property is set to true, so it is good practice to check whether another filter has already dealt with the problem, to avoid attempting to recover from a problem that another filter has resolved.

■ **Note**   If none of the exception filters for an action method set the ExceptionHandled property to true, the MVC Framework uses the default ASP.NET exception handling procedure which will display the dreaded "yellow screen of death."

The Result property is used by the exception filter to tell the MVC Framework what to do. The two main uses for exception filters are to log the exception and to display a message to the user. To demonstrate how this all fits together, I have created a new class file called RangeExceptionAttribute.cs in the Infrastructure folder. The contents of this file are shown in Listing 18-21.

Listing 18-21. The Contents of the RangeExceptionAttribute.cs File

```
using System;
using System.Web.Mvc;

namespace Filters.Infrastructure {
    public class RangeExceptionAttribute : FilterAttribute, IExceptionFilter {

        public void OnException(ExceptionContext filterContext) {
            if (!filterContext.ExceptionHandled &&
                filterContext.Exception is ArgumentOutOfRangeException) {
                filterContext.Result
                    = new RedirectResult("~/Content/RangeErrorPage.html");
                filterContext.ExceptionHandled = true;
            }
        }
    }
}
```

This exception filter handles ArgumentOutOfRangeException instances by redirecting the user's browser to a file called RangeErrorPage.html in the Content folder. Notice that I have derived the RangeExceptionAttribute class from the FilterAttribute class, in addition to implementing the IExceptionFilter interface. In order for a .NET attribute class to be treated as an MVC filter, the class has to implement the IMvcFilter interface. You can do this directly, but the easiest way to create a filter is to derive your class from FilterAttribute, which implements the required interface and provides some useful basic features, such as handling the default order in which filters are processed (which I will come to later in this chapter).

Applying the Exception Filter

I need to do some groundwork before I can test the exception filter. First, I need to create a Content folder in the example project and create the RangeErrorPage.html file within it. This is the file that I will direct users to when the exception is handled and you can see the contents of the file in Listing 18-22.

Listing 18-22. The Contents of the RangeErrorPage.html File

```
<!DOCTYPE html>
<html xmlns="http://www.w3.org/1999/xhtml">
<head>
    <title>Range Error</title>
</head>
<body>
    <h2>Sorry</h2>
    <span>One of the arguments was out of the expected range.</span>
</body>
</html>
```

Next, I need to add an action method to the Home controller which will throw the exception I want to demonstrate. You can see the addition in Listing 18-23.

Listing 18-23. Adding a New Action in the HomeController.cs File

```
using System;
using System.Web.Mvc;
using Filters.Infrastructure;

namespace Filters.Controllers {
    public class HomeController : Controller {

        [Authorize(Users = "admin")]
        public string Index() {
            return "This is the Index action on the Home controller";
        }

        [GoogleAuth]
        [Authorize(Users = "bob@google.com")]
        public string List() {
            return "This is the List action on the Home controller";
        }
```

```
        public string RangeTest(int id) {
            if (id > 100) {
                return String.Format("The id value is: {0}", id);
            } else {
                throw new ArgumentOutOfRangeException("id", id, "");
            }
        }
    }
}
```

You can see the default exception handling if you start the application and navigate to the /Home/RangeTest/50 URL. The default routing that Visual Studio creates for an MVC project has a segment variable called id which will be set to 50 for this URL, triggering the response shown in Figure 18-3. (See Chapters 15 and 16 for details of routing and URL segments.)

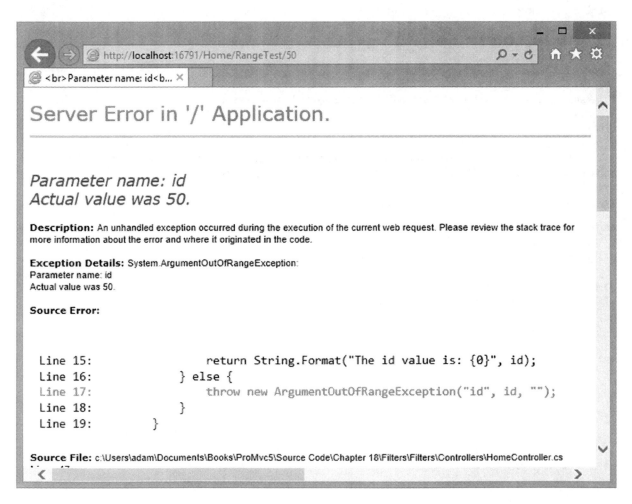

Figure 18-3. The default exception handling response

■ **Note**   Visual Studio will detect the exception and break the debugger to give you control of the execution of the application. Press F5 or click the Continue button to continue the execution of the application and see the default exception handling behavior.

I can apply the exception filter to either controllers or individual actions, as shown in Listing 18-24.

Listing 18-24. Applying the Filter in the HomeController.cs File

```
...
[RangeException]
public string RangeTest(int id) {
    if (id > 100) {
        return String.Format("The id value is: {0}", id);
    } else {
        throw new ArgumentOutOfRangeException("id");
    }
}
...
```

You can see the effect if you restart the application and navigate to the /Home/RangeTest/50 URL again, as shown in Figure 18-4.

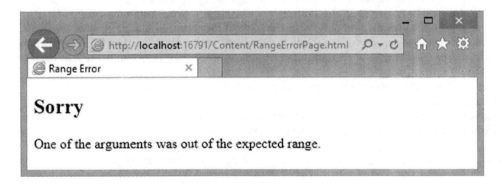

Figure 18-4. *The effect of applying the exception filter*

Using a View to Respond to an Exception

Depending on the exception you are dealing with, displaying a page of static content can be the simplest and safest thing to do. There is little chance of the process going wrong and causing additional problems. However, while you can be confident that the user will see the message, this approach is not especially useful to the user, who gets a generic warning and is dropped out of the application.

An alternative approach is to use a view to display details of the problem and present the user with some contextual information and options they can follow to sort things out. To demonstrate this, I have made some changes to the RangeExceptionAttribute class, as shown in Listing 18-25.

Listing 18-25. Returning a View from an Exception Filter in the RangeExceptionAttribute.cs File

```
using System;
using System.Web.Mvc;

namespace Filters.Infrastructure {
    public class RangeExceptionAttribute : FilterAttribute, IExceptionFilter {

        public void OnException(ExceptionContext filterContext) {

            if (!filterContext.ExceptionHandled &&
                    filterContext.Exception is ArgumentOutOfRangeException) {

                int val = (int)(((ArgumentOutOfRangeException)
                    filterContext.Exception).ActualValue);
                filterContext.Result = new ViewResult {
                    ViewName = "RangeError",
                    ViewData = new ViewDataDictionary<int>(val)};
                filterContext.ExceptionHandled = true;
            }
        }
    }
}
```

I create a ViewResult object and set the values of the ViewName and ViewData properties to specify the name of the view and the model object that will be passed to it. This is messy code because I am working with the ViewResult object directly, rather than relying on the View method defined by the Controller class that is used in action methods. I am not going to go into this code because I cover views in depth in Chapter 20 and the built-in exception filter, which I describe in the next section, can be used to achieve the same effect more elegantly. I just want you to see how things work behind the scenes.

The ViewResult object specifies a view called RangeError and passes the int value of the argument that caused the exception as the view model object.

To display details of the error, I created the Views/Shared folder to the Visual Studio project and created the RangeError.cshtml file within it, the contents of which you can see in Listing 18-26.

Listing 18-26. The Contents of the RangeError.cshtml view File

```
@model int

<!DOCTYPE html>
<html>
<head>
    <meta name="viewport" content="width=device-width" />
    <title>Range Error</title>
</head>
<body>
    <h2>Sorry</h2>
    <span>The value @Model was out of the expected range.</span>
    <div>
        @Html.ActionLink("Change value and try again", "Index")
    </div>
</body>
</html>
```

The view file uses standard HTML and Razor tags to present a (slightly) more useful message to the user. The example application is pretty limited, so there is not anything useful I can direct the user to do to resolve the problem. But I have used the `ActionLink` helper method to create a link that targets another action method, just to demonstrate that you have the full set of view features available. You can see the result if you restart the application and navigate to the /Home/RangeTest/50 URL, as shown in Figure 18-5.

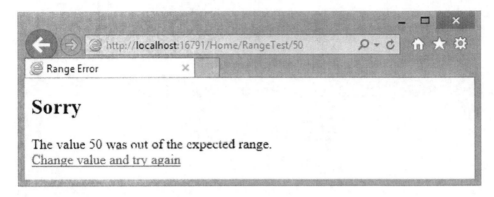

Figure 18-5. *Using a view to display an error message from an exception filter*

Avoiding the Wrong Exception Trap

The benefits of using a view to display an error are that you can use layouts to make the error message consistent with the rest of your application and generate dynamic content that will help the user understand what is going wrong and what they can do about it.

The drawback is that you must thoroughly test your view to make sure that you do not just generate another exception. I see this a lot, where the testing focus is on the main features of the application and does not properly cover the different error situations that can arise. As a simple demonstration, I have added a Razor code block to the `RangeError.cshtml` view that will throw an exception, as shown in Listing 18-27.

Listing 18-27. Adding Code That Will Throw an Exception to the RangeError.cshtml File

```
@model int

@{
    var count = 0;
    var number = Model / count;
}

<!DOCTYPE html>
<html>
<head>
    <meta name="viewport" content="width=device-width" />
    <title>Range Error</title>
</head>
<body>
    <h2>Sorry</h2>
    <span>The value @Model was out of the expected range.</span>
```

```
    <div>
        @Html.ActionLink("Change value and try again", "Index")
    </div>
</body>
</html>
```

When the view is rendered, the code will generate a `DivideByZeroException`. If you start the application and navigate to the `/Home/RangeTest/50` URL again, you will see the exception thrown while trying to render the view and not the one thrown by the controller, as shown in Figure 18-6.

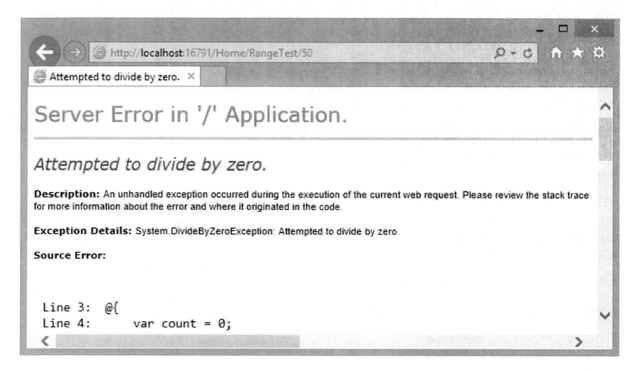

Figure 18-6. *An exception thrown while rendering a view*

This isn't a realistic scenario, but it demonstrates what happens when there are problems in the view. The user sees a bewildering error that does not relate to the problem he or she encountered in the application. When using an exception filter that relies on a view, be careful to test that view thoroughly.

Using the Built-in Exception Filter

I showed you how to create an exception filter because I think understanding what happens behind the scenes in the MVC Framework is a good thing. But you do not often need to create your own filters in real projects because Microsoft has included the `HandleErrorAttribute` in the MVC Framework, which is a built-in implementation of the `IExceptionFilter` interface. With it, you can specify an exception and the names of a view and layout using the properties described in Table 18-8.

Table 18-8. *HandleErrorAttribute Properties*

Name	Type	Description
ExceptionType	Type	The exception type handled by this filter. It will also handle exception types that inherit from the specified value, but will ignore all others. The default value is System.Exception, which means that, by default, it will handle all standard exceptions.
View	string	The name of the view template that this filter renders. If you do not specify a value, it takes a default value of Error, so by default, it renders /Views/<currentControllerName>/Error.cshtml or /Views/Shared/Error.cshtml.
Master	string	The name of the layout used when rendering this filter's view. If you do not specify a value, the view uses its default layout page.

When an unhandled exception of the type specified by ExceptionType is encountered, this filter will render the view specified by the View property (using the default layout or the one specified by the Master property).

Preparing to Use the Built-in Exception Filter

The HandleErrorAttribute filter works only when custom errors are enabled in the Web.config file, which is done by adding a customErrors attribute inside the <system.web> node, as shown in Listing 18-28.

Listing 18-28. Enabling Custom Error in the Web.config File

```
...
<system.web>
  <compilation debug="true" targetFramework="4.5.1" />
  <httpRuntime targetFramework="4.5.1" />
  <authentication mode="Forms">
    <forms loginUrl="~/Account/Login" timeout="2880">
      <credentials passwordFormat="Clear">
        <user name="user"  password="secret"/>
        <user name="admin" password="secret" />
      </credentials>
    </forms>
  </authentication>
  <customErrors mode="On" defaultRedirect="/Content/RangeErrorPage.html"/>
</system.web>
...
```

The default value for the mode attribute is RemoteOnly, which means that connections made from the local machine will always receive the standard yellow page of death errors, which is a problem because IIS Express will only allow local connections. By setting the mode attribute to On, I am specifying that my error handling policy should always be applied, irrespective of where the connections originate. The defaultRedirect attribute specifies a default content page that will be displayed if all else fails.

Applying the Built-in Exception Filter

You can see how I applied the HandleError filter to the Home controller in Listing 18-29.

Listing 18-29. Using the HandleErrorAttribute Filter in the HomeController.cs File

```
...
[HandleError(ExceptionType = typeof(ArgumentOutOfRangeException),
    View = "RangeError")]
public string RangeTest(int id) {
    if (id > 100) {
        return String.Format("The id value is: {0}", id);
    } else {
        throw new ArgumentOutOfRangeException("id", id, "");
    }
}
...
```

I have recreated the situation I had with the custom filter, which is that an ArgumentOutOfRangeException will be dealt with by displaying the RangeError view to the user.

When rendering a view, the HandleErrorAttribute filter passes a HandleErrorInfo view model object, which is a wrapper around the exception that provides additional information that you use in your view. Table 18-9 describes the properties defined by the HandleErrorInfo class.

Table 18-9. HandleErrorInfo Properties

Name	Type	Description
ActionName	string	Returns the name of the action method that generated the exception
ControllerName	string	Returns the name of the controller that generated the exception
Exception	Exception	Returns the exception

You can see how I have updated the RangeError.cshtml view to use this model object in Listing 18-30.

Listing 18-30. Using a HandleErrorInfo Model Object in the RangeError.cshtml File

```
@model HandleErrorInfo

@{
    ViewBag.Title = "Sorry, there was a problem!";
}

<!DOCTYPE html>
<html>
<head>
    <meta name="viewport" content="width=device-width" />
    <title>Range Error</title>
</head>
<body>
    <h2>Sorry</h2>
    <span>The value @(((ArgumentOutOfRangeException)Model.Exception).ActualValue)
        was out of the expected range.</span>
```

```
<div>
    @Html.ActionLink("Change value and try again", "Index")
</div>
</body>
</html>
```

I have to cast the value of the Model.Exception property to the ArgumentOutOfRangeException type to be able to read the ActualValue property because the HandleErrorInfo class is a general-purpose model object that is used to pass any exception to a view.

Using Action Filters

Action filters are filters that can be used for any purpose. The built-in class for creating this kind of filter, IActionFilter, is shown in Listing 18-31.

Listing 18-31. The IActionFilter Interface

```
namespace System.Web.Mvc {

    public interface IActionFilter {
        void OnActionExecuting(ActionExecutingContext filterContext);
        void OnActionExecuted(ActionExecutedContext filterContext);
    }
}
```

This interface defines two methods. The MVC Framework calls the OnActionExecuting method *before* the action method is invoked. It calls the OnActionExecuted method *after* the action method has been invoked.

Implementing the OnActionExecuting Method

The OnActionExecuting method is called before the action method is invoked. You can use this opportunity to inspect the request and elect to cancel the request, modify the request, or start some activity that will span the invocation of the action. The parameter to this method is an ActionExecutingContext object, which subclasses the ControllerContext class and defines the two additional properties described in Table 18-10.

Table 18-10. *ActionExecutingContext Properties*

Name	Type	Description
ActionDescriptor	ActionDescriptor	Provides details of the action method
Result	ActionResult	The result for the action method; a filter can cancel the request by setting this property to a non-null value

You can use a filter to cancel the request by setting the Result property of the parameter to an action result. To demonstrate this, I have created my own action filter class file called CustomActionAttribute.cs in the Infrastructure folder of the example project, as shown in Listing 18-32.

Listing 18-32. The Contents of the CustomActionAttribute.cs File

```
using System.Web.Mvc;

namespace Filters.Infrastructure {
    public class CustomActionAttribute : FilterAttribute, IActionFilter {

        public void OnActionExecuting(ActionExecutingContext filterContext) {
            if (filterContext.HttpContext.Request.IsLocal) {
                filterContext.Result = new HttpNotFoundResult();
            }
        }

        public void OnActionExecuted(ActionExecutedContext filterContext) {
            // not yet implemented
        }
    }
}
```

In this example, I use the OnActionExecuting method to check whether the request has been made from the local machine. If it has, I return a 404–Not Found response to the user.

■ **Note**   You can see from Listing 18-32 that you do not need to implement both methods defined in the IActionFilter interface to create a working filter. Be careful not to throw a NotImplementedException, which Visual Studio adds to a class when you implement an interface. The MVC Framework calls both methods in an action filter and if an exception is thrown then you will trigger the exception filters. If you do not need to add any logic to a method, then just leave it empty.

You apply an action filter as you would any other attribute. To demonstrate the action filter I created in Listing 18-32, I have added a new action method to the Home controller, as shown in Listing 18-33.

Listing 18-33. Adding a New Action in the HomeController.cs File

```
using System;
using System.Web.Mvc;
using Filters.Infrastructure;

namespace Filters.Controllers {
    public class HomeController : Controller {

        [Authorize(Users = "admin")]
        public string Index() {
            return "This is the Index action on the Home controller";
        }

        [GoogleAuth]
        [Authorize(Users = "bob@google.com")]
        public string List() {
            return "This is the List action on the Home controller";
        }
```

```
    [HandleError(ExceptionType = typeof(ArgumentOutOfRangeException),
        View = "RangeError")]
    public string RangeTest(int id) {
        if (id > 100) {
            return String.Format("The id value is: {0}", id);
        } else {
            throw new ArgumentOutOfRangeException("id", id, "");
        }
    }

    [CustomAction]
    public string FilterTest() {
        return "This is the FilterTest action";
    }
}
}
```

You can test the filter by starting the application and navigating to the /Home/FilterTest URL. The request from the browser will, of course, be a local connection and that will cause the custom action filter to generate a 404 error for the browser, as shown in Figure 18-7.

Figure 18-7. *The effect of using an action filter*

■ **Tip** If you want to be sure that it is the filter that is producing the error, simply remove the attribute from the FilterTest action method in the Home controller and try again.

Implementing the OnActionExecuted Method

You can also use the filter to perform some task that spans the execution of the action method. As a simple example, I have created a class file called ProfileActionAttribute.cs in the Infrastructure folder, and used it to define a class that measures the amount of time that an action method takes to execute. You can see the code for this filter in Listing 18-34.

Listing 18-34. The Contents of the ProFileActionAttribute.cs File

```
using System.Diagnostics;
using System.Web.Mvc;

namespace Filters.Infrastructure {

    public class ProfileActionAttribute : FilterAttribute, IActionFilter {
        private Stopwatch timer;

        public void OnActionExecuting(ActionExecutingContext filterContext) {
            timer = Stopwatch.StartNew();
        }

        public void OnActionExecuted(ActionExecutedContext filterContext) {
            timer.Stop();
            if (filterContext.Exception == null) {
                filterContext.HttpContext.Response.Write(
                    string.Format("<div>Action method elapsed time: {0:F6}</div>",
                        timer.Elapsed.TotalSeconds));
            }
        }
    }
}
```

In this example, I use the OnActionExecuting method to start a timer (using the high-resolution Stopwatch timer class in the System.Diagnostics namespace). The OnActionExecuted method is invoked when the action method has completed. Listing 18-35 shows how I applied the attribute to the Home controller. (I removed the previous filter I created so that local requests are not redirected.)

Listing 18-35. Applying the Action Filter in the HomeController.cs File

```
...
[ProfileAction]
public string FilterTest() {
    return "This is the ActionFilterTest action";
}
...
```

If you start the application and navigate to the /Home/FilterTest URL, you will see the results illustrated by Figure 18-8.

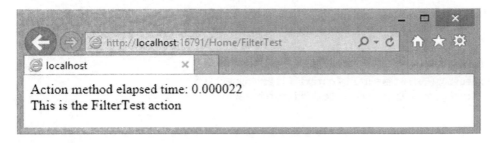

Figure 18-8. *Using an action filter to measure performance*

■ **Tip** Notice that the profile information is shown in the browser before the result of the action method. This is because the action filter is executed after the action method has completed but before the result is processed.

The parameter that is passed to the OnActionExecuted method is an ActionExecutedContext object. This class defines some useful properties, as shown in Table 18-11. The Exception property returns any exception that the action method has thrown, and the ExceptionHandled property indicates if another filter has dealt with it.

Table 18-11. *ActionExecutedContext Properties*

Name	Type	Description
ActionDescriptor	ActionDescriptor	Provides details of the action method
Canceled	bool	Returns true if the action has been canceled by another filter
Exception	Exception	Returns an exception thrown by another filter or by the action method
ExceptionHandled	bool	Returns true if the exception has been handled
Result	ActionResult	The result for the action method; a filter can cancel the request by setting this property to a non-null value

The Canceled property will return true if another filter has canceled the request (by setting a value for the Result property) since the time that the filter's OnActionExecuting method was invoked. The OnActionExecuted method will still be called, but only so that it can tidy up and release any resources the filter was using.

Using Result Filters

Result filters are general-purpose filters which operate on the results produced by action methods. Result filters implement the IResultFilter interface, which is shown in Listing 18-36.

Listing 18-36. The IResultFilter Interface

```
namespace System.Web.Mvc {

    public interface IResultFilter {
        void OnResultExecuting(ResultExecutingContext filterContext);
        void OnResultExecuted(ResultExecutedContext filterContext);
    }
}
```

In Chapter 17, I explained how action methods return action results, allowing separation between the intent of an action method and its execution. When I apply a result filter to an action method, the OnResultExecuting method is invoked *after* the action method has returned an action result but *before* the action result is executed. The OnResultExecuted method is invoked after the action result is executed.

The parameters to these methods are ResultExecutingContext and ResultExecutedContext objects, respectively, and they are similar to their action filter counterparts. They define the same properties, which have the same effects. (See Table 18-11.) To demonstrate a simple result filter, I created a class file called ProfileResultAttribute.cs in the Infrastructure folder and used it to define the class shown in Listing 18-37.

Listing 18-37. The Contents of the ProFileResultAttribute.cs File

```
using System.Diagnostics;
using System.Web.Mvc;

namespace Filters.Infrastructure {
    public class ProfileResultAttribute : FilterAttribute, IResultFilter {
        private Stopwatch timer;

        public void OnResultExecuting(ResultExecutingContext filterContext) {
            timer = Stopwatch.StartNew();
        }

        public void OnResultExecuted(ResultExecutedContext filterContext) {
            timer.Stop();
            filterContext.HttpContext.Response.Write(
                    string.Format("<div>Result elapsed time: {0:F6}</div>",
                        timer.Elapsed.TotalSeconds));
        }
    }
}
```

This result filter is the complement to the action filter I created in the previous section and measures the amount of time taken to execute the result. You can see how I applied this filter to the Home controller in Listing 18-38.

Listing 18-38. Applying the Result Filter in the HomeController.cs File

```
...
[ProfileAction]
[ProfileResult]
public string FilterTest() {
    return "This is the ActionFilterTest action";
}
...
```

Figure 18-9 shows the effect of starting the application and navigating to the /Home/FilterTest URL. You can see that both filters have added data to the response sent to the browser. The output from the result filter is shown after the result from the action method, of course, since the OnResultExecuted method cannot be executed by the MVC Framework until the result has been properly dealt with—which, in this case, means inserting a string value into the result.

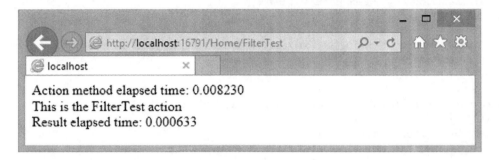

Figure 18-9. *The effect of applying a result filter*

Using the Built-in Action and Result Filter Class

The MVC Framework includes a built-in class that can be derived to create a class that is both an action and result filter. The class, called ActionFilterAttribute, is shown in Listing 18-39.

Listing 18-39. The ActionFilterAttribute Class

```
public abstract class ActionFilterAttribute : FilterAttribute, IActionFilter,
    IResultFilter{

        public virtual void OnActionExecuting(ActionExecutingContext filterContext) {
        }

        public virtual void OnActionExecuted(ActionExecutedContext filterContext) {
        }

        public virtual void OnResultExecuting(ResultExecutingContext filterContext) {
        }

        public virtual void OnResultExecuted(ResultExecutedContext filterContext) {
        }
    }
}
```

The only benefit to using this class is that you do not need to override and implement the methods that you do not intend to use. Otherwise, there is no advantage over implementing the filter interfaces directly.

To demonstrate the use of the ActionFilterAttribute class, I added a class file called ProfileAllAttribute.cs to the Infrastructure folder of the example project and used it to define the class shown in Listing 18-40.

Listing 18-40. The Contents of the ActionFilterAttribute.cs File

```
using System.Diagnostics;
using System.Web.Mvc;

namespace Filters.Infrastructure {
    public class ProfileAllAttribute : ActionFilterAttribute {
        private Stopwatch timer;

        public override void OnActionExecuting(ActionExecutingContext filterContext) {
            timer = Stopwatch.StartNew();
        }

        public override void OnResultExecuted(ResultExecutedContext filterContext) {
            timer.Stop();
            filterContext.HttpContext.Response.Write(
                    string.Format("<div>Total elapsed time: {0:F6}</div>",
                        timer.Elapsed.TotalSeconds));
        }
    }
}
```

The ActionFilterAttribute class implements the IActionFilter and IResultFilter interfaces, which means that the MVC Framework will treat derived classes as both types of filters, even if not all of the methods are overridden. In the example, I have implemented only the OnActionExecuting method from the IActionFilter interface and the OnResultExecuted method from the IResultFilter interface. This allows me to continue the profiling theme and measure the time it takes for the action method to execute and the result to be processed as a single unit. Listing 18-41 shows how I applied the filter to the Home controller.

Listing 18-41. Applying the Filter in the HomeController.cs File

```
...
[ProfileAction]
[ProfileResult]
[ProfileAll]
public string FilterTest() {
    return "This is the FilterTest action";
}
...
```

You can see the effect of all of these filters if you start the application and navigate to the /Home/FilterTest method. Figure 18-10 shows the result.

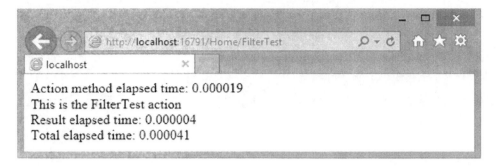

Figure 18-10. *The effect of adding the ProFileAll filter*

Using Other Filter Features

The previous examples have given you all the information you need to work effectively with filters. In the following sections, I will show you some of the advanced MVC Framework filtering capabilities, which are interesting but not as widely used.

Filtering Without Attributes

The normal way of using filters is to apply attributes, as I have demonstrated in the previous sections. However, there is an alternative. The Controller class implements the IAuthenticationFilter, IAuthorizationFilter, IActionFilter, IResultFilter, and IExceptionFilter interfaces. It also provides empty virtual implementations of each of the OnXXX methods you have already seen, such as OnAuthorization and OnException. In Listing 18-42 I have updated the Home controller to use this feature and create a self-profiling controller class.

Listing 18-42. Using the Controller Filter Methods in the HomeController.cs File

```
using System;
using System.Diagnostics;
using System.Web.Mvc;
using Filters.Infrastructure;

namespace Filters.Controllers {
    public class HomeController : Controller {
        private Stopwatch timer;

        [Authorize(Users = "admin")]
        public string Index() {
            return "This is the Index action on the Home controller";
        }

        [GoogleAuth]
        [Authorize(Users = "bob@google.com")]
        public string List() {
            return "This is the List action on the Home controller";
        }
```

```
    [HandleError(ExceptionType = typeof(ArgumentOutOfRangeException),              View =
"RangeError")]
    public string RangeTest(int id) {
        if (id > 100) {
            return String.Format("The id value is: {0}", id);
        } else {
            throw new ArgumentOutOfRangeException("id", id, "");
        }
    }

    public string FilterTest() {
        return "This is the FilterTest action";
    }

    protected override void OnActionExecuting(ActionExecutingContext filterContext) {
        timer = Stopwatch.StartNew();
    }

    protected override void OnResultExecuted(ResultExecutedContext filterContext) {
        timer.Stop();
        filterContext.HttpContext.Response.Write(
                string.Format("<div>Total elapsed time: {0}</div>",
                    timer.Elapsed.TotalSeconds));
    }
  }
}
```

I removed the filters from the FilterTest action method because they are no longer required. The Home controller will add the profile information to the response for any action method. Figure 18-11 shows the effect of starting the application and navigating to the /Home/RangeTest/200 URL, which targets the RangeTest action without causing the exception I set up to demonstrate the HandleError filter.

Figure 18-11. *The effect of implementing filter methods directly in the controller*

This technique is most useful when you are creating a base class from which multiple controllers in your project are derived. The whole point of filtering is to put code that is required *across* the application in one reusable location, so using these methods in a class that will not be used as a base for controllers does not make much sense.

■ **Tip**   I prefer to use attributes. I like the separation between the controller logic and the filter logic. If you are looking for a way to apply a filter to all of your controllers, continue reading to see how to do that with global filters.

Using Global Filters

Global filters are applied to all of the action methods in all of the controllers in your application. There is a convention for setting up global filters, which is created by Visual Studio automatically when you use the MVC project template but which must be set up manually with the Empty template.

Application-wide configuration is done in classes added to the App_Start folder, which is why I defined routes in Chapters 15 and 16 in the App_Start/RouteConfig.cs file. To create the equivalent for filters, I added a new class file called FilterConfig.cs to the App_Start folder with the content shown in Listing 18-43.

Listing 18-43. The Content of the FilterConfig.cs File

```
using System.Web;
using System.Web.Mvc;

namespace Filters {
    public class FilterConfig {
        public static void RegisterGlobalFilters(GlobalFilterCollection filters) {
            filters.Add(new HandleErrorAttribute());
        }
    }
}
```

This is the same content that Visual Studio would have created for the MVC template. The FilterConfig class defines a static method called RegisterGlobalFilters that receives the collection of global filters, expressed as a GlobalFilterCollection object, to which new filters can be added.

There are two conventions to note in this file. The first is that the FilterConfig class is defined in the Filters namespace and not Filters.App_Start, which is what Visual Studio will use when it creates the file. The second is that the HandleError filter, which I described earlier in the chapter, is always defined as a global filter by calling the Add method on the GlobalFilterCollection object.

■ **Note**   You don't have to set up the HandleError filter globally, but it defines the default MVC exception handling policy. This will render the /Views/Shared/Error.cshtml view when an unhandled exception arises. This exception handling policy is disabled by default for development. See the "Creating an Exception Filter" section earlier in the chapter for a note on how to enable it in the Web.config file.

I am going to apply my ProfileAll filter globally and I use the same method call that sets up the HandleError filter, as shown in Listing 18-44.

Listing 18-44. Adding a Global Filter to the FilterConfig.cs File

```
using System.Web;
using System.Web.Mvc;
using Filters.Infrastructure;
```

```
namespace Filters {
    public class FilterConfig {
        public static void RegisterGlobalFilters(GlobalFilterCollection filters) {
            filters.Add(new HandleErrorAttribute());
            filters.Add(new ProfileAllAttribute());
        }
    }
}
```

■ **Tip**   Notice that I register the filter globally by creating an instance of the filter class, which means that I need to refer to the class name, including the `Attribute` suffix. The rule is that you omit `Attribute` when applying the filter as an attribute, but include it when directly creating an instance of its class.

The next step is to ensure that the `FilterConfig.RegisterGlobalFilters` method is called from the `Global.asax` file when the application starts. You can see the addition I have made to this file in Listing 18-45.

Listing 18-45. Setting Up Global Filters in the Global.asax File

```
using System;
using System.Collections.Generic;
using System.Linq;
using System.Web;
using System.Web.Mvc;
using System.Web.Routing;

namespace Filters {
    public class MvcApplication : System.Web.HttpApplication {
        protected void Application_Start() {
            AreaRegistration.RegisterAllAreas();
            RouteConfig.RegisterRoutes(RouteTable.Routes);
            FilterConfig.RegisterGlobalFilters(GlobalFilters.Filters);
        }
    }
}
```

To demonstrate the global filter, I have created a new controller called `Customer`, as shown in Listing 18-46. I have created a new controller because I want to use code to which I have not previously applied a filter.

Listing 18-46. The Contents of the CustomerController.cs File

```
using System.Web.Mvc;

namespace Filters.Controllers {
    public class CustomerController : Controller {

        public string Index() {
            return "This is the Customer controller";
        }
    }
}
```

This is a simple controller whose Index action returns a `string`. Figure 18-12 illustrates the effect of the global filter, which I achieved by starting the application and navigating to the /Customer URL. Even though I have not applied a filter directly to the controller, the global filter adds the profiling information shown in the figure.

Figure 18-12. *The Effect of a Global Filter*

Ordering Filter Execution

I have already explained that filters are executed by type. The sequence is authentication filters, authorization filters, action filters, and then result filters. The framework executes exception filters at any stage if there is an unhandled exception. However, within each type category, you can take control of the order in which individual filters are used. Listing 18-47 shows a class file called `SimpleMessageAttribute.cs` that I added to the `Infrastructure` folder to define a simple filter so as to demonstrate ordering filter execution.

Listing 18-47. The Contents of the SimpleMessageAttribute.cs File

```
using System;
using System.Web.Mvc;

namespace Filters.Infrastructure {

    [AttributeUsage(AttributeTargets.Method, AllowMultiple=true)]
    public class SimpleMessageAttribute : FilterAttribute, IActionFilter {

        public string Message { get; set; }

        public void OnActionExecuting(ActionExecutingContext filterContext) {
            filterContext.HttpContext.Response.Write(
                string.Format("<div>[Before Action: {0}]<div>", Message));
        }

        public void OnActionExecuted(ActionExecutedContext filterContext) {
            filterContext.HttpContext.Response.Write(
                string.Format("<div>[After Action: {0}]<div>", Message));
        }
    }
}
```

This filter writes a message to the response when the OnActionExecuting and OnActionExecuted methods are invoked, part of which is specified using the Message property (which I will set when I apply the filter). I can apply multiple instances of this filter to an action method, as shown in Listing 18-48. (Notice that in the AttributeUsage attribute in Listing 18-47, I set the AllowMultiple property to true).

Listing 18-48. Applying Multiple Filters to an Action in the CustomerController.cs File

```
using System.Web.Mvc;
using Filters.Infrastructure;

namespace Filters.Controllers {
    public class CustomerController : Controller {

        [SimpleMessage(Message="A")]
        [SimpleMessage(Message="B")]
        public string Index() {
            return "This is the Customer controller";
        }
    }
}
```

I created two filters with different messages: the first has a message of A, and the other has a message of B. I could have used two different filters, but this approach allows me to demonstrate that you can configure global filters through properties. When you run the application and navigate to /Customer URL, you will see the result shown in Figure 18-13.

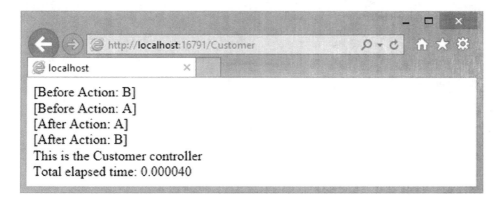

Figure 18-13. Multiple filters on the same action method

The MVC Framework executes the B filter before the A filter, but it could have been the other way around. The MVC Framework does not guarantee any particular order or execution. Most of the time, the order does not matter. When it does, you can use the Order property, as shown in Listing 18-49.

Listing 18-49. Using the Order Property in a Filter

```
using System.Web.Mvc;
using Filters.Infrastructure;

namespace Filters.Controllers {
    public class CustomerController : Controller {
```

```
        [SimpleMessage(Message = "A", Order = 1)]
        [SimpleMessage(Message = "B", Order = 2)]
        public string Index() {
            return "This is the Customer controller";
        }
    }
}
```

The Order parameter takes an int value, and the MVC Framework executes the filters in ascending order. In the listing, I have given the A filter the lowest value, so the framework executes it first, as shown in Figure 18-14.

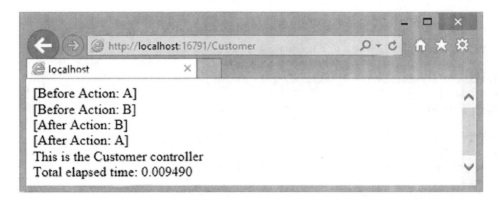

Figure 18-14. *Specifying the order of filter execution*

■ **Note**   Notice that the OnActionExecuting methods are executed in the order I specified, but the OnActionExecuted methods are executed in the reverse order. The MVC Framework builds up a stack of filters as it executes them before the action method, and then unwinds the stack afterward. This unwinding behavior cannot be changed.

If I do not specify a value for the Order property, it is assigned a default value of -1. This means that if you mix filters so that some have Order values and others do not, the ones without these values will be executed first, since they have the lowest Order value.

If multiple filters of the same type (say, action filters) have the same Order value (say 1), then the MVC Framework determines the execution order based on where the filter has been applied. Global filters are executed first, then filters applied to the controller class, and then filters applied to the action method.

■ **Note**   The order of execution is reversed for exception filters. If exception filters are applied with the same Order value to the controller and to the action method, the filter on the action method will be executed first. Global exception filters with the same Order value are executed last.

Overriding Filters

There will be occasions when you want to apply a filter globally or at the controller level, but use a different filter for a specific action method. To demonstrate what I mean, I have updated the SimpleMessage filter so that it can be applied to an entire controller, as shown in Listing 18-50.

Listing 18-50. Adding Controller-Level Application in the SimpleMessageAttribute.cs File

```
using System;
using System.Collections.Generic;
using System.Linq;
using System.Web;
using System.Web.Mvc;

namespace Filters.Infrastructure {

    [AttributeUsage(AttributeTargets.Class | AttributeTargets.Method,
        AllowMultiple = true)]
    public class SimpleMessageAttribute : FilterAttribute, IActionFilter {

        public string Message { get; set; }

        public void OnActionExecuting(ActionExecutingContext filterContext) {
            filterContext.HttpContext.Response.Write(
                string.Format("<div>[Before Action: {0}]<div>", Message));
        }

        public void OnActionExecuted(ActionExecutedContext filterContext) {
            filterContext.HttpContext.Response.Write(
                string.Format("<div>[After Action: {0}]<div>", Message));
        }
    }
}
```

This change means that the filter can be applied to individual action methods or to the entire controller class. In Listing 18-51, you can see how I have changed the way that the filter is applied to the Customer controller.

Listing 18-51. Updating the CustomerController.cs File

```
using System.Web.Mvc;
using Filters.Infrastructure;

namespace Filters.Controllers {
    [SimpleMessage(Message = "A")]
    public class CustomerController : Controller {

        public string Index() {
            return "This is the Customer controller";
        }
```

```
        [SimpleMessage(Message = "B")]
        public string OtherAction() {
            return "This is the Other Action in the Customer controller";
        }
    }
}
```

I have applied the SimpleMessage filter to the controller class, meaning that the message A will be added to the response when either of the action methods is invoked. I have added a new OtherAction method, to which I have applied the SimpleMessage filter again, but this time with the message B.

The problem is that, by default, the OtherAction method is affected by both applications of the filter: at the controller and method level. You can see how this works by starting the application and navigating to /Customer/OtherAction, as shown in Figure 18-15.

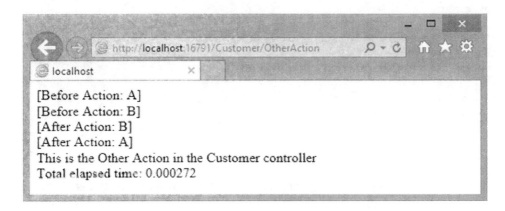

Figure 18-15. *The default filter behavior*

If you want an action method to just be affected by the filters that have been directly applied to it, then you can use a *filter override*. This tells the MVC Framework to ignore any filters that have been defined at a higher-level, such as the controller or globally. Filter overrides are attributes that implement the IOverrideFilter interface, which is shown in Listing 18-52.

Listing 18-52. The IOverrideFilter interface

```
namespace System.Web.Http.Filters {
    public interface IOverrideFilter : IFilter {

        Type FiltersToOverride { get; }
    }
}
```

The FiltersToOverride method returns the type of filter that will be overridden. I am interested in action filters for this example and to that end I created the CustomOverrideActionFiltersAttribute.cs file in the Infrastructure. As Listing 18-53 shows, I implemented the FiltersToOverride method so that my new attribute overrides the IActionFilter type.

■ **Caution**   The MVC Framework comes with some built-in filter overrides in the System.Web.Mvc.Filters namespace: OverrideAuthenticationAttribute, OverrideActionFiltersAttribute, and so on. As I write this, these filters do not work. This is because they are derived from Attribute and not FilterAttribute. I assume that this will be resolved in a later release, but in the meantime you should create custom filter override attributes like the one I demonstrate below.

Listing 18-53. The Contents of the CustomOverrideActionFiltersAttribute.cs File

```
using System;
using System.Web.Mvc;
using System.Web.Mvc.Filters;

namespace Filters.Infrastructure {

    [AttributeUsage(AttributeTargets.Class | AttributeTargets.Method,
        Inherited = true, AllowMultiple = false)]
    public class CustomOverrideActionFiltersAttribute : FilterAttribute,
            IOverrideFilter {
        public Type FiltersToOverride {
            get { return typeof(IActionFilter); }
        }
    }
}
```

I can apply this filter to my controller to prevent the global and controller level action filters from taking effect, as shown in Listing 18-54.

Listing 18-54. Applying a Filter Override in the CustomerController.cs File

```
using System.Web.Mvc;
using Filters.Infrastructure;

namespace Filters.Controllers {
    [SimpleMessage(Message = "A")]
    public class CustomerController : Controller {

        public string Index() {
            return "This is the Customer controller";
        }

        [CustomOverrideActionFilters]
        [SimpleMessage(Message = "B")]
        public string OtherAction() {
            return "This is the Other Action in the Customer controller";
        }
    }
}
```

As Figure 18-16 shows, only the SimpleMessage attribute which I have applied directly to the OtherAction method is run.

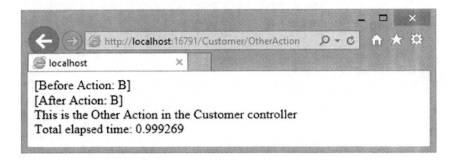

Figure 18-16. *The effect of overriding action filters*

Summary

In this chapter, you have seen how to encapsulate logic that addresses cross-cutting concerns as filters. I showed you the different kinds of filters available and how to implement each of them. You saw how filters can be applied as attributes to controllers and action methods, and how they can be applied as global filters. Filters are a means of extending the logic that is applied when a request is processed, without needing to include that logic in the action method. In the next chapter, I show you how to change and extend the way that the MVC Framework deals with controllers.

CHAPTER 19

Controller Extensibility

In this chapter, I am going to show you some of the advanced MVC features for working with controllers. I start this chapter by exploring the parts of the request handling process that lead to the execution of an action method and demonstrating the different ways to take control of it. Figure 19-1 shows the basic flow of control between components.

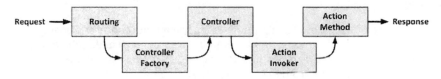

Figure 19-1. *Invoking an action method*

My focus for the first part of this chapter is the *controller factory* and the *action invoker*. The names of these components suggest their purpose. The controller factory is responsible for creating instances of controllers to service a request and the action invoker is responsible for finding and invoking the action method in the controller class. The MVC Framework includes default implementations of both of these components, and I will show you how to configure and control their behavior. I will also show you how to replace these components entirely and use custom logic. Table 19-1 provides the summary for this chapter.

Table 19-1. *Chapter Summary*

Problem	Solution	Listing
Create a custom controller factory	Implement the IControllerFactory interface	1–7
Prioritize namespaces in the default controller factory	Use the DefaultNamespaces collection	8
Create a custom controller activator	Implement the IControllerActivator interface	9–11
Create a custom action invoker	Implement the IActionInvoker interface	12–14
Specify an action name that is different from the action method name	Use the ActionName attribute	15
Control the selection of action methods	Apply action method selectors	16
Prevent a method from being used as an action	Use the NoAction attribute	17

(*continued*)

Table 19-1. (*continued*)

Problem	Solution	Listing
Create a custom action method selector	Derive from the ActionMethodSelectorAttribute class	18–21
Respond to requests for non-existent action methods	Override the HandleUnknownAction method in the controller	22
Control how controllers use the session feature	Return a value from the SessionStateBehavior enumeration in the IControllerFactory implementation or apply the SessionState attribute to the controller class	23, 24
Prevent controllers from blocking worker threads when waiting for input	Create an asynchronous controller	25–30

Preparing the Example Project

For this chapter, I created a project called ControllerExtensibility using the Empty template option and enabled the option to add the core MVC references and folders. I need some simple controllers to work with in this chapter, so that I can demonstrate the different kinds of extensibility features that are available. To get set up, I created the Result.cs file in the Models folder and used it to define the Result class shown in Listing 19-1.

Listing 19-1. The Contents of the Result.cs File

```
namespace ControllerExtensibility.Models {
    public class Result {
        public string ControllerName { get; set; }
        public string ActionName { get; set; }
    }
}
```

The next step is to create the /Views/Shared folder and add a new view called Result.cshtml. This is the view that all of the action methods in the controllers will render, and you can see the contents of this file in Listing 19-2.

Listing 19-2. The Contents of the Result.cshtml File

```
@model ControllerExtensibility.Models.Result

@{
    Layout = null;
}

<!DOCTYPE html>

<html>
<head>
    <meta name="viewport" content="width=device-width" />
    <title>Result</title>
```

```
</head>
<body>
    <div>Controller: @Model.ControllerName</div>
    <div>Action: @Model.ActionName</div>
</body>
</html>
```

This view uses the Result class that I defined in Listing 19-2 as its model and displays the values of the ControllerName and ActionName properties. Finally, I need to create some basic controllers. Listing 19-3 shows the Product controller.

Listing 19-3. The Contents of the Product Controller.cs File

```
using System.Web.Mvc;
using ControllerExtensibility.Models;

namespace ControllerExtensibility.Controllers {
    public class ProductController : Controller {

        public ViewResult Index() {
            return View("Result", new Result {
                ControllerName = "Product",
                ActionName = "Index"
            });
        }

        public ViewResult List() {
            return View("Result", new Result {
                ControllerName = "Product",
                ActionName = "List"
            });
        }
    }
}
```

Listing 19-4 shows the Customer controller.

Listing 19-4. The Contents of the CustomerController.cs File

```
using System.Web.Mvc;
using ControllerExtensibility.Models;

namespace ControllerExtensibility.Controllers {
    public class CustomerController : Controller {

        public ViewResult Index() {
            return View("Result", new Result {
                ControllerName = "Customer",
                ActionName = "Index"
            });
        }
```

531

```
        public ViewResult List() {
            return View("Result", new Result {
                ControllerName = "Customer",
                ActionName = "List"
            });
        }
    }
}
```

These controllers do not perform any useful actions other than to report that they have been called via the Result.cshtml view.

Setting the Start URL

I want Visual Studio to start with the root URL for the application rather than guess the URL based on the file that is being edited. Select ControllerExtensibility Properties from the Visual Studio Project menu, switch to the Web tab and check the Specific Page option in the Start Action section. You don't have to provide a value. Just checking the option is enough.

Creating a Custom Controller Factory

As with much of the MVC Framework, the best way to understand how controller factories work is to create a custom implementation. I do not recommend that you do this in a real project, as there are easier ways to create custom behavior by extending the built-in factory. But this is a nice way to demonstrate how the MVC framework creates instances of controllers. Controller factories are defined by the IControllerFactory interface, which is shown in Listing 19-5.

Listing 19-5. The IControllerFactory Interface

```
using System.Web.Routing;
using System.Web.SessionState;

namespace System.Web.Mvc {
    public interface IControllerFactory {

        IController CreateController(RequestContext requestContext,
            string controllerName);

        SessionStateBehavior GetControllerSessionBehavior(RequestContext requestContext,
            string controllerName);

        void ReleaseController(IController controller);
    }
}
```

In the sections that follow, I create a simple custom controller factory and walk you through implementations for each of the methods in the IControllerFactory interface. To begin, I created an Infrastructure folder and added a new class file called CustomControllerFactory.cs, which I used to create the custom controller factory shown in Listing 19-6.

Listing 19-6. The Contents of the CustomControllerFactory.cs File

```
using System;
using System.Web.Mvc;
using System.Web.Routing;
using System.Web.SessionState;
using ControllerExtensibility.Controllers;

namespace ControllerExtensibility.Infrastructure {

    public class CustomControllerFactory: IControllerFactory {

        public IController CreateController(RequestContext requestContext,
            string controllerName) {

            Type targetType = null;
            switch (controllerName) {
                case "Product":
                    targetType = typeof(ProductController);
                    break;
                case "Customer":
                    targetType = typeof(CustomerController);
                    break;
                default:
                    requestContext.RouteData.Values["controller"] = "Product";
                    targetType = typeof(ProductController);
                    break;
            }

            return targetType == null ? null :
                (IController)DependencyResolver.Current.GetService(targetType);
        }

        public SessionStateBehavior GetControllerSessionBehavior(RequestContext
            requestContext, string controllerName) {

            return SessionStateBehavior.Default;
        }

        public void ReleaseController(IController controller) {
            IDisposable disposable = controller as IDisposable;
            if (disposable != null) {
                disposable.Dispose();
            }
        }
    }
}
```

The most important method in the interface is CreateController, which the MVC Framework calls when it needs a controller to service a request. The parameters to this method are a RequestContext object, which allows the factory to inspect details of the request, and a string, which contains the controller value from the routed URL. The RequestContext class defines the properties described in Table 19-2.

Table 19-2. *RequestContext Properties*

Name	Type	Description
HttpContext	HttpContextBase	Provides information about the HTTP request
RouteData	RouteData	Provides information about the route that matches the request

One of the reasons that I do not recommend creating a custom controller this way is that finding controller classes in the web application and instantiating them is complicated. You need to be able to locate controllers dynamically and consistently and deal with all sorts of potential problems, such as disambiguating between classes with the same name in different namespaces, constructor exceptions and a whole lot more.

There are only two controllers in the example project and I am going to instantiate them directly, which means hard-wiring the class names into the controller factory, something which is obviously not a good idea for a real project, but which lets me side-step enormous amounts of complexity.

The purpose of the CreateController method is to create instances of controller classes that can handle the current request. There are no restrictions on how you do this. The only rule is that you *must* return an object that implements the IController interface as the method result.

The conventions that you have seen so far in this book exist because that's how the default controller factory has been written. As an example, I have implemented one of these conventions in my code: that when I receive a request for a controller, I append Controller to the class name, so that a request for Product leads to the ProductController class being instantiated.

You are free to follow the MVC Framework conventions when you write a controller factory or to discard them and create your own to suit your project needs. I do not think it is sensible to create your own conventions just for the sake of it, but it is useful to understand just how flexible the MVC Framework can be.

Dealing with the Fallback Controller

Custom controller factories must return an implementation of the IController interface as the result from the CreateController method, otherwise, an error will be displayed to the user. This means that you need to have a fallback position for when the request you are processing does not target any of the controllers in your project. You can create any policy you like for dealing with this situation: you could define a special controller that renders an error message, for example, or do as I have and map the request to a controller class that is known to always exist.

When I get a request that does not map to either of the controllers in the project, I target the ProductController class. This may not be the most useful thing to do in a real project, but it demonstrates that the controller factory has complete flexibility in how requests are interpreted. However, you do need to be aware of how the other points in the MVC Framework operate.

By default, the MVC Framework selects a view based on the controller value in the routing data, not the name of the controller class. So, in my example, if I want the fallback position to work with views that follow the convention of being organized by controller name, I need to change the value of the controller routing property, like this:

```
...
requestContext.RouteData.Values["controller"] = "Product";
...
```

This change will cause the MVC Framework to search for views associated with the fallback controller and not the controller that the routing system has identified based on the URL that the user requested.

There are two important points here: the first is that not only does the controller factory have sole responsibility for matching requests to controllers, but it can *change* the request to alter the behavior of subsequent steps in the request processing pipeline. This is pretty potent stuff and a critical characteristic of the MVC Framework.

The second point is that while you are free to follow whatever conventions you want in your controller factory, you still need to know what the conventions are for other parts of the MVC Framework. And, because those other components can be replaced with custom code as well (as I demonstrate for views in Chapter 20), it makes sense to follow as many of the conventions as possible to allow components to be developed and used independently of one another.

Instantiating Controller Classes

There are no rules about how you instantiate your controller classes, but it is good practice to use the dependency resolver that I introduced in Chapter 6. This allows you to keep your custom controller factory focused on mapping requests to controller classes, and leaves issues like dependency inject to be handled separately and for the entire application. You can see how I used the DependencyResolver class to create controllers instances:

```
...
return targetType == null ? null :
    (IController)DependencyResolver.Current.GetService(targetType);
...
```

The static DependencyResolver.Current property returns an implementation of the IDependencyResolver interface, which defines the GetService method. You pass a System.Type object to this method and get an instance of it in return. There is a strongly typed version of the GetService method, but because I do not know what type I am dealing with in advance, I have to use the version that returns an Object and then perform an explicit case to IController.

■ **Note**   Notice that I am not using the dependency resolver to address tight-coupling issues between classes. Instead, I am asking it to create instances of types that I specify so that it can examine the dependencies that the controller classes have declared and resolve them. I have not set up Ninject in this chapter, which means that the default resolver will be used and that simply creates instances by looking for parameterless constructors and invoking them. However, by building my controller factory to use the DependencyResolver class, I ensure that I can seamlessly take advantage of more advanced dependency resolvers like Ninject if one is added to the project.

Implementing the Other Interface Methods

Two other methods are in the IControllerFactory interface:

- The GetControllerSessionBehavior method is used by the MVC Framework to determine if session data should be maintained for a controller. I will come back to this in the "Using Sessionless Controllers" section later in this chapter.

- The ReleaseController method is called when a controller object created by the CreateController method is no longer needed. In my example implementation, I check to see if the class implements the IDisposable interface. If it does, I call the Dispose method to release any resources that can be freed.

My implementations of the GetControllerSessionBehavior and ReleaseController methods are suitable for most projects and can be used verbatim (although you should read the section on sessionless controllers later in this chapter to make sure you understand the options available).

Registering a Custom Controller Factory

I tell the MVC Framework to use the custom controller factory through the `ControllerBuilder` class. You need to register custom factory controllers when the application is started, which means using the `Application_Start` method in the `Global.asax.cs` file, as shown in Listing 19-7.

Listing 19-7. Registering a Custom Controller Factory in the Global.asax File

```
using System;
using System.Collections.Generic;
using System.Linq;
using System.Web;
using System.Web.Mvc;
using System.Web.Routing;
using ControllerExtensibility.Infrastructure;

namespace ControllerExtensibility {

    public class MvcApplication : System.Web.HttpApplication {

        protected void Application_Start() {
            AreaRegistration.RegisterAllAreas();
            RouteConfig.RegisterRoutes(RouteTable.Routes);

            ControllerBuilder.Current.SetControllerFactory(new
                CustomControllerFactory());
        }
    }
}
```

Once the controller factory has been registered, it will be responsible for handling all of the requests that the application receives. You can see the effect of the custom factory by starting the application. The browser will request the root URL, which will be mapped to the Home controller by the routing system. The custom factory will handle the request for the Home controller by creating an instance of the `ProductController` class, which will produce the result shown in Figure 19-2.

Figure 19-2. *Using the custom controller factory*

Working with the Built-in Controller Factory

I showed you how to create a custom controller factory because it is the most effective way of demonstrating what a controller factory does and how it functions. For most applications, however, the built-in controller factory class, called `DefaultControllerFactory`, is perfectly adequate. When it receives a request from the routing system, this factory looks at the routing data to find the value of the `controller` property and tries to find a class in the Web application that meets the following criteria:

- The class must be `public`.

- The class must be concrete (not `abstract`).

- The class must *not* take generic parameters.

- The name of the class must end with `Controller`.

- The class must implement the `IController` interface.

The `DefaultControllerFactory` class maintains a list of such classes in the application so that it does not need to perform a search every time a request arrives. If a suitable class is found, then an instance is created using the controller activator (I will come back to this in the upcoming "Customizing DefaultControllerFactory Controller Creation" section), and the job of the controller is complete. If there is no matching controller, then the request cannot be processed any further.

Notice how the `DefaultControllerFactory` class follows the convention-over-configuration pattern. You do not need to register your controllers in a configuration file, because the factory will find them for you. All you need to do is create classes that meet the criteria that the factory is seeking.

If you want to create custom controller factory behavior, you can configure the settings of the default factory or override some of the methods. This way, you are able to build on the useful convention-over-configuration behavior without having to re-create it, a task which, I noted earlier, is complicated and painful. In the sections that follow, I show you different ways to tailor controller creation.

Prioritizing Namespaces

In Chapter 16, I showed you how to prioritize one or more namespaces when creating a route. This was to address the ambiguous controller problem, where controller classes have the same name but reside in different namespaces. It is the `DefaultControllerFactory` that processes the list of namespaces and prioritizes them.

■ **Tip** Global prioritization is overridden by route-specific prioritization. This means you can define a global policy, and then tailor individual routes as required. See Chapter 16 for details on specifying namespaces for individual routes.

If you have an application that has a lot of routes, it can be more convenient to specify priority namespaces globally, so that they are applied to all of your routes. Listing 19-8 shows how to do this in the `Application_Start` method of the `Global.asax` file. (This is where I put these statements, but you can also use the `RouteConfig.cs` file in the `App_Start` folder if you prefer.)

Listing 19-8. Global Namespace Prioritization in the Global.asax File

```
using System;
using System.Collections.Generic;
using System.Linq;
using System.Web;
using System.Web.Mvc;
using System.Web.Routing;
using ControllerExtensibility.Infrastructure;
```

```
namespace ControllerExtensibility {

    public class MvcApplication : System.Web.HttpApplication {

        protected void Application_Start() {

            AreaRegistration.RegisterAllAreas();
            RouteConfig.RegisterRoutes(RouteTable.Routes);

            ControllerBuilder.Current.DefaultNamespaces.Add("MyControllerNamespace");
            ControllerBuilder.Current.DefaultNamespaces.Add("MyProject.*");
        }
    }
}
```

I use the static `ControllerBuilder.Current.DefaultNamespaces.Add` method to add namespaces that should be given priority. The order in which I add the namespaces does not imply any kind of search order or relative priority. All of the namespaces defined by the Add method are treated equally and the priority is relative to those namespaces which have not been specified by the Add method. This means that the controller factory will search the entire application if it can't find a suitable controller class in the namespaces defined by the Add method.

■ **Tip**   Notice that I used an asterisk character (*) in the second statement shown in bold in Listing 19-8. This allows me to specify that the controller factory should look in the `MyProject` namespace and any child namespaces that `MyProject` contains. Although this looks like regular expression syntax, it isn't; you can end your namespaces with `.*`, but you cannot use any other regular expression syntax with the `Add` method.

Customizing DefaultControllerFactory Controller Instantiation

There are a number of ways to customize how the `DefaultControllerFactory` class instantiates controller objects. By far, the most common reason for customizing the controller factory is to add support for DI. There are several different ways of doing this. The most suitable technique depends on how you are using DI elsewhere in your application.

Using the Dependency Resolver

The `DefaultControllerFactory` class will use a dependency resolver to create controllers if one is available. I covered dependency resolvers in Chapter 6 and showed you the `NinjectDependencyResolver` class, which implements the `IDependencyResolver` interface to provide Ninject DI support. I also demonstrated how to use the `DependencyResolver` class earlier in this chapter when I created my own custom controller factory. The `DefaultControllerFactory` will call the `IDependencyResolver.GetService` method to request a controller instance, which gives you the opportunity to resolve and inject any dependencies.

Using a Controller Activator

You can also introduce DI into controllers by creating a *controller activator*. You create this activator by implementing the `IControllerActivator` interface, as shown in Listing 19-9.

Listing 19-9. The IControllerActivator Interface

```
namespace System.Web.Mvc {
    using System.Web.Routing;

    public interface IControllerActivator {
        IController Create(RequestContext requestContext, Type controllerType);
    }
}
```

The interface contains one method, called Create, which is passed a RequestContext object describing the request and a Type that specifies which controller class should be instantiated.

To demonstrate an implementation of this interface, I added a new class file called CustomControllerActivator.cs in the Infrastructure folder and used it to define the class shown in Listing 19-10.

Listing 19-10. The Contents of the CustomControllerActivator.cs File

```
using System;
using System.Web.Mvc;
using System.Web.Routing;
using ControllerExtensibility.Controllers;

namespace ControllerExtensibility.Infrastructure {
    public class CustomControllerActivator : IControllerActivator {

        public IController Create(RequestContext requestContext,
            Type controllerType) {

            if (controllerType == typeof(ProductController)) {
                controllerType = typeof(CustomerController);
            }
            return (IController)DependencyResolver.Current.GetService(controllerType);
        }
    }
}
```

This IControllerActivator implementation is simple. If the ProductController class is requested, it responds with an instance of the CustomerController class. This is not something you would want to do in a real project, but it demonstrates how you can use the IControllerActivator interface to intercept requests between the controller factory and the dependency resolver.

To use a custom activator, I need to pass an instance of the implementation class to the DefaultControllerFactory constructor and register the result in the Application_Start method of the Global.asax file, as shown in Listing 19-11.

Listing 19-11. Registering a Custom Activator in the Global.asax File

```
using System;
using System.Collections.Generic;
using System.Linq;
using System.Web;
using System.Web.Mvc;
using System.Web.Routing;
using ControllerExtensibility.Infrastructure;
```

```
namespace ControllerExtensibility {

    public class MvcApplication : System.Web.HttpApplication {

        protected void Application_Start() {

            AreaRegistration.RegisterAllAreas();
            RouteConfig.RegisterRoutes(RouteTable.Routes);

            ControllerBuilder.Current.SetControllerFactory(new
                DefaultControllerFactory(new CustomControllerActivator()));
        }
    }
}
```

You can see the effect of the custom activator if you start the application and navigate to the /Product URL. The route will target the Product controller and the DefaultControllerFactory will ask the activator to instantiate the ProductFactory class, but my activator intercepts this request and creates an instance of the CustomerController class instead, as shown in Figure 19-3.

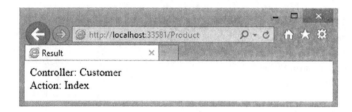

Figure 19-3. *Intercepting instantiation requests using a custom controller activator*

Overriding DefaultControllerFactory Methods

You can override methods in the DefaultControllerFactory class to customize the creation of controllers. Table 19-3 describes the three methods you can override, each of which performs a different role.

Table 19-3. *Overridable DefaultContollerFactory Methods*

Method	Result	Description
CreateController	IController	The implementation of the CreateController method from the IControllerFactory interface. By default, this method calls GetControllerType to determine which type should be instantiated, and then gets a controller object by passing the result to the GetControllerInstance method.
GetControllerType	Type	Maps requests to controller types. This is where most of the conventions listed earlier in the chapter are enforced.
GetControllerInstance	IController	Creates an instance of a specified type.

Creating a Custom Action Invoker

Once the controller factory has created an instance of a class, the framework needs a way of invoking an action on that instance. If you derived your controller from the Controller class, then this is the responsibility of an *action invoker*, which is the subject of this section.

■ **Tip** If you create a controller directly from the IController interface, then you are responsible for executing the action yourself. (See details of creating controllers in this way.) Action invokers are part of the functionality included in the Controller class.

An action invoker implements the IActionInvoker interface, which is shown in Listing 19-12.

Listing 19-12. The IActionInvoker Interface

```
namespace System.Web.Mvc {

    public interface IActionInvoker {

        bool InvokeAction(ControllerContext controllerContext, string actionName);
    }
}
```

The interface has only a single member: InvokeAction. The parameters are a ControllerContext object (which I described in Chapter 17) and a string that contains the name of the action to be invoked. The result type is a bool: a value of true indicates that the action was found and invoked and false indicates that the controller has no matching action.

Notice that I have not used the word *method* in this description. The association between actions and methods is strictly optional. Although this is the approach that the built-in action invoker takes, you are free to handle actions any way that you choose. Listing 19-13 shows an implementation of the IActionInvoker interface that takes a different approach, which I defined in a class file called CustomActionInvoker.cs in the Infrastructure folder.

Listing 19-13. The Contents of the CustomActionInvoker.cs File

```
using System.Web.Mvc;

namespace ControllerExtensibility.Infrastructure {

    public class CustomActionInvoker : IActionInvoker {

        public bool InvokeAction(ControllerContext controllerContext,
                string actionName) {

            if (actionName == "Index") {
                controllerContext.HttpContext.
                    Response.Write("This is output from the Index action");
                return true;
            } else {
                return false;
            }
        }
    }
}
```

This action invoker doesn't care about the methods in the controller class. In fact, it deals with actions itself. If the request is for the Index action, then the invoker writes a message directly to the Response. If the request is for any other action, then it returns false, which causes a 404–Not found error to be displayed to the user.

The action invoker associated with a controller is obtained through the Controller.ActionInvoker property. This means that different controllers in the same application can use different action invokers. To demonstrate this, I have added a new controller to the example project called ActionInvoker, the definition of which you can see in Listing 19-14.

Listing 19-14. The Contents of the ActionInvokerController.cs File

```
using ControllerExtensibility.Infrastructure;
using System.Web.Mvc;

namespace ControllerExtensibility.Controllers {

    public class ActionInvokerController : Controller {
        public ActionInvokerController() {
            this.ActionInvoker = new CustomActionInvoker();
        }
    }
}
```

There are no action methods in this controller. It depends on the action invoker to process requests. You can see how this works by starting the application and navigating to the /ActionInvoker/Index URL. The custom action invoker will generate the response shown in Figure 19-4. If you navigate to a URL that targets any other action on the same controller, you will see the 404 error page.

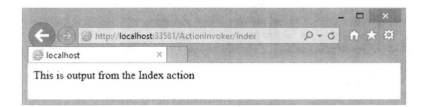

Figure 19-4. The effect of a custom action invoker

I am not suggesting that you implement your own action invoker. And, if you do, I do not suggest you follow this approach. Why? First, the built-in support has some useful features, as you will see shortly. Second, the example has some problems: a lack of extensibility, poor separation of responsibilities, and a lack of support for views of any kind. But the example shows how the MVC Framework fits together and demonstrates, once again, that almost every aspect of the request processing pipeline can be customized or replaced entirely.

Using the Built-in Action Invoker

The built-in action invoker, which is the ControllerActionInvoker class, has some sophisticated techniques for matching requests to actions. And, unlike my implementation in the previous section, the default action invoker operates on methods. To qualify as an action, a method must meet the following criteria:

- The method must be public.

- The method must *not* be static.

- The method must *not* be present in System.Web.Mvc.Controller or any of its base classes.

- The method must *not* have a special name.

The first two criteria are simple enough. For the next, excluding any method that is present in the Controller class or its bases means that methods such as ToString and GetHashCode are excluded, as are the methods that implement the IController interface. This is sensible, because the inner workings of controllers should not be exposed to the outside world. The last criterion means that constructors, property and event accessors are excluded. In fact, no class member that has the IsSpecialName flag from System.Reflection.MethodBase will be used to process an action.

■ **Note**   Methods that have generic parameters (such as MyMethod<T>()) meet all of the criteria, but the MVC Framework will throw an exception if you try to invoke such a method to process a request.

By default, the ControllerActionInvoker finds a method that has the same name as the requested action. So, for example, if the action value that the routing system produces is Index, then the ControllerActionInvoker will look for a method called Index that fits the action criteria. If it finds such a method, it will be invoked to handle the request. This behavior is exactly what you want almost all of the time, but as you might expect, the MVC Framework provides some opportunities to fine-tune the process.

Using a Custom Action Name

Usually, the name of an action method determines the action that it represents. The Index action method services requests for the Index action. You can override this behavior using the ActionName attribute, which I have applied to the Customer controller as shown in Listing 19-15.

Listing 19-15. Using a Custom Action Name in the CustomerController.cs File

```
using System.Web.Mvc;
using ControllerExtensibility.Models;

namespace ControllerExtensibility.Controllers {
    public class CustomerController : Controller {

        public ViewResult Index() {
            return View("Result", new Result {
                ControllerName = "Customer",
                ActionName = "Index"
            });
        }

        [ActionName("Enumerate")]
        public ViewResult List() {
            return View("Result", new Result {
                ControllerName = "Customer",
                ActionName = "List"
            });
        }
    }
}
```

In this listing, I have applied the attribute to the List method, passing in a parameter value of Enumerate. When the action invoker receives a request for the Enumerate action, it will now use the List method to service it. You can see the effect of the ActionName attribute by starting the application and navigating to the /Customer/Enumerate URL. You can see that the results shown by the browser in Figure 19-5 are those from the List method.

Figure 19-5. *The effect of the ActionName attribute*

Applying the attribute overrides the name of the action. This means that URLs which directly target the List method will no longer work, as shown in Figure 19-6.

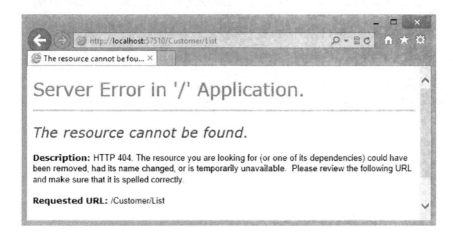

Figure 19-6. *Using the method name as the action when the ActionName attribute has been applied*

There are two main reasons why you might want to override a method name in this way:

- You can then accept an action name that wouldn't be legal as a C# method name (for example, [ActionName("User-Registration")]).

- If you want to have two different C# methods that accept the same set of parameters and should handle the same action name, but in response to different HTTP request types (for example, one with [HttpGet] and the other with [HttpPost]), you can give the methods different C# names to satisfy the compiler, but then use [ActionName] to map them both to the same action name.

Using Action Method Selection

It is often the case that a controller will contain several actions with the same name. This can be because there are multiple methods, each with different parameters, or because you used the `ActionName` attribute so that multiple methods represent the same action.

In these situations, the MVC Framework needs some help selecting the appropriate action with which to process a request. The mechanism for doing this is called *action method selection*. It allows you to define kinds of requests that an action is willing to process. You have already seen an example of action method selection when I restricted an action using the `HttpPost` attribute when I built the SportsStore application. I had two methods called `Checkout` in the `Cart` controller and I used the `HttpPost` attribute to indicate that one of them was to be used only for HTTP POST requests, as shown in Listing 19-16.

Listing 19-16. Using the HttpPost Attribute

```
using System.Linq;
using System.Web.Mvc;
using SportsStore.Domain.Abstract;
using SportsStore.Domain.Entities;
using SportsStore.WebUI.Models;

namespace SportsStore.WebUI.Controllers {

    public class CartController : Controller {
        private IProductRepository repository;
        private IOrderProcessor orderProcessor;

        public CartController(IProductRepository repo, IOrderProcessor proc) {
            repository = repo;
            orderProcessor = proc;
        }

        // ...other action methods omitted for brevity...

        public ViewResult Checkout() {
            return View(new ShippingDetails());
        }

        [HttpPost]
        public ViewResult Checkout(Cart cart, ShippingDetails shippingDetails) {
            if (cart.Lines.Count() == 0) {
                ModelState.AddModelError("", "Sorry, your cart is empty!");
            }

            if (ModelState.IsValid) {
                orderProcessor.ProcessOrder(cart, shippingDetails);
                cart.Clear();
                return View("Completed");
            } else {
                return View(shippingDetails);
            }
        }
    }
}
```

The action invoker uses action method selectors to resolve ambiguity when selecting an action. In Listing 19-16, there are two candidates for the Checkout action. The invoker gives preference to the actions that have selectors. In this case, the HttpPost selector is evaluated to see if the request can be processed. If it can, then this is the method that will be used. If not, then the *other* method, the one without the attribute, will be used.

There are built-in attributes that work as selectors for the different kinds of HTTP requests: HttpPost for POST requests, HttpGet for GET requests, HttpPut for PUT requests, and so on. Another built-in attribute is NonAction, which indicates to the action invoker that a method that would otherwise be considered a valid action method should not be used. You can see how I have applied the NonAction attribute in Listing 19-17, where I have defined a new action method in the Customer controller.

Listing 19-17. Using the NonAction Selector in the CustomerController.cs File

```
using System.Web.Mvc;
using ControllerExtensibility.Models;

namespace ControllerExtensibility.Controllers {
    public class CustomerController : Controller {

        public ViewResult Index() {
            return View("Result", new Result {
                ControllerName = "Customer",
                ActionName = "Index"
            });
        }

        [ActionName("Enumerate")]
        public ViewResult List() {
            return View("Result", new Result {
                ControllerName = "Customer",
                ActionName = "List"
            });
        }

        [NonAction]
        public ActionResult MyAction() {
            return View();
        }
    }
}
```

The MyAction method in the listing will not be considered as an action method, even though it meets all of the criteria that the invoker looks for. This is useful for ensuring that you do not expose the workings of your controller classes as actions. Of course, normally such methods should simply be marked private, which will prevent them from being invoked as actions; however, [NonAction] is useful if for some reason you must mark such a method as public. Requests for URLs that target NonAction methods will generate 404–Not Found errors, as shown in Figure 19-7.

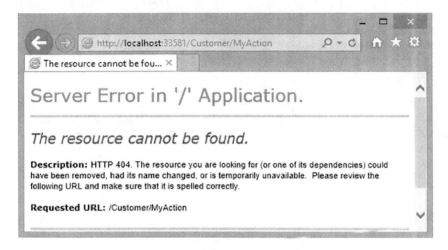

Figure 19-7. *The effect of requesting a URL that targets a NonAction method*

Creating a Custom Action Method Selector

Action method selectors are derived from the ActionMethodSelectorAttribute class, which is shown in Listing 19-18.

Listing 19-18. The ActionMethodSelectorAttribute Class

```
using System.Reflection;

namespace System.Web.Mvc {
    [AttributeUsage(AttributeTargets.Method, AllowMultiple = false, Inherited = true)]
    public abstract class ActionMethodSelectorAttribute : Attribute {

        public abstract bool IsValidForRequest(ControllerContext controllerContext,
            MethodInfo methodInfo);
    }
}
```

The ActionMethodSelectorAttribute is abstract and defines one abstract method: IsValidForRequest. The parameters for this method are a ControllerContext object, which allows you to inspect the request, and a MethodInfo object, which you can use to get information about the method to which your selector has been applied. You return true from IsValidForRequest if the method is able to process a request, and false otherwise. I created a simple custom action method selector in a class file, LocalAttribute.cs, that I added to the Infrastructure folder of the example project, as shown in Listing 19-19.

Listing 19-19. The Contents of the LocalAttribute.cs File

```
using System.Reflection;
using System.Web.Mvc;

namespace ControllerExtensibility.Infrastructure {
    public class LocalAttribute : ActionMethodSelectorAttribute {
```

```
        public override bool IsValidForRequest(ControllerContext controllerContext,
                MethodInfo methodInfo) {
            return controllerContext.HttpContext.Request.IsLocal;
        }
    }
}
```

I have overridden the IsValidForRequest method so that it returns true when the request originates from the local machine. To demonstrate the custom action method selector, I created a Home controller in the example project, as shown in Listing 19-20.

Listing 19-20. The Contents of the HomeController.cs File

```
using System.Web.Mvc;
using ControllerExtensibility.Infrastructure;
using ControllerExtensibility.Models;

namespace ControllerExtensibility.Controllers {
    public class HomeController : Controller {

        public ActionResult Index() {
            return View("Result", new Result {
                ControllerName = "Home", ActionName = "Index"
            });
        }

        [ActionName("Index")]
        public ActionResult LocalIndex() {
            return View("Result", new Result {
                ControllerName = "Home", ActionName = "LocalIndex"
            });
        }
    }
}
```

I have used the ActionName attribute to create a situation in which there are two Index action methods. At this point, the action invoker doesn't have any way to figure out which one should be used when a request for the /Home/ Index URL arrives and will generate the error shown in Figure 19-8 when such a request is received.

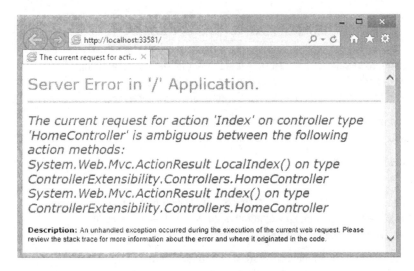

Figure 19-8. *The error shown when there are ambiguous action method names*

To resolve this situation, I can apply the custom method selection attribute to one of the ambiguous methods, as shown in Listing 19-21.

Listing 19-21. Applying the Method Selection Attribute to the HomeController.cs File

```
...
[Local]
[ActionName("Index")]
public ActionResult LocalIndex() {
    return View("Result", new Result {
        ControllerName = "Home", ActionName = "LocalIndex"
    });
}
...
```

If you restart the application and navigate to the root URL from a browser running on the local machine, you will see that the MVC Framework takes the method selection attribute into account to resolve the ambiguity between the methods in the controller class, as shown in Figure 19-9.

Figure 19-9. *Using a method selection attribute to resolve action method ambiguity*

THE ACTION METHOD DISAMBIGUATION PROCESS

Now that you have seen inside the action method selector base class, you can understand how the action invoker selects an action method. The invoker starts the process with a list of possible candidates, which are the controller methods that meet the action method criteria. Then it goes through the following process:

- The invoker discards any method based on name. Only methods that have the same name as the target action or have a suitable `ActionName` attribute are kept on the list.

- The invoker discards any method that has an action method selector attribute that returns `false` for the current request.

- If there is exactly one action method with a selector left, then this is the method that is used. If there is more than one method with a selector, then an exception is thrown, because the action invoker cannot disambiguate between the available methods.

- If there are no action methods with selectors, then the invoker looks at those without selectors. If there is exactly one such method, then this is the one that is invoked. If there is more than one method without a selector, an exception is thrown, because the invoker can't choose between them.

Handling Unknown Actions

If the action invoker is unable to find an action method to invoke, it returns `false` from its `InvokeAction` method. When this happens, the `Controller` class calls its `HandleUnknownAction` method. By default, this method returns a 404–Not Found response to the client. This is the most useful thing that a controller can do for most applications, but you can choose to override this method in your controller class if you want to do something special. Listing 19-22 provides a demonstration of overriding the `HandleUnknownAction` method in the `Home` controller.

Listing 19-22. Overriding the HandleUnknownAction Method in the HomeController.cs File

```
using System.Web.Mvc;
using ControllerExtensibility.Infrastructure;
using ControllerExtensibility.Models;

namespace ControllerExtensibility.Controllers {
    public class HomeController : Controller {

        // ...other action methods omitted for brevity...

        protected override void HandleUnknownAction(string actionName) {
            Response.Write(string.Format("You requested the {0} action", actionName));
        }
    }
}
```

If you start the application and navigate to a URL that targets a nonexistent action method, you will see the response shown in Figure 19-10.

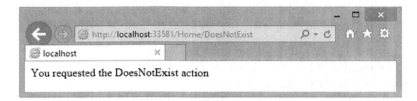

Figure 19-10. *Dealing with requests for action methods that do not exist*

Improving Performance with Specialized Controllers

The MVC Framework provides two special kinds of controllers that may improve the performance of your MVC web applications. Like all performance optimizations, these controllers represent compromises, either in ease of use or with reduced functionality. In the follow sections, I demonstrate both kinds of controllers and outline their benefits and shortcomings.

Using Sessionless Controllers

By default, controllers support *session state*, which can be used to store data values across requests, making life easier for the MVC programmer. Creating and maintaining session state is an involved process. Data must be stored and retrieved, and the sessions themselves must be managed so that they expire appropriately. Session data consumes server memory or space in some other storage location, and needing to synchronize the data across multiple Web servers makes it harder to run your application on a server farm.

In order to simplify session state, ASP.NET will process only one query for a given session at a time. If the client makes multiple overlapping requests, they will be queued up and processed sequentially by the server. The benefit is that you do not need to worry about multiple requests modifying the same data. The downside is that you do not get the request throughput you might like.

Not all controllers need the session state features. In such cases, you can improve the performance of your application by avoiding work involved in maintaining session state. You do this by using *sessionless controllers*. These are just like regular controllers, with two exceptions: the MVC Framework will not load or store session state when they are used to process a request, and overlapping requests can be processed simultaneously.

Managing Session State in a Custom IControllerFactory

At the start of this chapter, I showed you that the IControllerFactory interface contained a method called GetControllerSessionBehavior, which returns a value from the SessionStateBehavior enumeration. That enumeration contains four values that control the session state configuration of a controller, as described in Table 19-4.

Table 19-4. *The Values of the SessionStateBehavior Enumeration*

Value	Description
Default	Use the default ASP.NET behavior, which is to determine the session state configuration from HttpContext.
Required	Full read-write session state is enabled.
ReadOnly	Read-only session state is enabled.
Disabled	Session state is disabled entirely.

A controller factory that implements the IControllerFactory interface directly sets the session state behavior for controllers by returning SessionStateBehavior values from the GetControllerSessionBehavior method. The parameters to this method are a RequestContext object and a string containing the name of the controller. You can return any of the four values shown in the table, and you can return different values for different controllers. As a demonstration, I have changed the implementation of the GetControllerSessionBehavior method in the CustomControllerFactory class that I created earlier in the chapter, as shown in Listing 19-23.

Listing 19-23. Defining Session State Behavior for a Controller in the CustomControllerFactory.cs File

```
...
public SessionStateBehavior GetControllerSessionBehavior(RequestContext
        requestContext, string controllerName) {
    switch (controllerName) {
        case "Home":
            return SessionStateBehavior.ReadOnly;
        case "Product":
            return SessionStateBehavior.Required;
        default:
            return SessionStateBehavior.Default;
    }
}
...
```

Managing Session State Using DefaultControllerFactory

When you are using the built-in controller factory, you can control the session state by applying the SessionState attribute to individual controller classes, as shown in Listing 19-24 where I have created a new controller called FastController.

Listing 19-24. Using the SessionState Attribute in the FastController.cs File

```
using System.Web.Mvc;
using System.Web.SessionState;
using ControllerExtensibility.Models;

namespace ControllerExtensibility.Controllers {

    [SessionState(SessionStateBehavior.Disabled)]
    public class FastController : Controller {

        public ActionResult Index() {
            return View("Result", new Result {
                ControllerName = "Fast ",ActionName = "Index"
            });
        }
    }
}
```

The `SessionState` attribute is applied to the controller class and affects all of the actions in the controller. The sole parameter to the attribute is a value from the `SessionStateBehavior` enumeration. In the example, I disabled session state entirely, which means that if I try to set a session value in the controller, like this:

```
...
Session["Message"] = "Hello";
...
```

or try to read back from the session state in a view, like this:

```
...
Message: @Session["Message"]
...
```

The MVC Framework will throw an exception when the action is invoked or the view is rendered.

■ **Tip** When session state is `Disabled`, the `HttpContext.Session` property returns `null`.

If you have specified the `ReadOnly` behavior, then you can read values that have been set by other controllers, but you will still get a runtime exception if you try to set or modify a value. You can get details of the session through the `HttpContext.Session` object but trying to alter any values causes an error.

■ **Tip** If you are simply trying to pass data from the controller to the view, consider using the View Bag feature instead, which is not affected by the `SessionState` attribute.

Using Asynchronous Controllers

The underlying ASP.NET platform maintains a pool of .NET threads that are used to process client requests. This pool is called the *worker thread pool*, and the threads are called *worker threads*. When a request is received, a worker thread is taken from the pool and given the job of processing the request. When the request has been processed, the worker thread is returned to the pool, so that it is available to process new requests as they arrive. There are two key benefits of using thread pools for ASP.NET applications:

- By reusing worker threads, you avoid the overhead of creating a new one each time you process a request.
- By having a fixed number of worker threads available, you avoid the situation where you are processing more simultaneous requests than your server can handle.

The worker thread pool works best when requests can be processed in a short period of time. This is the case for most MVC applications. However, if you have actions that depend on other servers and take a long time to complete, then you can reach the point where all of your worker threads are tied up waiting for other systems to complete their work.

■ **Note** In this section, I assume that you are familiar with the Task Parallel Library (TPL). If you want to learn about the TPL, see my book on the topic, called *Pro .NET Parallel Programming in C#*, which is published by Apress.

Your server is capable of doing more work (after all, you are just waiting, which takes up little of your resources), but because you have tied up all of your worker threads, incoming requests are being queued up. You will be in the odd state of your application grinding to a halt while the server is largely idle.

■ **Caution**   At this point, some readers are thinking that they can write a worker thread pool that is tailored to their application. *Do not do it.* Writing concurrent code is easy. Writing concurrent code *that works* is difficult. If you are new to concurrent programming, then you lack the required skills. My advice is to stick with the default pool. If you are experienced in concurrent programming, then you already know that the benefits will be marginal compared with the effort of coding and testing a new thread pool.

The solution to this problem is to use an *asynchronous controller*. This increases the overall performance of your application, but does not bring any benefits to the execution of your asynchronous operations.

■ **Note**   Asynchronous controllers are useful only for actions that are I/O- or network-bound and *not* CPU-intensive. The problem you are trying to solve with asynchronous controllers is a mismatch between the pool model and the type of request you are processing. The pool is intended to ensure that each request gets a decent slice of the server resources, but you end up with a set of worker threads that are doing nothing. If you use additional background threads for CPU-intensive actions, then you will dilute the server resources across too many simultaneous requests.

Creating the Example

To begin the exploration of asynchronous controllers, I am going to show you an example of the kind of problem that they are intended to solve. Listing 19-25 shows a regular synchronous controller called RemoteData that I added to the example project.

Listing 19-25. The Contents of the RemoteDataController.cs File

```
using System.Web.Mvc;
using ControllerExtensibility.Models;

namespace ControllerExtensibility.Controllers {
    public class RemoteDataController : Controller {

        public ActionResult Data() {
            RemoteService service = new RemoteService();
            string data = service.GetRemoteData();
            return View((object)data);
        }
    }
}
```

This controller contains an action method, Data, which creates an instance of the model class RemoteService and calls the GetRemoteData method on it. This method is an example of a time-consuming, low-CPU activity. The RemoteService class, which I defined in a class file called RemoteService.cs in the Models folder, is shown in Listing 19-26.

Listing 19-26. The Contents of the RemoteService.cs File

```
using System.Threading;

namespace ControllerExtensibility.Models {
    public class RemoteService {

        public string GetRemoteData() {
            Thread.Sleep(2000);
            return "Hello from the other side of the world";
        }
    }
}
```

Okay, I admit it: I faked the GetRemoteData method. In the real world, this method could be retrieving complex data across a slow network connection, but to keep things simple, I used the Thread.Sleep method to simulate a two-second delay. The last addition I need is a new view. I created the Views/RemoteData folder and added the Data.cshtml view file to it, the contents of which are shown in Listing 19-27.

Listing 19-27. The Contents of the Data.cshtml File

```
@model string

@{
    Layout = null;
}

<!DOCTYPE html>

<html>
<head>
    <meta name="viewport" content="width=device-width" />
    <title>Data</title>
</head>
<body>
    <div>
        Data: @Model
    </div>
</body>
</html>
```

When you run the application and navigate to the /RemoteData/Data URL, the action method is invoked, the RemoteService object is created, and the GetRemoteData method is called. After two seconds (simulating a real operation), the data is returned from the GetRemoteData method, passed to the view and rendered as Figure 19-11.

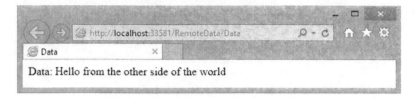

Figure 19-11. *Navigating to the /RemoteData/Data URL*

The problem here is that the worker thread that was handling the request was idle for two seconds. It wasn't doing anything useful, and it was not available for handling other requests while it was waiting.

■ **Caution**   Using an asynchronous controller frees up the worker thread so that it can process other queries. It doesn't prevent the user from experiencing a two-second wait. After all, that fake data still has to be obtained and processed. There are client-side techniques you can use to make such requests asynchronously in the browser, which allows you to at least keep the user informed about the progress of getting the data and allow them to continue working with another part of the application. See my *Pro ASP.NET MVC 5 Client* book, published by Apress in 2014, for details.

Creating an Asynchronous Controller

Having shown you the problem I was going to solve, I can now move on to create the asynchronous controller. There are two ways to create an asynchronous controller. One is to implement the System.Web.Mvc.Async. IAsyncController interface, which is the asynchronous equivalent of IController. I am not going to demonstrate that approach, because it requires so much explanation of the .NET concurrent programming facilities.

■ **Tip**   Not all actions in an asynchronous controller need to be asynchronous. You can include synchronous methods as well, and they will behave as expected.

I want to stay focused on the MVC Framework, which is why I will demonstrate the second approach: to use the new await and async keywords in a regular controller.

In previous versions of the .NET Framework, creating asynchronous controllers was a complex process and required deriving the controller from a special class and splitting actions into two methods. The new await and async keywords, which I described in Chapter 4, have simplified this process a lot: you create a new Task object and await its response, as shown in Listing 19-28.

■ **Tip**   The old method of creating asynchronous action methods is still supported, although the approach I describe here is much more elegant and the one I recommend. One artifact of the old approach is that you can't use action method names that end with Async (e.g., IndexAsync) or Completed (e.g., IndexCompleted).

Listing 19-28. Creating an Asynchronous Controller in the RemoteDataController.cs File

```
using System.Web.Mvc;
using ControllerExtensibility.Models;
using System.Threading.Tasks;

namespace ControllerExtensibility.Controllers {
    public class RemoteDataController : Controller {

        public async Task<ActionResult> Data() {
            string data = await Task<string>.Factory.StartNew(() => {
                return new RemoteService().GetRemoteData();
            });

            return View((object)data);
        }
    }
}
```

I have refactored the action method so that it returns a Task<ActionResult>, applied the async and await keywords, and created a Task<string>, which is responsible for calling the GetRemoteData method.

Consuming Asynchronous Methods in a Controller

You can also use an asynchronous controller to consume asynchronous methods elsewhere in your application. To demonstrate this, I have added an asynchronous method to the RemoteService class, as shown in Listing 19-29.

Listing 19-29. Adding an Asynchronous Method in the RemoteService.cs File

```
using System.Threading;
using System.Threading.Tasks;

namespace ControllerExtensibility.Models {
    public class RemoteService {

        public string GetRemoteData() {
            Thread.Sleep(2000);
            return "Hello from the other side of the world";
        }

        public async Task<string> GetRemoteDataAsync() {
            return await Task<string>.Factory.StartNew(() => {
                Thread.Sleep(2000);
                return "Hello from the other side of the world";
            });
        }
    }
}
```

The result from the GetRemoteDataAsync method is a Task<string>, which yields the same message as the synchronous method when it is completed. In Listing 19-30, you can see how I have consumed this asynchronous method in a new action method that I added to the RemoteData controller.

Listing 19-30. Consuming Asynchronous Methods in the RemoteData Controller

```
using System.Web.Mvc;
using ControllerExtensibility.Models;
using System.Threading.Tasks;

namespace ControllerExtensibility.Controllers {
    public class RemoteDataController : Controller {

        public async Task<ActionResult> Data() {
            string data = await Task<string>.Factory.StartNew(() => {
                return new RemoteService().GetRemoteData();
            });

            return View((object)data);
        }

        public async Task<ActionResult> ConsumeAsyncMethod() {
            string data = await new RemoteService().GetRemoteDataAsync();
            return View("Data", (object)data);
        }
    }
}
```

You can see that both action methods follow the same basic pattern and that the difference is where the Task object is created. The result of calling either action method is that the worker thread is not tied up while I wait for the GetRemoteData call to complete, which means that the thread is available to process other requests which can significantly improve the performance of your MVC Framework application.

Summary

In this chapter, you have seen how the MVC Framework creates controllers and invokes methods. I have explored and customized the built-in implementations of the key interfaces, and created custom versions to demonstrate how they work. You have learned how action method selectors can be used to differentiate between action methods and seen some specialized kinds of controllers that can be used to increase the request processing capability of your applications.

The underlying theme of this chapter is extensibility. Almost every aspect of the MVC Framework can be modified or replaced entirely. For most projects, the default behaviors are entirely sufficient. But having a working knowledge of how the MVC Framework fits together helps you to make informed design and coding decisions (and it is just plain interesting).

In the next chapter, I turn to views. I explain how they work and, as you will have come to expect by now, how to configure and customize the default behaviors.

■ ■ ■

CHAPTER 20

Views

In Chapter 17, you saw how action methods can return ActionResult objects. As you learned, the most commonly used action result is ViewResult, which causes a view to be rendered and returned to the client. You have seen views being used in many examples already, so you know roughly what they do. In this chapter, I focus and clarify that knowledge. I begin by showing you how the MVC Framework handles ViewResults using *view engines*, including demonstrating how to create a custom view engine. Next, I will describe techniques for working effectively with the built-in Razor View Engine. Then I will cover how to create and use partial views, child actions, and Razor sections, which are all essential topics for effective MVC development. Table 20-1 provides the summary for this chapter.

Table 20-1. *Chapter Summary*

Problem	Solution	Listing
Create a custom view engine	Implement the IViewEngine and IView interfaces	1–8
Customize the Razor view engine	Derive from the RazorViewEngine class	9–15
Define regions of content for use in a layout	Use Razor sections	16
Apply sections in a layout	Use the RenderSection and RenderBody helpers	17–22
Define reusable fragments of markup	Use partial views	23–26
Define reusable business logic	Use child actions	27–29

Creating a Custom View Engine

I am going to dive in at the deep end and create a custom view engine. You do not need to do this for most projects because the MVC Framework includes the Razor view engine, whose syntax I described in Chapter 5 and which I have been using for all of the examples so far in this book.

■ **Tip** Older versions of the MVC Framework supported views created using the same markup and view engine as ASP. NET Web Forms, which is why you will sometimes see references to .aspx files in debugging and error messages.

The value in creating a custom view engine is to demonstrate how the request processing pipeline works and complete your knowledge of how the MVC Framework operates. This includes understanding just how much freedom view engines have in translating a ViewResult into a response to the client. View engines implement the IViewEngine interface, which is shown in Listing 20-1.

Listing 20-1. The IViewEngine Interface from the MVC Framework

```
namespace System.Web.Mvc {
    public interface IViewEngine {

        ViewEngineResult FindPartialView(ControllerContext controllerContext,
            string partialViewName, bool useCache);

        ViewEngineResult FindView(ControllerContext controllerContext,
            string viewName, string masterName, bool useCache);

        void ReleaseView(ControllerContext controllerContext, IView view);
    }
}
```

The role of a view engine is to translate requests for views into ViewEngineResult objects. The first two methods in the interface, FindView and FindPartialView, are passed parameters that describe the request and the controller that processed it (a ControllerContext object), the name of the view and its layout, and whether the view engine is allowed to reuse a previous result from its cache. These methods are called when a ViewResult is being processed. The final method, ReleaseView, is called when a view is no longer needed.

■ **Note**   The MVC Framework support for view engines is implemented by the ControllerActionInvoker class, which is the built-in implementation of the IActionInvoker interface, as described in Chapter 17. You will not have automatic access to the view engines feature if you have implemented your own action invoker or controller factory directly from the IActionInvoker or IControllerFactory interfaces.

The ViewEngineResult class allows a view engine to respond to the MVC Framework when a view is requested. Listing 20-2 shows the ViewEngineResult class.

Listing 20-2. The ViewEngineResult Class from the MVC Framework

```
using System.Collections.Generic;

namespace System.Web.Mvc {
    public class ViewEngineResult {

        public ViewEngineResult(IEnumerable<string> searchedLocations) {
            if (searchedLocations == null) {
                throw new ArgumentNullException("searchedLocations");
            }
            SearchedLocations = searchedLocations;
        }

        public ViewEngineResult(IView view, IViewEngine viewEngine) {
            if (view == null) { throw new ArgumentNullException("view");}
            if (viewEngine == null) { throw new ArgumentNullException("viewEngine");}
            View = view;
            ViewEngine = viewEngine;
        }
```

```
        public IEnumerable<string> SearchedLocations { get; private set; }
        public IView View { get; private set; }
        public IViewEngine ViewEngine { get; private set; }
    }
}
```

You express a result by choosing one of the two constructors. If your view engine is able to provide a view for a request, then you create a ViewEngineResult using this constructor:

```
...
public ViewEngineResult(IView view, IViewEngine viewEngine)
...
```

The parameters to this constructor are an implementation of the IView interface and a view engine (so that the ReleaseView method can be called later). If your view engine cannot provide a view for a request, then you use this constructor:

```
...
public ViewEngineResult(IEnumerable<string> searchedLocations)
...
```

The parameter for this version is an enumeration of the places you searched to find a view. This information is displayed to the user if no view can be found, as I will demonstrate later.

■ **Note** You are not alone if you think that the ViewEngineResult class is a little awkward. Expressing outcomes using different versions of a class constructor is an odd approach and does not really fit with the rest of the MVC Framework design.

The last building block of the view engine system is the IView interface, which is shown in Listing 20-3.

Listing 20-3. The IView Interface from the MVC Framework

```
using System.IO;

namespace System.Web.Mvc {
    public interface IView {
        void Render(ViewContext viewContext, TextWriter writer);
    }
}
```

An IView implementation is passed to the constructor of a ViewEngineResult object, which is then returned from the view engine methods. The MVC Framework then calls the Render method. The ViewContext parameter provides information about the request from the client and the output from the action method. The TextWriter parameter is for writing output to the client.

The ViewContext object defines properties that give you access to information about the request and details of how the MVC Framework has processed it so far. I have described the most useful of these properties in Table 20-2.

Table 20-2. *Useful ViewContext Properties*

Name	Description
Controller	Returns the IController implementation that processed the current request
RequestContext	Returns details of the current request
RouteData	Returns the routing data for the current request
TempData	Returns the temp data associated with the request
View	Returns the implementation of the IView interface that will process the request. Obviously, this will be the current class if you are creating a custom view implementation.
ViewBag	Returns an object that represents the view bag
ViewData	Returns a dictionary of the view model data, which also contains the view bag and meta data for the model. See Table 20-3 for details.

The most interesting of these properties is ViewData, which returns a ViewDataDictionary object. The ViewDataDictionary class defines a number of useful properties that give access to the view model, the view bag and the view model metadata. I have described the most useful of these properties in Table 20-3.

Table 20-3. *Useful ViewDataDictionary Properties*

Name	Description
Keys	Returns a collection of key values for the data in the dictionary, which can be used to access view bag properties
Model	Returns the view model object for the request
ModelMetadata	Returns a ModelMetadata object that can be used to reflect on the model type
ModelState	Returns information about the state of the model, which I describe in detail in Chapter 25

As I said earlier, the simplest way to see how this works—how IViewEngine, IView, and ViewEngineResult fit together—is to create a view engine. I am going to create a simple view engine that returns one kind of view. This view will render a result that contains information about the request and the view data produced by the action method. This approach lets me demonstrate the way that view engines operate without getting bogged down in parsing view templates.

Preparing the Example Project

The example project for this part of the chapter is called Views and I created it using the Empty template, checking the option to add the core MVC folders and references. I created a Home controller, which you can see in Listing 20-4.

Listing 20-4. The Contents of the HomeController.cs File

```
using System;
using System.Web.Mvc;

namespace Views.Controllers {
    public class HomeController : Controller {
```

```
        public ActionResult Index() {
            ViewBag.Message = "Hello, World";
            ViewBag.Time = DateTime.Now.ToShortTimeString();
            return View("DebugData");
        }

        public ActionResult List() {
            return View();
        }
    }
}
```

I have not created any views for this project because I am going to implement a custom view engine rather than relying on Razor.

Creating a Custom IView

I am going to start by creating an implementation of the IView interface. I added an Infrastructure folder to the example project and created a new class file within it called DebugDataView.cs, which is shown in Listing 20-5.

Listing 20-5. The Contents of the DebugDataView.cs

```
using System.IO;
using System.Web.Mvc;

namespace Views.Infrastructure {
    public class DebugDataView : IView {

        public void Render(ViewContext viewContext, TextWriter writer) {

            Write(writer, "---Routing Data---");
            foreach (string key in viewContext.RouteData.Values.Keys) {
                Write(writer, "Key: {0}, Value: {1}",
                    key, viewContext.RouteData.Values[key]);
            }

            Write(writer, "---View Data---");
            foreach (string key in viewContext.ViewData.Keys) {
                Write(writer, "Key: {0}, Value: {1}", key,
                    viewContext.ViewData[key]);
            }
        }

        private void Write(TextWriter writer, string template, params object[] values) {
            writer.Write(string.Format(template, values) + "<p/>");
        }
    }
}
```

This view demonstrates the use of the two parameters to the Render method: I take values from the ViewContext and write a response to the client using the TextWriter. First I write out the routing data information and then the view bag data.

■ **Tip** The view data feature is a holdover from earlier versions of the MVC Framework that were released before C# had support for dynamic objects (which I described in Chapter 4). View data was a less flexible precursor to the view bag and isn't used directly any more, except when writing custom IView implementations when it provides easy access to the properties defined on the view bag object.

Creating an IViewEngine Implementation

Remember that the purpose of the view engine is to produce a ViewEngineResult object that contains either an IView or a list of the places that searched for a suitable view. Now that I have an IView implementation to work with, I can create the view engine. I added a class file called DebugDataViewEngine.cs in the Infrastructure folder, the contents of which are shown in Listing 20-6.

Listing 20-6. The Contents of the DebugDataViewEngine.cs File

```
using System.Web.Mvc;

namespace Views.Infrastructure {
    public class DebugDataViewEngine : IViewEngine {

        public ViewEngineResult FindView(ControllerContext controllerContext,
                string viewName, string masterName, bool useCache) {

            if (viewName == "DebugData") {
                return new ViewEngineResult(new DebugDataView(), this);
            } else {
                return new ViewEngineResult(new string[]
                    { "No view (Debug Data View Engine)" });
            }
        }

        public ViewEngineResult FindPartialView(ControllerContext controllerContext,
                string partialViewName, bool useCache) {

            return new ViewEngineResult(new string[]
                { "No view (Debug Data View Engine)" });
        }

        public void ReleaseView(ControllerContext controllerContext, IView view) {
            // do nothing
        }
    }
}
```

I am going to support only a single view, which is called DebugData. When I see a request for that view, I will return a new instance of the custom IView implementation, like this:

```
...
return new ViewEngineResult(new DebugDataView(), this);
...
```

If I were implementing a more serious view engine, I would use this opportunity to search for templates, taking into account the layout and provided caching settings. As it is, this simple example only requires a new instance of the DebugDataView class. If I receive a request for a view other than DebugData, I return a ViewEngineResult, like this:

```
...
return new ViewEngineResult(new string[] { "No view (Debug Data View Engine)" });
...
```

The IViewEngine interface presumes that the view engine has places it needs to look to find views. This is a reasonable assumption, because views are typically template files that are stored as files in the project. In this case, I do not have anywhere to look, so I just return a dummy location which will indicate that I was asked for a view that cannot be delivered.

The custom view engine doesn't support partial views, so I return a result from the FindPartialView method that indicates I do not have a view to offer. I return to the topic of partial views and how they are handled in the Razor engine later in the chapter. I have not implemented the ReleaseView method, because there are no resources that I need to release in the custom IView implementation, which is the usual purpose of this method.

Registering a Custom View Engine

I register view engines in the Application_Start method of Global.asax, as shown in Listing 20-7.

Listing 20-7. Registering a Custom View Engine Using Global.asax

```
using System;
using System.Collections.Generic;
using System.Linq;
using System.Web;
using System.Web.Mvc;
using System.Web.Routing;
using Views.Infrastructure;

namespace Views {

    public class MvcApplication : System.Web.HttpApplication {
        protected void Application_Start() {
            AreaRegistration.RegisterAllAreas();
            RouteConfig.RegisterRoutes(RouteTable.Routes);

            ViewEngines.Engines.Add(new DebugDataViewEngine());
        }
    }
}
```

The static `ViewEngine.Engines` collection contains the set of view engines that are installed in the application. The MVC Framework supports the idea of there being several engines installed in a single application. When a `ViewResult` is being processed, the action invoker obtains the set of installed view engines and calls their `FindView` methods in turn.

The action invoker stops calling `FindView` methods as soon as it receives a `ViewEngineResult` object that contains an `IView`. This means that the order in which engines are added to the `ViewEngines.Engines` collection is significant if two or more engines are able to service a request for the same view name. If you want your view to take precedence, then you can insert it at the start of the collection, like this:

```
...
ViewEngines.Engines.Insert(0, new DebugDataViewEngine());
...
```

Testing the View Engine

I am now in a position to test the custom view engine. When the application is started, the browser will automatically navigate to the root URL for the project, which will be mapped to the `Index` action in the `Home` controller. The action method uses the `View` method to return a `ViewResult` that specifies the `DebugData` view. You can see the result of this in Figure 20-1.

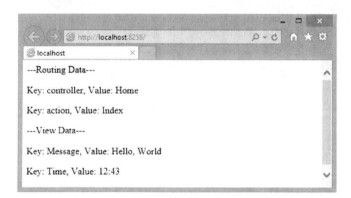

***Figure 20-1.** Using a custom view engine*

This is the result of the `FindView` method being called for a view that I am able to process. If you navigate to the `/Home/List` URL, the MVC Framework will invoke the `List` action method, which calls the `View` method to request its default view, which is not one that is supported. You can see the result in Figure 20-2.

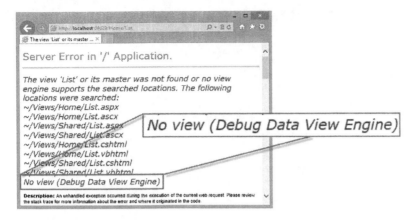

Figure 20-2. *Requesting an unsupported view*

You can see that my message is reported as one of the locations that have been searched for a view. Notice that Razor and ASPX views appear on the list as well. This is because those view engines are still being used. If I want to ensure that only my custom view engine is used, then I have to call the `Clear` method before I register my engine in the `Global.asax` file, as shown in Listing 20-8.

Listing 20-8. Removing the Other View Engines in the Global.asax File

```
using System;
using System.Collections.Generic;
using System.Linq;
using System.Web;
using System.Web.Mvc;
using System.Web.Routing;
using Views.Infrastructure;

namespace Views {

    public class MvcApplication : System.Web.HttpApplication {
        protected void Application_Start() {
            AreaRegistration.RegisterAllAreas();
            RouteConfig.RegisterRoutes(RouteTable.Routes);

            ViewEngines.Engines.Clear();
            ViewEngines.Engines.Add(new DebugDataViewEngine());
        }
    }
}
```

If you restart the application and navigate to /Home/List again, only the custom view engine will be used, as shown in Figure 20-3.

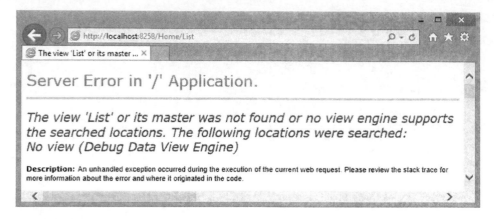

Figure 20-3. *Using only the custom view engine in the example application*

Working with the Razor Engine

In the previous section, I was able to create a custom view engine by implementing just two interfaces. Admittedly, I ended up with something simple that generated ugly views, but you saw how the concept of MVC extensibility continues throughout the request processing pipeline.

The complexity in a view engine comes from the system of view templates that includes code fragments and support layouts, and is compiled to optimize performance. I did not do any of these things in the simple custom view engine—and there isn't much need to—because the built-in Razor engine takes care of all of that for me. The functionality that almost all MVC applications require is available in Razor. Only a vanishingly small number of projects need to go to the trouble of creating a custom view engine. I gave you a primer on the Razor syntax in Chapter 5. In this chapter, I am going to show you how to use other features to create and render Razor views. You will also learn how to customize the Razor engine.

Preparing the Example Project

For this part of the chapter, I have created a new MVC project using the Empty template option, checking the option to add the core MVC folders and references. I called the project WorkingWithRazor and I added a Home controller, which is shown in Listing 20-9.

Listing 20-9. The Contents of the HomeController.cs File

```
using System.Web.Mvc;

namespace WorkingWithRazor.Controllers {
    public class HomeController : Controller {

        public ActionResult Index() {
            string[] names = { "Apple", "Orange", "Pear" };
            return View(names);
        }
    }
}
```

I also created a view called `Index.cshtml` in the `Views/Home` folder. You can see the contents of the view file in Listing 20-10.

Listing 20-10. The Contents of the Index.cshtml File

```
@model string[]

@{
    ViewBag.Title = "Index";
}

This is a list of fruit names:

@foreach (string name in Model) {
    <span><b>@name</b></span>
}
```

Understanding Razor View Rendering

The Razor View Engine compiles the views in your applications to improve performance. The views are translated into C# classes, and then compiled, which is why you are able to include C# code fragments so easily. It is instructive to look at the source code that Razor views generate, because it helps to put many of the Razor features in context.

The views in an MVC application are not compiled until the application is started, so to see the classes that are created by Razor, you need to start the application and navigate to the `/Home/Index` action. The initial request to MVC application triggers the compilation process for all views. You can see the output from the request in Figure 20-4.

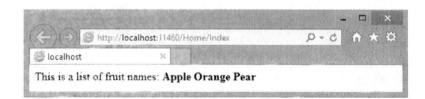

Figure 20-4. *The output from the Index action method on the Home controller*

Conveniently, classes generated from the view files are written to the disk as C# code files and then compiled, which means that you can see the C# statements that represent a view. You can find the generated files in `c:\Users\<yourLoginName>\AppData\Local\Temp\Temporary ASP.NET Files` on Windows 7 and Windows 8.

Finding the code file generated for a particular view requires a bit of poking around. There are usually a number of folders with cryptic names, and the names of the `.cs` files do not correspond to the names of the classes they contain. As an example, I found the generated class for the view in Listing 20-10 in a file called `App_Web_ihpp0d0l.0.cs` in the `root\7bbfc2bc\bd7485cd` folder. I have tidied up the class from my system to make it easier to read, as shown in Listing 20-11.

Listing 20-11. The Generated C# Class for a Razor View

```
namespace ASP {
    using System;
    using System.Collections.Generic;
    using System.IO;
    using System.Linq;
```

```
using System.Net;
using System.Web;
using System.Web.Helpers;
using System.Web.Security;
using System.Web.UI;
using System.Web.WebPages;
using System.Web.Mvc;
using System.Web.Mvc.Ajax;
using System.Web.Mvc.Html;
using System.Web.Optimization;
using System.Web.Routing;

public class _Page_Views_Home_Index_cshtml : System.Web.Mvc.WebViewPage<string[]> {

    public _Page_Views_Home_Index_cshtml() {
    }

    public override void Execute() {
        ViewBag.Title = "Index";
        WriteLiteral("\r\n\r\nThis is a list of fruit names:\r\n\r\n");

        foreach (string name in Model) {
            WriteLiteral("    <span><b>");
            Write(name);
            WriteLiteral("</b></span>\r\n");
        }
    }
}
}
```

First, note that the class is derived from `WebViewPage<T>`, where T is the model type: `WebViewPage<string[]>` for this example. This is how strongly typed views are handled. Also notice the name of the class that has been generated: `_Page_Views_Home_Index_cshtml`. You can see how the path of the view file has been encoded in the class name. This is how Razor maps requests for views into instances of compiled classes.

In the `Execute` method, you can see how the statements and elements in the view have been handled. The code fragments that I prefixed with the @ symbol are expressed directly as C# statements. The HTML elements are handled with the `WriteLiteral` method, which writes the contents of the parameter to the result as they are given. This is opposed to the `Write` method, which is used for C# variables and encodes the string values to make them safe for use in an HTML page.

Both the `Write` and `WriteLiteral` methods write content to a `TextWriter` object. This is the same object that is passed to the `IView.Render` method, which you saw at the start of the chapter. The goal of a compiled Razor view is to generate the static and dynamic content and send it to the client via the `TextWriter`. This is useful to keep in mind when I turn to HTML helper methods later in later chapters.

Configuring the View Search Locations

The Razor View Engine follows a standard convention when looking for a view. For example, if you request the Index view associated with the Home controller, Razor looks through this list of views:

- `~/Views/Home/Index.cshtml`

- `~/Views/Home/Index.vbhtml`

- ~/Views/Shared/Index.cshtml

- ~/Views/Shared/Index.vbhtml

As you now know, Razor is not really looking for the view files on disk, because they have already been compiled into C# classes. Razor looks for the compiled class that represents these views. The .cshtml files are templates containing C# statements (the kind I am using), and the .vbhtml files contain Visual Basic statements.

You can change the view files that Razor searches for by creating a subclass of RazorViewEngine. This class is the Razor IViewEngine implementation. It builds on a series of base classes that define a set of properties that determine which view files are searched for. These properties are described in Table 20-4.

Table 20-4. *Razor View Engine Search Properties*

Property	Description	Default Value
ViewLocationFormats MasterLocationFormats PartialViewLocationFormats	The locations to look for views, partial views, and layouts	~/Views/{1}/{0}.cshtml, ~/Views/{1}/{0}.vbhtml, ~/Views/Shared/{0}.cshtml, ~/Views/Shared/{0}.vbhtml
AreaViewLocationFormats AreaMasterLocationFormats AreaPartialViewLocationFormats	The locations to look for views, partial views, and layouts for an area	~/Areas/{2}/Views/{1}/{0}.cshtml, ~/Areas/{2}/Views/{1}/{0}.vbhtml, ~/Areas/{2}/Views/Shared/{0}.cshtml, ~/Areas/{2}/Views/Shared/{0}.vbhtml

These properties predate the introduction of Razor, which why each set of three properties has the same values. Each property is an array of strings, which are expressed using the composite string formatting notation. The following are the parameter values that correspond to the placeholders:

- {0} represents the name of the view.

- {1} represents the name of the controller.

- {2} represents the name of the area.

To change the search locations, you create a new class that is derived from RazorViewEngine and change the values for one or more of the properties described in Table 20-4.

To demonstrate how to change the locations that are searched, I added an Infrastructure folder to the project and created a class file called CustomLocationViewEngine.cs, which is shown in Listing 20-12.

Listing 20-12. The Contents of the CustomLocationViewEngine.cs File

```
using System.Web.Mvc;

namespace WorkingWithRazor.Infrastructure {
    public class CustomLocationViewEngine : RazorViewEngine {

        public CustomLocationViewEngine() {
            ViewLocationFormats = new string[]
                {"~/Views/{1}/{0}.cshtml", "~/Views/Common/{0}.cshtml"};
        }
    }
}
```

I have set a new value for the ViewLocationFormats. The new array contains entries only for .cshtml files. In addition, I have changed the location I look for shared views to be Views/Common, rather than Views/Shared. I register the derived view engine using the ViewEngines.Engines collection in the Application_Start method of Global.asax, as shown in Listing 20-13.

Listing 20-13. Registering the Custom View Engine in the Global.asax File

```
using System;
using System.Collections.Generic;
using System.Linq;
using System.Web;
using System.Web.Mvc;
using System.Web.Routing;
using WorkingWithRazor.Infrastructure;

namespace WorkingWithRazor {

    public class MvcApplication : System.Web.HttpApplication {
        protected void Application_Start() {
            AreaRegistration.RegisterAllAreas();
            RouteConfig.RegisterRoutes(RouteTable.Routes);

            ViewEngines.Engines.Clear();
            ViewEngines.Engines.Add(new CustomLocationViewEngine());
        }
    }
}
```

Remember that the action invoker goes to each view engine in turn to see if a view can be found. By the time that I am able to add the view to the collection, it will already contain the standard Razor View Engine. To avoid competing with that implementation, I call the Clear method to remove any other view engines that may have been registered, and then call the Add method to register the custom implementation.

To demonstrate the changed locations, I created the /Views/Common folder and added a view file called List.cshtml. You can see the contents of this file in Listing 20-14.

Listing 20-14. The Contents of the /Views/Common/List.cshtml File

```
@{
    ViewBag.Title = "List";
}

<h3>This is the /Views/Common/List.cshtml View</h3>
```

To display this view, I added a new action method to the Home controller, as shown in Listing 20-15.

Listing 20-15. Adding a New Action Method in the HomeController.cs File

```
using System.Web.Mvc;

namespace WorkingWithRazor.Controllers {
    public class HomeController : Controller {
```

```
        public ActionResult Index() {
            string[] names = { "Apple", "Orange", "Pear" };
            return View(names);
        }

        public ActionResult List() {
            return View();
        }
    }
}
```

When I start the application and navigate to the /Home/List URL, the custom locations will be used to locate the List.cshtml view file in the /Views/Common folder, as shown in Figure 20-5.

Figure 20-5. *The effect of custom locations in the view engine*

Adding Dynamic Content to a Razor View

The whole purpose of views is to allow you to render parts of your domain model as a user interface. To do that, you need to be able to add *dynamic content* to views. Dynamic content is generated at runtime, and can be different for each and every request. This is opposed to *static content*, such as HTML, which you create when you are writing the application and is the same for each and every request. You can add dynamic content to views in the different ways described in Table 20-5.

Table 20-5. *Adding Dynamic Content to a View*

Technique	When to Use
Inline code	Use for small, self-contained pieces of view logic, such as if and foreach statements. This is the fundamental tool for creating dynamic content in views, and some of the other approaches are built on it. I introduced this technique in Chapter 5 and you have seen countless examples in the chapters since.
HTML helper methods	Use to generate single HTML elements or small collections of them, typically based on view model or view data values. The MVC Framework includes a number of useful HTML helper methods, and it is easy to create your own. HTML helper methods are the topic of Chapter 21.
Sections	Use for creating sections of content that will be inserted into layout at specific locations.
Partial views	Use for sharing subsections of view markup between views. Partial views can contain inline code, HTML helper methods, and references to other partial views. Partial views do not invoke an action method, so they cannot be used to perform business logic.
Child actions	Use for creating reusable UI controls or widgets that need to contain business logic. When you use a child action, it invokes an action method, renders a view, and injects the result into the response stream.

Two of these options, inline code and HTML helper methods, are covered elsewhere in this book and I describe the others in the sections that follow.

Using Layout Sections

The Razor engine supports the concept of *sections*, which allow you to provide regions of content within a layout. Razor sections give greater control over which parts of the view are inserted into the layout and where they are placed. To demonstrate the sections feature, I have edited the /Views/Home/Index.cshtml file, as shown in Listing 20-16.

Listing 20-16. Defining a Section in the Index.cshtml File

```
@model string[]

@{
    ViewBag.Title = "Index";
    Layout = "~/Views/Shared/_Layout.cshtml";
}

@section Header {
    <div class="view">
        @foreach (string str in new [] {"Home", "List", "Edit"}) {
            @Html.ActionLink(str, str, null, new { style = "margin: 5px" })
        }
    </div>
}

<div class="view">
    This is a list of fruit names:

    @foreach (string name in Model) {
        <span><b>@name</b></span>
    }
</div>

@section Footer {
    <div class="view">
        This is the footer
    </div>
}
```

Sections are defined using the Razor @section tag followed by a name for the section. In this listing, I created sections called Header and Footer. The content of a section contains the usual mix of HTML markup and Razor tags. Sections are defined in the view, but applied in a layout with the @RenderSection helper method. To demonstrate how this works, I created the /Views/Shared/_Layout.cshtml file, the contents of which you can see in Listing 20-17.

Listing 20-17. Using Sections in the _Layout.cshtml File

```
<!DOCTYPE html>
<html>
<head>
    <meta charset="utf-8" />
    <meta name="viewport" content="width=device-width" />
```

```
    <style type="text/css">
        div.layout { background-color: lightgray;}
        div.view { border: thin solid black; margin: 10px 0;}
    </style>
    <title>@ViewBag.Title</title>
</head>
<body>
    @RenderSection("Header")

    <div class="layout">
        This is part of the layout
    </div>

    @RenderBody()

    <div class="layout">
        This is part of the layout
    </div>

    @RenderSection("Footer")

    <div class="layout">
        This is part of the layout
    </div>
</body>
</html>
```

■ **Tip**   My custom view engine locations are still in use, but I have specified the view explicitly in the Index.cshtml file, which means that my layout will be obtained from the /Views/Shared folder, even though shared views are located in the /Views/Common folder.

When Razor parses the layout, the RenderSection helper method is replaced with the contents of the section in the view with the specified name. The parts of the view that are not contained with a section are inserted into the layout using the RenderBody helper.

You can see the effect of the sections by starting the application, as shown in Figure 20-6. I added some basic CSS styles to help make it clear which sections of the output are from the view and which are from the layout. This result is not pretty, but it neatly demonstrates how you can put regions of content from the view into specific locations in the layout.

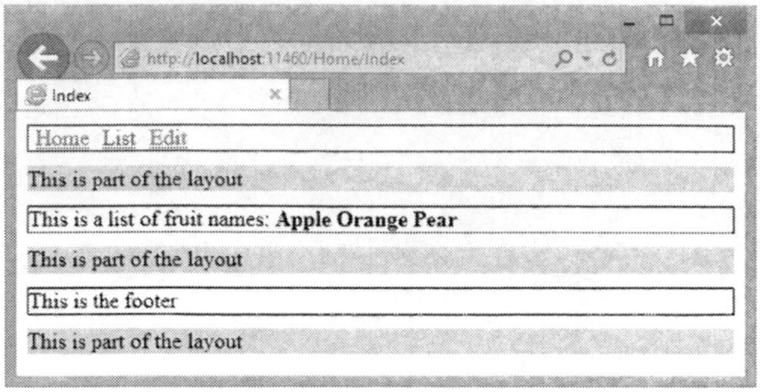

Figure 20-6. *Using sections in a view to locate content in a layout*

■ **Note**   A view can define only the sections that are referred to in the layout. The MVC Framework will throw an exception if you attempt to define sections in the view for which there is no corresponding @RenderSection helper call in the layout.

Mixing the sections in with the rest of the view is unusual. The convention is to define the sections at either the start or the end of the view, to make it easier to see which regions of content will be treated as sections and which will be captured by the RenderBody helper. Another approach, which I tend to use, is to define the view solely in terms of sections, including one for the body, as shown in Listing 20-18.

Listing 20-18. Defining a View in Terms of Razor Sections in the Index.cshtml File

```
@model string[]

@{
    ViewBag.Title = "Index";
    Layout = "~/Views/Shared/_Layout.cshtml";
}

@section Header {
    <div class="view">
        @foreach (string str in new [] {"Home", "List", "Edit"}) {
            @Html.ActionLink(str, str, null, new { style = "margin: 5px" })
        }
    </div>
}

@section Body {
    <div class="view">
        This is a list of fruit names:

        @foreach (string name in Model) {
            <span><b>@name</b></span>
        }
    </div>
}
```

```
@section Footer {
    <div class="view">
        This is the footer
    </div>
}
```

I find this makes for clearer views and reduces the chances of extraneous content being captured by RenderBody. To use this approach, I have to replace the call to the RenderBody helper with RenderSection("Body"), as shown in Listing 20-19.

Listing 20-19. Using RenderSection("Body") in the _Layout.cshtml File

```
<!DOCTYPE html>
<html>
<head>
    <meta charset="utf-8" />
    <meta name="viewport" content="width-device-width" />
    <style type="text/css">
        div.layout { background-color: lightgray;}
        div.view { border: thin solid black; margin: 10px 0;}
    </style>
    <title>@ViewBag.Title</title>
</head>
<body>
    @RenderSection("Header")

    <div class="layout">
        This is part of the layout
    </div>

    @RenderSection("Body")

    <div class="layout">
        This is part of the layout
    </div>

    @RenderSection("Footer")

    <div class="layout">
        This is part of the layout
    </div>
</body>
</html>
```

Testing For Sections

You can check to see if a view has defined a specific section from the layout. This is a useful way to provide default content for a section if a view does not need or want to provide specific content. I have modified the _Layout.cshtml file to check to see if a Footer section is defined, as shown in Listing 20-20.

Listing 20-20. Checking Whether a Section Is Defined in the _Layout.cshtml File

```
...
@if (IsSectionDefined("Footer")) {
    @RenderSection("Footer")
} else {
    <h4>This is the default footer</h4>
}
...
```

The IsSectionDefined helper takes the name of the section you want to check and returns true if the view you are rendering defines that section. In the example, I used this helper to determine if I should render some default content when the view does not define the Footer section.

Rendering Optional Sections

By default a view has to contain all of the sections for which there are RenderSection calls in the layout. If sections are missing, then the MVC Framework will report an exception to the user. To demonstrate this, I have added a new RenderSection call to the _Layout.cshtml file for a section called scripts, as shown in Listing 20-21. This is a section that Visual Studio adds to the layout by default when you create an MVC project using the MVC template.

Listing 20-21. A RenderSection Call for Which There Is No Corresponding Section in the _Layout.cshtml File

```
<!DOCTYPE html>
<html>
<head>
    <meta charset="utf-8" />
    <meta name="viewport" content="width=device-width" />
    <style type="text/css">
        div.layout { background-color: lightgray;}
        div.view { border: thin solid black; margin: 10px 0;}
    </style>
    <title>@ViewBag.Title</title>
</head>
<body>
    @RenderSection("Header")

    <div class="layout">
        This is part of the layout
    </div>

    @RenderSection("Body")

    <div class="layout">
        This is part of the layout
    </div>

    @if (IsSectionDefined("Footer")) {
        @RenderSection("Footer")
    } else {
        <h4>This is the default footer</h4>
    }
```

```
@RenderSection("scripts")

    <div class="layout">
        This is part of the layout
    </div>
</body>
</html>
```

When you start the application and the Razor engine attempts to render the layout and the view, you will see the error shown in Figure 20-7.

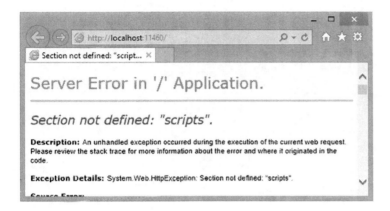

Figure 20-7. *The error shown when there is a missing section*

You can use the IsSectionDefined method to avoid making RenderSection calls for sections that the view does not define, but a more elegant approach is to use optional sections, which you do by passing an additional false value to the RenderSection method, as shown in Listing 20-22.

Listing 20-22. Making a Section Optional

```
...
@RenderSection("scripts", false)
...
```

This creates an optional section, the contents of which will be inserted into the result if the view defines it and which will not throw an exception otherwise.

Using Partial Views

You will often need to use the same fragments of Razor tags and HTML markup in several different places in the application. Rather than duplicate the content, you can use *partial views*, which are separate view files that contain fragments of tags and markup that can be included in other views. In this section, I show you how to create and use partial views, explain how they work, and demonstrate the techniques available for passing view data to a partial view.

Creating a Partial View

I am going to start by creating a partial view called MyPartial. Right-click on the Views/Shared folder, select Add ➤ View from the popup menu. Visual Studio will display the Add View dialog window, which you have seen in previous chapters. Set View Name to MyPartial, Template to Empty (without model) and check the Create as partial view option, as shown in Figure 20-8.

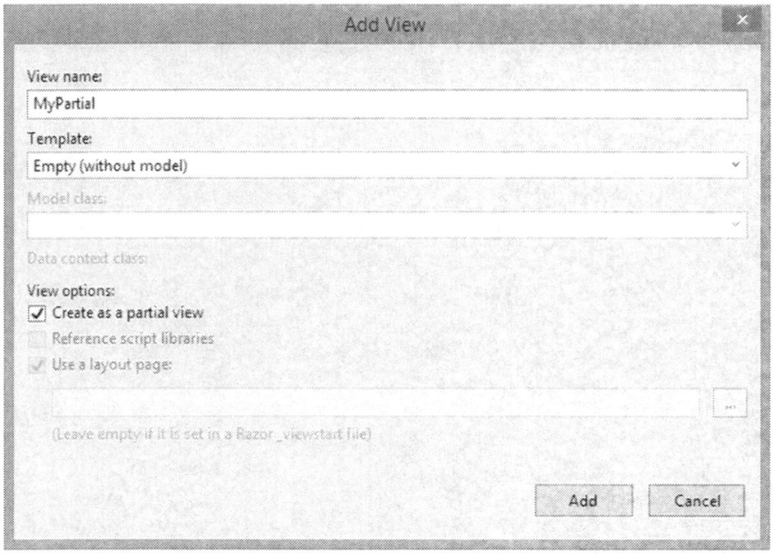

Figure 20-8. *Creating a partial view*

Click the Add button and Visual Studio will create the partial view, which is initially empty. I added the content shown in Listing 20-23.

Listing 20-23. The Content of the MyPartial.cshtml File

```
<div>
    This is the message from the partial view.
    @Html.ActionLink("This is a link to the Index action", "Index")
</div>
```

▪ **Tip** The scaffolding feature only sets the initial content for a file. What makes a view a partial is its content (it only contains a fragment of HTML, rather than a complete HTML document, and doesn't reference layouts) and the way that it is used (which I describe shortly). Once you are familiar with the different kinds of view, you can just use Add ➤ MVC 5 View Page (Razor) and set the contents you require directly.

I want to demonstrate that you can mix HTML markup and Razor tags in a partial view, so I have defined a simple message and a call to the ActionLink helper method. A partial view is consumed by calling the Html.Partial helper method from within another view. To demonstrate this, I have made the changes to the ~/Views/Common/List.cshtml view file shown in Listing 20-24.

Listing 20-24. Consuming a Partial View in the List.cshtml File

```
@{
    ViewBag.Title = "List";
    Layout = null;
}

<h3>This is the /Views/Common/List.cshtml View</h3>

@Html.Partial("MyPartial")
```

I specify the name of the partial view file without the file extension. The view engine will look for the partial view that I have specified in the usual locations, which means the /Views/Home and /Views/Shared folders for this example, since I called the Html.Partial method in a view that is being rendered for the Home controller. (I set the Layout variable to null so that I do not have to specify the sections I defined in the _Layout.cshtml file used earlier in the chapter.)

■ **Tip** The Razor View Engine looks for partial views in the same way that it looks for regular views (in the ~/Views/<controller> and ~/Views/Shared folders). This means that you can create specialized versions of partial views that are controller-specific and override partial views of the same name in the Shared folder. This may seem like an odd thing to do, but one of the most common uses of partial views is to render content in layouts, and this feature can be handy.

You can see the effect of consuming the partial view by starting the application and navigating to the /Home/List URL, as shown in Figure 20-9.

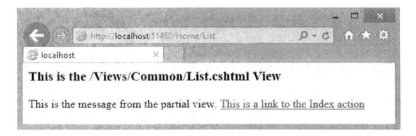

Figure 20-9. *The effect of consuming a partial view*

■ **Tip** The call I made to the ActionLink helper method in the partial view takes its controller information from the request that is being processed. That means that when I specified the Index method, the a element will refer to the Home controller, since that was the controller that led to the partial view being rendered. If I consume the partial view in a view being rendered for another controller, then the ActionLink would generate a reference to that controller instead. I come back to the topic of HTML helper methods in Chapter 21.

Using Strongly Typed Partial Views

You can create strongly typed partial views, and then pass view model objects to be used when the partial view is rendered. To demonstrate this feature, I created a new strongly typed partial view called MyStronglyTypedPartial.cshtml in the /Views/Shared folder. This time, rather than use the scaffold option, I selected Add ➤ MVC 5 View Page (Razor), set the name to MyStronglyTypedPartial and clicked the OK button to create the view. As I explained in the previous section, there is nothing about the file itself that denotes a partial view, just the content and the way it is used in the application. I removed the default content that Visual Studio adds to new view files and replaced it with the markup shown in Listing 20-25.

Listing 20-25. The Contents of the MyStronglyTypedPartial.cshtml File

```
@model IEnumerable<string>

<div>
    This is the message from the partial view.
    <ul>
        @foreach (string str in Model) {
            <li>@str</li>
        }
    </ul>
</div>
```

I use a Razor @foreach loop to display the contents of the view model object as items in an HTML list. To demonstrate the use of this partial view, I updated the /Views/Common/List.cshtml file, as shown in Listing 20-26.

Listing 20-26. Consuming a Strongly Typed Partial View in the List.cshtml File

```
@{
    ViewBag.Title = "List";
    Layout = null;
}

<h3>This is the /Views/Common/List.cshtml View</h3>

@Html.Partial("MyStronglyTypedPartial", new [] {"Apple", "Orange", "Pear"})
```

The difference from the previous example is that I pass an additional argument to the Partial helper method which defines the view model object. You can see the strongly typed partial view in use by starting the application and navigating to the /Home/List URL, as shown in Figure 20-10.

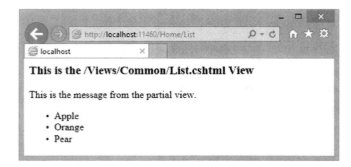

Figure 20-10. Consuming a strongly typed partial view

Using Child Actions

Child actions are action methods invoked from within a view. This lets you avoid repeating controller logic that you want to use in several places in the application. Child actions are to actions as partial views are to views. You can use a child action whenever you want to display some data-driven widget that appears on multiple pages and contains data unrelated to the main action that is running. I used this technique in the SportsStore example to include a data-driven navigation menu on every page, without needing to supply the navigation data directly from every action method. The navigation data was supplied independently by the child action.

Creating a Child Action

Any action can be used as a child action. To demonstrate the child action feature, I have added a new action method to the Home controller, as shown in Listing 20-27.

Listing 20-27. Adding a Child Action in the HomeController.cs File

```
using System;
using System.Web.Mvc;

namespace WorkingWithRazor.Controllers {
    public class HomeController : Controller {

        public ActionResult Index() {
            string[] names = { "Apple", "Orange", "Pear" };
            return View(names);
        }

        public ActionResult List() {
            return View();
        }

        [ChildActionOnly]
        public ActionResult Time() {
            return PartialView(DateTime.Now);
        }
    }
}
```

The action method is called Time and it renders a partial view by calling the PartialView method (which I described in Chapter 17). The ChildActionOnly attribute ensures that an action method can be called *only* as a child method from within a view. An action method doesn't need to have this attribute to be used as a child action, but I tend to use it to prevent the action methods from being invoked as a result of a user request.

Having defined an action method, I need to create the partial view that will be rendered when the action is invoked. Child actions are typically associated with partial views, although this is not compulsory. Listing 20-28 shows the /Views/Home/Time.cshtml view that I created for this demonstration. This is a strongly typed partial view whose view model is a DateTime object.

Listing 20-28. The Contents of the Time.cshtml File

```
@model DateTime

<p>The time is: @Model.ToShortTimeString()</p>
```

Rendering a Child Action

Child actions are invoked using the `Html.Action` helper. With this helper, the action method is executed, the `ViewResult` is processed, and the output is injected into the response to the client. Listing 20-29 shows the changes I have made to the `/Views/Common/List.cshtml` file to render the child action.

Listing 20-29. Calling a Child Action in the List.cshtml File

```
@{
    ViewBag.Title = "List";
    Layout = null;
}

<h3>This is the /Views/Common/List.cshtml View</h3>

@Html.Partial("MyStronglyTypedPartial", new [] {"Apple", "Orange", "Pear"})

@Html.Action("Time")
```

You can see the effect of the child action by starting the application and navigating to the /Home/List URL again, as shown in Figure 20-11.

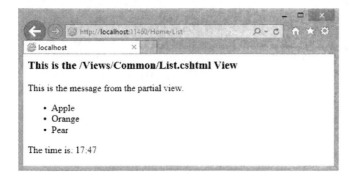

Figure 20-11. *Using a child action*

When I called the `Action` helper in Listing 20-29, I provided a single parameter that specified the name of the action method to invoke. This causes the MVC Framework to look for an action method in the controller that is handling the current request. To call action methods in other controllers, provide the controller name, like this:

```
...
@Html.Action("Time", "MyController")
...
```

You can pass parameters to action methods by providing an anonymously typed object whose properties correspond to the names of the child action method parameters. So, for example, if I have this child action:

```
...
[ChildActionOnly]
public ActionResult Time(DateTime time) {
    return PartialView(time);
}
...
```

then I can invoke it from a view as follows:

```
...
@Html.Action("Time", new { time = DateTime.Now })
...
```

Summary

In this chapter, I explored the details of the MVC view system and the Razor View Engine. You have seen how to create a custom view engine, how to customize the behavior of the default Razor engine and the different techniques available for inserting dynamic content into a view. In the next chapter, I focus on helper methods, which assist in generating content that you can insert into your views.

CHAPTER 21

■ ■ ■

Helper Methods

In this chapter, I look at the *helper methods*, which allow you to package up chunks of code and markup so that they can be reused throughout an MVC Framework application. I start by showing you how to create your own helper methods. The MVC Framework comes with a wide range of built-in helper methods, and I explore them in this chapter and the next two chapters, starting with the helper methods that you can use to create HTML form, input and select elements. Table 21-1 provides the summary for this chapter.

Table 21-1. *Chapter Summary*

Problem	Solution	Listing
Create a region of reusable markup within a view	Create an inline helper	1–4
Create markup that can be used within multiple views	Create an external helper	5–11
Generate a form element	Use the Html.BeginForm and Html.EndForm helpers	12–19
Generate a form element using a specific route	Use the Html.BeginRouteForm helper	20–21
Generate input elements	Use the input helpers	22–24
Generate input elements from model objects	Use the strongly typed input helpers	25
Generate select elements	Use the DropDownList and ListBox helpers and their strongly typed counterparts	26–27

Preparing the Example Project

For this chapter, I created a new Visual Studio MVC project called HelperMethods using the Empty template, checking the option to add the core MVC folders and references. I added a Home controller, which you can see in Listing 21-1

Listing 21-1. The Contents of the HomeController.cs File

```
using System.Web.Mvc;

namespace HelperMethods.Controllers {
    public class HomeController : Controller {

        public ActionResult Index() {

            ViewBag.Fruits = new string[] {"Apple", "Orange", "Pear"};
            ViewBag.Cities = new string[] { "New York", "London", "Paris" };
```

```
            string message = "This is an HTML element: <input>";

            return View((object)message);
        }
    }
}
```

In the Index action method, I pass a pair of `string` arrays to the view via the view bag and set the model object to be a `string`. I added a view called `Index.cshtml` to the `Views/Home` folder. You can see the contents of the view file in Listing 21-2. This is a strongly typed view (where the model type is `string`) and I have not used a layout.

Listing 21-2. The Contents of the Index.cshtml File

```
@model string

@{
    Layout = null;
}

<!DOCTYPE html>
<html>
<head>
    <meta name="viewport" content="width=device-width" />
    <title>Index</title>
</head>
<body>
    <div>
        Here are the fruits:
        @foreach (string str in (string[])ViewBag.Fruits) {
            <b>@str </b>
        }
    </div>
    <div>
        Here are the cities:
        @foreach (string str in (string[])ViewBag.Cities) {
            <b>@str </b>
        }
    </div>
    <div>
        Here is the message:
        <p>@Model</p>
    </div>
</body>
</html>
```

Setting the Start URL

I want Visual Studio to start with the root URL for the application rather than guess the URL based on the file that is being edited. Select `HelperMethods Properties` from the Visual Studio `Project` menu, switch to the `Web` tab and check the `Specific Page` option in the `Start Action` section. You don't have to provide a value. Just checking the option is enough.

Testing the Example Application

You can see how the view is rendered by starting the application. The default routing configuration added to the project by Visual Studio will map the root URL requested automatically by the browser to the Index action on the Home controller, as shown in Figure 21-1.

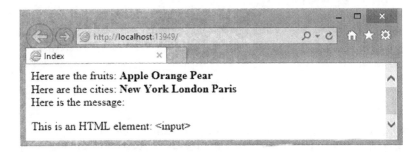

Figure 21-1. *Running the example application*

Creating Custom Helper Methods

I am going to follow the pattern I have established over the last few chapters and introduce you to helper methods by creating my own custom implementation. In the sections that follow, I will show you two different techniques for creating custom helper methods.

Creating an Inline Helper Method

The simplest kind of helper method is an *inline helper*, which is defined within a view. I can create an inline helper to simplify the example view using the @helper tag, as shown in Listing 21-3.

Listing 21-3. Creating an Inline Helper Method in the Index.cshtml File

```
@model string

@{
    Layout = null;
}

@helper ListArrayItems(string[] items) {
    foreach(string str in items) {
        <b>@str </b>
    }
}

<!DOCTYPE html>
<html>
<head>
    <meta name="viewport" content="width=device-width" />
    <title>Index</title>
</head>
```

```
<body>
    <div>
        Here are the fruits: @ListArrayItems(ViewBag.Fruits)
    </div>
    <div>
        Here are the cities: @ListArrayItems(ViewBag.Cities)
    </div>
    <div>
        Here is the message:
        <p>@Model</p>
    </div>
</body>
</html>
```

Inline helpers have names and parameters similar to regular C# methods. In the example, I defined a helper called ListArrayItems, which takes a string array as a parameter. Although an inline helper looks like a method, there is no return value. The contents of the helper body are processed and put into the response to the client.

■ **Tip**   Notice that I did not have to cast the dynamic properties from the ViewBag to string arrays when using the inline helper. One of the nice features of this kind of helper method is that it is happy to evaluate types at runtime.

The body of an inline helper follows the same syntax as the rest of a Razor view. Literal strings are regarded as static HTML, and statements that require processing by Razor are prefixed with the @ character. The helper in the example mixes static HTML and Razor tags to enumerate the items in the array, which produces the same output as the original view but has reduced the amount of duplication in the view.

The benefit of this approach is that I only have to make one change if I want to change the way that the array contents are displayed. As a simple example, in Listing 21-4 you can see how I have switched from just writing out the values to using the HTML unnumbered list elements.

Listing 21-4. Changing the Contents of a Helper Method in the Index.cshtml File

```
...
@helper ListArrayItems(string[] items) {
    <ul>
        @foreach(string str in items) {
            <li>@str</li>
        }
    </ul>
}
...
```

I only had to make the change in one place, which may seem like a trivial advantage in such a simple project, but this can be a useful way to keep your views simple and consistent in a real project. You can see the result of this change in Figure 21-2.

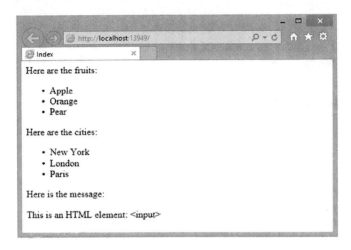

Figure 21-2. *Changing the markup in a helper method*

■ **Tip**   Notice that I had to prefix the foreach keyword with @ in this example but not in Listing 21-4. This is because the first element in the helper body changed to become an HTML element, which means I have to use @ to tell Razor that I am using a C# statement. In the previous example there was no HTML element, so Razor assumed the contents were code. It can be hard to keep track of these quirks, but the Visual Studio will flag up errors like this for you.

Creating an External Helper Method

Inline helpers are convenient, but they can be used only from the view in which they are declared and, if they are too complex, they can take over that view and make it hard to read.

The alternative is to create an external HTML helper method, which is expressed as a C# extension method. External helper methods can be used more widely, but are a little more awkward to write, because C# doesn't naturally handle HTML element generation elegantly. To demonstrate this feature, I added an Infrastructure folder to the example project and created a new CustomHelpers.cs class file within it. You can see the contents of this file in Listing 21-5.

Listing 21-5. The Contents of the CustomHelpers.cs File

```
using System.Web.Mvc;

namespace HelperMethods.Infrastructure {
    public static class CustomHelpers {

        public static MvcHtmlString ListArrayItems(this HtmlHelper html, string[] list) {

            TagBuilder tag = new TagBuilder("ul");
```

```
        foreach(string str in list) {
            TagBuilder itemTag = new TagBuilder("li");
            itemTag.SetInnerText(str);
            tag.InnerHtml += itemTag.ToString();
        }

        return new MvcHtmlString(tag.ToString());
    }
}
}
```

The helper method I created performs the same function as the inline helper in the previous example. It takes an array of strings and generates an HTML ul element, containing a li element for each string in the array.

The first parameter to the helper method is an HtmlHelper object, prefixed with the this keyword to tell the C# compiler that I am defining an extension method. The HtmlHelper provides access to information that can be useful when creating content, through the properties described in Table 21-2.

Table 21-2. *Useful Properties Defined by the HtmlHelper Class*

Property	Description
RouteCollection	Returns the set of routes defined by the application
ViewBag	Returns the view bag data passed from the action method to the view that has called the helper method
ViewContext	Returns a ViewContext object, which provides access to details of the request and how it has been handled (and which I describe below)

The ViewContext property is the most useful when you want to create content which adapts to the request being processed. In Table 21-3, I have described some of the most commonly used properties defined by the ViewContext class.

Table 21-3. *Useful Properties Defined by the ViewContext Class*

Property	Description
Controller	Returns the controller processing the current request
HttpContext	Returns the HttpContext object that describes the current request
IsChildAction	Returns true if the view that has called the helper is being rendered by a child action (see Chapter 20 for details of child actions)
RouteData	Returns the routing data for the request
View	Returns the instance of the IView implementation that has called the helper method

The information you can get about the request is fairly comprehensive, but for the most part helper methods are simple and used to keep formatting consistent. You can use the built-in helper methods for generating requests-specific content (I describe these helpers later in the chapter) and you can use partial views or child actions for more complex tasks (I provide guidance about which approach to use in next section of this chapter).

I do not need any information about the request in the example helper, but I do need to construct some HTML elements. The easiest way to create HTML in a helper method is to use the TagBuilder class, which allows you to build up HTML strings without needing to deal with all of the escaping and special characters. The TagBuilder class is part of the System.Web.WebPages.Mvc assembly but uses a feature called *type forwarding* to appear as though it is part of the System.Web.Mvc assembly. Both assemblies are added to MVC projects by Visual Studio, so you can use the TagBuilder class easily enough, but it does not appear in the Microsoft Developer Network (MSDN) API documentation.

I create a new TagBuilder instance, passing in name the HTML element I want to construct as the constructor parameter. I do not need to use the angle brackets (< and >) with the TagBuilder class, which means I can create a ul element, like this:

```
...
TagBuilder tag = new TagBuilder("ul");
...
```

The most useful members of the TagBuilder class are described in Table 21-4.

Table 21-4. Some Members of the TagBuilder Class

Member	Description
InnerHtml	A property that lets you set the contents of the element as an HTML string. The value assigned to this property will not be encoded, which means that is can be used to nest HTML elements.
SetInnerText(string)	Sets the text contents of the HTML element. The string parameter is encoded to make it safe to display.
AddCssClass(string)	Adds a CSS class to the HTML element
MergeAttribute(string, string, bool)	Adds an attribute to the HTML element. The first parameter is the name of the attribute, and the second is the value. The bool parameter specifies if an existing attribute of the same name should be replaced.

The result of an HTML helper method is an MvcHtmlString object, the contents of which are written directly into the response to the client. For the example helper, I pass the result of the TagBuilder.ToString method to the constructor of a new MvcHtmlString object, like this:

```
...
return new MvcHtmlString(tag.ToString());
...
```

This statement generates the HTML fragment that contains the ul and li elements and returns them to the view engine so that it can be inserted into the response.

Using a Custom External Helper Method

Using a custom external helper method is a little different to using an inline one. In Listing 21-6, you can see the changes I have made to the /Views/Home/Index.cshtml file to replace the inline helper with the external one.

Listing 21-6. Using a Custom External Helper Method in the Index.cshtml File

```
@model string
@using HelperMethods.Infrastructure

@{
    Layout = null;
}

<!DOCTYPE html>
<html>
<head>
    <meta name="viewport" content="width=device-width" />
    <title>Index</title>
</head>
<body>
    <div>
        Here are the fruits: @Html.ListArrayItems((string[])ViewBag.Fruits)
    </div>
    <div>
        Here are the cities: @Html.ListArrayItems((string[])ViewBag.Cities)
    </div>
    <div>
        Here is the message:
        <p>@Model</p>
    </div>
</body>
</html>
```

I need to ensure that the namespace that contains the helper extension method is in scope. I have done this using an @using tag, but if you are developing a lot of custom helpers then you will want to add the namespaces that contain them to the /Views/Web.config file so that they are always available in your views.

I refer to the helper using @Html.<helper>, where <helper> is the name of the extension method. In this case, I use @Html.ListArrayItems. The Html part of this expression refers to a property defined by the view base class, which returns an HtmlHelper object, which is the type to which I applied the extension method in Listing 21-5.

I pass data to the helper method as I would for an inline helper or a C# method, although I must take care to cast from the dynamic properties of the ViewBag object to the type defined by the external helper (in this case a string array). This syntax is not as elegant as using inline helpers, but it is part of the price that you must pay to create a helper that can be used in any view in your project.

KNOWING WHEN TO USE HELPER METHODS

Now that you have seen how helper methods work, you might be wondering when you should use them in preference to partial views or child actions, especially as there is overlap between what these features are capable of.

I only use helper methods to reduce the amount of duplication in views, just as I did in this example, and only for the simplest of content. For more complex markup and content I use partial views and I use a child action when I need to perform any manipulation of model data. I recommend that you follow the same approach and keep your use of helper methods as simple as possible. (If my helpers contain more than a handful of C# statements—or more C# statements that HTML elements—then I tend to switch to a child action.)

Managing String Encoding in a Helper Method

The MVC Framework makes an effort to protect you from malicious data by automatically encoding it so that it can be added to an HTML page safely. You can see an example of this in the Home controller in the example application where I pass a potentially troublesome string to the view as the model object, as shown in Listing 21-7.

Listing 21-7. The Contents of the HomeController.cs File

```
using System.Web.Mvc;

namespace HelperMethods.Controllers {
    public class HomeController : Controller {

        public ActionResult Index() {

            ViewBag.Fruits = new string[] { "Apple", "Orange", "Pear" };
            ViewBag.Cities = new string[] { "New York", "London", "Paris" };

            string message = "This is an HTML element: <input>";

            return View((object)message);
        }
    }
}
```

The model object contains a valid HTML element, but when the value is rendered by Razor, the following HTML is produced:

```
...
<div>
    Here is the message:
    <p>This is an HTML element: &lt;input&gt;</p>
</div>
...
```

This is a basic security precaution that prevents data values from being interpreted as valid markup by the browser. This is the foundation for a common form of attack in which malicious users will try to subvert the behavior of an application by trying to add their own HTML markup or JavaScript code. Razor encodes data values automatically when they are used in a view, but helper methods need to be able to generate HTML. As a consequence, they are given a higher level of trust by the view engine, and this can require some careful attention.

Demonstrating the Problem

To demonstrate the problem, I have created a new helper method in the CustomHelpers class, as shown in Listing 21-8. This helper takes a string as a parameter and generates the same HTML that I included in the Index view.

Listing 21-8. Defining a New Helper Method in the CustomHelpers.cs File

```
using System;
using System.Web.Mvc;

namespace HelperMethods.Infrastructure {
    public static class CustomHelpers {
```

```
        public static MvcHtmlString ListArrayItems(this HtmlHelper html, string[] list) {

            TagBuilder tag = new TagBuilder("ul");

            foreach(string str in list) {
                TagBuilder itemTag = new TagBuilder("li");
                itemTag.SetInnerText(str);
                tag.InnerHtml += itemTag.ToString();
            }

            return new MvcHtmlString(tag.ToString());
        }

        public static MvcHtmlString DisplayMessage(this HtmlHelper html, string msg) {
            string result = String.Format("This is the message: <p>{0}</p>", msg);
            return new MvcHtmlString(result);
        }
    }
}
```

I use the `String.Format` method to generate the HTML markup and pass the result as the argument to the `MvcHtmlString` constructor. In Listing 21-9, you can see how I have changed the `/View/Home/Index.cshtml` view to use the new helper method. (I also made some changes to emphasize the content that comes from the helper method.)

Listing 21-9. Using the DisplayMessage Helper Method in the Index.cshtml File

```
@model string
@using HelperMethods.Infrastructure

@{
    Layout = null;
}

<!DOCTYPE html>
<html>
<head>
    <meta name="viewport" content="width=device-width" />
    <title>Index</title>
</head>
<body>
    <p>This is the content from the view:</p>
    <div style="border: thin solid black; padding: 10px">
        Here is the message:
        <p>@Model</p>
    </div>

    <p>This is the content from the helper method:</p>
    <div style="border: thin solid black; padding: 10px">
        @Html.DisplayMessage(Model)
    </div>
</body>
</html>
```

You can see the effect the new helper method has by starting the application, as shown in Figure 21-3.

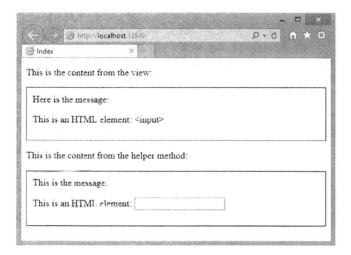

Figure 21-3. *Comparing how data values are encoded*

The helper method is trusted to generate safe content, which is unfortunate because it leads to the browser displaying an input element, which is the kind of behavior that can be exploited to subvert an application.

Encoding Helper Method Content

There are a couple of different ways to solve this problem and the choice between them depends on the nature of the content that your helper method produces. The simplest solution is to change the return type of the helper method to string, as shown in Listing 21-10. This alerts the view engine that your content is not safe and should be encoded before it is added to the view.

Listing 21-10. Ensuring that Razor Encodes Content in the CustomHelpers.cs File

```
using System.Web.Mvc;
using System;

namespace HelperMethods.Infrastructure {
    public static class CustomHelpers {

        public static MvcHtmlString ListArrayItems(this HtmlHelper html, string[] list) {

            TagBuilder tag = new TagBuilder("ul");

            foreach(string str in list) {
                TagBuilder itemTag = new TagBuilder("li");
                itemTag.SetInnerText(str);
                tag.InnerHtml += itemTag.ToString();
            }
```

```
            return new MvcHtmlString(tag.ToString());
        }

        public static string DisplayMessage(this HtmlHelper html, string msg) {
            return String.Format("This is the message: <p>{0}</p>", msg);
        }
    }
}
```

This technique causes Razor to encode all of the content that is returned by the helper, which is a problem when you are generating HTML elements (as I am in the example helper), but which is convenient otherwise. You can see the effect in Figure 21-4.

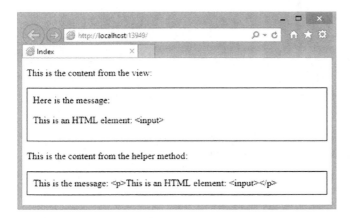

Figure 21-4. *Ensuring that the view engine encodes the response from a helper method*

I have solved the problem with the input element, but my p elements have been encoded as well, which is not what I need. In these situations, I need to be more selective and encode just the data values, as shown in Listing 21-11.

Listing 21-11. Selectively Encoding Data Values in the CustomHelpers.cs File

```
...
public static MvcHtmlString DisplayMessage(this HtmlHelper html, string msg) {
    string encodedMessage = html.Encode(msg);
    string result = String.Format("This is the message: <p>{0}</p>", encodedMessage);
    return new MvcHtmlString(result);
}
...
```

The HtmlHelper class defines an instance method called Encode, which solves the problem and encodes a string value so that it can be safely included in a view. The problem with this technique is that you have to remember to use it. I explicitly encode all of the data values at the start of the method as a reminder and I suggest that you adopt a similar approach.

You can see the result of this change in Figure 21-5, where you will see that the content generated by the external helper method matches that generated by using the model value directly in the view.

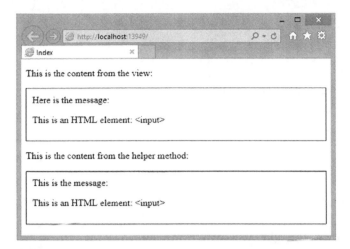

Figure 21-5. *The effect of selectively encoding content in an external helper method*

Using the Built-In Form Helper Methods

The MVC Framework includes a selection of built-in helper methods that help you manage the creating of HTML form elements. In the following sections, I will put these helpers in context and show you how they are used.

Creating Form Elements

One of the most common forms of interaction in a web application is the HTML form, which is the subject of a number of different helper methods. To demonstrate the form-related helpers, I made some additions to the example project. I started by creating a new class file called Person.cs in the Models folder. You can see the contents of this file in Listing 21-12. The Person type will be the view model class when I demonstrate the form-related helpers, and the Address and Role types will help me showcase some more advanced features.

Listing 21-12. The Contents of the Person.cs Model

```
using System;

namespace HelperMethods.Models {

    public class Person {
        public int PersonId { get; set; }
        public string FirstName { get; set; }
        public string LastName { get; set; }
        public DateTime BirthDate { get; set; }
        public Address HomeAddress { get; set; }
        public bool IsApproved { get; set; }
        public Role Role { get; set; }
    }
```

```
    public class Address {
        public string Line1 { get; set; }
        public string Line2 { get; set; }
        public string City { get; set; }
        public string PostalCode { get; set; }
        public string Country { get; set; }
    }

    public enum Role {
        Admin,
        User,
        Guest
    }
}
```

I also added new action methods to the Home controller to use the model objects, as shown in Listing 21-13.

Listing 21-13. Adding Action Methods in the HomeController.cs File

```
using System.Web.Mvc;
using HelperMethods.Models;

namespace HelperMethods.Controllers {
    public class HomeController : Controller {

        public ActionResult Index() {

            ViewBag.Fruits = new string[] { "Apple", "Orange", "Pear" };
            ViewBag.Cities = new string[] { "New York", "London", "Paris" };

            string message = "This is an HTML element: <input>";

            return View((object)message);
        }

        public ActionResult CreatePerson() {
            return View(new Person());
        }

        [HttpPost]
        public ActionResult CreatePerson(Person person) {
            return View(person);
        }
    }
}
```

This is the standard two-method approach to dealing with HTML forms, where I rely on model binding so that the MVC Framework will create a Person object from the form data and pass it to the action method with the HttpPost attribute. (I explained the HttpPost attribute in Chapter 19 and model binding is the topic of Chapter 24).

I am not processing the form data in any way because I am focused on how to generate elements in the view. The HttpPost action method just calls the View method and passes the Person object that it received as a parameter, which has the effect of redisplaying the form data to the user.

I am going to start with a standard manual HTML form and show you how to replace different parts of it using helper methods. You can see the initial version of the form in Listing 21-14, which shows the CreatePerson.cshtml view file that I added to the /Views/Home folder.

Listing 21-14. The Contents of the CreatePerson.cshtml File

```
@model HelperMethods.Models.Person

@{
    ViewBag.Title = "CreatePerson";
    Layout = "/Views/Shared/_Layout.cshtml";
}

<h2>CreatePerson</h2>

<form action="/Home/CreatePerson" method="post">
    <div class="dataElem">
        <label>PersonId</label>
        <input name="personId" value="@Model.PersonId"/>
    </div>
    <div class="dataElem">
        <label>First Name</label>
        <input name="FirstName" value="@Model.FirstName"/>
    </div>
    <div class="dataElem">
        <label>Last Name</label>
        <input name="lastName" value="@Model.LastName"/>
    </div>
    <input type="submit" value="Submit" />
</form>
```

This view contains a standard manually created form in which I have set the value of the value attribute of the input elements using the model object.

■ **Tip** Notice that I have set the name attribute on all of the input elements so that it corresponds to the model property that the input element displays. The name attribute is used by the MVC Framework default model binder to work out which input elements contain values for the model type properties when processing a post request. If you omit the name attribute, your form will not work properly. I describe model binding fully in Chapter 24, including how you can change this behavior.

I have created the Views/Shared folder and added a layout file called _Layout.cshtml with the contents shown in Listing 21-15. This is a simple layout with some CSS for the input elements in the form.

Listing 21-15. The Contents of the _Layout.cshtml File

```html
<!DOCTYPE html>
<html>
<head>
    <meta charset="utf-8" />
    <meta name="viewport" content="width=device-width" />
    <title>@ViewBag.Title</title>
    <style type="text/css">
        label { display: inline-block; width: 100px; }
        div.dataElem { margin: 5px; }
    </style>
</head>
<body>
    @RenderBody()
</body>
</html>
```

You can see the basic form functionality by starting the application and navigating to the /Home/CreatePerson URL, as shown in Figure 21-6. Because the form data is not used by the application in any way, clicking the Submit button will just cause whatever data is in the form to be redisplayed.

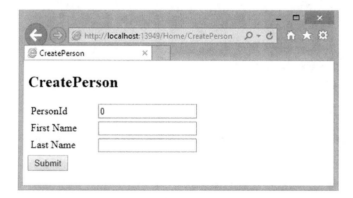

Figure 21-6. *Using the simple HTML form in the example application*

In Listing 21-16, you can see the HTML that the example MVC application has sent to the browser. I will use this to show you changes caused by helper methods.

Listing 21-16. The HTML Sent to the Browser for the Example Form

```html
<!DOCTYPE html>
<html>
<head>
    <meta charset="utf-8" />
    <meta name="viewport" content="width=device-width" />
    <title>CreatePerson</title>
```

```
    <style type="text/css">
        label { display: inline-block; width: 100px; }
        div.dataElem { margin: 5px; }
    </style>
</head>
<body>

<h2>CreatePerson</h2>

<form action="/Home/CreatePerson" method="post">
    <div class="dataElem">
        <label>PersonId</label>
        <input name="personId" value="0" />
    </div>
    <div class="dataElem">
        <label>First Name</label>
        <input name="FirstName" />
    </div>
    <div class="dataElem">
        <label>Last Name</label>
        <input name="lastName" />
    </div>
    <input type="submit" value="Submit" />
</form>
</body>
</html>
```

■ **Note**   Using the helper methods to generate HTML elements like form and input is not compulsory. If you prefer, you can code them using static HTML tags and populate values using view data or view model objects, just as I did in this section. The HTML that I generate from the helper methods in the following sections is clean and there are no special attribute values or sneaky tricks that mean you have to use them. But they make it easy to ensure that the HTML is in sync with the application so that, for example, changes in routing configuration will be reflected automatically in your forms. The helpers are there for convenience, rather than because they create essential or special HTML, and you do not have to use them if they do not suit your development style.

Creating Form Elements

Two of the most useful (and most commonly used) helpers are Html.BeginForm and Html.EndForm. These helpers create HTML form tags and generate a valid action attribute for the form that is based on the routing mechanism for the application.

There are 13 different versions of the BeginForm method, allowing you to be increasingly specific about how the resulting form element will be generated. I only need the most basic for the example application, which takes no arguments and creates a form element whose action attribute ensures that the form will be posted back to the same action method which led to the current view being generated. You can see how I have applied this overload of BeginForm and the EndForm helper in Listing 21-17. The EndForm helper has only one definition and it just closes the form element by adding </form> to the view.

Listing 21-17. Using the BeginForm and EndForm Helper Methods in the CreatePerson.cshtml File

```
@model HelperMethods.Models.Person

@{
    ViewBag.Title = "CreatePerson";
    Layout = "/Views/Shared/_Layout.cshtml";
}
<h2>CreatePerson</h2>

@{Html.BeginForm();}
    <div class="dataElem">
        <label>PersonId</label>
        <input name="personId" value="@Model.PersonId"/>
    </div>
    <div class="dataElem">
        <label>First Name</label>
        <input name="FirstName" value="@Model.FirstName"/>
    </div>
    <div class="dataElem">
        <label>Last Name</label>
        <input name="lastName" value="@Model.LastName"/>
    </div>
    <input type="submit" value="Submit" />
@{Html.EndForm();}
```

Notice that I had to treat the call to the helper methods as a C# statements. This is because of the way that the helper methods write their tags to the output. It is a pretty ugly result, but it doesn't matter because these helpers are rarely used in this way. A much more common approach is shown in Listing 21-18, which wraps the call to the BeginForm helper method in a using expression. At the end of the using block, the .NET runtime calls the Dispose method on the object returned by the BeginForm method, which calls the EndForm method for you. (You can see how this works by downloading the source code for the MVC Framework and taking a look at the System.Web.Mvc.Html.FormExtensions class.)

Listing 21-18. Creating a Self-Closing Form in the CreatePerson.cshtml File

```
@model HelperMethods.Models.Person

@{
    ViewBag.Title = "CreatePerson";
    Layout = "/Views/Shared/_Layout.cshtml";
}
<h2>CreatePerson</h2>

@using(Html.BeginForm()) {
    <div class="dataElem">
        <label>PersonId</label>
        <input name="personId" value="@Model.PersonId"/>
    </div>
    <div class="dataElem">
        <label>First Name</label>
        <input name="FirstName" value="@Model.FirstName"/>
    </div>
```

```
    <div class="dataElem">
        <label>Last Name</label>
        <input name="lastName" value="@Model.LastName"/>
    </div>
    <input type="submit" value="Submit" />
}
```

This approach, known as a self-closing form, is the one I use in my own projects. I like the way that the code block contains the form and makes it clear which elements will appear between the opening and closing form tags.

The other 12 variations for the BeginForm method allow you to change different aspects of the form element that is created. There is a lot of repetition in these overloads, as they allow you to be incrementally more specific about the details you provide. In Table 21-5 I have listed the most important overloads, which are the ones that you will use on a regular basis in an MVC application. The other overloads of the BeginForm method—which I have omitted—are provided for compatibility with the versions of the MVC Framework that were released before C# had support for creating dynamic objects.

Table 21-5. *The Overloads of the BeginForm Helper Method*

Overload	Description
BeginForm()	Creates a form which posts back to the action method it originated from
BeginForm(**action**, **controller**)	Creates a form which posts back to the action method and controller, specified as strings
BeginForm(action, controller, **method**)	As for the previous overload, but allows you to specify the value for the method attribute using a value from the System.Web.Mvc.FormMethod enumeration
BeginForm(action, controller, method, **attributes**)	As for the previous overload, but allows you to specify attributes for the form element an object whose properties are used as the attribute names
BeginForm(action, controller, **routeValues**, method, attributes)	As for the previous overload, but allows you to specify values for the variable route segments in your application routing configuration as an object whose properties correspond to the routing variables

I have shown you the simplest version of the BeginForm method, which is all I need for the example app, but in Listing 21-19 you can see the most complex, in which I specify additional information for how the form element should be constructed.

Listing 21-19. Using the Most Complex Overload of the BeginForm Method in the CreatePerson.cs File

```
@model HelperMethods.Models.Person

@{
    ViewBag.Title = "CreatePerson";
    Layout = "/Views/Shared/_Layout.cshtml";
}
<h2>CreatePerson</h2>

@using (Html.BeginForm("CreatePerson", "Home",
    new { id = "MyIdValue" }, FormMethod.Post,
    new { @class = "personClass", data_formType="person"})) {
```

```
    <div class="dataElem">
        <label>PersonId</label>
        <input name="personId" value="@Model.PersonId"/>
    </div>
    <div class="dataElem">
        <label>First Name</label>
        <input name="FirstName" value="@Model.FirstName"/>
    </div>
    <div class="dataElem">
        <label>Last Name</label>
        <input name="lastName" value="@Model.LastName"/>
    </div>
    <input type="submit" value="Submit" />
}
```

In this example, I have explicitly specified some details that would have been inferred automatically by the MVC Framework, such as the action name and the controller. I also specified that the form should be submitted using the HTTP POST method, which would have been used anyway.

The more interesting arguments are the ones that set values for the route variable and set attributes on the form element. I route values arguments to specify a value for the `id` segment variable in the default route added by Visual Studio to the `/App_Start/RouteConfig.cs` file when the project was created and I defined `class` and `data` attributes. (Data attributes are custom attributes which you can add to elements to make processing HTML content.) Here is the HTML `form` tag that this call to `BeginForm` produces:

```
...
<form action="/Home/CreatePerson/MyIdValue" class="personClass" data-formType="person"
    method="post">
...
```

You can see that the value for the `id` attribute has been appended to the target URL and that the class and data attributes have been applied to the element. Notice that I specified an attribute called `data_formType` in the call to `BeginForm` but ended up with a `data-formType` attribute in the output. You cannot specify property names in a dynamic object that contain hyphens, so I use an underscore that is then automatically mapped to a hyphen in the output, neatly side-stepping a mismatch between the C# and HTML syntaxes. (And, of course, I had to prefix the property name `class` with a @ so that I can use a C#-reserved keyword as a property name for the `class` attribute.)

Specifying the Route Used by a Form

When you use the `BeginForm` method, the MVC Framework finds the first route in the routing configuration that can be used to generate a URL that will target the required action and controller. In essence, you leave the route selection to be figured out for you. If you want to ensure that a particular route is used, then you can use the `BeginRouteForm` helper method instead. To demonstrate this feature, I have added a new route to the `/App_Start/RouteConfig.cs` file, as shown in Listing 21-20.

Listing 21-20. Adding a New Route to the RouteConfig.cs File

```
using System;
using System.Collections.Generic;
using System.Linq;
using System.Web;
using System.Web.Mvc;
using System.Web.Routing;
```

```
namespace HelperMethods {
    public class RouteConfig {
        public static void RegisterRoutes(RouteCollection routes) {
            routes.IgnoreRoute("{resource}.axd/{*pathInfo}");

            routes.MapRoute(
                name: "Default",
                url: "{controller}/{action}/{id}",
                defaults: new { controller = "Home", action = "Index",
                    id = UrlParameter.Optional }
            );

            routes.MapRoute(
                name: "FormRoute",
                url: "app/forms/{controller}/{action}"
            );
        }
    }
}
```

If I call the BeginForm method with this routing configuration, I will end up with a form element whose action attribute contains a URL which is created from the default route. In Listing 21-21, you can see how I have specified that the new route should be used through the BeginRouteForm method.

Listing 21-21. Specifying Which Route Should Be Used in the CreatePerson.cshtml File

```
@model HelperMethods.Models.Person

@{
    ViewBag.Title = "CreatePerson";
    Layout = "/Views/Shared/_Layout.cshtml";
}
<h2>CreatePerson</h2>

@using(Html.BeginRouteForm("FormRoute", new {}, FormMethod.Post,
    new { @class = "personClass", data_formType="person"})) {

    <div class="dataElem">
        <label>PersonId</label>
        <input name="personId" value="@Model.PersonId"/>
    </div>
    <div class="dataElem">
        <label>First Name</label>
        <input name="FirstName" value="@Model.FirstName"/>
    </div>
    <div class="dataElem">
        <label>Last Name</label>
        <input name="lastName" value="@Model.LastName"/>
    </div>
    <input type="submit" value="Submit" />
}
```

This produces the following form tag, whose action attribute corresponds to the structure of the new route:

```
...
<form action="/app/forms/Home/CreatePerson" class="personClass"
    data-formType="person" method="post">
...
```

■ Tip There are a range of different overloads for the BeginRouteForm method allowing you to specify differing degrees of details for the form element, just as with the BeginForm method. These follow the same structure as their BeginForm counterparts. See the API documentation for details.

Using Input Helpers

An HTML form is of no use unless you also create some input elements. Table 21-6 shows the basic helper methods that are available to create input elements and gives examples of the HTML they produce. For all of these helper methods, the first argument is used to set the value of the id and name attributes for the input element and the second argument is used to set the value attribute.

Table 21-6. *Basic Input HTML Helpers*

HTML Element	Example
Check box	Html.CheckBox("myCheckbox", false)

	Output:
	`<input id="myCheckbox" name="myCheckbox" type="checkbox" value="true" />`
	`<input name="myCheckbox" type="hidden" value="false" />`

Hidden field	Html.Hidden("myHidden", "val")
	Output: `<input id="myHidden" name="myHidden" type="hidden" value="val" />`
Radio button	Html.RadioButton("myRadiobutton", "val", true)

	Output:
	`<input checked="checked" id="myRadiobutton" name="myRadiobutton"`
	`type="radio" value="val" />`

Password	Html.Password("myPassword", "val")
	Output: `<input id="myPassword" name="myPassword" type="password" value="val" />`
Text area	Html.TextArea("myTextarea", "val", 5, 20, null)

	Output:
	`<textarea cols="20" id="myTextarea" name="myTextarea" rows="5">`
	`val</textarea>`

Text box	Html.TextBox("myTextbox", "val")
	Output: `<input id="myTextbox" name="myTextbox" type="text" value="val" />`

Each of these helpers is overloaded. The table shows the simplest version, but you can provide an additional object argument that you use to specify HTML attributes, just as I did with the form element in the previous section.

■ **Note**   Notice that the checkbox helper (Html.CheckBox) renders *two* input elements. It renders a checkbox and then a hidden input element of the same name. This is because browsers do not submit a value for checkboxes when they are not selected. Having the hidden control ensures that the MVC Framework will get a value from the hidden field when this happens.

You can see how I have used these basic input helper methods in Listing 21-22.

Listing 21-22. Using the Basic Input Element Helper Methods in the CreatePerson.cshtml File

```
@model HelperMethods.Models.Person

@{
    ViewBag.Title = "CreatePerson";
    Layout = "/Views/Shared/_Layout.cshtml";
}
<h2>CreatePerson</h2>

@using(Html.BeginRouteForm("FormRoute", new {}, FormMethod.Post,
    new { @class = "personClass", data_formType="person"})) {

    <div class="dataElem">
        <label>PersonId</label>
        @Html.TextBox("personId", @Model.PersonId)
    </div>
    <div class="dataElem">
        <label>First Name</label>
        @Html.TextBox("firstName", @Model.FirstName)
    </div>
    <div class="dataElem">
        <label>Last Name</label>
        @Html.TextBox("lastName", @Model.LastName)
    </div>
    <input type="submit" value="Submit" />
}
```

You can see the HTML input elements that this view produces in Listing 21-23. The output is similar to the original form element, but you can see some hints of the MVC Framework have appeared in the form of some data attributes which have been added to support form validation, which I describe in Chapter 25.

Listing 21-23. The Input Elements Created by the Basic Input Helper Methods

```
...
<form action="/app/forms/Home/CreatePerson" class="personClass" data-formType="person"
        method="post">
    <div class="dataElem">
        <label>PersonId</label>
        <input data-val="true" data-val-number="The field PersonId must be a number."
            data-val-required="The PersonId field is required." id="personId"
            name="personId" type="text" value="0" />
    </div>
    <div class="dataElem">
        <label>First Name</label>
        <input id="firstName" name="firstName" type="text" value="" />
    </div>
    <div class="dataElem">
        <label>Last Name</label>
        <input id="lastName" name="lastName" type="text" value="" />
    </div>
    <input type="submit" value="Submit" />
</form>
...
```

Generating the Input Element from a Model Property

The helper methods I used in the previous section are fine, but I still have to ensure that the value I pass as the first argument corresponds to the model value I pass as the second argument. If they are not consistent, then the MVC Framework will not be able to reconstruct the model object from the form data because the name attributes and the forms values of the input elements will not match. For each of the methods I listed in Table 21-6, there is an alternative overload which takes a single string argument, which I have used in Listing 21-24.

Listing 21-24. Generating the Input Element from the Model Property Name in the CreatePerson.cshtml File

```
@model HelperMethods.Models.Person

@{
    ViewBag.Title = "CreatePerson";
    Layout = "/Views/Shared/_Layout.cshtml";
}
<h2>CreatePerson</h2>

@using(Html.BeginRouteForm("FormRoute", new {}, FormMethod.Post,
    new { @class = "personClass", data_formType="person"})) {

    <div class="dataElem">
        <label>PersonId</label>
        @Html.TextBox("PersonId")
    </div>
```

```
<div class="dataElem">
    <label>First Name</label>
    @Html.TextBox("firstName")
</div>
<div class="dataElem">
    <label>Last Name</label>
    @Html.TextBox("lastName")
</div>
<input type="submit" value="Submit" />
}
```

The string argument is used to search the view data, ViewBag, and view model to find a corresponding data item that can be used as the basis for the input element. So, for example, if you call @Html.TextBox("DataValue"), the MVC Framework tries to find some item of data that corresponds with the key DataValue. The following locations are checked:

- ViewBag.DataValue

- @Model.DataValue

The first value that is found is used to set the value attribute of the generated HTML. (The last check, for @Model.DataValue, works only if the view model for the view contains a property or field called DataValue.)

If I specify a string like DataValue.First.Name, the search becomes more complicated. The MVC Framework will try different arrangements of the dot-separated elements, such as the following:

- ViewBag.DataValue.First.Name

- ViewBag.DataValue["First"].Name

- ViewBag.DataValue["First.Name"]

- ViewBag.DataValue["First"]["Name"]

Many permutations will be checked. Once again, the first value that is found will be used, terminating the search. There is an obvious performance consideration to this technique, but bear in mind that usually only a few items are in the view bag, so it does not take much time to search through them.

Using Strongly Typed Input Helpers

For each of the basic input helpers that I described in Table 21-6, there are corresponding *strongly typed* helpers. You can see these helpers in Table 21-7 along with samples of the HTML they produce. These helpers can be used only with strongly typed views. (Some of these helpers generate attributes that help with client-side form validation. I have omitted these from the table for brevity.)

Table 21-7. *Strongly Typed Input HTML Helpers*

HTML Element	Example
Check box	`Html.CheckBoxFor(x => x.IsApproved)`

	Output:
	`<input id="IsApproved" name="IsApproved" type="checkbox" value="true" />`
	`<input name="IsApproved" type="hidden" value="false" />`

Hidden field	`Html.HiddenFor(x => x.FirstName)`
	Output: `<input id="FirstName" name="FirstName" type="hidden" value="" />`
Radio button	`Html.RadioButtonFor(x => x.IsApproved, "val")`
	Output: `<input id="IsApproved" name="IsApproved" type="radio" value="val" />`
Password	`Html.PasswordFor(x => x.Password)`
	Output: `<input id="Password" name="Password" type="password" />`
Text area	`Html.TextAreaFor(x => x.Bio, 5, 20, new{})`
	Output: `<textarea cols="20" id="Bio" name="Bio" rows="5">Bio value</textarea>`
Text box	`Html.TextBoxFor(x => x.FirstName)`
	Output: `<input id="FirstName" name="FirstName" type="text" value="" />`

The strongly typed input helpers work on lambda expressions. The value that is passed to the expression is the view model object, and you can select the field or property that will be used to set the `value` attribute. You can see how I have used this kind of helper in the `CreatePerson.cshtml` view from the example application in Listing 21-25.

Listing 21-25. Using the Strongly Typed Input Helper Methods in the CreatePerson.cshtml File

```
@model HelperMethods.Models.Person

@{
    ViewBag.Title = "CreatePerson";
    Layout = "/Views/Shared/_Layout.cshtml";
}
<h2>CreatePerson</h2>

@using(Html.BeginRouteForm("FormRoute", new {}, FormMethod.Post,
    new { @class = "personClass", data_formType="person"})) {

    <div class="dataElem">
        <label>PersonId</label>
        @Html.TextBoxFor(m => m.PersonId)
    </div>
    <div class="dataElem">
        <label>First Name</label>
        @Html.TextBoxFor(m => m.FirstName)
    </div>
```

```
<div class="dataElem">
    <label>Last Name</label>
    @Html.TextBoxFor(m => m.LastName)
</div>
<input type="submit" value="Submit" />
}
```

The HTML generated by these helpers is not any different, but I use the strongly typed helper methods in my own projects because they reduce the chances of causing an error by mistyping a property name.

Creating Select Elements

Table 21-8 shows the helper methods that can be used to create select elements. These can be used to select a single item from a drop-down list or present a multiple-item select element that allows several items to be selected. As with the other form elements, there are versions of these helpers that are weakly and strongly typed.

Table 21-8. *HTML Helpers That Render Select Elements*

HTML Element	Example
Drop-down list	`Html.DropDownList("myList", new SelectList(new [] {"A", "B"}), "Choose")`

	Output:
	`<select id="myList" name="myList">`
	`    <option value="">Choose</option>`
	`    <option>A</option>`
	`    <option>B</option>`
	`</select>`

Drop-down list	`Html.DropDownListFor(x => x.Gender, new SelectList(new [] {"M", "F"}))`

	Output:
	`<select id="Gender" name="Gender">`
	`    <option>M</option>`
	`    <option>F</option>`
	`</select>`

Multiple-select	`Html.ListBox("myList", new MultiSelectList(new [] {"A", "B"}))`

	Output:
	`<select id="myList" multiple="multiple" name="myList">`
	`    <option>A</option>`
	`    <option>B</option>`
	`</select>`

Multiple-select	`Html.ListBoxFor(x => x.Vals, new MultiSelectList(new [] {"A", "B"}))`

	Output:
	`<select id="Vals" multiple="multiple" name="Vals">`
	`    <option>A</option>`
	`    <option>B</option>`
	`</select>`

The select helpers take SelectList or MultiSelectList parameters. The difference between these classes is that MultiSelectList has constructor options that let you specify that more than one item should be selected when the page is rendered initially.

613

Both of these classes operate on IEnumerable sequences of objects. In Table 21-8, I created inline arrays that contained the list items I wanted displayed, but a nice feature of SelectList and MultiSelectList is that they will extract values from objects, including the model object, for the list items. You can see how I have created a select element for the Role property of the Person model in Listing 21-26.

Listing 21-26. Creating a Select Element for the Person.Role Property in the CreatePerson.cshtml File

```
@model HelperMethods.Models.Person

@{
    ViewBag.Title = "CreatePerson";
    Layout = "/Views/Shared/_Layout.cshtml";
}
<h2>CreatePerson</h2>

@using(Html.BeginRouteForm("FormRoute", new {}, FormMethod.Post,
    new { @class = "personClass", data_formType="person"})) {

    <div class="dataElem">
        <label>PersonId</label>
        @Html.TextBoxFor(m => m.PersonId)
    </div>
    <div class="dataElem">
        <label>First Name</label>
        @Html.TextBoxFor(m => m.FirstName)
    </div>
    <div class="dataElem">
        <label>Last Name</label>
        @Html.TextBoxFor(m => m.LastName)
    </div>
    <div class="dataElem">
        <label>Role</label>
        @Html.DropDownListFor(m => m.Role,
            new SelectList(Enum.GetNames(typeof(HelperMethods.Models.Role))))
    </div>
    <input type="submit" value="Submit" />
}
```

I defined the Role property so that it is a value from the Role enumeration defined in the same class file. Because the SelectList and MultiSelectList objects operate on IEnumerable objects, I have to use the Enum.GetNames method to be able to use the Role enum as the source for the select element. You can see the HTML that the latest version of the view creates, including the select element, in Listing 21-27.

Listing 21-27. The HTML Generated by the CreatePerson View

```
<!DOCTYPE html>
<html>
<head>
    <meta charset="utf-8" />
    <meta name="viewport" content="width=device-width" />
    <title>CreatePerson</title>
```

```
    <style type="text/css">
        label { display: inline-block; width: 100px;}
        .dataElem { margin: 5px;}
    </style>
</head>
<body>

<h2>CreatePerson</h2>

<form action="/app/forms/Home/CreatePerson" class="personClass"
            data-formType="person" method="post">
    <div class="dataElem">
        <label>PersonId</label>
        <input data-val="true" data-val-number="The field PersonId must be a number." data-val-
required="The PersonId field is required." id="PersonId" name="PersonId" type="text" value="0" />
    </div>
    <div class="dataElem">
        <label>First Name</label>
        <input id="FirstName" name="FirstName" type="text" value="" />
    </div>
    <div class="dataElem">
        <label>Last Name</label>
        <input id="LastName" name="LastName" type="text" value="" />
    </div>
    <div class="dataElem">
        <label>Role</label>
        <select data-val="true" data-val-required="The Role field is required."
                id="Role" name="Role">
            <option selected="selected">Admin</option>
            <option>User</option>
            <option>Guest</option>
        </select>
    </div>
    <input type="submit" value="Submit" />
</form>
</body>
</html>
```

Summary

In this chapter, I introduced the concept of helper methods, which you can use in views to generate chunks of content in a reusable way. I started by showing you how to create custom inline and external helpers and then showed you the helpers that are available to create HTML form, input and select elements. In the next chapter, I continue on this theme and show you how to use *templated helpers*.

CHAPTER 22

■ ■ ■

Templated Helper Methods

The HTML helpers that I looked at in the previous chapter, such as `Html.CheckBoxFor` and `Html.TextBoxFor`, generate a specific type of element, which means that I have to decide in advance what kinds of elements should be used to represent model properties and to manually update the views if the type of a property changes.

In this chapter, I demonstrate the *templated helper methods*, with which I specify the property I want displayed and let the MVC Framework figure out what HTML elements are required. This is a more flexible approach to displaying data to the user, although it requires some initial care and attention to set up. Table 22-1 provides the summary for this chapter.

Table 22-1. *Chapter Summary*

Problem	Solution	Listing
Generate an element that can be used to edit a model property	Use the `Html.Editor` and `Html.EditorFor` helpers	1–5, 18
Generate labels for and read-only representations of model properties	Use the `Html.Label` and `Html.Display` helpers	6–8
Generate elements for a complete model object	Use the `DisplayForModel`, `EditorForModel` and `LabelForModel` helpers	9–10
Hide an element from the user when generating elements using a whole-model helper or prevent it from being edited	Apply the `HiddenInput` attribute to the property	11–12
Set the label that will be used to display model properties	Use the `DisplayName` and `Display` attributes	13
Specify the way in which model properties are displayed	Use the `DataType` attribute	14
Specify the template used to display a model property	Use the `UIHint` attribute	15
Define model metadata separately from the model type	Create a buddy class and use the `MetadataType` attribute	16–17
Change the elements that are generated for a model property	Create a custom template	19–22

Preparing the Example Project

In this chapter I am going to continue using the `HelperMethod` project that I created in Chapter 21. In that project, I created a `Person` model class along with a couple of supporting types. As a reminder, I have listed these in Listing 22-1.

Listing 22-1. The Contents of the Person.cs File

```
using System;

namespace HelperMethods.Models {

    public class Person {
        public int PersonId { get; set; }
        public string FirstName { get; set; }
        public string LastName { get; set; }
        public DateTime BirthDate { get; set; }
        public Address HomeAddress { get; set; }
        public bool IsApproved { get; set; }
        public Role Role { get; set; }
    }

    public class Address {
        public string Line1 { get; set; }
        public string Line2 { get; set; }
        public string City { get; set; }
        public string PostalCode { get; set; }
        public string Country { get; set; }
    }

    public enum Role {
        Admin,
        User,
        Guest
    }
}
```

The example project contains a simple Home controller that I use to display forms and receive form posts. You can see the definition of the HomeController class in Listing 22-2.

Listing 22-2. The Contents of the HomeController.cs File

```
using System.Web.Mvc;
using HelperMethods.Models;

namespace HelperMethods.Controllers {
    public class HomeController : Controller {

        public ActionResult Index() {

            ViewBag.Fruits = new string[] { "Apple", "Orange", "Pear" };
            ViewBag.Cities = new string[] { "New York", "London", "Paris" };

            string message = "This is an HTML element: <input>";

            return View((object)message);
        }
```

```
        public ActionResult CreatePerson() {
            return View(new Person());
        }

        [HttpPost]
        public ActionResult CreatePerson(Person person) {
            return View(person);
        }
    }
}
```

It is the two CreatePerson action methods that I will be using in this chapter, both of which render the /Views/Home/CreatePerson.cshtml view file. In Listing 22-3, you can see the CreatePerson view from the end of the last chapter, with a simple change.

Listing 22-3. The Contents of the CreatePerson.cshtml File

```
@model HelperMethods.Models.Person

@{
    ViewBag.Title = "CreatePerson";
    Layout = "/Views/Shared/_Layout.cshtml";
    Html.EnableClientValidation(false);
}
<h2>CreatePerson</h2>

@using (Html.BeginRouteForm("FormRoute", new { }, FormMethod.Post,
    new { @class = "personClass", data_formType = "person" })) {

    <div class="dataElem">
        <label>PersonId</label>
        @Html.TextBoxFor(m => m.PersonId)
    </div>
    <div class="dataElem">
        <label>First Name</label>
        @Html.TextBoxFor(m => m.FirstName)
    </div>
    <div class="dataElem">
        <label>Last Name</label>
        @Html.TextBoxFor(m => m.LastName)
    </div>
    <div class="dataElem">
        <label>Role</label>
        @Html.DropDownListFor(m => m.Role,
            new SelectList(Enum.GetNames(typeof(HelperMethods.Models.Role))))
    </div>
    <input type="submit" value="Submit" />
}
```

I made one addition, which I have marked in bold. By default, the helper methods will add data attributes to the HTML elements they generate to support the kind of form validation I showed you when I created the SportsStore application. I do not want those attributes in this chapter, so I have used the Html.EnableClientValidation method to disable them for the CreatePerson view. The client validation feature is still enabled for the rest of the application and I will explain how validation works in detail (including the purpose of the data attributes) in Chapter 25.

Using Templated Helper Methods

The first templated helper methods that I am going to look at are Html.Editor and Html.EditorFor. The Editor method takes a string argument that specifies the property for which editor element is required. The helper follows the search process that I described in Chapter 20 to locate a corresponding property in the view bag and model object. The EditorFor method is the strongly typed equivalent, which allows you to use a lambda expression to specify a model property that you want the editor element for.

In Listing 22-4, you can see how I have applied both the Editor and EditorFor helper methods to the CreatePerson view. As I mentioned in the last chapter, I prefer to use the strongly typed helpers because they reduce the chances of causing an error by mistyping the property name, but I have used both types in this listing just to demonstrate that you can mix and match as you see fit.

Listing 22-4. Using the Editor and EditorFor Helper Methods in the CreatePerson.cshtml File

```
@model HelperMethods.Models.Person

@{
    ViewBag.Title = "CreatePerson";
    Layout = "/Views/Shared/_Layout.cshtml";
    Html.EnableClientValidation(false);
}
<h2>CreatePerson</h2>

@using(Html.BeginRouteForm("FormRoute", new {}, FormMethod.Post,
    new { @class = "personClass", data_formType="person"})) {

    <div class="dataElem">
        <label>PersonId</label>
        @Html.Editor("PersonId")
    </div>
    <div class="dataElem">
        <label>First Name</label>
        @Html.Editor("FirstName")
    </div>
    <div class="dataElem">
        <label>Last Name</label>
        @Html.EditorFor(m => m.LastName)
    </div>
    <div class="dataElem">
        <label>Role</label>
        @Html.EditorFor(m => m.Role)
    </div>
    <div class="dataElem">
        <label>Birth Date</label>
        @Html.EditorFor(m => m.BirthDate)
    </div>
    <input type="submit" value="Submit" />
}
```

The HTML elements that are created by the Editor and EditorFor methods are the same. The only difference is the way that you specify the property that the editor elements are created for. You can see the effect of the changes that I have made by starting the example application and navigating to the /Home/CreatePerson URL, as shown in Figure 22-1.

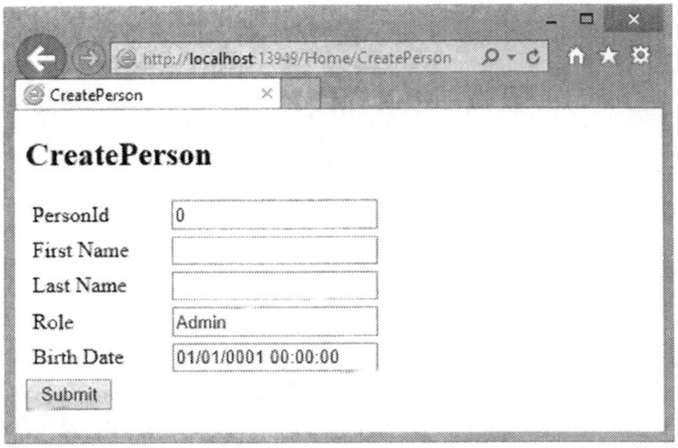

Figure 22-1. *Using the Editor and EditorFor helper methods in a form*

Other than the addition of the BirthDate property, this does not look different from the kind of form that I was creating in Chapter 21. However, there is a pretty substantial change, which you can see if you use a different browser. In Figure 22-2, you can see the same URL displayed in the Opera browser (which you can get from www.opera.com).

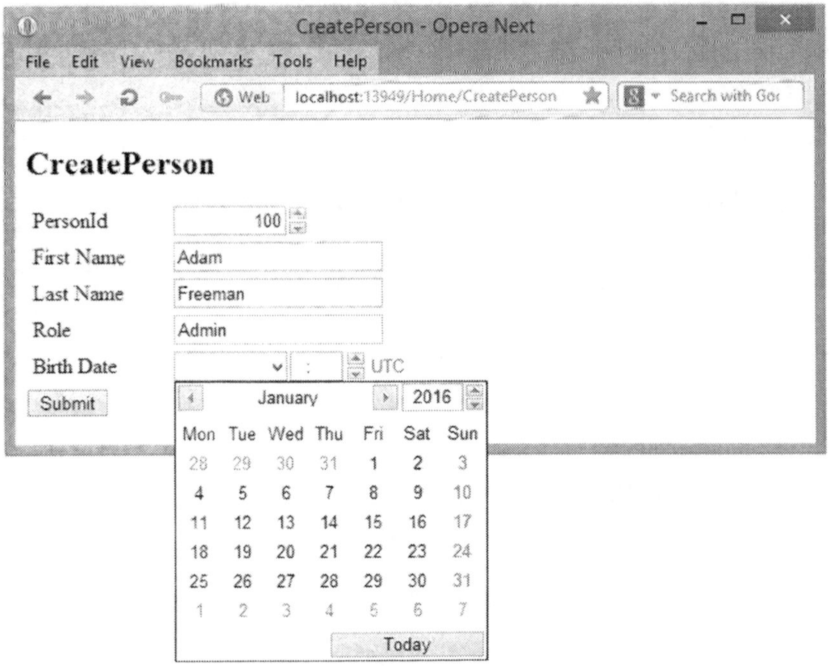

Figure 22-2. *Displaying a form created using the Editor and EditorFor helper methods*

Notice that the elements for the PersonId and BirthDate properties look different. The PersonId element has spinner arrows (allowing you to increment and decrement the value) and the BirthDate element is presented with a date picker.

The HTML5 specification defines different types of input element that can be used to edit common data types, such as numbers and dates. The Helper and HelperFor methods use the type of the property I want to edit to select one of those new input element types. You can see this in Listing 22-5, where I have shown the HTML that was generated for the form.

Listing 22-5. The HTML Input Elements Created by the Editor and EditorFor Helper Methods

```
<!DOCTYPE html>
<html>
<head>
    <meta charset="utf-8" />
    <meta name="viewport" content="width=device-width" />
    <title>CreatePerson</title>
    <style type="text/css">
        label { display: inline-block; width: 100px;}
        .dataElem { margin: 5px;}
    </style>
</head>
<body>

<h2>CreatePerson</h2>

<form action="/app/forms/Home/CreatePerson" class="personClass"
        data-formType="person" method="post">
    <div class="dataElem">
        <label>PersonId</label>
        <input class="text-box single-line" id="PersonId" name="PersonId"
            type="number" value="0" />
    </div>
    <div class="dataElem">
        <label>First Name</label>
        <input class="text-box single-line" id="FirstName" name="FirstName"
            type="text" value="" />
    </div>
    <div class="dataElem">
        <label>Last Name</label>
        <input class="text-box single-line" id="LastName" name="LastName"
            type="text" value="" />
    </div>
    <div class="dataElem">
        <label>Role</label>
        <input class="text-box single-line" id="Role" name="Role"
            type="text" value="Admin" />
    </div>
```

```
    <div class="dataElem">
        <label>Birth Date</label>
        <input class="text-box single-line" id="BirthDate" name="BirthDate"
            type="datetime" value="01/01/0001 00:00:00" />
    </div>
    <input type="submit" value="Submit" />
</form>
</body>
</html>
```

The type attribute specifies which kind of input element should be displayed by the browser. The helper methods have specified the number and datetime types for the PersonId and BirthDate properties and the text type, which is the default for the other properties. The reason that we only see these types in Opera is because the HTML5 features are still not widely supported, even in the latest version of Internet Explorer and Chrome.

■ **Tip**   Most web UI toolkits include date pickers that you can use instead of relying on the HTML5 input element types. If you have not already selected such a toolkit for a project, then I suggest you start with jQuery UI (http://jqueryui.com), which is an open-source toolkit, built on jQuery.

You can see that by using the templated helper methods I have been able to tailor the form elements to the content, although not in an especially useful way, in part because not all browsers can display the HTML5 input element types and in part because some properties, such as Role, are not displayed in a helpful way. I will show you how to provide the MVC Framework with additional information that will improve the HTML that the helper methods produce. But I am going to show you the other templated helpers that are available before I get into the detail. You can see the complete set of helpers in Table 22-2 and I demonstrate each of them in the sections that follow.

Table 22-2. *The MVC Templated HTML Helpers*

Helper	Example	Description
Display	Html.Display("FirstName")	Renders a read-only view of the specified model property, choosing an HTML element according to the property's type and metadata
DisplayFor	Html.DisplayFor(x => x.FirstName)	Strongly typed version of the previous helper
Editor	Html.Editor("FirstName")	Renders an editor for the specified model property, choosing an HTML element according to the property's type and metadata
EditorFor	Html.EditorFor(x => x.FirstName)	Strongly typed version of the previous helper
Label	Html.Label("FirstName")	Renders an HTML <label> element referring to the specified model property
LabelFor	Html.LabelFor(x => x.FirstName)	Strongly typed version of the previous helper

Generating Label and Display Elements

To demonstrate the other helper methods, I am going to add a new action method and view to the example that will display a read-only view of the data submitted from the HTML form. First, I have updated the HttpPost version of the CreatePerson action in the Home controller, as shown in Listing 22-6.

Listing 22-6. Specifying a Different View in the HomeController .cs File

```
using System.Web.Mvc;
using HelperMethods.Models;

namespace HelperMethods.Controllers {
    public class HomeController : Controller {

        public ActionResult Index() {

            ViewBag.Fruits = new string[] { "Apple", "Orange", "Pear" };
            ViewBag.Cities = new string[] { "New York", "London", "Paris" };

            string message = "This is an HTML element: <input>";

            return View((object)message);
        }

        public ActionResult CreatePerson() {
            return View(new Person());
        }

        [HttpPost]
        public ActionResult CreatePerson(Person person) {
            return View("DisplayPerson", person);
        }
    }
}
```

I added the DisplayPerson.cshtml view file to the /Views/Home folder, and you can see the contents of this file in Listing 22-7.

Listing 22-7. The Contents of the DisplayPerson.cshtml File

```
@model HelperMethods.Models.Person

@{
    ViewBag.Title = "DisplayPerson";
    Layout = "/Views/Shared/_Layout.cshtml";
}
<h2>DisplayPerson</h2>
<div class="dataElem">
    @Html.Label("PersonId")
    @Html.Display("PersonId")
</div>
```

```
<div class="dataElem">
    @Html.Label("FirstName")
    @Html.Display("FirstName")
</div>
<div class="dataElem">
    @Html.LabelFor(m => m.LastName)
    @Html.DisplayFor(m => m.LastName)
</div>
<div class="dataElem">
    @Html.LabelFor(m => m.Role)
    @Html.DisplayFor(m => m.Role)
</div>
<div class="dataElem">
    @Html.LabelFor(m => m.BirthDate)
    @Html.DisplayFor(m => m.BirthDate)
</div>
```

You can see the output that this new view produces by starting the application, navigating to the /Home/CreatePerson URL, filling in the form and clicking the Submit button. The result is shown in Figure 22-3 and you can see that I have taken a small step backward, because the Label and LabelFor helpers have just used the property names as the content for the labels.

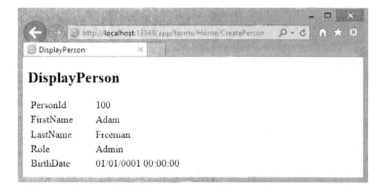

Figure 22-3. *Using helpers to generate a read-only view of the Person object*

You can see the output that these helper methods produce in Listing 22-8. Notice that the Display and DisplayFor methods do not generate an HTML element by default. They just emit the value of the property they operate on.

Listing 22-8. The HTML Generated from the DisplayPerson View

```
<!DOCTYPE html>
<html>
<head>
    <meta charset="utf-8" />
    <meta name="viewport" content="width=device-width" />
    <title>DisplayPerson</title>
```

```
    <style type="text/css">
        label { display: inline-block; width: 100px;}
        .dataElem { margin: 5px;}
    </style>
</head>
<body>

<h2>DisplayPerson</h2>
<div class="dataElem">
    <label for="PersonId">PersonId</label>
    100
</div>
<div class="dataElem">
    <label for="FirstName">FirstName</label>
    Adam
</div>
<div class="dataElem">
    <label for="LastName">LastName</label>
    Freeman
</div>
<div class="dataElem">
    <label for="Role">Role</label>
    Admin
</div>
<div class="dataElem">
    <label for="BirthDate">BirthDate</label>
    01/01/0001 00:00:00
</div>

</body>
</html>
```

Although these helpers may not seem especially useful at the moment, I will show you how to change their behavior shortly in order to produce output that is much more the kind of thing that you would want to display to users.

Using Whole-Model Templated Helpers

I have been using templated helpers which generate output for a single property, but the MVC Framework also defines helpers that operate on the entire objects, a process known as *scaffolding*. There are scaffolding helpers available, as shown in Table 22-3.

Table 22-3. *The MVC Scaffolding Templated Helper methods*

Helper	Example	Description
DisplayForModel	Html.DisplayForModel()	Renders a read-only view of the entire model object
EditorForModel	Html.EditorForModel()	Renders editor elements for the entire model object
LabelForModel	Html.LabelForModel()	Renders an HTML <label> element referring to the entire model object

> ▪ **Tip**   This is not the same kind of scaffolding that Microsoft added to Visual Studio to create MVC components like controllers and views, but the basic idea is the same in which output is generated based on the characteristics of a data type. In the case of Visual Studio, the output from the scaffolding is a class or Razor file and for the templated helpers, the output is HTML.

In Listing 22-9, you can see how I have used the `LabelForModel` and `EditorForModel` helper methods to simplify the `CreatePerson.cshtml` view.

Listing 22-9. Using the Scaffolding Helper Methods in the CreatePerson.cshtml File

```
@model HelperMethods.Models.Person

@{
    ViewBag.Title = "CreatePerson";
    Layout = "/Views/Shared/_Layout.cshtml";
    Html.EnableClientValidation(false);
}

<h2>CreatePerson: @Html.LabelForModel()</h2>

@using(Html.BeginRouteForm("FormRoute", new {}, FormMethod.Post,
    new { @class = "personClass", data_formType="person"})) {

    @Html.EditorForModel()

    <input type="submit" value="Submit" />
}
```

You can see the effect of the scaffold helpers in Figure 22-4. Once again, you can see what the helpers are trying to do but that things are not quite right yet. The `LabelForModel` helper has not generated a useful label. Although more properties from the `Person` model object are being shown than I defined manually in previous examples, not everything is visible (such as the `Address` property) and what is visible is not always useful (such as the `Role` property, which would be more usefully expressed as a `select` instead of an `input` element).

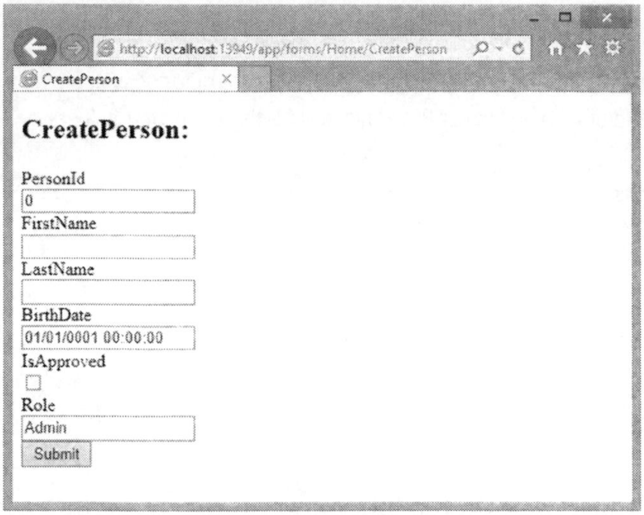

Figure 22-4. *Using the scaffolding helpers to create an editor for the Person model object*

Part of the problem is that the HTML that the scaffolding helpers generate doesn't correspond to the CSS styles that I defined in the /Views/Shared/_Layout.cshtml file in the previous chapter. Here is an example of the HTML generated to edit the FirstName property:

```
...
<div class="editor-label">
    <label for="FirstName">FirstName</label>
</div>
<div class="editor-field">
    <input class="text-box single-line" id="FirstName" name="FirstName"
        type="text" value="" />
</div>
...
```

I can tidy up the appearance of a view by adding styles to the layout that correspond to the CSS class values added to the div and input elements by the scaffolding helpers. In Listing 22-10, you can see the changes I made to the _Layout.cshtml file.

Listing 22-10. Making Changes to the CSS Styles Defined in the _Layout.cshtml File

```
<!DOCTYPE html>
<html>
<head>
    <meta charset="utf-8" />
    <meta name="viewport" content="width=device-width" />
    <title>@ViewBag.Title</title>
    <style type="text/css">
        label { display: inline-block; width: 100px; }
        div.dataElem { margin: 5px; }
        h2 > label { width: inherit; }
        .editor-label, .editor-field { float: left; margin-top: 10px;}
```

```
        .editor-field input { height: 20px; }
        .editor-label { clear: left;}
        .editor-field { margin-left: 10px;  }
        input[type=submit] { float: left; clear: both; margin-top: 10px; }
        .column { float: left; margin: 10px;}
    </style>
</head>
<body>
    @RenderBody()
</body>
</html>
```

These new styles produce something that is more in keeping with the layout I used in earlier examples, as shown in Figure 22-5.

Figure 22-5. *The effect of styling elements using the classes defined by the scaffolding helper methods*

Using Model Metadata

As you have seen, the templated helpers have no special knowledge about the application and its model data types, and so I end up with HTML that is not what exactly what I desire. I want the benefits that come with simpler views, but I need to improve the quality of the output that the helper methods generate before I can use them seriously.

I cannot blame the templated helpers in these situations; the HTML that is generated is based on a best guess about what I want. This is, of course, the problem I have with all scaffolding, which has to make a best-effort attempt based on a generic understanding of the application. Fortunately, the templated helpers can be improved by using model metadata to provide guidance about how to handle model types. Metadata is expressed using C# attributes, where attributes and parameter values provide a range of instructions to the view helpers. The metadata is applied to the model class, which the helper methods consult when they generate HTML elements. In the following sections, I show you how to use metadata to provide directions to the helpers for labels, displays, and editors.

Using Metadata to Control Editing and Visibility

In the Person class, the PersonId property is one that I do not want the user to be able to see or edit. Most model classes have at least one such property, often related to the underlying storage mechanism—a primary key that is managed by a relational database, for example, which I demonstrated when I created the SportsStore application. I can use the HiddenInput attribute, which causes the helper to render a hidden input field. You can see how I have applied the HiddenAttribute to the Person class in Listing 22-11.

Listing 22-11. Using the HiddenInput Attribute in the Person.cs File

```
using System;
using System.Web.Mvc;

namespace HelperMethods.Models {

    public class Person {
        [HiddenInput]
        public int PersonId { get; set; }
        public string FirstName { get; set; }
        public string LastName { get; set; }
        public DateTime BirthDate { get; set; }
        public Address HomeAddress { get; set; }
        public bool IsApproved { get; set; }
        public Role Role { get; set; }
    }

    // ...other types omitted for brevity...
}
```

When this attribute has been applied, the Html.EditorFor and Html.EditorForModel helpers will render a read-only view of the decorated property (which is the term used to describe a property to which an attribute has been applied), as shown in Figure 22-6, which shows the effect of starting the application and navigating to the /Home/CreatePerson URL.

Figure 22-6. *Creating a read-only representation of a property in an editor*

The value of the PersonId property is shown, but the user cannot edit it. The HTML that is generated for the property is as follows:

```
...
<div class="editor-field">
    0
    <input id="PersonId" name="PersonId" type="hidden" value="0" />
</div>
...
```

The value of the property (0 in this case) is rendered literally, but the helper also includes a hidden input element for the property, which is helpful for HTML forms because it ensures that a value for the property is submitted along with the rest of the form. This is something I will return to when I look at model binding in Chapter 24 and model validation in Chapter 25. If I want to hide a property entirely, then I can set the value of the DisplayValue property in the DisplayName attribute to false, as shown in Listing 22-12.

Listing 22-12. Using the HiddenInput Attribute to Hide a Property in the Person.cshtml File

```
...
public class Person {
    [HiddenInput(DisplayValue=false)]
    public int PersonId { get; set; }
    public string FirstName { get; set; }
    public string LastName { get; set; }
    public DateTime BirthDate { get; set; }
    public Address HomeAddress { get; set; }
    public bool IsApproved { get; set; }
    public Role Role { get; set; }
}
...
```

When I use the Html.EditorForModel helper on a Person object, a hidden input will be created so that the value for the PersonId property will be included in any form submissions, but the label and the value will be omitted. This has the effect of hiding the PersonId property from the user, as shown by Figure 22-7.

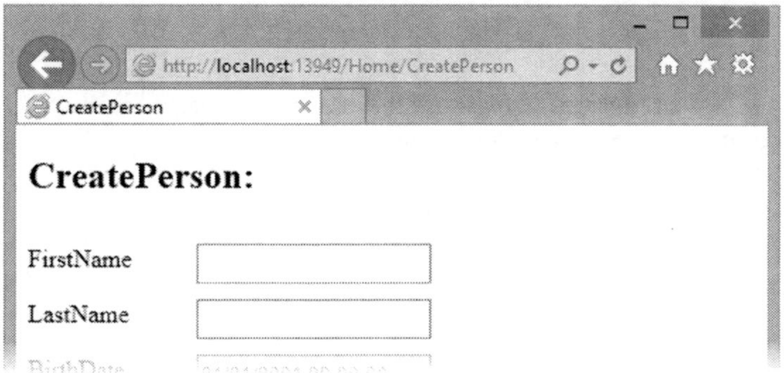

Figure 22-7. Hiding model object properties from the user

If I have chosen to render HTML for individual properties, I can still create the hidden input for the PersonId property by using the Html.EditorFor helper, like this:

```
...
@Html.EditorFor(m => m.PersonId)
...
```

The HiddenInput property is detected, and if DisplayValue is true, then the following HTML is generated:

```
...
<input id="PersonId" name="PersonId" type="hidden" value="1" />
...
```

EXCLUDING A PROPERTY FROM SCAFFOLDING

To completely exclude a property from the generated HTML, I can use the ScaffoldColumn attribute. Whereas the HiddenInput attribute includes a value for the property in a hidden input element, the ScaffoldColumn attribute can mark a property as being entirely off limits for the scaffolding process. Here is an example of the attribute in use:

```
...
[ScaffoldColumn(false)]
public int PersonId { get; set; }
...
```

When the scaffolding helpers see the ScaffoldColumn attribute applied in this way, they skip over the property entirely; no hidden input elements will be created, and no details of this property will be included in the generated HTML. The appearance of the generated HTML will be the same as if I had used the HiddenInput attribute, but no value will be returned for the property during a form submission. This has an effect on model binding, which I discuss in Chapter 24. The ScaffoldColumn attribute doesn't have an effect on the per-property helpers, such as EditorFor. If I call @Html.EditorFor(m => m.PersonId) in a view, then an editor for the PersonId property will be generated, even when the ScaffoldColumn attribute is present.

Using Metadata for Labels

By default, the Label, LabelFor, LabelForModel, and EditorForModel helpers use the names of properties as the content for the label elements they generate. For example, if I render a label like this:

```
...
@Html.LabelFor(m => m.BirthDate)
...
```

the HTML element that is generated will be as follows:

```
...
<label for="BirthDate">BirthDate</label>
...
```

Of course, the names given to properties are often not suitable for display to the user. To that end, I can apply the DisplayName attribute from the System.ComponentModel.DataAnnotations namespace, passing in the value I want as a value for the Name property. Listing 22-13 demonstrates this attribute applied to the Person class.

Listing 22-13. Using the DisplayName Attribute to Define a Label in the Person.cs File

```
using System;
using System.Web.Mvc;
using System.ComponentModel.DataAnnotations;
using System.ComponentModel;

namespace HelperMethods.Models {

    [DisplayName("New Person")]
    public class Person {
        [HiddenInput(DisplayValue=false)]
        public int PersonId { get; set; }

        [Display(Name="First")]
        public string FirstName { get; set; }

        [Display(Name = "Last")]
        public string LastName { get; set; }

        [Display(Name = "Birth Date")]
        public DateTime BirthDate { get; set; }

        public Address HomeAddress { get; set; }

        [Display(Name="Approved")]
        public bool IsApproved { get; set; }
        public Role Role { get; set; }
    }

    // ...other types omitted for brevity...
}
```

When the label helpers render a label element for the BirthDate property, they will detect the Display attribute and use the value of the Name parameter for the inner text, like this:

```
...
<label for="BirthDate">Birth Date</label>
...
```

The helpers also recognize the DisplayName attribute, which can be found in the System.ComponentModel namespace. This attribute has the advantage of being able to be applied to classes, which allows me to use the Html.LabelForModel helper. You can see how I have applied this attribute to the Person class in the listing. (I can apply the DisplayName attribute to properties as well, but I tend to use this attribute only for model classes, for no reason other than habit.) You can see the effect of the Display and DisplayName attributes in Figure 22-8.

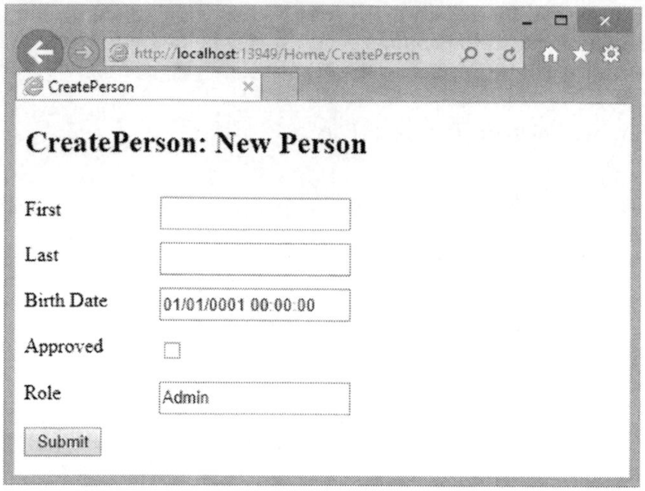

Figure 22-8. *Using the Display and DisplayName attributes to control labels*

Using Metadata for Data Values

I can also use metadata to provide instructions about how a model property should be displayed. I can use this to deal with the fact that the BirthDate property is displayed with a time when I really just want a date, for example. I control the way that data values are displaying using the DataType attribute, which you can see applied to the Person class in Listing 22-14.

Listing 22-14. Applying the DataType Attribute to the Person.cs File

```
...
[DisplayName("New Person")]
public class Person {
    [HiddenInput(DisplayValue=false)]
    public int PersonId { get; set; }

    [Display(Name="First")]
    public string FirstName { get; set; }

    [Display(Name = "Last")]
    public string LastName { get; set; }

    [Display(Name = "Birth Date")]
    [DataType(DataType.Date)]
    public DateTime BirthDate { get; set; }

    public Address HomeAddress { get; set; }

    [Display(Name="Approved")]
    public bool IsApproved { get; set; }
    public Role Role { get; set; }
}
...
```

The DataType attribute takes a value from the DataType enumeration as a parameter. In the example I have specified the DataType.Date value, which causes the templated helpers to render the value of the BirthDate property as a date without a time component, as shown in Figure 22-9.

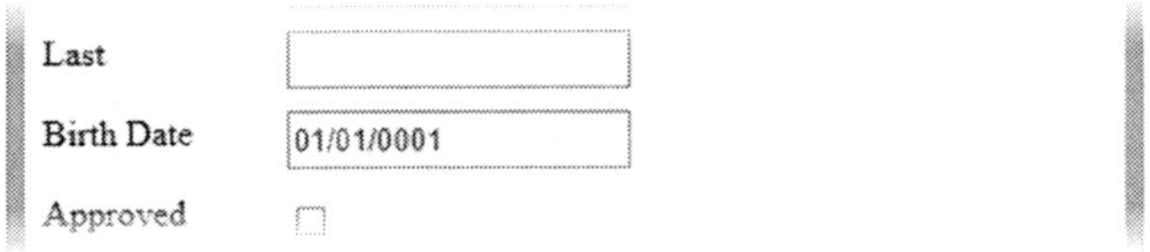

Last	
Birth Date	01/01/0001
Approved	☐

Figure 22-9. *Using the DataType attribute to control the display of a DateTime value*

■ **Tip** The change is more pronounced when the application is viewed using a Web browser that has better support for the HTML5 input element types.

Table 22-4 describes the most useful values of the DataType enumeration.

Table 22-4. *The Values of the DataType Enumeration*

Value	Description
DateTime	Displays a date and time (this is the default behavior for System.DateTime values)
Date	Displays the date portion of a DateTime
Time	Displays the time portion of a DateTime
Text	Displays a single line of text
PhoneNumber	Displays a phone number
MultilineText	Renders the value in a textarea element
Password	Displays the data so that individual characters are masked from view
Url	Displays the data as a URL (using an HTML a element)
EmailAddress	Displays the data as an e-mail address (using an a element with a mailto href)

The effect of these values depends on the type of the property they are associated with and the helper being used. For example, the MultilineText value will lead those helpers that create editors for properties to create an HTML textarea element but will be ignored by the display helpers. This makes sense. The textarea element allows the user to edit a value, which doesn't have a beating when displaying the data in a read-only form. Equally, the Url value has an effect only on the display helpers, which render an HTML a element to create a link.

Using Metadata to Select a Display Template

As their name suggests, templated helpers use display templates to generate HTML. The template that is used is based on the type of the property being processed and the kind of helper being used. I can use the UIHint attribute to specify the template used to render HTML for a property, as shown in Listing 22-15.

Listing 22-15. Using the UIHint Attribute in the Person.cshtml File

```
...
[DisplayName("New Person")]
public class Person {
    [HiddenInput(DisplayValue=false)]
    public int PersonId { get; set; }

    [Display(Name="First")]
    [UIHint("MultilineText")]
    public string FirstName { get; set; }

    [Display(Name = "Last")]
    public string LastName { get; set; }

    [Display(Name = "Birth Date")]
    [DataType(DataType.Date)]
    public DateTime BirthDate { get; set; }

    public Address HomeAddress { get; set; }

    [Display(Name="Approved")]
    public bool IsApproved { get; set; }
    public Role Role { get; set; }
}
...
```

In the listing, I specified the MultilineText template, which renders an HTML textarea element for the FirstName property when used with one of the editor helpers, such as EditorFor or EditorForModel. Table 22-5 shows the set of built-in templates that the MVC Framework includes.

Table 22-5. *The Built-In MVC Framework View Templates*

Value	Effect (Editor)	Effect (Display)
Boolean	Renders a checkbox for bool values. For nullable bool? values, a select element is created with options for True, False, and Not Set.	As for the editor helpers, but with the addition of the disabled attribute, which renders read-only HTML controls
Collection	Renders the appropriate template for each of the elements in an IEnumerable sequence. The items in the sequence do not have to be of the same type.	As for the editor helper
Decimal	Renders a single-line textbox input element and formats the data value to display two decimal places	Renders the data value formatted to two decimal places
DateTime	Renders an input element whose type attribute is datetime and which contains the complete date and time	Renders the complete value of a DateTime variable
Date	Renders an input element whose type attribute is date and that contains the date component (but not the time)	Renders the date component of a DateTime variable

(continued)

Table 22-5. (*continued*)

Value	Effect (Editor)	Effect (Display)
EmailAddress	Renders the value in a single-line textbox input element	Renders a link using an HTML a element and an href attribute that is formatted as a mailto URL
HiddenInput	Creates a hidden input element	Renders the data value and creates a hidden input element
Html	Renders the value in a single-line textbox input element	Renders a link using an HTML a element
MultilineText	Renders an HTML textarea element that contains the data value	Renders the data value
Number	Renders an input element whose type attribute is set to number	Renders the data value
Object	See explanation after this table	See explanation after this table
Password	Renders the value in a single-line textbox input element so that the characters are not displayed but can be edited	Renders the data value—the characters are not obscured
String	Renders the value in a single-line textbox input element	Renders the data value
Text	Identical to the String template	Identical to the String template
Tel	Renders an input element whose type attribute is set to tel	Renders the data value
Time	Renders an input element whose type attribute is time and which contains the time component (but not the date)	Renders the time component of a DateTime variable
Url	Renders the value in a single-line textbox input element	Renders a link using an HTML a element. The inner HTML and the href attribute are both set to the data value.

Caution Care must be taken when using the UIHint attribute. I will receive an exception if I select a template that cannot operate on the type of the property I have applied it to, for example, applying the Boolean template to a string property.

The Object template is a special case. It is the template used by the scaffolding helpers to generate HTML for a view model object. This template examines each of the properties of an object and selects the most suitable template for the property type. The Object template takes metadata such as the UIHint and DataType attributes into account.

Applying Metadata to a Buddy Class

It is not always possible to apply metadata to an entity model class. This is usually the case when the model classes are generated automatically, like sometimes with ORM tools such as the Entity Framework (although not the way I used Entity Framework in the SportsStore application). Any changes applied to automatically generated classes, such as applying attributes, will be lost the next time the classes are updated or regenerated.

The solution to this problem is to ensure that the model class is defined as partial and to create a second partial class that contains the metadata. Many tools that generate classes automatically create partial classes by default, including the Entity Framework. Listing 22-16 shows the Person class modified such that it could have been generated automatically. There is no metadata, and the class is defined as partial.

Listing 22-16. A Partial Model Class in the Person.cs File

```
using System;
using System.ComponentModel.DataAnnotations;

namespace HelperMethods.Models {

    [MetadataType(typeof(PersonMetaData))]
    public partial class Person {
        public int PersonId { get; set; }
        public string FirstName { get; set; }
        public string LastName { get; set; }
        public DateTime BirthDate { get; set; }
        public Address HomeAddress { get; set; }
        public bool IsApproved { get; set; }
        public Role Role { get; set; }
    }

    // ...other types omitted from listing for brevity...
}
```

I tell the MVC Framework about the buddy class through the MetadataType attribute, which takes the type of the buddy class as its argument. Buddy classes must be defined in the same namespace and must also be partial classes. To demonstrate how this works, I have added a new folder to the example project called Models/Metadata. In this folder, I created a new class file called PersonMetadata.cs, the contents of which are shown in Listing 22-17.

Listing 22-17. The Contents of the PersonMetadata.cs File

```
using System;
using System.ComponentModel;
using System.ComponentModel.DataAnnotations;
using System.Web.Mvc;

namespace HelperMethods.Models {

    [DisplayName("New Person")]
    public partial class PersonMetaData {
        [HiddenInput(DisplayValue=false)]
        public int PersonId { get; set; }

        [Display(Name="First")]
        public string FirstName { get; set; }

        [Display(Name = "Last")]
        public string LastName { get; set; }
```

```
        [Display(Name = "Birth Date")]
        [DataType(DataType.Date)]
        public DateTime BirthDate { get; set; }

        [Display(Name="Approved")]
        public bool IsApproved { get; set; }
    }
}
```

The buddy class only needs to contain properties to which metadata applies. I do not have to replicate all of the properties of the Person class, for example.

■ **Tip** Take particular care to change the namespace that Visual Studio adds to the new class file. The buddy class must be in the same namespace as the model class, which is HelperMethods.Models for the example project.

Working with Complex Type Properties

The template process relies on the Object template that I described in the previous section. Each property is inspected, and a template is selected to render HTML to represent the property and its data value.

You may have noticed that the HomeAddress property was not rendered as part of the Person class when I used the EditorForModel helper. This happens because the Object template operates only on *simple types*, which means those types that can be parsed from a string value using the GetConverter method of the System.ComponentModel.TypeDescriptor class. The supported types include the intrinsic C# types, such as int, bool, and double, and many common framework types, including Guid and DateTime.

The result is that scaffolding helpers are not recursive. Given an object to process, a scaffolding templated helper method will generate HTML only for simple property types and will ignore any properties that are complex objects.

Although it can be inconvenient, this is a sensible policy. The MVC Framework does not know how the model objects are created. If the Object template was recursive, then it could easily end up triggering an ORM lazy-loading feature, which would lead it to read and render every object in the underlying database. If I want to render HTML for a complex property, I have to do it explicitly by making a separate call to a templated helper method. You can see how I have done this in Listing 22-18, which shows the changes I have made to the CreatePerson.cshtml view.

Listing 22-18. Dealing with a Property That Is a Complex Type in the CreatePerson.cshtml File

```
@model HelperMethods.Models.Person

@{
    ViewBag.Title = "CreatePerson";
    Layout = "/Views/Shared/_Layout.cshtml";
    Html.EnableClientValidation(false);
}
<h2>CreatePerson: @Html.LabelForModel()</h2>

@using(Html.BeginRouteForm("FormRoute", new {}, FormMethod.Post,
    new { @class = "personClass", data_formType="person"})) {

    <div class="column">
        @Html.EditorForModel()
    </div>
```

```
<div class="column">
    @Html.EditorFor(m => m.HomeAddress)
</div>
<input type="submit" value="Submit" />
}
```

To display the HomeAddress property, I added a call to the strongly typed EditorFor helper method. (I also added some div elements to provide structure to the HTML that is generated, relying on the CSS style I defined for the column class back in Listing 22-10.) You can see the result in Figure 22-10.

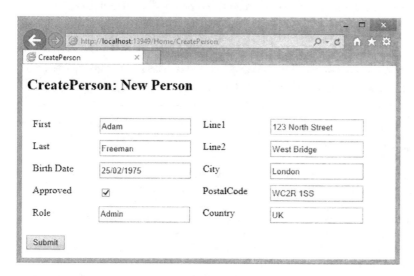

Figure 22-10. *Displaying a complex property*

■ **Tip** The HomeAddress property is typed to return an Address object, and I can apply all of the same metadata to the Address class as I did to the Person class. The Object template is invoked explicitly when I use the EditorFor helpers on the HomeAddress property, and so all of the metadata conventions are honored.

Customizing the Templated View Helper System

I have shown you how to use metadata to shape the way that the templated helpers render data, but this is the MVC Framework and so there are some advanced options that completely customize the templated helpers. In the following sections, I will show you how to supplement or replace the built-in support to create specific results.

Creating a Custom Editor Template

One of the easiest ways of customizing the templated helpers is to create a custom template. This allows me to render exactly the HTML I want for a model property.

To demonstrate how this feature works, I am going to create a custom template for the Role property in the Person class. This property is typed to be a value from the Role enumeration, but the way that this is rendered by default is problematic because the templated helpers just create a regular input element that allows the user to enter any value and not just the values defined by the enumeration.

The MVC Framework looks for custom editor templates in the /Views/Shared/EditorTemplates folder, so I created this folder in the example project and then created a new strongly typed partial view called Role.cshtml within it. You can see the contents of this file in Listing 22-19.

Listing 22-19. The Contents of the Role.cshtml File

```
@model HelperMethods.Models.Role

@Html.DropDownListFor(m => m,
    new SelectList(Enum.GetNames(Model.GetType()), Model.ToString()))
```

The model type for this view is the Role enumeration and I use the Html.DropDownListFor helper method to create a select with option elements for the values in the enumeration. I passed an additional value to the SelectList constructor, which specifies the selected value, which I obtained from the view model object. The DropDownListFor method and the SelectList object operate on string values, so I have to make sure that I cast the enumeration values and the view model value.

When I use any of the templated helper methods to generate an editor for the Role type, my /Views/Shared/EditorTemplates/Role.cshtml file will be used, ensuring that I present the user with a consistent and usable representation of the data type. You can see the effect of the custom template in Figure 22-11.

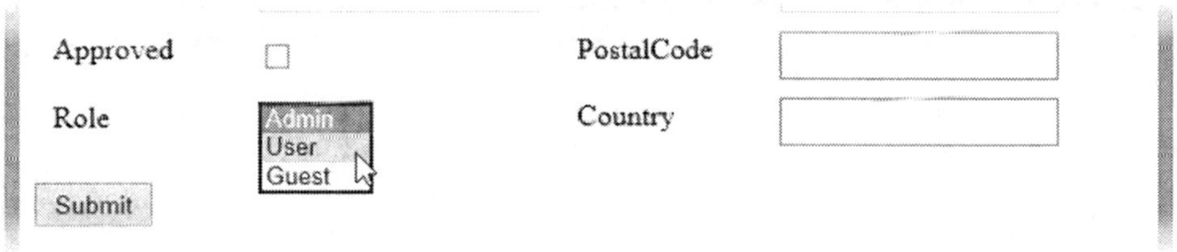

Figure 22-11. *The effect of a custom template for the Role enumeration*

UNDERSTANDING THE TEMPLATE SEARCH ORDER

The Role.cshtml template works because the MVC Framework looks for custom templates for a given C# type before it uses one of the built-in templates. In fact, there is a specific sequence that the MVC Framework follows to find a suitable template:

1. The template passed to the helper. For example, Html.EditorFor(m => m.SomeProperty, "MyTemplate") would lead to MyTemplate being used.

2. Any template that is specified by metadata attributes, such as UIHint

3. The template associated with any data type specified by metadata, such as the DataType attribute

4. Any template that corresponds to the .NET class name of the data type being processed

5. The built-in String template if the data type being processed is a simple type

6. Any template that corresponds to the base classes of the data type

641

7. If the data type implements IEnumerable, then the built-in Collection template will be used.

8. If all else fails, the Object template will be used, subject to the rule that scaffolding is not recursive.

Some of these steps rely on the built-in templates, which are described in Table 22-5. At each stage in the template search process, the MVC Framework looks for a template called EditorTemplates/<name> for editor helper methods or DisplayTemplates/<name> for display helper methods. For the Role template, I satisfied step 4 in the search process; I created a template called Role.cshtml and placed it in the /Views/Shared/EditorTemplates folder.

Custom templates are found using the same search pattern as regular views, which means I can create a controller-specific custom template and place it in the ~/Views/<controller>/EditorTemplates folder to override the templates found in the ~/Views/Shared/EditorTemplates folder.

Creating a Generic Template

I am not limited to creating type-specific templates. I can, for example, create a template that works for all enumerations and then specify that this template be selected using the UIHint attribute. If you look at the template search sequence in the "Understanding the Template Search Order" sidebar, you will see that templates specified using the UIHint attribute take precedence over type-specific ones.

To demonstrate how this works, I have created a new view file called Enum.cshtml in the /Views/Shared/EditorTemplates folder. The contents of this file are shown in Listing 22-20.

Listing 22-20. The Contents of the Enum.cshtml

```
@model Enum

@Html.DropDownListFor(m => m, Enum.GetValues(Model.GetType())
    .Cast<Enum>()
    .Select(m => {
        string enumVal = Enum.GetName(Model.GetType(), m);
        return new SelectListItem() {
            Selected = (Model.ToString() == enumVal),
            Text = enumVal,
            Value = enumVal
        };
    }))
```

The model type for this template is Enum, which allows me to work with any enumeration. For variety, I have used some LINQ to generate the strings that are required to create the select and option elements (although this is not a requirement for a generic template: I just like LINQ).

I can then apply the UIHint attribute. The example project defines a metadata buddy class, so I have applied the attribute to the PersonMetadata class, as shown in Listing 22-21. (As a reminder, you can find this class defined in the /Models/Metadata/PersonMetadata.cs file.)

Listing 22-21. Using the UIHint Attribute to Specify a Custom Template in the PersonMetadata.cs File

```
using System;
using System.ComponentModel;
using System.ComponentModel.DataAnnotations;
using System.Web.Mvc;

namespace HelperMethods.Models {

    [DisplayName("New Person")]
    public partial class PersonMetaData {
        [HiddenInput(DisplayValue=false)]
        public int PersonId { get; set; }

        [Display(Name="First")]
        public string FirstName { get; set; }

        [Display(Name = "Last")]
        public string LastName { get; set; }

        [Display(Name = "Birth Date")]
        [DataType(DataType.Date)]
        public DateTime BirthDate { get; set; }

        [Display(Name="Approved")]
        public bool IsApproved { get; set; }

        [UIHint("Enum")]
        public Role Role { get; set; }
    }
}
```

This approach gives a more general solution that you can apply throughout an application to ensure that all Enum properties are displayed using a select element. I prefer to create model type-specific custom templates, but it can be more convenient to have one template that you can apply widely.

Replacing the Built-in Templates

If I create a custom template that has the same name as one of the built-in templates, the MVC Framework will use the custom version in preference to the built-in one. Listing 22-22 shows the contents of the Boolean.cshtml file that I added to the /Views/Shared/EditorTemplates folder. This view replaces the built-in Boolean template which is used to render bool and bool? values.

Listing 22-22. The Contents of the Boolean.cshtml File

```
@model bool?

@if (ViewData.ModelMetadata.IsNullableValueType && Model == null) {
    @:(True) (False) <b>(Not Set)</b>
} else if (Model.Value) {
    @:<b>(True)</b> (False) (Not Set)
} else {
    @:(True) <b>(False)</b> (Not Set)
}
```

In this view, I display all of the possible values and highlight the one that corresponds to the model object. You can see the effect of this template in Figure 22-12.

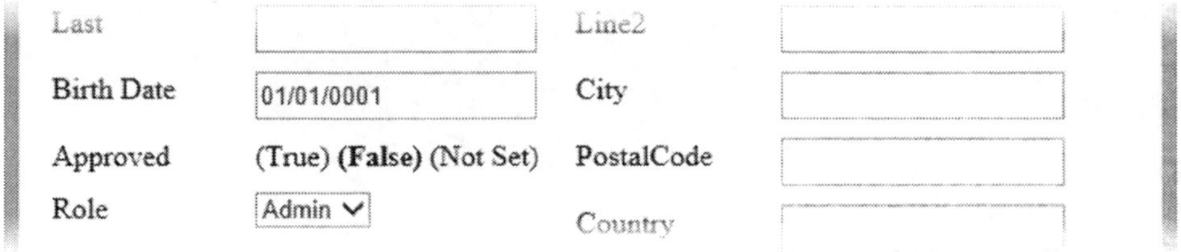

Figure 22-12. *The effect of overriding a built-in editor template*

You can see the flexibility that custom templates offer, even if the example I have shown is not especially useful and does not let the user change the property value. As you have seen, there are a number of different ways that you can control how your model properties are displayed and edited, and you can pick the approach that suits your programming style and application best.

Summary

In this chapter, I have shown you the system of model templates that are accessible through the templated view helper methods. It can take a little while to set up the metadata and to create custom templates, but the result is closely tailored to your application and gives you complete flexibility in how your view model data is displayed and edited.

CHAPTER 23

URL and Ajax Helper Methods

In this chapter, I am going to complete my coverage of the MVC Framework helper methods by showing you those methods that are able to generate URLs, links, and Ajax-enabled elements. Ajax is a key feature of any rich Web application and the MVC Framework includes some useful features that are based on the jQuery library. I'll show you how this works and demonstrate how you can use it to create Ajax-enabled forms and links. Table 23-1 provides the summary for this chapter.

Table 23-1. *Chapter Summary*

Problem	Solution	Listing
Generate links and URLs	Use the `Url.Content`, `Url.Action`, `Url.RouteUrl`, `Html.ActionLink`, `Html.RouteLink` helpers.	1–3
Submit form data via Ajax	Use the unobtrusive Ajax package and the `Ajax.BeginForm` helper.	4–10
Ensure that non-JavaScript browsers do not display HTML fragments	Set the `Url` Ajax option.	11
Provide the user with feedback during an Ajax request	Use the `LoadingElementId` and `LoadingElementDuration` Ajax options.	12
Prompt the user before making an Ajax request	Use the `Confirm` Ajax option.	13
Create an Ajax enabled link	Use the `Ajax.ActionLink` helper.	14, 15
Receive notifications about the progress and outcome of Ajax requests	Use the Ajax callback options.	16
Use JSON data in Ajax requests	Use the `JsonResult` action result.	17–19
Detect Ajax requests in the controller	Use the `Request.IsAjaxRequest` method.	20, 21

> **Note**   You will need to clear the browser history as you go from one example in this chapter to the next. This is just because I build features incrementally and isn't something you would need to worry about in a real project. I have added notes to remind you at key points in the chapter, but if you don't get the result you are expecting from an example then the first thing to try is clearing the history.

Preparing the Example Project

I am going to continue using the HelperMethods project that I created in Chapter 21 and added to in Chapter 22. For this chapter, I have created a new controller called People, shown in Listing 23-1. This controller defines a collection of Person model objects that I will use to demonstrate different helper features.

Listing 23-1. The Contents of the PeopleController.cs File

```
using System;
using System.Linq;
using System.Web.Mvc;
using HelperMethods.Models;

namespace HelperMethods.Controllers {
    public class PeopleController : Controller {
        private Person[] personData = {
            new Person {FirstName = "Adam", LastName = "Freeman", Role = Role.Admin},
            new Person {FirstName = "Jacqui", LastName = "Griffyth", Role = Role.User},
            new Person {FirstName = "John", LastName = "Smith", Role = Role.User},
            new Person {FirstName = "Anne", LastName = "Jones", Role = Role.Guest}
        };

        public ActionResult Index() {
            return View();
        }

        public ActionResult GetPeople() {
            return View(personData);
        }

        [HttpPost]
        public ActionResult GetPeople(string selectedRole) {
            if (selectedRole == null || selectedRole == "All") {
                return View(personData);
            } else {
                Role selected = (Role)Enum.Parse(typeof(Role), selectedRole);
                return View(personData.Where(p => p.Role == selected));
            }
        }
    }
}
```

I have not used any new techniques in this controller. The Index action method returns the default view. I will use the two GetPeople action methods to handle a simple form. The new features in this chapter appear in the views, which I create as I demonstrate different helper methods.

Defining Additional CSS Styles

I also need to add some new CSS styles to the project, which I have done in the Views/Shared/_Layout.cshtml file, as shown in Listing 23-2. I will define the elements the new styles apply to as I go through the chapter.

Listing 23-2. Adding Styles to the _Layout.cshtml File

```
<!DOCTYPE html>
<html>
<head>
    <meta charset="utf-8" />
    <meta name="viewport" content="width=device-width" />
    <title>@ViewBag.Title</title>
    <style type="text/css">
        label { display: inline-block; width: 100px; }
        div.dataElem { margin: 5px; }
        h2 > label { width: inherit; }
        .editor-label, .editor-field { float: left; margin-top: 10px; }
        .editor-field input { height: 20px; }
        .editor-label { clear: left; }
        .editor-field { margin-left: 10px; }
        input[type=submit] { float: left; clear: both; margin-top: 10px; }
        .column { float: left; margin: 10px; }
        table, td, th { border: thin solid black; border-collapse: collapse;
            padding: 5px; background-color: lemonchiffon;
            text-align: left; margin: 10px 0; }
        div.load { color: red; margin: 10px 0; font-weight: bold; }
        div.ajaxLink { margin-top: 10px; margin-right: 5px; float: left; }
    </style>
</head>
<body>
    @RenderBody()
</body>
</html>
```

Installing the NuGet Packages

The MVC Framework relies on the Microsoft *Unobtrusive Ajax* package to make and process Ajax requests. To install this package, select Package Manager Console from the Visual Studio Tools ➤ Library Package Manager menu and enter the following command:

```
Install-Package jQuery -version 1.10.2
Install-Package Microsoft.jQuery.Unobtrusive.Ajax -version 3.0.0
```

NuGet will install the package—and the jQuery library it depends on—into the project, creating a Scripts folder that contains a number of JavaScript files.

Creating Basic Links and URLs

One of the most fundamental tasks in a view is to create a link or URL that the user can follow to another part of the application. In previous chapters, you saw most of the helper methods that you can use to create links and URLs, but I want to take a moment to recap before moving on to some of the more advanced helpers that are available. Table 23-2 describes the available HTML helpers and it shows examples of each of them.

Table 23-2. HTML Helpers That Render URLs

Description	Example
Application-relative URL	`Url.Content("~/Content/Site.css")`
	Output: `/Content/Site.css`
Link to named action/controller	`Html.ActionLink("My Link", "Index", "Home")`
	Output: `<a href="/">My Link</a>`
URL for action	`Url.Action("GetPeople", "People")`
	Output: `/People/GetPeople`
URL using route data	`Url.RouteUrl(new {controller = "People", action="GetPeople"})`
	Output: `/People/GetPeople`
Link using route data	`Html.RouteLink("My Link", new {controller = "People",` `    action="GetPeople"})`
	Output: `<a href="/People/GetPeople">My Link</a>`
Link to named route	`Html.RouteLink("My Link", "FormRoute", new {controller = "People",` `    action="GetPeople"})`
	Output: `<a href="/app/forms/People/GetPeople">My Link</a>`

■ **Tip**   As a reminder, the benefit of using these helpers to generate links and URLs is that the output is derived from the routing configuration, which means that a change in routes is automatically reflected in the links and URLs.

To demonstrate these helpers in action, I added an `Index.cshtml` view file to the `Views/People` folder, the contents of which you can see in Listing 23-3.

Listing 23-3. The Contents of the Index.cshtml File

```
@{
    ViewBag.Title = "Index";
    Layout = "/Views/Shared/_Layout.cshtml";
}
<h2>Basic Links & URLs</h2>
<table>
    <thead><tr><th>Helper</th><th>Output</th></tr></thead>
    <tbody>
        <tr>
            <td>Url.Content("~/Content/Site.css")</td>
            <td>@Url.Content("~/Content/Site.css")</td>
        </tr>
```

```
        <tr>
            <td>Html.ActionLink("My Link", "Index", "Home")</td>
            <td>@Html.ActionLink("My Link", "Index", "Home")</td>
        </tr>
        <tr>
            <td>Url.Action("GetPeople", "People")</td>
            <td>@Url.Action("GetPeople", "People")</td>
        </tr>
        <tr>
            <td>Url.RouteUrl(new {controller = "People", action="GetPeople"})</td>
            <td>@Url.RouteUrl(new {controller = "People", action="GetPeople"})</td>
        </tr>
        <tr>
            <td>Html.RouteLink("My Link", new {controller = "People",
                action="GetPeople"})</td>
            <td>@Html.RouteLink("My Link", new {controller = "People",
                action-"GetPeople"})</td>
        </tr>
        <tr>
            <td>Html.RouteLink("My Link", "FormRoute", new {controller = "People",
                action="GetPeople"})</td>
            <td>@Html.RouteLink("My Link", "FormRoute", new {controller = "People",
                action="GetPeople"})</td>
        </tr>
    </tbody>
</table>
```

This view contains the same set of helper calls that I listed in Table 23-2 and presents the results in an HTML table. You can see the effect by starting the application and navigating to the /People/Index URL, as shown in Figure 23-1. I have included this example because it makes it easy to experiment with routing changes and immediately see the effect.

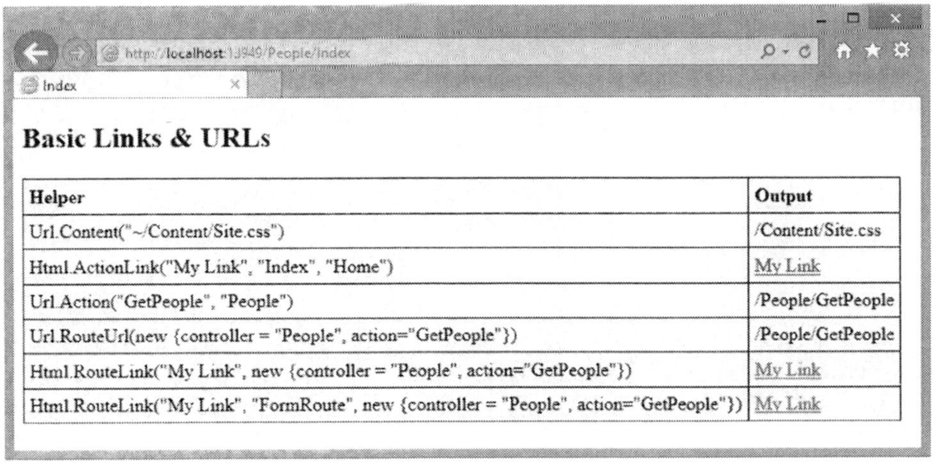

Figure 23-1. *Using helpers to create links and URLs*

Using MVC Unobtrusive Ajax

Ajax (or, if you prefer, *AJAX*) is shorthand for *Asynchronous JavaScript and XML*. The XML part is not as significant as it used to be, but the asynchronous part is what makes Ajax useful. It is a model for requesting data from the server in the background, without having to reload the Web page. The MVC Framework contains built-in support for *unobtrusive* Ajax, which means that you use helper methods to define your Ajax features, rather than having to add blocks of code throughout your views.

■ **Tip**   The MVC Framework unobtrusive Ajax feature is based on jQuery. If you are familiar with the way that jQuery handles Ajax, then you will understand the MVC Ajax features.

Creating the Synchronous Form View

I am going to begin this section by creating the view for the `GetPeople` action in the controller, which I created as the `/Views/People/GetPeople.cshtml` file. You can see the contents of this file in Listing 23-4.

Listing 23-4. The Contents of the GetPeople.cshtml View File

```
@using HelperMethods.Models
@model IEnumerable<Person>
@{
    ViewBag.Title = "GetPeople";
    Layout = "/Views/Shared/_Layout.cshtml";
}
<h2>Get People</h2>
<table>
    <thead><tr><th>First</th><th>Last</th><th>Role</th></tr></thead>
    <tbody>
        @foreach (Person p in Model) {
            <tr>
                <td>@p.FirstName</td>
                <td>@p.LastName</td>
                <td>@p.Role</td>
            </tr>
        }
    </tbody>
</table>

@using (Html.BeginForm()) {
    <div>
        @Html.DropDownList("selectedRole", new SelectList(
            new [] {"All"}.Concat(Enum.GetNames(typeof(Role)))))
        <button type="submit">Submit</button>
    </div>
}
```

This is a strongly typed view whose model type is IEnumerable<Person>. I enumerate the Person objects in the model to create rows in an HTML table and use the Html.BeginForm helper to create a form that posts back to the action and controller that the view was generated by. The form contains a call to the Html.DropDownList helper, which I use to create a select element that contains option elements for each of the values defined by the Role enumeration, plus the value All. (I have used LINQ to create the list of values for the option elements by concatenating the values in the enum with an array that contains a single All string.)

The form contains a button that submits the form. The effect is that you can use the form to filter the Person objects that I defined in the controller in Listing 23-1, as shown in Figure 23-2. To test, start the application and navigate to the /People/GetPeople URL.

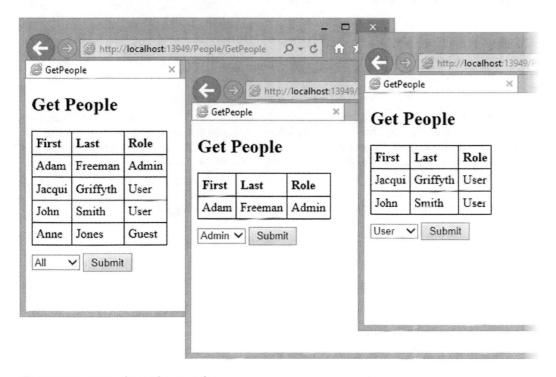

Figure 23-2. *A simple synchronous form*

This is a simple demonstration of a fundamental limitation in HTML forms, which is that the entire page is reloaded when the form is submitted. It means that the entire content of the Web page has to be regenerated and loaded from the server (which can be an expensive operation for complex views) and while this is happening, users cannot perform any other task with the application. They have to wait until the new page is generated, loaded, and then displayed by the browser.

For a simple application like this one, where the browser and server are running on the same machine, the delay is hardly noticeable. But for real applications over real internet connections, synchronous forms can make using a Web application frustrating for the user and expensive in terms of server bandwidth and processing power.

Preparing the Project for Unobtrusive Ajax

The unobtrusive Ajax feature is set up in two places in the application. First, in the Web.config file (the one in the root folder of the project) the configuration/appSettings element contains an entry for the UnobtrusiveJavaScriptEnabled property, which must be set to true, as shown in Listing 23-5. (This property is set to true by default when Visual Studio creates the project.)

Listing 23-5. Enabling the Unobtrusive Ajax Feature in the Web.config File

```xml
<?xml version="1.0" encoding="utf-8"?>

<configuration>
  <appSettings>
    <add key="webpages:Version" value="3.0.0.0" />
    <add key="webpages:Enabled" value="false" />
    <add key="ClientValidationEnabled" value="true" />
    <add key="UnobtrusiveJavaScriptEnabled" value="true" />
  </appSettings>
  <system.web>
    <compilation debug="true" targetFramework="4.5.1" />
    <httpRuntime targetFramework="4.5.1" />
  </system.web>
</configuration>
```

In addition to checking the Web.config setting, I need to add references to the jQuery JavaScript libraries that implement the unobtrusive Ajax functionality from the NuGet package I added at the start of the chapter. You can reference the libraries from individual views, but a more common approach is to do this in a layout file so that it affects all of the views that use that layout. In Listing 23-6, you can see how I have added references for two JavaScript libraries to the /Views/Shared/_Layout.cshtml file.

Listing 23-6. Adding References for the Unobtrusive Ajax JavaScript Libraries to the _Layout.cshtml File

```html
<!DOCTYPE html>
<html>
<head>
    <meta charset="utf-8" />
    <meta name="viewport" content="width=device-width" />
    <title>@ViewBag.Title</title>
    <style type="text/css">
        label { display: inline-block; width: 100px; }
        div.dataElem { margin: 5px; }
        h2 > label { width: inherit; }
        .editor-label, .editor-field { float: left; margin-top: 10px; }
        .editor-field input { height: 20px; }
        .editor-label { clear: left; }
        .editor-field { margin-left: 10px; }
        input[type=submit] { float: left; clear: both; margin-top: 10px; }
        .column { float: left; margin: 10px; }
        table, td, th { border: thin solid black; border-collapse: collapse;
            padding: 5px; background-color: lemonchiffon;
            text-align: left; margin: 10px 0; }
        div.load { color: red; margin: 10px 0; font-weight: bold; }
        div.ajaxLink { margin-top: 10px; margin-right: 5px; float: left; }
    </style>
    <script src="~/Scripts/jquery-1.10.2.js"></script>
    <script src="~/Scripts/jquery.unobtrusive-ajax.js"></script>
</head>
```

```
<body>
    @RenderBody()
</body>
</html>
```

The files that I have referenced with the script elements were added to the Scripts folder by the NuGet package. The jquery-1.10.2.js file contains the core jQuery library and the jquery.unobtrusive-ajax.js file contains the Ajax functionality (which relies on the main jQuery library).

Creating an Unobtrusive Ajax Form

I am now ready to start applying unobtrusive Ajax features to the example application, starting with an unobtrusive Ajax form. In the sections that follow, I go through the process of replacing a regular synchronous form with an Ajax equivalent and explain how the unobtrusive Ajax feature works.

Preparing the Controller

The goal is that only the data in the HTML table element is replaced when the user clicks on the Submit button in the example application. That means that the first thing that I need to do is refactor the action methods in the People controller so that I can get just the data I want through a child action. You can see the changes I have made to the People controller in Listing 23-7.

Listing 23-7. Refactoring the Action Methods in the PeopleController.cs File

```
using System;
using System.Collections.Generic;
using System.Linq;
using System.Web;
using System.Web.Mvc;
using HelperMethods.Models;

namespace HelperMethods.Controllers {
    public class PeopleController : Controller {
        private Person[] personData = {
            new Person {FirstName = "Adam", LastName = "Freeman", Role = Role.Admin},
            new Person {FirstName = "Jacqui", LastName = "Griffyth", Role = Role.User},
            new Person {FirstName = "John", LastName = "Smith", Role = Role.User},
            new Person {FirstName = "Anne", LastName = "Jones", Role = Role.Guest}
        };

        public ActionResult Index() {
            return View();
        }

        public PartialViewResult GetPeopleData(string selectedRole = "All") {
            IEnumerable<Person> data = personData;
            if (selectedRole != "All") {
                Role selected = (Role)Enum.Parse(typeof(Role), selectedRole);
                data = personData.Where(p => p.Role == selected);
            }
            return PartialView(data);
        }
```

```
        public ActionResult GetPeople(string selectedRole = "All") {
            return View((object)selectedRole);
        }
    }
}
```

I have added a GetPeopleData action that selects the Person objects that I need to display, and passes them to the PartialView method to generate the table rows that are required. Because the selection of the data is handled in the GetPeopleData action method, I have been able to simplify the GetPeople action method and remove the HttpPost version entirely. The purpose of this method is to pass the selected role as a string to its view.

I created a new partial view file, /Views/People/GetPeopleData.cshtml, for the new GetPeopleData action method. You can see the contents of the view in Listing 23-8. This view is responsible for generating the tr elements that will populate the table using the enumeration of Person objects that are passed from the action method.

Listing 23-8. The Contents of the GetPeopleData.cshtml File

```
@using HelperMethods.Models
@model IEnumerable<Person>

@foreach (Person p in Model) {
    <tr>
        <td>@p.FirstName</td>
        <td>@p.LastName</td>
        <td>@p.Role</td>
    </tr>
}
```

I also had to update the /Views/People/GetPeople.cshtml view, which you can see in Listing 23-9.

Listing 23-9. Updating the GetPeople.cshtml File

```
@using HelperMethods.Models
@model string
@{
    ViewBag.Title = "GetPeople";
    Layout = "/Views/Shared/_Layout.cshtml";
}
<h2>Get People</h2>
<table>
    <thead><tr><th>First</th><th>Last</th><th>Role</th></tr></thead>
    <tbody>
        @Html.Action("GetPeopleData", new {selectedRole = Model })
    </tbody>
</table>

@using (Html.BeginForm()) {
    <div>
        @Html.DropDownList("selectedRole", new SelectList(
            new [] {"All"}.Concat(Enum.GetNames(typeof(Role)))))
        <button type="submit">Submit</button>
    </div>
}
```

I have changed the view model type to `string`, which I pass to the `Html.Action` helper method to invoke the `GetPeopleData` child action. This renders the partial view and generates the table rows.

Creating the Ajax Form

I still have a synchronous form in the application after these changes, but I have separated out the functionality in the controller so that I can request just the table rows through the `GetPeopleData` action. This new action method will be the target of the Ajax request and the next step is to update the `GetPeople.cshtml` view so that posting the form is handled through Ajax, as shown in Listing 23-10.

Listing 23-10. Creating an Unobtrusive Ajax Form in the GetPeople.cshtml File

```
@using HelperMethods.Models
@model string
@{
    ViewBag.Title = "GetPeople";
    Layout = "/Views/Shared/_Layout.cshtml";
    AjaxOptions ajaxOpts = new AjaxOptions {
        UpdateTargetId = "tableBody"
    };
}
<h2>Get People</h2>
<table>
    <thead><tr><th>First</th><th>Last</th><th>Role</th></tr></thead>
    <tbody id="tableBody">
        @Html.Action("GetPeopleData", new {selectedRole = Model })
    </tbody>
</table>

@using (Ajax.BeginForm("GetPeopleData", ajaxOpts)) {
    <div>
        @Html.DropDownList("selectedRole", new SelectList(
            new [] {"All"}.Concat(Enum.GetNames(typeof(Role)))))
        <button type="submit">Submit</button>
    </div>
}
```

At the heart of the MVC Framework support for Ajax forms is the `Ajax.BeginForm` helper method, which takes an `AjaxOptions` object as its argument. I like to create the `AjaxOptions` objects at the start of the view in a Razor code block, but you can create them inline when you call `Ajax.BeginForm` if you prefer.

The `AjaxOptions` class, which is in the `System.Web.Mvc.Ajax` namespace, defines properties that let me configure how the asynchronous request to the server is made and what happens to the data that comes back. These properties are described in Table 23-3.

Table 23-3. *AjaxOptions Properties*

Property	Description
Confirm	Sets a message to be displayed to the user in a confirmation window before making the Ajax request
HttpMethod	Sets the HTTP method that will be used to make the request—must be either Get or Post
InsertionMode	Specifies the way in which the content retrieved from the server is inserted into the HTML. The three choices are expressed as values from the InsertionMode enum: InsertAfter, InsertBefore and Replace (which is the default).
LoadingElementId	Specifies the ID of an HTML element that will be displayed while the Ajax request is being performed
LoadingElementDuration	Specifies the duration of the animation used to reveal the element specified by LoadingElementId
UpdateTargetId	Sets the ID of the HTML element into which the content retrieved from the server will be inserted
Url	Sets the URL that will be requested from the server

In the listing, I have set the UpdateTargetId property to tableBody. This is the id I assigned to the tbody HTML element in the view in Listing 23-10. When the user clicks the Submit button, an asynchronous request will be made to the GetPeopleData action method and the HTML fragment that is returned is used to replace the existing elements in the tbody.

■ **Tip** The AjaxOptions class also defines properties that specify callbacks for different stages in the request life cycle. See the "Working with Ajax Callbacks" section later in this chapter for details.

That's all there is to it: I replace the Html.BeginForm method with Ajax.BeginForm and ensure that I have a target for the new content. Everything else happens automatically and the result is an asynchronous form.

It can be hard to detect when you are testing with the browser and the server on the same machine, but you can tell that the browser is making Ajax requests for fragments of HTML by using the browser F12 tools. These tools allow you to monitor the network requests that the browser makes and in Figure 23-3, you can see the Internet Explorer tools showing a call to the GetPeopleData action method.

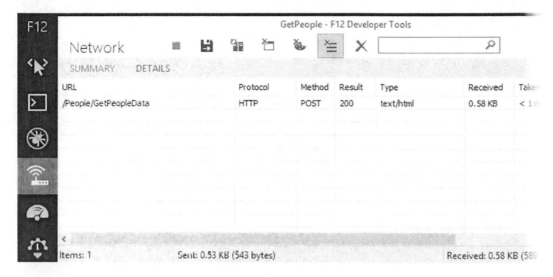

Figure 23-3. *Confirming that Ajax requests are being made*

Understanding How Unobtrusive Ajax Works

When I call the Ajax.BeginForm helper method, the options that I specify using the AjaxOptions object are transformed into attributes applied to the form element. The view in Listing 23-10 produces the following form element:

```
...
<form action="/People/GetPeopleData" data-ajax="true" data-ajax-mode="replace"
    data-ajax-update="#tableBody" id="form0" method="post">
...
```

When the HTML page rendered from the GetPeople.cshtml view is loaded by the browser, the JavaScript in the jquery.unobtrusive-ajax.js library scans the HTML elements and identifies the Ajax form by looking for elements that have a data-ajax attribute with a value of true.

The other attributes whose names start with data-ajax contain the values I specified using the AjaxOptions class. These configuration options are used to configure jQuery, which has built-in support for managing Ajax requests.

■ **Tip**   You don't have to use the MVC Framework support for unobtrusive Ajax. There are plenty of alternatives available, including using jQuery directly. That said, pick a technique and stick to it. I recommend against mixing the MVC Framework unobtrusive Ajax support with other techniques and libraries in the same view, as there can be some unfortunate interactions, such as duplicated or dropped Ajax requests.

Setting Ajax Options

I can fine-tune the behavior of the Ajax requests by setting values for the properties of the AjaxOptions object that I pass to the Ajax.BeginForm helper method. In the following sections, I explain what each of these options does and why they can be useful.

Ensuring Graceful Degradation

When I set up the Ajax-enabled form in Listing 23-10, I passed in the name of the action method that I wanted to be called asynchronously. In the example, this was the GetPeopleData action, which generates a partial view containing a fragment of HTML.

One problem with this approach is that it doesn't work well if the user has disabled JavaScript (or is using a browser that doesn't support it). In such cases, when the user submits the form, the browser display discards the current HTML page and replaces it with the fragment returned by the target action method. The effect can be seen in Figure 23-4.

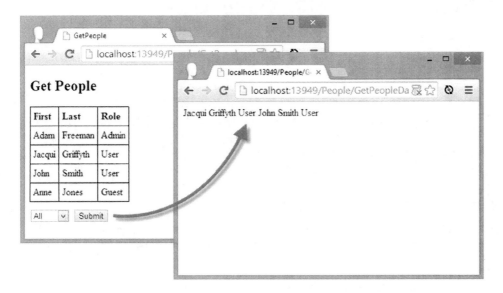

Figure 23-4. *The effect of using the Ajax.BeginForm helper without browser JavaScript support*

■ **Note**   I used Google Chrome for this figure because it makes it easy to toggle JavaScript.

The simplest way to address this problem is to use the AjaxOptions.Url property to specify the target URL for the asynchronous request rather than specifying the action name as an argument to the Ajax.BeginForm method, as shown in Listing 23-11.

Listing 23-11. Ensuring Gracefully Degrading Forms in the GetPeople.cshtml File

```
@using HelperMethods.Models
@model string
@{
    ViewBag.Title = "GetPeople";
    Layout = "/Views/Shared/_Layout.cshtml";
    AjaxOptions ajaxOpts = new AjaxOptions {
        UpdateTargetId = "tableBody",
        Url = Url.Action("GetPeopleData")
    };

}
```

```
<h2>Get People</h2>
<table>
    <thead><tr><th>First</th><th>Last</th><th>Role</th></tr></thead>
    <tbody id="tableBody">
        @Html.Action("GetPeopleData", new {selectedRole = Model })
    </tbody>
</table>

@using (Ajax.BeginForm(ajaxOpts)) {
    <div>
        @Html.DropDownList("selectedRole", new SelectList(
            new [] {"All"}.Concat(Enum.GetNames(typeof(Role)))))
        <button type="submit">Submit</button>
    </div>
}
```

I have used the Url.Action helper method to create a URL that will invoke the GetPeopleData action, and used the version of the Ajax.BeginForm method that takes only an AjaxOptions parameter. This has the effect of creating a form element that posts back to the originating action method if JavaScript isn't enabled, like this:

```
...
<form action="/People/GetPeople" data-ajax="true" data-ajax-mode="replace"
    data-ajax-update="#tableBody" data-ajax-url="/People/GetPeopleData" id="form0"
    method="post">
...
```

If JavaScript is enabled, then the unobtrusive Ajax library will take the target URL from the data-ajax-url attribute, which refers to the child action. If JavaScript is disabled, then the browser will use the regular form posting technique, which takes the target URL from the action attribute, which points back at the action method that will generate a complete HTML page.

■ **Caution**   You might be wondering why I am making such a big deal about users who have disabled JavaScript. After all, who does that? In fact, it is prevalent in two groups of users. The first group consists of those users who take their IT security seriously and disable anything that could be used as the basis for an attack, something that JavaScript has been known for over the years. The second group is users in large corporations, which apply incredibly restrictive policies in the name of IT security (although, in my experience, corporate PCs are so poorly set up that security is nonexistent and the restrictions just annoy the users). You can ignore graceful degradation if you feel you can ignore IT security experts and people who work for big companies. But, since these can be affluent and tech-savvy users, I always take the time to make sure I support them.

Providing the User with Feedback While Making an Ajax Request

One drawback of using Ajax is that it isn't obvious to the user that something is happening, because the request to the server is made in the background. I can inform the user that a request is being performed by using the AjaxOptions.LoadingElementId and AjaxOptions.LoadingElementDuration properties. Listing 23-12 shows how I have applied these properties in the GetPeople.cshtml view file.

Listing 23-12. Giving Feedback to the User in the GetPeople.cshtml File

```
@using HelperMethods.Models
@model string
@{
    ViewBag.Title = "GetPeople";
    Layout = "/Views/Shared/_Layout.cshtml";
    AjaxOptions ajaxOpts = new AjaxOptions {
        UpdateTargetId = "tableBody",
        Url = Url.Action("GetPeopleData"),
        LoadingElementId = "loading",
        LoadingElementDuration = 1000
    };

}
<h2>Get People</h2>

<div id="loading" class="load" style="display:none">
    <p>Loading Data...</p>
</div>

<table>
    <thead><tr><th>First</th><th>Last</th><th>Role</th></tr></thead>
    <tbody id="tableBody">
        @Html.Action("GetPeopleData", new {selectedRole = Model })
    </tbody>
</table>

@using (Ajax.BeginForm(ajaxOpts)) {
    <div>
        @Html.DropDownList("selectedRole", new SelectList(
            new [] {"All"}.Concat(Enum.GetNames(typeof(Role)))))
        <button type="submit">Submit</button>
    </div>
}
```

The AjaxOptions.LoadingElementId property specifies the id attribute value of a hidden HTML element that will be shown to the user while an Ajax request is performed. To demonstrate this feature, I added a div element to the view that I hid from the user by setting the CSS display property to none. I gave this div element an id attribute of loading and used this id as the value for the LoadingElementId property and the unobtrusive Ajax feature will display the element to the user for the duration of the request, as shown in Figure 23-5. The LoadingElementDuration property specifies the duration of the animation that is used to reveal the loading element to the user. I specified a value of 1000, which denotes one second.

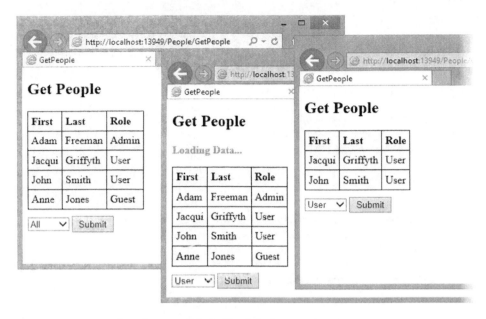

Figure 23-5. *Providing the user with feedback during an Ajax request*

Prompting the User Before Making a Request

The AjaxOptions.Confirm property lets me specify a message that will be used to prompt the user before each asynchronous request. The user can elect to proceed with or cancel the request. Listing 23-13 shows how I have applied this property to the GetPeople.cshtml file.

Listing 23-13. *Promoting the User Before Making an Asynchronous Request in the GetPeople.cshtml File*

```
...
@{
    ViewBag.Title = "GetPeople";
    Layout = "/Views/Shared/_Layout.cshtml";
    AjaxOptions ajaxOpts = new AjaxOptions {
        UpdateTargetId = "tableBody",
        Url = Url.Action("GetPeopleData"),
        LoadingElementId = "loading",
        LoadingElementDuration = 1000,
        Confirm = "Do you wish to request new data?"
    };
}
...
```

With this addition, the user is prompted each time they submit the form, as shown in Figure 23-6. The user is prompted for *every* request, which means that this feature should be used sparingly to avoid irritating the user.

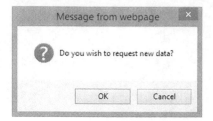

Figure 23-6. *Prompting the user before making a request*

Creating Ajax Links

In addition to forms, unobtrusive Ajax can be used to create a elements that will be followed asynchronously. The mechanism for this is similar to the way that Ajax forms work. You can see how I have added Ajax links to the GetPeople.cshtml view in Listing 23-14.

Listing 23-14. *Creating Ajax-Enabled Links in the GetPeople.cshtml File*

```
@using HelperMethods.Models
@model string
@{
    ViewBag.Title = "GetPeople";
    Layout = "/Views/Shared/_Layout.cshtml";
    AjaxOptions ajaxOpts = new AjaxOptions {
        UpdateTargetId = "tableBody",
        Url = Url.Action("GetPeopleData"),
        LoadingElementId = "loading",
        LoadingElementDuration = 1000,
        Confirm = "Do you wish to request new data?"
    };
}
<h2>Get People</h2>

<div id="loading" class="load" style="display:none">
    <p>Loading Data...</p>
</div>

<table>
    <thead><tr><th>First</th><th>Last</th><th>Role</th></tr></thead>
    <tbody id="tableBody">
        @Html.Action("GetPeopleData", new {selectedRole = Model })
    </tbody>
</table>

@using (Ajax.BeginForm(ajaxOpts)) {
    <div>
        @Html.DropDownList("selectedRole", new SelectList(
            new [] {"All"}.Concat(Enum.GetNames(typeof(Role)))))
        <button type="submit">Submit</button>
    </div>
}
```

```
<div>
    @foreach (string role in Enum.GetNames(typeof(Role))) {
        <div class="ajaxLink">
            @Ajax.ActionLink(role, "GetPeopleData",
                new {selectedRole = role},
                new AjaxOptions {UpdateTargetId = "tableBody"})
        </div>
    }
</div>
```

I have used a foreach loop to call the Ajax.ActionLink helper for each of the values defined by the Role enumeration, creating a set of Ajax-enabled a elements. The a elements that are produced have the same kind of data attributes you saw when working with forms, like this:

```
...
<a data-ajax="true" data-ajax-mode="replace" data-ajax-update="#tableBody"
    href="/People/GetPeopleData?selectedRole=Guest">Guest</a>
...
```

The routing configuration in the project does not have an entry for the selectedRole variable, so the URL that has been generated for the href attribute specifies the role that the link represents using the query string component of the URL.

You can see the links I added to the view in Figure 23-7. Clicking one of these links will call the GetPeopleData action method and replace the contents of the tbody element with the HTML fragment that is returned. This creates the same effect of filtering the data that I achieved using the Ajax-enabled form earlier in the chapter.

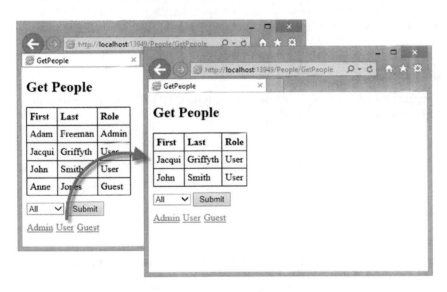

Figure 23-7. Adding Ajax-enabled links to a view

■ **Tip** You may have to clear your browser history to see the changes for this example.

Ensuring Graceful Degradation for Links

I face the same problem with the Ajax-enabled links as I did with the forms. When there is no JavaScript support on the browser, clicking one of the links will just display the HTML fragment that the `GetPeopleData` action method generates.

I can address this using the `AjaxOptions.Url` property to specify the URL for the Ajax request. For this example, I have specified the `GetPeople` action to the `Ajax.ActionLink` helper method, as shown in Listing 23-15.

Listing 23-15. Creating Graceful Ajax-Enabled Links in the GetPeople.cshtml File

```
...
<div>
    @foreach (string role in Enum.GetNames(typeof(Role))) {
        <div class="ajaxLink">
            @Ajax.ActionLink(role, "GetPeople",
                new {selectedRole = role},
                new AjaxOptions {
                    UpdateTargetId = "tableBody",
                    Url = Url.Action("GetPeopleData", new {selectedRole = role})
                })
        </div>
    }
</div>
...
```

This is why I created a new `AjaxOptions` object for each of the links rather than using the one I created in the Razor code block for the `form` element. Independent `AjaxOptions` allow me to specify a different value for the `Url` property for each link and support graceful degradation for non-JavaScript browsers.

Working with Ajax Callbacks

The `AjaxOptions` class defines a set of properties that specify JavaScript functions that will be called at various points in the Ajax request life cycle. These properties are described in Table 23-4.

Table 23-4. AjaxOptions Callback Properties

Property	jQuery Event	Description
OnBegin	beforeSend	Called immediately prior to the request being sent
OnComplete	complete	Called if the request is successful
OnFailure	error	Called if the request fails
OnSuccess	success	Called when the request has completed, irrespective of whether the request succeeded or failed

Each of the `AjaxOptions` callback properties correlates to an Ajax event supported by the jQuery library. I have listed the jQuery events in Table 23-4 for those readers who have used jQuery before. You can get details on each of these events and the parameters that will be passed to your functions at `http://api.jquery.com/jQuery.ajax` or in my book, *Pro jQuery 2.0*, also published by Apress.

In Listing 23-16, you can see how I have used a `script` element to define some basic JavaScript functions that will report on the progress of the Ajax request and use the properties shown in Table 23-4 to specify the functions as handlers for the Ajax events.

Listing 23-16. Using the Ajax Callbacks in the GetPeople.cshtml File

```
@using HelperMethods.Models
@model string
@{
    ViewBag.Title = "GetPeople";
    Layout = "/Views/Shared/_Layout.cshtml";
    AjaxOptions ajaxOpts = new AjaxOptions {
        UpdateTargetId = "tableBody",
        Url = Url.Action("GetPeopleData"),
        LoadingElementId = "loading",
        LoadingElementDuration = 1000,
        Confirm = "Do you wish to request new data?"
    };
}

<script type="text/javascript">
    function OnBegin() {
        alert("This is the OnBegin Callback");
    }

    function OnSuccess(data) {
        alert("This is the OnSuccessCallback: " + data);
    }

    function OnFailure(request, error) {
        alert("This is the OnFailure Callback:" + error);
    }

    function OnComplete(request, status) {
        alert("This is the OnComplete Callback: " + status);
    }
</script>

<h2>Get People</h2>

<div id="loading" class="load" style="display:none">
    <p>Loading Data...</p>
</div>

<table>
    <thead><tr><th>First</th><th>Last</th><th>Role</th></tr></thead>
    <tbody id="tableBody">
        @Html.Action("GetPeopleData", new {selectedRole = Model })
    </tbody>
</table>
```

```
@using (Ajax.BeginForm(ajaxOpts)) {
    <div>
        @Html.DropDownList("selectedRole", new SelectList(
            new [] {"All"}.Concat(Enum.GetNames(typeof(Role)))))
        <button type="submit">Submit</button>
    </div>
}

<div>
    @foreach (string role in Enum.GetNames(typeof(Role))) {
        <div class="ajaxLink">
            @Ajax.ActionLink(role, "GetPeople",
                new {selectedRole = role},
                new AjaxOptions {
                    UpdateTargetId = "tableBody",
                    Url = Url.Action("GetPeopleData", new {selectedRole = role}),
                    OnBegin = "OnBegin",
                    OnFailure = "OnFailure",
                    OnSuccess = "OnSuccess",
                    OnComplete = "OnComplete"
                })
        </div>
    }
</div>
```

I have defined four functions, one for each of the callbacks. For this example, I have kept things simple and simply display a message to the user in each of the functions. With these changes, clicking one of the links will display a sequence of alters that report on the progress of the Ajax request, as shown in Figure 23-8.

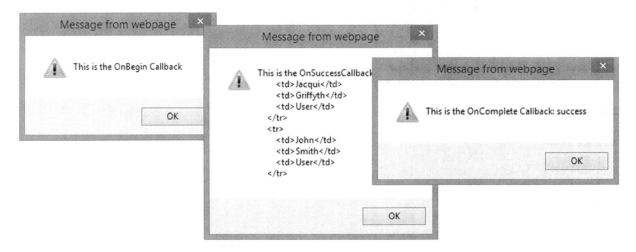

Figure 23-8. *The series of dialog boxes shown in response to the Ajax callbacks*

Displaying dialog boxes to the user for each callback isn't the most useful thing to do with the Ajax callbacks, but it demonstrates the sequence in which they are called. These JavaScript functions can be used for any purpose: manipulate the HTML DOM, trigger additional requests, and so forth. One of the most useful things to do with the callbacks is handle JSON data, which I describe in the next section.

Working with JSON

In the Ajax examples so far, the server has rendered fragments of HTML and sent them to the browser. This is a perfectly acceptable technique, but it is verbose (because the server is sending the HTML elements along with the data) and it limits what can be done with the data at the browser.

One way to address both of these issues is to use the *JavaScript Object Notation* (JSON) format, which is a language-independent way of expressing data. It emerged from the JavaScript language, but has long since taken on a life of its own and is widely used. In this section, I'll show you how to create an action method that returns JSON data, as well as how to process that data in the browser.

■ **Tip** In Chapter 27, I describe the Web API feature, which is an alternative approach for creating Web services.

Adding JSON Support to the Controller

The MVC Framework makes creating an action method that generates JSON data simple. You can see how I have added such an action method to the People controller in Listing 23-17.

Listing 23-17. An Action Method That Returns JSON Data in the PeopleController.cs File

```
using System;
using System.Collections.Generic;
using System.Linq;
using System.Web;
using System.Web.Mvc;
using HelperMethods.Models;

namespace HelperMethods.Controllers {
    public class PeopleController : Controller {
        private Person[] personData = {
            new Person {FirstName = "Adam", LastName = "Freeman", Role = Role.Admin},
            new Person {FirstName = "Jacqui", LastName = "Griffyth", Role = Role.User},
            new Person {FirstName = "John", LastName = "Smith", Role = Role.User},
            new Person {FirstName = "Anne", LastName = "Jones", Role = Role.Guest}
        };

        public ActionResult Index() {
            return View();
        }

        private IEnumerable<Person> GetData(string selectedRole) {
            IEnumerable<Person> data = personData;
            if (selectedRole != "All") {
                Role selected = (Role)Enum.Parse(typeof(Role), selectedRole);
                data = personData.Where(p => p.Role == selected);
            }
            return data;
        }
```

```
    public JsonResult GetPeopleDataJson(string selectedRole = "All") {
        IEnumerable<Person> data = GetData(selectedRole);
        return Json(data, JsonRequestBehavior.AllowGet);
    }

    public PartialViewResult GetPeopleData(string selectedRole = "All") {
        return PartialView(GetData(selectedRole));
    }

    public ActionResult GetPeople(string selectedRole = "All") {
        return View((object)selectedRole);
    }
    }
}
```

Since I want to present the same data in two different formats (HTML and JSON), I have refactored the controller so that there is a common (and private) GetData method that is responsible for performing the filtering.

I have added a new action method called GetPeopleDataJson, which returns a JsonResult object. This is a special kind of ActionResult that tells the view engine that I want to return JSON data to the client, rather than HTML. (You can learn more about the ActionResult class and the role it plays in the MVC Framework in Chapter 17.)

I create a JsonResult by calling the Json method in the action method, passing in the data that I want converted to the JSON format, like this:

```
...
return Json(data, JsonRequestBehavior.AllowGet);
...
```

In this case, I have also passed in the AllowGet value from the JsonRequestBehavior enumeration. By default, JSON data will only be sent in response to POST requests, but by passing this value as a parameter to the Json method, I tell the MVC Framework to respond to GET requests as well.

■ **Caution**   You should only use JsonRequestBehavior.AllowGet if the data you are returning is not private. Due to a security issue in many Web browsers, it's possible for third-party sites to intercept JSON data that you return in response to a GET request, which is why JsonResult will not respond to GET requests by default. In most cases, you will be able to use POST requests to retrieve the JSON data instead, avoiding the problem. For more information, see http://haacked.com/archive/2009/06/25/json-hijacking.aspx.

Processing JSON in the Browser

To process the JSON I retrieve from the MVC Framework application server, I specify a JavaScript function using the OnSuccess callback property in the AjaxOptions class. In Listing 23-18, you can see how I have updated the GetPeople.cshtml view file to remove the handler functions I defined in the last section and use the OnSuccess callback to process the JSON data.

Listing 23-18. Working with JSON Data in the GetPeople.cshtml File

```
@using HelperMethods.Models
@model string
@{
    ViewBag.Title = "GetPeople";
    Layout = "/Views/Shared/_Layout.cshtml";
    AjaxOptions ajaxOpts = new AjaxOptions {
        UpdateTargetId = "tableBody",
        Url = Url.Action("GetPeopleData"),
        LoadingElementId = "loading",
        LoadingElementDuration = 1000,
        Confirm = "Do you wish to request new data?"
    };
}

<script type="text/javascript">
    function processData(data) {
        var target = $("#tableBody");
        target.empty();
        for (var i = 0; i < data.length; i++) {
            var person = data[i];
            target.append("<tr><td>" + person.FirstName + "</td><td>"
                + person.LastName + "</td><td>" + person.Role + "</td></tr>");
        }
    }
</script>

<h2>Get People</h2>

<div id="loading" class="load" style="display:none">
    <p>Loading Data...</p>
</div>

<table>
    <thead><tr><th>First</th><th>Last</th><th>Role</th></tr></thead>
    <tbody id="tableBody">
        @Html.Action("GetPeopleData", new {selectedRole = Model })
    </tbody>
</table>

@using (Ajax.BeginForm(ajaxOpts)) {
    <div>
        @Html.DropDownList("selectedRole", new SelectList(
            new [] {"All"}.Concat(Enum.GetNames(typeof(Role)))))
        <button type="submit">Submit</button>
    </div>
}
```

```
<div>
    @foreach (string role in Enum.GetNames(typeof(Role))) {
        <div class="ajaxLink">
            @Ajax.ActionLink(role, "GetPeople",
                new {selectedRole = role},
                new AjaxOptions {
                    Url = Url.Action("GetPeopleDataJson", new {selectedRole = role}),
                    OnSuccess = "processData"
                })
        </div>
    }
</div>
```

I have defined a new function called processData, which contains some basic jQuery code that processes the JSON objects and uses them to create the tr and td elements needed to populate the table.

■ **Tip**   I don't go into jQuery in this book because it is a topic in and of itself. I love jQuery, though, and if you want to learn more about it, then I have written *Pro jQuery* 2.0 (Apress, 2013).

Notice that I have removed the value for the UpdateTargetId property from the AjaxOptions objects I created for the links. If you forget to do this, the unobtrusive Ajax feature will try and treat the JSON data it retrieves from the server as HTML. You can usually tell this is happening because the contents of the target element will be removed but not replaced with any new data.

You can see the result of the switch to JSON by starting the application, navigating to the /People/GetPeople URL, and clicking one of the links. As Figure 23-9 shows, I don't get quite the right result. In particular, the information displayed in the Role column of the table isn't correct. I will explain why this happens and show you how to make it right in the next section.

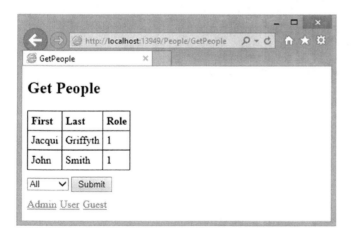

Figure 23-9. *Working with JSON data instead of HTML fragments*

Preparing Data for Encoding

When I called the Json method from within the GetPeopleDataJson action method, I left the MVC Framework to figure out how to encode People objects in the JSON format. The MVC Framework doesn't have any special insights into the model types in an application, and so it makes a best-effort guess about what it needs to do. Here is how the MVC Framework expresses a single Person object in JSON:

```
...
{"PersonId":0,"FirstName":"Adam","LastName":"Freeman",
    "BirthDate":"\/Date(62135596800000)\/","HomeAddress":null,"IsApproved":false,"Role":0}
...
```

It looks like a bit of a mess, but the result is actually pretty clever—it just isn't quite what I need. First, all the properties defined by the Person class are represented in the JSON, even though I did not assign values to some of them in the People controller. In some cases, the default value for the type has been used (false is used for IsApproved, for example), and in others null has been used (such as for HomeAddress). Some values are converted into a form that can be readily interpreted by JavaScript, such as the BirthDate property, but others are not handled as well, such as using 0 for the Role property rather than Admin.

VIEWING JSON DATA

It can be useful to see what JSON data your action methods return and the easiest way to do this is to enter a URL that targets the action in the browser, like this:

```
http://localhost:13949/People/GetPeopleDataJson?selectedRole=Guest
```

You can do this in pretty much any browser, but most will force you to save and open a text file before you can see the JSON content. I like to use the Google Chrome browser for this because it helpfully displays the JSON data in the main browser window, which makes the process quicker and means you don't end up with dozens of open text file windows. I also recommend Fiddler (www.fiddler2.com), which is an excellent Web debugging proxy that allows you to dig right into the details of the data sent between the browser and the server.

The MVC Framework has made a good attempt, but I end up sending properties to the browser that I don't subsequently use and the Role value isn't expressed in a useful way. This is a typical situation when relying on the default JSON encoding, and some preparation of the data you want to send the client is usually required. In Listing 23-19, you can see how I have revised the GetPeopleDataJson action method in the People controller to prepare the data I pass to the Json method.

Listing 23-19. Preparing Data Objects for JSON Encoding in the PeopleController.cs File

```
...
public JsonResult GetPeopleDataJson(string selectedRole = "All") {
    var data = GetData(selectedRole).Select(p => new {
        FirstName = p.FirstName,
        LastName = p.LastName,
        Role = Enum.GetName(typeof(Role), p.Role)
    });
    return Json(data, JsonRequestBehavior.AllowGet);
}
...
```

I have used LINQ to create a sequence of new objects that contain just the `FirstName` and `LastName` properties from the `Person` objects, along with the string representation of the `Role` value. The effect of this change is that I get JSON data that contains just the properties I want, expressed in a way that is more useful to the jQuery code, like this:

```
...
{"FirstName":"Adam","LastName":"Freeman","Role":"Admin"}
...
```

Figure 23-10 shows the change in the output displayed in the browser. You can't tell the unused properties are not sent, of course, but you can see that the `Role` column contains the right values.

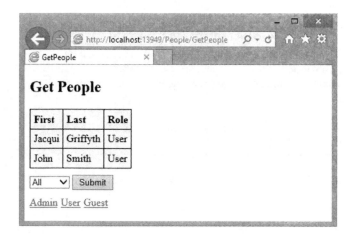

Figure 23-10. *The effect of preparing the data objects for JSON encoding*

■ **Tip** You may have to clear your browser history to see the changes for this example.

Detecting Ajax Requests in the Action Method

The `People` controller presently contains two action methods so that I can support requests for HTML and JSON data. This is usually how I build controllers, because I like lots of short and simple actions, but you don't have to work this way. The MVC Framework provides a simple way of detecting Ajax requests, which means that you can create a single action method that handles multiple data formats. In Listing 23-20, you can see how I have refactored the `Person` controller to contain a single action that handles both JSON and HTML.

Listing 23-20. Creating a Single Action Method in the PersonController.cs File

```
using System;
using System.Collections.Generic;
using System.Linq;
using System.Web;
using System.Web.Mvc;
using HelperMethods.Models;
```

```
namespace HelperMethods.Controllers {
    public class PeopleController : Controller {
        private Person[] personData = {
            new Person {FirstName = "Adam", LastName = "Freeman", Role = Role.Admin},
            new Person {FirstName = "Jacqui", LastName = "Griffyth", Role = Role.User},
            new Person {FirstName = "John", LastName = "Smith", Role = Role.User},
            new Person {FirstName = "Anne", LastName = "Jones", Role = Role.Guest}
        };

        public ActionResult Index() {
            return View();
        }

        public ActionResult GetPeopleData(string selectedRole = "All") {
            IEnumerable<Person> data = personData;
            if (selectedRole != "All") {
                Role selected = (Role)Enum.Parse(typeof(Role), selectedRole);
                data = personData.Where(p => p.Role == selected);
            }
            if (Request.IsAjaxRequest()) {
                var formattedData = data.Select(p => new {
                    FirstName = p.FirstName,
                    LastName = p.LastName,
                    Role = Enum.GetName(typeof(Role), p.Role)
                });
                return Json(formattedData, JsonRequestBehavior.AllowGet);
            } else {
                return PartialView(data);
            }
        }

        public ActionResult GetPeople(string selectedRole = "All") {
            return View((object)selectedRole);
        }
    }
}
```

I used the Request.IsAjaxRequest method to detect Ajax requests and deliver the JSON format if the result is true. There are a couple of limitations that you should be aware of before you follow this approach. First, the IsAjaxRequest methods returns true if the browser has included the X-Requested-With header in its request and set the value to XMLHttpRequest. This is a widely used convention, but it isn't universal and so you should consider whether your users are likely to make requests that require JSON data without setting this header.

The second limitation is that it assumes that all Ajax requests require JSON data. Your application may be better served by separating the way that a request has been made from the data format that the client seeks. This is my preferred approach and the reason I tend to define separate action methods for data formats.

I also need to make two changes to the GetPeople.cshtml view to support the single action method, as shown in Listing 23-21.

Listing 23-21. Supporting a Single Data Action Method in the GetPeople.cshtml File

```
@using HelperMethods.Models
@model string
@{
    ViewBag.Title = "GetPeople";
    Layout = "/Views/Shared/_Layout.cshtml";
    AjaxOptions ajaxOpts = new AjaxOptions {
        Url = Url.Action("GetPeopleData"),
        LoadingElementId = "loading",
        LoadingElementDuration = 1000,
        OnSuccess = "processData"
    };
}

<script type="text/javascript">
    function processData(data) {
        var target = $("#tableBody");
        target.empty();
        for (var i = 0; i < data.length; i++) {
            var person = data[i];
            target.append("<tr><td>" + person.FirstName + "</td><td>"
                + person.LastName + "</td><td>" + person.Role
                + "</td></tr>");
        }
    }
</script>

<h2>Get People</h2>

<div id="loading" class="load" style="display:none">
    <p>Loading Data...</p>
</div>

<table>
    <thead><tr><th>First</th><th>Last</th><th>Role</th></tr></thead>
    <tbody id="tableBody">
        @Html.Action("GetPeopleData", new {selectedRole = Model })
    </tbody>
</table>

@using (Ajax.BeginForm(ajaxOpts)) {
    <div>
        @Html.DropDownList("selectedRole", new SelectList(
            new [] {"All"}.Concat(Enum.GetNames(typeof(Role)))))
        <button type="submit">Submit</button>
    </div>
}
```

```
<div>
    @foreach (string role in Enum.GetNames(typeof(Role))) {
        <div class="ajaxLink">
            @Ajax.ActionLink(role, "GetPeople",
                new {selectedRole = role},
                new AjaxOptions {
                    Url = Url.Action("GetPeopleData", new {selectedRole = role}),
                    OnSuccess = "processData"
                })
        </div>
    }
</div>
```

The first change is to the AjaxOptions object I use for the Ajax-enabled form. Because I am no longer able to receive an HTML fragment via an Ajax request, I had to use the same processData function to handle the JSON server response that I created for the Ajax-enabled links. The second change is to the value of the Url property for the AjaxOptions objects created for the links. The GetPeopleDataJson action no longer exists and I target the GetPeopleData action instead.

Summary

In this chapter, I looked at the MVC Framework's unobtrusive Ajax feature, taking advantage of the functionality of the jQuery library in a simple and elegant way and without needing to add lots of code to views. If you are able to work with HTML fragments, then you don't need to add any JavaScript code to your views at all. But I like working with JSON, which means that I tend to need small JavaScript functions that use jQuery to process the data and generate the HTML elements I require. In the next chapter, I look at one of the most interesting and useful aspects of the MVC Framework: model binding.

CHAPTER 24

Model Binding

Model binding is the process of creating .NET objects using the data sent by the browser in an HTTP request. I have been relying on the model binding process each time I have defined an action method that takes a parameter. The parameter objects are created through model binding from the data in the request. In this chapter, I'll show you how the model binding system works and demonstrate the techniques required to customize it for advanced use. Table 24-1 provides the summary for this chapter.

***Table 24-1.** Chapter Summary*

Problem	Solution	Listing
Bind to a simple type or a collection	Add a parameter to an action method.	1–6, 21–27
Provide a fallback value for model binding	Use a nullable type for the action method parameter or use a default value.	7–8
Bind to a complex type	Ensure that the HTML generated by your views contains nested property values.	9–13
Override the default approach to locating nested complex types	Use the Prefix property Bind attribute applied to the action method parameter.	14–18
Selectively bind properties	Use the Include or Exclude properties of the Bind attribute, applied either to the action method parameter or to the model class.	19–20
Manually invoke model binding	Call the UpdateModel or TryUpdateModel methods.	28–32
Create a custom value provider	Implement the IValueProvider interface.	33–37
Create a custom model binder	Implement the IModelBinder interface.	38–40

Preparing the Example Project

I have created a new Visual Studio project called MvcModels using the Empty template option and checking the option to include the core MVC folders and references. I will be using the same model class that you have seen in previous chapters, so create a new class file called Person.cs in the Models folder and ensure that the contents match Listing 24-1.

Listing 24-1. The Contents of the Person.cs File

```
using System;

namespace MvcModels.Models {

    public class Person {
        public int PersonId { get; set; }
        public string FirstName { get; set; }
        public string LastName { get; set; }
        public DateTime BirthDate { get; set; }
        public Address HomeAddress { get; set; }
        public bool IsApproved { get; set; }
        public Role Role { get; set; }
    }

    public class Address {
        public string Line1 { get; set; }
        public string Line2 { get; set; }
        public string City { get; set; }
        public string PostalCode { get; set; }
        public string Country { get; set; }
    }

    public enum Role {
        Admin,
        User,
        Guest
    }
}
```

I have also defined a Home controller, as shown in Listing 24-2. This controller defines a collection of sample Person objects and defines the Index action, which allows me to select a single Person by the value of the PersonId property.

Listing 24-2. The Contents of the HomeController.cs File

```
using System.Linq;
using System.Web.Mvc;
using MvcModels.Models;

namespace MvcModels.Controllers {
    public class HomeController : Controller {
        private Person[] personData = {
            new Person {PersonId = 1, FirstName = "Adam", LastName = "Freeman",
                Role = Role.Admin},
            new Person {PersonId = 2, FirstName = "Jacqui", LastName = "Griffyth",
                Role = Role.User},
            new Person {PersonId = 3, FirstName = "John", LastName = "Smith",
                Role = Role.User},
            new Person {PersonId = 4, FirstName = "Anne", LastName = "Jones",
                Role = Role.Guest}
        };
```

```
        public ActionResult Index(int id) {
            Person dataItem = personData.Where(p => p.PersonId == id).First();
            return View(dataItem);
        }
    }
}
```

I have created a view file called /Views/Home/Index.cshtml to support the action method. You can see the contents of this file in Listing 24-3. I have used the templated display helper to show some of the property values of the Person view model.

Listing 24-3. The Contents of the /Views/Home/Index.cshtml File

```
@model MvcModels.Models.Person
@{
    ViewBag.Title = "Index";
    Layout = "~/Views/Shared/_Layout.cshtml";
}
<h2>Person</h2>
<div><label>ID:</label>@Html.DisplayFor(m => m.PersonId)</div>
<div><label>First Name:</label>@Html.DisplayFor(m => m.FirstName)</div>
<div><label>Last Name:</label>@Html.DisplayFor(m => m.LastName)</div>
<div><label>Role:</label>@Html.DisplayFor(m => m.Role)</div>
```

Finally, I created the Views/Shared folder and added a layout called _Layout.cshtml to it, the contents of which can be seen in Listing 24-4.

Listing 24-4. The Contents of the _Layout.cshtml File

```
<!DOCTYPE html>

<html>
<head>
    <meta name="viewport" content="width=device-width" />
    <title>@ViewBag.Title</title>
    <style>
        label { display: inline-block; width: 100px; font-weight: bold; margin: 5px; }
        form label { float: left; }
        input.text-box { float: left; margin: 5px; }
        button[type=submit] { margin-top: 5px; float: left; clear: left; }
        form div { clear: both; }
    </style>
</head>
<body>
    <div>
        @RenderBody()
    </div>
</body>
</html>
```

Understanding Model Binding

Model binding is an elegant bridge between the HTTP request and the C# methods that define actions. Most MVC Framework applications rely on model binding to some extent, including the simple example application that I created in the previous section. To see model binding at work, start the application and navigate to /Home/Index/1. The result is illustrated in Figure 24-1.

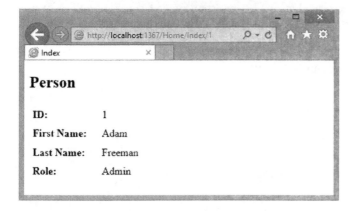

Figure 24-1. *A simple demonstration of model binding*

The URL contained the value of the PersonId property of the Person object I wanted to view, like this:

```
/Home/Index/1
```

The MVC Framework translated that part of the URL and used it as the argument when it called on the Index method in the Home controller class to service the request:

```
...
public ActionResult Index(int id) {
...
```

The process by which the URL segment was converted into the int method argument is an example of model binding. In the sections that follow, I show the process that this simple demonstration initiated, and then move on to explain some of the more complex model binding features. The process that leads to model binding begins when the request is received and processed by the routing engine. I have not changed the routing configuration for the example application, and the default route that Visual Studio adds to the /App_Start/RouteConfig.cs file was used to process the request. As a reminder, you can see the default route in Listing 24-5.

Listing 24-5. The Contents of the RouteConfig.cs File

```
using System;
using System.Collections.Generic;
using System.Linq;
using System.Web;
using System.Web.Mvc;
using System.Web.Routing;
```

```
namespace MvcModels {
    public class RouteConfig {
        public static void RegisterRoutes(RouteCollection routes) {
            routes.IgnoreRoute("{resource}.axd/{*pathInfo}");

            routes.MapRoute(
                name: "Default",
                url: "{controller}/{action}/{id}",
                defaults: new { controller = "Home", action = "Index",
                    id = UrlParameter.Optional }
            );
        }
    }
}
```

I described how routes are defined and how they work in detail in Chapters 15 and 16, so I am not going to repeat that information here. For the model binding process, the important part is the id optional segment variable. When I navigated to the /Home/Index/1 URL, the last segment of the URL, which specifies the Person object I am interested in, is assigned to the id routing variable.

The action invoker, which I introduced in Chapter 17, used the routing information to figure out that the Index action method was required to service the request, but it couldn't call the Index method until it had some useful values for the method argument.

The default action invoker, ControllerActionInvoker, (introduced in Chapter 17), relies on *model binders* to generate the data objects that are required to invoke the action. Model binders are defined by the IModelBinder interface, which is shown in Listing 24-6. I'll come back to this interface later in the chapter when I show you how to create a custom model binder.

Listing 24-6. The IModelBinder Interface from the MVC Framework

```
namespace System.Web.Mvc {

    public interface IModelBinder {
        object BindModel(ControllerContext controllerContext,
            ModelBindingContext bindingContext);
    }
}
```

There can be multiple model binders in an MVC application, and each binder can be responsible for binding one or more model types. When the action invoker needs to call an action method, it looks at the parameters that the method defines and finds the responsible model binder for the type of each one.

For the example in this section, the action invoker would examine the Index method and find that it has one int parameter. It would then locate the binder responsible for int values and call its BindModel method.

The model binder is responsible for providing an int value that can be used to call the Index method. This usually means transforming some element of the request data (such as form or query string values), but the MVC Framework doesn't put any limits on how the data is obtained.

I will show you some examples of custom binders later in this chapter. I will also show you some of the features of the ModelBindingContext class, which is passed to the IModelBinder.BindModel method.

Using the Default Model Binder

Although an application can define custom model binders, most just rely on the built-in binder class, DefaultModelBinder. This is the binder that is used by the action invoker when it cannot find a custom binder to bind the type. By default, this model binder searches four locations, shown in Table 24-2, for data matching the name of the parameter being bound.

Table 24-2. *The Order in Which the DefaultModelBinder Class Looks for Parameter Data*

Source	Description
Request.Form	Values provided by the user in HTML form elements
RouteData.Values	The values obtained using the application routes
Request.QueryString	Data included in the query string portion of the request URL
Request.Files	Files that have been uploaded as part of the request (see Chapter 12 for a demonstration of uploading files)

The locations are searched in order. For example, in my simple example, the DefaultModelBinder looks for a value for the id parameter as follows:

1. Request.Form["id"]

2. RouteData.Values["id"]

3. Request.QueryString["id"]

4. Request.Files["id"]

The search is stopped as soon as a value is found. In the example, the form data is searched without success, but a routing variable is found with the right name. This means that the query string and the names of uploaded files will not be searched at all.

■ **Tip** When replying on the default model binder, it is important that the parameters for your action method match the data property you are looking for. My example application works because the name of the action method parameter corresponds to the name of a routing variable. If I had named the action method parameter personId, for example, the default model binder would not have been able to locate a matching data value and my request would have failed.

Binding to Simple Types

When dealing with simple parameter types, the DefaultModelBinder tries to convert the string value, which has been obtained from the request data into the parameter type using the System.ComponentModel.TypeDescriptor class. If the value cannot be converted (for example, if I have supplied a value of apple for a parameter that requires an int value), then the DefaultModelBinder won't be able to bind to the model. You can see the problem that this creates by starting the example application and navigating to the URL /Home/Index/apple. Figure 24-2 illustrates the response from the server.

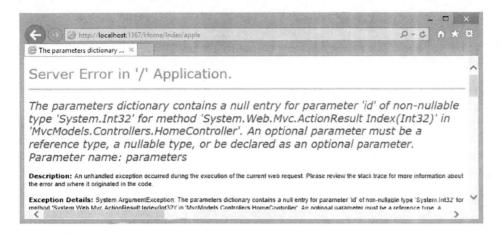

Figure 24-2. *An error processing a model property*

The default model binder is a little dogged. It sees that an int value is required and it tries to convert the value I provided in the URL, apple, into an int, which causes the error shown by the figure. I can make things easier for the model binder by using a nullable type, which provides a fallback position. Instead of requiring a numeric value, a nullable int parameter gives the model binder the choice of setting the action method argument to null when invoking the action. You can see how I have applied a nullable type to the Index action in Listing 24-7.

Listing 24-7. Using a Nullable Type for an Action Method Parameter in the HomeController.cs File

```
...
public ActionResult Index(int? id) {
    Person dataItem = personData.Where(p => p.PersonId == id).First();
    return View(dataItem);
}
...
```

If you run the application and navigate to /Home/Index/apple, you can see that I only changed, rather than solved, the problem, as shown by Figure 24-3.

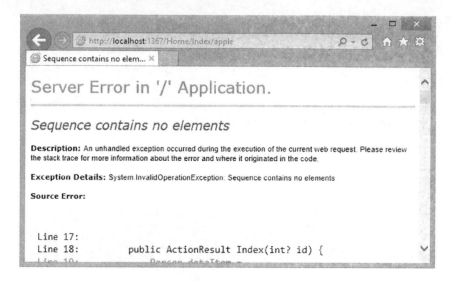

Figure 24-3. A request for a null value

The model binder is able to use null as the value for the id argument to the Index method, but the code inside the action method doesn't check for null values. I could fix that by explicitly checking for null values, but I can also set a default value for the parameter that will be used instead of null. You can see how I have applied a default parameter value to the Index action method in Listing 24-8.

Listing 24-8. Applying a Default Parameter Value in the HomeController.cs File

```
...
public ActionResult Index(int id = 1) {
    Person dataItem = personData.Where(p => p.PersonId == id).First();
    return View(dataItem);
}
...
```

Whenever the model binder is unable to find a value for the id parameter, the default value of 1 will be used instead, which has the effect of selecting the Person object whose PersonId property has a value of 1, as shown in Figure 24-4.

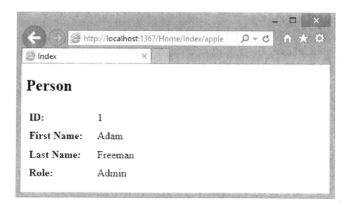

Figure 24-4. The effect of using a default parameter value in an action method

684

■ **Tip** Bear in mind that I have solved the problem of non-numeric values for the model binder, but that I can still get `int` values for which there are no valid `Person` objects defined by the `Home` controller. For example, the model binder will happily convert the final segment of the URLs `/Home/Index/-1` and `/Home/Index/500` to `int` values. This will allow the action method to call the `Index` method with a real value, but will still result in an error because I don't perform any additional checks in the controller. I recommend you pay attention to the range of parameter values your action method may receive, and test accordingly.

CULTURE-SENSITIVE PARSING

The `DefaultModelBinder` class uses culture-specific settings to perform type conversions from different areas of the request data. The values that are obtained from URLs (the routing and query string data) are converted using culture-insensitive parsing, but values obtained from form data are converted taking culture into account.

The most common problem that this causes relates to `DateTime` values. Culture-insensitive dates are expected to be in the universal format `yyyy-mm-dd`. Form date values are expected to be in the format specified by the server. This means that a server set to the UK culture will expect dates to be in the form `dd-mm-yyyy`, whereas a server set to the US culture will expect the format `mm-dd-yyyy`, though in either case `yyyy-mm-dd` is acceptable, too.

A date value won't be converted if it isn't in the right format. This means that you must make sure that all dates included in the URL are expressed in the universal format. You must also be careful when processing date values that users provide. The default binder assumes that the user will express dates in the format of the server culture, something that is unlikely to always happen in an MVC application that has international users.

Binding to Complex Types

When the action method parameter is a complex type (i.e., any type which cannot be converted using the `TypeConverter` class), then the `DefaultModelBinder` class uses reflection to obtain the set of public properties and then binds to each of them in turn. To demonstrate how this works, I have added two new action methods to the `Home` controller, as shown in Listing 24-9.

Listing 24-9. Adding New Action Methods to the HomeController.cs File

```
using System.Linq;
using System.Web.Mvc;
using MvcModels.Models;

namespace MvcModels.Controllers {
    public class HomeController : Controller {
        private Person[] personData = {
            new Person {PersonId = 1, FirstName = "Adam", LastName = "Freeman",
                Role = Role.Admin},
            new Person {PersonId = 2, FirstName = "Jacqui", LastName = "Griffyth",
                Role = Role.User},
            new Person {PersonId = 3, FirstName = "John", LastName = "Smith",
                Role = Role.User},
```

```
                new Person {PersonId = 4, FirstName = "Anne", LastName = "Jones",
                    Role = Role.Guest}
        };

        public ActionResult Index(int? id = 1) {
            Person dataItem = personData.Where(p => p.PersonId == id).First();
            return View(dataItem);
        }

        public ActionResult CreatePerson() {
            return View(new Person());
        }

        [HttpPost]
        public ActionResult CreatePerson(Person model) {
            return View("Index", model);
        }
    }
}
```

The CreatePerson overload without any parameters creates a new Person object and passes it to the view method, which has the effect of rendering the /Views/Home/CreatePerson.cshtml view, which I created to support the action method and the contents of which you can see in Listing 24-10.

Listing 24-10. The Contents of the CreatePerson.cshtml File

```
@model MvcModels.Models.Person
@{
    ViewBag.Title = "CreatePerson";
    Layout = "~/Views/Shared/_Layout.cshtml";
}
<h2>Create Person</h2>
@using (Html.BeginForm()) {
    <div>@Html.LabelFor(m => m.PersonId)@Html.EditorFor(m => m.PersonId)</div>
    <div>@Html.LabelFor(m => m.FirstName)@Html.EditorFor(m => m.FirstName)</div>
    <div>@Html.LabelFor(m => m.LastName)@Html.EditorFor(m => m.LastName)</div>
    <div>@Html.LabelFor(m => m.Role)@Html.EditorFor(m => m.Role)</div>
    <button type="submit">Submit</button>
}
```

This view renders a simple set of labels and editors for the properties of a Person object and contains a form element that posts the editor data back to the CreatePerson action method (the version decorated with the HttpPost attribute). This action method uses the /Views/Home/Index.cshtml view to display the data that the form contained. You can see how the new action methods work by starting the application and navigating to /Home/CreatePerson, as shown in Figure 24-5.

Figure 24-5. *Using the CreatePerson action methods*

I create a different kind of model binding situation when I post the form back to the CreatePerson method. The default model binder discovers that the action method requires a Person object and process each of the properties in turn. For each simple type property, the binder tries to locate a request value, just as it did in the previous example. So, for example, when it encounters the PersonId property, the binder will look for a PersonId data value, which it finds in the form data in the request.

If a property requires another complex type, then the process is repeated for the new type. The set of public properties are obtained and the binder tries to find values for all of them. The difference is that the property names are nested. For example, the HomeAddress property of the Person class is of the Address type, which is shown in Listing 24-11.

Listing 24-11. A Nested Model Class in the Person.cs File

```
...
public class Address {
    public string Line1 { get; set; }
    public string Line2 { get; set; }
    public string City { get; set; }
    public string PostalCode { get; set; }
    public string Country { get; set; }
}
...
```

When looking for a value for the Line1 property, the model binder looks for a value for HomeAddress.Line1, as in the name of the property in the model object combined with the name of the property in the property type.

Creating Easily-Bound HTML

The use of prefixes means that I have to design views that take them into account, although the helper methods make this easy to do. In Listing 24-12, you can see how I have updated the CreatePerson.cshtml view file so that I capture some of the properties for the Address type.

Listing 24-12. Updating the CreatePerson.cshtml File

```
@model MvcModels.Models.Person
@{
    ViewBag.Title = "CreatePerson";
    Layout = "~/Views/Shared/_Layout.cshtml";
}
<h2>Create Person</h2>
@using(Html.BeginForm()) {
    <div>@Html.LabelFor(m => m.PersonId)@Html.EditorFor(m=>m.PersonId)</div>
    <div>@Html.LabelFor(m => m.FirstName)@Html.EditorFor(m=>m.FirstName)</div>
    <div>@Html.LabelFor(m => m.LastName)@Html.EditorFor(m=>m.LastName)</div>
    <div>@Html.LabelFor(m => m.Role)@Html.EditorFor(m=>m.Role)</div>
    <div>
        @Html.LabelFor(m => m.HomeAddress.City)
        @Html.EditorFor(m=> m.HomeAddress.City)
    </div>
    <div>
        @Html.LabelFor(m => m.HomeAddress.Country)
        @Html.EditorFor(m=> m.HomeAddress.Country)
    </div>
    <button type="submit">Submit</button>
}
```

I have used the strongly typed EditorFor helper method, and specified the properties I want to edit from the HomeAddress property. The helper automatically sets the name attributes of the input elements to match the format that the default model binder uses, as follows:

```
...
<input class="text-box single-line" id="HomeAddress_Country" name="HomeAddress.Country"
    type="text" value="" />
...
```

As a consequence of this feature, I don't have to take any special action to ensure that the model binder can create the Address object for the HomeAddress property. I can demonstrate this by editing the /Views/Home/Index.cshtml view to display the HomeAddress properties when they are submitted from the form, as shown in Listing 24-13.

Listing 24-13. Displaying the HomeAddress.City and HomeAddress.Country Properties in the Index.cshtml File

```
@model MvcModels.Models.Person
@{
    ViewBag.Title = "Index";
    Layout = "~/Views/Shared/_Layout.cshtml";
}
<h2>Person</h2>
<div><label>ID:</label>@Html.DisplayFor(m => m.PersonId)</div>
<div><label>First Name:</label>@Html.DisplayFor(m => m.FirstName)</div>
<div><label>Last Name:</label>@Html.DisplayFor(m => m.LastName)</div>
<div><label>Role:</label>@Html.DisplayFor(m => m.Role)</div>
<div><label>City:</label>@Html.DisplayFor(m => m.HomeAddress.City)</div>
<div><label>Country:</label>@Html.DisplayFor(m => m.HomeAddress.Country)</div>
```

If you start the application and navigate to the /Home/CreatePerson URL, you can enter values for the City and Country properties, and check that they are being bound to the model object by submitting the form, as shown in Figure 24-6.

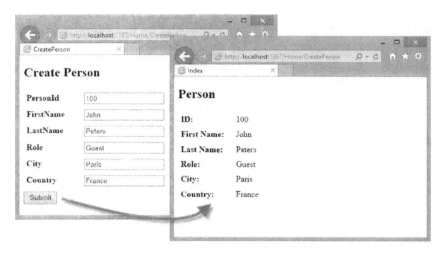

Figure 24-6. *Binding to properties in complex objects*

Specifying Custom Prefixes

There are occasions when the HTML you generate relates to one type of object, but you want to bind it to another. This means that the prefixes containing the view won't correspond to the structure that the model binder is expecting and your data won't be properly processed. To demonstrate this situation, I have created a new class file called AddressSummary.cs in the Models folder. You can see the contents of this file in Listing 24-14.

Listing 24-14. The Contents of the AddressSummary.cs File

```
namespace MvcModels.Models {
    public class AddressSummary {
        public string City { get; set; }
        public string Country { get; set; }
    }
}
```

I have added a new action method in the Home controller that uses the AddressSummary class, as shown in Listing 24-15.

Listing 24-15. Adding a New Action Method in the HomeController.cs File

```
using System.Linq;
using System.Web.Mvc;
using MvcModels.Models;
```

689

```
namespace MvcModels.Controllers {
    public class HomeController : Controller {

        // ...other methods and statements omitted for brevity...

        public ActionResult DisplaySummary(AddressSummary summary) {
            return View(summary);
        }
    }
}
```

The new action method is called DisplaySummary. It has an AddressSummary parameter, which it passes to the View method so that it can be displayed by the default view. I created the DisplaySummary.cshtml file in the /Views/Home folder and you can see the contents in Listing 24-16.

Listing 24-16. The Contents of the DisplaySummary.cshtml File

```
@model MvcModels.Models.AddressSummary
@{
    ViewBag.Title = "DisplaySummary";
    Layout = "~/Views/Shared/_Layout.cshtml";
}
<h2>Address Summary</h2>
<div><label>City:</label>@Html.DisplayFor(m => m.City)</div>
<div><label>Country:</label>@Html.DisplayFor(m => m.Country)</div>
```

This view displays the values of the two properties defined by the AddressSummary class. To demonstrate the problem with prefixes when binding to different model types, I will change the call to the BeginForm helper method in the /Views/Home/CreatePerson.cshtml file so that the form is submitted back to the new DisplaySummary action method, as shown in Listing 24-17.

Listing 24-17. Changing the Target of the Form in the CreatePerson.cshtml File

```
@model MvcModels.Models.Person
@{
    ViewBag.Title = "CreatePerson";
    Layout = "~/Views/Shared/_Layout.cshtml";
}
<h2>Create Person</h2>
@using(Html.BeginForm("DisplaySummary", "Home")) {
    <div>@Html.LabelFor(m => m.PersonId)@Html.EditorFor(m=>m.PersonId)</div>
    <div>@Html.LabelFor(m => m.FirstName)@Html.EditorFor(m=>m.FirstName)</div>
    <div>@Html.LabelFor(m => m.LastName)@Html.EditorFor(m=>m.LastName)</div>
    <div>@Html.LabelFor(m => m.Role)@Html.EditorFor(m=>m.Role)</div>
    <div>
        @Html.LabelFor(m => m.HomeAddress.City)
        @Html.EditorFor(m=> m.HomeAddress.City)
    </div>
    <div>
        @Html.LabelFor(m => m.HomeAddress.Country)
        @Html.EditorFor(m=> m.HomeAddress.Country)
    </div>
    <button type="submit">Submit</button>
}
```

690

You can see the problem if you start the application and navigate to the /Home/CreatePerson URL. When you submit the form, the values that you entered for the City and Country properties are not displayed in the HTML generated by the DisplaySummary view.

The problem is that the name attributes in the form have the HomeAddress prefix, which is not what the model binder is looking for when it tries to bind the AddressSummary type. I can fix this by applying the Bind attribute to the action method parameter, which tells the binder which prefix to look for, as shown in Listing 24-18.

Listing 24-18. Applying the Bind Attribute in the HomeController.cs File

```
...
public ActionResult DisplaySummary([Bind(Prefix="HomeAddress")]AddressSummary summary) {
    return View(summary);
}
...
```

The syntax is a bit nasty, but the effect is useful. When populating the properties of the AddressSummary object, the model binder will look for HomeAddress.City and HomeAddress.Country data values in the request. In this example, I displayed editors for properties of the Person object, but used the model binder to create an instance of the AddressSummary class when the form data was posted, as shown in Figure 24-7. This may seem like a long setup for a simple problem, but the need to bind to a different kind of object is surprisingly common and you are likely to need this technique in your projects.

Figure 24-7. Binding to the properties of a different object type

Selectively Binding Properties

Imagine that the Country property of the AddressSummary class is especially sensitive and that I don't want the user to be able to specify values for it. The first thing I can do is prevent the user from seeing the property or even prevent the property from being included in the HTML sent to the browser, using the attributes I showed you in Chapter 22, or simply by not adding editors for that property to the view.

However, a nefarious user could simply edit the form data sent to the server when submitting the form data and pick the value for the Country property that suits them. What I really want to do is tell the model binder not to bind a value for the Country property from the request, which I can do by using the Bind attribute on the action method parameter. In Listing 24-19, you can see how I have used the attribute to prevent the user from providing a value for Country property in the DisplaySummary action method in the Home controller.

Listing 24-19. Excluding a Property from Model Binding in the HomeController.cs File

```
...
public ActionResult DisplaySummary(
    [Bind(Prefix="HomeAddress", Exclude="Country")]AddressSummary summary) {
    return View(summary);
}
...
```

The `Exclude` property of the `Bind` attribute allows you to exclude properties from the model binding process. You can see the effect by navigating to the /Home/CreatePerson URL, entering some data and submitting the form. You will see that there is no data displayed for the `Country` property. (As an alternative, you can use the `Include` property to specify only those properties that should be bound in the model; all other properties will be ignored.)

When the `Bind` attribute is applied to an action method parameter, it only affects instances of that class that are bound for that action method; all other action methods will continue to try and bind all the properties defined by the parameter type. If you want to create a more widespread effect, then you can apply the `Bind` attribute to the model class itself, as shown in Listing 24-20, where I have applied the `Bind` method to the `AddressSummary` class so that only the `City` property is included in the bind process.

Listing 24-20. Applying the Bind Attribute in the AddressSummary.cs File

```
using System.Web.Mvc;

namespace MvcModels.Models {
    [Bind(Include="City")]
    public class AddressSummary {
        public string City { get; set; }
        public string Country { get; set; }
    }
}
```

■ **Tip**   When the `Bind` attribute is applied to the model class *and* to an action method parameter, a property will be included in the bind process only if neither application of the attribute excludes it. This means that the policy applied to the model class cannot be overridden by applying a less restrictive policy to the action method parameter.

Binding to Arrays and Collections

The default model binder includes some nice support for binding request data to arrays and collections. I demonstrate these features in the following sections, before moving on to show you how to customize the model binding process.

Binding to Arrays

One elegant feature of the default model binder is how it supports action method parameters that are arrays. To demonstrate this, I have added a new method to the `Home` controller called `Names`, which you can see in Listing 24-21.

Listing 24-21. Adding the Names Action Method in the HomeController.cs File

```
using System.Linq;
using System.Web.Mvc;
using MvcModels.Models;

namespace MvcModels.Controllers {
    public class HomeController : Controller {

        // ...other methods and statements omitted for brevity...

        public ActionResult Names(string[] names) {
            names = names ?? new string[0];
            return View(names);
        }
    }
}
```

The Names action method takes a string array parameter called names. The model binder will look for any data item that is called names and create an array that contains those values.

▌ **Tip**   Notice that I have to check to see if the parameter is null in the action method for this example. You can only use constant or literal values as defaults for parameters.

In Listing 24-22, you can see the /Views/Home/Names.cshtml view file, which I created to show array binding.

Listing 24-22. The Contents of the Names.cshtml File

```
@model string[]
@{
    ViewBag.Title = "Names";
    Layout = "~/Views/Shared/_Layout.cshtml";
}
<h2>Names</h2>
@if (Model.Length == 0) {
    using(Html.BeginForm()) {
        for (int i = 0; i < 3; i++) {
            <div><label>@(i + 1):</label>@Html.TextBox("names")</div>
        }
        <button type="submit">Submit</button>
    }
} else {
    foreach (string str in Model) {
        <p>@str</p>
    }
    @Html.ActionLink("Back", "Names");
}
```

This view displays different content based on the number of items there are in the view model. If there are no items, then I display a form that contains three identical input elements, like this:

```
...
<form action="/Home/Names" method="post">
    <div><label>1:</label><input id="names" name="names" type="text" value="" /></div>
    <div><label>2:</label><input id="names" name="names" type="text" value="" /></div>
    <div><label>3:</label><input id="names" name="names" type="text" value="" /></div>
    <button type="submit">Submit</button>
</form>
...
```

When I submit the form, the default model binder sees that the action method requires a string array and looks for data items that have the same name as the parameter. For this example, this means the contents of all of the input elements is gathered together to populate an array. You can see how the action method and view operate in Figure 24-8.

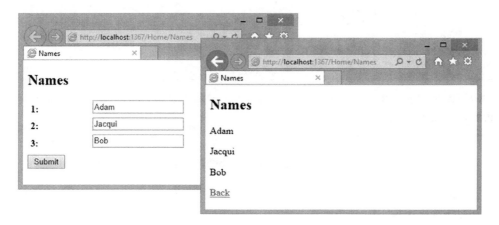

Figure 24-8. *Model binding for arrays*

Binding to Collections

It isn't just arrays that I can bind to. I can also use the .NET collection classes. In Listing 24-23, you can see how I have changed the type of the Names action method parameter to be a strongly typed List.

Listing 24-23. Using a Strongly Typed Collection in the HomeController.cs File

```
using System.Collections.Generic;
using System.Linq;
using System.Web.Mvc;
using MvcModels.Models;

namespace MvcModels.Controllers {
    public class HomeController : Controller {

        // ...other methods and statements omitted for brevity...
```

```
        public ActionResult Names(IList<string> names) {
            names = names ?? new List<string>();
            return View(names);
        }
    }
}
```

Notice that I have used the IList interface. I didn't need to specify a concrete implementation class (although I could have if I preferred). In Listing 24-24, you can see how I have modified the Names.cshtml view file to use the new model type.

Listing 24-24. Using a Collection As the Model Type in the Names.cshtml File

```
@model IList<string>
@{
    ViewBag.Title = "Names";
    Layout = "~/Views/Shared/_Layout.cshtml";
}
<h2>Names</h2>
@if (Model.Count == 0) {
    using(Html.BeginForm()) {
        for (int i = 0; i < 3; i++) {
            <div><label>@(i + 1):</label>@Html.TextBox("names")</div>
        }
        <button type="submit">Submit</button>
    }
} else {
    foreach (string str in Model) {
        <p>@str</p>
    }
    @Html.ActionLink("Back", "Names");
}
```

The functionality of the Names action is unchanged, but I am now able to work with a collection class rather than an array.

Binding to Collections of Custom Model Types

I can also bind individual data properties to an array of custom types, such as the AddressSummary model class. In Listing 24-25, you can see that I have added a new action method to the Home controller called Address, which has a strongly typed collection parameter that relies on a custom model class.

Listing 24-25. Defining an Action Method in the HomeController.cs File

```
using System.Collections.Generic;
using System.Linq;
using System.Web.Mvc;
using MvcModels.Models;
```

```
namespace MvcModels.Controllers {
    public class HomeController : Controller {

        // ...other methods and statements omitted for brevity...

        public ActionResult Address(IList<AddressSummary> addresses) {
            addresses = addresses ?? new List<AddressSummary>();
            return View(addresses);
        }
    }
}
```

The view that I created for this action method is the /Views/Home/Address.cshtml file, which you can see in Listing 24-26.

Listing 24-26. The Contents of the Address.cshtml File

```
@using MvcModels.Models
@model IList<AddressSummary>
@{
    ViewBag.Title = "Address";
    Layout = "~/Views/Shared/_Layout.cshtml";
}
<h2>Addresses</h2>
@if (Model.Count() == 0) {
    using (Html.BeginForm()) {
        for (int i = 0; i < 3; i++) {
            <fieldset>
                <legend>Address @(i + 1)</legend>
                <div><label>City:</label>@Html.Editor("[" + i + "].City")</div>
                <div><label>Country:</label>@Html.Editor("[" + i + "].Country")</div>
            </fieldset>
        }
        <button type="submit">Submit</button>
    }
} else {
    foreach (AddressSummary str in Model) {
        <p>@str.City, @str.Country</p>
    }
    @Html.ActionLink("Back", "Address");
}
```

This view renders a form element if there are no items in the model collection. The form consists of pairs of input elements whose name attributes are prefixed with an array index, like this:

```
...
<fieldset>
    <legend>Address 1</legend>
    <div>
        <label>City:</label>
        <input class="text-box single-line" name="[0].City" type="text" value="" />
    </div>
```

```
    <div>
        <label>Country:</label>
        <input class="text-box single-line" name="[0].Country" type="text" value="" />
    </div>
</fieldset>
<fieldset>
    <legend>Address 2</legend>
    <div>
        <label>City:</label>
        <input class="text-box single-line" name="[1].City" type="text" value="" />
    </div>
    <div>
        <label>Country:</label>
        <input class="text-box single-line" name="[1].Country" type="text" value="" />
    </div>
</fieldset>
...
```

When the form is submitted, the default model binder realizes that it needs to create a collection of AddressSummary objects and uses the array index prefixes in the name attributes to obtain values for the object properties. The properties prefixed with [0] are used for the first AddressSummary object, those prefixed with [1] are used for the second object, and so on.

The Address.cshtml view defines input elements for three such indexed objects and displays them when the model collection contains items. Before I can demonstrate this, I need to remove the Bind attribute from the AddressSummary model class, as shown in Listing 24-27; otherwise, the model binder will ignore the Country property.

Listing 24-27. Removing the Bind Attribute from the AddressSummary.cs File

```
using System.Web.Mvc;

namespace MvcModels.Models {
    // This attribute has been commented out
    //[Bind(Include="City")]
    public class AddressSummary {
        public string City { get; set; }
        public string Country { get; set; }
    }
}
```

You can see how the binding process for custom object collections works by starting the application and navigating to the /Home/Address URL. Enter some cities and countries, and then click the Submit button to post the form to the server. The model binder will find and process the indexed data values and use them to create the collection of AddressSummary objects that are then passed back to the view and displayed to you, as shown in Figure 24-9.

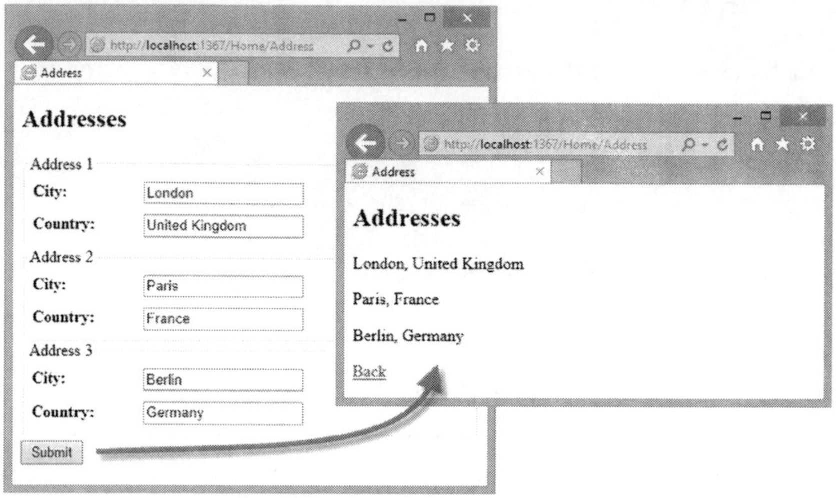

Figure 24-9. *Binding collections of custom objects*

Manually Invoking Model Binding

The model binding process is performed automatically when an action method defines parameters, but I can take direct control of the process if I want to. This gives more explicit control over how model objects are instantiated, where data values are obtained from, and how data parsing errors are handled. Listing 24-28 demonstrates how I have changed the Address action method in the Home controller to manually invoke the binding process.

Listing 24-28. Manually Invoking the Model Binding Process in the HomeController.cs File

```
using System.Collections.Generic;
using System.Linq;
using System.Web.Mvc;
using MvcModels.Models;

namespace MvcModels.Controllers {
    public class HomeController : Controller {

        // ...other methods and statements omitted for brevity...

        public ActionResult Address() {
            IList<AddressSummary> addresses = new List<AddressSummary>();
            UpdateModel(addresses);
            return View(addresses);
        }
    }
}
```

The UpdateModel method takes a model object that I was previously defining as a parameter and tries to obtain values for its public properties using the standard binding process.

When I manually invoke the binding process, I am able to restrict the binding process to a single source of data. By default, the binder looks in four places: form data, route data, the query string, and any uploaded files. Listing 24-29 shows how to restrict the binder to searching for data in a single location—in this case, the form data.

Listing 24-29. Restricting the Binder to the Form Data in the HomeController.cs File

```
...
public ActionResult Address() {
    IList<AddressSummary> addresses = new List<AddressSummary>();
    UpdateModel(addresses, new FormValueProvider(ControllerContext));
    return View(addresses);
}
...
```

This version of the UpdateModel method takes an implementation of the IValueProvider interface, which becomes the sole source of data values for the binding process. Each of the four default data locations is represented by an IValueProvider implementation, as shown in Table 24-3.

Table 24-3. *The Built-in IValueProvider Implementations*

Source	IValueProvider Implementation
Request.Form	FormValueProvider
RouteData.Values	RouteDataValueProvider
Request.QueryString	QueryStringValueProvider
Request.Files	HttpFileCollectionValueProvider

Each of the classes listed in Table 24-3 takes a ControllerContext constructor parameter, which I obtain through the property called ControllerContext that is defined by the Controller class, as shown in the listing. The most common way of restricting the source of data is to look only at the form values. There is a neat binding trick that I can use so that I don't have to create an instance of FormValueProvider, as shown in Listing 24-30.

Listing 24-30. Restricting the Binder Data Source in the HomeController.cs File

```
...
public ActionResult Address(FormCollection formData) {
    IList<AddressSummary> addresses = new List<AddressSummary>();
    UpdateModel(addresses, formData);
    return View(addresses);
}
...
```

The FormCollection class implements the IValueProvider interface, and if I define the action method to take a parameter of this type, the model binder will provide me with an object that I can pass directly to the UpdateModel method.

■ **Tip** There are other overloaded versions of the UpdateModel method that specify a prefix to search for and which model properties should be included in the binding process.

Dealing with Binding Errors

Users will inevitably supply values that cannot be bound to the corresponding model properties—invalid dates or text for numeric values, for example. When I invoke model binding explicitly, I am responsible for dealing with any errors. The model binder expresses binding errors by throwing an InvalidOperationException. Details of the errors can be found through the ModelState feature, which I describe in Chapter 25. But when using the UpdateModel method, I must be prepared to catch the exception and use the ModelState to express an error message to the user, as shown in Listing 24-31.

Listing 24-31. Dealing with Model Binding Errors in the HomeController.cs File

```
...
public ActionResult Address(FormCollection formData) {
    IList<AddressSummary> addresses = new List<AddressSummary>();
    try {
        UpdateModel(addresses, formData);
    } catch (InvalidOperationException ex) {
        // provide feedback to user
    }
    return View(addresses);
}
...
```

As an alternative approach, I can use the TryUpdateModel method, which returns true if the model binding process is successful and false if there are errors, as shown in Listing 24-32.

Listing 24-32. Using the TryUpdateModel Method in the HomeController.cs File

```
...
public ActionResult Address(FormCollection formData) {
    IList<AddressSummary> addresses = new List<AddressSummary>();
    if (TryUpdateModel(addresses, formData)) {
        // proceed as normal
    } else {
        // provide feedback to user
    }
    return View(addresses);
}
...
```

The only reason to favor TryUpdateModel over UpdateModel is if you don't like catching and dealing with exceptions. There is no functional difference in the model binding process.

■ **Tip**   When model binding is invoked automatically, binding errors are not signaled with exceptions. Instead, you must check the result through the ModelState.IsValid property. I explain ModelState in Chapter 25.

Customizing the Model Binding System

I have shown you the default model binding process. As you might expect by now, there are some different ways in which the binding system can be customized. I show you some examples in the following sections.

Creating a Custom Value Provider

By defining a custom value provider, I can add my own source of data to the model binding process. Value providers implement the IValueProvider interface, which is shown in Listing 24-33.

Listing 24-33. The IValueProvider Interface from the MVC Framework

```
namespace System.Web.Mvc {
    public interface IValueProvider {

        bool ContainsPrefix(string prefix);

        ValueProviderResult GetValue(string key);
    }
}
```

The ContainsPrefix method is called by the model binder to determine if the value provider can resolve the data for a given prefix. The GetValue method returns a value for a given data key, or null if the provider doesn't have any suitable data.

I have added an Infrastructure folder to the example project and created a new class file called CountryValueProvider.cs, which I will use to provide values for the Country property. You can see the contents of this file in Listing 24-34.

Listing 24-34. The Contents of the CountryValueProvider.cs File

```
using System.Globalization;
using System.Web.Mvc;

namespace MvcModels.Infrastructure {
    public class CountryValueProvider : IValueProvider {

        public bool ContainsPrefix(string prefix) {
            return prefix.ToLower().IndexOf("country") > -1;
        }

        public ValueProviderResult GetValue(string key) {
            if (ContainsPrefix(key)) {
                return new ValueProviderResult("USA", "USA",
                    CultureInfo.InvariantCulture);
            } else {
                return null;
            }
        }
    }
}
```

This value provider only responds to requests for values for the Country property and it always returns the value USA. For all other requests, I return null, indicating that I cannot provide data.

I have to return the data value as a ValueProviderResult class. This class has three constructor parameters. The first is the data item that I want to associate with the requested key. The second parameter is a version of the data value that is safe to display as part of an HTML page. The final parameter is the culture information that relates to the value; I have specified the InvariantCulture.

To register the value provider with the application, I need to create a factory class that will create instances of the provider when they are required by the MVC Framework. The factory class must be derived from the abstract ValueProviderFactory class. In Listing 24-35, you can see the contents of the CustomValueProviderFactory.cs class file that I added to the Infrastructure folder.

Listing 24-35. The Contents of the CustomValueProviderFactory.cs File

```
using System.Web.Mvc;

namespace MvcModels.Infrastructure {
    public class CustomValueProviderFactory : ValueProviderFactory {

        public override IValueProvider GetValueProvider(ControllerContext
                controllerContext) {
            return new CountryValueProvider();
        }
    }
}
```

The GetValueProvider method is called when the model binder wants to obtain values for the binding process. This implementation simply creates and returns an instance of the CountryValueProvider class, but you can use the data provided through the ControllerContext parameter to respond to different kinds of requests by creating different value providers.

I need to register the factory class with the application, which I do in the Application_Start method of Global.asax, as shown in Listing 24-36.

Listing 24-36. Registering a Value Provider Factory in the Global.asax File

```
using System;
using System.Collections.Generic;
using System.Linq;
using System.Web;
using System.Web.Mvc;
using System.Web.Routing;
using MvcModels.Infrastructure;

namespace MvcModels {

    public class MvcApplication : System.Web.HttpApplication {
        protected void Application_Start() {
            AreaRegistration.RegisterAllAreas();
            RouteConfig.RegisterRoutes(RouteTable.Routes);

            ValueProviderFactories.Factories.Insert(0, new CustomValueProviderFactory());
        }
    }
}
```

I register the factory class by adding an instance to the static ValueProviderFactories.Factories collection. The model binder looks at the value providers in sequence, which means I have to use the Insert method to put the custom factory at the first position in the collection if I want to take precedence over the built-in providers.

If I want the custom provider to be a fallback that is used when the other providers cannot supply a data value, then I can use the Add method to append the factory class to the end of the collection, like this:

```
...
ValueProviderFactories.Factories.Add(new CustomValueProviderFactory());
...
```

I want the custom value provider to be used before any other provider, and so I used the Insert method. I need to modify the Address action method before I can test the value provider, so that the model binder doesn't just look at the form data for model property values. In Listing 24-37, you can see how I have removed the restriction on the source for values in the call to the TryUpdateModel method.

Listing 24-37. Removing the Restriction on the Sources of Model Property Values in the HomeController.cs File

```
using System.Collections.Generic;
using System.Linq;
using System.Web.Mvc;
using MvcModels.Models;

namespace MvcModels.Controllers {
    public class HomeController : Controller {

        // ...other methods and statements omitted for brevity...

        public ActionResult Address() {
            IList<AddressSummary> addresses = new List<AddressSummary>();
            UpdateModel(addresses);
            return View(addresses);
        }
    }
}
```

You can see the custom value provider at work if you start the application and navigate to the /Home/Address URL. Enter city and country data, and then press the Submit button. You will see that the custom value provider, which has precedence over the built-in providers, has been used to generate values for the Country property in each of the AddressSummary objects that the model binder has created, as shown in Figure 24-10.

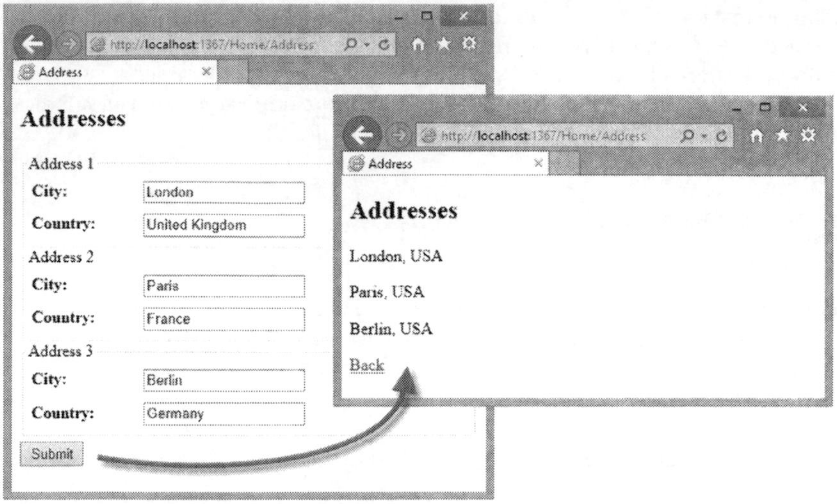

Figure 24-10. *The effect of the custom value provider*

Creating a Custom Model Binder

I can override the default binder's behavior by creating a custom model binder for a specific type. Custom model binders implement the IModelBinder interface, which I showed you earlier in the chapter. To demonstrate how to create a custom binder, I have added the AddressSummaryBinder.cs class file to the Infrastructure folder, the contents of which you can see in Listing 24-38.

Listing 24-38. The Contents of the AddressSummaryBinder.cs File

```
using MvcModels.Models;
using System.Web.Mvc;

namespace MvcModels.Infrastructure {
    public class AddressSummaryBinder : IModelBinder {

        public object BindModel(ControllerContext controllerContext,
                ModelBindingContext bindingContext) {

            AddressSummary model = (AddressSummary)bindingContext.Model
                ?? new AddressSummary();
            model.City = GetValue(bindingContext, "City");
            model.Country = GetValue(bindingContext, "Country");
            return model;
        }

        private string GetValue(ModelBindingContext context, string name) {
            name = (context.ModelName == "" ? "" : context.ModelName + ".") + name;
```

```
                ValueProviderResult result = context.ValueProvider.GetValue(name);
                if (result == null || result.AttemptedValue == "") {
                    return "<Not Specified>";
                } else {
                    return (string)result.AttemptedValue;
                }
            }
        }
    }
}
```

The MVC Framework will call the BindModel method when it wants an instance of the model type that the binder supports. I will show you how to register a model binder shortly, but the AddressSummaryBinder class will only be used to create instances of the AddressSummary class, which makes the code a lot simpler. (You can create custom binders that support multiple types, but I prefer one binder for each type.)

■ **Tip** I don't perform any input validation in this model binder, meaning that I blithely assume that the user has provided valid values for all of the Person properties. I discuss validation in Chapter 25, but for the moment, I want to focus on the basic model binding process.

The parameters to the BindModel method are a ControllerContext object that you can use to get details of the current request and a ModelBindingContext object, which provides details of the model object that is sought, as well as access to the rest of the model binding facilities in the MVC application. In Table 24-4, I have described the most useful properties defined by the ModelBindingContext class.

Table 24-4. *The Most Useful Properties Defined by the ModelBindingContext Class*

Property	Description
Model	Returns the model object passed to the UpdateModel method if binding has been invoked manually
ModelName	Returns the name of the model that is being bound
ModelType	Returns the type of the model that is being created
ValueProvider	Returns an IValueProvider implementation that can be used to get data values from the request

The custom model binder is simple. When the BindModel method is called, I check to see if the Model property of the ModelBindingContext object has been set. If it has, this is the object that I will generate data value for, and if not, then I create a new instance of the AddressSummary class. I get the values for the City and Country properties by calling the GetValue method and return the populated AddressSummary object.

In the GetValue method, I use the IValueProvider implementation obtained from the ModelBindingContext.ValueProvider property to get values for the model object properties.

The ModelName property tells me if there is a prefix I need to append to the property name I am looking for. You will recall that the action method is trying to create a collection of AddressSummary objects, which means that the individual input elements will have name attribute values that are prefixed [0] and [1]. The values I am looking for in the request will be [0].City, [0].Country, and so on. As a final step, I supply a default value of <Not Specified> if I can't find a value for a property or the property is the empty string (which is what is sent to the server when the user doesn't enter a value in the input elements in the form).

Registering the Custom Model Binder

I have to register the custom model binder so that the MVC application knows which types it can support. I do this in the Application_Start method of Global.asax, as demonstrated by Listing 24-39.

Listing 24-39. Registering a Custom Model Binder

```
using System;
using System.Collections.Generic;
using System.Linq;
using System.Web;
using System.Web.Mvc;
using System.Web.Routing;
using MvcModels.Infrastructure;
using MvcModels.Models;

namespace MvcModels {

    public class MvcApplication : System.Web.HttpApplication {
        protected void Application_Start() {
            AreaRegistration.RegisterAllAreas();
            RouteConfig.RegisterRoutes(RouteTable.Routes);

            // This statement has been commented out
            //ValueProviderFactories.Factories.Insert(0,
            //    new CustomValueProviderFactory());

            ModelBinders.Binders.Add(typeof(AddressSummary), new AddressSummaryBinder());
        }
    }
}
```

I register the binder through the ModelBinders.Binders.Add method, passing in the type that the binder supports and an instance of the binder class. Notice that I have removed the statement that registers the custom value provider. You can test the custom model binder by starting the application, navigating to the /Home/Address URL, and filling in only some of the form elements. When you submit the form, the custom model binder will use <Not Specified> for all of the properties for which you didn't enter a value, as shown in Figure 24-11.

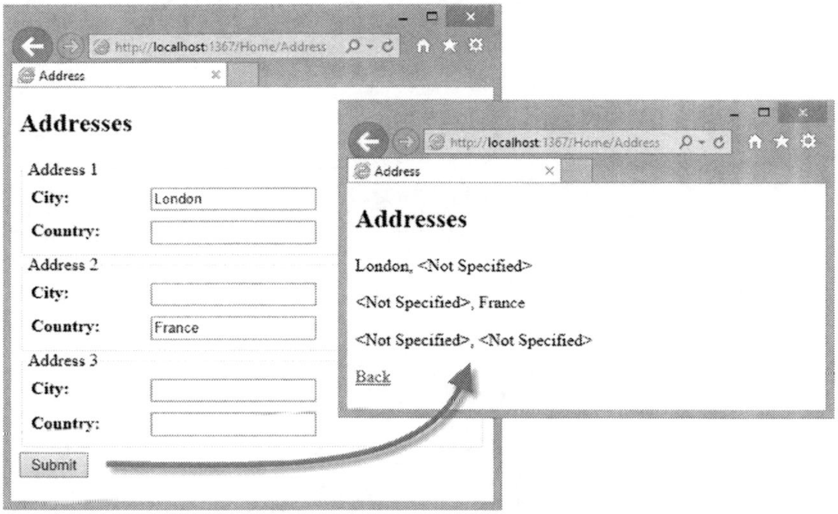

Figure 24-11. *The effect of using a custom model binder*

Registering a Model Binder with an Attribute

You can also register custom model binders by decorating the model class with the `ModelBinder` attribute, which means that you don't need to use the `Global.asax` file. In Listing 24-40, you can see how I have specified `AddressSummaryBinder` as the binder for the `AddressSummary` class.

Listing 24-40. Using the ModelBinder Attribute in the AddressSummary.cs File

```
using System.Web.Mvc;
using MvcModels.Infrastructure;

namespace MvcModels.Models {

    [ModelBinder(typeof(AddressSummaryBinder))]
    public class AddressSummary {
        public string City { get; set; }
        public string Country { get; set; }
    }
}
```

Summary

In this chapter, I introduced you to the workings of the model binding process, showing you how the default model binder operates and the different ways in which the process can be customized. Many MVC Framework applications will only need the default model binder, which works nicely to process the HTML that the helper methods generate. But for more advanced applications, it can be useful to use custom binders that create model objects in a more efficient or specific way. In the next chapter, I show you how to validate model objects and how to present the user with meaningful errors when invalid data is received.

CHAPTER 25

■ ■ ■

Model Validation

In the previous chapter, I showed you how the MVC Framework creates model objects from HTTP requests through the model binding process. Throughout that chapter, I worked on the basis that the data the user supplied was valid. The reality is that users will often enter data that isn't valid and cannot be used, which leads me to the topic of this chapter: *model validation*.

Model validation is the process of ensuring the data received by the application is suitable for binding to the model and, when this is not the case, providing useful information to the user that will help explain the problem.

The first part of the process, checking the data received, is one of the key ways to preserve the integrity of the domain model. Rejecting data that doesn't make sense in the context of the domain can prevent odd and unwanted states arising in the application. The second part, helping the user correct the problem, is equally important. Without the information and feedback they need to interact with the application, users become frustrated and confused. In public-facing applications, this means users will simply stop using the application. In corporate applications, this means the user's workflow will be hindered. Neither outcome is desirable. Fortunately, the MVC Framework provides extensive support for model validation. I will show you how to use the basic features and then demonstrate some advanced techniques to fine-tune the validation process. Table 25-1 provides the summary for this chapter.

Table 25-1. *Chapter Summary*

Problem	Solution	Listing
Explicitly validate a model	Use the ModelState object to record validation errors.	1–7
Generate a summary of validation errors	Use the Html.ValidationSummary helper method.	8–10
Display property-level validation errors	Use the Html.ValidationMessageFor helper method.	11
Define validation rules within the model class	Apply attributes to the properties of the model class.	12
Create a custom validation attribute	Derive from the ValidationAttribute class.	13–19
Define a self-validating model	Implement the IValidatableObject interface.	20
Use client-side validation	Add the Microsoft unobtrusive validation package to the application.	21–23
Perform remote validation	Define an action method that returns a JsonResult and add the Remote attribute to the model property to be validated.	24, 25

Preparing the Example Project

For this chapter, I created a new project called ModelValidation using the Visual Studio Empty template, checking the option to add the core MVC folders and references. Having created the project, I added a new class file called Appointment.cs, which you can see in Listing 25-1, to the Models folder.

Listing 25-1. The Contents of the Appointment.cs File

```
using System;
using System.ComponentModel.DataAnnotations;

namespace ModelValidation.Models {
    public class Appointment {

        public string ClientName { get; set; }

        [DataType(DataType.Date)]
        public DateTime Date { get; set; }

        public bool TermsAccepted { get; set; }
    }
}
```

The Appointment model class defines three properties and I have used the DataType attribute to indicate that the Date property should be expressed as a date without a time component. I also created a Home controller for the example project and defined action methods that operate on the Appointment model class, as shown in Listing 25-2.

Listing 25-2. The Contents of the HomeController.cs File

```
using System;
using System.Web.Mvc;
using ModelValidation.Models;

namespace ModelValidation.Controllers {
    public class HomeController : Controller {

        public ViewResult MakeBooking() {
            return View(new Appointment { Date = DateTime.Now });
        }

        [HttpPost]
        public ViewResult MakeBooking(Appointment appt) {

            // statements to store new Appointment in a
            // repository would go here in a real project

            return View("Completed", appt);
        }
    }
}
```

I have defined two versions of the MakeBooking action method. The one that is of most interest is the version to which the HttpPost attribute has been applied, since this is the version where model binding will be used to construct the Appointment parameter object.

Notice that I added a comment to indicate where, in a real application, statements would be placed to store the details of the Appointment object that the model binder will create. I am not going to create a repository because I want to focus on the model binding and validation process. But it is important to bear in mind that the main reason to validate a model is to prevent bad or meaningless data from being placed in the repository and causing problems (either when trying to store the data or when trying to process the data later).

Creating the Layout

I will need a simple layout for some of the examples in this chapter. I created the Views/Shared folder and added the _Layout.cshtml file to it, the contents of which you can see in Listing 25-3.

Listing 25-3. The Contents of the _Layout.cshtml File

```
<!DOCTYPF html>
<html>
<head>
    <meta charset="utf-8" />
    <meta name="viewport" content="width=device-width" />
    <title>@ViewBag.Title</title>
    <style type="text/css">
        .field-validation-error { color: #f00;}
        .validation-summary-errors { color: #f00; font-weight: bold;}
        .input-validation-error { border: 2px solid #f00; background-color: #fee; }
        input[type="checkbox"].input-validation-error { outline: 2px solid #f00; }
    </style>
</head>
<body>
    @RenderBody()
</body>
</html>
```

I also created a view start file so that the layout is applied to views automatically. I added a new view file called _ViewStart.cshtml to the Views folder and you can see the contents of the new file in Listing 25-4. (I introduced view start files in Chapter 5 as part of the overview of Razor functionality.)

Listing 25-4. The Contents of the _ViewStart.cshtml File

```
@{
    Layout = "~/Views/Shared/_Layout.cshtml";
}
```

Creating the Views

To complete the preparation, I created two views to support the action methods, both of which are located in the /Views/Home folder. In Listing 25-5, you can see the contents of the MakeBooking.cshtml file, which contains a form that allows the user to create a new appointment.

Listing 25-5. The Contents of the MakeBooking.cshtml File

```
@model ModelValidation.Models.Appointment
@{
    ViewBag.Title = "Make A Booking";
}
<h4>Book an Appointment</h4>

@using (Html.BeginForm()) {
    <p>Your name: @Html.EditorFor(m => m.ClientName)</p>
    <p>Appointment Date: @Html.EditorFor(m => m.Date)</p>
    <p>@Html.EditorFor(m => m.TermsAccepted) I accept the terms & conditions</p>
    <input type="submit" value="Make Booking" />
}
```

When the form is posted back to the application, the MakeBooking action method displays the details of the appointment that the user has created using the Completed.cshtml view, which you can see in Listing 25-6.

Listing 25-6. The Contents of the Completed.cshtml File

```
@model ModelValidation.Models.Appointment
@{
    ViewBag.Title = "Completed";
}
<h4>Your appointment is confirmed</h4>
<p>Your name is: <b>@Html.DisplayFor(m => m.ClientName)</b></p>
<p>The date of your appointment is: <b>@Html.DisplayFor(m => m.Date)</b></p>
```

As you may have gathered, the example for this chapter is based around creating appointments. You can see how it works by starting the application and navigating to the /Home/MakeBooking URL. Entering details into the form and clicking the Submit button will send the data to the server, which performs the model-binding process to create an Appointment object, the details of which are then rendered using the Completed.cshtml view, as shown in Figure 25-1.

Figure 25-1. Using the example application

As it stands, the application will accept any data the user submits, but to preserve the integrity of the application and domain model, I need three things to be true before I know that the user has provided an acceptable Appointment object:

- The user must provide a name.

- The user must provide a date (in the mm/dd/yyyy format) that is in the future.

- The user must have checked the check box to accept the terms and conditions.

Model validation is the process of enforcing these requirements. In the following sections, I will show you the different techniques available for checking the data that the user has provided and to give the user feedback when the application cannot use the data they have submitted.

Explicitly Validating a Model

The most direct way of validating a model is to do so in the action method. Listing 25-7 shows how I have added explicit checks for each property defined by the Appointment class in the HttpPost version of the MakeBooking action method.

Listing 25-7. Explicitly Validating a Model in the HomeController.cs File

```
using System;
using System.Web.Mvc;
using ModelValidation.Models;

namespace ModelValidation.Controllers {
    public class HomeController : Controller {

        public ViewResult MakeBooking() {
            return View(new Appointment { Date = DateTime.Now });
        }

        [HttpPost]
        public ViewResult MakeBooking(Appointment appt) {

            if (string.IsNullOrEmpty(appt.ClientName)) {
                ModelState.AddModelError("ClientName", "Please enter your name");
            }

            if (ModelState.IsValidField("Date") && DateTime.Now > appt.Date) {
                ModelState.AddModelError("Date", "Please enter a date in the future");
            }

            if (!appt.TermsAccepted) {
                ModelState.AddModelError("TermsAccepted", "You must accept the terms");
            }

            if (ModelState.IsValid) {
                // statements to store new Appointment in a
                // repository would go here in a real project
                return View("Completed", appt);
```

```
            } else {
                return View();
            }
        }
    }
}
```

I check the values that the model binder has assigned to the properties of the parameter object and register any errors I find with the ModelState property, which the controller inherits from its base class. As an example, consider how I check the ClientName property:

```
...
if (string.IsNullOrEmpty(appt.ClientName)) {
    ModelState.AddModelError("ClientName", "Please enter your name");
}
...
```

I want a value from the user for this property, so I use the static string.IsNullOrEmpty method to check the property. If I have not received a value, I use the ModelState.AddModelError method to specify the name of the property for which there is a problem (ClientName) and a message that should be displayed to the user to help them correct the problem (Please enter your name).

I can check to see whether the model binder was able to assign a value to a property by using the ModelState.IsValidField property. I do this for the Date property to make sure that the model binder was able to parse the value the user submitted; there is no point performing additional checks or reporting additional errors if no value could be parsed from the request data.

After I have validated all the properties in the model object, I read the ModelState.IsValid property to see whether there were errors. This method returns true if I called the Model.State.AddModelError method during the checks or if the model binder had any problems creating the Appointment object:

```
...
if (ModelState.IsValid) {
    // statements to store new Appointment in a
    // repository would go here in a real project
    return View("Completed", appt);
} else {
    return View();
}
...
```

I know I have a valid Appointment object if there are no problems reported by the IsValid property and I can render the Completed.cshtml view (and, in a real project, store the Appointment object in the repository). If the IsValue property returns false, then I know that I have a problem, which I deal with by calling the View method to render the default view.

Displaying Validation Errors to the User

It may seem odd to deal with a validation error by calling the View method, but the templated view helpers that I used to generate input elements in the MakeBooking.cshtml view check the view model for validation errors.

The helpers add a CSS class called input-validation-error to the input elements if an error has been reported for the corresponding properties, which is why I added these CSS styles to the layout when I created the example project:

```
...
.input-validation-error { border: 2px solid #f00; background-color: #fee; }
input[type="checkbox"].input-validation-error { outline: 2px solid #f00; }
...
```

The first style creates the effect of setting a red border and a pink background on any element for which there is an error. The second style applies a red border to checkbox elements. These elements are hard to style and usually require special attention. You can test the explicit validation approach by starting the application, navigating to the /Home/MakeBooking URL, and clicking the Make Booking button without entering any data in the form. The result is shown in Figure 25-2.

Figure 25-2. *Errors result in highlighted elements*

STYLING CHECK BOXES

Styling checkboxes can be difficult, especially with older browsers. An alternative to the CSS styles I defined in the _Layout.cshtml is to replace the Boolean editor template with a custom template (as the ~/Views/Shared/EditorTemplates/Boolean.cshtml file) and to wrap the check box in another element that can be more easily styled. Here is the sort of template that I use, which you can tailor to your own application:

```
@model bool?

@if (ViewData.ModelMetadata.IsNullableValueType) {
    @Html.DropDownListFor(m => m, new SelectList(new[] { "Not Set", "True", "False" },
Model))
} else {
    ModelState state = ViewData.ModelState[ViewData.ModelMetadata.PropertyName];
    bool value = Model ?? false;

    if (state != null && state.Errors.Count > 0) {
        <span class="input-validation-error" style="padding: 0; margin: 1px">
            @Html.CheckBox("", value)
        </span>
```

```
        } else {
            @Html.CheckBox("", value)
        }
    }
```

This template will wrap a check box in a `span` element to which the `input-validation-error` style has been applied if there are any model errors associated with the property that the template has been applied to. You can learn more about replacing editor templates in Chapter 22.

When you submit the form without any data, errors are highlighted for the `ClientName` and `TermsAccepted` properties because values are not provided. The default value that displayed for the `Date` property is a valid date, but it is not in the future and so is also flagged as a validation error.

The user will not be shown the `Completed.cshtml` view until the form is submitted with data that can be parsed by the model browser and which passes the explicit validation checks in the `MakeBooking` action method. Until that happens, submitting the form will cause the `MakeBooking.cshtml` view to be rendered with the current validation errors.

Displaying Validation Messages

The classes that the templated helper methods apply to `input` elements indicate that there are problems with a field, but they do not tell the user what the problem is. Fortunately, there are some convenient helper methods that assist in doing this. Listing 25-8 shows one of these helper methods, which I have applied to the `MakeBooking.cshtml` view (since this is where the validation errors are shown to the user).

Listing 25-8. Using the Validation Summary Helper Method in the MakeBooking.cshtml File

```
@model ModelValidation.Models.Appointment
@{
    ViewBag.Title = "Make A Booking";
}
<h4>Book an Appointment</h4>

@using (Html.BeginForm()) {
    @Html.ValidationSummary()
    <p>Your name: @Html.EditorFor(m => m.ClientName)</p>
    <p>Appointment Date: @Html.EditorFor(m => m.Date)</p>
    <p>@Html.EditorFor(m => m.TermsAccepted) I accept the terms & conditions</p>
    <input type="submit" value="Make Booking" />
}
```

The `Html.ValidationSummary` helper adds a summary of the validation errors to the user. If there are no errors, then the helper doesn't generate any HTML. Figure 25-3 demonstrates the validation summary in use. I produced this effect by clearing the data fields and submitting the form.

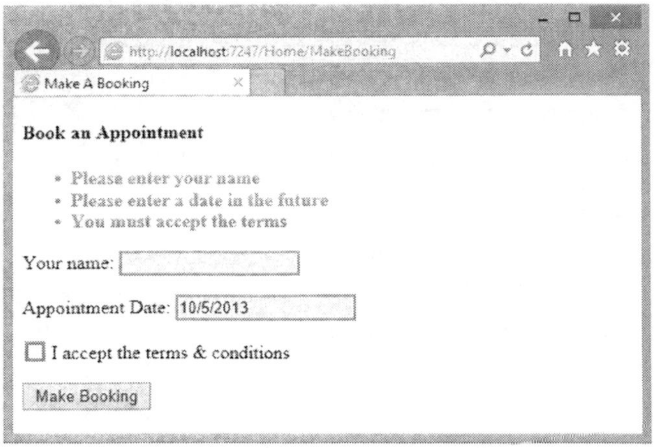

Figure 25-3. *Displaying a validation summary*

■ **Note**   The values that I have shown for the Date property in this chapter follow the US date format of month/day/year. If you are in a different locale, then you can either enter valid dates in your local format (such as day/month/year, which is used widely in Europe) or add ⟨globalization culture="en-US" uiCulture="en-US"/⟩ to the system.web element in the Web.config file for the example project to force the MVC application to use US date formats.

The validation summary displays the error messages that I registered with the ModelState in the MakeBooking action method. Here is the HTML that the helper method generates:

```
...
<div class="validation-summary-errors" data-valmsg-summary="true">
    <ul>
        <li>Please enter your name</li>
        <li>Please enter a date in the future</li>
        <li>You must accept the terms</li>
    </ul>
</div>
...
```

The errors are expressed as a list contained in a div element, to which the validation-summary-errors class is applied. This class corresponds to one of the styles that I defined in the _Layout.cshtml file when I created the project at the start of the chapter:

```
...
.validation-summary-errors { color: #f00; font-weight: bold;}
...
```

There are a number of overloaded versions of the ValidationSummary method and Table 25-2 shows the most useful. Some of the overloads of the ValidationSummary helper method allow me to specify that only *model-level errors* should be displayed. The errors that I have registered with ModelState so far have been *property-level errors*, meaning there is a problem with the value supplied for a given property and changing that value can address the problem.

Table 25-2. *Useful Overloads of the ValidationSummary Helper Method*

Overloaded Method	Description
Html.ValidationSummary()	Generates a summary for all validation errors
Html.ValidationSummary(bool)	If the bool parameter is true, then only model-level errors are displayed (see the explanation after the table). If the parameter is false, then all errors are shown.
Html.ValidationSummary(string)	Displays a message (contained in the string parameter) before a summary of all the validation errors
Html.ValidationSummary(bool, string)	Displays a message before the validation errors. If the bool parameter is true, only model-level errors will be shown.

By contrast, model-level errors can be used when there is some problem arising from an interaction between two or more property values. As a simple example, let's imagine that customers named Joe cannot make appointments on Mondays. Listing 25-9 shows how I can enforce this rule with an explicit validation check in the MakeBooking action method and report problems as model-level validation errors.

Listing 25-9. A Model-Level Validation Error in the HomeController.cs File

```
...
[HttpPost]
public ViewResult MakeBooking(Appointment appt) {

    if (string.IsNullOrEmpty(appt.ClientName)) {
        ModelState.AddModelError("ClientName", "Please enter your name");
    }

    if (ModelState.IsValidField("Date") && DateTime.Now > appt.Date) {
        ModelState.AddModelError("Date", "Please enter a date in the future");
    }

    if (!appt.TermsAccepted) {
        ModelState.AddModelError("TermsAccepted", "You must accept the terms");
    }

    if (ModelState.IsValidField("ClientName") && ModelState.IsValidField("Date")
        && appt.ClientName == "Joe" && appt.Date.DayOfWeek == DayOfWeek.Monday) {
        ModelState.AddModelError("", "Joe cannot book appointments on Mondays");
    }

    if (ModelState.IsValid) {
        // statements to store new Appointment in a
        // repository would go here in a real project
        return View("Completed", appt);
    } else {
        return View();
    }
}
...
```

Before I check to see whether Joe is trying to book on a Monday, I use the ModelState.IsValidField method to ensure that I have valid ClientName and Date values to work with. This means I will not generate a model-level error unless the previous checks on the properties have been successful. I register a model-level error by passing the empty string ("") as the first parameter to the ModelState.AddModelError method, like this:

```
...
ModelState.AddModelError("", "Joe cannot book appointments on Mondays");
...
```

I can then update the MakeBooking.cshtml view file to use the version of the ValidationSummary helper method that takes a bool parameter to display only the model-level errors, as shown in Listing 25-10.

Listing 25-10. Display Only Model-Level Errors in the MakeBooking.cshtml File

```
@model ModelValidation.Models.Appointment
@{
    ViewBag.Title = "Make A Booking";
}
<h4>Book an Appointment</h4>

@using (Html.BeginForm()) {
    @Html.ValidationSummary(true)
    <p>Your name: @Html.EditorFor(m => m.ClientName)</p>
    <p>Appointment Date: @Html.EditorFor(m => m.Date)</p>
    <p>@Html.EditorFor(m => m.TermsAccepted) I accept the terms & conditions</p>
    <input type="submit" value="Make Booking" />
}
```

You can see the result of these changes in Figure 25-4, where I have entered the name Joe and specified a date, which is a Monday.

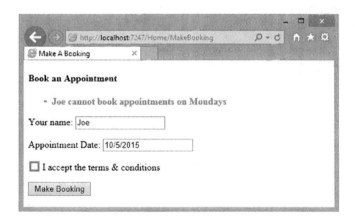

Figure 25-4. *Displaying validation summary information for model-level errors*

You can see from the figure that there are two validation errors. The first is the model-level error that arises from Joe trying to get a Monday appointment. The second is that the terms and conditions check box is unchecked. Since I am displaying only model-level errors in the validation summary, the user will not see any information about the second problem in the summary, something I will address in the next section.

Displaying Property-Level Validation Messages

The reason you might want to restrict the validation summary to model-level errors is to display property-level errors alongside the fields themselves, in which case you will not want to duplicate the property-specific messages. Listing 25-11 shows how I updated the MakeBooking.cshtml view to display model-level errors in the summary and to display property-level errors alongside the corresponding input field.

Listing 25-11. Using Property-Specific Validation Error Messages in the MakeBooking.cshtml File

```
@model ModelValidation.Models.Appointment
@{
    ViewBag.Title = "Make A Booking";
}
<h4>Book an Appointment</h4>

@using (Html.BeginForm()) {
    @Html.ValidationSummary(true)
    <p>@Html.ValidationMessageFor(m => m.ClientName)</p>
    <p>Your name: @Html.EditorFor(m => m.ClientName)</p>
    <p>@Html.ValidationMessageFor(m => m.Date)</p>
    <p>Appointment Date: @Html.EditorFor(m => m.Date)</p>
    <p>@Html.ValidationMessageFor(m => m.TermsAccepted)</p>
    <p>@Html.EditorFor(m => m.TermsAccepted) I accept the terms & conditions</p>
    <input type="submit" value="Make Booking" />
}
```

The Html.ValidationMessageFor helper displays validation errors for a single model property. You can see the effect it has on the MakeBooking view in Figure 25-5.

Figure 25-5. *Using the per-property validation message helper*

The helper only inserts HTML into the response if there is a validation error for the property it is applied to and generates elements like this:

```
...
<p>
    <span class="field-validation-error" data-valmsg-for="ClientName"
            data-valmsg-replace="true">
        Please enter your name
    </span>
</p>
...
```

The class that the elements are assigned to corresponds to the one of the styles that I defined in the _Layout.cshtml file:

```
...
.field-validation-error { color: #f00;}
...
```

Using Alternative Validation Techniques

Performing model validation in the action method is only one of the validation techniques available in the MVC Framework. In the following sections, I show different approaches.

Performing Validation in the Model Binder

The default model binder performs validation as part of the binding process. As an example, Figure 25-6 shows what happens if I clear the Date field and submit the form.

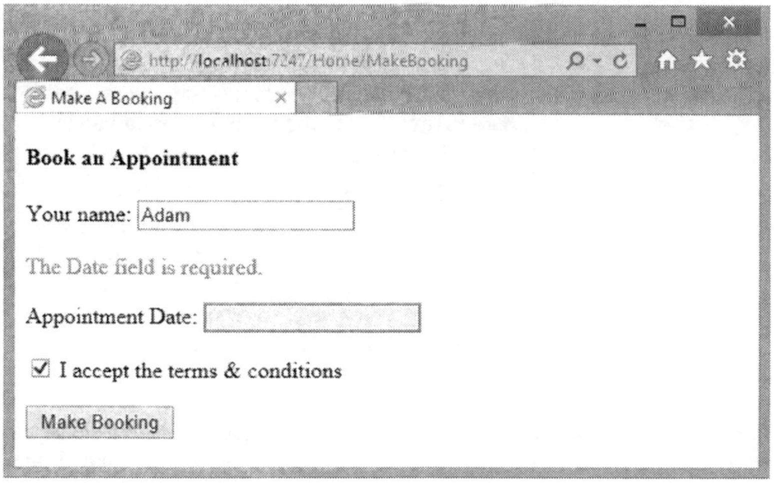

Figure 25-6. *A validation message from the model binder*

The error displayed for the Date field has been added by the model binder because it wasn't able to create a DateTime object from the empty field posted in the form. The model binder performs basic validation for each of the properties in the model object. If a value has not been supplied, the message shown in Figure 25-6 will be displayed. If I supply a value that cannot be parsed into the model property type, then a different message is displayed, as shown in Figure 25-7.

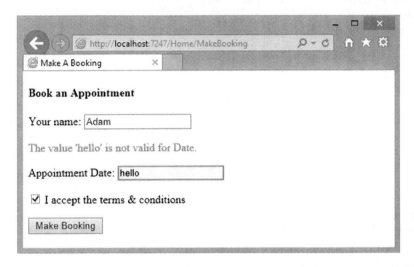

Figure 25-7. *A format validation error displayed by the model binder*

The built-in default model binder class, DefaultModelBinder, provides some useful methods that can be overridden to add validation to a binder. Table 25-3 describes these methods.

Table 25-3. *DefaultModelBinder Methods for Adding Validation to the Model Binding Process*

Method	Description	Default Implementation
OmModelUpdated	Called when the binder has tried to assign values to all of the properties in the model object	Applies the validation rules defined by the model metadata and registers any errors with ModelState. I describe the use of metadata for validation later in this chapter.
SetProperty	Called when the binder wants to apply a value to a specific property	If the property cannot hold a null value and there was no value to apply, then the The <name> field is required error is registered with ModelState. If there is a value but it cannot be parsed, then the The value <value> is not valid for <name> error is registered.

I can override the methods shown in Table 25-3 to push validation logic into the binding process when creating a custom model binder, which I demonstrated in Chapter 24. This is not a technique I like, however, because it feels like the wrong place in the MVC pattern to put the validation logic—although, as with so much in an MVC application, it is a matter of personal taste and preference. I prefer to handle validation using metadata applied to the model class, which I demonstrate in the next section.

Specifying Validation Rules Using Metadata

The MVC Framework supports the use of metadata to express model validation rules. The advantage of using metadata is that the validation rules are enforced anywhere that the binding process is applied throughout the application, not just in a single action method. The validation attributes are detected and enforced by the built-in default model binder class, DefaultModelBinder, which I described in Chapter 24. In Listing 25-12, you can see how I have applied some validation attributes to the Appointment model class.

Listing 25-12. Validation Rules in the Appointment.cs File

```
using System;
using System.ComponentModel.DataAnnotations;

namespace ModelValidation.Models {
    public class Appointment {

        [Required]
        public string ClientName { get; set; }

        [DataType(DataType.Date)]
        [Required(ErrorMessage="Please enter a date")]
        public DateTime Date { get; set; }

        [Range(typeof(bool), "true", "true", ErrorMessage = "You must accept the terms")]
        public bool TermsAccepted { get; set; }
    }
}
```

I used two validation attributes in the listing: Required and Range. The Required attribute specifies that it is a validation error if the user doesn't submit a value for a property. The Range attribute specifies a subset of acceptable values. Table 25-4 shows the set of built-in validation attributes available in an MVC application.

Table 25-4. *The Built-in Validation Attributes*

Attribute	Example	Description
Compare	[Compare("MyOtherProperty")]	Two properties must have the same value. This is useful when you ask the user to provide the same information twice, such as an e-mail address or a password.
Range	[Range(10, 20)]	A numeric value (or any property type that implement IComparable) must not lie beyond the specified minimum and maximum values. To specify a boundary on only one side, use a MinValue or MaxValue constant—for example, [Range(int.MinValue, 50)].
RegularExpression	[RegularExpression("pattern")]	A string value must match the specified regular expression pattern. Note that the pattern has to match the *entire* user-supplied value, not just a substring within it. By default, it matches case sensitively, but you can make it case insensitive by applying the (?i) modifier—that is, [RegularExpression("(?i)mypattern")].

(continued)

Table 25-4. (*continued*)

Attribute	Example	Description
Required	[Required]	The value must not be empty or be a string consisting only of spaces. If you want to treat whitespace as valid, use [Required(AllowEmptyStrings = true)].
StringLength	[StringLength(10)]	A string value must not be longer than the specified maximum length. You can also specify a minimum length: [StringLength(10, MinimumLength=2)].

All of the validation attributes support specifying a custom error message by setting a value for the ErrorMessage property, like this:

```
...
[Required(ErrorMessage="Please enter a date")]
...
```

If there is no custom error message, then the default messages will be used, such as the ones I showed you earlier in the chapter. The built-in validation attributes are basic, and they only do property-level validation. Even so, some sleight of hand if required to get things working consistently. As an example, consider the validation attribute I applied to the TermsAccepted property:

```
...
[Range(typeof(bool), "true", "true", ErrorMessage="You must accept the terms")]
...
```

I want to make sure that the user checks the box to accept the terms. I cannot use the Required attribute, because the templated helper for bool values generates a hidden HTML element to ensure that I get a value even when the box isn't checked. To work around this, I use a feature of the Range attribute that lets me provide a Type and specify the upper and lower bounds as string values. By setting both bounds to true, I create the equivalent of the Required attribute for bool properties that are edited using check boxes.

■ **Tip** The DataType attribute cannot be used to validate user input, only to provide hints for rendering values using the templated helpers (described in Chapter 22). So, for example, do not expect the DataType(DataType.EmailAddress) attribute to enforce a specific format.

Creating a Custom Property Validation Attribute

The trick of using the Range attribute to re-create the behavior of the Required attribute is a little awkward. Fortunately, validation isn't limited to just the built-in attributes; I can also create my own by deriving from the ValidationAttribute class and implementing custom validation logic. This is a lot more useful and to demonstrate how this works, I have added an Infrastructure folder to the example project and created a class file called MustBeTrueAttribute.cs within it. Listing 25-13 shows the contents of the new class file.

Listing 25-13. A Custom Property Validation Attribute in the MustBeTrueAttribute.cs File

```
using System.ComponentModel.DataAnnotations;

namespace ModelValidation.Infrastructure {
    public class MustBeTrueAttribute : ValidationAttribute {

        public override bool IsValid(object value) {
            return value is bool && (bool)value;
        }
    }
}
```

This class defines a new attribute that I have called MustBeTrueAttribute and which overrides the IsValid method of the base class. This is the method that the model binder will call to validate properties to which the attribute is applied, passing in the value that the user has provided as the parameter.

The validation logic is simple; a value is valid if it is a bool that has a value of true. I indicate that a value is valid by returning true from the IsValid method. In Listing 25-14, you can see how I have replaced the Range attribute with the custom MustBeTrue attribute in the Appointment class.

Listing 25-14. Applying a Custom Validation Attribute in the Appointment.cs File

```
using System;
using System.ComponentModel.DataAnnotations;
using ModelValidation.Infrastructure;

namespace ModelValidation.Models {
    public class Appointment {

        [Required]
        public string ClientName { get; set; }

        [DataType(DataType.Date)]
        [Required(ErrorMessage="Please enter a date")]
        public DateTime Date { get; set; }

        [MustBeTrue(ErrorMessage="You must accept the terms")]
        public bool TermsAccepted { get; set; }
    }
}
```

This is neater and easier to make sense of than abusing the Range attribute. You can see the effect of the custom model validation attribute in Figure 25-8.

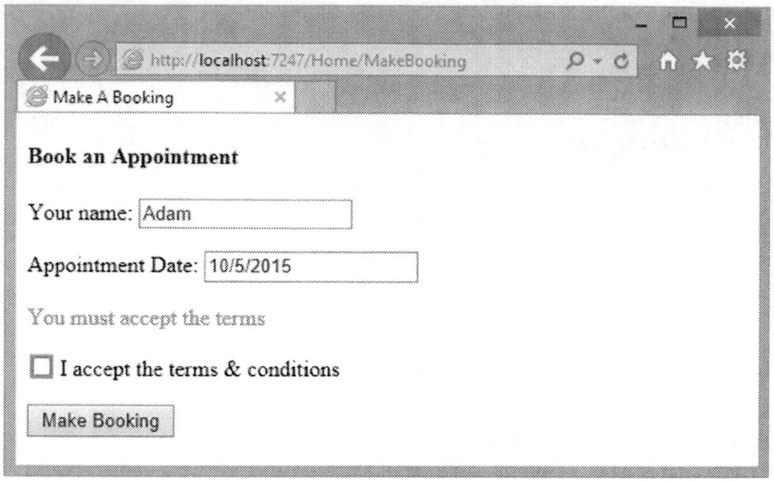

Figure 25-8. *The error message from a custom validation attribute*

Deriving from the Built-In Validation Attributes

In the previous example, I built a validation attribute from scratch, but I can also derive new classes from the built-in attributes, which gives me the ability to extend their behavior. In Listing 25-15, you can see the contents of a new class file called FutureDateAttribute.cs that I added to the Infrastructure folder.

Listing 25-15. The Contents of the FutureDateAttribute.cs Class File

```
using System;
using System.ComponentModel.DataAnnotations;

namespace ModelValidation.Infrastructure {
    public class FutureDateAttribute : RequiredAttribute {

        public override bool IsValid(object value) {
            return base.IsValid(value) && ((DateTime)value) > DateTime.Now;
        }
    }
}
```

I have derived the new FutureDataAttribute class from RequiredAttribute and overridden the IsValid method to validate that the date is in the future. Since I have called the base implementation of the IsValid method, the custom attribute will perform all of the basic validation steps contained in the Required attribute. You can see how I have applied the new attribute to the Appointment model class in Listing 25-16.

Listing 25-16. Applying a Custom Model Validation Attribute in the Appointment.cs File

```
using System;
using System.ComponentModel.DataAnnotations;
using ModelValidation.Infrastructure;
using System.Web.Mvc;
```

```
namespace ModelValidation.Models {
    public class Appointment {

        [Required]
        public string ClientName { get; set; }

        [DataType(DataType.Date)]
        [FutureDate(ErrorMessage="Please enter a date in the future")]
        public DateTime Date { get; set; }

        [MustBeTrue(ErrorMessage="You must accept the terms")]
        public bool TermsAccepted { get; set; }
    }
}
```

Creating a Model Validation Attribute

The custom validation attributes I have created so far are applied to individual model properties and this means they are only able to raise property-level validation errors. I can use attributes to validate the entire model as well, which allows me to raise model-level errors. As a demonstration, I have created the NoJoeOnMondaysAttribute.cs class file in the Infrastructure folder. The contents of the new file are shown in Listing 25-17.

Listing 25-17. The Contents of the NoJoeOnMondaysAttribute.cs File

```
using System;
using System.ComponentModel.DataAnnotations;
using ModelValidation.Models;

namespace ModelValidation.Infrastructure {
    public class NoJoeOnMondaysAttribute : ValidationAttribute {

        public NoJoeOnMondaysAttribute() {
            ErrorMessage = "Joe cannot book appointments on Mondays";
        }

        public override bool IsValid(object value) {
            Appointment app = value as Appointment;
            if (app == null || string.IsNullOrEmpty(app.ClientName) ||
                    app.Date == null) {
                // I don't have a model of the right type to validate, or I don't have
                // the values for the ClientName and Date properties I require
                return true;
            } else {
                return !(app.ClientName == "Joe" &&
                    app.Date.DayOfWeek == DayOfWeek.Monday);
            }
        }
    }
}
```

When I apply a validation attribute to the model class, as opposed to a single property, the object parameter that the model binder will pass to the IsValid method will be the model object—an Appointment in this example. The validation attribute checks to make sure that I really do have an Appointment object and, if so, that I have values for the ClientName and Date properties that I can work with. If I have the data I need, then I make sure that Joe isn't trying to get a booking on a Monday. In Listing 25-18, you can see how I applied the custom attribute to the Appointment class.

Listing 25-18. Applying a Model-Level Custom Validation Attribute in the Appointment.cs File

```
using System;
using System.ComponentModel.DataAnnotations;
using ModelValidation.Infrastructure;

namespace ModelValidation.Models {
    [NoJoeOnMondays]
    public class Appointment {

        [Required]
        public string ClientName { get; set; }

        [DataType(DataType.Date)]
        [FutureDate(ErrorMessage="Please enter a date in the future")]
        public DateTime Date { get; set; }

        [MustBeTrue(ErrorMessage="You must accept the terms")]
        public bool TermsAccepted { get; set; }
    }
}
```

At this point, I am performing the same kinds of validation in the action method and the validation attributes, which means that the user will see two similar error messages for the same validation problem. To resolve this, I have removed the explicit validation checks from the MakeBooking action method in the Home controller, as shown in Listing 25-19, which has the effect of making the validation attributes solely responsible for performing the custom validation checks.

Listing 25-19. Removing the Explicit Validation Checks from the HomeController.cs File

```
using System;
using System.Web.Mvc;
using ModelValidation.Models;

namespace ModelValidation.Controllers {
    public class HomeController : Controller {

        public ViewResult MakeBooking() {
            return View(new Appointment { Date = DateTime.Now });
        }

        [HttpPost]
        public ViewResult MakeBooking(Appointment appt) {
            if (ModelState.IsValid) {
                // statements to store new Appointment in a
                // repository would go here in a real project
                return View("Completed", appt);
```

```
        } else {
            return View();
        }
    }
}
}
```

An important point to note is that model-level validation attributes will not be used when a property-level problem is detected. To see how this works, start the application and navigate to the /Home/MakeBooking URL. Enter Joe as the name, 10/5/2020 as the date, and leave the check box unchecked. When you submit the form, you will see only the warning about the check box. Check the box and submit again. Only now will you see the model-level error, as illustrated in Figure 25-9.

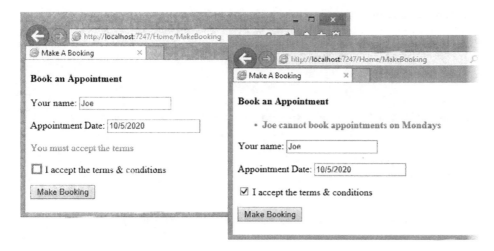

Figure 25-9. *Property-level errors being displayed before model-level errors*

The problem from the user's perspective is that I have implicitly accepted the name and data values by not flagging up errors for them in the first panel. This may seem like a minor issue, but it is worth paying careful attention to any situation that may frustrate users.

Defining Self-Validating Models

Another validation technique is to create *self-validating models*, where the validation logic is part of the model class. A self-validating model implements the IValidatableObject interface, as shown in Listing 25-20.

Listing 25-20. Adding Self-Validation to the Appointment.cs File

```
using System;
using System.Collections.Generic;
using System.ComponentModel.DataAnnotations;
using ModelValidation.Infrastructure;
```

```
namespace ModelValidation.Models {
    public class Appointment : IValidatableObject {

        public string ClientName { get; set; }

        [DataType(DataType.Date)]
        public DateTime Date { get; set; }

        public bool TermsAccepted { get; set; }

        public IEnumerable<ValidationResult> Validate(ValidationContext
                validationContext) {

            List<ValidationResult> errors = new List<ValidationResult>();

            if (string.IsNullOrEmpty(ClientName)) {
                errors.Add(new ValidationResult("Please enter your name"));
            }

            if (DateTime.Now > Date) {
                errors.Add(new ValidationResult("Please enter a date in the future"));
            }

            if (errors.Count == 0 && ClientName == "Joe"
                && Date.DayOfWeek == DayOfWeek.Monday) {

                errors.Add(
                    new ValidationResult("Joe cannot book appointments on Mondays"));
            }

            if (!TermsAccepted) {
                errors.Add(new ValidationResult("You must accept the terms"));
            }

            return errors;
        }
    }
}
```

The IValidatableObject interface defines one method, Validate. This method takes a ValidationContext parameter, although this type isn't MVC-specific and isn't a great deal of use. The result of the Validate method is an enumeration of ValidationResult objects, each of which represents a validation error.

If the model class implements the IValidatableObject interface, then the Validate method will be called after the model binder has assigned values to each of the model properties. This approach has the benefit of combining the flexibility of putting the validation logic in the action method, but with the consistency of being applied any time the model binding process creates an instance of the model type.

One benefit of this approach is that the model- and property-level validation is combined in one place, which means that all of the errors are displayed together, as shown in Figure 25-10. Some programmers don't like putting the validation logic in the model class, but I think it sits nicely in the MVC design pattern—and I like the flexibility and consistency, of course.

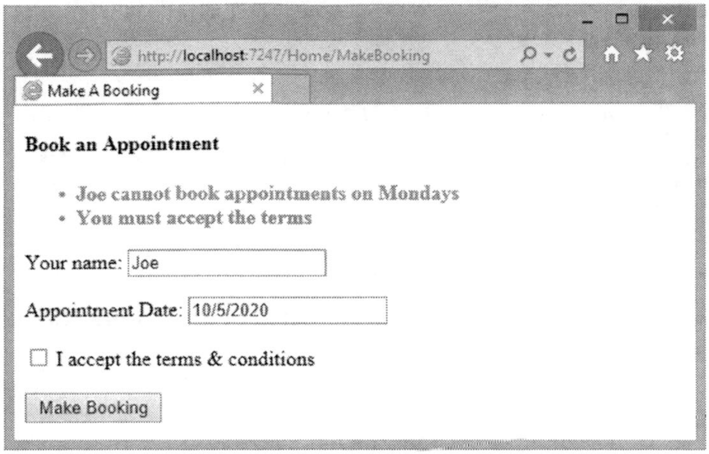

Figure 25-10. *The effect of a self-validating model class*

Performing Client-Side Validation

The validation techniques I have demonstrated so far have all been examples of server-side validation. This means the user submits their data to the server, and the server validates the data and sends back the results of the validation (either success in processing the data or a list of errors that need to be corrected).

In Web applications, users typically expect immediate validation feedback—without having to submit anything to the server. This is known as *client-side validation* and is implemented using JavaScript. The data that the user has entered is validated before being sent to the server, providing the user with immediate feedback and an opportunity to correct any problems.

The MVC Framework supports unobtrusive client-side validation. The term *unobtrusive* means that validation rules are expressed using attributes added to the HTML elements that views generate. These attributes are interpreted by a JavaScript library that is included as part of the MVC Framework that, in turn, configures the jQuery Validation library, which does the actual validation work. In the following sections, I will show you how the built-in validation support works and demonstrate how I can extend the functionality to provide custom client-side validation.

■ **Tip**   Client-side validation is focused on validating individual properties. In fact, it is hard to set up model-level client-side validation using the built-in support that comes with the MVC Framework. To that end, most MVC applications use client-side validation for property-level issues and rely on server-side validation for the overall model.

Enabling Client-Side Validation

Client-side validation is controlled by two settings in the Web.config file, as shown in Listing 25-21.

Listing 25-21. Controlling Client-Side Validation in the Web.config File

```
...
<appSettings>
  <add key="webpages:Version" value="3.0.0.0" />
  <add key="webpages:Enabled" value="false" />
```

```
    <add key="ClientValidationEnabled" value="true" />
    <add key="UnobtrusiveJavaScriptEnabled" value="true" />
</appSettings>
...
```

Both of these settings must be true for client-side validation to work. When you first created your MVC project, Visual Studio created these entries and set them to true.

■ **Tip**   You can also configure client-side validation on a per-view basis by setting the
HtmlHelper. ClientValidationEnabled and HtmlHelper.UnobtrusiveJavaScriptEnabled in a Razor code block.

Adding the NuGet Packages

Ensuring that the MVC Framework will generate the attributes required for validation is only part of the setup process. I also have to add the JavaScript packages that process those attributes and check the data that the user has entered into the form. All of the required packages are available through NuGet, so select Package Manager Console from the Visual Studio Tools ➤ Library Package Manager menu and enter the following commands:

```
Install-Package jQuery –version 1.10.2
Install-Package jQuery.Validation –version 1.11.1
Install-Package Microsoft.jQuery.Unobtrusive.Validation –version 3.0.0
```

These packages add files to the Scripts folder, which I then need to add to the layout with script elements, as shown in Listing 25-22.

Listing 25-22. Adding Script Elements for the Validation Libraries to the _Layout.cshtml File

```
<!DOCTYPE html>
<html>
<head>
    <meta charset="utf-8" />
    <meta name="viewport" content="width=device-width" />
    <title>@ViewBag.Title</title>
    <style type="text/css">
        .field-validation-error { color: #f00;}
        .validation-summary-errors { color: #f00; font-weight: bold;}
        .input-validation-error { border: 2px solid #f00; background-color: #fee; }
        input[type="checkbox"].input-validation-error { outline: 2px solid #f00; }
    </style>
    <script src="~/Scripts/jquery-1.10.2.js"></script>
    <script src="~/Scripts/jquery.validate.js"></script>
    <script src="~/Scripts/jquery.validate.unobtrusive.js"></script>
</head>
<body>
    @RenderBody()
</body>
</html>
```

■ **Tip** In Chapter 26, I'll show you the bundles feature, which makes it easier to manage JavaScript and CSS files in a project.

The order in which the script elements are added to the layout is important. You must add the jQuery library first, followed by the jQuery Validation library and only then can you add the Microsoft unobtrusive validation library.

Using Client-Side Validation

Once I have enabled client-side validation and ensured that the JavaScript libraries are referenced in the layout, I can start to perform client-side validation. The simplest way of doing this is to apply the metadata attributes that I previously used for server-side validation, such as Required, Range, and StringLength. Listing 25-23 shows the Appointment model class with these annotations applied. (I have removed the implementation of the IValidatableObject interface, which has no effect on client-side validation.)

Listing 25-23. Validation Attributes Applied in the Appointment.cs File

```
using System;
using System.ComponentModel.DataAnnotations;

namespace ModelValidation.Models {
    public class Appointment {

        [Required]
        [StringLength(10, MinimumLength = 3)]
        public string ClientName { get; set; }

        [DataType(DataType.Date)]
        public DateTime Date { get; set; }

        public bool TermsAccepted { get; set; }
    }
}
```

That's all I have to do to get the basic client-side validation working. I have applied a slightly different mix of the built-in validation attributes so that I can demonstrate some of the client-side validation features. But once you have the JavaScript libraries included in the HTML that is sent to the client, everything just starts to work. You can see the effect of the client-side validation by starting the application, navigating to the /Home/MakeBooking URL and entering the letter X into the name field. Hit the tab key or click one of the other input elements and you will immediately see a validation message produced by the JavaScript running in the browser, as shown in Figure 25-11.

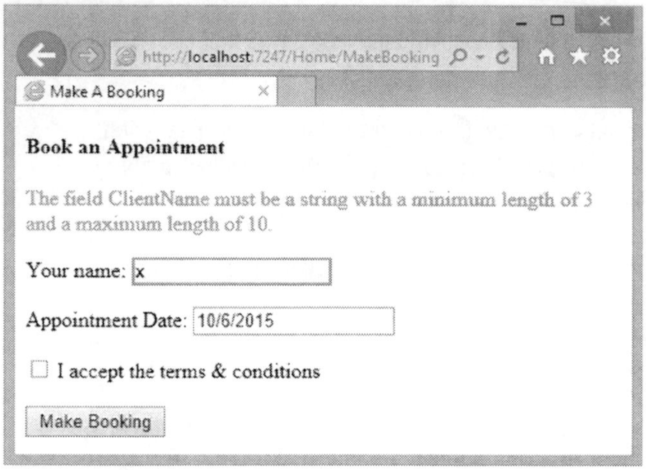

Figure 25-11. *Immediate feedback from the client-side validation feature*

I applied the `StringLength` validation attribute to the `Appointment` class in Listing 25-23 and it is the error message from that attribute that you can see in the figure. The feedback presented in the browser is immediate and no request has been made to the server. In fact, the JavaScript code that is performing the validation will prevent the form from being submitted until there are no outstanding validation errors.

The feedback is also immediate when the user corrects the error. If you return to the name field and keep typing, the validation error will be removed when the name you have entered is three or more characters long. But if you keep typing until you get to the eleventh character, you will see the error reappear. This is because I specified a minimum length of three characters and a maximum length of ten for the `ClientName` property with the `StringLength` attribute. This kind of dynamic feedback helps the user to provide the data that the application requires without having to submit the form to the server and wait for a response.

Understanding How Client-Side Validation Works

One of the benefits of using the MVC Framework client-side validation feature is that I do not have to write any JavaScript. Instead, the validation rules are expressed using HTML attributes. Here is the HTML that is rendered by the `Html.EditorFor` helper for the `ClientName` property when client-side validation is disabled:

```
...
<input class="text-box single-line" id="ClientName" name="ClientName" type="text"
    value="" />
...
```

And here is the HTML rendered for the same property when client-side validation is switched on:

```
...
<input class="text-box single-line" data-val="true"
    data-val-length="The field ClientName must be a string with a minimum length of 3 and
        a maximum length of 10." data-val-length-max="10" data-val-length-min="3"
    data-val-required="The ClientName field is required." id="ClientName"
    name="ClientName" type="text" value="" />
...
```

The MVC client-side validation support doesn't generate any JavaScript or JSON data to direct the validation process; like much of the rest of the MVC Framework, validation relies on convention. The first attribute that was added is data-val. The jQuery Validation library identifies those fields that require validation by looking for this attribute.

Individual validation rules are specified using an attribute in the form data-val-<name>, where name is the rule to be applied. So, for example, the Required attribute I applied to the model class has resulted in a data-val-required attribute in the HTML. The value associated with the attribute is the error message associated with the rule. Some rules require additional attributes. You can see this with the length rule, which has data-val-length-min and data-val-length-max attributes to let me specify the minimum and maximum string lengths that are allowed. The interpretation of the required and length validation rules is provided by the jQuery Validation library, on which the MVC client validation features are built.

AVOIDING CONFLICTS WITH BROWSER VALIDATION

Some of the current generation of HTML5 browsers support simple client side validation based on the attributes applied to input elements. The general idea is that, say, an input element to which the required attribute has been applied, for example, will cause the browser to display a validation error when the user tries to submit the form without providing a value.

If you are generating form elements from models, as I have been doing in this chapter, then you won't have any problems with browser validation because the MVC Framework generates and uses data attributes to denote validation rules (so that, for example, an input element that must have a value is denoted with the data-val-required attribute, which browsers do not recognize).

However, you may run into problems if you are unable to completely control the markup in your application, something that often happens when you are passing on content generated elsewhere. The result is that the jQuery validation and the browser validation can both operate on the form, which is just confusing to the user. To avoid this problem, you can add the novalidate attribute to the form element.

One of the nice features about the MVC client-side validation is that the same attributes used to specify validation rules are applied at the client *and* at the server. This means that data from browsers that do not support JavaScript are subject to the same validation as those that do, without requiring any additional effort.

MVC CLIENT VALIDATION VERSUS JQUERY VALIDATION

The MVC client-validation features are built on top of the jQuery Validation library. If you prefer, you can use the Validation library directly and ignore the MVC features. The Validation library is flexible and feature-rich. It is well worth exploring, if only to understand how to customize the MVC features to take best advantage of the available validation options. I cover the jQuery Validation library in depth in my *Pro jQuery* 2.0 book, also published by Apress.

Performing Remote Validation

The last validation feature I will look at in this chapter is remote validation. This is a client-side validation technique that invokes an action method on the server to perform validation.

A common example of remote validation is to check whether a username is available in applications when such names must be unique; the user submits the data, and the client-side validation is performed. As part of this process, an Ajax request is made to the server to validate the username that has been requested. If the username has been taken, a validation error is displayed so that the user can enter another value.

This may seem like regular server-side validation, but there are some benefits to this approach. First, only some properties will be remotely validated; the client-side validation benefits still apply to all the other data values that the user has entered. Second, the request is relatively lightweight and is focused on validation, rather than processing an entire model object.

The third difference is that the remote validation is performed in the background. The user doesn't have to click the submit button and then wait for a new view to be rendered and returned. It makes for a more responsive user experience, especially when there is a slow network between the browser and the server.

That said, remote validation is a compromise. It strikes a balance between client-side and server-side validation, but it does require requests to the application server, and it is not as quick to validate as normal client-side validation.

The first step toward using remote validation is to create an action method that can validate one of the model properties. I am going to validate the Date property of the Appointment model to ensure that the requested appointment is in the future. (This is one of the original validation rules I used at the start of the chapter, but which isn't possible to validate using the standard client-side validation features.) In Listing 25-24, you can see the ValidateDate action method that I added to the Home controller.

Listing 25-24. Adding a Validation Action Method to the HomeController.cs File

```
using System;
using System.Web.Mvc;
using ModelValidation.Models;

namespace ModelValidation.Controllers {
    public class HomeController : Controller {

        public ViewResult MakeBooking() {
            return View(new Appointment { Date = DateTime.Now });
        }

        [HttpPost]
        public ViewResult MakeBooking(Appointment appt) {
            if (ModelState.IsValid) {
                // statements to store new Appointment in a
                // repository would go here in a real project
                return View("Completed", appt);
            } else {
                return View();
            }
        }

        public JsonResult ValidateDate(string Date) {
            DateTime parsedDate;

            if (!DateTime.TryParse(Date, out parsedDate)) {
                return Json("Please enter a valid date (mm/dd/yyyy)",
                    JsonRequestBehavior.AllowGet);
            } else if (DateTime.Now > parsedDate) {
                return Json("Please enter a date in the future",
                    JsonRequestBehavior.AllowGet);
```

```
        } else {
            return Json(true, JsonRequestBehavior.AllowGet);
        }
    }
    }
}
}
```

Actions methods that support remote validation must return the JsonResult type, which tells the MVC Framework that I am working with JSON data, as explained in Chapter 23. In addition to the result, validation action methods must define a parameter that has the same name as the data field being validated: this is Date for the example. I make sure that I can parse a DateTime object from the value that the user has submitted and, if I can, check to see that the date is in the future.

■ **Tip** I could have taken advantage of model binding so that the parameter to my action method would be a DateTime object, but doing so would mean that the validation method wouldn't be called if the user entered a nonsense value like apple, for example. This is because the model binder wouldn't have been able to create a DateTime object from apple and throws an exception when it tries. The remote validation feature doesn't have a way to express that exception and so it is quietly discarded. This has the unfortunate effect of *not* highlighting the data field and so creating the impression that the value that the user has entered is valid. As a general rule, the best approach to remote validation is to accept a string parameter in the action method and perform any type conversion, parsing, or model binding explicitly.

I express validation results using the Json method, which creates a JSON-formatted result that the client-side remote validation script can parse and process. If the value that I am processing meets my requirements, then I pass true as the parameter to the Json method, like this:

```
...
return Json(true, JsonRequestBehavior.AllowGet);
...
```

If I am unhappy with the value, I pass the validation error message that the user should see as the parameter, like this:

```
...
return Json("Please enter a date in the future", JsonRequestBehavior.AllowGet);
...
```

In both cases, I must also pass the JsonRequestBehavior.AllowGet value as a parameter. This is because the MVC Framework disallows GET requests that produce JSON by default, and I have to override this behavior to handle the validation request. Without this additional parameter, the validation request will quietly fail, and no validation errors will be displayed to the client.

To use the remote validation method, I apply the Remote attribute to the property I want to validate in the model class. In Listing 25-25, you can see how I have applied the attribute to the Date property.

Listing 25-25. Using the Remote Attribute in the Appointment.cs File

```
using System;
using System.ComponentModel.DataAnnotations;
using System.Web.Mvc;
```

```
namespace ModelValidation.Models {
    public class Appointment {

        [Required]
        [StringLength(10, MinimumLength = 3)]
        public string ClientName { get; set; }

        [DataType(DataType.Date)]
        [Remote("ValidateDate", "Home")]
        public DateTime Date { get; set; }

        public bool TermsAccepted { get; set; }
    }
}
```

The arguments for the attribute are the name of the action and the controller that should be used to generate the URL that the JavaScript validation library will call to perform the validation—in this case, the ValidateDate action on the Home controller. The actual URL used will be created according to the application routing configuration.

You can see how the remote validation works by starting the application, navigating to the /Home/MakeBooking URL, and entering a date that is in the past. As you type, you will see the validation message appear, as shown in Figure 25-12.

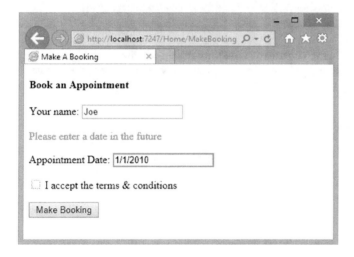

Figure 25-12. *Performing remote validation*

■ **Caution**   The validation action method will be called when the user first submits the form and then again each time he or she edits the data. In essence, every keystroke will lead to a call to the server. For some applications, this can be a significant number of requests and must be taken into account when specifying the server capacity and bandwidth that an application requires in production. Also, you might choose *not* to use remote validation for properties that are expensive to validate (for example, if you have to query a slow Web service to determine whether a username is unique).

Summary

In this chapter, I examined the wide range of techniques available to perform model validation, ensuring that the data that the user has provided is consistent with the constraints imposed on the data model.

Model validation is an important topic, and getting the right validation in place for an application is essential to ensuring that the users have a good and frustration-free experience. Equally important is the fact that the integrity of the domain model is preserved. In the next chapter I show you the bundles feature, which is used to manage JavaScript and CSS files.

CHAPTER 26

Bundles

In this chapter, I am going to look at the *bundles* feature, which the MVC Framework provides to organize and optimize the CSS and JavaScript files that views and layouts cause the browser to request from the server. Table 26-1 provides the summary for this chapter.

Table 26-1. *Chapter Summary*

Problem	Solution	Listing
Define bundles	Create instances of the StyleBundle and ScriptBundle classes and add them to the bundle table.	1–6
Prepare an application for bundles	Ensure that the Views/web.config file includes a reference for the System.Web.Optimization namespace.	7
Add a bundle to a view or layout	Use the Styles.Render and Scripts.Render helpers.	8
Enable concatenation and minification of bundles	Set the debug attribute of the compilation attribute in the Web.config file to false.	9

Preparing the Example Application

For this chapter, I have created a new MVC project called ClientFeatures using the Empty template option, checking the option to add the core MVC folders and references.

Adding the NuGet Packages

The bundles feature that I describe in this chapter makes it easier to manage JavaScript and CSS files. To that end, I am going to install a number of NuGet packages that are commonly used for client-side development. Select Package Manager Console from the Visual Studio Tools ➤ Library Package Manager menu and enter the following commands:

```
Install-Package jQuery -version 1.10.2
Install-Package jQuery.Validation -version 1.11.1
Install-Package Microsoft.jQuery.Unobtrusive.Validation -version 3.0.0
Install-Package Bootstrap -version 3.0.0
Install-Package Microsoft.jQuery.Unobtrusive.Ajax -version 3.0.0
```

Creating the Model and Controller

I am going to create a variation on the application that I used in the previous chapter, so I started by creating a new class file called Appointment.cs in the Models folder. You can see the contents of this file in Listing 26-1.

Listing 26-1. The Contents of the Appointment.cs File

```
using System;
using System.ComponentModel.DataAnnotations;

namespace ClientFeatures.Models {
    public class Appointment {

        [Required]
        public string ClientName { get; set; }

        public bool TermsAccepted { get; set; }
    }
}
```

I created a Home controller that operates on the Appointment model class, as shown in Listing 26-2.

Listing 26-2. The Contents of the HomeController.cs File

```
using System;
using System.Web.Mvc;
using ClientFeatures.Models;

namespace ClientFeatures.Controllers {
    public class HomeController : Controller {

        public ViewResult MakeBooking() {
            return View(new Appointment {
                ClientName = "Adam",
                TermsAccepted = true
            });
        }

        [HttpPost]
        public JsonResult MakeBooking(Appointment appt) {
            // statements to store new Appointment in a
            // repository would go here in a real project
            return Json(appt, JsonRequestBehavior.AllowGet);
        }
    }
}
```

There are two version of the MakeBooking method in this controller. The version with no parameters creates an Appointment object and passes it to the View method to render the default view. The HttpPost version of the MakeBooking method relies on the model binder to create an Appointment object and uses the Json method to encode the Appointment and send it back to the client in the JSON format.

I am focused on an MVC Framework feature that support client-side development in this chapter, so I have taken some shortcuts in the controller that wouldn't be sensible or useful in a real project. Most importantly, I do not perform any kind of validation when I receive a POST request and just send the details of the object created by the model binder back to the browser as JSON (with no support for HTML responses).

Creating the Layout and View

I created the Views/Shared folder and added a view file called _Layout.cshtml to it, the content of which you can see in Listing 26-3. The main purpose of this the layout is to import the JavaScript and CSS files that I added via NuGet so that they can be used in views.

Listing 26-3. The Contents of the _Layout.cshtml File

```
@{
    Layout = null;
}

<!DOCTYPE html>

<html>
<head>
    <meta name="viewport" content="width=device-width" />
    <title>@ViewBag.Title</title>
    <style>
        .field-validation-error { color: #f00; }
        .validation-summary-errors { color: #f00; font-weight: bold; }
        .input-validation-error { border: 2px solid #f00; background-color: #fee; }
        input[type="checkbox"].input-validation-error { outline: 2px solid #f00; }
        div.hidden { display: none; }
        div.visible { display: block; }
    </style>
    <link href="~/Content/bootstrap.css" rel="stylesheet" />
    <link href="~/Content/bootstrap-theme.css" rel="stylesheet" />
    <script src="~/Scripts/jquery-1.10.2.js"></script>
    <script src="~/Scripts/jquery.validate.js"></script>
    <script src="~/Scripts/jquery.validate.unobtrusive.js"></script>
    <script src="~/Scripts/jquery.unobtrusive-ajax.js"></script>
    @RenderSection("Scripts", false)
</head>
<body>
    @RenderSection("Body")
</body>
</html>
```

I defined two Razor sections in the view. The Scripts section will allow views to add JavaScript code to the head element section of the HTML response to the server, and the Body section allows the view to add content to the body element. (I explained how Razor sections worked in Chapter 20.) I added a view file called MakeBooking.cshtml to the Home/Views folder, as shown in Listing 26-4.

Listing 26-4. The Contents of the MakeBooking.cshtml File

```
@model ClientFeatures.Models.Appointment

@{
    ViewBag.Title = "Make Appointment";
    Layout = "~/Views/Shared/_Layout.cshtml";
    AjaxOptions ajaxOpts = new AjaxOptions {
        OnSuccess = "processResponse"
    };
}

@section Scripts {

<script type="text/javascript">

    function switchViews() {
        $(".hidden, .visible").toggleClass("hidden visible");
    }

    function processResponse(appt) {
        $('#successClientName').text(appt.ClientName);
        switchViews();
    }

    $(document).ready(function () {
        $('#backButton').click(function (e) {
            switchViews();
        });
    });
</script>

}

@section Body {

<div id="formDiv" class="visible well">
    @using (Ajax.BeginForm(ajaxOpts)) {
        @Html.ValidationSummary(true)
        <div class="form-group">
            <label for="ClientName">Your name:</label>
            <p>@Html.ValidationMessageFor(m => m.ClientName)</p>
            @Html.TextBoxFor(m => m.ClientName, new  {@class = "form-control" })
        </div>
        <div class="checkbox">
            <label>
                @Html.CheckBoxFor(m => m.TermsAccepted)
                I accept the terms & conditions
            </label>
        </div>
        <input type="submit" value="Make Booking" class="btn btn-primary"/>
    }
</div>
```

```
<div id="successDiv" class="hidden well">
    <h4 class="lead">Your appointment is confirmed</h4>
    <p>Your name is: <b id="successClientName"></b></p>
    <button id="backButton" class="btn btn-primary">Back</button>
</div>

}
```

My goal in this view is just to use all of the JavaScript and CSS files that I defined in the layout. To that end, I have defined an Ajax form that uses the unobtrusive Ajax library (described in Chapter 23) and that relies on the unobtrusive client-side validation library (described in Chapter 25). Both of these libraries depend on jQuery and I have used Bootstrap CSS classes to style the content.

I have taken advantage of the `Scripts` section I defined in the layout to include some JavaScript code that responds to the JSON response from the controller and manipulates the markup to display the results using some simple jQuery. This lets me deal with a single view for the example.

I want to create a typical scenario for a complex view file without needing to create a complex application, which is why I have added lots of JavaScript and CSS files for such a simple example. The key idea is that there are lots of files to be managed. When you are writing real applications, you will be struck by just how many script and style files you have to deal with in your views.

You can see how the example application works by starting the application and navigating to the /Home/MakeBooking URL. The form is pre-populated with data so that you can just click the Make Booking button to submit the form data to the server using Ajax. When the response is received, you will see a summary of the Appointment object that was created by the model binder from the form data, along with a button element that will return you to the form, as illustrated in Figure 26-1.

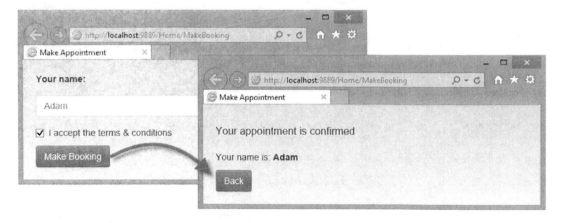

Figure 26-1. *Using the example application*

The project contains a number of JavaScript and CSS files, which are combined with inline JavaScript code and CSS styles to generate HTML for the browser. This is a typical mix that you will encounter in most MVC Framework projects.

Developers tend to write view files just as they would write HTML pages, which is fine but isn't the most effective approach. As I will show you in the sections that follow, there are some hidden problems in the MakeBooking.cshtml view file and I show you a number of improvements in the way that scripts and style sheets are managed.

Profiling Script and Style Sheet Loading

When considering any kind of optimization in any kind of project, you need to start by taking some measurements. I am all for efficient and optimized applications, but my experience is that people rush to optimize problems that don't have much impact and, in doing so, make design decisions that cause problems later.

For the problems that I am going to look at in this chapter, I am going to take the measurements using the Internet Explorer *F12 tools* (so called because you access them by pressing the F12 key).

I want to focus just on the HTTP requests that are made in the normal execution of the application, and that means disabling the Visual Studio Browser Link feature, which works by adding JavaScript code to the HTML sent to the browser, leading to additional HTTP requests.

Click on the small down arrow next to the Browser Link button on the Visual Studio toolbar and uncheck the `Enable Browser Link` menu item, as shown in Figure 26-2.

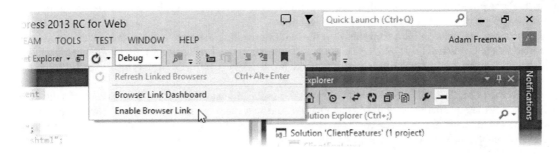

***Figure 26-2.** Disabling the browser link feature in Visual Studio*

Load the application, navigate to the /Home/MakeBooking URL, and then press the F12 key. When the tools window opens, navigate to the `Network` tab and click the green arrow button to start capturing the HTTP requests that the browser makes. Then click the `Clear Browser Cache` button, which will ensure that the browser requests the contents of all of the JavaScript and CSS files that are referenced in the layout. Reload the contents of the browser tab (right-click in the browser window and select `Refresh`), and you will see the results shown in Figure 26-3.

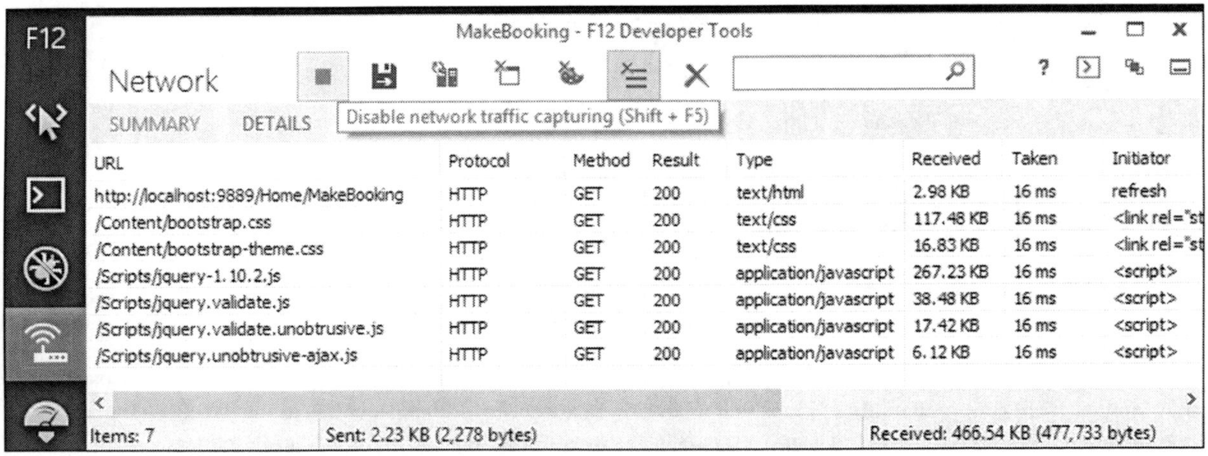

URL	Protocol	Method	Result	Type	Received	Taken	Initiator
http://localhost:9889/Home/MakeBooking	HTTP	GET	200	text/html	2.98 KB	16 ms	refresh
/Content/bootstrap.css	HTTP	GET	200	text/css	117.48 KB	16 ms	<link rel="st
/Content/bootstrap-theme.css	HTTP	GET	200	text/css	16.83 KB	16 ms	<link rel="st
/Scripts/jquery-1.10.2.js	HTTP	GET	200	application/javascript	267.23 KB	16 ms	<script>
/Scripts/jquery.validate.js	HTTP	GET	200	application/javascript	38.48 KB	16 ms	<script>
/Scripts/jquery.validate.unobtrusive.js	HTTP	GET	200	application/javascript	17.42 KB	16 ms	<script>
/Scripts/jquery.unobtrusive-ajax.js	HTTP	GET	200	application/javascript	6.12 KB	16 ms	<script>

Items: 7   Sent: 2.23 KB (2,278 bytes)   Received: 466.54 KB (477,733 bytes)

***Figure 26-3.** Profiling script and style sheet loading for the example application*

The F12 tools allow you to profile the network requests that your application makes. (All of the mainstream browsers offer similar developer tools and there are other alternatives. My favorite is Fiddler, which you can get from www.fiddler2.com).

So that I can assess the optimizations that I make in this chapter, I will use the data shown in Figure 26-3 as the baseline. Here are the key figures:

- The browser made seven requests for the /Home/MakeBooking URL.

- There were two requests for CSS files.

- There were four requests for JavaScript files.

- A total of 2,278 bytes were sent from the browser to the server.

- A total of 477,733 bytes were sent from the server to the browser

This is the worst-case profile for the example application because I cleared the browser's cache before I reloaded the view. I have done this because it allows me to easily create a measurable starting point, even though I know that real-world use would be improved by the browser caching files from previous requests.

If I reload the /Home/MakeBooking URL without clearing the cache, then I get the following results:

- The browser made seven requests for the /Home/MakeBooking URL.

- There were two requests for CSS files.

- There were four requests for JavaScript files.

- A total of 2,086 bytes were sent from the browser to the server.

- A total of 5,214 bytes were sent from the server to the browser.

This is the best-case scenario, where all the requests for CSS and JavaScript files were able to be serviced using previously cached files.

■ **Note**   In a real project, I would stop at this point and ask myself if I have a problem to solve or if the current state of the application is acceptable. It may seem that 473K is a lot of bandwidth for a simple Web page, but context is everything. I might be developing an application for Intranet use where bandwidth is cheap and plentiful, and optimizations of any sort are outweighed by the cost of the developer, who could be working on more important projects. Equally, I could be writing an application that operates over the Internet with high-value customers in countries with low-speed connections, in which case it is worth spending the time to optimize every aspect of the application. The point is that you shouldn't automatically assume that you have to squeeze every optimization into every application. There will often be better things you could be doing. (This is *always* the case if you are sneakily optimizing your application without telling anyone. Stealth optimization is a bad idea and will catch up with you eventually.)

Using Script and Style Bundles

My goal is to turn the JavaScript and CSS files into *bundles*, which allows me to treat several related files as a single unit. I walk through the steps required to set up and apply bundles in the sections that follow.

Adding the NuGet Package

The bundles feature requires a NuGet package that isn't included in the Visual Studio Empty template. Select Package Manager Console from the Visual Studio Tools ➤ Library Package Manager menu and enter the following command:

```
Install-Package Microsoft.AspNet.Web.Optimization -version 1.1.1
```

Defining the Bundles

The convention is to define bundles in a file called BundleConfig.cs, which is placed in the App_Start folder. In Listing 26-5, you can see the contents of the BundleConfig.cs file that I added to the example project. (You won't need to create this file yourself if you are using some of the other Visual Studio project templates because it will be added automatically.)

Listing 26-5. The Contents of the BundleConfig.cs File

```
using System.Web.Optimization;

namespace ClientFeatures {

    public class BundleConfig {

        public static void RegisterBundles(BundleCollection bundles) {

            bundles.Add(new StyleBundle("~/Content/css").Include(
                "~/Content/*.css"));

            bundles.Add(new ScriptBundle("~/bundles/clientfeaturesscripts")
                .Include("~/Scripts/jquery-{version}.js",
                    "~/Scripts/jquery.validate.js",
                    "~/Scripts/jquery.validate.unobtrusive.js",
                    "~/Scripts/jquery.unobtrusive-ajax.js"));
        }
    }
}
```

■ **Tip** Notice that I have changed the namespace in which the class is defined in this file. The convention is that the classes defined in the files in the App_Start folder are defined in the top-level namespace for the application, which is ClientFeatures for this project.

The static RegisterBundles method is called from the Application_Start method in Global.asax—which I'll set up in the next section—when the MVC Framework application first starts. The RegisterBundles method takes a BundleCollection object, which I use to register new bundles of files through the Add method.

■ **Tip** The classes that are used for creating bundles are contained in the System.Web.Optimization namespace and, as I write this, the MSDN API documentation for this namespace isn't easy to find. You can navigate directly to http://msdn.microsoft.com/en-us/library/system.web.optimization.aspx if you want to learn more about the classes in this namespace.

I can create bundles for script files and for style sheets and it is important that I keep these types of files separate because the MVC Framework optimizes the files differently. Styles are represented by the StyleBundle class and scripts are represented by the ScriptBundle class.

When you create a new bundle, you create an instance of either StyleBundle or ScriptBundle, both of which take a single constructor argument that is the path that the bundle will be referenced by. The path is used as a URL for the browser to request the contents of the bundle, so it is important to use a scheme for your paths that won't conflict with the routes your application supports. The safest way to do this is to start your paths with ~/bundles or ~/Content. (The importance of this will become apparent as I explain how bundles work.)

Once you have created the StyleBundle or ScriptBundle objects, you use the Include method to add details of the style sheets or script files that the bundle will contain. There are some nice features available for making your bundles flexible.

I started by creating a StyleBundle with the ~/Content/css path. I want this bundle to include all the CSS files in the application, so I passed the value ~/Content/*.css as the argument to the Include method. The asterisk (*) character is a wild card, which means that the bundle refers to all of the CSS files in the /Content folder of the project. This is an excellent way of ensuring that files in a directory are automatically included in a bundle and where the order in which the files are loaded isn't important.

■ **Tip** The order in which the browser loads the Bootstrap CSS files isn't important, so using a wildcard is just fine. But if you are relying on the CSS style precedence rules, then you need to list the files individually to ensure a specific order, which is what I did for the JavaScript files.

The other bundle in the BundleConfig.cs file is a ScriptBundle whose path I set to ~/bundles/clientfeaturesscripts. You will see the paths for both bundles again when I apply them to the application shortly. I used the Include method for this bundle to specify individual JavaScript files, separated by commas. I could have used another wildcard, but the order in which JavaScript files are processed usually matters and so I have listed out the individual files. Notice how I specified the jQuery library file:

```
...
~/Scripts/jquery-{version}.js
...
```

The {version} part of the file name is pretty handy because it matches any version of the file specified and it uses the configuration of the application to select either the regular or minified version of the file (which I'll explain shortly). The version I installed of the jQuery library is 1.10.2, which means that the bundle will include the /Scripts/jquery-1.10.2.js file

The benefit of using {version} is that you can update the libraries you use to new versions without having to redefine your bundles. The drawback is that the {version} token isn't able to differentiate between two versions of the same library in the same directory. So, for example, if I were to add the jquery-2.0.2.js file to the Scripts folder, I would end up with both the 1.10.2 and 2.0.2 files being shipped to the client. Since this would undermine the goal of the optimization, I must ensure that only one version of the library is in the /Scripts folder.

> ■ **Note** The jQuery team has done something unusual with their version numbering and is maintaining two different development branches. As of jQuery 1.9, the jQuery 1.x and 2.x branches have the same API, but the jQuery 2.x release doesn't support older Microsoft browsers. You should use the 1.x release in your projects unless you are sure that none of your users are stuck with Internet Explorer versions 6, 7 or 8. For more details see my *Pro jQuery 2.0* book, published by Apress.

Since I used the Empty template to create the example project, I need to add a statement to the Global.asax file to call the RegisterBundles method in the BundleConfig class, as shown in Listing 26-6.

Listing 26-6. Setting Up the Bundles in the Global.asax File

```
using System;
using System.Collections.Generic;
using System.Linq;
using System.Web;
using System.Web.Mvc;
using System.Web.Routing;
using System.Web.Optimization;

namespace ClientFeatures {

    public class MvcApplication : System.Web.HttpApplication {
        protected void Application_Start() {
            AreaRegistration.RegisterAllAreas();
            RouteConfig.RegisterRoutes(RouteTable.Routes);
            BundleConfig.RegisterBundles(BundleTable.Bundles);;,bv
        }
    }
}
```

Applying Bundles

The first thing I need to do, before I can apply the bundles, is make sure that the namespace that contains the bundle-related classes is available for use within my view. To do this, I added an entry to the pages/namespaces element in the Views/web.config file, as shown in Listing 26-7.

Listing 26-7. Adding the Bundles Namespace to the Web.config File

```
...
<pages pageBaseType="System.Web.Mvc.WebViewPage">
  <namespaces>
    <add namespace="System.Web.Mvc" />
    <add namespace="System.Web.Mvc.Ajax" />
    <add namespace="System.Web.Mvc.Html" />
    <add namespace="System.Web.Routing" />
    <add namespace="System.Web.Optimization"/>
    <add namespace="ClientFeatures" />
  </namespaces>
</pages>
...
```

You won't need to do this if you are using one of the more complex Visual Studio project templates, but Visual Studio doesn't set this up automatically when the Empty template is used.

The next step is to apply the bundles to the layout. You can see the changes I made to the _Layout.cshtml file in Listing 26-8.

Listing 26-8 Applying Bundles to the _Layout.cshtml File

```
@{
    Layout = null;
}

<!DOCTYPE html>

<html>
<head>
    <meta name="viewport" content="width=device-width" />
    <title>@ViewBag.Title</title>
    <style>
        .field-validation-error { color: #f00; }
        .validation-summary-errors { color: #f00; font-weight: bold; }
        .input-validation-error { border: 2px solid #f00; background-color: #fee; }
        input[type="checkbox"].input-validation-error { outline: 2px solid #f00; }
        div.hidden { display: none; }
        div.visible { display: block; }
    </style>
    @Styles.Render("~/Content/css")
    @Scripts.Render("~/bundles/clientfeaturesscripts")
    @RenderSection("Scripts", false)
</head>
<body>
    @RenderSection("Body")
</body>
</html>
```

Bundles are added using the @Scripts.Render and @Styles.Render helper methods and you can see how I have used these helpers to replace the link and script elements with the combined bundles of files.

■ **Tip** Notice that I have left the Scripts section in the layout so that the view can define its inline code. You can mix and match bundles and regular script and link elements freely, although you should consider moving inline code and styles to external files to maximize the optimization that the MVC Framework can perform, which I describe shortly.

You can see the HTML that these helper methods generate by starting the application, navigating to the /Home/MakeBooking URL, and viewing the page source. Here is the output produced by the Styles.Render method for the ~/Content/css bundle:

```
...
<link href="/Content/bootstrap-theme.css" rel="stylesheet"/>
<link href="/Content/bootstrap.css" rel="stylesheet"/>
...
```

And here is the output produced by the `Scripts.Render` method:

```
...
<script src="/Scripts/jquery-1.10.2.js"></script>
<script src="/Scripts/jquery.unobtrusive-ajax.js"></script>
<script src="/Scripts/jquery.validate.js"></script>
<script src="/Scripts/jquery.validate.unobtrusive.js"></script>
...
```

Optimizing the JavaScript and CSS Files

Organizing JavaScript and CSS files into related groups is a useful way to make sure that you don't forget to include a file and that your layouts include whatever version of a file that is included in the project. But the real magic of bundles is that they can be used to optimize the delivery of JavaScript and CSS content to the browser.

The key to this is contained in the `Web.config` file (the one in the root folder this time) and the debug attribute of the `compilation` element. Open the `Web.config` file and set the attribute value to `false`, as shown in Listing 26-9.

Listing 26-9. Disabling Debug Mode in the Web.config File

```
...
<system.web>
    <compilation debug="false" targetFramework="4.5.1" />
    <httpRuntime targetFramework="4.5.1" />
</system.web>
...
```

When the debug attribute is set to `true`, the HTML sent to the browser contains `link` and `script` elements for individual files. When the attribute is `false`, the minified versions of the files are selected and concatenated together so that they can be delivered to the client as a blob.

■ **Note** Minification processes a JavaScript or CSS file to remove whitespace and, in the case of JavaScript files, shortens the variable and function names so that the files require less bandwidth to transfer. Most libraries provide both debug (i.e., human-readable) and minified versions of their files, which is why the `Scripts` folder contains, for example, the `jquery-validate.js` and `jquery-validate.min.js` file. The extra `.min` in the file name denotes the minified file. The selection between the files is automatic and, for the most part, minification is a simple and successful process. Some advanced libraries (such as one of my favorites, AngularJS), however, require a special minification process. Caution is recommended.

Select `Start Without Debugging` from the Visual Studio Debug menu. (You can't run the debugger when the debug attribute is set to `false`.) Navigate to the `/Home/MakeBooking` URL and press the F12 key to bring up the developer tools. Switch to the network tab, clear the browser cache and then click the green arrow button to start recording the requests made by the browser. Reload the page to see the effect of setting the debug attribute to `false`, which Figure 26-4 illustrates.

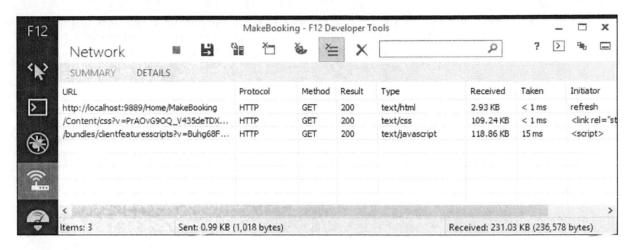

Figure 26-4. *Profiling with bundles*

Here is the summary of the profile information:

- The browser made three requests for the /Home/MakeBooking URL.

- There was one request for a CSS file.

- There was one request for a JavaScript file.

- A total of 1,018 bytes were sent from the browser to the server.

- A total of 236,578 bytes were sent from the server to the browser.

That's not bad. I have shaved about 50 percent off the amount of data that is sent to the browser just by letting ASP.NET and the MVC Framework optimize my JavaScript and CSS files. You can see how this works if you look at the HTML that the application renders. Here is the HTML that the Styles.Render method has produced:

```
...
<link href="/Content/css?v=PrAOvG90Q_V435deTDX5p8RzKE4Gs8_LEeYxl29skhc1"
    rel="stylesheet"/>
...
```

And here is the HTML produced by the Scripts.Render method:

```
...
<script
    src="/bundles/clientfeaturesscripts?v=Buhg68FkCPk3xjXtPsE87M94MTb7DCZx3zKAYDoxRIA1">
</script>
...
```

These long URLs are used to request the contents of a bundle in a single blob of data. The MVC Framework minifies CSS data differently from JavaScript files, which is why I have to keep style sheets and scripts in different bundles.

The impact of the optimizations is significant. I have far fewer requests from the browser (which reduces the amount of data sent to the client) and I have less data sent in return—all of which helps keep down the cost of running the web application.

This is the point where I usually stop optimizing the requests. I could go further: moving the inline scripts into separate files so that they can be minified, for example. But I don't like to optimize too heavily unless I have a tangible problem to solve. Each optimization makes the application harder to debug and harder to maintain.

Summary

In this chapter, I showed you the bundles feature, which can help manage the JavaScript and CSS files in an application and optimize their delivery to the client. In the next chapter, I will show you the Web API (which makes it easy to create Web services that clients can consume), which is the foundation for *single page applications*.

CHAPTER 27

∎ ∎ ∎

Web API and Single-page Applications

In this chapter, I describe the Web API feature, which is a relatively new addition to the ASP.NET platform that allows you to quickly and easily create Web services that provide an API to HTTP clients, known as *Web APIs*.

The Web API feature is based on the same foundation as the MVC Framework applications, but is not part of the MVC Framework. Instead, Microsoft has taken some key classes and characteristics that are associated with the System.Web.Mvc namespace and duplicated them in the System.Web.Http namespace. The idea is that Web API is part of the core ASP.NET platform and can be used in other types of Web applications or used as a stand-alone Web services engine. I have included Web API in this book because one of the main uses for it is to create *single-page applications* (SPAs) by combining the Web API with MVC Framework features you have seen in previous chapters. I'll explain what SPAs are and how they work later in the chapter.

That is not to take away from the way that Web API simplifies creating Web services. It is a huge improvement over the other Microsoft Web service technologies that have been appearing over the last decade or so. I like the Web API and you should use it for your projects, not least because it is simple and built on the same design that the MVC Framework uses.

I start this chapter by creating a regular MVC Framework application and then using the Web API to transform it into a single-page application. This is a surprisingly simple example, so I have treated the process like an extended example and applied some of the relevant techniques from earlier chapters because you can never have enough examples. Table 27-1 provides the summary for this chapter.

Table 27-1. *Chapter Summary*

Problem	Solution	Listing
Create a RESTful web service	Add a Web API controller to an MVC Framework application.	1–10
Map between HTTP methods and action names in a Web API controller	Apply attributes such as HttpPut and HttpPost to the methods.	11
Create a single-page application	Use Knockout and jQuery to obtain data via Ajax and bind it to HTML elements.	12–17

Understanding Single-page Applications

The term *single-page application* (SPA) is a broadly applied term. The most consistently-used definition is a web application whose initial content is delivered as a combination of HTML and JavaScript and whose subsequent operations are performed using a RESTful web service that delivers data via JSON in response to Ajax requests.

This differs from the kind of application I have been building in most of the chapters of this book, where operations performed by the user result in new HTML documents being generated in response to synchronous HTTP requests, which I will refer to as round-trip applications (RTAs).

The advantages of a SPA are that less bandwidth is required and that the user receives a smoother experience. The disadvantages are that the smoother experience can be hard to achieve and that the complexity of the JavaScript code required for a SPA demands careful design and testing.

Most applications mix and match SPA and RTA techniques, where each major functional area of the application is delivered as a SPA, and navigation between functional areas is managed using standard HTTP requests that create a new HTML document.

Preparing the Example Application

For this chapter, I created a new ASP.NET project called WebServices using the Empty template. I checked the options to add the folders and references for both MVC and Web API applications, as shown in Figure 27-1.

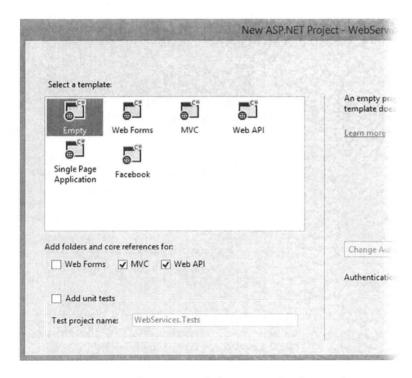

Figure 27-1. *Creating the project with the MVC and Web API references*

I will use this project to create a regular MVC Framework application and then use the Web API to create a web service. Once the web service is complete, I'll return to the MVC Framework application and make it into a single-page application.

Creating the Model

This application will create and maintain a series of reservations. I want to keep the application simple so that I can focus on the mechanics of the features I describe, and so these reservations will consist of just a name and a location. I added a class file called Reservation.cs to the Models folder, the contents of which are shown in Listing 27-1.

Listing 27-1. The Contents of the Reservation.cs File

```
namespace WebServices.Models {
    public class Reservation {
        public int ReservationId { get; set; }
        public string ClientName { get; set; }
        public string Location { get; set; }
    }
}
```

I am going to create a simple in-memory collection of Reservation objects to act as the model repository. I don't want to go to the trouble of setting up a database, but I do need to be able to perform CRUD operations on a collection of model objects so that I can demonstrate some important aspects of the Web API. I added a class file called ReservationRepository.cs to the Models folder and you can see the contents of the new file in Listing 27-2.

Listing 27-2. The Contents of the ReservationRespository.cs File

```
using System.Collections.Generic;
using System.Linq;

namespace WebServices.Models {
    public class ReservationRespository {
        private static ReservationRespository repo = new ReservationRespository();

        public static ReservationRespository Current {
            get {
                return repo;
            }
        }

        private List<Reservation> data = new List<Reservation> {
            new Reservation {
                ReservationId = 1, ClientName = "Adam", Location = "Board Room"},
            new Reservation {
                ReservationId = 2, ClientName = "Jacqui", Location = "Lecture Hall"},
            new Reservation {
                ReservationId = 3, ClientName = "Russell", Location = "Meeting Room 1"},
        };

        public IEnumerable<Reservation> GetAll() {
            return data;
        }

        public Reservation Get(int id) {
            return data.Where(r => r.ReservationId == id).FirstOrDefault();
        }

        public Reservation Add(Reservation item) {
            item.ReservationId = data.Count + 1;
            data.Add(item);
            return item;
        }
```

```
    public void Remove(int id) {
        Reservation item = Get(id);
        if (item != null) {
            data.Remove(item);
        }
    }

    public bool Update(Reservation item) {
        Reservation storedItem = Get(item.ReservationId);
        if (storedItem != null) {
            storedItem.ClientName = item.ClientName;
            storedItem.Location = item.Location;
            return true;
        } else {
            return false;
        }
    }
  }
}
```

■ **Tip** In a real project, I would be concerned about tight coupling between classes and introduce interfaces and dependency injection into the application. My focus in this chapter is just on the Web API and SPA applications, so I am going to take some shortcuts when it comes to other standard techniques.

The repository class has an initial list of three Reservation objects and defines methods that allow me to view, add, delete and update the collection. Since there is no persistent storage, any changes that are made to the repository will be lost when the application is stopped or restarted, but this example is all about the way in which content can be delivered and not how it is stored by the server. To ensure that there is some persistence between requests, I have created a static instance of the ReservationRespository class, which is accessible through the Current property.

Adding the NuGet Packages

I am going to rely on three NuGet packages in this chapter: jQuery, Bootstrap and Knockout. I have already described and used jQuery and Bootstrap in earlier chapters. Knockout is the library that Microsoft has adopted for single-page applications. It was created by Steve Sanderson, whom I worked with on an earlier edition of this book and who works for the Microsoft ASP.NET team. Even though Steve works for Microsoft, the Knockout package is open source and widely used and you can learn more about it at http://knockoutjs.com. I'll explain how Knockout works later in the chapter, but for the moment I just need to install the NuGet packages. Select Package Manager Console from the Visual Studio Tools ➤ Library Package Manager menu and enter the following commands:

```
Install-Package jquery -version 1.10.2
Install-Package bootstrap -version 3.0.0
Install-Package knockoutjs -version 3.0.0
```

Adding the Controller

I added a controller called Home to the example project, the definition of which you can see in Listing 27-3.

Listing 27-3. The Contents of the HomeController.cs File

```
using System.Web.Mvc;
using WebServices.Models;

namespace WebServices.Controllers {

    public class HomeController : Controller {
        private ReservationRespository repo = ReservationRespository.Current;

        public ViewResult Index() {
            return View(repo.GetAll());
        }

        public ActionResult Add(Reservation item) {
            if (ModelState.IsValid) {
                repo.Add(item);
                return RedirectToAction("Index");
            } else {
                return View("Index");
            }
        }

        public ActionResult Remove(int id) {
            repo.Remove(id);
            return RedirectToAction("Index");
        }

        public ActionResult Update(Reservation item) {
            if (ModelState.IsValid && repo.Update(item)) {
                return RedirectToAction("Index");
            } else {
                return View("Index");
            }
        }
    }
}
```

This is a fairly typical controller for such a simple application. Each of the action methods corresponds directly to one of the methods in the repository and the only value that the controller adds is to perform model validation, to select views, and perform redirections. In a real project, there would be more business domain logic, of course, but because the example application I am using is so basic, the controller ends up being little more than a wrapper around the repository.

Adding the Layout and Views

To generate the content for the application, I started by creating the Views/Shared folder and adding a view file called _Layout.cshtml to it, the contents of which are shown by Listing 27-4.

Listing 27-4. The Contents of the _Layout.cshtml File

```
@{
    Layout = null;
}

<!DOCTYPE html>

<html>
<head>
    <meta name="viewport" content="width=device-width" />
    <title>@ViewBag.Title</title>
    <link href="~/Content/bootstrap.css" rel="stylesheet" />
    <link href="~/Content/bootstrap.min.css" rel="stylesheet" />
    @RenderSection("Scripts")
</head>
<body>
    @RenderSection("Body")
</body>
</html>
```

This is a basic layout that has link elements for the Bootstrap CSS files. I have defined two layout sections, Scripts and Body, that I will use to insert content into the layout. My next step was to create the top-level view for the application. Although I am going through the process of creating a regular MVC Framework application, I know that I am going to end up with a single-page application and the transformation will be made easier if I create a single view that contains all the HTML that the application will require, even if it results in an odd appearance initially. I added a view file called Index.cshtml to the Views/Home folder, the contents of which you can see in Listing 27-5.

Listing 27-5. The Contents of the Index.cshtml File

```
@using WebServices.Models

@model IEnumerable<Reservation>
@{
    ViewBag.Title = "Reservations";
    Layout = "~/Views/Shared/_Layout.cshtml";
}

@section Scripts {

}

@section Body {
    <div id="summary" class="section panel panel-primary">
        @Html.Partial("Summary", Model)
    </div>
```

```
    <div id="editor" class="section panel panel-primary">
        @Html.Partial("Editor", new Reservation())
    </div>
}
```

The view model for this view is an enumeration of Reservation objects and I rely on two partial views to provide the functional building blocks that the user will see. The first partial view file is called Summary.cshtml. I created the file in the Views/Home folder and you can see the contents of the file in Listing 27-6.

Listing 27-6. The Contents of the Summary.cshtml File

```
@model IEnumerable<WebServices.Models.Reservation>

<div class="panel-heading">Reservation Summary</div>
<div class="panel-body">
    <table class="table table-striped table-condensed">
        <thead>
            <tr><th>ID</th><th>Name</th><th>Location</th><th></th></tr>
        </thead>
        <tbody>
            @foreach (var item in Model) {
                <tr>
                    <td>@item.ReservationId</td>
                    <td>@item.ClientName</td>
                    <td>@item.Location</td>
                    <td>
                        @Html.ActionLink("Remove", "Remove",
                                new { id = item.ReservationId },
                                new { @class = "btn btn-xs btn-primary" })
                    </td>
                </tr>
            }
        </tbody>
    </table>
</div>
```

The view model for the partial view is the same enumeration of Reservation object and I use it to generate a Bootstrap-styled table element that displays the object property values. I use the Html.ActionLink helper method to generate a link that will invoke the Remove action on the Home controller and use Bootstrap to style it as a button.

The other partial view is called Editor.cshtml and I put this in the Views/Home folder as well. Listing 27-7 shows the contents of this file. This partial view contains a form that can be used to create new reservations. Submitting the form invokes the Add action on the Home controller.

Listing 27-7. The Contents of the Editor.cshtml File

```
@model WebServices.Models.Reservation

<div class="panel-heading">
    Create Reservation
</div>
```

```
<div class="panel-body">
    @using(Html.BeginForm("Add", "Home")) {
        <div class="form-group">
            <label>Client Name</label>
            @Html.TextBoxFor(m => m.ClientName, new {@class = "form-control"})
        </div>
        <div class="form-group">
            <label>Location</label>
            @Html.TextBoxFor(m => m.Location, new { @class = "form-control" })
        </div>
        <button type="submit" class="btn btn-primary">Save</button>
    }
</div>
```

Setting the Start Location and Testing the Example Application

The last preparatory step is to set the location that Visual Studio will navigate to when the application is started. Select WebServices Properties from the Visual Studio Project menu, switch to the Web tab and check the Specific Page option in the Start Action section. You don't have to provide a value. Just checking the option is enough. To test the application in its classic MVC Framework form, select Start Debugging from the Visual Studio Debug menu. You will see the (slightly odd) all-in-one layout that provides the user with a list of the current reservations and the ability to create and delete items, as shown in Figure 27-2.

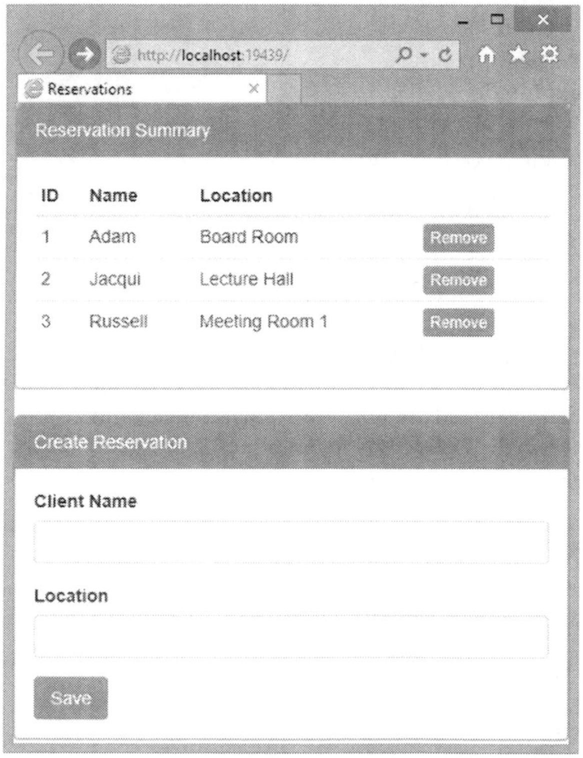

Figure 27-2. *Testing the example application*

Using Web API

The Web API feature is based on adding a special kind of controller to an MVC Framework application. This kind of controller, called an *API Controller*, has two distinctive characteristics:

1. Action methods return model, rather than `ActionResult`, objects.

2. Action methods are selected based on the HTTP method used in the request.

The model objects that are returned from an API controller action method are encoded as JSON and sent to the client. API controllers are designed to deliver Web data services, so they do not support views, layouts, or any of the other features that I used to generate HTML in the example application.

■ **Tip**   The inability of an API controller to generate HTML from views is the reason that single-page applications combine standard MVC Framework techniques with the Web API. The MVC Framework performs the steps required to deliver HTML content to the user (including authentication, authorization, and selecting and rendering a view). Once the HTML is delivered to the browser, the Ajax requests generated by the JavaScript it contains are handled by the Web API controller.

As I demonstrated in Chapter 23, you can create action methods in regular controllers that return JSON data to support Ajax, but the API controller offers an alternative approach that separates the data-related actions in your application from the view-related actions, and makes creating a general-purpose Web API quick and simple.

Creating the Web API Controller

Adding Web API to an application is incredibly simple. In part this is because I am creating a basic web service, but also because the integration with the underpinnings of the MVC Framework means that little work is required. I created the `WebController.cs` class file in the `Controllers` folder of the project and used it to define the controller shown in Listing 27-8.

Listing 27-8. The Contents of the WebController.cs File

```
using System.Collections.Generic;
using System.Web.Http;
using WebServices.Models;

namespace WebServices.Controllers {

    public class WebController : ApiController {
        private ReservationRespository repo = ReservationRespository.Current;

        public IEnumerable<Reservation> GetAllReservations() {
            return repo.GetAll();
        }

        public Reservation GetReservation(int id) {
            return repo.Get(id);
        }
```

```
        public Reservation PostReservation(Reservation item) {
            return repo.Add(item);
        }

        public bool PutReservation(Reservation item) {
            return repo.Update(item);
        }

        public void DeleteReservation(int id) {
            repo.Remove(id);
        }
    }
}
```

That is all that is required to create a Web API. The API controller has a set of five action methods that map to the capabilities of the repository and provide web service access to the Reservation objects.

Testing the API Controller

I will explain how the API controller works shortly, but first I am going to perform a simple test. Start the application. Once the browser loads the root URL for the project, navigate to the /api/web URL. The result that you see will depend on the browser that you are using. If you are using Internet Explorer, then you will be prompted to save or open a file that contains the following JSON data:

```
[{"ReservationId":1,"ClientName":"Adam","Location":"Board Room"},
 {"ReservationId":2,"ClientName":"Jacqui","Location":"Lecture Hall"},
 {"ReservationId":3,"ClientName":"Russell","Location":"Meeting Room 1"}]
```

If you navigate to the same URL using a different browser, such as Google Chrome, then the browser will display the following XML data:

```
<ArrayOfReservation>
    <Reservation>
        <ClientName>Adam</ClientName>
        <Location>Board Room</Location>
        <ReservationId>1</ReservationId>
    </Reservation>
    <Reservation>
        <ClientName>Jacqui</ClientName>
        <Location>Lecture Hall</Location>
        <ReservationId>2</ReservationId>
    </Reservation>
    <Reservation>
        <ClientName>Russell</ClientName>
        <Location>Meeting Room 1</Location>
        <ReservationId>3</ReservationId>
    </Reservation>
</ArrayOfReservation>
```

There are a couple of interesting things to note here. The first is that the request for the /api/web URL has produced a list of all of the model objects and their properties, from which we can infer that the GetAllReservations action method in the Reservation controller was called.

The second point to note is that different browsers received different data formats. You might get different results if you try this yourself because later versions of the browsers may change the way they make requests, but you can see that one of requests has produced JSON and the other has produced XML. (You can also see why JSON has largely replaced XML for Web services. XML is more verbose and harder to process, especially when you are using JavaScript.)

The different data formats are used because the Web API uses the HTTP Accept header contained in the request to work out what data type the client would prefer to work with. Internet Explorer got JSON because this is the Accept header it sends:

```
...
Accept: text/html, application/xhtml+xml, */*
...
```

The browser specified that it would like text/html content most of all, and then application/xhtml+xml. The final part of the Accept header is */*, which means the browser will accept any data type if the first two are not available.

The Web API supports JSON and XML, but it gives preference to JSON, which is what it used to respond to the */* part of the IE Accept header. Here is the Accept header that Google Chrome sent:

```
...
Accept:text/html,application/xhtml+xml,application/xml;q=0.9,*/*;q=0.8
...
```

I have highlighted the important part: Chrome has said that it prefers to receive application/xml data in preference to the */* catchall. The Web API controller honored this preference and delivered the XML data. I mention this because a common problem with Web API is getting an undesired data format. This happens because the Accept header gives unexpected preference to a format, or it is missing from the request entirely.

Understanding How the API Controller Works

You will understand a lot more about how the API controller works by navigating to the /api/web/3 URL. You will see the following JSON (or the equivalent XML if you are using another browser):

```
{"ReservationId":3,"ClientName":"Russell","Location":"Meeting Room 1"}
```

This time, the Web API controller has returned details of the Reservation object whose ReservationId value corresponds to the last segment of the URL I requested. The format of the URL and the use of the URL segment should remind you of Chapter 15, where I explained how MVC Framework routes work.

API controllers have their own routing configuration, which is completely separate from the rest of the application. You can see the default configuration that Visual Studio creates for new projects by looking at the /App_Start/WebApiConfig.cs file, which I have shown in Listing 27-9. This is one of the files that Visual Studio adds to the project when you check the Web API box during project creation.

Listing 27-9. The Contents of the WebApiConfig.cs File

```
using System;
using System.Collections.Generic;
using System.Linq;
using System.Web.Http;

namespace WebServices {
    public static class WebApiConfig {
        public static void Register(HttpConfiguration config) {

            config.MapHttpAttributeRoutes();

            config.Routes.MapHttpRoute(
                name: "DefaultApi",
                routeTemplate: "api/{controller}/{id}",
                defaults: new { id = RouteParameter.Optional }
            );
        }
    }
}
```

The WebApiConfig.cs file contains the routes used for API Controllers, but uses different classes from the regular MVC routes defined in the RouteConfig.cs file. The Web API feature is implemented as a stand-alone ASP.NET feature and it can be used outside of the MVC Framework, which means that Microsoft has duplicated some key MVC Framework functionality in the System.Web.Http namespace to keep MVC and Web API features separate. (This seems oddly duplicative when writing an MVC Framework application but makes sense since Microsoft is trying to target non-MVC developers with Web API, too.) Visual Studio also adds a call from the Application_Start method in the Global.asax class so that the Web API routes are added to the application configuration, as shown in Listing 27-10.

Listing 27-10. The Contents of the Global.asax File

```
using System;
using System.Collections.Generic;
using System.Linq;
using System.Web;
using System.Web.Mvc;
using System.Web.Routing;
using System.Web.Security;
using System.Web.SessionState;
using System.Web.Http;

namespace WebServices {
    public class Global : HttpApplication {
        void Application_Start(object sender, EventArgs e) {
            AreaRegistration.RegisterAllAreas();
            GlobalConfiguration.Configure(WebApiConfig.Register);
            RouteConfig.RegisterRoutes(RouteTable.Routes);
        }
    }
}
```

The result is that the application has two sets of routes: those used for MVC Framework controllers and those used for Web API controllers.

Understanding API Controller Action Selection

The default Web API route, which you can see in Listing 27-9, has a static api segment, and controller and id segment variables, the latter being optional. They key difference from a regular MVC route is that there is no action segment variable, and this is where the behavior of API controllers takes shape.

When a request comes in to the application that matches a Web API route, the action is determined from the HTTP method used to make the request. When I tested the API controller by requesting /api/reservation using the browser, the browser specified the GET method.

The ApiController class, which is the base for API controllers, knows which controller it needs to target from the route and uses the HTTP method to look for suitable action methods.

The convention when naming API controller action methods is to prefix the name with the action method that it supports and include some reference to the model type that it operates on. But this is just a convention because Web API will match any action method whose name contains the HTTP method used to make the request.

For the example, that means that a GET request results in a choice between the GetAllReservations and GetReservation, but method names like DoGetReservation or just ThisIsTheGetAction would also be matched.

To decide between the two action methods, the controller looks at the arguments that the contenders accept and uses the routing variables to make the best match. When requesting the /api/reservation API, there were no routing variables except for controller, and so the GetAllReservations method was selected because it has no arguments. When requesting the /api/reservation/3 URL, I supplied a value for the optional id segment variable, which made the GetReservation the better match because it accepts an id argument.

The other actions in the Web API controller are targeted using other HTTP methods: POST, DELETE, and PUT. This is the foundation for the *Representation State Transfer* (REST) style of Web API, known more commonly as a *RESTful* service, where an operation is specified by the combination of a URL and the HTTP method used to request it.

■ **Note**   REST is a style of API rather than a well-defined specification, and there is disagreement about what exactly makes a Web service RESTful. One point of contention is that purists do not consider Web services that return JSON as being RESTful. Like any disagreement about an architectural pattern, the reasons for the disagreement are arbitrary and dull. I try to be pragmatic about how patterns are applied, and JSON services are RESTful as far as I am concerned.

Mapping HTTP Methods to Action Methods

I explained that the ApiController base class uses the HTTP method to work out which action methods to target. It is a nice approach, but it does mean that you end up with some unnatural method names that are inconsistent with conventions you might be using elsewhere. For example, the PutReservation method might be more naturally called UpdateReservation. Not only would UpdateReservation make the purpose of the method more obvious, but it may allow for a more direct mapping between the actions in your controller and the methods in your repository.

■ **Tip**   You might be tempted to derive your repository class from ApiController and expose the repository methods directly as a Web API. I recommend against that and strongly suggest you create a separate controller, even as simple as the one I created in the example. At some point, the methods you want to offer via your API and the capabilities of your repository will diverge, and having a separate API controller class will make that easier to manage.

The System.Web.Http namespace contains a set of attributes that you can use to specify which HTTP methods an action should be used for. You can see how I have applied two of these attributes in Listing 27-11 to create a more natural set of method names.

Listing 27-11. Applying Attributes in the WebController.cs File

```
using System.Collections.Generic;
using System.Web.Http;
using WebServices.Models;

namespace WebServices.Controllers {

    public class WebController : ApiController {
        private ReservationRespository repo = ReservationRespository.Current;

        public IEnumerable<Reservation> GetAllReservations() {
            return repo.GetAll();
        }

        public Reservation GetReservation(int id) {
            return repo.Get(id);
        }

        [HttpPost]
        public Reservation CreateReservation(Reservation item) {
            return repo.Add(item);
        }

        [HttpPut]
        public bool UpdateReservation(Reservation item) {
            return repo.Update(item);
        }

        public void DeleteReservation(int id) {
            repo.Remove(id);
        }
    }
}
```

You can see the duplication with the MVC Framework features and the Web API. The HttpPost and HttpPut attributes that I used in Listing 27-11 have the exact same purpose as the attributes with the same name that I used in Chapter 19, but they are defined in the System.Web.Http namespace and not System.Web.Mvc. Duplication aside, the attributes work in the same way and I have ended up with more useful method names that will still work for the POST and PUT HTTP methods. (There are, of course, attributes for all of the HTTP methods, including GET, DELETE and so on.)

Using Knockout for Single-page Applications

The purpose of creating the Web API web service is to refactor the example application so that operations on the application data can be performed using Ajax requests whose JSON results will be used to update the HTML in the browser. The overall functionality of the application will be the same, but I won't be generating complete HTML documents for each interaction between the client and the server.

The transition to a single-page application puts more of a burden on the browser because I need to preserve application state at the client. I need a data model that I can update, a series of logic operations that I can perform to transform the data and a set of UI elements that allows the user to trigger those operations. In short, I need to recreate a miniature version of the MVC pattern in the browser.

The library that Microsoft has adopted for single-page applications is Knockout, which creates a JavaScript implementation of the MVC pattern (or, more accurately, the MVVM pattern which I described in Chapter 3 and is sufficiently close to the MVC pattern that I am going to treat them as the same thing). In the sections that follow, I am going to return to the MVC Framework side of the example application and apply the Knockout library to create a simple SPA.

■ **Note**   Knockout does a lot more than I am going to demonstrate here and I recommend you explore the library in more depth to see what it is capable of. You can learn more at `http://knockoutjs.com` or from my *Pro JavaScript for Web Apps* book, which is published by Apress. I like Knockout, but for more complex applications I prefer AngularJS. It has a steeper learning curve, but the investment is worthwhile. You can learn more at `http://angularjs.org` or read my *Pro AngularJS* book, which—as you might have guessed by now—is also published by Apress.

Adding the JavaScript Libraries to the Layout

The first step is to add the Knockout and jQuery files to the layout so that they are available in the view. You can see the script element I added in Listing 27-12.

Listing 27-12. Adding the Knockout JavaScript File to the _Layout.cshtml File

```
@{
    Layout = null;
}

<!DOCTYPE html>

<html>
<head>
    <meta name="viewport" content="width=device-width" />
    <title>@ViewBag.Title</title>
    <link href="~/Content/bootstrap.css" rel="stylesheet" />
    <link href="~/Content/bootstrap.min.css" rel="stylesheet" />
    <script src="~/Scripts/jquery-1.10.2.js"></script>
    <script src="~/Scripts/knockout-3.0.0.js"></script>
    @RenderSection("Scripts")
</head>
<body>
    @RenderSection("Body")
</body>
</html>
```

I will be using Knockout to create the MVC implementation and jQuery to handle the Ajax requests.

Implementing the Summary

The first major change I will make is to replace the Summary partial view with some inline Knockout and jQuery. You don't have to use Knockout in a single file, but I want to leave the partial views intact so you can see the difference between the standard MVC Framework way of working and the SPA techniques. In Listing 27-13, you can see the changes that I made to the Index.cstml view file.

Listing 27-13. Using Knockout and jQuery to Implement the Summary in the Index.cshtml File

```
@using WebServices.Models
@{
    ViewBag.Title = "Reservations";
    Layout = "~/Views/Shared/_Layout.cshtml";
}

@section Scripts {
    <script>
        var model = {
            reservations: ko.observableArray()
        };

        function sendAjaxRequest(httpMethod, callback, url) {
            $.ajax("/api/web" + (url ? "/" + url : ""), {
                type: httpMethod, success: callback
            });
        }

        function getAllItems() {
            sendAjaxRequest("GET", function(data) {
                model.reservations.removeAll();
                for (var i = 0; i < data.length; i++) {
                    model.reservations.push(data[i]);
                }
            });
        }

        function removeItem(item) {
            sendAjaxRequest("DELETE", function () {
                getAllItems();
            }, item.ReservationId);
        }

        $(document).ready(function () {
            getAllItems();
            ko.applyBindings(model);
        });
    </script>
}
```

```
@section Body {
    <div id="summary" class="section panel panel-primary">
        <div class="panel-heading">Reservation Summary</div>
        <div class="panel-body">
            <table class="table table-striped table-condensed">
                <thead>
                    <tr><th>ID</th><th>Name</th><th>Location</th><th></th></tr>
                </thead>
                <tbody data-bind="foreach: model.reservations">
                    <tr>
                        <td data-bind="text: ReservationId"></td>
                        <td data-bind="text: ClientName"></td>
                        <td data-bind="text: Location"></td>
                        <td>
                            <button class="btn btn-xs btn-primary"
                                    data-bind="click: removeItem">Remove</button>
                        </td>
                    </tr>
                </tbody>
            </table>
        </div>
    </div>
    <div id="editor" class="section panel panel-primary">
        @Html.Partial("Editor", new Reservation())
    </div>
}
```

There is a lot going on here, so I am going to break down the changes and explain each of them in turn. The overall effect of the changes, however, is that the browser uses the Web API controller to get details of the current reservations.

■ **Note**   Notice that I have removed the @model expression from the Index view in Listing 27-13. I am not using the view model objects to generate the content in the view, which means that I don't need a view model. The controller is still obtaining the Reservation objects from the repository and passing them to the view, but I'll fix this later in the chapter.

Defining the Ajax Functions

jQuery has excellent support for making Ajax requests. To that end, I have defined a function called sendAjaxRequest that I will use to target methods on the Web API controller, as follows:

```
...
function sendAjaxRequest(httpMethod, callback, url) {
    $.ajax("/api/web" + (url ? "/" + url : ""), {
        type: httpMethod, success: callback
    });
}
...
```

The $.ajax function provides access to the jQuery Ajax functionality. The arguments are the URL you want to request and an object that contains configuration parameters. The sendAjaxRequest function is a wrapper around the jQuery functionality and its arguments are the HTTP method that should be used for the request (which affects the action method selected by the controller), a callback function that will be invoked when the Ajax request has succeeded and an optional URL suffix. Using the sendAjaxRequest function as a foundation, I defined functions to get all of the data available and to delete a reservation, like this:

```
...
function getAllItems() {
    sendAjaxRequest("GET", function(data) {
        model.reservations.removeAll();
        for (var i = 0; i < data.length; i++) {
            model.reservations.push(data[i]);
        }
    });
}

function removeItem(item) {
    sendAjaxRequest("DELETE", function () {
        getAllItems();
    }, item.ReservationId);
}
...
```

The getAllItems function targets the GetAllReservations controller action method and retrieves all of the reservations from the server. The removeItem function targets the DeleteReservation action method and calls the getAllItems function to refresh the data after a deletion.

Defining the Model

Underpinning the Ajax functions is the model, which I defined like this:

```
...
var model = {
    reservations: ko.observableArray()
};
...
```

Knockout works by creating *observable objects* that it monitors for changes and uses to update the HTML displayed by the browser. My model is simple. It consists of an observable array, which is just like a regular JavaScript array, but is wired up so that any changes I made are detected by Knockout. You can see how I use the model in the Ajax functions, like this:

```
...
function getAllItems() {
    sendAjaxRequest("GET", function(data) {
        model.reservations.removeAll();
        for (var i = 0; i < data.length; i++) {
            model.reservations.push(data[i]);
        }
    });
}
...
```

The two statements I highlighted are how I get the data from the server into the model. I call the removeAll method to remove any existing data from the observable array and then iterate through the results I get from the server with the push method to populate the array with the new data.

Defining the Bindings

Knockout applies changes in the data model to HTML elements via *data bindings*. Here are the most important data bindings in the Index view:

```
...
<tbody data-bind="foreach: model.reservations">
    <tr>
        <td data-bind="text: ReservationId"></td>
        <td data-bind="text: ClientName"></td>
        <td data-bind="text: Location"></td>
        <td>
            <button class="btn btn-xs btn-primary"
                    data-bind="click: removeItem">Remove</button>
        </td>
    </tr>
</tbody>
...
```

Knockout is expressed using the data-bind attribute and there is a wide range of bindings available, three of which I have used in the view. The basic format for a data-bind attribute is:

```
data-bind="type: expression"
```

The types of the three bindings in the listing are foreach, text and click, and I picked these three because they represent the different ways in which Knockout can be used.

The first two, the foreach and text bindings, generate HTML elements and content from the data model. When the foreach binding is applied to an element, Knockout generates the child elements for each object in the expression, just like the Razor @foreach that I was using in the partial view.

The text binding inserts the value of the expression as the text of the element that it is applied to. This means that when I use this binding, for example:

```
...
<td data-bind="text: ClientName"></td>
...
```

Knockout will insert the value of the ClientName property of the current object being processed by the foreach binding, which has the same effect as the Razor @Model.ClientName expression I used previously.

The click directive is different: it sets up an even handler for the click event on the element to which it has been applied. You don't have to use Knockout to set up events, of course, but the click binding is integrated with the other bindings and the function you specify to call when the event is triggered is passed the data object that was being processed by the foreach binding when the binding was applied. This is why the removeItem function is able to define an argument that receives a Reservation object (or its JavaScript representation, anyway).

Processing the Bindings

Knockout bindings are not processed automatically, which is why I included this code in the `script` element:

```
...
$(document).ready(function () {
    getAllItems();
    ko.applyBindings(model);
});
...
```

The `$(document).ready` call is a standard jQuery technique to defer execution of a function until all of the HTML elements in the document have been loaded and processed by the browser. Once that happens, I call the `getAllItems` function to load the data from the server and then the `ko.applyBindings` function to use the data model to process the `data-bind` attributes. This final call is the one that connects the data objects to the HTML elements, generates the content I require, and sets up the event handlers.

Testing the Summary Bindings

You might be wondering why I have gone to all this trouble, given that I have essentially replaced Razor expressions with their equivalent Knockout bindings. There are three important differences and to demonstrate them fully, I am going to use the browser F12 tools.

The first difference is that the model data is no longer included in the HTML that is sent to the browser. Instead, once the HTML has been processed, the browser makes an Ajax request to the Web API controller and gets the list of reservations expressed as JSON. You can see this by starting the application and using the F12 tools to monitor the requests that the browser makes (as described in Chapter 26). Figure 27-3 shows the results.

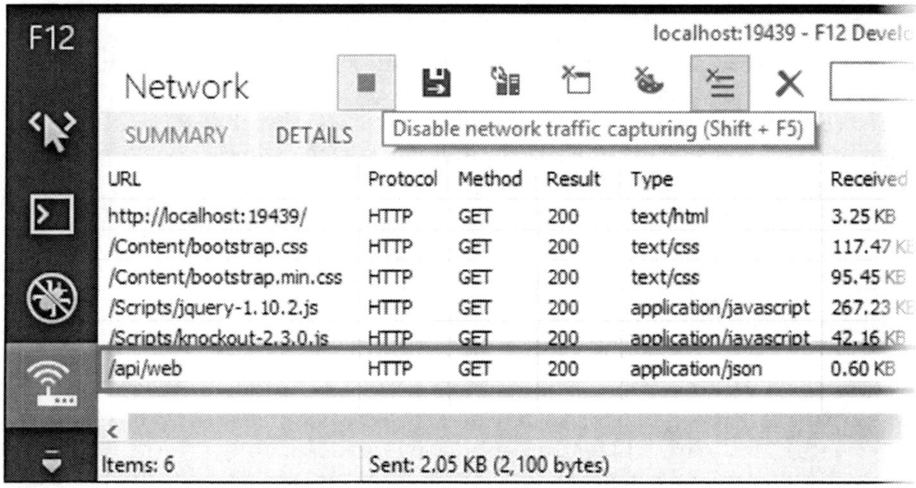

Figure 27-3. *Monitoring the connections made by the browser*

The second difference is that the data is processed by the browser, rather than at the server, as the view is rendered. To test this, you can edit the getAllItems function so that it doesn't make the Ajax request or process the data it receives, like this:

```
...
function getAllItems() {
    return;
    sendAjaxRequest("GET", function(data) {
        model.reservations.removeAll();
        for (var i = 0; i < data.length; i++) {
            model.reservations.push(data[i]);
        }
    });
}
...
```

The function will return before the Ajax request is made and you can see the effect by restarting the application, as shown in Figure 27-4. This may seem obvious, but it is an important characteristic of SPAs that the browser does a lot more work, including processing data and generating HTML content.

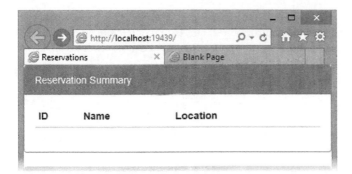

Figure 27-4. *Demonstrating that the data is retrieved and processed by the browser*

The final difference is that the data bindings are *live*, meaning that changes in the data model are reflected in the content that the foreach and text bindings generate. To test this, ensure that you return the getAllItems function to its working state and reload the application. Once the browser has requested, received and processed the data, open the F12 tools and switch to the Console section. Enter the following command into the console and hit Enter:

```
model.reservations.pop()
```

This expression removes the last item from the array of data objects in the model and as soon as you enter the command, the layout of the HTML page will reflect the change, as shown in Figure 27-5. The overall effect is that I have shifted some of the complexity of generating the HTML from the server to the client.

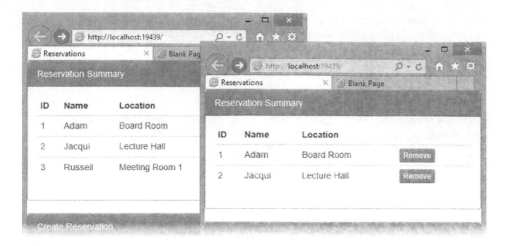

Figure 27-5. *Manipulating the model via the JavaScript console*

Improving the Delete Feature

Now that you have seen how applying Knockout has changed the nature of the client, I am going to quickly loop back and remove a shortcut that I took when I defined the Ajax methods for the application. The removeItem function is badly written:

```
...
function removeItem(item) {
    sendAjaxRequest("DELETE", function () {
        getAllItems();
    }, item.ReservationId);
}
...
```

I have highlighted the problem: the function makes two Ajax requests to the server—the first to perform the deletion and the second to request the contents of the repository to update the data model. Now that I have demonstrated that the client maintains its own model and that live bindings reflect model changes in the HTML, I can improve upon this function, as shown in Listing 27-14.

Listing 27-14. Improving the RemoveItem Function in the Index.cshtml File

```
...
function removeItem(item) {
    sendAjaxRequest("DELETE", function () {
        for (var i = 0; i < model.reservations().length; i++) {
            if (model.reservations()[i].ReservationId == item.ReservationId) {
                model.reservations.remove(model.reservations()[i]);
                break;
            }
        }
    }, item.ReservationId);
}
...
```

When the request to the server succeeds, I remove the corresponding data object from the model, which means that the second Ajax request is no longer required.

GETTING USED TO THE KNOCKOUT SYNTAX

There are some syntax quirks when working with Knockout observable arrays and two of them can be seen in Listing 27-14. To get an item from the array, I have to treat `model.reservations` like a function, as follows:

```
...
model.reservations()[i].ReservationId
...
```

And when it comes to removing items from the array, I use a function that is not standard JavaScript:

```
...
model.reservations.remove(model.reservations()[i]);
...
```

Knockout tries to maintain the standard JavaScript syntax, but there are some compromises required to track changes to data objects, such as these quirks. They can be confusing when you first start working with Knockout, but you soon get used to them. And you learn that when you don't get the effect you require, the likely cause is a mismatch between the standard JavaScript syntax and that required for a Knockout observable object or array. You can get further information about the Knockout API at `http://knockoutjs.com`.

Implementing the Create Feature

The next step is to use Knockout to replace the `Editor` partial view. Once again, I could have updated the partial view to contain the Knockout functionality, but I have chosen to include everything in the `Index.cshtml` file, as shown in Listing 27-15.

Listing 27-15. Implementing the Create Feature in the Index.cshtml File

```
@using WebServices.Models
@{
    ViewBag.Title = "Reservations";
    Layout = "~/Views/Shared/_Layout.cshtml";
}

@section Scripts {
    <script>
        var model = {
            reservations: ko.observableArray(),
            editor: {
                name: ko.observable(""),
                location: ko.observable("")
            }
        };
```

```
        function sendAjaxRequest(httpMethod, callback, url, reqData) {
            $.ajax("/api/web" + (url ? "/" + url : ""), {
                type: httpMethod,
                success: callback,
                data: reqData
            });
        }

        // ...other functions omitted for brevity...

        function handleEditorClick() {
            sendAjaxRequest("POST", function (newItem) {
                model.reservations.push(newItem);
            }, null, {
                ClientName: model.editor.name,
                Location: model.editor.location
            });
        }

        $(document).ready(function () {
            getAllItems();
            ko.applyBindings(model);
        });
    </script>
}

@section Body {
    <div id="summary" class="section panel panel-primary">
        <!-- elements omitted for brevity -->
    </div>
    <div id="editor" class="section panel panel-primary">
        <div class="panel-heading">
            Create Reservation
        </div>
        <div class="panel-body">
            <div class="form-group">
                <label>Client Name</label>
                <input class="form-control" data-bind="value: model.editor.name" />
            </div>
            <div class="form-group">
                <label>Location</label>
                <input class="form-control" data-bind="value: model.editor.location" />
            </div>
            <button class="btn btn-primary"
                data-bind="click: handleEditorClick">Save</button>
        </div>
    </div>
}
```

To create the editor, I have used Knockout in a different way, as I'll explain step-by-step in the sections that follow.

Extending the Model

I need to collect two pieces of information from the user in order to create a new Reservation in the repository: the name of the client (corresponding to the ClientName property) and the location (corresponding to the Location property). My first step is to extend the model so that I define variables that I can use to capture these values, like this:

```
...
var model = {
    reservations: ko.observableArray(),
    editor: {
        name: ko.observable(""),
        location: ko.observable("")
    }
};
...
```

The ko.observable function creates an observable value, which I will rely on later in the chapter. Changes to these values will be reflected in any bindings that use the name and location properties.

Implement the Input Elements

The next step is to create the input elements through which the user will supply values for my new model properties. I have used the Knockout value binding, which sets the value attribute on an element, as follows:

```
...
<input class="form-control" data-bind="value: model.editor.name" />
...
```

The value bindings ensure that the values entered by the user into the input elements will be used to set the model properties.

■ **Tip** Notice that I don't need a form element anymore. I will be using an Ajax request to send the data values to the server in response to a button click, none of which relies on the standard browser support for forms.

Creating the Event Handler

I used the click binding to handle the click event from the button element displayed under the input elements, as follows:

```
...
<button class="btn btn-primary" data-bind="click: handleEditorClick">Save</button>
...
```

The binding specifies that the handleEditorClick function should be called when the button is clicked and I defined this function in the script element, as follows:

```
...
function handleEditorClick() {
    sendAjaxRequest("POST", function (newItem) {
            model.reservations.push(newItem);
        }, null, {
            ClientName: model.editor.name,
            Location: model.editor.location
        });
}
...
```

The event handler function calls the sendAjaxRequest function. The callback adds the newly created data object sent back from the server to the model. I send an object containing the new model properties to the sendAjaxRequest function, which I have extended so that it will send them to the server as part of the Ajax request, using the data option property.

Testing the Create Feature

You can see how the Knockout implementation of the create feature works by starting the application, entering a name and location into the input elements and clicking the Save button, as illustrated by Figure 27-6.

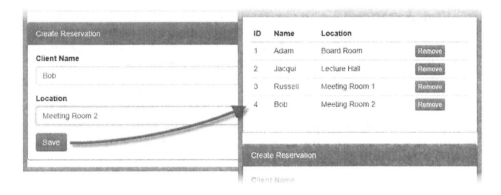

Figure 27-6. *Creating a new reservation*

Completing the Application

Now that you have seen how I can apply Knockout and the Web API to create a single-page application, I am going to finish this chapter by completing the application to add some missing features and remove some of the quirks.

Simplify the Home Controller

The Home controller is still set up with action method to manipulate the repository to retrieve and manage Reservation objects, even though all of the data displayed by the client is being requested via Ajax to the Web API controller. In Listing 27-16, you can see how I have updated the controller to remove the action methods that the Web API controller has replaced. I have also updated the Index action method so that it no longer passes a view model object.

Listing 27-16. Removing the Data Selection from the HomeController.cs File

```
using System.Web.Mvc;
using WebServices.Models;

namespace WebServices.Controllers {

    public class HomeController : Controller {

        public ViewResult Index() {
            return View();
        }
    }
}
```

Manage Content Visibility

The final change I am going to make is to manage the visibility of the elements in the HTML document so that only the summary or the editor is visible. You can see how I have done this in Listing 27-17.

Listing 27-17. Managing Element Visibility in the Index.cshtml File

```
@using WebServices.Models
@{
    ViewBag.Title = "Reservations";
    Layout = "~/Views/Shared/_Layout.cshtml";
}

@section Scripts {
    <script>
        var model = {
            reservations: ko.observableArray(),
            editor: {
                name: ko.observable(""),
                location: ko.observable("")
            },
            displaySummary: ko.observable(true)
        };

        function sendAjaxRequest(httpMethod, callback, url, reqData) {
            $.ajax("/api/web" + (url ? "/" + url : ""), {
                type: httpMethod,
                success: callback,
                data: reqData
            });
        }
```

781

```
        function getAllItems() {
            sendAjaxRequest("GET", function(data) {
                model.reservations.removeAll();
                for (var i = 0; i < data.length; i++) {
                    model.reservations.push(data[i]);
                }
            });
        }

        function removeItem(item) {
            sendAjaxRequest("DELETE", function () {
                for (var i = 0; i < model.reservations().length; i++) {
                    if (model.reservations()[i].ReservationId == item.ReservationId) {
                        model.reservations.remove(model.reservations()[i]);
                        break;
                    }
                }
            }, item.ReservationId);
        }

        function handleCreateClick() {
            model.displaySummary(false);
        }

        function handleEditorClick() {
            sendAjaxRequest("POST", function (newItem) {
                model.reservations.push(newItem);
                model.displaySummary(true);
            }, null, {
                ClientName: model.editor.name,
                Location: model.editor.location
            });
        }

        $(document).ready(function () {
            getAllItems();
            ko.applyBindings(model);
        });
    </script>
}

@section Body {
    <div id="summary" class="section panel panel-primary"
            data-bind="if: model.displaySummary">
        <div class="panel-heading">Reservation Summary</div>
        <div class="panel-body">
            <table class="table table-striped table-condensed">
                <thead>
                    <tr><th>ID</th><th>Name</th><th>Location</th><th></th></tr>
                </thead>
```

```
            <tbody data-bind="foreach: model.reservations">
                <tr>
                    <td data-bind="text: ReservationId"></td>
                    <td data-bind="text: ClientName"></td>
                    <td data-bind="text: Location"></td>
                    <td>
                        <button class="btn btn-xs btn-primary"
                                data-bind="click: removeItem">Remove</button>
                    </td>
                </tr>
            </tbody>
        </table>
        <button class="btn btn-primary"
            data-bind="click: handleCreateClick">Create</button>
    </div>
</div>
<div id="editor" class="section panel panel-primary"
    data-bind="ifnot: model.displaySummary">
<div class="panel-heading">
    Create Reservation
</div>
<div class="panel-body">
    <div class="form-group">
        <label>Client Name</label>
        <input class="form-control" data-bind="value: model.editor.name" />
    </div>
    <div class="form-group">
        <label>Location</label>
        <input class="form-control" data-bind="value: model.editor.location" />
    </div>
    <button class="btn btn-primary"
        data-bind="click: handleEditorClick">Save</button>
</div>
</div>
}
```

I have added a property to the model that specifies whether the summary should be shown. I use this property with the if and ifnot bindings, which add and remove elements to and from the DOM based on their expression. If the displaySummary property is true, then the data summary will be shown and if it is false, then the editor will be shown. The final changes I made were to add a Create button that calls a function that changes the displaySummary property and an addition to the callback function that processes new items that changes it back again. You can see the final result in Figure 27-7.

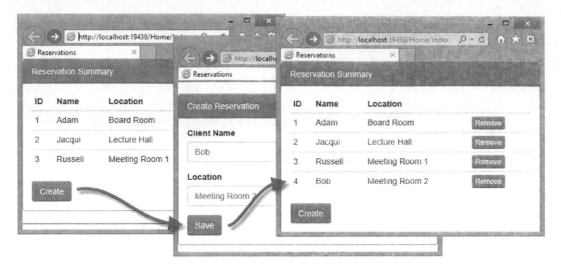

Figure 27-7. *Adding a reservation using the final application*

Summary

In this chapter, I showed you how to use the Web API and Knockout to create a single-page application that performs data operations using RESTful Web service. While not part of the MVC Framework, the Web API is modeled so closely on the nature and structure of MVC that it is familiar to MVC developers and, as I demonstrated, Web API controllers can be added alongside regular MVC controllers in an application.

And that is all I have to teach you about the MVC Framework. I started by creating a simple application, and then took you on a comprehensive tour of the different components in the framework, showing you how they can be configured, customized, or replaced entirely. I wish you every success in your MVC Framework projects and I can only hope that you have enjoyed reading this book as much as I enjoyed writing it.

Index

■ D

■ Q

■ R

Get the eBook for only $10!

> Now you can take the weightless companion with you anywhere, anytime. Your purchase of this book entitles you to 3 electronic versions for only $10.

This Apress title will prove so indispensible that you'll want to carry it with you everywhere, which is why we are offering the eBook in 3 formats for only $10 if you have already purchased the print book.

Convenient and fully searchable, the PDF version enables you to easily find and copy code—or perform examples by quickly toggling between instructions and applications. The MOBI format is ideal for your Kindle, while the ePUB can be utilized on a variety of mobile devices.

Go to www.apress.com/promo/tendollars to purchase your companion eBook.

CPSIA information can be obtained at www.ICGtesting.com
Printed in the USA
LVOW09s1003301114

416259LV00005B/13/P

9 781430 265290